"The most influential scholar of the last gener[a] Testament, was without rival, Gordon Fee. Mar and pastorally carries forward the work of Fee—extending and expanding it—to the distinctive need for so many of us. Keown probes the questions, 'What does the Spirit do?', 'How does the Spirit do what the Spirit does?', and 'How much does the Spirit do?' *Pneumaformity*, taking a cue many have taken, turns to Michael Gorman and his thesis of 'cruciformity' and then explores how cruciformity occurs in the life of the believer: only in the power of the Spirit. At once academically respectable and pastorally useful, *Pneumaformity* will be a generational book. Those conformed to the Spirit will be formed into the Christ of the cross."

—Scot McKnight,
Professor of New Testament

"The idea that the Christian life is one of 'cruciformity' and 'Christoformity' has become prominent in conversations about Paul's understanding of God's goal for people in Christ. In the tradition of Gordon Fee's *God's Empowering Presence*, Keown brings to the conversation a welcome emphasis on the agency of the Holy Spirit in this process and demonstrates well-nigh exhaustively the importance of the Spirit in Paul's understanding of the Christian life. Readers will find here both a summons and guide to becoming more attuned to, and zealous for, what the Spirit—and *only* the Spirit—can accomplish in them and through them."

—David A. deSilva,
Trustees' Distinguished Professor of New Testament and Greek,
Ashland Theological Seminary

"Mark Keown has written an interesting and challenging book that thoroughly examines the importance of the Holy Spirit in Paul's thought and writing. We know about Paul's God and the importance of Jesus Christ, but Keown gives us a strong endorsement of the centrality of the Holy Spirit in Paul's theology. More than that, Keown calls us to think again about what it means to live the Christian life in conformity to the Spirit."

—Stanley E. Porter,
President, Dean, and Professor of New Testament,
Roy A. Hope Chair in Christian Worldview,
McMaster Divinity College, Hamilton, Ontario, Canada

"In this inspiring work, Mark Keown focuses on the amazing breadth and depth of the Spirit's work. Written with verve and great clarity, and with a strong concern for the church and its witness, this book leads us to a much deeper understanding of the Spirit's role in transforming those who place their faith in Jesus Christ as Lord and Savior. Packed with scriptural insight and wisdom, this book discusses the fullness of the Spirit's work in our lives, in the church, and in the world. But it is also written with the hope that it will encourage us all to be filled with the Spirit and to live by the Spirit that we might be conformed to Christ. May it be so!"

—Paul Trebilco,
Professor of New Testament Studies,
University of Otago, Dunedin, New Zealand

"Following in the footsteps of Gordon Fee and Michael Gorman, Keown forges a new path in Pauline studies by focusing on the Holy Spirit as central to Christian spiritual formation. By expanding the study to passages where the Spirit is not specifically mentioned, he shows that it is through the Holy Spirit that the Father transforms his people into the image of his Son. In this clear and scholarly work, Keown challenges pneumaform people to be devoted to worship and to participate in God's mission in the world. I highly recommend this thorough study of the Holy Spirit in Paul's letters."

—Phillip J. Long,
Professor of Biblical Studies,
Grace Christian University

"In this monumental work, Mark Keown convincingly demonstrates that Paul's understanding of the Christian life is thoroughly pneumatological. Building on the prior studies of notable scholars such as Michael Gorman, Scot McKnight, and Gordon Fee, Keown offers fresh insight related to Paul's understanding of the work of the Spirit in the life of the believer. Readers will appreciate his careful exegetical analysis, thoughtful theological reflection, and the impressive breadth of subjects explored in the volume that together provide a fuller picture of the role of the Spirit in Paul's thinking. Thoroughly researched yet accessible, this impressive volume will serve as a valuable resource for the study of Pauline theology and the doctrine of the Holy Spirit."

—Benjamin P. Laird,
Associate Professor of Biblical Studies
John W. Rawlings School of Divinity, Liberty University

"Themes such as 'cruciformity' (conformity to the crucified Christ) and 'Christoformity' (conformity to Christ) are most certainly helpful. But so is Keown's important emphasis on 'pneumaformity,' which focuses on the Spirit's transformational role in the life of the believer. Readers will benefit from the rich exegesis of relevant Pauline texts and application to the Christian life!"

—Miguel Echevarría,
Associate Professor of New Testament and Greek,
Southeastern Baptist Theological Seminary

"Building upon the pioneering works of scholars such as Gordon Fee, Michael Gorman, Scot McKnight, and Jimmy Dunn, Mark Keown rightly suggests that, in the *Corpus Paulinum*, the Holy-Spirit-empowered apostle issued a clarion call to his hearers and readers toward what Keown calls 'pneumaformity.' For Keown, 'pneumaformity' is not merely some catchy buzzword or specialized lens through which to read and understand Paul and his letters, but the diachronic, ethical, and Pauline basis for living the Christian life—a life that is to be lived, led, conformed, and transformed by God's Spirit and fully realized in the eschaton. While Keown gives sufficient detail and precision when necessary, he helpfully synthesizes big-picture concepts, so readers do not miss the proverbial forest for the trees. An example of such synthesis is Keown's holistic treatment of the Spirit's work, which serves as a beneficial corrective to myopic, imbalanced pneumatological perspectives. Thus, Keown clarifies the Spirit's cosmic scope in Christian living—simultaneously impacting individuals, churches, communities, and the world. Moreover, Keown explores the entirety of Paul's epistles and not just his larger letters, which are so often the focus in delimited surveys of the Spirit. In sum, Keown's readers—scholars, students, and busy pastors alike—will greatly benefit from his keen, yet approachable, exegetical insights throughout this work. I highly recommend this book for all those wishing to 'keep in step' with the Holy Spirit!"

—Gregory Lamb,
Adjunct Professor of New Testament Greek,
Southeastern Baptist Theological Seminary

"We have heard about 'cruciformity' and being 'Christo-centric,' but 'pneumaformity' is quite another thing! Or is it? Keown brings a complementary Spirit perspective to Paul's Christological work and in doing so revives what Irenaeus spoke of as God's two hands at work in the world. Keown's work makes for a welcome biblical companion to the many theological works on the Trinity, updating in many ways the seminal work of its stated inspiration, Gordon Fee's *God's Empowering Presence*."

— Myk Habets,
Head of Theology, Laidlaw College,
Auckland, New Zealand

"In *Pneumaformity* the reader is presented with the riches of a believer and scholar who has immersed himself for years in Paul's letters and strived to uncover both their historical meaning and contemporary significance. Mark Keown stands on the shoulders of giants like Gordon Fee and Michael Gorman, but he brings his own passion and insights to the exegetical and theological task in order to present a compelling vision of the Christian life as one shaped from beginning to end by the Spirit of Christ. This book lays out a cohesive and wide-ranging discussion of Christian conversion, sanctification, discipleship, witness, and future hope in Paul's letters, all under the unifying theme of *pneumaformity*. Not just a work of scholarship, this book is an exhortation to Christian life and community that is more fully shaped by the work of God's Spirit."

—Jonathan Robinson,
Lecturer in New Testament at Carey Baptist College, New Zealand,
Author of *Markan Typology*

"In this stimulating new book, Pauline scholar and seminary professor Mark Keown builds on Michael Gorman's work on 'cruciformity' and Scot McKnight's work on 'Christoformity.' For Keown, 'pneumaformity' expresses the Spirit's work in producing both cruciformity and Christoformity in the lives of believers. Another conversation partner is Gordon Fee and his classic work *God's Empowering Presence*, now thirty years old. In updating Fee's work, Keown approaches the work of the Spirit in Paul not by working through Paul's letters chronologically, as Fee did, but topically. This is a systematic biblical theology of the work of the Spirit in Paul. Those who are familiar with Mark Keown's writings will be eagerly waiting to get their hands on this superb book. It is a must-read for anyone interested in the work of the Spirit in the theology of Paul (and that should be all of us)."

—Philip Church,
Senior Research Fellow,
Laidlaw College

"It is one thing to talk of how our lives as Christians should reflect Christ's life. It is another to explore exactly how we can increasingly live that way. Through the terminology of 'pneumaformity' and exploring its many aspects and implications, Keown brings the Spirit's role in our ongoing transformation to the forefront of our consideration. His exploration of this theme is biblically grounded, thorough, at times controversial, and often compelling. May an increased understanding and application of the Spirit's crucial role in our ongoing transformation lead to us enjoying more and more the fullness of life that God has for us."

—Gregory J. Liston,
Senior Lecturer in Theology, Laidlaw College,
Author of *The Anointed Church* and *Kingdom Come*

"This book is a follow-up to Michael Gorman's *Cruciformity* and Scot McKnight's *Christoformity*, with the focus on Paul's teaching of the Holy Spirit. Keown's analysis of Paul's pneumatology is broader than linguistic research that is usually limited to the word *Pneuma* ('Spirit'). His reading of Paul is constructed upon Paul's trinitarian view of God. This extends the scope of pneumatology to include segments of Paul's writing that were previously ignored. As such, Keown provides an integrated study of Pauline pneumatology in relation to the works of the Father and the Son. He carefully and systematically presents the roles of the Spirit in every stage of the Christian life by drawing connections within the Pauline corpus and beyond. This book is an excellent addition to Pauline scholarship and pneumatology research."

—Tat Yan Lee,
President, Bible College of Malaysia

"Mark Keown's *Pneumaformity: Transformation by the Spirit in Paul* is a comprehensive discussion of the Spirit's intersection with all areas of cruciform life. It is full of theological detail that will enrich learning for both scholars and students. I highly recommend this valuable work."

—Sarah Harris,
Research Fellow,
Carey Baptist College and Graduate School

"Building upon the works of Gorman and McKnight on cruciformity and Christoformity, Keown continues the conversation by placing the rightful emphasis on the role of the Holy Spirit in the process of the transformation of God's people. By using the term, 'pneumaformity,' Keown traces the work of the Spirit in a thematic fashion drawn from the thirteen letters of Paul. Written in an engaging and inspiring manner, Keown guides the reader into deeper insights on the role the Spirit plays in a believer's life, with special attention given to suffering and mission engagement, themes rarely touched on by studies in pneumatology. Keown's *Pneumaformity* is a rare gift, and I am excited to recommend it to pastors and students who desire a deeper understanding of the Holy Spirit and how to live a Christian life in total submission to God's Spirit."

— Kar Yong Lim,
Lecturer in New Testament Studies,
Seminari Theoloji Malaysia

PNEUMAFORMITY

Transformation

by the Spirit

in Paul

MARK J. KEOWN

Printed in the United States of America

24 25 26 27 28 / 5 4 3 2 1

To my God—Father, Son, and Spirit—
and to my beloved wife, Emma.
I cannot thank you enough
for your goodness to me.

CONTENTS

ACKNOWLEDGMENTS

I want to acknowledge God—Father, Son, and Spirit—first, and I pray that this work pleases you and reflects who you are and how we are to live in response. I also thank my wife, the wonderful Emma, for her endless patience with me as I stumble and falter, seeking to follow the Lord. Thanks also to Kregel for working with me on this project. I also pay tribute to the late Gordon Fee, a great scholar and inspiration. I met Gordon once after he had completed *God's Empowering Presence*. He addressed a room full of people skeptical of the Pentecostal and charismatic movements at Otago University, Dunedin, New Zealand. He spoke powerfully and brilliantly, and I suggested that he should have given an altar call afterward. He was my leading conversation partner in this book. As such, I do hope this work honors and supplements his magisterial effort. I also pay tribute to all others I engaged with in this, including the apostle Paul, through whom the Spirit speaks today. I also honor Michael Gorman and pray that this adds to his ongoing appeal to the church to be cruciform and, similarly, Scot McKnight's appeal that we be Christoform. I also pay tribute to the late James Dunn, whose book *Jesus and the Spirit* proved very useful. I never met him, but I owe him a lot as he is my *Doktorvater* through Paul Trebilco. I pray that the Spirit-led ideas will stick and the others drop away as they are exposed as flawed or imbalanced. I ask, Lord, that you might bless this book and use it to inspire your people to live by the Spirit. Amen.

ABBREVIATIONS

acc.   accusative

ANF[1]   Roberts, Alexander, James Donaldson, and A. Cleveland Coxe, eds. *The Apostolic Fathers with Justin Martyr and Irenaeus*. Vol. 1 of *The Ante-Nicene Fathers*. Buffalo, NY: Christian Literature, 1885.

aor.   aorist

AYB   Anchor Yale Bible

BDAG   Bauer, Walter, Frederick W. Danker, William Arndt, and F. Wilbur Gingrich. *A Greek-English Lexicon of the New Testament and Other Early Christian Literature*. 3rd ed. Chicago: University of Chicago Press, 2000.

BDB   Brown, Francis, Samuel Rolles Driver, and Charles Augustus Briggs. *Enhanced Brown-Driver-Briggs Hebrew and English Lexicon*. Oxford: Clarendon, 1977.

BECNT   Baker Exegetical Commentary on the New Testament

BGD   Arndt, William, F. Wilbur Gingrich, Frederick W. Danker, and Walter Bauer. *A Greek-English Lexicon of the New Testament and Other Early Christian Literature: A Translation and Adaption of the Fourth Revised and Augmented Edition of Walter Bauer's Griechisch-Deutsches Worterbuch Zu Den Schrift En Des Neuen Testaments Und Der Ubrigen Urchristlichen Literatur*. Chicago: University of Chicago Press, 1979.

BGPPM   Gorman, Michael J. *Becoming the Gospel: Paul, Participation, and Mission*. GOCS. Grand Rapids: Eerdmans, 2015.

BNTC   Black's New Testament Commentary

BrillDAG   Montanari, Franco. *The Brill Dictionary of Ancient Greek*. Edited by Madeleine Goh and Chad Schroeder. Leiden: Brill, 2015.

BSac   *Bibliotheca Sacra*

CBQ	*Catholic Biblical Quarterly*
CCGNT	Classic Commentaries on the Greek New Testament
COQG	Christian Origins and the Question of God
CPNIVC	College Press New International Version Commentary
CPNSC	Gorman, Michael J. *Cruciformity: Paul's Narrative Spirituality of the Cross.* Grand Rapids: Eerdmans, 2001.
dat.	dative
DJG2	Green, Joel B., Jeannine K. Brown, and Nicholas Perrin, eds. *Dictionary of Jesus and the Gospels.* 2nd ed. Downers Grove, IL: IVP Academic, 2013.
DLNTD	Martin, Ralph P., and Peter H. Davids, eds. *Dictionary of the Later New Testament and Its Developments.* Downers Grove, IL: InterVarsity Press, 1997.
DNTB	Evans, Craig A., and Stanley E. Porter, eds. *Dictionary of New Testament Background: A Compendium of Contemporary Biblical Scholarship.* Downers Grove, IL: InterVarsity Press, 2000.
DPL	Hawthorne, Gerald F., Ralph P. Martin, and Daniel G. Reid, eds. *Dictionary of Paul and His Letters.* Downers Grove, IL: InterVarsity Press, 1993.
ECHC	Early Christianity in Its Hellenistic Context
EDEJ	Collins, John J., and Daniel C. Harlow, eds. *The Eerdmans Dictionary of Early Judaism.* Grand Rapids: Eerdmans, 2010.
EEC	Evangelical Exegetical Commentary
EJ	Neusner, Jacob, Alan J. Avery-Peck, and William Scott Green, eds. *The Encyclopedia of Judaism.* Leiden: Brill, 2000.
esp.	especially
ESV	English Standard Version
EVV	English version or verse numbers
fut.	future
gen.	genitive
GEP	Fee, Gordon D. *God's Empowering Presence: The Holy Spirit in the Letters of Paul.* Grand Rapids: Baker Academic, 2011.
GGNTLHR	Robertson, A. T. *A Grammar of the Greek New Testament in the Light of Historical Research.* 3rd ed. Bellingham, WA: Logos Bible Software, 2006.
GNT	Greek New Testament
GOCS	The Gospel and Our Culture Series
HALOT	Koehler, Ludwig, Walter Baumgartner, M. E. J. Richardson, and Johann Jakob Stamm. *The Hebrew and Aramaic Lexicon of the Old Testament.* Leiden: Brill, 1994–2000.
ICC	International Critical Commentary
inf.	infinitive

ITCG	Gorman, Michael J. *Inhabiting the Cruciform God: Kenosis, Justification, and Theosis in Paul's Narrative Soteriology.* Grand Rapids: Eerdmans, 2009.
JBL	*Journal of Biblical Literature*
JSNT	*Journal for the Study of the New Testament*
JSPL	*Journal for the Study of Paul and His Letters*
L&N	Louw, Johannes P., and Eugene Albert Nida. *Greek-English Lexicon of the New Testament: Based on Semantic Domains.* New York: United Bible Societies, 1996.
LEB	Lexham English Bible
LES	Lexham English Septuagint
lit.	literally
LSJ	Liddell, Henry George, Robert Scott, Henry Stuart Jones, and Roderick McKenzie. *A Greek-English Lexicon.* Oxford: Clarendon, 1996.
LXX	The Septuagint
masc.	masculine
mid.	middle
MM	Moulton, James Hope, and George Milligan. *The Vocabulary of the Greek Testament.* London: Hodder and Stoughton, 1930.
MT	Masoretic Text
NA28	Aland, Kurt, Barbara Aland, Johannes Karavidopoulos, Carlo M. Martini, and Bruce M. Metzger. *Novum Testamentum Graece.* 28th ed. Stuttgart: Deutsche Bibelgesellschaft, 2012.
NAC	New American Commentary
NCB	The New Century Bible Commentary
NCCS	New Covenant Commentary Series
NET	The NET Bible
neut.	neuter
NICNT	The New International Commentary on the New Testament
NIDNTTE	Silva, Moisés, ed. *New International Dictionary of New Testament Theology and Exegesis.* Grand Rapids: Zondervan, 2014.
NIGTC	New International Greek Testament Commentary
NIV	New International Version
NovTSup	Supplements to Novum Testamentum
n.p.	no page
NRSV	New Revised Standard Version
NT	New Testament
NTL	The New Testament Library
NTS	*New Testament Studies*
opt.	optative
OT	Old Testament

part.	participle
pass.	passive
PBM	Paternoster Biblical Monographs
perf.	perfect
plur.	plural
PNTC	Pillar New Testament Commentary
PPNCCC	McKnight, Scot. *Pastor Paul: Nurturing a Culture of Christo-formity in the Church.* Theological Explorations for the Church Catholic. Grand Rapids: Brazos, 2019.
pres.	present
PTMS	Princeton Theological Monograph Series
SBLDS	Society of Biblical Literature Dissertation Series
SNTSMS	Society for New Testament Studies Monograph Series
subj.	subjective
subjn.	subjunctive
TCGNT	Metzger, Bruce Manning. *A Textual Commentary on the Greek New Testament, Second Edition: A Companion Volume to the United Bible Societies' Greek New Testament (4th Rev. Ed.).* London: United Bible Societies, 1994.
TDNT	Theological Dictionary of the New Testament
TECC	Theological Explorations for the Church Catholic
TENTS	Texts and Editions for New Testament Study
TNTC	Tyndale New Testament Commentary
TynBul	*Tyndale Bulletin*
UBS5	Aland, Barbara, Kurt Aland, Johannes Karavidopoulos, Carlo M. Martini, and Bruce M. Metzger, eds. *The Greek New Testament.* 5th rev. ed. Stuttgart: Deutsche Bibelgesellschaft, 2014.
WBC	Word Biblical Commentary
ZECNT	Zondervan Exegetical Commentary on the New Testament.[1]

---

1.   Ancient text abbreviations can be found in the SBL Handbook of Style.

INTRODUCTION

This book is motivated by six things. First, in studying and teaching Paul for the last three decades, it is clear to me that Paul's understanding of the Christian life was profoundly pneumatological.[1] The pneumatic aspect is especially apparent in Galatians and Romans. In Galatians 1–4, Paul challenges the ideas of Judaizers who argue that Christian life and ethics must be shaped by obedience to the Torah, especially its boundary markers (as in Second Temple Judaism). Paul's response is to repudiate the notion that believers are "under the law" and assert that justification is by faith alone. Then, in Galatians 5–6, he expounds the basis for the Christian ethical life: being led by the Spirit.

Similarly, in Romans, while acknowledging the law is spiritual,[2] Paul asserts that the Christian life is not lived out of self-effort to conform oneself to an external code that has no power to transform a sinner's heart. Instead, as God's children, believers live their lives in Christ (esp. Romans 6), led by the Spirit (esp. Rom. 7:6; 8:1–17). For Paul, then, authentic Christian living is an inside-out life empowered by God's Spirit. The Spirit of God brings about the transformation of God's people. The Christian quest, then, is to understand what it means to be led by the Spirit and how this can come

---

1.   Readers should consider Gordon Fee's section "A 'Theology' of the Spirit" in Gordon D. Fee, *God's Empowering Presence: The Holy Spirit in the Letters of Paul* (Grand Rapids: Baker Academic, 2011), 2–5 (hereafter *GEP*). I share his interests and perspective to a large degree.

2.   The problem lies not with the law. For Paul, the law is "spiritual" (Rom. 7:14), likely meaning that the law originates from God and at its heart expresses the will of God, his Son, and his Spirit. See also Douglas J. Moo, *The Letter to the Romans*, 2nd ed., NICNT (Grand Rapids: Eerdmans, 2018), 477. Moo connects connects it to 2 Cornthians 10:3–4. I also note this parallels Romans 7:12, where the "spiritual" nature of the law is explicated as its being "holy, righteous, and good." Fee makes the same connection. For him, the law is "of the Spirit" with the human problem sin and the flesh (*GEP*, 512). Similarly, Dunn writes, "the law is 'spiritual' in the sense that it derives from the Spirit (given to men by inspiration/revelation) and was intended to address men at the level of the Spirit." James D. G. Dunn, *Jesus and the Spirit: A Study of the Religious and Charismatic Experience of Jesus and the First Christians as Reflected in the New Testament* (Grand Rapids: Eerdmans 1997), 208.

about and then, when the Spirit's will is perceived, to live in step with the Spirit.

CRUCIFORMITY, CHRISTOFORMITY, RESURRECTIFORMITY

A second reason for the book is a love of the notion of cruciformity and the desire to emphasize the Spirit's role in bringing it to pass in a person's life. "Cruciformity" may be defined as "conformity to the crucified Christ."[3] Much has been written on the concept, particularly in the writings of Michael Gorman. His focus is appropriate as Paul explicitly refers to believers being conformed to the image of God's Son (Rom. 8:29). Moreover, the notion of believers living lives conformed to the sacrifice of Jesus on the cross is "a concept commonly believed to be central to Paul's theology and ethics."[4] Furthermore, Christ and the cross are central to Paul's theology. In my writings, particularly my EEC *Philippians* commentary, I describe this as conforming to the "pattern of Christ."[5]

Gorman in *CPNSC* devotes chapter 4 to the Spirit and cruciformity.[6] Gorman acknowledges the implicit connection between the Spirit and Christ's death and people living in the present with Christ's "self-giving, self-sacrificing love" that is found in Paul's letters.[7] He sees this in Galatians, 1 Corinthians, 2 Corinthians, and Romans 5–8. He correctly identifies Paul as an uncharismatic charismatic who featured spiritual gifts and experiences, tongues, signs and wonders, and revelatory experiences.[8] Nevertheless, as an uncharismatic, he was not interested in rhetoric or an impressive presence.[9] He also says, "Understanding Paul's experience of the Spirit enables us to comprehend this paradox. The distinctive feature of Paul's experience of the Spirit, and his resulting understanding of the essence of this Spirit, is the paradoxical symbiosis (union) of power and weakness, of power and cruciformity."[10] Individual Christians and communities of the Spirit experience this tension. For him, "The charismatic criterion of cruciformity—especially the need for edifying love—is grounded in part in Paul's conviction that the Spirit dwells in our midst, not just in our hearts. The Spirit of cruciformity is the Spirit of Christian community, and it is by means of cruciformity that the Spirit produces unity."[11] He agrees that for Paul, "God is cruciform, that the crucified Jesus is the exalted Lord, and that the Spirit of God and of Christ is the Spirit of cruciformity."[12]

---

3. Michael J. Gorman, *Cruciformity: Paul's Narrative Spirituality of the Cross* (Grand Rapids: Eerdmans, 2001), 4 (hereafter *CPNSC*).
4. Gorman, *CPNSC*, 4.
5. Mark J. Keown, *Philippians*, EEC (Bellingham, WA: Lexham, 2017), 1:1.
6. Gorman, *CPNSC*, 50–63.
7. Gorman, *CPNSC*, 58.
8. I would put myself in this category.
9. Gorman, *CPNSC*, 50–52.
10. Gorman, *CPNSC*, 51.
11. Gorman, *CPNSC*, 61.
12. Gorman, *CPNSC*, 62.

Gorman also acknowledges, "the presence and power of the Spirit is a fundamental dimension of the experience of Paul and his communities." Steeped in the Hebrew Scriptures, Paul assumes the presence of the Spirit in the Christian life from start to finish.[13] He acknowledges the role of the Spirit in his own ministry and that of others. As it was for Israel as God led them, Christian life was "walking . . . according to the Spirit" and being "led by the Spirit." "Life" is generated in believers by the Spirit as they receive the Spirit as a down payment for their future resurrection. The Spirit generates fruit and especially love in believers, who are to live according to the Spirit and not the flesh. The Spirit assures believers of their identity as God's children. The Spirit helps believers in their weaknesses. The reality of life in the Spirit, however, includes death and suffering. Yet, the Spirit also generates hope. Indeed, as Gorman says, "The Spirit is the Spirit of cruciformity. The Spirit marks and 'seals' people as God's own children, God's own 'possession'" (2 Cor. 1:22, 5:5), but only inasmuch as they are marked by conformity to the death of Christ.

However, cruciformity as a descriptor of Paul's understanding of the transformation of believers is not without weaknesses. In particular, "cruciformity" speaks of conformity to *an event* and a moment in Christ's life rather than the whole life and being of the person of Jesus. It also fails to account for the resurrection, without which the cross would be null and void. Another weakness is that the term gives no hint at the crucial role of the Spirit in this process (although Gorman does include this in his analysis).

As such, another recent way of describing conformity to Christ is "Christoformity," a term used by Scot McKnight, who admits to standing on Gorman's shoulders as he uses the term. For McKnight, "Christoformity" means being "conformed to Christ." McKnight writes with pastors as his intended audience: "Pastors are nurturers of Christoformity in this sense: we are formed by his life, by his death, and by his resurrection and ascension."[14] McKnight's term has advantages, as it speaks of believers being conformed to the whole person of Christ, including the cross, rather than an event.

McKnight's fuller definition of Christoformity includes the Spirit:

We are not only to believe the gospel but also to embody it. To use the Greek and Latin terms no one uses, *bio*-formity, *cruci*-formity, and *anastasi*-formity. Add those together and you get Christoformity, but the way we become Christoform is through participation in Christ: through baptism, through faith, through indwelling and being indwelled by Christ, *through the Spirit*, through being clothed with Christ, through

---

13.   Gorman, *CPNSC*, 52–53.
14.   Scot McKnight, *Pastor Paul: Nurturing a Culture of Christoformity in the Church*, TECC (Grand Rapids: Brazos, 2019), 6 (hereafter *PPNCCC*).

fellowship, through transformation, and through sharing all the events in Christ's life.[15]

Again, he writes,

> Rather, Christ is present in our world at its core through the Spirit, and the grace of God operating through the Spirit is the only path of Christoformity. Speaking theologically, Christocentricity is only possible through Pneumacentricity: we can only find Christ at the center if we are open to the Spirit taking us there. . . . So, let's make this clear: Christoformity in us and in others only happens through the Spirit.[16]

However, as with cruciformity, the label does not indicate that the Spirit (of Christ) does this work in God's people.

Another term utilized in this area is "Resurrectiformity"[17] (or *anastasiformity*, above), which focuses on a believer being conformed to the life of the resurrected Christ. This idea helps highlight Paul's eschatological understanding of ethics. In the eschaton, believers will be free from sin and able to live fully in their "spiritual bodies." As they have the foretaste of this eternity in their beings—the Spirit—and as they yield to him, they live the life God wills for them in the present and which will be completed in the new creation. Such a life is that of the eschaton for which they are destined in this ruptured world. In particular, they must live by the greatest of these that continues from this age into the next: love (1 Cor. 13:13).

While deSilva does not use these -formity terms in his discussion of the heart of Paul's gospel, he uses "transformation" in a parallel sense. He challenges the standard Romans Road understanding of Paul's theology, arguing transformation lies at the heart of Paul's gospel.[18] DeSilva sees the Spirit as central to this work of God in believers and the world. "God offers you the means to become reconciled with him and to become a new person who will want and love and do what is pleasing to him *because the Spirit of his Son will live in you* and *change* you."[19] He goes on,

> The good news is nothing less than that God has set in motion the forces and factors that can transform all of creation and make it new, good, and right once again—including *us*. This transformation remains from begin-

---

15. McKnight, *PPNCCC*, 4 (emphasis original).

16. McKnight, *PPNCCC*, 193.

17. Michael J. Gorman, "Cruciform or Resurrectiform? Paul's Paradoxical Practice of Participation in Christ," *Ex Auditu: An International Journal for the Theological Interpretation of Scripture* 33 (2017): 60–83; Markus Nikkanen, "Response to Gorman," *Ex Auditu: An International Journal for the Theological Interpretation of Scripture* 33 (2017): 84–91.

18. David A. deSilva, *Transformation: The Heart of Paul's Gospel* (Bellingham, WA: Lexham, 2014), 1–5.

19. DeSilva, *Transformation*, 2, emphasis mine.

ning to end a work of God's favor or "grace," for it begins at God's initiative; it transpires through the working and the power of the gift that God has given, namely the Spirit; and it is brought to completion because of God's commitment and faithfulness.[20]

In sum, "cruciformity" as a term does draw a person's focus to the zenith of Jesus's sacrifice for humankind and a desire to emulate his example *to the point of death*. "Christoformity" is helpful because it points us in the direction of the whole life of Christ as something to be emulated, not just its final moments. "Resurrectiformity" is also helpful in that it highlights that the present Christian life is the life of love experienced in the eschaton and lived in the present. "Transformation" is another helpful way to delineate the change God is bringing in individuals, the church, and the world. However, while advocates of these various ideas acknowledge the Spirit's role, what is not fully developed and explored is that this change is the work of the Spirit on behalf of the Father and the Son.

If these things Gorman, McKnight, and deSilva have said are true, and indeed they are, an entire monograph devoted to the role of the Spirit in cruciformity/Christoformity is appropriate. My broader perspective includes not only the death of Jesus but participation in his mission, power, and the exercise of spiritual gifts.[21] For Paul, there are not two sides to the Spirit's work, there is one—Christoformity—forming us to be like Jesus. Yes, there is a paradox, but we must not read Paul in a binary way—death and resurrection are fused. Gorman's analysis will be helpful as I look at Paul's Spiritual[22] Christoform understanding.

GOD'S EMPOWERING PRESENCE

A third factor in writing this book is the monumental work on the Spirit by Gordon Fee. Fee wrote his outstanding work *God's Empowering Presence (GEP)* in 1994. Most work on cruciformity in Paul has been written after the beginning of the millennium, and so cruciformity does not receive much attention in Fee's work. As such, another look at Paul's doctrine of the Spirit in light of ideas such as cruciformity, Christoformity, and resurrectiformity is justified. Indeed, I begin with Fee's premise, "Life in the present is empowered by the God who dwells among us and in us. As the personal presence of God, the Spirit is not merely some 'force' or 'influence.' The living God is a God of power; and by the Spirit the power of the living God is present with and for us."[23]

---

20.   DeSilva, *Transformation*, 2. See also the section "God Makes This Transformation Possible through the Gift of the Holy Spirit" (pp. 58–63).

21.   To give credit where due, Gorman presents a fuller picture in *Becoming the Gospel: Paul, Participation, and Mission*, GOCS (Grand Rapids: Eerdmans, 2015); (hereafter *BGPPM*).

22.   Or as he sometimes puts it, "Spirit-ual." Gorman, *BGPPM*, 31. I was tempted to use this throughout the book; however, as with Gorman, it is implied when talking about Christian spirituality.

23.   Fee, *GEP*, 8. He astutely adds, "Person, presence, power: these three realities are what the Holy Spirit meant for the apostle Paul."

THE SPIRIT AS GOD'S POWER

A fourth motivation for writing such a book is methodological. Most discussions of the Spirit, including Fee's, focus on references to πνεῦμα that apply to God in Paul's writings.[24] Such a narrow linguistic approach directs us to texts where the Holy Spirit is definitely in view (where the references are of God's Spirit). However, the approach is too simple and produces a reductionist picture of Paul's pneumatology. I say this because Paul uses the language of (what we call) the Godhead interchangeably. When talking about the work of God in the life of a believer, Paul sometimes uses πνεῦμα. Elsewhere, he uses other theological language (God), christological language,[25] and, at times, general language. I claim this because it is *by the Spirit* that God acts on the lives of those in Christ. God and his Son are present in the lives of believers and his people. Hence, it is inadequate merely to focus on πνεῦμα language, even if it must be central to such a study as this.

I argued such an approach in my commentary on Philippians. Paul does mention the present work of the Spirit in the letter four times.[26] However, in the letter, Paul has much more to say about the power of God working in believers using other language.[27] Sometimes Paul stresses *God's* power and action in the believer, as in Philippians 2:13.[28] The present work of Christ is stated at other times.[29] Finally, he uses ambiguous language that can apply to any member of the Trinity (or two or all).[30] Perhaps the best example is Philippians 1:6, where "he" who began the good work in or through the Philippians is usually recognized as God. However, it can be Christ, the Spirit, or, better, God through Christ by the work of the Spirit given at their conversion (or the beginning of the church or its mission). The process of God's completion of what he began can be God, Christ, the Spirit, or all three members of the Godhead working in harmony in the believer.[31]

---

24. I commend to readers the section "The Holy Spirit or a Holy Spirit" in Fee, *GEP*, 15–24, where Fee discusses Paul's uses of πνεῦμα in different cases, rightly concluding, "The evidence confirms that Paul knows no such thing as 'a spirit' or 'a holy spirit' when using πνεῦμα to refer to divine activity. He only and always means the Spirit of the living God, the Holy Spirit himself" (p. 24). However, there are many texts Fee does not consider that I believe fill out Paul's pneumatology.

25. Jesus, Christ, Lord, Savior, and some others.

26. Phil. 1:19, 27; 2:1; 3:3.

27. Fee, *GEP*, 82: "For Paul the terms 'Spirit' and 'power' are at times nearly interchangeable; to speak of the Spirit is also to speak of power."

28. See also Phil. 1:2; 2:27; 3:8, 9, 12, 14, 15; 4:1, 2, 4, 5, 7, 9, 10, 19, 21, 23.

29. Not always using "Christ," but a range of other descriptors including "Jesus," "Christ," "Lord," "Son," and "Savior" (and combinations thereof), in particular. See Phil. 1:2, 8, 11, 14, 21; 2:1, 5, 19, 29, 30; 3:1.

30. See Keown, *Philippians*, 1:135–37, and in discussions on the texts referenced throughout the commentary.

31. Gorman notes that Paul's ease of "speaking of the Spirit as the Spirit of God as well as the Spirit of Christ demonstrates how closely he associates the Spirit with both God the Father and the Lord Jesus, and how difficult it is for him to distinguish them and their present activities from one another." Gorman, *CPNSC*, 71.

Befitting a book focused on the Spirit, discussing explicit references will play a prominent role. However, careful attention will be paid to other language used of the present work of God in the believer and church. While this will complicate the work required, it will provide a fuller perspective on God's transforming work by the Spirit in the life of his people.

LIVING BY THE SPIRIT

The fifth reason to write this book is my personal quest to understand more fully how to live by the Spirit so that I may live in a way that pleases the God who saved me and called me to his service. I remember vividly working over Philippians 2:1–11 and 3:10, 20–21 and weeping as I grasped more of what Paul was saying in these majestic passages. Recognizing that Paul was an apostle of Christ and his Spirit, I hope readers are helped in their journey toward being the people God created them to be.

PNEUMAFORMITY

The final reason for this work is a conviction that the Spirit does the work of conforming us to Christ in the present age. While Paul urges believers to be conformed to the image of Christ and the pattern of his life (esp. Phil. 2:5), and while the work of God is to transform people into the image of God's Son (esp. Rom. 8:29), the agency for this in the present age is the Holy Spirit. I am not suggesting that the Spirit does this work independently of the Father and Son. The Father and Son do this work through the agency of the Spirit. For Paul, it is *in and by the Holy Spirit* that saving faith is born, that God and his Son reside in believers, and that believers participate in the anointing of Christ and are sealed for eternal life (2 Cor. 1:21; Eph. 1:13–14). It is in and by the Spirit that the Father transforms people through the Son into people that are more and more like Jesus in their being and Spirit-led in their praxis.[32] This work will focus on the role of the Spirit in bringing believers into conformity with God's Son. It will consider the Spirit's role in the transformation to live in the pattern of Christ. In a sense, then, it is a study of spirituality.[33]

With all this in mind, in this book, standing on the shoulders of Gorman, McKnight, and others, and engaging particularly with the work of Gordon Fee on the Spirit, I am using the term *pneumaformity* to define the process of God's transformation of his people. The term draws on the Greek word for "Spirit," πνεῦμα, and blends it with "form" language.[34] Pneumaformity is not an idea that opposes cruciformity, Christoformity, or resurrectiformity. Still, it comes at it from another angle, focusing on the Spirit's role in transforming

---

32. E.g., Rom. 1:4; 8:9; 15:19; 2 Cor. 3:3; Gal. 3:5.
33. Gorman defines it crisply: "*Spirit*uality can also be described, of course, as life in the Spirit." Gorman, *CPNSC*, 3.
34. Originally, "form" finds its origins in Latin language *forma*, meaning a "fashion or form," a "pattern or example." J. M. Harden, *Dictionary of the Vulgate New Testament* (London: SPCK, 1921), 49.

a person who places their faith in Jesus Christ as Lord and Savior. Indeed, for Paul, a person who does not have a saving faith in God does not have the Spirit residing in them in that unique way only a believer can know. When a person believes in Jesus with a faith that God deems genuine, through his Son, God pours the Spirit into that person's inner being. By the Spirit, God, Father and Son, dwells in the believer. The Spirit, in that instant, begins the work of transforming the believer, conforming them to the image of Jesus Christ, God's Son.

In my view, a monograph entirely devoted to this dimension of the process of transformation a believer undergoes is not only justified but essential, as in this age, it is by the Spirit that God and Jesus encounter a believer. Jewish writings anticipated the coming of the Spirit—"the promised Holy Spirit." Jesus lived from somewhere between 6 and 4 BC until AD 30 or 33.[35] The Gospel writers agree that his ministry was preceded by God pouring his Spirit into Jesus.[36] Especially in Luke's Gospel, the whole life of Jesus, including his being, character, and ministry, is empowered by the Spirit. While Matthew and Mark's gospels only hint at the reception of the Spirit by believers in the period after Jesus's resurrection, Luke is clear: believers are to wait in Jerusalem, and they will receive the gift of the Spirit who will clothe them with power from on high (Luke 24:49; Acts 1:8). John summarizes the receipt of the Spirit in association with the commissioning of the disciples by Jesus breathing on them (John 20:21). The book of Acts traces the early days of God's people, empowered by the Spirit for witness to the world.

One of the overarching emphases of today's studies is ethics. This ethical focus makes sense to a degree, for a core aspect of Paul's understanding of the work of the Spirit is ethical (esp. Gal. 5:14–6:10). Yet, the work of the Spirit is far broader than mere ethics, whether social or behavioral, as by the Spirit and through the Son, God calls people into fellowship with him (e.g., 1 Cor. 1:9). It is by the Spirit that God through Christ transforms people to be those devoted to worship and the service of God and Christ.[37] The Spirit summons them into deep κοινωνία with God's holy people (a temple of the Spirit).[38] The Spirit also engifts them and impels them into mission to the world.[39] This study will seek to argue that the πνεῦμα-formation of a person involves an initial relationship with God and relationships with one another in God's ἐκκλησία, with those who do not believe in God and his Son, and with the creation itself.

---

35. See for a discussion, H. W. Hoehner and J. K. Brown, "Chronology," *DJG2*, 134–38.
36. Matt. 3:16; Mark 1:10; Luke 3:22; John 1:32–33.
37. Rom. 6:18, 22; 12:1; Phil. 1:1; 3:3.
38. 1 Cor. 3:16; 6:19; 12:5; Eph. 2:19–22.
39. E.g., Rom. 15:16; 1 Cor. 4:1; 2 Cor. 4:5; 6:4.

THIS BOOK'S APPROACH

To achieve this, I will conduct a thematic study in which each Pauline letter is considered. This study will not be as exhaustive as Fee's work on the Spirit but will cover the same material from the perspective of God's work in formation. Obviously, it is essential to engage with the specific uses of πνεῦμα in Paul's letters.[40] I will leave aside references that do not refer to God's Spirit.[41]

As mentioned, aside from explicit πνεῦμα texts, other texts that specifically refer to the agency of God,[42] Christ,[43] or ambiguous agency are considered with equal interest.[44] I do so because, as I have observed, Paul uses the language of the Godhead fluidly and interchangeably while retaining the individuality of the three persons of the Godhead. As such, while Paul does

---

40. Explicit references to God's Spirit include Rom. 1:4, 9; 2:29; 3:25; 4:24; 5:5; 7:6; 8:2–17, 23, 26–27; 9:1; 12:11; 14:7; 15:13, 16, 19, 30; 1 Cor. 1:8–9; 2:4, 10–16; 3:16; 4:21; 6:11, 19; 7:40; 8:3; 12:3–4, 7–11, 13; 14:2, 12; 2 Cor. 1:22; 3:3, 6, 8, 17–18; 5:5; 6:6; 13:14; Gal. 3:2, 3, 5, 14; 4:6, 29; 5:5, 16–18, 22–25; 6:1, 8; Eph. 1:13, 17; 2:18, 22; 3:5, 16; 4:3–4, 30; 5:18; 6:17–18; Phil. 1:19, 27; 2:1; 3:3. Col. 1:8; 1 Thess. 1:5–6; 4:8; 5:19; 2 Thess. 2:13; 1 Tim. 3:16; 4:1; 2 Tim. 1:7, 14; Titus 3:5.

41. These include the spirit of a person implanted by God (and so in a sense, the Spirit of God), giving them life, and the point of connection between God's Spirit and that of believers (Rom. 1:9; 8:16; 1 Cor. 2:11; 5:4; 7:34; 14:14–16; 16:18; 2 Cor. 2:13; 7:1, 13; Gal. 6:18; Phil. 4:23; 1 Thess. 5:23; 2 Tim. 4:22; Philem. 25); a person's spirit as metonymy for the whole person represented by their inner spirit now in union with God's Spirit (1 Cor. 5:5); a person's spirit joined to the Holy Spirit partaking in one spiritual entity (1 Cor. 6:17); a spirit, God's or otherwise, influencing prophets who speak in church (1 Cor. 14:32; cf. 2 Thess. 2:2); a false spirit (generating slavery [Rom. 8:15], causing stupor [Rom. 11:8], of the world [1 Cor. 2:12], at work in unbelievers [Eph. 2:2], who bring influence and false messages [1 Cor. 12:10; 2 Thess. 2:2; 1 Tim. 4:8 (2nd)], and false gospels [2 Cor. 11:4]). Contentious passages I take as God's Spirit include Rom. 12:11; 1 Cor. 4:21; 5:3 (Paul cannot be with the Corinthians in his spirit; across time and space demands this is the Spirit, also Col. 2:5); 15:45 (not saying Jesus is a Spirit, but presently gives life through his Spirit, cf. 2 Cor. 3:6); 2 Cor. 4:13; 12:18; Gal. 6:1; Eph. 1:17; 4:23; Phil. 1:27; 2 Thess. 2:8; 2 Tim. 1:7. I agree with Fee's categorization other than 2 Thess. 2:2 (not the Spirit but an evil spirit, or a double entendre); 2:8 (Christ's breath as his Spirit).

42. Such texts worthy of consideration as indicators of God's work by the Spirit include Rom. 1:1–2, 4, 7, 16, 19–21, 24, 26, 28; 2:4–11; 3:29–30; 4:17, 21, 24; 8:20, 28–30, 37–39; 9:18, 22–24; 10:9, 13, 20–21; 11:18, 21, 23, 25–26; 12:1–8; 14:4; 15:5, 13, 15–26, 33; 16:25–27; 1 Cor. 1:1–4, 8–9, 18, 21, 24, 27–28; 2:5; 3:6–7, 17; 4:9; 7:7, 15, 17–24; 10:5, 13; 12:6, 18, 24, 28; 14:25; 15:10, 15, 27–28, 38; 2 Cor. 1:1–4, 9–10, 12, 21; 2:14, 17; 3:5, 7; 4:6–7, 14; 5:18–21; 6:1–2, 7; 7:6; 8:1, 16; 9:8–11, 14; 10:13; 12:9; 13:4, 11, 14; Gal. 1:1, 3, 6, 15, 20; 2:6, 8; 3:18; 4:7; 5:8; Eph. 1:1–11, 17–22; 2:4–10, 19–22; 3:16–21; 4:6–11, 24; Phil. 1:2, 6; 2:13, 27; 3:14–15, 21; 4:7, 19; Col. 1:1–2, 16–17, 19, 27; 2:12, 13, 19; 3:15; 4:3; 1 Thess. 1:1, 4, 10; 2:2, 4–5, 10, 12; 3:11–12; 4:7, 9; 5:23–24; 2 Thess. 1:1–2, 12; 2:11, 13–14, 16; 3:3, 5; 1 Tim. 1:1–2, 12; 6:17; 2 Tim. 1:1–2, 6, 8–9, 18; 2:9, 25; Titus 1:4; Philem. 3.

43. Texts that reference Christ's active role potentially indicating the Spirit include Rom. 1:7, 8; 5:1–2, 11, 17, 21; 7:25; 8:10, 37; 10:12, 17; 11:25–26; 15:18; 16:20; 1 Cor. 1:3–5, 17, 24, 30; 2:16; 3:5; 8:6; 12:5; 15:25; 16:7, 23; 2 Cor. 1:2, 5, 10, 20; 2:10, 12, 14–15, 17; 3:3, 4, 14, 16–18; 4:4, 10–11, 14; 5:17–21; 6:1; 8:9; 10:1, 5, 8; 11:10; 12:1, 9, 19; 13:3, 5, 10, 14; Gal. 1:1, 6; 2:8, 20; 3:26–28; 4:19; 5:6; 6:18; Eph. 1:2–14; 2:5–7, 10, 13–16, 18, 20–22; 3:17, 19; 4:7–16, 17; 5:26–27, 29; 6:8, 10, 23–24; Phil. 1:2, 6, 8, 11, 21; 2:1; 3:10, 21; 4:5, 19, 23; Col. 1:17, 20, 22; 2:6–7, 10; 3:4, 11, 15–17; 4:12–13; 1 Thess. 3:11–13; 4:2; 5:9, 28; 2 Thess. 1:2, 12; 2:16; 3:1, 3–5, 16, 18; 1 Tim. 1:2, 12–14; 2 Tim. 1:2, 12, 16, 18; 2:1; 3:11; 4:17, 22; Titus 1:4; 3:5; Philem. 3, 25.

44. Texts that are nonspecific but potentially indicate the role of the Spirit include Rom. 1:27; 2:4; Gal. 2:9; Phil. 4:13; Col. 1:9; 2 Thess. 2:6–7; 2 Tim. 1:12.

not use the language of the Spirit in these texts, these implicitly speak of the Spirit's role to an equal degree as those with specific πνεῦμα language. To fully understand the Spirit's role in the believer's life, one must explore all passages that speak of God and Christ's present work in the believer and world. Such a study is required because Paul understands that it is by the Spirit, through Christ, that God is transforming people, communities, and the cosmos.

Where specific language is concerned, aside from πνεῦμα, I will consider other terms from the word group. Of particular interest is πνευματικός, which, as Dunn notes, means "spiritual" and is used of people (e.g., 1 Cor. 2:13, 15; 14:37; Gal. 6:1), in contrast to "fleshly" (1 Cor. 9:11), and overlaps with χάρισμα.[45] Grace language is also important, especially χάρισμα, which speaks of a manifestation of "divine grace" broadly and more specifically of spiritual gifts.[46] Like Fee, I will take note of points in Paul's letters where "power" language is used; however, my study extends beyond merely that to any text in which divine influence is implied, regardless of which member of the Trinity is most explicit.

Like Fee, I will work with the thirteen-letter Pauline corpus. However, the study will not track through each book (as with Fee) but will arrange the material in the following thematic manner.[47]

In chapter 1, I will consider the promise of the Spirit in the OT. I will explore references to רוּחַ from the MT and πνεῦμα in the LXX and draw together a picture of the possibilities concerning the Spirit in Israel's writings. My attention focuses on passages that I consider to speak of the Spirit, even if many are disputed. I do this to create a backdrop for Paul's understanding of God's action in believers.

Chapter 2 will explore the Spirit's participation in the conversion of a person and that person's inclusion in the life of God in Christ.[48] Of real interest here are those texts in Paul that speak of the work of the Spirit in drawing

---

45. See Dunn, *Jesus and the Spirit*, 208–9, for more detail. Other terms include the associated adverb πνευματικῶς, "Spirit-ually" of Spirit-ual discernment unbelievers cannot attain (1 Cor. 2:14). The other important term is θεόπνευστος, "God-breathed, God-Spirited," that will be discussed in regard to the Scriptures in 2 Timothy 3:16. See further, chapter 3, "The Spirit Who Sanctifies." Martin, among others, takes it as "spiritual gifts." See Ralph P. Martin, *The Spirit and the Congregation: Studies in 1 Corinthians 12–15* (Grand Rapids: Eerdmans, 1984), 8. But as Fee points out, this is too narrow. Fee, *GEP*, 152.

46. See Dunn, *Jesus and the Spirit*, 207–8, for more detail. He goes on to add, "*Charisma is an event, an action enabled by divine power; charisma is divine energy accomplishing a particular result (in word and deed) through the individual*" (p. 209, emphasis original; see also pp. 254–58).

47. As Fee and I see eye to eye on so many things, such a study would not be that different. However, by arranging the book thematically, I can apply exegetical insights across Paul's letters while indicating where I agree and disagree with Fee.

48. I use the term *conversion* recognizing that it can be argued to be an extrabiblical notion. I use it to describe that moment when an unbeliever sincerely believes in Christ, or where someone comes to realize that they believe in Christ.

people to God, the proclamation and hearing of the gospel, the call and election of people by God the Father, their inclusion in Christ the Son, and their receipt of the Spirit.

Chapter 3 continues the study of the Spirit's involvement in conversion. Paul writes that the immediate impact of the Spirit is to liberate, justify, impart love and life, provide strength to proclaim, seal and guarantee salvation, and so on.

I will focus in chapter 4 on the Spirit's role in integrating people into God's people (his family), Christ, and his temple. While I hold that conversion is necessarily individual in Paul's theology, at conversion, a person is integrated into a people in and by the Spirit. I will discuss how Paul speaks of this and the Spirit's function in this regard. Consequently, I will discuss how Paul speaks of the collective aspects of the Spirit's work at and after individual conversion.

Chapter 5 focuses on the Spirit's role in forming people devoted to God in Christ. Here, I will look at texts in Paul's letters that speak of worshipping God and the Spirit's explicit and implicit role in forming believers for whom worship of God is central to their understanding of their faith. To control the extent of this and stop overlap with later sections, the vertical aspects of the Spirit's role will be central (worship and service *of* God and Son).

In a sense, chapter 6 is the heart of the book. In it, I give attention to the role of the Spirit in the formation of the Christian person with a Christlike character. I will take note of passages that focus on shaping believers and forming them into the people God created them to be.

Chapter 7 builds on chapter 6, considering the more traditional aspects of ethics and virtue in terms of Christian formation. These form the ethical basis by which a believer is to live. The paraenetic passages of Paul are important for this chapter and especially the role of the Spirit in conforming people to the ethics of Christ. However, the whole Pauline corpus will be explored to see various aspects of character formation by God in Christ through the work of the Spirit.

Chapter 8 discusses the Spirit and suffering. I will note that Paul accepts that suffering is undeniably an unavoidable aspect of being human. Christians are not suddenly immune from this suffering when they convert. They continue to live in a creation ravaged by sin, subject to frustration and yearning for release. I will then explore the somewhat unique idea that the Spirit increases human suffering as the person is swept up into Christ's being and mission and summoned to the life of the Spirit. Then the way in which the Spirit supports believers in suffering will be considered.

Chapter 9 will focus on the Spirit and participation in church life. The main interest will be spiritual gifts and their expression within the community. Building on chapter 9, in chapter 10, I will consider the language of the Godhead and missional engagement. The chapter will not be purely interested in evangelistic mission but will have an equal interest in social justice, transformation, and ecology (as the texts indicate).

In chapter 11, I will consider the Spirit's place in the final eschatological transformation of the believer. Here, I will explore those passages that look to the future completion of the individuals' transformation concerning the Spirit's function.

Finally, in chapter 12, I will land the study with some thoughts concerning ongoing life in the Spirit.

The structure of the project will follow the above explanation and is as follows:

1. The Promised Holy Spirit

2. The Spirit Leads to Conversion

3. The Immediate Impact of the Spirit

4. The Spirit and the Christian Community

5. The Spirit and Worship

6. The Spirit and Christoformity

7. The Spirit, Ethics, and Virtue

8. The Spirit and Suffering

9. The Spirit and Participation in Church Life

10. The Spirit and Mission

11. The Spirit and the Eschaton

12. Living by the Spirit

CHAPTER 1

THE PROMISED HOLY SPIRIT

A s a Pharisaic Jew, Paul entered Christian life as a monotheist believing in one God, something he no doubt said daily in the Shema (Deut. 6:4–5). However, like others in Second Temple Judaism, he longed for the coming of the Spirit of God. Thus, he refers to "the promised Spirit" (Gal. 3:14) and "the promised Holy Spirit" (Eph. 1:13). As Fee says, for Paul, "the Spirit is the fulfillment of the promises found in Jeremiah and Ezekiel."[1]

What did the idea of the promised Holy Spirit mean to Paul? Paul does not cite an OT text with the term πνεῦμα.[2] However, there are indications of his drawing together OT ideas that he understood to allude to the Spirit. Although there is no explicit connection between circumcision of the heart and the Spirit in the OT,[3] the link of the Spirit and renewed and softened hearts in Ezekiel is suggestive of the role of the Spirit in circumcision (Ezek. 11:19; 18:31; 36:26–27). It is no surprise that Paul links the ideas together (Rom. 2:29; Phil. 3:3; cf. 2 Cor. 3:3). It is unclear whether he made this connection before his conversion. However, it is an important set of connections, as it speaks to the expectation of pneumaformity in the OT. God would give his people a new heart, one circumcised by the Spirit.

The motif of the church as the "temple of the Holy Spirit" in Paul is suggestive of the hopes of God's glory filling the tabernacle, the Jerusalem temple at its Solomonic consecration, and the future hope found in Ezekiel and Haggai (1 Cor. 3:16; 6:19; Eph. 2:19–22).[4] It is certain that, like other Second Temple

---

1. Fee, *GEP*, 6. I would add that the Spirit's coming is a fulfillment of the expectations in other OT prophetic documents, e.g., Joel. See also *GEP*, 395, 670.
2. Ephesians 3:5 can be read as Paul believing that God revealed the gospel to the OT prophets by the Spirit. However, as in Ephesians 2:20 and 4:11, this speaks of early church prophets, not the OT. See the discussion in Ernest Best, *A Critical and Exegetical Commentary on Ephesians*, ICC (Edinburgh: T&T Clark, 1998), 282. Fee, *GEP*, 692 does not directly comment but implies he agrees with this perspective.
3. Deut. 10:16; 30:6; Jer. 4:4; 9:25.
4. Exod. 40:34–35; Lev. 9:23; Num. 14:10; 16:19, 42; 20:6; 1 Kings 8:1; 2 Chron. 7:1, 3; 2 Chron. 5:14; 7:2; Ps. 26:8; Ezek. 43:4, 5; 44:4; Hag. 2:7, 9.

Jews, Paul yearned for God's glory to fill the temple. This promise is likely an aspect of the "promised Holy Spirit."

The sentence τὴν ἐπαγγελίαν τοῦ πνεύματος λάβωμεν διὰ τῆς πίστεως in Galatians 3:14 is nestled in Paul's defense of "justification by faith" in light of the promises and blessings associated with Abraham and the inability of people to fulfill the law.[5] Here, Paul draws together a range of OT texts associated with Abraham, covenant, blessing, promise, faith, law, human failure, the "bondage to the law," Christ (the seed of Abraham), descent from Abraham, baptism,[6] and the promise of the Spirit.[7] As will be discussed in this chapter, the coming of a Messiah imbued with the Spirit and the outpouring of the Spirit at the culmination of this age were aspects of Jewish expectation. Perhaps Paul now sees these things occurring in Jesus, the crucified Messiah, which he decidedly did not anticipate.

The association of the Spirit and wisdom in Ephesians 1:17 calls to mind Isaiah 11:2, where the Spirit rests on the stump of Jesse, a messianic expectation. Ephesians stresses the "in-Christ" status of believers, and so Paul's hope of a Spirit-anointed, wise Messiah has metamorphosed into one for a Spirit-anointed, wise people.[8]

All in all, there is very little explicit OT connection in Paul's pneumatology. We are left to consider what else he expected in the phrase "the promised [Holy] Spirit." As such, here I will consider relevant uses of πνεῦμα in the LXX; Pseudepigrapha, in the works of Josephus, and Philo; the use of רוּחַ in

---

5.   On Galatians 3:13–14, see Fee, *GEP*, 390–95. He argues that τὴν ἐπαγγελίαν τοῦ πνεύματος is not "appositional in the strict sense, meaning either 'the promise, that is, the Spirit' or 'the promised Holy Spirit'" (p. 394). Instead, he recognizes that for Paul, "the Spirit is the way the promised blessing made to Abraham has been realized in all of Abraham's true children, who are 'by faith in Christ Jesus'" (pp. 394–95). Still, Fee accepts that has in view "'the promised Holy Spirit' of the prophetic tradition" (p. 395).

6.   Contra Fee, who takes it as an ambiguous reference to water baptism (*GEP*, 861), I take baptism here to be Spirit-baptism. See Mark J. Keown, *Galatians: A Commentary for Students* (Auckland: Morphe, 2020), 499–503 (also see further chapter 2).

7.   Especially the blessing to the nations in Genesis 12:3 (Gal. 3:8); the cursedness on humankind for failing to live the law in Deuteronomy 27:26 (Gal. 3:10); the need to live by faith in Habakkuk 2:4 (Gal. 3:11; cf. Rom. 1:17); Christ's taking of the curse in Deuteronomy 21:23 (Gal. 3:13); the singular offspring of Abraham through Genesis (Gen. 12:7; 13:15; 15:5, 13, 18; 16:10; 17:7–9; 21:12, see Gal. 3:6, 19) that becomes multiple in Christ (Gal. 3:29); the coming of the law (Gal. 3:17; cf. Exod. 19:1–20:19); the Abrahamic and Sinaitic covenants (Gal. 3:17–18); the law (Gal. 3:2, 5, 10–13, 17–19, 21, 23–24); faith (Gal. 3:2, 5–9, 11, 12, 14, 22–26); and christological language (Gal. 3:1, 13–14, 16, 22, 24, 26–28).

8.   McKnight avers, "One doesn't acquire wisdom simply by attending a seminary or by reading a great book about wisdom; wisdom is more than knowledge and intellectual growth. Pastoral wisdom in Paul is Spirit prompted, for in his list of Spirit-prompted gifts, we read, 'To one is given *through the Spirit* the utterance of wisdom, and to another the utterance of knowledge *according to the same Spirit*' (1 Cor. 12:8). Paul's understanding of wisdom is thus Pneumacentric too. Wisdom is a gift of God for which Paul is praying for his churches (Eph. 1:8–9, 17; Col. 1:9, 28)." McKnight, *PPNCCC*, 178–79 (emphasis original).

the writings of Qumran; and the Spirit in the Mishnah as a representative of rabbinic writings (albeit recognizing that they were written later and only give us tentative insights into the Spirit at the time of Paul).

Current scholarship debates which of these references refer to God's Spirit. However, this is not relevant to Paul's understanding but is a contemporary matter of debate. Consequently, rather than complicate this study with such considerations, I will consider those uses of πνεῦμα where God is the agent or implied.[9] Although there are many exceptions (see Appendix 1), πνεῦμα in the LXX usually translates רוּח. The interest of this discussion is where πνεῦμα is used for God's Spirit (for other uses, see Appendix 2). This examination is supplemented in places with consideration of the use of "glory"[10] language and other ways in which the Jewish writings speak of the hope of God being with his people in a fresh and dynamic way.[11] As we look at this material, we find a rich LXX pneumatology anticipating the work of the Spirit in Paul's letters.

THE SPIRIT OF CREATION AND RENEWAL

Genesis 1:2 speaks of the πνεῦμα θεοῦ (וְרוּחַ אֱלֹהִים) rushing ("hovering," MT) over the waters of the deep.[12] Nothing is specified concerning the actions of God's Spirit here. The placement of this between mentions of God's overall creative act in Genesis 1:1 and his creative speech in what follows in Genesis 1:3–27 suggests the Spirit's active agency with and on behalf of God.[13] After the flood, God's Spirit is described as a wind blowing over the land, causing the waters to abate (Gen. 8:1).[14] This speaks of God's re-creation and reordering of the primordial chaos. In this regard, Philo writes of the life-creating spirit force in rich soil (*Spec.* 4.217).

In the LXX, at the exodus, God dried up the Red Sea (Josh. 2:10). Similarly, he held back the Jordan as Israel entered the land (Josh. 4:5, 7, 23; 5:1).

---

9. My analysis can be criticized by my own methodology in looking in the NT for theological, christological, and ambiguous references to God's action in believers while talking about pneumatology. Still, I have chosen to focus on *pneuma* references in Jewish Greek sources to control the scope of this study. More could be added on expectations surrounding God and eschatological agents working in the lives of God's people in their hoped-for eschatological future. This can be an area of future additional research.

10. No consideration has been given to obviously Christianized texts. These include: Christ's first coming not in glory but as a man (Sib. Or. 8:256); Christ will come in glory (Sib. Or. 2:242); glory ascribed to the triune God (Gk. Apoc. Ezra 7:16; T. Ab (A) 20:15; T. Ab. (B) 14:9); glory ascribed to Christ (Apoc. Dan. 14:16); and glory of the Lord burst forth on a priest of God and "the Spirit of understanding and supplication shall rest upon him in the water" (T. Levi 18:7).

11. The Spirit and glory are linked at Qumran: "And the substance of the spirit of glory is like work from Ophir, which diffuses [lig]ht" (4Q405 Frag. 23 ii:9).

12. See also Josephus, *Ant.* 1:27; Philo, *Leg.* 1:33.

13. See also Job 12:9 of "the hand of the LORD" causing creation. Philo also speaks of God as the divine and invisible Spirit (*Plant.* 18). The Spirit is a substance and the invisible spirit has a voice (*Somn.* 2:252).

14. We can also note Psalm 29:3, where the voice of God is over the waters fully of thunder and power.

Similarly, Psalm 17:16 sees creation affected by "the breathing of the wind of your wrath" (LES, 18:15 EVV).[15] In Judith 16:14, God sent his Spirit to establish creation. God's πνεῦμα also sustains creation (Ps. 32:6 [33:6 EVV], see also Wis. 1:7).

The blowing of his Spirit or wind causes waters to flow (Ps. 147:7 [147:18 EVV]). Isaiah envisages the Spirit poured out from God (on high), the wilderness transformed into a fruitful field, then into a forest (Isa. 32:15). He also anticipates the Spirit gathering animals to fill the habitations of the destroyed nations (Isa. 34:16). The "hand of the LORD," the creator, brings life to the desert (Isa. 41:20). The presence of God causes rocks and flint to become water; hence, people should tremble (Ps. 114:6). He causes mountains to quake (Judg. 5:5; Isa. 64:1, 3; Ezek. 38:20) and to melt like wax (Ps. 97:5), and sends rain (1 Kings 17:14).[16] By his arm, the Lord created the heavens and earth (Jer. 32:17).

The hope of the prophets is the renewal of Judah and Israel. In Isaiah 44:3, God says he will pour his Spirit and blessing on Israel's offspring, causing them to spring up like grass and trees beside streams so that they call on the Lord. While Israel has provoked the Spirit, God remembers putting his Spirit in their midst and saving them in the exodus (Isa. 63:11) and the way he guided them (Isa. 63:14). In Joseph and Asenath 8:9, Joseph prays that he would renew Asenath by his Spirit.[17]

THE SPIRIT AS SOURCE OF LIFE

In Genesis 6:3, God limits the period his πνεῦμα (רוּחַ) resides in people to 120 years. This limitation presupposes that the Spirit is the source of all physical life (also Eccl. 3:19), including the spirit of living creatures and animals (Eccl. 3:21; Ezek. 1:20–21; 10:17). As such, all that lives is sustained by the Spirit, the source and sustainer of life. Consequently, Job says, "In his hand is the life of every living thing and the breath of all mankind" (Job 12:10). Builders of idols "did not know the one who formed him and who inspired an energizing soul into him and breathed in a living spirit" (Wis. 15:11 LES). Elsewhere, this is described as the πνεῦμα ζωῆς, "breath of life" (רוּחַ חַיִּים).[18] The Hebrew phrase is used earlier in Genesis 1:30 of all the animal

---

15. ESV: "at the blast of the breath of your nostrils."

16. See the creational acts in 1 Kings 19:11 before God is heard in a whisper.

17. See also Buchanan, who discusses the new creation theme in Galatians. Key texts include Gen. 1:1–2; 2:7; Ps. 33:6–9; 104; Jub. 1:23–25, 29; 2:1; Wis. 1:5–7; 7:22; 9:17; 15:11; Isa. 42:5; 65:17; Ezek. 36:26–27; 37:1–14; 1Q422; 1QS3; 1QS4, 20–22; 11Q19, 29:7–10 among others. Grant David Buchanan, "The Spirit, New Creation, and Christian Identity in Galatians: Toward a Pneumatological Reading of Galatians" (PhD diss., University of Divinity, Melbourne, 2021), 33–71.

18. Gen. 6:17; 7:15, 22; Jdt. 10:13; 2 Macc. 7:22; Job 12:10; 33:4; Isa. 57:16; 1 En. 14:2. Similar here is the idea of the spirit (or life) of a person (Gen. 45:27). See also the end of life as the absence of breath (3 Kgdms. 17:17); God removing a person's spirit (Ps. 103:29 [104:29 EVV]); an idol with no breath or spirit (Ps. 134:17 [135:17 EVV]; Hab. 2:19; Jer. 10:14; 28:17; Ep. Jer. 24; 1QpHab XII, 17); when

world. Again, in Genesis 2:7, it is employed in the creation of Adam from dust as God breathed into his nostrils.[19] For Josephus, God implanted the Spirit and the soul in Adam (*Ant.* 1:34).

God is thus, on occasion, labeled "God of the spirits of all flesh."[20] In Psalm 104:30, God sends forth his Spirit, and people are created. When Job says, "the spirit of God is in my nostrils," he is referring to God's Spirit, who animates his life (Job 27:3). Isaiah speaks of God giving breath and spirit to those who walk in the earth (Isa. 42:5).[21] The LXX of Daniel 5:4 refers to God as "the one who held the life-force of their breath" (LES, cf. Dan. 5:23 LXX). Humankind is distinct from the divine because they borrow a spirit but cannot make gods, despite their idolatrous attempts to do so (Wis. 15:16).

For Philo, humans are composed of divine spirit or breath at creation and generally.[22] This breath is "the essence of life" (*Det.* 80, 81), which is "the fountain of reason" (*Det.* 83). "The man is stamped with the spirit which is after the image of God and differs not a whit" (*Plant.* 44). This spirit is named the soul (*Det.* 84). It remains in the soul (*Gig.* 28). Philo says of the Spirit: "And therefore the lawgiver held that the substance of the soul is twofold, blood being that of the soul as a whole, and the divine breath or spirit that of its most dominant part." Thus he says plainly, "The soul of every flesh is the blood" (*Her.* 55; Lev. 17:11; see also *Spec.* 4:123, Loeb).

Philo speaks of the impossibility of the Spirit remaining in flesh and cites Genesis 6:3 (*Gig.* 19, 28, 29, 53; *Deus.* 2). The Spirit can remain a long time in the likes of Moses (*Gig.* 47). God is the God of the spirits and of all flesh (*Agr.* 44; Virt. 58, citing Num. 27:16). Philo considers that the Spirit causes cohesion by returning to itself (*Deus.* 35).[23]

SPIRIT OF MARRIAGE

Malachi 2:15 suggests that Malachi understood God's Spirit was apportioned to a married couple to enable the forming of their marriage union in

---

a person's spirit or breath departs, they return to the earth (Ps. 145:4 [146:4 EVV]); the spirit that sustains life returns to God who gave it (Eccl. 12:7); the spirit dissolves like empty air at death (Wis. 2:3). When a person dies, the spirit leaves and a person cannot restore it (Wis. 16:14, see also Sir. 38:23; Bar. 2:17). Death is described as a command "to take up my spirit" (Tob. 3:6). The Spirit is the Spirit of life (T. Reu. 2:4). In m. 'Ohal. 1:6A, a person is unclean through death when the spirit goes forth.

19.   Other passages speak of the glory of Adam (T. Ab. (A) 11:8, 9; T. Ab. (B) 8:7; Apoc. Mos. 21; CD–A Col. iii:20); his glory and abundance of days (1QHa Col. iv:15); and the deposit of God's glory in Adam (4Q511 Frags. 52, 54–55, 57–59:2). This deposit is akin to the Spirit. Adam is also fashioned in the image of God's glory (4Q504 Frag. 8 recto:4).

20.   Num. 16:22; 27:16; 2 Macc. 3:24; 14:46; Jub. 10:3; Philo, *Post.* 67; *Virt.* 58.

21.   Other texts speak of the spirit giving human life. See also Job 32:8; 33:4; 34:14; Zech. 12:1; Isa. 38:12; 57:16.

22.   *Opif.* 135, 144; *Leg.* 1:33, 37; 3:161; *Det.* 80.

23.   For Josephus, building on the idea of "the life is in the blood," blood contains the soul and spirit (*Ant.* 3:260; Lev. 17:11).

the hope of godly offspring.[24] Malachi then declares that God hates divorce and violence. He reasons that Israel, married as she is to God, must be attentive to her spirit and faithful to him (Mal. 2:16). His injunction may indicate that Malachi understands that "Marriage is not only a union of flesh that can be dissolved but one of the divine Spirit."[25]

THE EVER-PRESENT SPIRIT

In the pre-fall paradise, God's "presence" (פָּנֶה) is in the garden (Gen. 3:8; 4:16).[26] As will be discussed further below, he is present with his people in his tabernacle and temple. The covenants between God and Israel suggest God's agency to limit flooding and his constant presence with his people.[27] He sees human goodness, sin, and capabilities, and people walk with him.[28] His presence is assumed at other places of worship (1 Sam. 1:22, see below "The Spirit in the Tabernacle and Temple"), and his servants grow and minister in his presence (Josh. 22:27; 1 Sam. 2:11, 21),[29] and execute justice (or injustice) in his presence (Lam. 3:35). He leads Moses and Israel by cloud and fire and is in their midst (Exod. 13:21; 34:5; Num. 14:14). He hears Israel's grumbling and responds, indicating his presence with them (Exod. 16:9). He descends on Sinai in fire (Exod. 19:18). He meets with Moses above the mercy seat (note 73). In Exodus 33:11, this kind of encounter is described as "presence to presence" (my translation).[30] God passes his goodness before him (Exod. 33:19; 34:6). Israel stands before him (Deut. 4:10; 29:10). Israel need not be afraid, for the great and awesome God is in their midst (Deut. 7:21). God will pass over the Jordan before Israel into the promised land, the ark of the covenant symbolizing his presence (Josh. 3:11).[31] Sometimes, the "hand of the LORD"

---

24. The LXX adapts the Hebrew to the women who have the residue of "his breath," which is ambiguous.
25. See Richard A. Taylor and E. Ray Clendenen, *Haggai, Malachi*, NAC 21A (Nashville: Broadman & Holman Publishers, 2004), 355.
26. Angels are also associated with God's presence (e.g., Isa. 63:9) and also indicate God's presence with people (e.g., Gen. 24:40; Judg. 6:22; 13:20; 1 Chron. 21:16, 30; 2 Chron. 32:21). This should not be confused with the Spirit's presence (although God's Spirit may be with the angel).
27. E.g., Gen. 6:18; 9:6, 11; 15:8; 17:4, 21; Exod. 2:24; 6:4; 24:8; 26:28; Lev. 6:24; Deut. 29:25; 31:16; 2 Kings 17:35; Isa. 59:21; 61:8; Jer. 32:40; Ezek. 37:26. The ark of the covenant also symbolizes God's presence (see further below).
28. Gen. 6:11; 7:1; 10:9; 17:1, 18; 18:22; 19:13, 27; 24:40; Mal. 2:6. "Walked with God": Gen. 5:22, 24; 6:9. See also walking before God: Gen. 24:40; 48:15; 1 Kings 8:25; 2 Chron. 6:16; Isa. 38:3; walking in God's commandments: 2 Chron. 6:16; 7:14; Jer. 9:13; Ezek. 5:7; 11:12.
29. See also 1 Sam. 26:20; 2 Chron. 29:11.
30. See also Exod. 34:34; Deut. 5:4; 34:10.
31. See also the ark's role in the destruction of Jericho (Josh. 6:6–8, 13, 26) and after the catastrophe of Ai (Josh. 7:6–13, 23). Uzzah's death speaks of God's holy presence, which he inadvertently violated (1 Chron. 13:20). To minister before the ark is to minister before God (1 Chron. 16:4, 37). Mention of the mercy seat and God's presence speaks of the same (Lev. 16:2).

has positive connotations of God's presence,[32] as does the "arm of the LORD."[33] Other language is used of God's presence with people and Israel.[34]

There are many examples of God being with Israel. Other people recognize his presence with Abraham (Gen. 21:22) and Isaac (Gen. 26:28). God is with Isaac (Gen. 26:3, 24),[35] as he is with Jacob,[36] Joseph (Gen. 39:3, 23; 48:21), Moses,[37] Joshua,[38] Samuel (1 Sam. 3:19), Saul (1 Sam. 10:7), David,[39] Phinehas (1 Chron. 9:20), Solomon (1 Kings 11:38; 1 Chron. 28:20; 2 Chron. 1:1), those building the temple (1 Chron. 22:18; Hab. 2:4), priests and Levites working in the temple (1 Chron. 28:21), Asa (2 Chron. 15:2, 9), judges (2 Chron. 19:2), Job (Job 29:5), Hezekiah (2 Kings 18:7; 20:3), Jabez (1 Chron. 4:10), Cyrus (2 Chron. 36:23), Jeremiah (Jer. 1:8, 19; 15:20), and Haggai (Hag. 1:13).

God was with Israel for the forty-year wilderness journey (Num. 23:21; Deut. 2:7). Moses promises God's presence to the Israelites as they enter and live in the land (Num. 32:29; Ezek. 34:30). God is also with Israel as they go to war and gives them victory (Deut. 20:1, 4; 2 Chron. 32:8).[40] His presence and peace are conveyed through blessing (Num. 6:25, 26; Ps. 89:15). As God's people meet, they are in his presence (e.g., 2 Chron. 20:13). He is with Israel in trouble to hear prayer (Ps. 91:15).

However, when Israel fails to follow God, he will not be with them (Num. 14:43; Josh. 7:12). Similarly, an unclean person is cut off from God's presence (Lev. 22:3). For Isaiah, such people should hide "before the terror of the LORD" (Isa. 2:10).[41] Still, this withdrawal from God is not absolute, for as it says in Deuteronomy 31:6, God is with Israel and will never leave or forsake them (also Deut. 31:6, 8). What they are really doing is "defying his glorious presence" (Isa. 3:8). Hence, Amos tells Israel if they seek good, God will be present with them (Amos 5:14, also 2 Chron. 30:9). Jeremiah tells Israel to remove their detestable things from their midst (Jer. 4:1). Even in exile, cast away from God's presence (Jer. 23:29; 52:3),[42] God is with his

---

32. E.g., 2 Sam. 24:14; 1 Kings 18:46; 1 Chron. 21:13; 28:18; Ezra 7:6, 28; Pss. 89:1; 118:15–16; Prov. 21:1; Isa. 62:3; 66:13.

33. See earlier on "The Spirit of Judgment" and "The Spirit Who Protects and Delivers." See also 2 Chron. 32:8; Isa. 33:2; 40:10; 53:1; 62:8.

34. E.g., God's faithfulness and love with him (Ps. 89:24).

35. See also Gen. 27:20.

36. See Gen. 28:15, 20; 31:3; 46:4.

37. See Gen. 31:5, 11; 35:3; Exod. 3:12; 31:18; Deut. 5:4; 9:10. Also ironically by Pharaoh to Moses (Exod. 10:10). Prayer-wishes asking for God's presence are common (Exod. 18:19; Ruth 2:4; 1 Sam. 17:37; 20:13; 2 Sam. 14:17; 1 Chron. 22:11, 16).

38. See Deut. 31:23; Josh. 1:5, 9, 17; 3:7.

39. E.g., 1 Sam. 16:18; 18:12, 14; 2 Sam. 5:10; 7:3, 9; 1 Chron. 11:9; 17:2, 8; Ps. 23:4.

40. Also Judg. 1:22; 6:12, 16; 2 Chron. 20:17; Zech. 10:5. See also Jer. 20:11: "But the LORD is with me as a dread warrior."

41. Also Isa. 2:19, 21.

42. Also 2 Kings 17:18, 20, 23; 23:27; 24:3, 20.

people and will be with them when they return (Isa. 41:10; 43:2, 5).[43] Jonah, too, seeks to flee God's presence, but God reaches him in the fish (Jon. 1:3, 10). Though Jeremiah doesn't reference the Spirit, we see that God is with Israel to save them.[44] Zechariah foresees the day when Gentiles seek Jews out because the Greeks have heard that God is with them (Zech. 8:23). Ezekiel pictures the establishment of an everlasting covenant and God's sanctuary in their midst forever (Ezek. 37:26–27).

The Psalms are replete with references to God's presence (פָּנֶה) with people (Ps. 41:12), especially the upright (Pss. 11:7; 140:13). Before him enemies perish (Ps. 9:3); people experience joy (Pss. 16:11; 21:6), vindication (Ps. 17:3), protection (Ps. 39:20), and conviction (Ps. 90:8).[45] Prayers are raised to experience his presence.[46] When experiencing God's presence, people are to respond with such things as rejoicing (Deut. 12:12, 18), seeking his presence (1 Chron. 16:11, Ps. 105:2, 4), worshipping (1 Chron. 16:29), being humble (2 Kings 22:19),[47] kneeling (Ps. 85:6), giving thanks with music and song,[48] trembling,[49] being silent (Hab. 2:20, Zeph. 1:7, Zech. 2:13), and fulfilling vows (Ps. 116:14, 18). So, after his sin, David pleads that God will not cast him away from his presence or take his Holy Spirit from him, indicating the link between God's presence and the Spirit (Ps. 51:11). Similarly, in Psalm 138:7–10 (139:7–10 EVV), David sings of his inability to flee the Spirit whether into heaven or Sheol. At any time of the day, the Spirit is with him, leads him, and holds him fast. In Haggai, via the prophet, God assures Israel that "my Spirit remains in your midst" and urges them not to fear (Hag. 2:5). Wisdom 1:7 speaks of the spirit of the Lord filling the world and holding all things together. Again, in Wisdom 12:1 (LES): "For your incorruptible spirit is in all things." In Sibylline Oracles 3:701, the Spirit of God that knows no falsehood is throughout the world.

THE SPIRIT WHO SPEAKS

Many OT texts refer to God speaking to people.[50] Examples include God speaking to Adam in the garden, Abraham (Gen. 17:22), Jacob (Gen. 35:13–15), Moses,[51] and Israel (Neh. 9:13); God's presence found in a low whisper for Elijah (1 Kings 19:12); and God's instructions to Elisha (2 Kings 3:17). God

---

43. Compare 2 Kings 13:23.
44. See Jer. 15:19; 30:11; 42:11; 46:28.
45. Similarly, the corruption of the earth is seen by God's presence (פָּנֶה) at the time of the flood (Gen. 6:11).
46. E.g., Pss. 4:6; 13:1; 27:8; 80:19. Prayers questioning why God hides his face also indicate a desire for God's presence (Job 13:10, 24; Pss. 13:1; 44:24; 88:14; 102:2; 104:29; cf. Ps. 30:7; Isa. 54:8; 57:17; Ezek. 39:23–24).
47. Also 2 Chron. 33:12; 34:27; cf. 2 Chron. 33:23; 36:12.
48. E.g., 1 Chron. 16:33; Pss. 95:2; 98:6; 100:2.
49. E.g., Pss. 96:9; 114:7; Lam. 2:19.
50. At times this is expressed as an angel (e.g., Dan. 9:22; Zech. 1:9, 13, 14, 19; 2:3; 4:1, 4, 5; 5:5, 10; 6:4); however, this is not the Spirit of God directly speaking.
51. E.g., Exod. 19:9; 20:22; 34:32–35; Num. 12:6–8.

is present with Israel by his word, again invoking ideas of the presence of the Spirit (Jer. 27:18).

At times in the OT, God's communication to people is through the agency of the Spirit (1 Kings 22:24; 2 Chron. 18:23).[52] The Spirit also speaks through people. For example, in 2 Samuel 23:2, David sings, "The Spirit of the LORD speaks by me; his word is on my tongue." He speaks through his prophets (see "The Spirit of Prophecy"). Similarly, Ezekiel testifies that "the Spirit entered into me and set me on my feet, and I heard him speaking to me" (Ezek. 2:2, also Ezek. 3:24; 11:5). Joel anticipates God speaking to his people in dreams and visions when the Spirit is poured out on them (Joel 2:28–29). The Spirit is also the Spirit of instruction, seen when Nehemiah recalls God giving his good Spirit to instruct Israel in the wilderness (Neh. 9:20).

THE SPIRIT IN GOD-ANOINTED LEADERS

In the Pentateuch, there are references to God's glory manifesting in various ways in Israel's experience. God's glory appears in cloud and fire (Exod. 16:10; Deut. 5:24) and on Mount Sinai in a cloud like a devouring fire (Exod. 24:16, 17). People tremble at God's glory on Sinai (4Q377 Frag. 1 recto ii:9). God's glory is partially revealed to Moses as he passes by him (Exod. 33:18, 22 LXX). His glory is seen in his exertion of power, for example, giving quail and manna (Exod. 16:7).

God is with a range of Israel's leaders (see "The Ever-Present Spirit" above). Still, the first explicit reference to a person filled with God's Spirit is Joseph. As a result of Joseph's extraordinary leadership and wisdom, Pharaoh asks, "Can we find a man like this, in whom is the Spirit (רוּחַ, πνεῦμα) of God?" (Gen. 41:38). At the appointment of the seventy in Numbers 11, the Spirit on Moses is apportioned to the elders. This distribution to others assumes the previous anointing of Moses (Num. 11:17). The effect of receiving the Spirit is seen in their prophesying (Num. 11:25). The anointing of two others, Eldad and Medad, along with Moses's desire that all have this experience, shows that this can extend beyond consecrated leaders and anticipates Paul's mention that all can prophesy (Num. 11:26–30; 1 Cor. 14:24, 31).

Something akin to Eldad and Medad's experience occurs to messengers of Saul sent to seize David; when they encounter Samuel and a band of prophesying prophets, the Spirit of God comes upon them, and they too prophesy (1 Sam. 19:20–21). Even Saul, who had previously had the Spirit of God withdraw from him and who is afflicted with an evil spirit, experiences the same, causing people to question whether he was among the prophets (1 Sam. 19:24). The OT gives witness to the Spirit spontaneously overflowing from those Spirit-filled onto others so that they prophesy.

---

52. See also Neh. 9:20, 30; Isa. 59:21; 61:1. False spirits also have the faculty of speech, e.g., 1 Kings 22:21; 2 Chron. 18:20. They also speak through false prophets (e.g., 2 Chron. 18:21).

The "Spirit of God" enables Balaam's prophecy (Num. 23:7 LXX; 24:2). Joshua is described as "a man in whom is the Spirit" (Num. 27:18). In Deuteronomy 34:9, Joshua is "filled with a spirit of understanding."

The Spirit also comes upon, stirs, springs upon, and leaps upon the judges, who lead Israel to victory and peace; hence, this is a spirit of victory in war and establishing shalom.[53] Similarly, the Spirit rushed upon Israel's first king, Saul, enabling him to prophesy (1 Sam. 10:6). The Spirit will also transform him into another man (below). In 1 Samuel 11:6, the Spirit leaps on him, and he leads Israel to victory. The Spirit withdraws from Saul due to his disobedience, and an evil spirit torments him. The Spirit of the Lord comes upon David at his anointing (1 Sam. 16:13–15) and also on David's mighty warriors (1 Chron. 12:19).

In the Pseudepigrapha (T. Sim. 4:4; Jos. Asen. 4:9), the Spirit is sent upon Isaac (T. Ab. (A) 4:7). Solomon bemoans the Spirit of God leaving him so that his words became idle talk, and he was convinced to build temples to idols (T. Sol. 26:6).

THE SPIRIT WHO LISTENS AND SEES

Not only does the Spirit speak, but God listens to his people, implying the Spirit's presence to hear his people. The Spirit's presence is symbolized anthropomorphically, whereby God has ears that hear.[54] Hence, he heard Leah and the wife of Manoah, and they bore children.[55] God hears human cries.[56] God heard Israel's cries from Egypt and, remembering his covenant, brought them out of Egypt.[57] He heard Moses's intercession for Aaron, and Aaron was spared (Deut. 9:19).[58] In the judges period, he heard Israel's cries and raised judges (e.g., Judg. 2:18; 6:6). God heard Solomon's prayer and consecrated his temple with his presence ("my eyes and my heart") permanently (1 Kings 9:3).[59] Hezekiah's prayers were also heard, and Israelites were healed (2 Chron. 30:20; Isa. 38:5); the prayers of the poor are heard, and they are saved (Ps. 34:6), as were those of Job (Job 42:9).[60] At other times, God hears of Israel's grumbling or sin and acts in judgment.[61]

From creation, God has seen his world.[62] His eyes "run to and fro throughout the whole earth," and "his eyes see."[63] Zechariah's vision of a stone

---

53. See Judg. 3:10; 11:29; 13:25; 14:6, 19; 15:14.
54. E.g., 1 Sam. 8:12; 2 Sam. 22:7; Pss. 18:2; 130:2.
55. E.g., Gen. 29:33; 30:17, 22; Judg. 13:9.
56. Gen. 21:17; Pss. 4:3; 18:6; 34:17; 61:5; 69:33; 78:59; Prov. 15:29.
57. E.g., Exod. 2:24–25; 3:7; Num. 20:16; Deut. 26:7.
58. See also Deut. 5:28. Similarly, God heard Daniel's prayer (Dan. 10:12).
59. See also 2 Sam. 22:7.
60. There are many other instances of God hearing; see e.g., 2 Kings 5:8; 19:4, 20; 20:5; 2 Chron. 33:13; 34:27; Isa. 37:4.
61. Exod. 16:7–9, 12; Num. 11:1; 12:1–2; Deut. 1:34; Ps. 78:21, 59.
62. Gen. 1:4, 10, 12, 18, 21, 25, 31.
63. 2 Chron. 16:9; Ps. 11:4. Also 2 Sam. 7:19; 1 Chron. 17:17; 14:2; 34:2; Prov. 15:3; 22:12.

with seven eyes speaks of God's eyes that range through the world (Zech. 3:9; 4:10). God's eyes see the righteous, and he bestows favor.[64] He watches over all humankind (Pss. 14:2; 33:13; 53:2) and especially over his people (Job 29:2). Similarly, his eyes are on the land (Deut. 11:12).[65] He sees sin and responds, calling people to repentance (e.g., Jonah 3:10) or bringing judgment.[66] He sees injustice and acts for the oppressed (Ps. 146:9). As such, people pray that God will see and respond (e.g., 2 Kings 19:16).

THE SPIRIT OF JUDGMENT

God comes in judgment to the earth (Pss. 96:13; 98:9). He fights for Israel (Exod. 14:25). The notion of "the hand of the LORD" recurs of judgment, suggesting God's action via his Spirit.[67] Similarly, the "arm of the Lord" speaks of God's judgment on Israel and his enemies.[68] In Exodus 15, twice πνεῦμα (רוּחַ) is used for God's destruction of Egypt's forces in the Red Sea. In v. 8, the "blast of God's anger" (my translation) causes the waters to gather.[69] This event is similar to God's Spirit participating in bringing creation and order from the chaos of the primordial waters, but here not to bring life but instead take it where it violates God's creation and threatens his people (see also v. 10).[70] Fire explodes from heaven to destroy Nadab and Abihu for unauthorized offerings (Lev. 10:1–2; Num. 3:4; 26:61) while the Korahites are swallowed up by the ground (Num. 16:31–35).

At times, רוּחַ is the force of the Spirit or wind in judgment (Ps. 47:8 [48:8 EVV]).[71] The use of the Urim speaks of God's presence to bring judgment (Num. 27:21). In Psalm 106:25 (107:25 EVV), God causes the wind to rise, creating waves and bringing death. God is a jealous God whose anger can be riled so that he moved against his own people (Deut. 6:15; 28:25). He brings hornets against Israel's enemies, which invokes a picture of God's wind blowing insects into enemies (Deut. 7:20). The Lord also throws enemies into panic (Josh. 10:10). He is a consuming fire (Deut. 9:3). Second Kingdoms 22:16 LXX mentions God uncovering the foundations of the world by his breath (πνεῦμα) of his anger. God causes leprosy to break out on priests that defy him (2 Chron. 26:19). With his arm, he fights

---

64. E.g., Gen. 6:8; Exod. 15:26; 1 Sam. 20:3; 2 Sam. 15:25; 1 Kings 15:5, 11; 2 Kings 10:30; 12:2; 14:3; 15:3, 34; 16:2; 18:3; 22:2; 2 Chron. 24:2; 25:2; 26:4; 27:2; 28:1; 29:2; Ps. 34:15; Prov. 5:21; Isa. 49:5.

65. See also Amos 9:8.

66. Gen. 6:2, 5, 12; 31:42; Deut. 32:19; Isa. 59:15.

67. Also Exod. 16:3; Deut. 2:15; Josh. 4:24; 22:31; Judg. 2:15; Ruth 1:13; 1 Sam. 5:6, 9; 7:13; 12:15; Ps. 75:8; Isa. 25:10; 51:17; Ezek. 8:1. Compare Acts 13:11; cf. Luke 1:66; Acts 11:21.

68. Exod. 6:6; 15:16; Deut. 4:34; 26:8; Isa. 48:14; Ezek. 20:33; 30:22.

69. See also "the wind of his anger" (Job 4:9 LES). Similarly, see Odes Sol. 1:8, 10.

70. Another aspect of judgment is God sending an evil spirit to Saul after withdrawing his Spirit from him (1 Sam. 16:14; 19:9). Similarly, God sends a spirit of deep sleep on Jerusalem's leaders, closing the eyes of the prophets and covering the heads of the seers (Isa. 29:9). See also 1QapGen ar XX, 16.

71. See also Wis. 11:20.

with and for Israel (Isa. 30:32). He visits nations in judgment and deliverance (Isa. 23:17; Jer. 27:22; 32:5). Israel's justice system implies God's presence in his chosen priests and judges to make judgments on his behalf (Deut. 19:17).

The Spirit's role in judgment is important in Isaiah. Isaiah predicts the blood of the people of Zion being cleansed with a spirit of judgment and burning (Isa. 4:4). He also looks to the Spirit-imbued Messiah coming and God bringing a violent wind of judgment on the Sea of Egypt (Isa. 11:15).[72] God's breath is likened to a flooded stream reaching the neck and sifting the nations for destruction and bridling people by the jaw (Isa. 30:28). The nations tremble at his presence (Isa. 64:2).

Isaiah 26:18 speaks of evil as an act of God's breath and east wind (or wind of anger, LXX). When God's redemption comes to his people, God will be a spirit of judgment, preventing destruction (Isa. 28:6 LXX).[73] The enemies of Israel will fear God and his glory, and he will come like a rushing stream driven by God's רוּחַ (Isa. 59:19).

For Ezekiel, God will set and display his glory among the nations in God's judgment (Ezek. 39:21). In Testament of Abraham (A) 4:10, God sends an all-devouring spirit to consume food on a table.[74] With the heavy involvement of the Spirit in Ezekiel's movement and speech in Ezekiel 11, it is implied in Ezekiel 11:13 that the Spirit brings about the death of Pelatiah. This event arguably anticipates the deaths of Ananias and Sapphira in Acts 5.

THE SPIRIT WHO PROTECTS AND DELIVERS

Associated with the judgment of enemies is God's protection. His safekeeping is seen in the victories referred to above, especially the exodus (Exodus 15). It is also evident in the destruction of Egypt (Isa. 11:15). God's presence brings victory (Num. 10:9) and is the basis for courage and fearlessness before enemies (Num. 14:9). Defeat leads to the conclusion that God is not with Israel (Judg. 6:13). Solomon's prayer for God's presence as with their ancestors is no doubt motivated with hopes of God's protection (1 Kings 8:57). God is seen to be with Israel as they entered war, symbolized by the priests leading them into battle (2 Chron. 13:12). He is with Israel "to fight our battles" (2 Chron. 32:8). So the psalmist twice states, "The Lord of Hosts is with us; the God of Jacob is our fortress" (Ps. 46:7, 11). Isaiah warns the nations that God is with Israel, so their plans are futile (Isa. 8:10). Although the telling doesn't mention the Spirit, Egyptian idols tremble at God's presence as he rides on a cloud to them (Isa. 19:1, 16). The

---

72. The upper end of the Gulf of Suez. See John D. W. Watts, *Isaiah 1–33*, WBC 24 (Dallas: Word, 1985), 179.

73. In the Hebrew, God is a Spirit of justice for the one who sits in judgment and strengthens those resisting enemies at the gate.

74. God's glory is also expressed in judgment (Isa. 10:16).

anthropomorphic arm of the Lord is used for both God's judgment (above) and his deliverance (especially from Egypt).[75]

THE GUIDING SPIRIT

God was not only present with Israel, but spiritually guided him from Egypt (Deut. 4:37) and traveled with him in the wilderness (Exod. 33:14–15; Isa. 63:14). The pillar of cloud and fire signifies the presence of the Lord and his glory, leading Israel or being with him.[76] God goes before Israel (Deut. 1:30) and guides him (Deut. 32:12). The casting of lots is a means by which God guides (Josh. 18:6, 8, 10; 19:51).[77] In Psalm 138:10 (139:10 EVV), God's hand holds and leads the psalmist (139:10 EVV), and the ever-present Spirit (above) is likened to a hand leading David. In Psalm 5:8 and again in Psalm 142:10 (143:10 ESV), the Holy Spirit guides David in a straight (or level) way. We see here the Spirit's guidance, a common Pauline theme. Isaiah critiques Israel's leaders for forming political alliances rather than being led by the Spirit (Isa. 30:1). He speaks of God guiding Israel by the Spirit through the wilderness. For Philo, the Divine Spirit guides people into the way of truth (*Mos.* 2:265).

THE SPIRIT OF PROVISION

It is apparent in the OT that the promised land is given to Israel (e.g., Deut. 2:31).[78] Although the Spirit is not mentioned in these references, God's agency in military victories suggests his presence, giving Israel triumph.[79] In Numbers 11:31, God sends a wind (πνεῦμα, רוּחַ) that causes quail to fall, from which the people ate.

THE SPIRIT WHO PERFORMS MIRACLES

Reference has been made to the wind of God causing quail to fall for the people to eat (Num. 11:31). In contexts where Spirit language is not used, the role of the Spirit is implied as God's glory is seen in his miracles in Egypt (Num. 14:22) and his other marvelous works (Ps. 96:3). The Spirit is associated with miracles more explicitly in Joel 2. The result of the Lord pouring out his Spirit is women and men prophesying, people dreaming dreams and visions that bring God's word to his people, and God revealing his wonders (מוֹפֵת) in the heavens and on the earth—for instance, in blood, fire, and columns of smoke, and the sun darkened and the moon bloodied. Such portents will precede the day of the Lord. Such portents will precede

---

75. E.g., Exod. 6:6; 15:16; Deut. 4:34; 5:15; 7:19; 11:2; 26:8; 2 Kings 17:36; Ps. 98:1; Isa. 30:30, 32; 51:9; 52:10.
76. See Exod. 13:21–22; 14:19, 24; 16:10; 19:9; 24:16; 33:9–10; 34:5; 40:34–35, 38; Lev. 16:2; Num. 9:18–20; 10:34; 11:25; 12:5; 14:14; 16:42; 31:15; Deut. 5:22; 31:15; 1 Kings 8:10–11; 2 Chron. 5:13–14; Neh. 9:12, 19; Pss. 99:7; 105:39; Isa. 4:5; Ezek. 10:4. See also 2 Chron. 5:14; Isa. 19:1; Ezek. 1:28.
77. See also Acts 1:26.
78. See also Deut. 2:33, 36; Josh. 2:9; 2 Chron. 28:3; 33:2.
79. E.g., Deut. 7:1–2, 22–23; 9:4–5; 31:3; Josh. 23:3, 5, 9, 13, 18; 2 Chron. 33:9.

the day of the Lord from which those who call on the Lord's name will be saved (cf. Rom 10:13).[80]

THE SPIRIT OF PROPHECY

In some passages already referenced, prophecy is associated with the Spirit.[81] In 2 Samuel 23:2, the Spirit speaks in or by (ἐν, בְּ) David, and God's word is on his tongue. This verse indicates God placing the capacity to prophesy in David. God's warnings to Israel via prophets are recalled in Nehemiah 9:30. The writings of the prophets are considered Spirit-commanded in Zechariah 1:6 LXX (also Zech. 7:12).

False prophecies emanate from false spirits (1 Kings 22:22–24). Elijah's spirit is doubled on Elisha (2 Kings 2:9, 15; cf. Luke 1:17).[82] Prophets stand and minister before God's presence.[83] Other examples of God's Spirit coming on people who prophesy include Azariah, son of Obed (2 Chron. 15:1); Uzziel (2 Chron. 20:14); and Azariah, son of Jehoiada (2 Chron. 24:20). Nehemiah writes of God bearing with Israel and warning them through the prophets for many years (Neh. 9:30). Isaiah declares that he is sent by God, who also sent his Spirit (Isa. 48:16). Jeremiah speaks of the fullness of wind coming on him, leading him to speak words of judgment to Israel (Jer. 4:12).

Ezekiel's pneumatology is evident. The Spirit comes upon him and gives him visions of Jerusalem, causes him to experience heat in his spirit, and transports him to the temple and to the bodies of those exiled in Babylon.[84] While Daniel does not associate it with the Spirit, God's hand writes on the wall, warning Nebuchadnezzar of the end of his empire (Dan. 5:24–29). Men and women prophesy and have dreams and visions due to the eschatological outpouring envisaged by Joel (Joel 2:28–29). As such, God speaks to people and through them to others through his Spirit.

In apocryphal writings, Elisha is filled with God's Spirit (Sir. 48:12) and by a great spirit. Isaiah saw the final things and comforted Zion (Sir. 48:24). Philo describes God's Spirit as the divine and prophetical spirit (*Fug.* 186). God enables prophecy (*Mos.* 1:175, 277) and fills prophets with his divine spirit (*Decal.* 175). The prophet does not speak from his thoughts but interprets

---

80. See also texts where God is the agent of miraculous signs (מוֹפֵת: Exod. 4:21; 7:3; 11:9–10; Deut. 4:34; 6:22; 7:19; 13:1; 26:8; 29:3; 34:11; 1 Kings 13:3, 5; 1 Chron. 16:12; 2 Chron. 32:24; Neh. 9:10; Pss. 71:7; 78:43; 105:5, 27; 135:9; Isa. 8:18; Jer. 32:20–21; אוֹת: Exod. 7:3; 10:1, 2; 14:11, 22; Deut. 4:34; 6:22; 7:19; 11:3; 13:2; 26:8; 29:3; 34:11; Josh. 24:17; 1 Sam. 2:34; 10:9; 2 Kings 20:9; Neh. 9:10; Pss. 65:8; 78:34; 105:27; 135:9; Isa. 7:11, 14; Jer. 32:20–21). See also works of his glory (4Q405 Frag. 23 ii:12).
81. Num. 11:25–30; 23:6; 24:2; 1 Sam 10:9–13; 19:20–24.
82. Even though this is "your spirit" and "the spirit of Elijah," clearly this is the Lord's Spirit which with Elijah, God's prophet, was imbued.
83. E.g., 1 Kings 17:1; 18:15; 2 Kings 5:16. See also "the hand of the LORD" on Elijah (1 Kings 18:46), Elisha, interestingly conveyed with music (2 Kings 3:15), and Ezekiel (Ezek. 1:3; 3:14, 22; 8:1; 37:1).
84. Ezek. 2:2; 3:12, 14, 24; 11:1, 5, 24; 37:1; 43:5.

what God inspires and says; his reasoning has departed his soul, and the divine spirit enters and affects his voice speaking the prophecies (*Spec.* 4:49).

In Josephus, the Spirit met Balaam's donkey (*Ant.* 4:108) and inspired Balaam's oracle (*Ant.* 4:118). The "Spirit of God" seized Balaam (*Ant.* 4:119). The Spirit left Saul and came upon David, who began to prophesy (*Ant.* 6:166). The Spirit came upon a group of prophets, who then prophesy (*Ant.* 6:222). A true prophet has the power of the Spirit in him (*Ant.* 8:408). Daniel has the Divine Spirit, seen by his wisdom (*Ant.* 10:239).

THE SPIRIT WHO TRANSPORTS

In 1 Kings 18:12, Obadiah anticipates Elijah being transported by the Spirit of the Lord to "I know not where." Although this is on the lips of Obadiah and could simply mean that the Spirit guides Elijah away, it potentially points to an expectation of the Spirit's power to transport or translate someone across time and space. Later, Elijah flees Ahab, is sustained for forty days by a meal from an angel, and eventually reaches Mount Horeb (1 Kings 19:1–8). The Spirit also transports Elisha onto a mountain or into a valley in 2 Kings 2:16, where the prophet speaks with God.

The Spirit also transports Ezekiel. The Spirit enters Ezekiel, sets him on his feet, and speaks to him (Ezek. 2:2). By the Spirit, he is lifted and taken away, and the hand of the Lord is strongly on him (Ezek. 3:12, 14). The Spirit again enters him and directs him to shut himself in his house (Ezek. 3:24). In Ezekiel 8, a humanlike figure lifted him by the hair, and the Spirit transported him to the temple, where he saw the glory of God and heard God speak (Ezek. 8:3–4). Similarly, in Ezekiel 11, he is brought again to the temple and told to prophesy, which he does when the Spirit falls on him (Ezek. 11:1–19). The Spirit also transports Ezekiel to exiles in Babylon (Ezek. 11:24). Later, "the hand of the LORD," which is specifically associated with the Spirit, takes Ezekiel to the valley of the dry bones, where he sees the extraordinary vision of their reanimation (Ezek. 37:1). The work of the Spirit is seen as Ezekiel is transported by the "hand of the LORD" (Ezek. 40:1) to behold the glory of God filling the restored temple (Ezek. 43:5). This capacity of the Spirit to translate people instantly across space potentially anticipates Christ's Spirit-empowered ability to move through time[85] and space, as well as Philip's translation (Acts 8:39–40).

GIFTS OF THE SPIRIT

The NT idea of *charismata* is anticipated in Exodus 28:3, where those skilled in craftsmanship with the πνεύματος αἰσθήσεως, "spirit of perception," will sew clothing for Aaron. Similarly, God has filled Bezalel with the Spirit of God (LXX: spirit divine), giving him the ability, intelligence, wisdom, and understanding for craftsmanship (Exod. 31:2–3; 35:31; Philo, *Gig.* 23).

---

85. Luke 24:31, 36; John 20:19, 26. See also Matt. 28:8.

As mentioned above, prophesying is associated with the spiritual anointing of leaders (Num. 11:25). The gift of tongues is anticipated in the Testament of Job 48:1–3, where Hemera speaks ecstatically in an angelic dialect and her clothing is inscribed with the Spirit.

THE SPIRIT IN THE TABERNACLE AND TEMPLE

The presence of the Lord in his tabernacle and temple is symbolized by the bread of the Presence (פֶּנֶה לֶחֶם).[86] His presence is also indicated by the priests and Levites who serve before him in the tent and temple.[87] Sacrifices and rituals are performed before him.[88] Firstfruit offerings are made before the Lord (Deut. 26:10). Festivals remind people of God's presence (Num. 10:10), and people come into this presence at the pilgrimage festivals (Exod. 34:24).[89] Habakkuk 2:20 states, "But the LORD is in his holy temple." Because God is present in his temple, the presence of the Lord is in Jerusalem (Jer. 3:17).

Rather than Spirit language, OT writers commonly use glory to describe God's presence. As such, Jerusalem is a place of God's glory (Pss. Sol. 2:21 [wreath of glory]; 11:7). Josephus considers the glory of God entering the temple as the Spirit (Ant. 8:114). He is present in his glory at the tabernacle.[90] Writers at Qumran speak of the glory in the tent of the God of knowledge (4Q405 Frags. 20 ii–21–22:7; 11Q17 Col. vii:10).

Glory language is also used concerning the temple. His glory fills the temple at its commissioning and the entry of the ark (1 Kings 8:11; 2 Chron. 5:14; 7:1, 3 [fire]; Ant. 8.106). God sanctifies the temple with his glory, and his glory resides in the temple (11Q19 Col. xxix:8). So the temple is where God's glory dwells (Ps. 26:8, also 63:2). Ultimately, God will fill his house with glory (Hag. 2:7). It is thus a temple of glory (T. Levi 18:6; 11Q17 Col. x:6).[91]

God's glory fills the temple at its consecration, causing the priests to be unable to stand to minister (1 Kings 8:11). Similarly, Ezekiel sees God's glory in the temple which fills it as the cloud, and the brightness of God's presence filled the tabernacle (Ezek. 3:12; 10:4).[92] The glory that fills the temple is even seen over Jerusalem and Zion (4Q380 Frag. 1 i:6). God's glory moves and encounters Ezekiel (Ezek. 3:23; 8:4; 10:4) and travels on a cherub away from

---

86.   Exod. 25:30; 35:13; 39:36; Num. 4:7; 1 Sam. 21:6; 1 Kings 7:48; 2 Chron. 4:19. In 1 Chron. 28:15, "the hand of the LORD" conveys the very plan of the temple to David, suggesting the Spirit's guidance (1 Chron. 28:19).

87.   E.g., Exod. 27:21; 28:12, 29, 30, 35, 38; Num. 17:7, 9; Deut. 18:7; 1 Chron. 6:32; 16:39; 23:13; 2 Chron. 29:11. See also earlier references to the ark ("The Ever-Present Spirit").

88.   E.g., Exod. 29:11, 23–26, 42; 30:8, 16; 40:23, 25; Lev. 1:3, 5, 11; Num. 15:28; 16:7; Deut. 27:7; 1 Kings 8:64–65; 1 Chron. 23:31. See especially "before the Lord" (8 times in Genesis; 23 times in Exodus; 63 times in Leviticus; 40 times in Numbers; 30 times in Deuteronomy; 51x in Judges–2 Kings).

89.   See also Deut. 14:23, 26; 15:20; 16:11, 16; 31:11.

90.   See Exod. 40:34–35; Lev. 9:6, 23; Num. 14:10; 16:10, 42; 20:6.

91.   Compare 3 Macc. 2:14; Liv. Proph. 12:10.

92.   In Ezekiel 9:3 the glory moves from a cherub to the threshold of the house.

the temple (Ezek. 10:18–19; 11:22, 23). The Spirit is mentioned in Ezekiel 11:24 and carries Ezekiel to Babylon.

THE SPIRIT WHO OVERCOMES EVIL SPIRITS

In 1 Samuel 16:13–15, God's Spirit comes upon David and withdraws from Saul, to whom God sends an evil spirit. David's worshipful lyre playing causes the evil spirit to depart from Saul (1 Sam. 16:23). However, later, as David played, Saul sought to kill him (1 Sam. 19:9).

THE SPIRIT WHO STRENGTHENS

The presence of the Lord who will never leave or forsake Israel means Israel must be strong and courageous as they enter the promised land (Deut. 31:6). In David's contrite lament, he pleads that God would strengthen or uphold him with a willing (MT) or guiding spirit (Ps. 50:14 [51:12 EVV]). Similarly, the Spirit provides Micah with strength and capacities of judgment and might (Mic. 3:8). As noted above, the Spirit provides courage in times of fear (Hag. 2:5).

THE SPIRIT AND THE MIND

For Philo, "The mind is evicted at the arrival of the divine Spirit, but when that departs the mind returns to its tenancy. Mortal and immortal may not share the same home. And therefore the setting of reason and the darkness which surrounds it produce ecstasy and inspired frenzy" (*Her.* 265). We see this transformation in Caleb. Philo cites Numbers 14:24: "There was another spirit in him." He then states that Caleb experienced a total change so that "the ruling mind in him was changed to supreme perfection" (*Mut.* 123). The mind is the fervent and kindled spirit (*Fug.* 134). "Therefore, the face, which is the dominant portion of the soul; making the spirit, which is calculated for seeing, reach to the eyes, that which has the power of hearing reach the ears, the spirit of smelling reach the nostrils, that of taste the mouth, and causing that of touch to pervade the whole surface of the body" (*Fug.* 182).

Breath within the heart generates thoughts (*Spec.* 1:6). A person's rational spirit is fashioned after the model of the divine image (*Spec.* 1:171). This fashioning is seen in Moses. This spirit was imparted to the seventy elders. They were confirmed as leaders by the all-wise spirit, whereas without the Spirit, they could not be leaders (*Gig.* 24; Num. 11:17; see also *Fug.* 186). It is not the individual spirit of Moses that could be diluted (*Gig.* 26) but the Spirit of God: wise, divine, indivisible, undistributable, good, and everywhere diffused. He fills the universe and is not reduced when given to others or added to where understanding, knowledge, and wisdom are concerned (*Gig.* 28). In *Gig.* 55, Moses always has "the divine spirit at his side, taking the lead in every journey of righteousness." The Spirit communicates the things of God inwardly (*Somn.* 2:252) and enables Moses to prophesy (*Mos.* 1:175, 277). Philo describes it as "the most pure spirit of Moses" (*Mos.* 2:40).

The Spirit is on Abraham (*Ios.* 116). In *Virt.* 217, the divine spirit was breathed upon him from on high and dwelt in his soul and "invested his body with singular beauty, his voice with persuasiveness, and his hearers with understanding."

THE SPIRIT OF WISDOM

Wisdom is associated with the Spirit where the Messiah is concerned (Isa. 11:2, see also Pss. Sol. 18:7). In Wisdom 1:6, wisdom is a kindly spirit; in Wisdom 7:22, wisdom is a spirit full of excellent attributes.[93] Again, in Wisdom 9:17, wisdom comes from the Holy Spirit sent from on high. If God is willing, the scribe is filled with a spirit of understanding so that he pours forth wisdom (Sir. 39:6). The Spirit is the spirit of wisdom that came to Solomon (Wis. 7:7). For Philo, the Spirit is the divine spirit of wisdom (*Gig.* 47). The Spirit elevates the mind (*Plant.* 24). Similar to this is the spirit of understanding (T. Levi 2:3; 18:7).

THE SPIRIT WHO EFFECTS GOD'S PURPOSES

It is implied throughout the OT Scriptures that where God's Spirit is in action, the will of God comes to pass. A good example is the memorable Zechariah 4:6, where an angel tells Zechariah to pass on the word of the Lord to Zerubbabel that God's purposes will come to pass, "not by might, nor by power, but *by my Spirit*, says the LORD of hosts" (emphasis mine).

THE SPIRIT-ANOINTED MESSIAH

Isaiah 11:1–2 predicts the coming of a descendent of Jesse (and so of David) who will bear fruit. On him, the Spirit will rest: a Spirit of wisdom, understanding, counsel, might, knowledge, and the fear of the Lord (in which he will delight). Clearly, the Spirit generates these things in him. With the breath of his lips—perhaps referring to Spirit-empowered speech—God will bring his just and fair judgment, destroying the wicked (Isa. 3–4). He will be faithful and righteous and will establish shalom in the natural order (Isa. 11:5–8). The earth will be full of God's knowledge, which will be a sign to all nations as he rests in his glorious place (Isa. 11:9–10). When he comes, God will gather his people from the world (Isa. 11:11–12), and Israel's enemies will be subdued (Isa. 11:13–16).

In Isaiah 61:1, the prophet declares that God's Spirit is upon a messianic figure because the Messiah is anointed by God to liberate people in great suffering (the poor, brokenhearted, captives, prisoners), to declare the year of God's favor and the day of vengeance, and to bring comfort, gladness, and

---

93. "Intelligent, holy, unique, manifold, subtle, agile, clear, unpolluted, distinct, invulnerable, loving the good, keen, irresistible, beneficent, humane, steadfast, sure, free from anxiety, all-powerful, overseeing all, and penetrating through all spirits that are intelligent, pure, and altogether subtle" (NRSV).

praise to those who mourn or are weak in spirit. Those people will stand firm and rebuild the devastated cities. People of other nations will serve them, and they will be priests of God. Their shame will become honor and joy. This restoration is linked to the eternal (new) covenant (v. 8). The children of God's people will be known in the nations. The prophet will rejoice in the Lord. In verse 10, the figure will rejoice because he is beautifully adorned with salvation and righteousness. Praise will arise before the nations. In Luke 4, Jesus assumes the place of this figure.

The Messiah of Psalms of Solomon 17–18 is made powerful in the Holy Spirit (Pss. Sol. 17:37) and is imbued with the wisdom of spirit (Pss. Sol. 18:7). In the Mishnah, the Holy Spirit informs the priests that the people are forgiven for shedding blood (*m. Sota* 9:6G).[94]

THE SPIRIT-ANOINTED SERVANT

In Isaiah 42:1, God places his Spirit on his servant so that he brings forth justice to the nations with gentleness and mercy. While Israel—and presumably the pre-Christian Paul before his Damascus Road experience—did not connect this to the Messiah, this is read as the Servant-Messiah by the early Christians and Paul.

THE SPIRIT OUTPOURED

In Isaiah 32:15, the Spirit is poured out from on high, and the wilderness and fields flourish into new life. Isaiah 59:21–22 associates the Spirit resting on God's people forever with his eternal covenant with his people (cf. Isa. 61:8). God assures Israel through the prophets that his Spirit and his words will never again depart from his people. As Peter preached on the Day of Pentecost (Acts 2:17–18), the prophet Joel anticipated God pouring his Spirit on all flesh, something Peter connects to the day of Pentecost (Joel 2:28–29 [3:1–2 LXX]; Acts 2:17–18). The outpouring of the Spirit of grace is anticipated in the Pseudepigrapha and will cause people to be children of truth and walk in God's decrees (T. Jud. 24:2–3). In Qumran, God places his glory "in them," which comes after a reference to the Messiah. Hence, this speaks of Spirit-imbued, renewed, messianic people of God (4Q369 Frag. 1 ii:12).

THE HOLY SPIRIT WHO SANCTIFIES

The phrase "Holy Spirit" (רוּחַ קָדְשׁ, τὸ πνεῦμα τὸ ἅγιόν), which is so prevalent in the NT, is found only three times in the Hebrew OT and once in Wisdom.[95] It describes God's Spirit as holy, consecrated, pure, and purifying. In terms of pneumaformity, by this Holy Spirit, God sanctifies people. The Holy Spirit is also referenced in the Pseudepigrapha. God sends the Spirit on

---

94. Relatedly, in Qumran, the glory of clouds are placed on the Messiah (4Q381 Frag. 15:7).
95. Ps. 50:13; Wis. 9:17; Isa. 63:10, 11. See also Dan. 5:9; 6:4 (LXX).

Isaac (T. Ab. (A) 4:7; also T. Levi 16:8).[96] Other references include the Spirit of sanctification (T. Levi 18:7) and the Spirit of holiness gifted to the saints who eat of the tree of life (T. Levi 18:11). Philo stresses the holy nature of the Spirit that cannot be polluted by unclean sacrifices (*Virt.* 135). In Qumran, prophecy was revealed to prophets by the Holy Spirit (1QS VIII, 15). Related to the notion of the "Holy Spirit" are mentions of God's glory (קְדֹשׁ) sanctifying the tabernacle (Exod. 16:17; 31:3),[97] God's people (Exod. 29:43–44),[98] and Aaron and his sons (Exod. 29:44).[99]

SIN AGAINST THE SPIRIT

First Enoch 20:6 speaks of humans who sin in the spirit, perhaps anticipating Jesus's condemnation of the blasphemy of the Spirit (Mark 3:29).

A SPIRIT NOT TO BE PROVOKED

There are instances of God's anger with people and Israel.[100] Failure to live to please God provokes him.[101] Judgment is also linked to the provocation of the Spirit. In Micah 2:7 LXX, "The house of Jacob provoked the spirit of the Lord," bringing judgment. Similarly, Isaiah speaks of Israel rebelling and provoking the Holy Spirit, causing God to turn in enmity against Israel (Isa. 63:10).

THE SPIRIT WHO RESURRECTS AND TRANSFORMS

The power of the Spirit to transform has been seen above in a range of categories, especially creation, leaders, and those who can prophesy. In 1 Samuel 10, at the anointing of Saul, Samuel predicts that the Spirit will rush upon Saul (as upon the judges) so that he will prophesy, which he then does (1 Sam. 10:10). He will "be turned into another man" (1 Sam. 10:6). In the LXX, the passive of στρέφω indicates the agency of the Spirit. We see here the transforming power of the Spirit. Ezekiel predicts God giving his people "a new spirit" and replacing their hearts of stone with hearts of flesh. So we learn that while God will punish those who persist in evil, those who obey his

---

96. See also Ass. Mos. 11:15. The Holy Spirit is also mentioned in obviously christianized texts: the spirit on Jesus (Sib. Or. 6:7; 7:67). Similarly, the Holy Spirit (Trinitarian text) (Sib. Or. 7:69). Also Clement of Alexandria, Strom. 5.11.77 (Apoc. Zeph. 1). Also Gk. Apoc. Ezra 7:16 (Trinity); divine spirit entering believers converting them to baptism (Apoc. Sedr. 14:5; 15:4). The Spirit of God pouring on people when the temple curtain was torn (T. Benj. 9:2). See also T. Ab. (A) 20:15; T. Ab. (B) 14:9; Mart. Ascen. Isa. 3:16, 25.

97. Compare 1 Kings 9:3; 2 Chron. 7:16, 20; 30:8; 36:14 of Solomon's temple.

98. Compare Lev. 21:8, 15; 21:23; 22:9, 16, 32; Ezek. 37:28, where God sanctifies his people (also Num. 3:13; 8:17, of the firstborn).

99. Compare Num. 16:37.

100. E.g., Deut. 1:37; 3:26; 4:21; Isa. 12:1; Jer. 18:23.

101. Deut. 4:25; 31:29; 32:21; Judg. 2:12; 1 Kings 15:30; 16:2, 7, 13, 26, 33; 20:20, 22, 54; 2 Kings 17:11, 17; 21:6, 15, 17; 23:19, 26; 28:25; 2 Chron. 33:6, 25; Ezra 5:12; Jdt. 11:11; Pss. 77:40, 58; 105:32; Zech. 8:14; Jer. 7:18, 19; 8:19; 11:17; 25:6; Ezek. 16:26; Bar. 4:6; Pss. Sol. 4:1, 25.

law will be God's people (Ezek. 11:19–20). This hope is repeated more fully in Ezekiel 36:22–32 with renewed, purified, and rebuilt Israel living in the land in repentance and in the abundance and peace of the garden of Eden (cf. Ezek. 18:31).

In Ezekiel 37, the Spirit gives Ezekiel the stunning vision of a valley full of dry bones of the long-dead. He is urged to prophesy over the bones, that God will fill them with his breath and cause them to grow flesh and come alive. This Ezekiel does, and an army is formed. The bones are then likened to Israel without hope, but God will renew Israel by placing his Spirit in his people.

In Sirach 34:13, the spirits of those who fear the Lord shall live, for their hope is upon the one who saves them. The Spirit of life enters the dead to make them alive again (T. Ab. (A) 18:11). The Spirit of God rests on those who repudiate evil, corruption, hatred, and illicit sexual relations and instead pursue goodness and love. The Spirit ensures that the person has no pollution in their heart (T. Benj. 8:3). In pseudepigraphal writings, the Spirit is described as the Spirit of truth (T. Jud. 20:1, 5), the Spirit of love (T. Gad 4:7), the Spirit of goodness (T. Benj. 4:5), and the Spirit of perseverance (*Det.* 17). Philo speaks of two types of people: some live by the divine Spirit and reason, while others live by blood and carnal pleasure (*Her.* 57).

THE SPIRIT WHO FILLS ISRAEL

The OT regularly states that exile resulted from Israel's sin, and such exile is also associated with the Spirit. Although Spirit language is not used, the use of glory language when God sends Israel into exile implies the work of the Spirit (Zech. 2:8). Indeed, the glory of God departed from Israel when the ark was removed (1 Sam. 4:21–22).

Still, the prophets dreamed of God's Spirit filling Israel. Isaiah foresees God's glory over all of Mount Zion in the eschaton (Isa. 4:5; 24:23). Moreover, as they return from exile, God's glory guards them from behind (Isa. 58:8; also 52:12). His glory will dwell in the land (Ps. 85:9). God will be the glory in Jerusalem (Zech. 2:5). The glory of God will rise from Israel and will be seen by the nations, and their leaders will come, drawn to it (Isa. 60:1–2; 62:2). They will come and see God's glory in Jerusalem and declare it to the nations (Isa. 66:18–19). Psalms of Solomon 11:6 speaks of Israel proceeding under the supervision of God's glory as Jerusalem is restored. Prayers are made at Qumran that God's glory will fill the land and inheritance.[102]

THE SPIRIT WHO FILLS THE WHOLE EARTH

Isaiah's extraordinary temple vision speaks of God's glory filling the earth (Isa. 6:3). Mention has also been made of the Spirit anointing the Messiah, resulting in the whole earth being flooded with the knowledge of the earth (Isa. 11:9). The dream of the glory of God filling the earth is

---

102. 1Q33 Col. xii:12; 1Q33 Col. xix:4; 4Q492 Frag. 1:1.

also attested (Num. 14:21; Ps. 72:19; 4Q434a Frags. 1 + 2:3). The vision of God's Spirit and glory filling Israel is transcended by the same hope for all of humankind. Isaiah sees the day when the new heavens and earth will remain before God, speaking of his permanent presence (Isa. 66:22). The knowledge of the glory of the Lord will fill the earth as waters cover the sea (Hab. 2:14, also 1QpHab Col. x:14–15). Hence, the psalmists pray for the glory of God to be over all the earth (Pss. 57:5, 11; 72:19; 108:5). They see the day when all the nations will come and worship before God (Ps. 86:9; Isa. 66:23; Zech. 8:22). In the writings of Qumran, the nations will ultimately know and honor God's glory (1QHa Col. xiv:12; 11Q5 Col. xxiv:9), and God's glory will appear in the world (4Q369 Frag. 1 ii:3).

CONCLUSION

Paul inherited a rich array of ideas concerning the Spirit from his Jewish heritage. Within Israel's monotheistic framework, he understood the Spirit's role in creation, participating with God in creating the universe and earth with its stunning geography, flora, fauna, and humankind. Paul recognized that within every living creature is a spirit breathed into them by God. This Spirit, or breath of God, is life. The marriage union was created to reflect the love relationship between the Trinity and is not merely a human relationship but is spiritual.

The Spirit is always with God's people and guides them. Paul recognized the Spirit's work in speaking to them on God's behalf and inscribing the Holy Scriptures. He was aware of the Spirit coming upon God-appointed leaders in Israel's story. The Spirit empowered the kings, and particularly the prophets. Paul knew God's Spirit could act in judgment, chastising sinful humankind and Israel when they strayed from God's ways. The Spirit guides God's people. The Spirit could provide, as with quail and manna in the wilderness. The Spirit empowered the prophets. Paul was aware that those with unique gifts, like the craftsman Bezalel, were gifted by the Spirit.

The Spirit inhabits the temple of God. Paul knew of evil spirits dangerous to creation, to God's purposes, and to his people. Yet he knew that God's Spirit was supreme over such forces. He recognized the work of the Spirit in generating God's life in people and strengthening them for the challenges of living in a hostile world. The Spirit generates wisdom in people. His Spirit's presence on earth enacts God's purposes.

Before his conversion, Paul looked forward to a Spirit-anointed Messiah imbued with wisdom, understanding, counsel, might, knowledge, and the fear of the Lord. This Messiah would rule the nations with justice and bring God's shalom. He would not have grasped that the Servant of Isaiah would represent this same figure. Paul would have looked forward to the last days when God would pour out his Spirit on the men and women of Israel. However, he had no idea this Messiah would be anointed with the Spirit and be crucified, rise again, and pour out his Spirit on the people of God. He is the Holy Spirit, utterly pure in every sense, and powerful to sanctify. The Spirit is not to be provoked or blasphemed.

Paul believed that God with the Spirit, his other spiritual forces, and Israel would subjugate the nations, conquer God's enemies, raise the righteous dead, grant them eternal life, and renew the cosmos with Jerusalem as its religious, cultural, economic, and political center. He did not envisage God pouring out his Spirit on uncircumcised Gentile sinners. To experience the Spirit, they had to believe in God and become Jews living under the law. He did not anticipate that genuine faith in Jesus, crucified and raised, would cause God to instantaneously pour his Spirit into that believer, Jew or Greek, slave or free, male or female.

He dreamed of the day God would see his temple not only rebuilt (as it was through Herod) but filled with his Spirit. Paul did not envisage God forming a temple of living people on the cornerstone and foundation of Jesus Christ the Lord. He did not understand that God's temple would transcend Jerusalem and become every believer and gathering of believers across the world, who would become one giant family of God, the body of Christ, the temple of the Spirit.

Paul anticipated God's redemption coming at the consummation of the age, when the nexus of events Israel dreamed of would come, including the pouring out of the Spirit, the resurrection of the dead, and the renewal of all things. He did not see the Spirit coming in time, forming temples of the Spirit who, propelled and empowered by the Spirit, would carry the message of God to the world so that the world would believe and receive the Spirit. He retained his view of a renewed humanity and world, but now it would be reshaped around the death and resurrection of Jesus and Pentecost. To the details of his view of the Spirit I now turn.

CHAPTER 2

THE SPIRIT LEADS TO CONVERSION

As discussed, as a Jewish Pharisee, Paul is well aware of the role of the Spirit in the creation of the world and every human being. He believed that, in some sense, the Spirit animated all life and that the Spirit is the force of life animating all fleshly creatures. In line with this, he believed in the existence of Adam and knew the story of God breathing life into him (1 Cor. 15:45). This breath is the Spirit of God. He knew that God had provided Adam and Eve with the source of eternal life within the garden of delight. However, he also knew that because of Eve's deception and their sin, they (and all their descendants) were deprived of access to the tree and everlasting life (Rom. 5:12; 2 Cor. 11:3).

Hence, after the flood, God limited the lifespan of humans to 120 years. So, while all people have received a spirit from God giving them life, they are mortal and perishable—at the point of death, this spirit of life has been withdrawn or has faded to nothing. While the spirit of life maintains them until their bodies can no longer support life, the close intimate connection with God, made possible by God's Spirit after Pentecost, did not exist for people prior to Pentecost. They were cut off from him in the close, personal sense Christians know today. Furthermore, Paul knew that the sin of Adam and Eve had introduced death into all humankind and had brought the whole creation into bondage to decay (Rom. 5:12; 8:21).

Before Christian conversion, Paul would have believed in the potential of salvation and hope of eternal life at the final resurrection of the dead, when all would face God in judgment. For a Jew, this came through birth into the people of God elected by grace—the covenant community formed with Abraham, codified at Sinai, recast and given monarchial leadership with David, and continued in the law-observant people of Israel submitted to God and his covenantal requirements, the law. Such faith was expressed in the daily recitation of the Shema and by careful observance of those laws that marked off Israel as distinct: Sabbath and the Jewish calendar, maintaining ritual purity, kosher eating, and the like. Righteous Jews knew of the presence of God's

Spirit prior to Christ, but not with the qualitative power experienced by all believers since Christ's death.

Where a Gentile was concerned, this person was welcome to gather with Israel at the synagogue and participate to a limited degree in worship. Such God-worshipers are found across Acts.[1] However, Gentiles had to join the covenant community by becoming proselytes to hold this hope of eternal life in God's coming reign. Their conversion involved faith in Yahweh expressed through Judaizing—by adhering to the rituals of circumcision (for men), ceremonial washing, and submission to the Torah, especially the boundary markers.[2] Culturally speaking, they had to become Jews and hope God would raise them after judgment. The assumption was that these Gentiles could only hope to receive the Spirit alongside Jews in the eschaton. Of course, God could still encounter non-Jews, as in the case of the Gentile Abram (Gen. 15:6; Rom. 4:3; Gal. 3:6). Still, for Israel, for a Gentile to be fully included in God's people required Judaizing. As the following discussion explores, Paul's understanding of what we call "conversion" and the Spirit was transformed in Christ.

THE SPIRIT SENDS GOSPEL COMMUNICATORS

Paul's use of sending and other language in the movement of God's missionaries is also relevant to this discussion, as it precedes and leads to conversion. His God is a sending God, including sending Jesus (Rom. 8:3; 4:4; cf. Eph. 2:17), the Spirit (Gal. 4:6), and preachers with the gospel (Rom. 10:15).[3] Their sending is missional—the Spirit sends so people hear, believe, and receive the Spirit.

Evangelism is a creative act of reaching into the world God made (2 Cor. 4:5–6). Philippians 1:6 can refer to salvation, or as is more likely, to God's beginning and completion of his mission.[4] Second Corinthians 2:14–15 evocatively expresses how Paul understands that God and Christ lead mission. God, in Christ, *leads* Paul's team in triumphal procession and spreads the fragrance of the knowledge of Christ everywhere through them. It suggests the gradual spread of the gospel as the fragrance of perfume fills a home (John 12:3; cf. Song 1:3; Jer. 25:10), or the smell of a burnt offering permeates the place of sacrifice (Eph. 5:2; cf. Exod. 29:18).[5] Notably, the scope of movement is ἐν παντὶ τόπῳ (in every place), even if not all find the smell pleasing

---

1. Acts 13:43, 50; 16:14; 17:4, 17; 18:7.
2. On Jewish conversion see Joshua Ezra Burns, "Conversion and Proselytism," *EDEJ* 484–86. Converts were also expected to integrate into local Jewish communities and observe Jewish law and cultic expectations. Women may take an elaborate penitential process including rejection of original religion (Jos. Asen. 10:10–13) and sometimes immersion.
3. He also sent the prophets throughout the Old Testament. See Judg. 6:8; 2 Sam. 12:25; 2 Kings 17:13; 24:2; 2 Chron. 24:19; 25:15; Jer. 7:5; 25:4; 28:9; 29:19; 35:15; 44:4; Amos 3:7; Hag. 1:12; Zech. 7:12.
4. Keown, *Congregational*, 216–23.
5. Ὀσμή is used frequently in the LXX of sweet-smelling sacrifices (e.g., Lev. 1:9; Num. 15:3; Ezek. 20:28).

(2 Cor. 2:15; cf. Exod. 5:21; 2 Macc. 9:9; Isa. 34:3). Christ sent Paul to preach the gospel of a crucified Messiah (1 Cor. 1:17); he is commissioned by God to speak in Christ (2 Cor. 2:17).

There is also a range of indicators of the Spirit's involvement in gospel proclamation. Paul knew that his ministry was Christ by the Spirit working in and through him as he preached, did good works, performed miracles, and established churches from Jerusalem to Illyricum "by the power of the Spirit of God" (Rom. 15:18–19).[6] He and his team preached such a gospel with words "taught by the Spirit" (1 Cor. 2:13). In Troas, "a door was opened for me in the Lord" (2 Cor. 2:12). While Paul did not take the opportunity because he had no peace in his spirit and deemed it more important to find Titus, it is God in Christ by his Spirit who opened the opportunity. And when these doors open, the preacher, empowered and led by the Spirit, is to preach the mystery of Christ clearly (Col. 4:4). Injunctions follow this to the Colossians concerning their gospel conversation—they also are to be led by the Spirit as they share the word (λόγος) wisely, opportunely, gracefully, winsomely, and responsively (Col. 4:5–6).

The process of pneumaformity begins with conversion and the reception of the Spirit. Conversion is preceded by the Spirit impelling people toward others to love them and share the faith with them verbally, actively, and spiritually.

He carried God's authority to build up God's people on his behalf (2 Cor. 10:8; 12:19; 13:10), Christ was speaking in and through him (2 Cor. 13:3), and Christ appointed him to serve him (1 Tim. 1:12). Paul and those in his orbit had been "entrusted [by God] with the gospel" (1 Thess. 2:4; 2 Tim. 1:12). With all of Christ's energy working powerfully in him, he toiled in the gospel—another implicit reference to the Spirit (Col. 1:29).[7]

Like Peter's ministry to the circumcised, Paul recognized (by the Spirit, implied) that God was working in him as he ministered to the Gentiles (Gal. 2:8).[8] Through his (and his team's) ministry, God spreads the fragrance of the knowledge of Christ everywhere—another metaphor pertaining to the Spirit (2 Cor. 2:14).

His speech to the Corinthians did not involve rhetorical brilliance but preaching the foolishness of Christ and Christ crucified (1 Cor. 2:2). This message came with a "demonstration of the Spirit and of power" as the power of the "foolish" gospel cut into the hearts of the Corinthians (1 Cor. 2:4).

---

6. See also texts where all spiritual gifts and activities are empowered by God, Father, Son, and Spirit (cf. 1 Cor. 12:18, 24, 28; Eph. 4:6–7).

7. Similarly see Fee, *GEP*, 645. He rightly avers that this is "yet another 'power' text which has the Holy Spirit as its unexpressed presupposition." He notes how ἐν δυνάμει ("with power") is related to Paul's apostolic ministry (Rom. 15:18–19; 2 Cor. 1:4–5; 6:7; 1 Thess. 1:5). Paul's ministry, despite his labor, "is ultimately empowered by God, who is at work in him by the Spirit."

8. The participle ὁ ἐνεργήσας can be God, Christ, or God in Christ working in Peter and Paul. In any case, this is done by the Spirit.

Paul also reminds the Thessalonians of how the message that converted them came with the word, power, much conviction, and the Spirit (1 Thess. 1:5). His ministry, then, is "the ministry of the Spirit" that completely transcends the "ministry of death" (2 Cor. 3:7).[9] He is commended as a servant of God by such reliance on the Holy Spirit (2 Cor. 6:6).

God, who began the mission in the world and Philippi by his Spirit, will complete it. God's election of the first Christians, such as the Thessalonians, who are "the firstfruits to be saved," refers to God's leading Paul to them to preach and their yielding to Christ (2 Thess. 2:13).

Paul's notion of "gospel doors" supports that for him, believers are led by the Spirit in mission. In 1 Corinthians 16:9, a wide door was opened for Paul in Corinth. The agent of this was God through Christ by the Spirit. Paul's decision to put Titus's needs ahead of this opportunity shows that Paul recognized that the Spirit might direct a person away from such opportunities to help another Christian in need. Paul's request for prayer that such doors are opened to the word in Colossians 4:3 indicates that God is the one who does this by his Spirit. Hence, all missional plans for Paul are subject to the Spirit's leading.

Paul's plan to remain in Ephesus until Pentecost and then travel to Macedonia and then Corinth is premised on the caveat "if the Lord permits" (1 Cor. 16:7). When he has to defend himself against accusations of vacillating in his mission plans, Paul speaks of God's leading him in Christ (2 Cor. 2:14–15). He needed to defend himself because instead of going to Macedonia, he resolved to go first to Corinth, only to change his mind again (2 Cor. 1:15–16). He did so because, after leaving Ephesus for Troas, and despite a gospel door opened to him, Paul became unsettled in his *spirit* and changed his mind to go and find Titus in Macedonia (rather than to Corinth). The mention of "my spirit" suggests the inward part of his being, where God's Spirit speaks and nudges the believer's life (cf. Rom. 8:26)—the Spirit caused Paul to adjust his plans.

For the convert, pneumaformity includes being open to the Spirit's lead in their particular missional vocation. All Christians are caught up in the Spirit's

---

9.   On 2 Corinthians 3:7, see Fee, *GEP*, 307–8. Paul uses three *a fortiori* (if one . . . how much more the other) arguments in the paragraph with this as an example of *a minori ad maius*, "from the lesser to the greater." He notes three aspects: (1) continue the contrast of new and Mosaic covenants; (2) emphasize the ministry of each; and (3) despite the impotency of the Mosaic covenant in salvation terms, recognize there was a glory attached to the covenant. The new covenant of the Spirit has come and the old is obsolete in eschatological terms. Paul uses διακονία throughout, contrasting how what is now (Christ and the Spirit having come) is of greater glory than that which was then (the glory of Moses's face after receiving the Law). "Now, the Spirit gives life as people are justified by faith" (v. 9). Fee correctly notes that while Christ brought justification, not the Spirit, this justification was effected in the Corinthian lives by the Spirit (cf. 1 Cor. 6:11). Thus, Paul can elide the "ministry of the Spirit" into the "the ministry of justification." See also Gorman, *ITCG*, 69, who argues Galatians 3:1–5 indicates that "the Spirit somehow effected the Galatians' experience of co-crucifixion and co-resurrection."

mission and have their part to play with their various gifts. The Spirit is leading a critical aspect of development in their engagement with others.

THE SPIRIT PRE-CONVERSION

Thus far, it is established that God leads people into and during mission.
It is *his* mission and by the Spirit that he appoints and sends people. What
about God's work in unbelievers before conversion? While Paul does not clarify the work of the Spirit in lives prior to conversion, he gives us some clues
that indicate the pre-conversion work of the Spirit in a life.

Traces of the Spirit in People

Paul's analysis of the human condition in Romans leads me to conclude
that God's Spirit is active in the world and people before salvation. First, Paul
posits that some things that can be known about God are plain to all people,
despite their universal ungodliness and unrighteousness. These things are
plain because "God made it clear to them" (Rom. 1:19 LEB). Paul elaborates
in Romans 1:20: "For from the creation of the world, his invisible attributes,
both his eternal power and deity, are discerned clearly, being understood in
the things created" (LEB). Two things that people can perceive of God's invisible attributes are singled out: his eternal power and his deity (or divinity).
The creation is so clearly designed, astonishingly glorious, and intricate that
people recognize aspects of God.

Moo says, "This text asserts that God has revealed something of himself
to all people in the world he has made."[10] Sadly, as Moo goes on to say, "It
is equally obvious that this revelation is universally rejected, as people turn
from knowledge of God to gods of their own making."[11] As God has made
himself plain to the world and as they know it and reject him, people are without excuse before God. God is fair to exercise his wrath against them (Rom.
1:18; 2:8–9).

The agent of revelation here is God, who "made it clear to them"
(ἐφανέρωσεν, 1:19). I postulate that it is by the Spirit that God makes
himself known to people through the glories of his creation. As people
ponder the wonders of creation, God's Spirit is tugging on their minds and
hearts, summoning them to recognize God's power and deity and then to
believe. Sadly, their universal problem is that while they may recognize the
activity of a creator, they universally fail to acknowledge him and appropriately honor him and thank him—their thinking is futile, their hearts darkened, and they rely on human wisdom and resort to idolatry. Exchanging
God's truth for a lie, they worship idolatrous created things rather than the
creator (Rom. 1:24).

---

10.   Moo, *Romans*, 117.
11.   Moo, *Romans*, 117.

The second passage that hints at the Spirit's work in all people despite their sin is Romans 2:14. Jews and Gentiles alike have sinned and will be judged and perish (Rom. 2:12; cf. 3:9, 23). Having heard the law, Jews have failed to observe it and are not justified before God based on the law (Rom. 2:13). Paul shifts focus to Gentiles in vv. 14–15. Gentiles do not have the law but do what the law requires despite not having it. Details are not given here, but Paul may be referring to Gentiles whom Jews encounter who embody love and goodness. These may include God-worshipers like Cornelius, Lydia, Titius Justus, and others who do not submit to the Jewish boundary markers but are good people who participate in the life of the synagogue. He may also be thinking of others in broader society. In doing what the law requires, implicitly, they demonstrate that "the work of the law is written on their hearts." Paul restates this in terms of their conscience bearing witness with them. However, like Jews, as Paul has just stated in v. 12, Gentiles do not observe the law flawlessly. They experience a cognitive dissonance relating to their behavior, their thoughts accusing or excusing them. These verses speak of the imprint of God to a degree inscribed on Gentiles who have no relationship with the God of Israel or his law.

The language of the law written on hearts and revealed in the Gentiles unwittingly doing the good required of the law is suggestive of God's work by the Spirit. Indeed, for Paul, the law itself is spiritual (Rom. 7:14).[12] The law on the heart recalls Jeremiah 31:33, where God says he will make a new covenant with Israel and write the law on their hearts. Other prophets link obedience to God's law and the Spirit, including Isaiah and Ezekiel (Isa. 59:21; Ezek. 36:26–27).[13] Later in the passage, Paul tells the Romans that what matters is not literal circumcision but that of the heart by the Spirit (Rom. 2:25–29). Paul also links the heart and Spirit in 2 Corinthians 3:3, where the Corinthian church is a letter from Christ written not with ink but with the Spirit of the living God, on tablets of human hearts.

As we draw the threads together, we sense that although for Paul, humankind is sinful and corrupted and, without exception, unable to attain righteousness through their works (law or otherwise), traces of the Spirit's work are on their darkened hearts. These traces suggest the power of the Spirit to tug on the human heart as people contemplate God's creation and indicate a common human morality. Upon hearing the gospel, they also must yield in faith to experience the fullness of the Spirit, poured out to indwell them and begin their pneumaformation. When they do, the Spirit circumcises their hearts, and transformation begins. They are new creations, the old has gone, and the new has come (2 Cor. 5:17; cf. Gal. 6:15). Indeed, the metaphor "new

---

12.   On this see Fee, *GEP*, 510.
13.   Also Ezek. 11:19; 18:31.

creation" calls to mind the hovering of the Spirit and God's renewal of those who yield.[14]

Before the Creation of the World

Paul believes that God is omniscient and all things are predestined. Predestination is found in a range of texts. In Romans 8:28–30, the foreknown who are also the called, justified, and glorified are predestined to be conformed to Christ's image. In the next chapter, Paul writes that God has prepared beforehand people destined for destruction or glory (Rom. 9:22–23; cf. 1 Peter 2:8). Believers are chosen in Christ before the foundation of the world to be holy in his sight and predestined for adoption (Eph. 1:4–5). God chose believers (us) in Christ "before the foundation of the world" to be his holy people, and in love and according to his will, he predestined believers (us) for adoption as children through Jesus Christ (Eph. 1:4–5, 11; cf. Rev 13:8).[15]

These passages are consistent with the Hebrew view of the absolute sovereignty of God.[16] This viewpoint is also found outside Paul in some NT texts.[17] As I have written elsewhere, I see no reason to diminish the fullness of God's sovereignty over individuals and every event. However, we must also recognize that NT writers like Paul hold that humans retain volition and the capability to say yes or no to God (see further below).[18]

These deterministic passages point to God's prior actions in people's lives, whether their destiny is salvation or destruction. I see no reason to see this as anything but indicative of God's action in history via the Spirit over and in every life. One can view this determinism harshly, with the Spirit's role direct and the Spirit the sole agent preparing people for salvation or destruction (without human agency). However, considering the evidence that Paul believes in human culpability for failing to yield to God (further below), it is better to posit that Paul understood that God is actively summoning all people to salvation by his Spirit. Some yield and receive the salvation for which they are predestined. Paul would call these the called and elect.[19] However, others who hear the summons of God through the word reject it. In their resistance to God's summons by his Spirit via the word, they become guilty of disobedience and liable to God's judgment. If they never yield, they receive the sentence of eternal condemnation.

---

14. See Myk Habets, *The Progressive Mystery: Tracing the Elusive Spirit in Scripture and Tradition* (Bellingham, WA: Lexham, 2019), 83–84.

15. See also Col. 3:12–13; 1 Thess. 1:4; 2 Thess. 2:14; 2 Tim. 1:9; Titus 1:1.

16. See, e.g., Exod. 4:21; Deut. 7:6; 14:2; Prov. 16:4; Isa. 48:3–5; Dan. 4:35.

17. See, e.g., John 6:44; 15:16; Acts 2:23; 13:48; 1 Peter 1:2.

18. Mark J. Keown, *Romans and the Mission of God* (Eugene, OR: Wipf & Stock, 2021), 293–306.

19. For *called* in a salvation sense, see Rom. 1:6, 7; 8:28, 30; 9:24; 1 Cor. 1:2, 9, 24, 26; 7:17, 18, 20, 21, 22, 24; Gal. 1:6; 5:8, 13; Eph. 1:18; 4:1, 4; Phil. 3:14; Col. 3:15; 1 Thess. 2:12; 4:7; 5:24; 2 Thess. 1:11; 2:14; 1 Tim. 6:12; 2 Tim. 1:9. On people as the elect, see Rom. 8:33; 11:7; 2 Tim. 2:10; Titus 1:1.

As God's foreknowledge is absolute, this is what they were created for (in that God knew the outcome and chose to create *this* world rather than another [that we know of]). God tolerated them, giving them time to repent. Sadly, they did not. By the Spirit, they were summoned to pneumaformity, but they resisted. As such, Paul's theology of the sovereignty of God strongly suggests that the Spirit is at work in all places and at all times in every life, summoning people to believe.

The Spirit Before and in the Womb

The work of the Spirit in calling and preparing people in the womb is an OT prophetic motif found in the NT of John the Baptist and Paul. Isaiah reminds Israel (Jacob) of its election, formed as it was by God from the womb (Isa. 44:1). David sings of his devotion to God from his mother's womb (Pss. 22:10; 71:6). God tells Jeremiah that before he formed him in the womb, God knew him and, before his birth, consecrated him and appointed him a prophet to the nations (Jer. 1:5). Isaiah's Servant, agreed in the NT to be Jesus, was called from the womb and named in his mother's body (Isa. 49:1). In Luke, Gabriel tells Zechariah that John will be filled with the Spirit from his mother's womb (Luke 1:15; cf. 1:41). Paul reminds the Galatians of his Damascus Road experience, describing God as the one who set him apart from his mother's womb and called him by his grace to his mission (Gal. 1:15).

This setting apart by God occurs at his period of gestation in his mother's womb, which aligns with OT texts where people are formed in the womb by God, including Job (Job 31:15) and David (Ps. 139:13–14).[20] The case of Paul's own setting apart is critical. He appears to say that even though he resisted the Christian message from the day he first heard it (from the likes of Stephen),[21] God had been working in his life, shaping it for the day when he would experience Christ, become a Christian, and serve God as his apostle. God's work in Paul raises the possibility of the work of the Spirit from conception in the lives of all people, even during their lives as unbelievers. We can surmise then that God prepares them to hear the gospel and to have the opportunity to believe. When they do believe, the Spirit inhabits them and transforms them into the instruments of God's work on earth (inasmuch as they are prepared to yield to his Spirit). They are condemned when they do not believe and reject God's summons.[22]

---

20. See also Psalm 58:3, where the wicked are estranged from the womb; Hosea 12:3, where Jacob grasped Esau's heel (cf. Gen. 25:26).

21. It is likely Paul encountered Stephen as a member of the Synagogue of the Freedmen, which included Cilicians, and engaged in fierce debate with him. This culminated in Stephen's death. Mark J. Keown, *Discovering the New Testament: An Introduction to Its Background, Theology, and Themes: The Pauline Letters* (Bellingham, WA: Lexham, 2021), 16.

22. I believe Fee, *GEP*, is lacking in discussing the potential work of the Spirit in terms of human formation from conception in the womb.

The Spirit and Life

Another thing we can say is that God, by his Spirit, sustains life in every living and breathing human and creature.[23] Also evident is that people have a spirit gifted by God that leaves them at death.[24] The Spirit of God has the power to speak and teach (Rom. 8:26; 1 Cor. 2:13; Gal. 4:6; 1 Tim. 4:1). It is not clear if Paul agrees with the likes of Philo as to whether the spirit in humans is actually the Spirit of God that returns to God at death or whether something gifted by God that ceases to exist at death. Either way, Paul likely understands that the Spirit communicates with the human spirit inwardly. Where a person is without faith, the mechanism of God speaking is undefined.

The Spirit's Communication and Human Sinfulness

I have touched on the issue of God's sovereignty and the human capability to hear and believe. Is it possible for the Spirit to speak to a person corrupted by sin? One possibility is that all humankind cannot respond to God's Word for salvation because of their total depravity. If so, we can postulate that the Spirit works *only* on those God has predetermined will receive salvation, those predestined.[25] Thus, only in those God has predetermined to believe does the Spirit interact inwardly with the human spirit, enabling faith to flower in the chosen. In my view, this creates a range of problems.

Paul strongly asserts the impartiality of God.[26] He also emphasizes God's justness.[27] As an impartial God, it is unconscionable to think that God would not give people the same opportunity to respond.

As noted previously, in Romans 1:19–21, Paul speaks of the wrath of God revealed against the ungodliness and unrighteousness of humankind. Yet he then asserts that God's existence and power should be discerned by people, despite their fallenness. Hence, they are "without excuse"; "they did not see fit to acknowledge God" (Rom. 1:28a). Consequently, God "gives them up" to their sinfulness (Rom. 1:24, 26, 28b). Paul, then, assumes that people, although fallen, should be able to perceive God and worship him. Sadly, they do not and are culpable. God, then, impartially renders to each person according to their works (Rom. 2:6–11).

Again, as discussed above, the presence of the law on the hearts of Gentiles, even if it doesn't enable them to live it out, demonstrates that within

---

23. Rom. 1:20–22; 8:19–23; 1 Cor. 8:6; 11:9; Eph. 3:9; Col. 1:15–16.
24. See those places Paul uses πνεῦμα of the human spirit (Rom. 1:9; 8:16 [second use]; 1 Cor. 2:11 [first use]; 5:3–5; 7:34; 14:14–16; 16:18; 2 Cor. 2:13; 7:1; Gal. 6:18 [a collective singular, also Phil. 4:23; 2 Tim. 4:22; Philem. 25]; Eph. 4:23; 1 Thess. 5:23).
25. See for example Rom. 8:29–30; 9:18, 22–23; Eph. 1:4, 5, 11, which can suggest predestination regardless of human response. Similarly, 2 Thessalonians 2:11 speaks of God sending a delusion on people. However, see also human responsibility in Romans 9:30–33.
26. Rom. 2:11; Gal. 2:6; Eph. 6:9; Col. 3:25.
27. Rom. 1:17; 3:5, 21–22, 25–26; 10:3; 2 Cor. 1:30; 5:21; cf. 2 Thess. 1:5–6. Indeed, as God reached out to the whole world through Christ, Israel was ignorant of this act of impartial justice in Christ (Rom. 10:3).

fallen humankind, there is some remnant of the law inscribed on their hearts (Rom. 2:14–15).

The blindness of unbelievers is attributed to Satan's (the god of this world) power to veil the gospel among those who are perishing. The god of this world blinds unbelievers' minds and stops them from seeing "the light of the gospel of the glory of Christ, who is the image of God" (2 Cor. 4:3–4; cf. 3:14, 16). The gospel is like light shining into human hearts that are hardened and "darkened in their understanding, alienated from the life of God because of the ignorance that is in them" (Eph. 4:18). The light of the gospel shines into foolish, lustful, hardened, veiled, blinded, and impenitent hearts,[28] and hardened, debased, futile, materialistic, alienated, hostile, sensuous, depraved, corrupted, defiled minds,[29] giving "the knowledge of the glory of God in the face of Jesus Christ" (2 Cor. 4:5–6).[30] The work of the Spirit is like light, shining into the heart and mind (cf. Eph. 1:17–18). Satan's work seeks to block that light.

Elsewhere, Paul touches on Satan's power to stop the reception of the gospel, mainly through disrupting Paul's mission (2 Cor. 2:11; 1 Thess. 2:18), through false gospels and preachers deceiving believers (2 Cor. 11:14; 1 Tim. 4:1; cf. Rom. 16:18), through enticing believers into temptation and his snares,[31] and through the lawless one who deceives others (2 Thess. 2:9).[32]

Paul also employs other vocabulary to describe demonic forces that interfere with God's communication. The plural of στοιχεῖον, "elemental principles," is used to describe the false ideologies and spiritual forces that keep unbelievers in bondage (Gal. 4:3, 9; Col. 2:8, 20).[33]

In Romans 8:38–39, Paul mentions rulers, powers, height, and depth, likely referring to demonic forces that can afflict people. Believers need not fear because God's love in Christ (by the Spirit) is present with them (cf. Rom. 5:5). The Corinthians must only participate in the Lord's Supper and not in idol feasts, or they will be exposed to demons (1 Cor. 10:20–21).

These evil spirits can speak through people (as does the Holy Spirit), even in Christian assemblies. Their power to mislead is confirmed in 1 Timothy 4:1–3, where the teaching of deceitful demons through insincere, conscience-seared false teachers causes some to desert the faith. Hence, God imparts the gift of discernment to enable believers to determine when a message is false (1 Cor. 12:10). All such messages are subject to the assessment of those with the prophetic gift (1 Cor. 14:32).

---

28. Rom. 1:21, 24; 2:5; 11:7; 2 Cor. 3:14, 15; 4:4; Eph. 4:18.

29. Rom. 1:28; 2 Cor. 3:14; Eph. 4:17; Phil. 3:19; Col. 1:21; 1 Tim. 6:5; 2 Tim. 3:8; Titus 1:15.

30. See also 2 Corinthians 3:14, "their minds were hardened" and veiled. The veil is removed when a person turns to the Lord (2 Cor. 3:16).

31. See 1 Cor. 7:5; Eph. 4:27; 1 Tim. 3:6–7; 5:15; 2 Tim. 2:26; cf. Eph. 6:11–17; 2 Thess. 3:3. See also Luke's accounts in Acts 13:10; 26:18 (cf. Acts 5:3; 10:38).

32. See also Rom. 16:20; 1 Cor. 5:5; 2 Cor. 6:15; 12:7; 1 Tim. 1:20; 3:6.

33. See for my view on the *stoicheia*, Keown, *Galatians*, 407–12, and "The Spirit Who Participates in Rebirth."

The spiritual forces of evil in Ephesians 6 scheme against believers and wage war against them. They must be wrestled with, and their threats extinguished by believers together resisting, clad with God's truth, righteousness, gospel readiness, faith, salvation, the Spirit and God's Word, and Spirit-led and empowered prayer. The failure of humankind, then, is due to a combination of their sinfulness, their preference for idolatry and desire, and the spiritual interference of Satan, who veils human hearts and minds from recognizing the truth of the gospel and yielding to God's beckoning in it.

Accordingly, we can speculate that while humankind is fallen and corrupted by sin, due to the spirit breathed into them to give them life, the spirit-presence within their heart and mind (even if corrupted by sin) retains a capacity to be touched by the Spirit as they encounter God's revelation. However, the Spirit does not overpower the person's will but invites people to yield by faith, with that person retaining the capacity (enabled by the spirit breathed into them) to yield or to resist.

As the word is heard and the Spirit impresses God's love and desire for relationship onto the human heart and mind, the person may remain hardened due to spiritual interference and their own misunderstanding and preferences and reject the word. Alternatively, as God desires, they may yield to the word with faith (see below). Such a view can be argued to threaten Paul's theology of God's sovereignty and grace's irresistibility. However, one can hold that the world, including its every detail, including those saved, is predestined by an omniscient, creating God. At the same time, Paul's letters affirm that human volition and response are part and parcel of the predetermined world people inhabit (even if we struggle to explain this easily). Predestination defines God's view of history as a completed event in his mind before creation. Human volition plays out in real time as people respond to God. Satan seeks to block the sword of the Spirit. People's responses are assured from the perspective of an omniscient God, but each individual is acting volitionally in the moment across time.[34]

Assuming Pauline authorship of the Pastorals, Paul unambiguously says that God "desires all people to be saved and to come to the knowledge of the truth" (1 Tim. 2:4). Such a passion drove Paul's relentless itinerant ministry to see all people saved (1 Cor. 9:19–22; 10:33).

Pneumaphanies

All this suggests that just as Jesus came into Israel to seek and save the lost (Luke 19:10), God's Spirit is perpetually at work in the world, reaching

---

34. See further Keown, *Romans and the Mission of God*, 293–306. I discuss God's sovereignty and human volition as Paul lays them out in Romans and colloquially define my position as "Calviminianism" (p. 304n24). We live in the dialectical tension between two truths whereby God is utterly sovereign so that everything is predestined. Still, we also have sufficient volition to choose and be accountable for our choices. God can create a world like this because he is God.

out to all people and beckoning them in their spirits to come to him. Satan seeks to disrupt God's invitations. The Spirit summons humankind through God's revelation in the magnificence of creation and his undeniable work in history so that people are without excuse. Across history, he has done this more directly by encountering the likes of Noah, Abraham and the patriarchs, Moses, Samuel, and the prophets and prophetesses of Israel, imparting "special revelation" of his being. In Jesus's life and ministry, he did so through christophanies as thousands of people ministered to him in person. As Luke so powerfully emphasizes, the Spirit was at work in and through Jesus, summoning people to enter God's reign through repentance and faith (Luke 4:14, 18–20). After the pivotal and foundational acts of the death and resurrection, Jesus appeared to Mary Magdalene, the Emmaus Road pair, Peter, Jesus's brother James, groups of disciples, and the apostle Paul.

All these encounters from before Christ's incarnation to his ascension involved God's revelation *plus* the inward work of the Spirit as he encountered people in what might be called "pneumaphanies." As God desired, despite all these people being flawed and Satan's efforts to hinder him, all such people yielded by faith and became God's children.

Pentecost marked the decisive turning point where Israel's dream of the Spirit being outpoured came to pass for those who had responded to God's theophany—in christophany and pneumaphany—with faith. According to Luke, the first group experienced an overwhelming rush of the πνεῦμα of God and spoke in tongues, and Peter preached to the crowds. Three thousand responded, were baptized, and were filled with the Spirit (Acts 2).

Since Pentecost, pneumaphanies continue as God reaches out to humankind with love, simultaneously inviting every person into a relationship with him. Pneumaformity begins when the pneumaphany is experienced, the recipient yields to the summons of God through his word, faith flowers, and the Spirit indwells the believer and engages with the believer's inward spirit previously breathed into them. People now "in Christ," and so "in God," by the power of the Spirit begin the journey of theoformity,[35] Christoformity, and cruciformity through the agency of the Spirit (pneumaformity). Since Adam, the vehicle of God's invitation into a relationship has been God's word. Word empowered by the Spirit is God's pattern of pneumaphany.

The Spirit works in harmony with and on behalf of God through his Son, bringing a person to conversion and converting them, and at that moment pneumaformation begins. The first aspect of the Spirit's role in a person's life is the Spirit's sovereign action in their lives before they hear the Christian message. While people communicating God's message to others is essential, the role of the Spirit in conversion cannot be limited only to the proclamation of the gospel by people imbued with the Spirit. The Spirit is sovereign and acts as God wills.

---

35. Similarly, Gorman, *ITCG*, 38. He speaks of "Spirit-enabled theoformity."

I suggest that the work of the Spirit is seen in Paul's Damascus Road experience. In Galatians 1:12, he encountered a "revelation of Jesus Christ," where he received the gospel. God called him by his grace (Gal. 1:15).[36] He was pleased to reveal his Son not merely to Paul, as if in an experience of seeing, but *into* (ἐν) Paul. The unexpected preposition speaks of the penetration of God into the mind and heart of the apostle, that is, the work of the Spirit.[37] Indeed, this was a fully triune experience. Something similar is expressed in the conversion of Lydia in Luke's writings: as "the Lord opened her heart to pay attention to what was said by Paul," she believed and was baptized (Acts 16:14). As seen in the non-Pauline biblical data and the history of the church, sometimes with a theophanic or christophanic experience, and through the speech and penetration of the Spirit ("pneumaphanic"), God summons people to him.[38]

THE SPIRIT IN CONVERSION

As discussed, Paul's conversion was the result of not only Christ's dynamic revelation to him but the work of the Spirit piercing *into* his inner being, enabling him to recognize Christ and his significance and hear God's call through his Son. His subsequent empowerment speaks of the receipt of the Spirit after this moment. And his ministry that followed testifies to the work of the Spirit in his mission (see "The Spirit Sends Gospel Communicators").

Spiritual Truths

In 1 Corinthians 2:13, Paul calls the Corinthians back to living faithfully to the gospel of a crucified Messiah, which he preached among them when he came to the city. By conforming their lives to the mind of the crucified Christ implanted in them by the Spirit, they will mature into a unified church (not one divided over their immature preferences for this or that preacher). To facilitate their maturation, Paul reminds them of his commitment to preach Christ and him crucified, without rhetorical flamboyancy but with the Spirit's power to convert them (2:1–5). It was the hidden wisdom of the message of the crucified

---

36. I find it interesting that Fee discusses Galatians 2:2 where ἀποκάλυψις, "revelation," is mentioned, but writes off 1:12, where the same term is used of his Damascus Road experience. Fee, *GEP*, 372. In my view, he misses Paul's hint at the Spirit's role especially in the passage confirmed by ἐν ἐμοί, "in me," in v. 16, which speaks of the same event and uses the cognate verb ἀποκαλύπτω. For consideration of grace in relation to Spirit, see Dunn, *Jesus and the Spirit*, 202–5.

37. "His choice to use ἐν here is likely intended to denote that the revelation of God's Son had a transformative power 'in' his very being." Douglas J. Moo, *Galatians*, BECNT (Grand Rapids: Baker Academic, 2013), 104. The same language is used in Galatians 4:6 of Spirit reception; see Richard N. Longenecker, *Galatians*, WBC 41 (Dallas: Word, 1990), 32. Compare Galatians 4:19, where Paul uses the image of childbirth and Christ being formed in the Galatians.

38. Examples of theophanies include Gen. 12:7; 26:24–25; 28:12–19; 32:30; Exod. 19:16–25; 33:11; Num. 24:9–18; Deut. 5:4; 34:10; 2 Chron. 7:12; Isa. 6:1; Ezek. 1:26; Rev. 4:2; 20:11. Christophanies are found in the resurrection accounts of Matthew, Luke (also Acts 1), John, and 1 Corinthians 15, as well as Paul's conversion (Acts 9:1–7; 26:12–18), and meeting the Lord in Acts 23:11 (also Acts 9:10–16; 10:3–6, 10–16).

Messiah Paul preached in Corinth that the world rulers failed to understand (2:6–8). The mystery of a crucified Messiah as the world's savior has now been revealed to believers (2:9–10).[39] However, the Spirit of and from God who knows God intimately searches and understands such things. (2:11–12b).

In v. 12, God has given this Spirit to believers "in order that [ἵνα] we may know the things [τά] freely given to us by God" (LEB). The things Paul has in mind are explained in v. 13: "things [ἅ] which we also speak, not in words taught by human wisdom, but in words taught by the Spirit, explaining spiritual things [plur. neut. Πνευματικός] to spiritual people [plur. masc. πνευματικός]" (LEB). The "spiritual things" here are the things of the gospel, mainly Christ and him crucified. As they are spiritual, we see, as we will see in the texts that follow, that the gospel and its truths are infused with God's Spirit.

Paul distinguishes between the fleshly person (ψυχικός) and spiritual (πνευματικῶς), with the former unable to discern the things of the Spirit of God, and the latter capable of doing so because they have the Spirit. As people who have received the Spirit, the Corinthians should be able to grasp Paul's meaning here and be renewed into pneumaform (or Christoform) people who have the mind of Christ and are unified in the Spirit.

Spiritual Things

In 1 Corinthians 9, Paul responds to the Corinthians' criticism by renouncing financial support from the Corinthians.[40] To defend his practice, Paul lays out six arguments for why a preacher of the gospel should be financially supported by other Christians (1 Cor. 9:7–14).[41] My interest lies in his description of his ministry among the Corinthians in his defense in vv. 9–12, based on Deuteronomy 25:4,[42] which instructs that an ox may eat from the grain it is treading.[43]

In v. 10,[44] Paul states that the Deuteronomic text was written for the sake of Christians (our sake). Before showing how this text applies to contemporary Christians, he returns to the farming context, stating that those who sow and thresh in the harvest field do so rightfully, hoping to receive a share of the produce.

Then, in v. 11, he applies the sowing motif to mission with a conditional rhetorical question. He writes, "If we have sown *spiritual things* [τὰ πνευματικὰ] in you, is it a greater thing if from you we reap fleshly things [τὰ

---

39.   See chapter 3, "The Spirit Who Reveals."
40.   Fee, *GEP*, 140. See also 2 Cor. 11:7–12; 12:13.
41.   "One of the strangest arguments on record." Fee, *GEP*, 140.
42.   His first three arguments in v. 7 come from the military and regular farming practice.
43.   See David E. Garland, *1 Corinthians*, BECNT (Grand Rapids: Baker Academic, 2003), 410–11, for consideration of the rabbinic background.
44.   This is not a quote from a noncanonical source, but explains why the law was written "on account of us." Garland, *1 Corinthians*, 411.

σαρκικὰ]?"[45] (my translation). Earlier in the letter, his and Apollos's ministries were seen as planting and watering (3:6). Here, by describing the work of
missionaries as "sowing spiritual things," Paul confirms that the gospel and its
things that bring transformation are spiritual matters.

The Word of God, the Sword of the Spirit

In Ephesians 6:17, Paul writes τὴν μάχαιραν τοῦ πνεύματος, ὅ ἐστιν
ῥῆμα θεοῦ. Here, a weapon in the Christian's armory is the sword of the
Spirit, the Word of God. Undoubtedly, πνεύματος here speaks of God's Spirit
rather than that of a person or the church. The image envisages God's Spirit
as a warrior holding in his hand a μάχαιρα, which, while at times is used of
a relatively short sword or dagger, here indicates a sword (one of the standard
weapons in the armory of an ancient warrior). The image invokes thoughts of
soldiers of the day, including the Romans and ancient gods and their weapons. More important, it calls to mind the commander of the armies of the
Lord and the armed God of armies (hosts) in Israel's tradition.

In Israel's tradition, God is the head of his armies that fight his enemies on
his behalf. He empowers the armies of Israel for military engagement, subdu-
ing Israel's enemies among the nations (e.g., Ps. 59:5).[46] In citing Isaiah 1:9,
which recalls God's destruction of Sodom and Gomorrah and anticipates the
Babylonian exile that came after Isaiah's ministry, Paul assumes this notion in
Romans 9:29, which serves as a warning to Israel in their rejection of Jesus
through unbelief (Rom. 9:30–32).

Old Testament passages link the Lord of Hosts with the redemption of
Israel and the Messiah. In Isaiah 9:7, the future messianic reign of God is
enacted by the "zeal of the Lord of hosts."[47] Again, in Psalm 89, the Davidic

---

45. Fee, GEP, 141, does not see Paul's use of τὰ σαρκικά (the things of the flesh) as pejorative. In a
    sense, I agree, as in the passage, Paul roundly endorses the church financially supporting its workers.
    However, two things indicate that there is a taint of his usual use of σάρξ as fleshly, worldly, and
    opposed to the Spirit. First, for Paul, money is a necessary evil that enables people to live, as seen
    in his injunctions to contentment with "food and clothing" and rejection of riches and people who
    peddle the gospel. Second, in this passage he renounces the "right" to this money, even rejecting a
    command of Jesus in this regard (9:14). Clearly, for Paul, things of the Spirit are really what matters,
    while money is needed to allow people to continue to live, and do so by the Spirit.

46. The Hebrew צָבָא, ṣā·ḇā(') has as its basis military ideas (HALOT 995). It is used of human armies
    (e.g., Gen. 21:22; 1 Sam. 12:9; 2 Kings 5:31), including Israel's arrangement in military formation
    for travel through the wilderness (Num. 1:52; Josh. 4:13; 5:14–15). It is transliterated into Greek as
    σαβαώθ and used in the NT in Romans 9:29 (see also James 5:4). God is called the God of hosts or
    armies some 240 times in the OT (e.g., 1 Sam. 1:3; 1 Chron. 12:8; Ps. 24:10).

47. See also Psalm 84:8–9, where the psalmist prays to the "Lord of Hosts," describing him as "our shield"
    and urging him to "look on the face of your anointed!" In Isaiah 37:32–38, the zeal of the Lord of
    Hosts defeats Sennacherib's Assyrian forces "for the sake of my servant David," giving an idea of how
    Israel understood God's military power, which many believed would be exercised in the messianic
    reign of the future Davidic king. See also the use of "anointed" language of Cyrus, who through the
    "Lord of Hosts" liberates Israel (Isa. 45:1–13).

covenant, the anointing of the king, and its eternal reign are affirmed.[48] Then God is addressed as "the LORD God of hosts" who rules the world and crushes enemies, establishing righteousness (esp. vv. 8–13).[49] The nations will bring tribute to the Lord of Hosts in Mount Zion (Isa. 18:7). He will protect Jerusalem (Isa. 31:4–5). In Jeremiah 30:8–9, the Lord of Hosts will break the yoke of the nations from Israel's neck, and they will serve God and the Davidic king (see also Jer. 33:12–22). In Zechariah 9:9–15, the messianic king comes on a donkey to remove war from Jerusalem, and he will protect them (v. 15). The Lord of Hosts strengthens Jerusalem and brings salvation so that all are like David, and the house of David is like God (12:1–9). The nations will come to Jerusalem and worship the Lord of Hosts at the Feast of Booths (14:16–19).

In some Old Testament texts, this Lord of Hosts or "man of war" (Exod. 15:3; Isa. 42:13) carries a sword, as do angels. Cherubim with a sword protected the tree of life (Gen. 3:24), and an angel with a sword blocked the way of Balaam's donkey (Num. 22:23, 31). The commander of the Lord's army meets Joshua with his drawn sword in his hand (Josh. 5:13; also 1 Chron. 21:27, 30). God then is portrayed as a warrior violently enacting his will on earth.[50] Swords are also associated with words, the mouth, and tongues. For example, the servant of Yahweh declares, "He made my mouth like a sharp sword" (Isa. 49:2).[51] Such texts potentially inform Paul's idea of the word as the sword of the Spirit.

The sword of the Spirit issuing forth from the mouth of God and his Son is the Word of God. In this era, between the resurrection and return of Christ,

---

48. See esp. Ps. 89:3–4, 20, 35, 38, 49–51.

49. See also Psalm 48, which begins celebrating Jerusalem as a fortress and describes it as "the city of the Lord of Hosts . . . which God will establish forever" (vv. 1–2, 8). Similarly, in Psalm 84, the Lord of Hosts dwells in Zion and shields and looks on the face of his anointed (vv. 1, 3, 7–9, 12). Micah's vision of Jerusalem as world center and cosmic peace is declared by "the LORD of hosts" (Mic. 4:1–5) who will rescue Zion (Mic. 4:6–13). In Micah 5:2, a ruler is born in Bethlehem who for Paul lies at the heart of this redemption. See also Psalms 97; 110; Zech. 8:1–23 (esp. v. 23 where ten men from every language will hold the robe of a Jew knowing God is with them).

50. Deuteronomy 32:41–42: God is a warrior who sharpens his flashing sword and takes bloody vengeance on his enemies and devours flesh; Isaiah 34:5–6: the LORD has a sword, which has drunk its full in the heavens, and falls on Edom, which is "sated with blood; it is gorged with fat"; Psalm 7:12 predicts that "God will whet his sword." In Isaiah 66:16, God's sword will judge all flesh "and those slain by the LORD shall be many." For Jeremiah "the sword of the LORD devours from one end of the land to the other; no flesh has peace" (Jer. 12:12). He cries out, "Ah, sword of the LORD! How long till you are quiet? Put yourself into your scabbard; rest and be still! How can it be quiet when the LORD has given it a charge? Against Ashkelon and against the seashore he has appointed it" (Jer. 47:6–7). Ezek. 21:3–5: "Behold, I am against you and will draw my sword from its sheath and will cut off from you both righteous and wicked. Because I will cut off from you both righteous and wicked, therefore my sword shall be drawn from its sheath against all flesh from south to north. And all flesh shall know that I am the LORD. I have drawn my sword from its sheath; it shall not be sheathed again." See also Ezek. 30:24–25; 32:1, 10; Zeph. 2:12.

51. See Job 5:15; Pss. 57:4; 59:7; 64:3; Prov. 12:18.

the Lord is enacting his will on earth by the sword of the Spirit. Because Jesus has taken humankind's judgment, God delays the final verdict, cutting the hearts of humankind with the Word of God. Those who yield will escape the retributive sword of God as the sword circumcises their hearts by the Spirit and marks them as God's people.

The neuter relative pronoun ὅ does not agree in gender with the feminine μάχαιραν or in case with πνεύματος and so, as in other such instances, finds its antecedent in the whole construct: the sword wielded by the Spirit is the ῥῆμα θεοῦ.[52] While some older interpreters tried to find a distinction between ῥῆμα and λόγος, this is unlikely with the ῥῆμα θεοῦ simply meaning "the message of God, the gospel," whether written or proclaimed.[53] Ῥῆμα is used of God's Word declared by John the Baptist (Luke 3:2; Acts 11:16), Jesus (e.g., John 6:63, 68), and Peter (Acts 11:14).[54] As with other NT writers who employ it of God's message,[55] Paul utilizes it four times in Romans 10 (below, Rom. 10:8, 17–18) and once in Ephesians 5:26. It is parallel to similar constructs using λόγος including "the word of truth," the gospel, preached in earlier times to the Ephesians (Eph. 1:13).[56]

Hence, Paul sees the gospel as the sword of the Spirit. The genitive can be one of source ("given by the Spirit [on God's behalf]") or is possessive ("belonging to the Spirit [on God's behalf]").[57] Either way, Paul paints a vivid image whereby the Spirit holds the sword in his hand.

The sword was used in battle with opponents, whether in defense when attacked or when going on the offensive. Some interpreters note the emphasis on "standing" throughout Ephesians 6 and assume it indicates the purpose here is primarily defensive.[58] If so, it would speak of believers gripping the gospel and defending themselves against the attacks from false teachers and

---

52. Similarly, Lincoln, *Ephesians*, 451.

53. Contra Fee, *GEP*, 728. He accepts that they are interchangeable synonyms but suggests that ῥῆμα emphasizes what is spoken at a particular time, while λόγος focuses on the content. He posits the distinction may hold here. I find this doubtful with ῥῆμα semantically broad enough to include the spoken and written word.

54. See also Matt. 4:4; Luke 1:38; 2:29; Acts 2:14; 5:20.

55. Heb. 1:3; 6:5; 11:3; 1 Peter 1:25; 2 Peter 3:2; Jude 17. Ῥῆμα is also commonly used of God's Word in the LXX (e.g., Gen. 15:1; Exod. 9:20–21; Num. 14:41; Deut. 5:5; 2 Chron. 36:22; 1 Esdr. 2:1; Isa. 66:5; Jer. 6:12).

56. In Paul: "the word of God" (Rom. 9:6; 1 Cor. 14:36; Col. 1:25; 1 Thess. 2:13; 1 Tim. 4:5; 2 Tim. 2:9; Titus 2:5); "the word of the cross" (1 Cor. 1:18); "the word" (1 Cor. 15:2; Gal. 6:6; Eph. 5:6; Phil. 1:14; Col. 4:3; 1 Thess. 1:6; 2 Tim. 4:2); the "word of truth" (Eph. 1:13; Col. 1:5; 2 Tim. 2:15); "the word of life" (Phil. 2:16); "the word of Christ" (Col. 3:16); and "the word of the Lord" (1 Thess. 1:8; 2 Thess. 3:1).

57. Fee, *GEP*, 728. Other possibilities might be attributive (spiritual sword), production ("produced by the Spirit [on God's behalf]").

58. See Markus Barth, *Ephesians* (New York: Doubleday, 1984), 798; Dickson, *Mission-Commitment*, 118–19.

others who repudiate God's Word (cf. Luke 4:1–11). Yet, while it undoubtedly includes defense, limiting it is inadequate for several reasons.[59]

First, the imagery of soldiers is not static but includes moving in formation to defend and, if possible, to attack.[60] Second, the parallel phrase "word of truth" in Ephesians 1:13 speaks of the initial evangelization of the Ephesians. This initial work was done by the likes of Priscilla, Aquila, Paul, and Apollos, moving with the gospel into the city, preaching the Word of God, the sword of the Spirit. Indeed, the evangelization of the world that Jesus endorsed and Paul sought to enact is premised on centripetal mission.

"The word of truth" is further defined as "the gospel (εὐαγγέλιον) of your salvation." Εὐαγγέλιον language is featured seven times in Ephesians, and each implies the movement of a preacher to communicate the gospel. In 2:17, Jesus "*came* and preached (εὐαγγελίζω) peace" to those near and those far off. "Came" (ἔρχομαι) implies movement to preach; here, sent from his eternal existence to earth (Gal. 4:6). As we see elsewhere, this is Spirit impelled.

In 3:6, 8, and 6:19, εὐαγγ-language is used of Paul's gospel preaching to the Gentiles and in Roman prison, again speaking of movement and a desire to advance the gospel. Although not specified, the evangelist in 4:11 is likely someone who moves with the gospel. The only person labeled (εὐαγγελιστής) in the NT is Philip, who, led by the Spirit, traveled *from* Jerusalem *to* Samaria and then *to* western Judea, *moving* north to Caesarea Maritima with the gospel (Acts 8).[61] According to Ephesians 6:15, all Christians are to put on their feet the readiness of the gospel of peace. While some thinkers see this as defensive and static, it instead speaks of feet ready to stand on the gospel, defend the faith, and move with the gospel.[62] Finally, the use of εὐαγγ-language in wider Greek sources speaks of the delivery of the good news of the prophet or herald of the empire.[63] As such, the Word of God here speaks of advancing the gospel through sharing it with others so that they may come to believe in Jesus, and defending oneself with the word against false ideas (cf. 4:14).

---

59.   See also Keown, *Congregational*, 288–92.

60.   Similarly, Fee, *GEP*, 728.

61.   Indeed, according to Acts 8:40, Philip was translated by the Spirit. If the baptismal river of the Ethiopian was the Wadi el-Hesi as is traditional (F. F. Bruce, *The Book of the Acts*, NICNT [Grand Rapids: Eerdmans, 1988], 177), this meant a translation of some fifty to one hundred kilometers to Azotus.

62.   Keown, *Congregational*, 286–91.

63.   All OT examples include someone bearing good news to another: news of military victories (1 Kgdms. 31:9); Israel's glory must not be proclaimed in Gath and Ashkelon (2 Kgdms. 1:20); the news that an enemy (Saul, Absalom) is dead (2 Kgdms. 4:10; 18:19–20, 26, 31; 1 Chron. 10:9); hoped for good news delivered (3 Kgdms. 1:42); good news of righteousness brought in the assembly (Ps. 39:10 [40:9 EVV]); people announcing God's Word as he commands (Ps. 67:12 [68:11]; Joel 2:32); people from all the earth singing God's salvation daily (Ps. 95:2 [96:2]); a herald on the mountain proclaiming good news (Nah. 1:15; Isa. 40:9; 52:7); people coming from Sheba to declare the Lord's salvation (Isa. 60:6); the sent anointed one of Isaiah 61:1 (cf. Luke 4:18–19); and the bearer of the news of a child (Jer. 20:15). See also Pss. Sol. 11:2.

So, the sword wielded by God's Spirit is the word of the gospel. As will now be discussed, when the word is communicated by a person to another and received through hearing or reading, God empowers the message to connect with the spirit breathed into all people. At that moment, either faith for salvation is ignited, or the word is rejected and the recipient remains lost to God.

The Gospel, the Power of God for Salvation

A range of passages in Paul inform us concerning the process whereby the Spirit, wielding his sword, penetrates the human heart and faith is born; justification is declared; and a person is reconciled to God, included in Christ, adopted into his family, and indwelt by the Spirit who anoints them, seals them for redemption, and incorporates them into the temple of the Spirit. We begin with Romans 1:16.

Twice Paul describes the gospel as the power of God. First, in Romans 1:16, the gospel is the power of God for salvation to everyone who believes, including first the Jews and also (or then) the Gentiles (all cultures in the same way). While the Spirit is not mentioned directly in either text, the "power of God" suggests the engagement of the Spirit noted in previous sections.[64] This perspective is easily demonstrated through a look at δύναμις in Paul. In Romans 1:4, the power of the Spirit of holiness brings about the declaration of Jesus's divine sonship at his resurrection from death (cf. 2 Cor. 13:4).[65] The power of God brings insight into the gospel to preachers (Eph. 3:7). The same Spirit-power is at work in the proclamation of the gospel, where at the moment of saving faith, those dead in sins and transgressions die in Christ and are spiritually resurrected. Ultimately, this power will raise perishable and mortal people to imperishable immortality (1 Cor. 6:14; 15:43; 2 Cor. 13:4).

By the power of the Spirit, believers abound in hope (Rom. 15:13). The power of the Spirit is exercised as the gospel is preached and miracles are performed (Rom. 15:19).[66] By the Spirit's power, believers find strength from God during suffering.[67] Believers are empowered for ministry by the Spirit (Col. 1:29). By the Spirit, their good purposes that come from their faith

---

64. "Paul believes that ultimately the gospel as divine power (see Rom. 1:16–17)—we might even say as the power behind the barking—ensures that a community filled with the gospel and thus *with the Spirit of God* will in fact bear witness." Gorman, *BGPPM*, 45.

65. Contra Fee, *GEP*, 132, who consistently argues God raised Christ without the use of the Spirit, which I find problematic. For example, on pp. 359–60, despite arguing consistently through the book that power language supposes the Spirit, he decries this is the case in 2 Corinthians 13:4. Yet, if Fee is consistent, he would concede the possibility the Spirit is the agency for God's power (which I believe to be the case).

66. Cf. 1 Cor. 12:10, 28–29; 2 Cor. 12:12; Gal. 3:5. Dunn rightly suggests, "What these *dunameis* included we are unfortunately now unable to determine." Dunn, *Jesus and the Spirit*, 210.

67. 2 Cor. 4:7; 12:9; Eph. 3:16; Col. 1:11.

are fulfilled (2 Thess. 1:11), their gifts are energized (2 Tim. 1:7), and they unashamedly participate in suffering for the gospel (2 Tim. 1:8). The resurrection power enables cruciform life; indeed, as this book will show, rightly understood, cruciformity or Christoformity *is* pneumaformity (Phil. 3:10).

Paul links Spirit, power, and proclamation in 1 Corinthians 2:4. The message of Christ crucified is the power of God for salvation (1 Cor. 1:18). The Spirit convicts human hearts not through fancy rhetoric or elaborate philosophy but through generating faith in the hearts of people who formerly did not believe. The power of the gospel is the power of God, not human persuasion (1 Cor. 2:5). The gospel preached by Paul came not merely in words but in power and the Spirit with full conviction (1 Thess. 1:5).[68]

So, when Paul says that the gospel is the power of God for salvation, he is speaking of the Spirit meeting the inward being of the person as the word is communicated. For those with ears to hear, salvation is the outcome as they believe and are justified. Such occurrences assume the power of the word to generate life from the Old Testament and to bring to pass God's purposes (Isa. 55:10–11).

The Word of the Cross, the Power of God (1 Corinthians 1:18)

First Corinthians 1:18 avers that the "word of the cross is folly to those who are perishing, but to us who are being saved it is the power of God." Whereas in Romans 1:16, the gospel's function in generating salvation is asserted, here, the dualizing power of the gospel is referenced. The "word of the cross" speaks of the gospel message that focuses on the death of Jesus as the point at which Jesus died for the sins of humankind.

The first group hears the gospel as foolishness or nonsense. Jews are unimpressed with a crucified Messiah and demand signs. Greeks who reject bodily resurrection find the notion of a raised Christ nonsense (1 Cor. 1:22).[69] The term for "perishing" is one of Paul's favored terms for destruction, ἀπόλλυμι,[70] and so as they do not respond with faith, their destiny is destruction. Although the Spirit's power comes on them, bidding them to yield in faith as they hear the word, they are blinded by Satan, have stubborn hearts and minds, and reject it. Faith is not born. However, conversely, "those who are being saved" refers to those who hear the message, who believe, and in

---

68.   Fee, *GEP*, 40–45, notes this is the earliest mention of conversion in the NT. He discusses whether v. 5 refers to Paul's preaching, signs and wonders, their conversion, or some combination thereof. He opts for the final option, which may be true due to the place of miracles in Paul's work (Rom. 15:19; 2 Cor. 12:12; Gal. 3:5). However, as Fee goes on to note (45), the emphasis here is on the power of the proclamation of the Pauline group.

69.   See also Tacitus, *Nero* 16, who describes Christians as holding a "new and impious superstition" (*superstitionis novae et maleficae*), and Pliny the Younger, who held it to be "a perverse and immoderate superstition" (*superstitionem pravam, immodicam*) (*Ep.* 10.96).

70.   See Rom. 2:2; 14:15; 1 Cor. 1:19; 8:11; 15:18; 2 Cor. 2:15; 4:3; 2 Thess. 2:10.

whom the Spirit of God takes up residence. Christ, for them, is "the power of God and the wisdom of God" (1 Cor. 1:24).

Further signs are not required for such people. The revelation of a crucified Messiah by the Spirit makes perfect sense, for in the Messiah's death, the love of God in the ultimate sacrifice to save them is understood. God's power is revealed in Christ to liberate them from their sin and all condemnation and shame. They recognize that God is inverting the power paradigms of their fallen world, and now power is seen in weakness, humiliation, and crucifixion, liberating the other. They experience the joy of God's pardon, the conferral of holiness, and redemption. Whereas their cultures demean the weak and broken, the gospel summons them to a place alongside the powerful in Jesus, the Son of God. Christ, the wisdom of God, becomes the epicenter of their philosophical (theological) reflections. While faith remains, their destiny is eternal life.

A Demonstration of the Spirit and Power

The Spirit's power unleashed when the gospel is shared is not proportionate to the preacher's rhetorical skill and philosophical brilliance. Paul knows this, so, especially in a place like Corinth, which was obsessed with status gained through rhetorical flair,[71] he does not seek to use his brilliant rhetoric and philosophical skill to win people to Christ. Instead, he focuses on making the story of Christ and his crucifixion for the world crystal clear. The apostle self-consciously embraces weakness, fear, and trembling, all seen as inadequacies in contemporary rhetoric.[72] He embodies the pattern of the cross as he preaches and makes the cross the center of his preaching. The preaching then becomes a demonstration of the Spirit and power as this ludicrous and foolish message of a humiliated and crucified so-called Son of God cuts the hearts of hearers. Their hearts respond to the Spirit's invitation through the word, and they believe.[73] Their faith was not some shallow momentary response based on Paul's persuasive oratory but was a deep-seated, yielding allegiance to God's invitation in the word by the Spirit. The Spirit did the

---

71. See Garland, *1 Corinthians*, 33.
72. Fee, *GEP*, 93, rightly states that "the power of Paul's 'nonrhetoric'" subverted the Corinthian triumphalism, their emphasis on power and Spirit, and rejection of weakness. Paul stresses power in weakness, a power that converts and sees them receive the Spirit.
73. Fee, *GEP*, 92–93, discusses what is constituted by "Spirit and power" here. He rightly rejects that this refers to "signs and wonders" based on Romans 15:19 and 2 Corinthians 12:12. Here, "in keeping with 1 Thes 1:5–6, it refers to their actual conversion, with its coincident gift of the Spirit." He suggests that this receipt was "probably evidenced by Spirit manifestations, especially tongues." I agree with him that they likely experienced various manifestations of the Spirit. However, I do not concur with "*especially* tongues." Tongues was likely one of the manifestations, but only one. Indeed, he will reject that "all speak in tongues" in 12:29. Still, his overall point and critique of overstating tongues in this context is appropriate.

converting through his sword, the Word of God, not Paul's presentation. And then the Spirit flooded the soul of the new convert.[74]

Word, Power, the Holy Spirit, and Conviction

Paul (with Silvanus and Timothy) begin 1 Thessalonians with a collective thanksgiving for the whole Thessalonian church. They recall their conversion when Paul and his team visited Thessalonica only a few months previously (Acts 17:1–10). God has chosen the Thessalonians because (ὅτι) of the preaching of Paul and his team. While his letter lacks the apologetic power of 2 Corinthians and Galatians, 1 Thessalonians 2:1–12 suggests that, Paul is gently but firmly defending his ministry and gospel against some challenging his authority. He does so by reminding them of how he and his team brought the gospel to the Thessalonians.

"Our gospel" means the gospel of God that Paul and his team hold dear and preach throughout the world.[75] It contrasts other false "gospels" that constantly threaten his churches. The Thessalonians should listen to the Pauline gospel, which is *the* gospel, and not alternatives. The coming of the gospel "to you" speaks of the initial proclamation in Thessalonica, summarized neatly by Luke in Acts 17:1–10 (cf. 1 Thess. 2:1–12). Paul explains that his gospel did not come merely with speech, "in word" (ἐν λόγῳ). But (ἀλλά) it came ἐν δυνάμει καὶ ἐν πνεύματι ἁγίῳ καὶ [ἐν] πληροφορίᾳ πολλῇ.

There is a range of options to translate ἐν in the three prepositional phrases. It can be translated as "in," as if the gospel came "clothed" in power, the Holy Spirit, and full conviction.[76] However, it is better to see it as a "marker introducing means or instrument, *with*" in an impersonal sense:[77] the word of the gospel came with power and the Holy Spirit. This use is found militarily with a blending of associative and instrumental ideas.[78] This idea takes us in the direction of Ephesians 6:17, with the preached gospel empowered by the Spirit.

The final phrase uses πληροφορία, a rare term that means, literally, "supreme fullness," and in the wider literature, "certainty."[79] Absent from the LXX, its three other NT uses carry the sense of full assurance (Col. 2:2;

---

74. See further on this passage, Mark J. Keown, "Preaching Christ Crucified: Cruciformity in Content and Delivery," in *Text Messages: Preaching God's Word in a Smartphone World*, ed. John Tucker (Eugene, OR: Wipf & Stock, 2017), 217–29.

75. In 1 Thessalonians, Paul variously describes the gospel as "our gospel" (1 Thess. 1:5), "the word" (1 Thess. 1:6), "the word of the Lord" (1 Thess. 1:8), "the gospel of God" (1 Thess. 2:2, 8, 9, 13), "the gospel" (1 Thess. 2:4), and "the gospel of Christ" (1 Thess. 3:2). All refer to the same gospel as, for Paul, there is only one (Gal. 1:6–9).

76. See BDAG, s.v. "ἐν," 327, meaning 2 (a).

77. BDAG, s.v. "ἐν," 328, meaning 5.

78. BDAG, s.v. "ἐν," 328, meaning 5, (a),α.

79. Gerhard Delling, "Πλήρης, Πληρόω, Πλήρωμα, Ἀναπληρόω, Ἀνταναπληρόω, Ἐκπληρόω, Ἐκπλήρωσις, Συμπληρόω, Πληροφορέω, Πληροφορία," *TDNT* 6:310.

Heb. 6:11; 10:22).[80] Here, it more likely speaks of much (πολλῇ) conviction that flows from complete assurance.[81] This usage refers to Paul and his team's absolute conviction in the truth of the gospel they preach, a conviction no doubt strengthened by the Spirit. Earlier, we read of Paul's rejection of flowery rhetoric or philosophical brilliance. Such a limitation should not be misunderstood as preaching without passion and conviction. Sharing the gospel includes words given with conviction and the empowerment of the Spirit. Again, the Spirit's role in evangelism is evident.

Faith Comes from Hearing the Word

The Spirit empowers the word as it is communicated to the recipient. What about the Spirit's role in the hearer? Romans 10:14–17 is primarily concerned with whether Jews have heard the gospel message and so can be justly held accountable. Yet, it also has a broader application indicating Paul's understanding of the process of evangelism, especially with his mention in Romans of his Gentile mission and desire to continue to Spain. With four overlapping rhetorical questions, Paul creates a sequence that must be satisfied for Israel (or anyone) to be accountable for not hearing and believing the gospel.[82]

As the gospel is shared, the Spirit is at work in the hearer. Romans 10:14–15 gives a neat summary of the process of evangelism saturated with God's Spirit. A person is sent by God (by the Spirit), they preach (empowered by the Spirit), the gospel is heard (as the Spirit summons and calls), the gospel is believed (enabled by the Spirit [or not, as in the case of Israel rejecting Jesus]), and the believer calls on the name of the Lord (v. 13) and is saved.[83]

For Paul and Isaiah (Isa. 52:7), the feet of such a preacher are "beautiful," for they bring God's redemption.[84] Paul summarizes the way in which faith is born in Romans 10:17: ἄρα ἡ πίστις ἐξ ἀκοῆς, ἡ δὲ ἀκοὴ διὰ ῥήματος Χριστοῦ. Faith comes from hearing the word (ῥημα, cf. Eph. 6:17). Faith is generated as the gospel empowered by the Spirit is heard. Humans either put up shields to the sword of the Spirit and it is blocked by the evil one (2 Cor. 4:4), or they allow it to penetrate their inner beings and faith wells

---

80. Fee, *GEP*, 44, argues that this speaks of the gospel's effectiveness. However, the term does not carry this meaning. For Paul, the gospel has effect whether someone is converted or not.
81. The verb *plērophoreō* is used six times in the NT. Luke uses it of "fully accomplished" (Luke 1:1). The other five uses are in Paul. In Romans 4:21: Abraham was "fully convinced" God was able to do what he promised. In Romans 14:5, again it speaks of being "fully convinced" in one's own mind concerning nonessential matters of the faith. In Colossians 4:12, Epaphras prays that the Colossians would be "fully assured" in all the will of God. In 2 Timothy 4:5, it has a slightly different sense of "fulfilling" a ministry, while in 2 Timothy 4:17, the message is "fulfilled" or "fully proclaimed."
82. A sorites is a sequence of propositions where one established predicate noun becomes the subject in the next (cf. Rom. 5:3–5).
83. See further Keown, *Romans and the Mission of God*, 146–47.
84. While ὡραῖος can have the meaning "timely," here it has the sense "beautiful, lovely." See Keown, *Romans and the Mission of God*, 193–94.

up. As they believe, they become "the called" and "the chosen" (or "elect"). They then respond by "call[ing] on the name of the Lord" (Rom. 10:13), which speaks of a prayerful cry to God their Father.[85] They are then "being saved," and if faith is maintained as they cooperate with God's power, they "will be saved."

Hearing and Believing

Another passage that supplements our understanding of the Spirit's role in conversion is Ephesians 1:13–14, which we have touched on while discussing Ephesians 6:17. The prepositional clause ἐν ᾧ can speak of the sphere in which the Ephesians heard the word of truth. Alternatively, if we supply the verb "to be," which is missing, and read the participle ἀκούσαντες temporally, it describes the moment of inclusion in Christ when they heard the gospel; "and in him [you were] when you heard . . ." Thus, the NIV reads, "And you also were included in Christ *when you heard* the message of truth . . ." (emphasis added).

The "word of truth" is a phrase emphasizing the fidelity of the good news in the face of alternative false gospels (Col. 1:5; 2 Tim. 2:15).[86] It is then clarified as "the gospel of your salvation." It is a moot point whether salvation here is present or future.[87] It carries both timings in Paul's thought, as hearing and believing takes a person into the salvation gifted by God at the moment of faith that will be complete at the consummation.

Ephesians 1:13b begins with the dative phrase ἐν ᾧ, which can be attached to the participle πιστεύσαντες, "having believed, when you believed" and so "having believed in him, you were sealed." Alternatively, it can be attached to the main verb ἐσφραγίσθητε, "you were sealed," and so "in him, you were sealed." The latter is preferable, although the participle "refers to an action coincident in time with that of the main verb."[88]

The participle πιστεύσαντες speaks of that moment when the letter's recipients heard the gospel and believed. In terms of this discussion, the sword of the Spirit pierced them, slipping past Satan's stratagems (Eph. 6:11, 16), and was received with willing submission to Jesus Christ the Lord. As will be discussed, the Spirit was downloaded into their inner beings at that moment of faith, sealing them in Christ for redemption.

---

85. Keown, *Romans and the Mission of God*, 146–47.
86. Paul repeatedly uses ἀλήθεια in regard to the gospel and its fidelity in relation to all other claims and claimants: "the truth" (Rom. 1:18, 25; 2:8; 1 Cor. 13:6; 2 Cor. 4:2; 12:6; 13:8; Gal. 4:16; 5:7; Eph. 4:15; 2 Thess. 2:10, 12, 13; 1 Tim. 2:4, 7; 3:15; 4:3; 6:5; 2 Tim. 2:18, 25; 3:7, 8; 4:4; Titus 1:1, 14); "God's truth" (Rom. 3:7); "the truth of Christ is in me" (2 Cor. 11:10); "the truth of the gospel" (Gal. 2:5, 14); "the truth is in Jesus" (Eph. 4:21); "the grace of God in truth" (Col. 1:6).
87. With its more realized eschatology, Ephesians emphasizes the present experience of eternal salvation (see Eph. 2:5, 8; see also Eph. 5:23; 6:17).
88. Lincoln, *Ephesians*, 39 (cf. Acts 19:2).

The Spirit and Faith

In discussing suffering and hope for those in Christ, Paul draws attention to the importance of faith (2 Cor. 4:13). The participle ἔχοντες is causal, "because." Strictly speaking, the plural refers to Paul identifying with the psalmist's words he will cite. However, what follows the quote draws in the Corinthians with Paul and his team, and so what he said applies to all believers. Τὸ αὐτὸ πνεῦμα, "the *same* Spirit," the divine Spirit who inspired the psalmist, stirs Paul[89] and arouses the Corinthians, who also believe and speak. The genitive is one of production—"the Spirit who produces faith."

Using κατά, "in accordance with," and the extremely common perfect of γράφω, τὸ γεγραμμένον,[90] Paul cites Psalm 116:10a, which are the first words of Psalm 115 in the LXX.[91] The quote connects faith and speech. In the original context, the second part of the verse stresses suffering. In Hebrew, Psalm 116 stresses the psalmist's love for God, cries of supplication, and God's response to his prayers (vv. 1–2, 4) amid a near-death ordeal (vv. 3, 8). Yahweh's goodness, mercy, and care are stressed (vv. 5–6a). The psalmist suffered, but God gave him victory, and so his soul should return to its resting place because God has been so generous (v. 7), and he lives (v. 9). Verse 10 states that when the psalmist cried out to God, "I am afflicted greatly" (LEB), he believed in God.[92] The remainder of the psalm speaks of what the psalmist can do in response to God, whom he trusted for deliverance and received it.

Paul likely chose this psalm here because of the link of Spirit, faith, speech, and suffering. Just as the psalmist spoke out in prayer during a time of extreme suffering, and through his words in the psalm, so Paul speaks out in his ministry of the gospel and to the Corinthians in the letter. By the Spirit, in accordance with faith, despite being in a sea of extreme suffering, Paul and his team speak out the gospel. They do so all the more because they know that the God who raised Jesus from death will also raise them and the Corinthians from the dead.

We see here that the Spirit enables initial faith. He generates ongoing faith. Prayer has the effect of enhancing this power as God responds to faith. This faith sustains believers in suffering. This faith leads the likes of Paul and

---

89. See also Fee, *GEP*, 323. He adds these reasons: (1) this continues the section from 2:14 where the Spirit has been the dominant theme; (2) if he is speaking of a disposition he could have said "the same faith as the Psalmist"; (3) for Paul Scripture is inspired by the Spirit; (4) Spirit and faith belong together in the new covenant.

90. Martin notes this is an unusual introductory formula found in legal documents and in rabbinic writings. Ralph P. Martin, *2 Corinthians*, 2nd ed., WBC 40 (Nashville: Thomas Nelson, 2014), 82–83.

91. While some Hebrew MSS have a break at v. 11, the original Hebrew was one psalm. S. Edward Tesh and Walter D. Zorn, *Psalms*, CPNIVC (Joplin, MO: College Press, 1999), 2:357.

92. Tesh and Zorn, *Psalms*, 2:357. Arguing the *kî* is concessive, they translate it "I believed [Yahweh] even though I was saying [over and over again!], 'I am greatly afflicted.'" In contrast, to the psalmist's dismay, "All people are liars."

his group to speak out in terms of the gospel that others may believe. It should do so for the Corinthians and us.

RECEIVING THE SPIRIT

In this first section, the focus will be on texts that speak of the Spirit's reception. I begin with four texts emphasizing God's role in initiating the distribution of the Spirit—the Spirit sent, given, supplied, and baptizing. Then I will consider the ideas that stress the recipient's perspective.

The Spirit Sent into the Human Heart

One way Paul speaks of the Spirit's entry into a person's life is the idea of the Spirit being sent. Something sent demands a sender, and so this concept emphasizes God's initiative and role in being the imparter of the Spirit. God's Spirit is an apostolic being, and God is the sender.

In Galatians 4:4–6,[93] Paul speaks of two climactic moments in salvation history. The first was when God sent out[94] (ἐξαπέστειλεν) his Son. The verb compounding ἐκ (from) and ἀποστέλλω (sent) implies Jesus existed previously and was sent from there, and in Paul's thought, his sending was from God in heaven.[95] He was born of a woman, indicating his natural birth by Mary. He was born under the law, indicating he was born a Jew, and in Paul's broader theology, lived in sinless obedience to it (2 Cor. 5:21; Phil. 2:8). The purpose of his sending was to redeem other Jews under the law (which cannot save), that they and all people might receive adoption as children (sons) of God.

The second sending uses the same verb: "and because you are children, God sent out/forth [ἐξαποστέλλω] the Spirit of his Son."[96] God sends his Spirit because they are now his children by faith and not works of the law.[97] In that Jesus is at the right hand of God (Rom. 8:34; Col. 3:1), the verb implies the sending of the Spirit from heaven.[98] The genitive τοῦ υἱοῦ αὐτοῦ indicates

---

93. On the context and relationship to the argument in Galatians 3 and the contrast with being "under Torah," see Fee, *GEP*, 399–401.
94. Or "sent out," Fee, *GEP*, 402.
95 This verse implies Christ's preexistence as God's Son. Similarly, Fee, *GEP*, 403.
96. Gorman, *CPNSC*, 220, rightly stresses that God sent his Son, and believers are to live by this Spirit that issues forth in Spirit fruit. On sending here, see Buchanan, "Spirit," 142–44.
97. See esp. Gal. 2:16, 20; 3:2, 5–9, 11–12, 14, 22–26; 5:5–6. I am not convinced with Fee's rejection that Paul here is not recounting the "individual believer's personal salvation history" nor "giving a chronology of personal salvation history." Fee, *GEP*, 407. Despite this, in my view, a chronology is implied in chapters 2–4. Christ the Son completes the work of salvation. A person hears the gospel of the Son and believes. That person is declared righteous by faith by God. God floods that person with the Spirit, who, as Fee himself says, appropriates the work of Christ the Son and their sonship experientially in their lives (p. 409). While these moments are all coterminous and instantaneous, there is a sequence implied here. "Because you are sons" implies "because you believe in the Son and are so God's children." Still, he is right to say, "Christ is the 'cause' and the Spirit the 'effect' as far as 'sonship' is concerned" (p. 408).
98. As with Christ (above), Paul presupposes the preexistence of the Spirit.

that the Spirit sent is the Spirit who indwelt Jesus and is both the Spirit of God and Christ (Rom. 8:9; Phil. 1:19; cf. 2 Cor. 3:17–18).[99] This Spirit enters crying, "Abba! Father!"[100] a familial cry of God's fatherhood bringing assurance of the believers' status as God's children.[101] They are then no longer slaves to "so-called gods," religious systems bound to the Torah (including Judaism), or the emperor (even if they are slaves in a worldly sense); they are members of God's family.[102] They have full inheritance rights as his children.

The Spirit Given

God giving the Spirit highlights God's initiative and generosity as a gift-giving God. God giving his Spirit comes at the climax of the chain of ideas (*litotes*) in Romans 5:3–5: Paul rejoices in suffering because it produces perseverance, character, and hope. The hope produced by experiencing suffering, learning perseverance through the struggle, and having one's character refined through it does not bring shame in the present or at the judgment. This confidence is premised on the love of God that has been poured out (ἐκχέω) into believers' hearts. The verb is most often used for liquids poured out, like blood.[103] Sometimes, it is used of God pouring out his wrath[104] or good things.[105] At other times, significantly, prophets anticipate God pouring out his Spirit.[106]

Here, God pours his love out *through* (διὰ) the Spirit. As such, love is poured into the human heart as the Spirit enters. This love is likened to a

---

99. "These three passages, besides saying something significant in terms of Christology (it is no small thing that the Spirit *of God* can so easily also be called the Spirit *of Christ*), also say something significant about the Spirit (that the indwelling Spirit, whom believers know as an experienced reality, is the way both the Father and the Son are present in the believer's life)." Fee, *GEP*, 405 (emphasis his).

100. This contrasts with Romans 8:15, where believers cry out at their adoption. Yet, as Fee says, the two passages mean much the same thing with the emphasis here on the Spirit's role through the Son. Fee, *GEP*, 406.

101. I concur completely with Fee's rejection of "cry" as evidence of ecstasy and any spiritual takeover. See Fee, *GEP*, 409–10. I also agree with his view on Abba, despite the debates over its meaning—while it is not to be translated as "daddy," as Fee says, "it was probably the language of intimacy and endearment" (*GEP*, 411), and "such a cry comes from the heart [suggesting] that for Paul a form of intimacy with God is involved" (*GEP*, 412).

102. Fee, *GEP*, 412.

103. Gen. 9:6; Exod. 29:12; Lev. 4:7; Deut. 12:16; 1 Kgdms. 25:31; 1 Macc. 1:37; Pss. 13:3 LXX; 78:3 [79:3 EVV]; Hos. 12:15; Joel 4:19; Zeph. 1:17; Isa. 59:7; Jer. 7:6; Lam. 4:13; Ezek. 16:38; Pss. Sol. 8:24; Sib. Or. 3:312; T. Zeb. 2:2; Liv. Pro. 21:1. Other things poured out include semen (Gen. 38:9), water (e.g., Exod. 4:9; 1 Kgdms. 7:6; Amos 5:8), rain (Eccl. 11:3), oil (Apoc. Mos. 40:2), ashes (e.g., Lev. 4:12), soil (4 Kgdms. 19:32), bread (Tob. 4:17), entrails (2 Kgdms. 20:10), and light (Opif. 71). It is used figuratively of souls being poured out (e.g., 1 Kgdms. 1:15; Ps. 41:5 [42:4 EVV]; Job 30:16; 1 En. 9:1), pouring out one's heart before God in prayer (Pss. 61:9 [62:8 EVV]; 101:1 [102:1 EVV]; 141:3 [142:2 EVV]; Sir. 35:14).

104. Ps. 68:25 [69:24 EVV]; Sir. 16:11; 36:6; Pss. Sol. 2:24; Hos. 5:10; Jer. 6:11; 10:25; Ezek. 7:5; 9:8; 14:19; 20:8, 13, 21; 21:36; 22:22, 31; 30:15; 36:18, or anger (Zeph 3:8; Lam. 2:4; 4:11), or powerful force in judgment (Jer. 6:6), or evil (Jer. 14:16); pour out contempt (Ps. 106:40 [107:40 EVV]; Job 12:21).

105. His blessing (Mal. 3:10) or grace (Ps. 44:3 [45:2 EVV]).

106. See Joel 3:1, 2; Zech. 12:10; Ezek. 39:29; T. Jud. 24:2; 32:15; 44:3. See in the NT Acts 2:33; 10:45.

liquid that pours into the believer, quenching their spiritual thirst and yearnings and filling them. The idea of the Spirit being poured out is found in Acts (Acts 2:33; 10:45). It fulfills the prophetic hope of the Spirit poured out onto Israel, bringing abundant life (Isa. 44:3) and intimate relationship with God (Ezek. 39:29) and causing Israel's people to prophesy (Joel 2:28–29).

In 1 Thessalonians 4:8, Paul again speaks of God giving his Spirit to believers in a continuous sense (present tense).[107] This verse is set in a passage that draws out a critical ethical implication of receiving the Spirit—renouncing sexual immorality and living holy lives, including sexual fidelity. As with the metaphor of sending, the idea of God giving the Spirit speaks of God's initiative and grace. The Spirit is a gift God gives believers. Furthermore, the Spirit in us is far more powerful than sin and the flesh, enabling us to be freed from inertia and move away from all that is wrong with our old selves into the life for which we were created.[108]

The Spirit Supplied

In Galatians 3:5, Paul speaks of the supply or provision of the Spirit. The verb used is ἐπιχορηγέω, which has the sense of providing, supplying, or supporting.[109] Paul uses it of God supplying seed to a sower (2 Cor. 9:10) or nourishing the body (Col. 2:19), while Peter uses it of supporting one's own faith and God providing a way into his kingdom (2 Peter 1:5, 11).[110] God supplies or provides the Spirit for believers. The present tense speaks of an ongoing, continuous provision of the Spirit.

The same sense may be in view in Philippians 1:19, where the prayers of the Philippians and "the supply [or help] of the Spirit of Jesus Christ" (ἐπιχορηγίας τοῦ πνεύματος Ἰησοῦ Χριστοῦ) will ensure Paul's salvation (and deliverance).[111] The metaphor speaks of God as the supreme patron, wanting the best for his children and supplying them with the Spirit who will sustain them and support them through situations like Paul's in prison. He will deliver them or sustain them through the trial.

Baptized in the Spirit

With their love of rhetoric, the Corinthians were obsessed with gifts of speaking. Alongside elevating their favorite preacher over others (1 Cor. 1:12), some delighted in the gift of tongues above other gifts. This favoritism

107. With Fee, GEP, 52.
108. DeSilva, Transformation, 49.
109. The verb has its background in "generous public service" and so speaks of God's giving, his benefaction. It also has the senses of furnishing, supplying, or "to provide what is necessary for the well-being of another, support" (BDAG, s.v. "ἐπιχορηγέω," 387).
110. A wife supporting a husband (Sir. 25:22), people providing for giants (1 En. 7:3).
111. Fee, GEP, 739–41, takes it as "supply." Despite Fee's rejection of the meaning "help," it can equally mean "help" as I have argued elsewhere and which I consider preferable. To be fair, the difference is minimal. See Keown, Philippians, 1:231; also chapter 5, "Relevant Prayer Texts."

led to relational discord over speaking gifts, including tongues. The matter of spiritual gifts was an aspect of the letter they sent to Paul (1 Cor. 12:1).

Three chapters, 1 Corinthians 12–14, focus on spiritual gifts. Paul stresses that all gifts are of value and all come from God. He emphasizes the need for loving others as they express their different gifts, even those who have gifts that seem insignificant. He tells them that if they want speaking gifts, they should opt for prophecy as it is the greatest speaking gift—it is not self-centered but builds up others with love, as the gospel summons believers to do.

Recalling 1 Corinthians 10:2–4,[112] in 1 Corinthians 12:13, Paul uses a chiasm to stress their common receipt of the Spirit and so their unity and social equality.

A1   καὶ γὰρ ἐν ἑνὶ πνεύματι ἡμεῖς πάντες εἰς ἓν σῶμα ἐβαπτίσθημεν
       for in one Spirit we were also all baptized into one body

       B   εἴτε Ἰουδαῖοι εἴτε Ἕλληνες εἴτε δοῦλοι εἴτε ἐλεύθεροι,
             Whether Jews or Greeks or slaves or freedpeople,

A2   καὶ πάντες ἓν πνεῦμα ἐποτίσθημεν.[113]
       And we were given one Spirit to drink.[114]

The chiasm throws stress onto the social oneness of the body of Christ.[115] The framing statements state that believers are baptized into *one* Spirit (who summons people into social oneness).

The church is a single entity, a body, albeit with a diversity of members and spiritual giftedness (v. 12). The dative phrase ἐν ἑνὶ πνεύματι in v. 13 is likely a dative of sphere that also includes agency or means and so should be translated "in one Spirit."[116] Alternatively, due to the Spirit being both the sphere of a Christian's existence and the instrument or means by which God acts, it may be translated "in and by one Spirit."[117]

---

112. Paul Gardner, *1 Corinthians*, ZECNT (Grand Rapids: Zondervan, 2018), 542. He notes the parallel of the baptism into Moses in the cloud and all drinking the same spiritual drink with the common baptism in one Spirit and drinking of the Spirit here.

113. The alternative readings εις (D² L 326. 614. 945. 2464 pm f vg^{cl}), πομα εποτισθημεν (630. 1505. 1881 sy^h; Cl), and σωμα εσμεν (A) can be rejected based on the inferiority of the external attestation.

114. Translation mine.

115. On the center of the chiasm and emphasis, see Ronald E. Man, "The Value of Chiasm for New Testament Interpretation," *BSac* 141 (1984): 148–51.

116. Carson, *Showing*, 47.

117. Scholars err when they create a binary here. Believers live in the Spirit in whom they are melded to God and his Son. The Spirit acts in their lives, and they yield or resist. Hence, it is best translated "in the Spirit" or "by the Spirit." Another option is "in and by the Spirit."

"We all" (ἡμεῖς πάντες) speaks of all believers in all places and all times, including people from the whole range of social backgrounds mentioned. "One body" (ἓν σῶμα) refers to the church of God, whether the specific church gathering in Corinth, in another locale, or throughout the world. Believers are baptized into (εἰς) one body.

The verb ἐβαπτίσθημεν can refer to water baptism. The verb βαπτίζω, the intensive of βάπτω, can sometimes mean "to bathe" or "to wash" but generally means "to immerse."[118] The verb is used for ritual washing (Mark 7:4; Luke 11:38), people baptized into Moses in the Red Sea (1 Cor. 10:2), people in Corinth baptized on behalf of the dead (1 Cor. 15:29), John's baptism for repentance and forgiveness,[119] and a baptism of suffering.[120] Commonly, it refers to Christian water baptism.[121]

The verb is ambiguous and is often used for water baptism. However, in Paul's thinking, while water baptism is essential,[122] Paul is clear that it is at the point of believing in Jesus that the Spirit is received rather than at the point of water baptism.[123] As faith determines justification and inclusion by God in Christ, Spirit baptism is more likely in view.[124]

In fact, in no other Pauline text is it suggested that the Spirit is received at baptism. So, in Galatians 3:2, the Galatians received the Spirit by *hearing with faith* (see also Gal. 3:5, emphasis mine). Similarly, in Galatians 3:14, believers "receive the promised Spirit *through faith*" (emphasis mine). The Ephesians were sealed with the Spirit when they heard the gospel and believed in Jesus (Eph. 1:13; cf. 2 Cor. 1:21–22; 5:5). Paul repudiated the requirement of adherence to Jewish boundary markers for salvation and inclusion in God's people. Arguing that passages like this and Galatians 3:27 refer to water baptism and that Paul required water baptism to receive the Spirit establishes a new boundary marker, meaning salvation and inclusion requires water baptism. Paul rejects such notions. All that is required is faith, even if all believers *should* undergo water baptism as a critical mark of inclusion in God's church.

As in Galatians 3:27, Spirit baptism is in mind in 1 Corinthians. This view should not come as a surprise. John declared that he baptizes with water but

---

118. Albrecht Oepke, "Βάπτω, Βαπτίζω, Βαπτισμός, Βάπτισμα, Βαπτιστής," *TDNT* 1:530.

119. See Matt. 3:6, 13, 14; Mark 1:4, 5, 8, 9; Luke 3:7, 12, 16, 21; 7:29, 30; John 1:25, 26, 28, 31, 33; 3:23; 10:40; Acts 1:5; 11:16; 19:3–4. The participle is used as a descriptor of John as the Baptizer (Mark 6:14, 24).

120. Mark 10:38, 39; 12:40.

121. Matt. 28:19; Acts 2:38, 41; 8:12, 13, 16, 36, 38; 9:18; 10:47, 48; 16:15, 33; 18:8; 19:5; 22:16; Rom. 6:3; 1 Cor. 1:13–17, also Mark 16:16. Jesus's disciples also baptized (John 3:22, 26; 4:1–2).

122. Paul's words in 1 Corinthians 1:13–16 could be misread as suggesting baptism is unimportant for Paul. Paul still ensured all new converts were baptized and affirms water baptism (Rom. 6:3–4; 1 Cor. 1:13–16; Eph. 4:5; Col. 2:12). He was also baptized (Acts 9:18; 22:16) and baptized Lydia (Acts 16:15), the Roman jailor's family (Acts 16:33), the first converts in Corinth (Acts 18:8; 1 Cor. 1:14, 16), and Ephesus Christians (Acts 19:5).

123. Of this verse, Dunn notes: "He is that baptismal water in which the whole person is publicly plunged." Dunn, *Jesus and the Spirit*, 202.

124. So also, Fee, *GEP*, 179–82.

that one who baptizes with the Holy Spirit (and with fire) would come.[125] By describing the receipt of the Spirit as a baptism, as with love being "poured out" as the Spirit is given (Rom. 5:5), the Spirit is likened to a liquid falling from above, like precipitation or a waterfall of God's presence poured onto and into the believer. The believer then is "filled" with the Spirit in their every part, as if they have drunk their fill (Eph. 5:18).[126]

Considering 1 Corinthians 12:13a, baptism in the Spirit leads to the question of what other Pauline references to baptism might refer to Spirit baptism. Clearly, as Paul speaks of different Christians baptizing the Corinthians, baptism in 1 Corinthians 1:13–17 is water baptism,[127] as is 1 Corinthians 15:29.[128]

Romans 6:3–4 may also refer to baptism in the Spirit.[129] As in Galatians, Paul's emphasis in Romans is justification by faith, not works of the law. As such, the moment of inclusion in Christ is faith, something water baptism symbolizes and enacts as believers' death, burial, and resurrection are visibly demonstrated in the baptism waters. Colossians 2:12 speaks of being buried with Christ in baptism and may be the same. The baptism in Ephesians 4:5 is intriguing, as it could go either way.

Indwelt by the Spirit

God was pleased to allow his fullness to dwell (κατοικέω) in Christ (Col. 1:19) so that the "whole fullness of deity dwells [pres. κατοικέω] bodily" (Col. 2:9 LEB). The present tense implies the continual and ongoing nature of God's indwelling, including currently, as Jesus sits exalted at God's right hand.

For Paul, those who are not justified by faith and indwelt by the Spirit of God are indwelt by sin (Rom. 7:17–18, 20). Now that Christ has died for the sins of humankind, those who have faith in God and his Son are indwelt by the Spirit. As with God's indwelling of Christ (above), Paul uses οἰκος-language to make this point. So, "the Spirit of God dwells (pres. οἰκέω) in [believers]" (Rom. 8:9), and "the Spirit of him who raised Jesus from the dead dwells [pres. οἰκέω] in [believers]" (Rom. 8:11). Again, in 1 Corinthians 3:16 when describing the Corinthian church as the temple of God, he states that "God's Spirit dwells [pres. οἰκέω] in you."[130]

While Galatians 2:19c–20 does not mention the Spirit, Fee correctly states that "'Christ lives in me' most likely is a kind of shorthand for 'Christ by his

---

125. "With the Holy Spirit": Mark 1:7; John 1:33; "Holy Spirit and fire": Matt. 3:11; Luke 3:16; Acts 1:5.
126. Luke 1:15, 41, 67; Acts 2:4; 4:8, 31; 9:17; 13:9, 53.
127. Obviously, baptism in 1 Corinthians 10:2 is not Christian baptism, but analogous with it for Paul.
128. However we understand baptism here, it is not Spirit baptism. Similarly, Fee, *GEP*, 179–82.
129. For example, Habets says of Romans 6:3, "Paul in particular uses the language of being baptized into Christ by the Holy Spirit." Myk Habets, *The Anointed Son: A Trinitarian Spirit Christology*, PTMS (Eugene, OR: Pickwick, 2010), 261.
130. The plural ὑμῖν indicates all the Corinthians individually (1 Cor. 6:19) are indwelt by the Spirit and so form the church, the temple of the Spirit. Similarly, see Gardner, *1 Corinthians*, 179.

Spirit lives in me.'"[131] Fee also appropriately rejects that this suggests the melding of the Spirit and the risen Lord into one entity but aligns with other texts that speak of the Spirit as the Spirit of Christ (Rom. 8:9).[132] Paul's life is now lived by faith in Jesus, the Son of God.

In Ephesians 2:22, again, while considering the people of God as God's temple, the church is being "built together into a dwelling place [κατοικητήριον] for God by the Spirit." In the next chapter, describing the same reality, Paul prays for the Ephesians that "Christ may dwell [κατοικέω] in your hearts through faith" (3:17). This shows that Paul is comfortable describing the same presence of God in believers with spiritual or christological language.[133] Paul also urges Timothy to guard the good deposit (the gospel)[134] entrusted to him "by the Holy Spirit who dwells [pres. part. τοῦ ἐνοικοῦντος] within us" (2 Tim. 1:14).[135] The gospel is entrusted to preachers by the Spirit. The Spirit gives the power to guard it if God's people yield to his unction and stand for the gospel when necessary.

Elsewhere, again speaking of the church as God's temple, Paul sees the hope of Leviticus 26:12—that God will make his dwelling (ἐνοικέω) among his people and walk with them—fulfilled in the age of the Spirit (2 Cor. 6:16).[136] The regular use of the present tense of associated verbs in these references indicates Paul is speaking of an ongoing experience of the indwelling of the Spirit of God.

Made to Drink the One Spirit

As will be discussed in chapter 5, the εἴτε . . . εἴτε string Paul inserts in 1 Corinthians 12:13b indicates that all people, whether Jew or Gentile (Greek),

---

131. Fee, *GEP*, 374. Fee also correctly reasons that Paul prefers Christ language here to emphasize his overall point that new Gentile converts do not need to yield to Jewish law. (I take it more broadly than Fee's "Jewish identity markers," but the contrast remains the same—the law or Christ/Spirit.) As he says, "As far as the Torah is concerned, death has brought an end to that relationship altogether because of the believer's intimate relationship with Christ, whose death brought an end to the time of the Torah" (p. 376). See also Charles H. Cosgrove, *The Cross and the Spirit: A Study in the Argument and Theology of Galatians* (Macon, GA: Mercer University Press, 1989), 173, 193–94; David A. deSilva, *The Letter to the Galatians*, NICNT (Grand Rapids: Eerdmans, 2018), 248.

132. Fee, *GEP*, 374. See also Myk Habets, *Anointed Son*, 136. He writes, "There is no reason to equate the 'Spirit of Christ' (Rom. 8:9) with 'Christ in you' (Rom. 8:10) *simpliciter*. The point is that the Spirit of Christ in believers develops 'Christ' in them."

133. Similarly, Colossians 3:16, where believers are to let the word of Christ dwell (pres. ἐνοικέω) in them richly. The present implies doing so habitually and continually.

134. "In view of the way in which it is called 'the good deposit' in v. 14, the reference must be to the gospel rather than to the task of proclaiming it." I. Howard Marshall and Philip H. Towner, *A Critical and Exegetical Commentary on the Pastoral Epistles*, ICC (London: T&T Clark, 2004), 711. See also 1 Tim. 6:20; 2 Tim. 1:12.

135. On this passage, see Fee, *GEP*, 790–92. He notes this is "the last explicit mention of the Holy Spirit in the Pauline corpus" (p. 791). That the "deposit" is the gospel is clear from vv. 9–10.

136. God "walking among them" also speaks of the presence of the Spirit recalling God walking with the saints of the OT (Gen. 5:22, 24; 6:8; Mic. 6:8; Mal. 2:6).

slave or free (citizens), receive the same Spirit. As such, there is no room for status divisions within the body of Christ. The receipt of the Spirit means the breaking down of such divisions. This clause chiastically restates 1 Corinthians 12:13a, discussed above. The metaphor for receiving the Spirit continues the theme of the Spirit as a fluid but shifts from God's pouring water over (or immersing) believers with the one Spirit to the receipt of the Spirit as a drink.

The verb ποτίζω is used literally of giving a drink or drinking as in Romans 12:20.[137] Paul uses it metaphorically for Christian nurture, as being fed milk (1 Cor. 3:2) or watering a seed (1 Cor. 3:6–8).[138] Here, the Spirit is a gift given to believers. The chiastic structure and the aorist passives of ἐποτίσθημεν and ἐβαπτίσθημεν clearly indicate that we should not read the baptism and drinking as two separate events. Instead, they describe the exact moment of receipt of the Spirit from God at conversion.

John imagines the Spirit as a liquid flowing from Christ into the beings of believers and from whom flows streams of living water.[139] John's idea of "the water of life" speaks of the Spirit drinking in God's life (John 4:14; Rev. 21:6; 22:1, 17). The crowds thinking the disciples were drunk on wine invokes the notion of drinking the Spirit, as does Paul's contrast between being drunk on wine and being filled with the Spirit (Acts 2:13; Eph. 5:18).[140]

So the giving of the Spirit is likened to God giving believers the water of life to drink. Believers, whether Jews or Gentiles, slave or free, or part of other analogous social divisions (cf. Gal. 3:28; Col. 3:11), receive the same Spirit of God. This image affirms that the reception of the Spirit can be likened to the outpouring of a liquid onto and into humankind and receiving it like drinking in God's presence. The combination of the baptism and drinking motifs stresses that the Spirit utterly fills and overwhelms believers in every part—body, soul, spirit, heart, and mind. Knowing this leads to a mind and body and all-of-life pneumatology.

The Spirit Received

At times, Paul uses λαμβανω language, which speaks of receiving the Spirit. Whereas the ideas above speak of God's initiative, the language speaks

---

137. Matt. 10:42; 25:35, 37, 42; 27:48; Mark 9:41; 15:36; Luke 13:15.
138. See also of the Babylonian prostitute making the nations drink of the wine of her passion (Rev. 14:8). Metaphorical uses in the LXX: drinking of God's luxury (Ps. 35:9 [36:8 EVV]); to drink the wine of bewilderment (Ps. 59:5 [60:3 EVV]); the drink of tears (Ps. 79:6 [80:6 EVV]); the water of wisdom (Sir. 15:3); a drinking cup of unmixed wine of error (Pss. Sol. 8:14, also Jer. 32:15, 17); to drink a wind of bewilderment (Isa. 29:10); to give water with gall as a symbol of judgment (Jer. 8:14; 9:14, also Jer. 23:15); a cup of comfort (Jer. 16:7); a cup of pain (Jer. 23:15); and to drink from excrement (Ezek. 32:6).
139. John 7:37–39. Alternatively, this speaks of streams of the Spirit as living water flowing out of Christ. See the discussion in D. A. Carson, *The Gospel according to John*, PNTC (Grand Rapids: Eerdmans, 1991), 323–26.
140. Interestingly, in 1 Thessalonians 5:19 Paul mixes ideas speaking of quenching (dousing with liquid) the Spirit (as if fire).

of believers *receiving* what God sends, gives, supplies, baptizes with, and gives to drink—the Spirit. While λαμβανω language can mean "to take," when used of the Spirit, it carries the softer meaning of "receive." God initiates the giving of the Spirit as a gift;[141] he is simply received into one's being when a person believes.

In 1 Corinthians 2:12, Paul reminds the Corinthians that believers (we) have not received a "spirit of the world" but "the Spirit who is from God."[142] The purpose for which the Spirit is given is "so that we might know the things from God that have been gifted to us" (my translation). The Spirit brings knowledge of the things of God, including the Spirit himself, the gifts he gives, and what God has done in human lives in creation and history to the present.

The language of receiving the Spirit is found in 2 Corinthians 11:4 in Paul's response to the Corinthian flirtation with false Jewish teachers. The verse is a chiastic conditional sentence with a threefold protasis culminating in a short apodosis.

A1   εἰ μὲν γὰρ ὁ ἐρχόμενος ἄλλον Ἰησοῦν κηρύσσει ὃν οὐκ ἐκηρύξαμεν,
    For if someone comes preaching another Jesus whom we did not preach,
    B   ἢ πνεῦμα ἕτερον λαμβάνετε ὃ οὐκ ἐλάβετε
        or you receive another spirit that you did not receive
A2   ἢ εὐαγγέλιον ἕτερον ὃ οὐκ ἐδέξασθε, καλῶς ἀνέχεσθε.
    or another gospel that you did not accept,
C   (Apodosis) καλῶς ἀνέχεσθε
    You put up with it quite easily.[143]

Parts A1 and A2 stress their reception of a false gospel of Christ. Part B indicates and emphasizes that in receiving this false gospel, the Corinthians receive a spirit other than the Holy Spirit received at conversion (cf. 2 Cor. 1:21–22). This passage stresses two things of interest. First, false gospels have their source in demonic beings who corrupt the gospel and deceive those who proclaim it. Second, the Spirit is received from God.

Again, in Galatians 3:2, Paul refers to the Galatians' experience of receiving the Spirit.[144] The context is Judaizers asserting that new Gentile converts must yield to the Torah, especially its boundary markers. He asks rhetorically whether they "received [ἐλάβετε] the Spirit by works of the law or by hearing [the gospel] with faith." The implied answer is the latter. As such, the gospel is received at the moment of hearing and believing the gospel.[145]

---

141. Also Martin, *Spirit*, 10–11.
142. On this being the Spirit of God, see Fee, *GEP*, 27; Keown, *Philippians*, 1:290–93.
143. BDAG, s.v. "ἀνέχω," 78; my translation.
144. This assumes it was a significant experience remembered by them all. Dunn, *Jesus and the Spirit*, 202.
145. Further on 3:2, see Fee, *GEP*, 383–84. See also Buchanan, "Spirit," 80–86.

Later in Galatians 3:14, with two parallel ἵνα clauses, Paul states the purpose and result[146] of Christ becoming a curse (on the cross) and redeeming believers (us)[147] from the curse of the law (cf. Deut. 21:23).[148] First, Jesus took the curse of the law on himself on the cross, "so that/with the result that the blessing of Abraham would come to the Gentiles in Christ Jesus." Second, Christ became the curse "so that/with the result that we would receive [λαμβανω] the promise of the Spirit through faith" (my translation).[149] Again, the Spirit is given based on faith. The first clause indicates the Spirit is imparted to those "in Christ." The promise refers to OT passages anticipating the outpouring of the Spirit (see chapter 1). It implies that believers participate in the same anointing Jesus received as his Spirit is imparted to believers (cf. 2 Cor. 1:21).

What follows in vv. 15–22 does not mention the Spirit but speaks of the promise of the inheritance that the law could not fulfill. The giving of the Spirit is the first installment of the inheritance that guarantees its ultimate completion. The law could "give life" (v. 21) but imprisoned all things so that the promise could be given to believers in the seed, Jesus Christ (v. 22). This promise is experienced in the Spirit and will be completed in the eschaton.[150]

CONCLUSION

The Spirit is intimately involved in Christian conversion. Before that moment of faith and Christian conversion, the Spirit actively sends the word to the soon-to-be-saved (often through a gospel communicator), shaping the person's life for future Christian vocation from conception, setting up the conditions for salvation, and beckoning them to follow. Whether God invites people to believe through the preaching of the gospel of Jesus Christ accompanied by the persuasive power of the Spirit or as he acts sovereignly, believ-

---

146. This is one of Paul's uses of ἵνα where it is difficult to discern whether it is a result or a purpose clause. Likely, this includes both: the purpose of Christ's crucifixion was that the blessing would come to the Gentiles in him, and it is also the result (as seen in Galatia as they received the Spirit, cf. 3:2).

147. Fee correctly observes the soteriological importance of "us/we" here, shifting from a focus on the Gentiles to all believers, including Paul himself. See GEP, 292.

148. Fee suggests this is a kind of "constructive" synonymous parallelism. However, he suggests the second takes the first a step further to the fulfillment of the promise by the Spirit. Fee, GEP, 394.

149. Here I agree with Buchanan, who defends that the ἵνα clauses referred to are both result clauses (although I would modify this to both being result and purpose as they define both the outcome and ongoing process through mission). Buchanan, "Spirit," 125–27.

150. In his discussion of the Spirit and inheritance, Fee overstates when he says, "But as v. 14 and 4:4–7 indicate, the 'inheritance' is to be understood as *having been realized* through the coming of the Spirit." Fee, GEP, 396–97, emphasis mine. It is not the inheritance realized in its fullest sense, but the first installment of what is to come. He also overstates when he says, "The Spirit is for Paul *the* means by which all the concerns of the letter are held together: righteousness by faith, Gentile inclusion, the blessing of Abraham, the promise(s) of God, the inheritance" (emphasis mine). God's action and Christ's redemptive death must be put on equal terms with the Spirit. Still, Fee is right to emphasize the role of the Spirit as concomitant to God's action and Christ's death.

ers are the elect. As those called by God, they experience a pneumaphany as the Spirit fills their beings. The Spirit is sent, gifted, and supplied. They are baptized, indwelt—they receive and drink of the Spirit. They are one with the Lord by the Spirit.

CHAPTER 3

THE IMMEDIATE IMPACT
OF THE SPIRIT

In the previous chapter, I explored the work of the Spirit leading to conversion and the receipt of the Spirit after the moment of faith. The next thing to discuss is what happens when the Spirit is poured into the hearts of believers. In other words, what is the effect of the Spirit? This chapter explores the many facets of transformation that flows from the moment the Spirit is downloaded by God into the hearts of those justified by faith.

SPIRIT BAPTISM

The Spirit Sealing and Guaranteeing Salvation
Some texts speak of the reception of the Spirit. Several emphasize that the Spirit is received at the moment of believing the gospel and propose the idea of a seal and guarantee (2 Cor. 1:21–22; 5:5; Eph. 1:13c–14; 4:30).[1] These texts will now be discussed.

2 CORINTHIANS 1:21–22
The first verses to be considered are 2 Corinthians 1:21–22.[2] In 2 Corinthians 1:19, Paul reminds the Corinthians that he, Silvanus (Silas), and Timothy preached to them Jesus Christ, the Son of God—a neat reminder that Christ is at the center of Paul's message (cf. 1 Cor. 2:1–2; 3:11). In Christ, the promises of God find their fulfillment, leading Spirit-responsive believers to respond with an amen to God's glory.

In v. 21, Paul affirms to the Corinthians that while Christ was preached by Paul, Silvanus, and Timothy (v. 19), God established both Paul's team and the Corinthians in (εἰς) Christ. He speaks of the receipt of the Spirit in three successive clauses—as the one who establishes (pres. part. βεβαιῶν) believers

---

1. Or immediately after (in earthly time). In that God functions in a dimension beyond time, I am not sure debates about timing are particularly relevant—faith and receiving the Spirit are effectively coterminous.
2. This is a nominal sentence (without a verb). Fee, *GEP*, 289.

in Christ[3]—(1) God also anointed us;[4] (2) he also sealed us; and (3) he gave the guarantee (ἀρραβῶν) of the Spirit in our hearts. These three are not consecutive actions of God but refer to the one event of Spirit-reception (cf. Rom. 5:5; Gal. 4:6). This moment comes at conversion, not water baptism.[5] The second and third of these reiterate what Paul says in Ephesians 1:13c–14 (considered below).

The first clause uses the verb χρίω, a cognate of Χριστός, "Christ," the Messiah, or "Anointed One." The verb is used across Jewish Greek literature in various ways of spreading a liquid substance over a person or object.[6] Commonly it is used sacrally of spreading oil on sacrifices[7] and on the tabernacle and its implements.[8] Frequently, it is used for anointing priests and kings.[9] The verb is applied to the future hope of a Messiah in Isaiah 61:1.[10]

In the NT, Luke uses χρίω when Jesus claims to be the messianic anointed one of Isaiah 61:1 (Luke 4:18; Acts 4:27). In Acts 10:38, Jesus is described as the one God anointed (χρίω) with the Holy Spirit and power.

---

3. Paul's "us with you in Christ" and the choice of the present tense "not only reaffirms the absolute interconnectedness between his ministry and their existence as believers, but also launches him into a moment of reflection on their mutual present 'confirmation' as predicated on the past event of their reception of the Spirit, presumably at conversion. Thus, the one who 'confirms' is the very God who previously 'anointed us.'" Fee, *GEP*, 290.

4. With the three clauses focused on God's action, Fee rightly notes that "one of the most God-centered, God-focused paragraphs in the Pauline corpus . . . emphasizes the absolutely central and crucial role taken by God." Fee, *GEP*, 289.

5. To quote Fee, "There seem to be no grounds in the text, therefore, for viewing this passage as also referring to water baptism. In fact, not one of its several metaphors is ever used in the NT, either individually or together, to refer to or allude to Christian baptism; moreover, in this text and others Paul designates the Spirit, not baptism, as God's 'seal' of ownership. The linkage itself is circuitous: one begins with mid-to-late-second century evidence for the imagery of 'seal' as referring directly to baptism, then presupposes the (questionable) assumption that Paul understood believers to receive the Spirit at baptism, then finally assumes the metaphors (especially 'anointing' and 'seal') to have baptism *inherently* in them." Fee, *GEP*, 294–95.

6. Also of basting bread with olive oil (Exod. 29:2; Num. 6:15); in the covenantal curses, no anointing with olive oil (Deut. 28:40); anointing a shield with oil (2 Kgdms. 1:21); anointing a garment (Jdt. 10:3); anointing with perfume like myrrh (Amos 6:6; Isa. 25:6); paint (Jer. 22:14; Josephus, *Ant.* 4.200); covering a boat in slime (Josephus, *Ant.* 2.220).

7. For example, the anointing of a bull for sin offering (Exod. 29:36). Holy anointing oil is not to be put on human flesh (Exod. 30:32).

8. For example, anointing the tabernacle and its implements with oil including the altar (Exod. 30:26; 40:9, 10; Lev. 8:11; Num. 7:1, 10, 84; Philo, *Spec.* 1.233); God's anointing of Israel (Ezek. 16:9).

9. Of anointing priests (Exod. 28:41; 29:7; 29:29; 30:30; 40:13; Lev. 6:13; 7:36; 8:12; 16:32; Num. 7:88; 35:25; Sir. 45:15; T. Levi 17:2; Josephus, *Ant.* 3.198; Philo, *Fug.* 110; *Mos.* 2:150). The high priest is the "anointed high priest" (Lev. 4:3) or "the anointed one" (T. Levi 17:3). Of anointing a king (Judg. 9:8, 15; 1 Kgdms. 9:16; 10:1; 11:15; 15:1, 17; 16:3, 12, 13; 2 Kgdms. 2:4, 7; 5:3, 17; 12:7; 19:11; 3 Kgdms. 1:34, 39, 45; 5:15; 19:15, 16; 4 Kgdms. 9:3, 6, 12; 11:12; 23:30; 1 Chron. 11:3; 14:8; 29:22; 2 Chron. 23:11; 36:1; Pss. 26:1; 44:8 [45:7 EVV]; 88:21 [89:20 EVV]; 151:4; Sir. 46:13; 48:8; Hos. 8:10; Josephus, *Ant.* 6.83, 157, 159; 7.357, 382; 9.106, 149, 239).

10. It is also used of being anointed with the "blessed ointment of incorruptibility" (Jos. Asen. 8:5; 15:4); to anoint oneself with the ointment of destruction (Jos. Asen. 8:5); and the anointing of the renewed city of Jerusalem (Ezek. 43:3 LXX).

The author of Hebrews cites Psalm 45:7 of Jesus as the one God anointed "with the oil of gladness." Some reject seeing "oil of gladness" as the Spirit with which Jesus was anointed at his baptism, preferring to link this to "the joy set before him" in Hebrews 12:3.[11] However, here it speaks of Jesus's anointing as Messiah, which occurred at his baptism. As such, "oil of gladness" speaks of the Spirit.[12]

Here, in 2 Corinthians 1:21, χρίω refers figuratively to the anointing of the Corinthians by God when they believed. As the Corinthians believed, just as Jesus received the Spirit at his baptism, they were anointed with the same Spirit. When they heard the message and believed it, God's response was to pour the oil of his Spirit onto and into them. As Paul says in Ephesians 4:30 (below), believers are anointed for the day of redemption. The Spirit guarantees their eternal life if they persevere in faith.

The second aspect of the Spirit's work is sealing the believer. The verb σφραγίζω is used across comparative literature of an official seal.[13] In the wider NT, it is used of sealing the tomb of Christ (Matt. 27:66), God setting his seal on Christ (John 6:27), believers sealing, or confirming, that God is true by receiving Christ's testimony (John 3:33), and God sealing things in Revelation.[14] Thus, it speaks of God's seal and carries deep solemnity and commitment.[15]

---

11. For example, F. F. Bruce, *The Epistle to the Hebrews*, NICNT (Grand Rapids: Eerdmans, 1990), 61.

12. As argues John Owen, *An Exposition of the Epistle to the Hebrews*, ed. W. H. Goold (Edinburgh: T&T Clark, 1862), 153.

13. In the LXX, of money sealed in royal treasury (4 Kgdms 22:5); vengeance stored in God's treasury (Deut. 32:34; Odes Sol. 2:34); the abyss sealed (Odes Sol. 12:3); a garden locked, symbolizing a woman sealed from sexual relationships (Song 4:12); transgressions sealed in a bag before God (Job 14:17); adulterers sealed up in the day (Job 24:12); a door locked and sealed (Bel. 13); royal and other letters, documents, decrees, marriage contracts, prophetic messages, deeds of purchase sealed with the ring in wax (3 Kgdms. 20:8 [1 Kings EVV 21:8]; 1 Esd. 3:8; 2 Esd. 20:3 [Neh. 10:1 EVV]; Tob. 7:13–14; Add. Esth. 3:10; 8:8, 10; Isa. 8:16; 29:11; Jer. 39:10, 11, 25; 32:44; Dan. 6:18; 12:4, 9). The Pseudepigrapha, aside from clearly Christianized texts (*Apoc. Dan.* 2:15; *Liv. Proph.* 2:15), speaks of Job sealed (locked up) by an angel (Test. Job 5:1); sealing up the grave of Adam (L.A.E. 48:3); God sealing periods of time (4 Bar. 3:9); God sealing the abyss (Pr. Man. 3); and the sealing up of demons (Test. Sol. 2:5; 4:12; 7:3; 8:12; 9:3; 10:6–7; 12:5; 16:7; 22:11). Josephus uses it of Darius sealing the lion's den (*Ant.* 10.258). Philo applies it to people with property sealed (*Mos.* 1.30); God sealing on the soul impressions of truth (*Opif.* 172), and soul given as a seal (*Somn.* 2.45); God sealing treasuries of evil things for judgment (*Alleg. Interp.* 3.105–6); then sealed (*Agr.* 169); and diplomatic letters (*Legat.* 330). Wider Greek uses include sealing with a ring (Aristot., *Mem. rem.* 450.1.30–34); sealed out of a house (Euripides, *Her.* 53); people sealed with war injuries (Euripides, *Iph. taur.* 1372); sealing a storeroom (Diogenes Laertius, *Lives* 4.59: Lacydes [435]; Athenaeus, *Deipn.* 6.265); the house where Zeus's thunderbolt is sealed (Aeschylus, *Eum.* 828); and of documents including sacred poems sealed in a temple (Diogenes Laertius, *Lives* 4.25: Zeno [402]); diplomatic letters (Polybius, *Hist.* 5.38.1; 31.13.9; Appian, *Bell. civ.* 1.4.41 [Iberica]; Euripides, *Iph. aul.* 38; Diodorus Siculus, *Hist.* 16.52.6), a will (Appian, *Bell. civ.* 3.1.105); sealing a security (Epictetus, *Diatr.* 2.13.7).

14. This includes the 144,000 sealed from the twelve tribes (Rev. 7:3–8); sealing God's words (Rev. 10:4); Satan sealed in the abyss (Rev. 20:3); and the seer instructing John not to seal up the words of prophecy in the Apocalypse (Rev. 22:10).

15. It is indeed a commercial metaphor, as are βεβαιῶν and ἀρραβῶνα. Fee, *GEP*, 292, however, suggests

God's role as the agent is emphasized in the middle participle.[16] The aorist participle grammaticalizes the past moment of sealing. Paul uses ἡμᾶς, which is inclusive of all believers. Paul speaks similarly of the sealing work of God by the Spirit in Ephesians 1:13 and 4:30. The latter text indicates this sealing is "for the day of redemption." The link to eternity suggests that the sealing is permanent. At the judgment, the seal will be broken and the "children of God" revealed (cf. Rom. 8:23).[17] Paul, then, likens the giving of the Spirit to God pouring hot wax onto the human heart and pressing the signet ring on the finger and hand of his power into it to seal the believer. With what follows, believers are assured that they are under God's protection and care and will be sustained to ultimate salvation.[18]

The third statement describes the Spirit as ἀρραβών "the down payment in our hearts." In Jewish Greek literature, it is used as a pledge or promise (deposit) for future payment and, more broadly, of a down payment for something to be fully paid later.[19] The two other NT uses of the Spirit as ἀρραβών are also in Paul. First, in 2 Corinthians 5:5 (below), as here, the Spirit is given as a guarantee of future salvation. Similarly, in Ephesians 1:14, the Spirit is the "guarantee" or "down payment" of the readers' inheritance for their redemption as God's possession.[20]

The giving (aor. δίδωμι)[21] of the Spirit then is likened by Paul to a first installment of the inheritance believers are guaranteed to receive at the consummation. The giving of the Spirit then gives certainty of future

---

that to push that too far is to overstate the transactional dimension and remove the deep relational intimacy implied in God's sealing.

16. Wallace, *Greek Grammar*, 414.

17. Fee suggests that structurally it is implied in the seal metaphor that the Spirit functions as a down payment on the inheritance to be received. Fee, *GEP*, 293. However, my analysis does not indicate that σφραγίζω itself points in this direction. However, τὸν ἀρραβῶνα most definitely does. We should not, in my view, confuse the metaphors. God seals his people, and the Spirit is *also* a down payment guaranteeing future salvation.

18. It is, of course, debated whether this means that believers can become unsealed through unbelief. If we push the metaphor, then clearly the answer is no. Once sealed, a believer is ensured salvation. However, this is challenged by Paul, who seems to argue that people can fall from salvation in some texts (although he never states that absolutely). Either way, the Spirit is within believers, sealing them, marking them as God's children, and providing the spiritual power to enable them to persevere.

19. Ἀρραβών is a loanword from the Hebrew עֵרָבוֹן, *'ērābôn*, used in Genesis 38. It is employed for the giving of personal items (signet, cord, staff) by Judah to Tamar as a *pledge guaranteeing* future payment of a goat promised for sexual services (Gen. 38:17–20; also *Test. Jud.* 12:5, 7). See also Philo, who allegorizes this ethically (*Fug.* 149–151). It is also used in Athenaeus, *Deipn.* 11.486d; 13.596b in the context of prostitution. See also MM, 79, who notes P Par 58[14], where a woman is given one thousand drachmae as a ἀραβῶνα for a cow (also P Lond 143[13]; P Fay 91[14]; P Oxy 2.299[2f] and other examples).

20. See Lincoln, *Ephesians*, 40, for the view that this is the believers as God's possession rather than believers possessing the inheritance.

21. The aorist grammaticalizes as a punctiliar past verb pointing to the moment God gave his Spirit to the Corinthians at the moment of faith.

salvation.[22] As Fee puts it, "It both establishes the contractual obligation and guarantees its fulfillment."[23] The combination of the two motifs applied to the Spirit ("sealing" and "down payment or guarantee") gives assurance to Christians. Furthermore, as Fee also says, "For Paul the gift of the Spirit is the first part of the redemption of the whole person, the beginning of the process that will end when believers assume their 'spiritual' bodies (enter into a mode of existence determined solely by the Spirit; see 1 Cor. 15:44)."[24]

For Fee, the Spirit is not the agency of final transformation; this is the work of God. However, the Spirit begins the work within the believer. This genesis begins in the hearts of his people (ἐν ταῖς καρδίαις ἡμῶν), the whole inner being of the believer.[25] As such, the believer's redemption has begun, to be completed in the eschaton. It stands to reason that the same Spirit is the agent of the final transformation of believers by the Father through the Son.[26] The use of the verb δίδωμι, "give," indicates that the Spirit is a gift of God. The ἀρραβών was an initial payment, down payment, or deposit paid in advance to secure the legal claim in question or secure a contract.[27]

2 Corinthians 5:5

In 2 Corinthians 5:1–5, Paul states that while believers groan in suffering and longing for eternal life, they can be utterly confident in their future resurrection into eternal life in which "what is mortal" is "swallowed up by life" (v. 4).[28] In v. 5a, he assures the Corinthians that God has prepared believers for this life. The article ὁ refers to θεός (God). God has given (aor. δίδωμι) believers (ἡμῖν, "us") the "guarantee of the Spirit" (τὸν ἀρραβῶνα τοῦ πνεύματος). As in 2 Corinthians 1:22, the Spirit is a down payment, deposit, or guarantee.

---

22. As with σφραγίζω, Paul's use leads into the debate concerning whether this guarantee can be withdrawn. Some would say so, as this is legal and business terminology of guarantee. However, it is gifted on the basis of faith, and so, if faith fails, then it is possible that God would then view the arrangement null. Either way, this is all tremendously assuring to readers.
23. Fee, *GEP*, 293.
24. Fee, *GEP*, 293.
25. "The presence of the Spirit as God's seal and down payment is the unmistakable evidence of salvation as 'already but not yet.' The future is already in evidence through the 'down payment,' the present guarantee; but he is present only as 'down payment'; the final inheritance, which he guarantees, is yet to be realized." Fee, *GEP*, 294.
26. See Fee, *GEP*, 293–94, on the powerful Trinitarian dynamic in the text.
27. BDAG, s.v. "ἀρραβών," 134.
28. For a bibliography on this contentious passage that he describes as "one of the thorniest passages in the Pauline corpus," see Fee, *GEP*, 324n125. Like Fee, I see no need to deal with the difficult issues raised by the text. I concur with the two threads he sees in the passage: (1) this passage "spells out the outcome" for the life and body of Paul's experience of ongoing death and internally God's life (by the Spirit); and (2) Paul is recapitulating what he said in 1 Corinthians 15 rather than presenting an alternative view.

What the Spirit guarantees is the saint's inheritance in eternity. A human marked by God's Spirit will live forever. The Spirit is given at the moment of faith. Here, Paul envisages the believer's present body being "overclothed" with another body which, as Fee observes, is the "spiritual body" in 1 Corinthians 15:44.[29]

Fee also astutely notes that in this passage, Paul affirms Christian corporeal existence in the interim between Christ's comings. He states, "As in 1 Cor. 6:19–20 and 1 Cor. 15:44–45, the Spirit is also the affirmation of our present bodily existence. We may 'groan' a bit in it; but it is not to be despised."

EPHESIANS 1:13c–14

As noted, ἐν ᾧ is again "in Christ" and is connected to ἐσφραγίσθητε, "in him you were sealed." The aorist participle πιστεύσαντες is temporal, "and when you believed," referring to the Ephesians' response to the gospel they heard. As the Spirit invited them to believe the message, they yielded, and the sword of the Word of God pierced their hearts. At that moment of faith, their hearts opened to God as Lydia's did in Philippi (Acts 16:14), and the Spirit poured into their beings, flooding them with God's love and presence (Rom. 5:5). The seal is a mark of ownership; hence, they become God's possession.[30] The Spirit then is likened to hot wax poured onto the heart, on which God's imprint is sealed, their hearts so sealed "for the day of redemption" (Eph. 4:30).

In v. 14, the Spirit is further defined as the ἀρραβὼν τῆς κληρονομίας ἡμῶν, "who is the guarantee of our inheritance." The inheritance is eternal life and the renewed cosmos to be shared with Christ. As noted regarding 2 Corinthians 1:21–22, the ἀρραβών is like a down payment, deposit, or guarantee of this inheritance to be possessed at the consummation. At the moment of the Spirit's entry, pneumaformity begins as God begins to conform the believer into the image of the Son.

EPHESIANS 4:30

In his ethical teaching in Ephesians 4, Paul urges the Ephesians not to grieve the Holy Spirit of God (which will be discussed in chapter 7, "Life Worthy of God's Calling"). He adds the detail concerning the Spirit: ἐν ᾧ ἐσφραγίσθητε εἰς ἡμέραν ἀπολυτρώσεως, "in whom you have been sealed for the day of redemption." The dative ἐν ᾧ is either instrumental ("by whom," ESV)[31] or, as is preferable, a dative of sphere ("in whom")[32]—God is

---

29. Fee, *GEP*, 327.
30. Fee, *GEP*, 670. He correctly notes also that there is no mention of water baptism and "nothing that suggests a baptismal motif" here. The Spirit and not baptism is the seal of ownership. Nor is there anything suggesting an experience subsequent to conversion, but one that is coterminous with it.
31. Fee, *GEP*, 716.
32. Lincoln, *Ephesians*, 291.

the agent, and he seals his people in, with, and by the Spirit.[33] This verse is crucial, as it explains the reason the believer is sealed. "The day of redemption" here is futuristic, speaking of the consummation at which Jesus returns, all are judged, and believers are fully pneumaformed and are gifted eternal life (Rom. 8:23). As such, the Spirit is God's seal indicating his ownership and vindication of believers for eternal life.

The Spirit Who Justifies

While justification is primarily the declaration of God the Father that a believer is justified or righteous in his sight through being in Christ by faith, the Spirit is not uninvolved in this, as evidenced by 1 Corinthians 6:11d.[34] Later in this chapter, I will discuss this verse concerning the Spirit's involvement in washing and sanctifying the Corinthian believers at conversion. Here, I consider the believer's justification.

In 1 Corinthians 6, Paul deals with two problems in the Corinthian church: (1) taking one another before unrighteous Roman judicial authorities on trivial matters (1 Cor. 6:1–8); and (2) sexual immorality, particularly sexual relations with prostitutes (1 Cor. 6:12–20). First Corinthians 6:9–10 bridges the two passages, reminding the Corinthians that the unrighteous (those who are unbelievers and not justified by faith) will not inherit the kingdom of God. Paul then breaks down the unrighteous into ten groups who will not do so.[35]

The list is not exhaustive but carefully chosen because these are things the Corinthians used to engage in and to which some were returning. The careful choosing of the list is suggested in v. 11a, where Paul states that these are the sort of things that the Corinthians used to do before becoming Christians. Four concern unchristian sexual relationships,[36] one focuses on idolatry,[37] one on alcohol abuse,[38] another on self-satiation,[39] and three relate to the relational abuse of the others.[40] Some were falling prey to these things again. Paul's intent here is not primarily to warn them they will not

---

33. Of course, all of these are implied in one way or another.

34. Habets correctly observes, "Salvation is new life in Christ in the Spirit; salvation not only involves justification by Christ but also justification by the Spirit." Habets, *Anointed Son*, 264.

35. The key to this interpretation is Paul's use of ἄδικοι, "unrighteous" (v. 10), and the parallel between θεοῦ βασιλείαν οὐ κληρονομήσουσιν (v. 10a) and βασιλείαν θεοῦ κληρονομήσουσιν (v. 11d). The list of sinful people explicates ἄδικοι. These are those who are not "justified," unlike the Corinthians who are (ἐδικαιώθητε, v. 11). In 6:1 he describes those in the Roman courts as τῶν ἀδίκων and again as ἀπίστων, "unbelievers," which helps to define Paul's intent in vv. 9–11—to call the Corinthians to the Christoform, pneumaform life.

36. Πόρνοι (sexually immoral people), μοιχοὶ (adulterers), μαλακοὶ (passive male homosexual partners), and ἀρσενοκοῖται (dominant male homosexual partners, LEB).

37. Εἰδωλολάτρης (idolators, LEB).

38. Μέθυσοι (abusers of alcohol, my translation).

39. πλεονέκται (greedy people). This is also seen by Paul as idolatry (Col. 3:5).

40. Κλέπται (thieves), πλεονέλοίδοροι (abusive people), and ἅρπαγες (robbers).

inherit the kingdom of God (as they are saved by faith and not works)[41] but to call them away from these things the unrighteous (and they) used to do and to live by the Spirit.[42]

To call them away from such behaviors, Paul reminds them of their conversion.[43] The third aspect of the Spirit's involvement is his reminder that they have been justified in the name of the Lord Jesus Christ and by the Holy Spirit. Paul uses δικ- language some 146 times, and 1 Corinthians 6:11 is unique in attributing God's justification, albeit alongside Christ's power, to the Spirit. Elsewhere justification is linked to faith,[44] God's grace (Rom. 3:24; Titus 3:7), Christ's blood (Rom. 5:9), or God (Rom. 8:33).

The link between justification and Spirit could mean the Spirit is the agent of declaring the person righteous. However, Paul uses the aorist passive for all three verbs, implying God's agency (divine passive).[45] The final two prepositional clauses modify all three verbs so that "God has effected the salvation expressed by these rich metaphors 'in the name of the Lord Jesus Christ and by his Spirit.'"[46] The two clauses are instrumental.[47]

Considering Paul's broader theology, "justified" here speaks of the moment of God's declaration that a person believes and is justified, and so is "in Christ," and is a recipient of the Spirit. They are washed and sanctified by the Spirit and in the name of the Lord Jesus. Fee avers,

> It is not that the Spirit saves; that is the work of the Father through the Son. But the Spirit appropriates God's salvation in the life of the believer in such a way that new life and behavior are the expected result; and without the latter, the effective work of the Spirit in the believer's life, there has been no true salvation—in any meaningful sense for Paul.[48]

---

41.   Contra Fee, *GEP*, 128, who writes, "His point, of course, is that some within the believing community are behaving just like those who will not inherit the kingdom. They must change their behavior or come under the same threat of judgment." While there may be a point where someone sins so grossly that God disinherits them, Paul's point here is not warning of destruction, but wooing them to the life of God, the life that should characterize the person "justified by faith." See further Mark J. Keown, "Redeeming Paul," in *Scriptural Sexuality*, eds. Zohar Hadromi-Allouche, Nirmal Fernando, and Keren Abbou Hershkovits, forthcoming.

42.   See further Keown, "Redeeming Paul." Here, I agree with Fee, *GEP*, 128, who rightly paraphrases it thusly: "'Your own conversion, effected by God through the work of Christ and the Spirit, is what has removed you from being among the wicked, who will not inherit the kingdom.' An inherent imperative is implied: 'Therefore, live out this new life in Christ and stop being like the wicked.'"

43.   Fee, *GEP*, 128, is not strictly correct to see here latent Trinitarian language whereby "God the Father saves, through the work of Christ, effected experientially by the Spirit." Here, God is not the agent of these actions, but Christ and the Spirit. Rather, while Fee is correct broadly speaking, this verse shows Paul's fluidity in terms of assigning salvation to the members of the Godhead.

44.   Rom. 1:17; 3:22, 26, 28, 30; 4:3, 5, 9, 11, 13, 22; 5:1; 9:30; 10:4, 6, 10; Gal. 2:16; 3:6, 8, 11, 24; Phil. 3:9.

45.   Fee, *GEP*, 527.

46.   Fee, *GEP*, 129.

47.   Fee, *GEP*, 129.

48.   Fee, *GEP*, 131–32.

DeSilva also notes of justification, "the transformation of which Paul speaks is Spirit-empowered and Spirit-directed. It all depends on God's gracious gift of the Holy Spirit, lavished upon us because of Jesus's death on our behalf."[49]

The mention is also relevant because the Spirit becomes the power in the believer for ongoing transformation. Mentioning the Spirit's role makes sense in context because Paul is urging the Corinthians away from the unrighteous vices he mentions, especially the vice list of vv. 9–10. As he says in Romans 6, they are slaves of righteousness who are to live out this righteous status (cf. Phil. 1:11). They do so by the Spirit. He is then calling the Corinthians to live pneumaformly by reminding them of God's justifying work via the Spirit.

Liberated from Bondage to the Law

Two verses link the Spirit to the liberation of believers from bondage to the law: Romans 7:6 and 8:2. Having drawn an analogy between a widow liberated from a marriage at her husband's death with a believer's freedom from the law, Paul sums up in Romans 7:6. For Paul, the adverbial phrase νυνὶ δὲ indicates a sharp change that has happened through God's redemption.[50]

The verb used in v. 6 (see also v. 2) for the believer's release from the law is strong, used elsewhere of destruction.[51] Believers are entirely discharged from the law and its requirements, having died to that which held them captive (cf. Gal. 3:22–23).[52] The result of this liberation is that believers can serve in the newness (καινότητι) of the Spirit (πνεύματος) and not in the oldness (παλαιότητι) of the written code of the law. The contrast between newness and oldness is that of life and death, the new covenant era of the Spirit and the Mosaic covenantal era of the law and sin. Believers, then, are liberated by the Spirit from bondage to the impossible task of seeking salvation and inclusion in God's people through law observance. Christ has come. Justification is by faith. The Spirit is received where justification is declared. Believers are to voluntarily enslave themselves to Jesus through submission to God's Spirit and the service of others. This willingness lies at the heart of pneumaformity.

After his long reflection on the cognitive dissonance caused by life under the law and his expression of gratitude to Jesus for his deliverance from the

---

49. DeSilva, *Transformation*, 14. He also rightly challenges the idea that the work of transformation becomes "'our righteousness' as something we achieve on our own or establish for ourselves."

50. See Rom. 3:21; 6:22; 7:6, 17; 1 Cor. 12:18; 13:13; 15:20; Eph. 2:13; Col. 1:22; 3:8. It can also be an important transition point in his travel plans (Rom. 15:23, 25), a shift of focus (2 Cor. 8:11, 22; Philem. 11), or a transition of life stage (Philem. 9).

51. The destruction of the rulers of the age (1 Cor. 2:6), of the stomach and food (1 Cor. 6:13), of all powers in enmity of God, including death (1 Cor. 15:24, 26; see also 2 Tim. 1:10), and of the lawless one (2 Thess. 2:8).

52. The verb κατέχω here is used with the sense "confine," as in being imprisoned (BDAG, s.v. "κατέχω," 533).

law (Rom. 7:12–25),[53] in Romans 8:1–2, Paul declares that a person "in Christ" (by faith implied) experiences no condemnation for breaking the law. The reason is given in v. 2: because the law of the Spirit of life has set the believer free (ἐλευθερόω) from the law of sin and death. The law of the Spirit of life is not necessarily the Mosaic law, the gospel, or a new norm here but is used as a play on words where νόμος carries the idea of "power" and so produces the idea of the "'law' of the Spirit who confers life."[54] The law of sin and death could be the Mosaic law that exposes sin and brings death temporally and eternally. Alternatively, it is used in the sense of "power" or "authority" and speaks of the "law" of sin that produces death. Here, the Mosaic law fits, for it reveals and amplifies the experience of the sin that brings death. The believer who receives the Spirit is liberated from the requirements of the Mosaic law (now fulfilled by Christ) and the effects of sin which produce death and destruction. The Spirit is the great emancipator of believers from the law and its consequences. They can now live the pneumaform life by the Spirit putting to death the misdeeds of the flesh (Rom. 8:4–16).

The Spirit Who Sets People Free from Sin

Not only does the Spirit liberate people from living under the law but it also sets people free from sin itself. Those baptized into Christ (which I have argued is baptism in the Spirit) have died in Christ and are now "freed from sin" (Rom. 6:7). Those who have yielded to the gospel are "set free from sin" and are now "enslaved to righteousness" (Rom. 6:17–18). They are not free *to* sin but are to work out the declaration of righteousness over them in Christ by yielding in obedience to Christ's summons to live by the Spirit. By doing this, the flesh is defeated,[55] and they now produce the fruit of righteousness, leading to sanctification and eternal life (Rom. 6:20, 22). Such ethical living is increasingly possible because the law of the Spirit of life in Christ Jesus has set them free from the law of sin and death (Rom. 8:2).

Hence, Paul can say in 2 Corinthians 3:17, "Now the Lord is the Spirit, and where the Spirit of the Lord is, there is freedom." Here, Paul states that Christ the Lord is experienced in the present via the Spirit. In and by the Spirit, believers are free from bondage to the Mosaic covenant, its condemnation,

---

53. N. T. Wright, "Romans," in *The New Interpreters Bible: A Commentary in Twelve Volumes*, vol. 10 (Nashville: Abingdon, 2002), 551–54.

54. Fee, *GEP*, 523–24; Moo, *Romans*, 498. See in context Romans 8:10–11, whereby in the present, the body remains dead in that it is subject to decay and ultimately death, but the Spirit is generating life. Ultimately, this Spirit will raise the believer (Rom. 8:11). This is what Wallace calls a genitive of production. See Daniel B. Wallace, *Greek Grammar Beyond the Basics: Exegetical Syntax of the New Testament* (Grand Rapids: Zondervan, 1996), 105.

55. "Thus, to live 'according to' the Spirit is not merely to have an external norm, but a power within, a power that acts to override, indeed to replace, the power of 'the flesh,' the power of sin (Rom. 7:17, 20)." Gorman, *CPNSC*, 54.

impotence to save, and legal requirements.[56] With unveiled faces, they can now see the light of the glory of God in Christ Jesus.

Similarly, in Galatians 5:1, Paul declares, "For freedom, Christ has set us free." Having asserted the Galatians' freedom from law's tyranny, Paul says they must not yield to the Judaizers' demands so that Christ's death no longer profits them for salvation and they are severed from grace (vv. 2–4). They must persevere in faith, love, and hope (vv. 5–6) and express their freedom through serving one another in love (v. 13).[57]

The Spirit Who Circumcises the Heart

Three passages arguably speak of the idea of circumcision of the heart (Rom. 2:25–29; Phil. 3:3; Col. 2:9). The focus of the first is circumcision, which, as is well known, was a critical covenantal boundary marker in Judaism. Paul argues that physical circumcision is only of value when a person maintains the law (Rom. 2:25; cf. 1 Cor. 7:19). In Romans 2:28, being a Jew is based not merely on the physical rite of circumcision but also on a heart circumcised by the Spirit rather than the letter of the law. Paul here picks up texts in Deuteronomy and Jeremiah urging Israel's people to circumcise the foreskins of their hearts, remove their stubbornness, love God completely, and renounce evil deeds.[58] In verse 29, the Spirit, and not the law, circumcises the heart.[59] This text anticipates what Paul will say concerning the Spirit's receipt in the remainder of Romans (esp. Rom. 5:5; 7:6; 8:1–16).

In Philippians 3:3, amid his declaration of who Christians are in contrast to the Judaizers (the dogs, the evil workers, the mutilators of the flesh [3:2]), with a play on κατατομή (mutilators), Paul declares that "we are the circumcision (περιτομή)."[60] "We" includes the Pauline group, consisting of Jews and Gentiles (cf. Col. 4:7–14), and the exclusively Gentile Philippians to whom he writes. All such believers place no confidence in their fleshly ability to fulfill the requirements of the law but trust in Jesus, through whom they are declared righteous (3:4–5, 9). These people make up "the circumcision." Paul follows this quickly with "who worship by the Spirit of God and boast in Christ Jesus" (LEB), linking their identity as God's circumcised people with the Spirit, in and by whom they worship, and with Jesus, in whom they exist and of whom they boast. Patently,

56. See the excellent discussion of the popularly abused idea of "freedom" in Fee, *GEP*, 313–14. He notes that it is a freedom for the things the Spirit does for believers "in appropriating the work of Christ to our lives." "The Spirit is the power that liberates from a rule-book mentality of casuistry and fear." Dunn, *Jesus and the Spirit*, 202.
57. "If freedom from sin and the gift of the Spirit that is able to work transformation within us were gained for us by Jesus's giving of himself over to death on our behalf, we are *not* ethically free to neglect this freedom and this gift in any of its aspects. Something that cost so much *must* be valued and made use of appropriately." DeSilva, *Transformation*, 42.
58. See Deut. 10:6; 30:6; Jer. 4:4; 9:25; cf. Acts 7:51.
59. On this, see further Fee, *GEP*, 489–93.
60. See also Fee, *GEP*, 751–52.

Paul is not speaking here about physical circumcision, as the chapter is devoted to refuting the false teachers who demand this very thing. Instead, it speaks of those whose hearts are circumcised by the Spirit based on their response of faith to the one who was obedient to death on the cross and who is their Savior (Phil. 2:8; 3:20). These people, believing Jews and Gentiles, are "the circumcision."

Turning to Colossians 2:9, as Paul begins his challenge to false teaching, he reminds the Colossians that Jesus embodies the fullness of God and that they have been filled in him who is supreme over all creation (Col. 2:9). Paul's declaration in Colossians 2:10, that the Colossians are "filled in him" speaks of their receipt of the Spirit (even if πνεῦμα is not used).

In v. 11, those in Christ and filled with him are circumcised "with a circumcision made without hands," that is, by the Spirit with whom they are filled. The putting off of the flesh is typical of Paul's flesh-Spirit antithesis. The flesh is put off *in Christ*. "The circumcision of Christ" is effectively equivalent to the circumcision of the heart by the Spirit. Believers are buried with him in baptism and raised with him by faith through God's power. Formerly dead in sin, they are made alive with him, forgiven, with all debts dealt with and nailed to the cross, and God's enemies disarmed (Col. 1:13–15).

Circumcision in these passages is not literal, although considering Paul's use of the sword language for the Spirit (Eph. 6:17),[61] it can lead to the image of God circumcising with the sword of the Spirit as it pierces the heart and faith is born. However, this pushes the metaphor too far. Instead, the passages speak of God flooding the person's inner being with his divine presence and power.

Paul considers circumcision by the Spirit entirely adequate, meaning that there is no need for a new male Gentile believer to be physically circumcised for salvation and inclusion in God's people (Gal. 5:2). To Judaize means to come under an obligation to keep the whole law (Gal. 5:3). A believer with a circumcised heart does not need circumcision, for they are a new creation (Gal. 6:15). They should live out this identity by holding firm in faith and expressing it through love (Gal. 5:6). Consequently, with Spirit-circumcision in mind and with Judaizers in view, Paul declares all Christians are "the circumcision" (Phil. 3:3) whether circumcised as he was (Phil. 3:5) or not.

The Spirit with Whom Christ Inscribes the Human Heart

ROMANS 2:15

Romans 2:14 and 15 have been discussed in terms of the work of the Spirit on the human heart before conversion. It is worth taking a second look at this passage from the perspective of Christ's inscribing work on the human heart.

---

61. Especially when it is remembered that the μάχαιρα can mean "a dagger" (BDAG, s.v. "μάχαιρα," 622). See Gen. 22:6, 10 (Abraham's near-sacrifice of Isaac); Josh. 5:2–3 (where flint knives are made to circumcise Israel); Judg 3:16, 21 (Ehud's knife, a cubit in length, or 17 inches/45 cm). See also Sib. Or. 7:77.

Romans 2:15 is found in Paul's long argument to establish the premise that Jews and Gentiles alike are under the power of sin (Rom. 3:9) and so are subject to God's wrath (Rom. 1:18; 2:5–11)—"all have sinned and fall short of the glory of God" (Rom. 3:23). In Romans 2:12–16, Paul explains how both Jew and Gentile are in this same place before God. Israel's people, who have the law, will perish due to their universal failure to practice its requirements. Gentiles, who sin without the law, will perish without the law. In Romans 2:14, Paul takes note of Gentiles who, while not having the law, "by nature do what the law requires." This verse can be read as if there are Gentiles who fulfill the law and fulfill meeting God's requirements, and so are saved. However, Paul is moving inexorably to the conclusion that no one is in this position, and so this is a false conclusion (3:23).

Alternatively, Paul is looking forward to Gentile Christians who are in Christ who has completed the law. However, this conclusion is also flawed, as Paul will not head into that space until Romans 3:20. What he is talking about here is the readily observable righteous Gentiles of Paul's world who might be likened to people today who are good but do not profess the Christian faith.[62] They are good people to a degree, and they even reflect God's image to a noticeable degree, but they still fall well short of the glory of God. Such people are "a law to themselves, even though they do not have the law."

Verse 15 tells us how this can be the case. In the behavior of such virtuous people, they show that the work of the law is written on their hearts. As argued earlier, this concept speaks of the inscription of the law on the human heart through God's creational work and when God breathes life into people. While all humanity is corrupted, there remain vestiges of the law on the human heart. Some people, although not Christians, respond to this intuitively (by nature) and do good. Their failure to uphold the law is seen in what follows—"their conscience bearing witness and their thoughts one after another accusing or even defending them" (LEB). In other words, such people perceive the law of God inwardly and respond; however, they do so imperfectly, as they accuse and excuse themselves as they sin.

I must say, on a personal note, that I recall such things before my conversion as a young man. Intuitively, I sensed the inward call of God to goodness (despite being an unbeliever and not recognizing its source). At times I sought to yield. Sometimes I did. Whether I did or didn't submit to the good I knew I should do, I could not do it consistently. I felt the accusation of my conscience and found all sorts of excuses for my failure. Such conflicting thoughts demonstrate that the law was written on my heart.[63]

---

62. Good examples might be the Roman centurion (Luke 7:1–10) and Cornelius (Acts 10:1–4). A Jewish gospel example is the lawyer in Mark 12:34, who is "not far from the kingdom of God."

63. Although I hold that Romans 7 is Paul looking back over his life as a Jew under the law and recognizing what it constituted, the passage also applies to wider humankind when they become aware of God's requirements. They go through a cognitive dissonance that stems from knowing the

While this passage does not speak of the present work of the Spirit in believers, it anticipates what happens at conversion. The Spirit enters the human heart, and the law of God is fully inscribed into the heart along with God's power, enabling the believer to yield to the law in an amplified manner. The heart is renewed, and the works of the law already on the heart are lit up in neon, perceived with new clarity, and the power to yield to a new degree is released. Where the person previously did not have the strength to obey, God's power is implanted, generating a new power to do so, even if God is not obeyed completely.

By the Spirit, believers who yield to him are increasingly able to please God and fulfill the law's intent, particularly love. I am not speaking of perfection, for Christians remain fleshly creatures prone to sin and destined for physical death. But now, the heart of God's law is lit up large on the believer's heart, and the power to obey more and more is present. Hence, Christians who habitually put to death the flesh and are persistent in seeking to please God by the Spirit increasingly obey God as they practice submitting to him.

2 Corinthians 3:3

This verse forms a part of Paul's defense of his apostolic integrity in the face of the criticism of false teachers. These teachers clearly have letters commending their ministry. They are also accusing Paul and his team and probably critiquing their failure to produce their own letters of commendation.

Rather than commend himself with letters of recommendation as the false teachers do, Paul tells the Corinthians that he needs no written letter, as their character and ministry in Corinth are sufficient; *they* are his coworkers' letters of recommendation. *They* are written on the hearts of the apostolic team of Timothy, Silas, Paul, and others unnamed.[64] This figure of speech implies that the Pauline team and the Corinthians were bound together in love—the Corinthians were inscribed on the hearts of the Pauline team.

This inscription is "to be known and read by all." Not only were the Corinthians etched on the hearts of Paul and his team, but others can also read what is written. This reading, of course, is not done by ripping open Paul and his coworkers' chests but by observing the existence of the Corinthian church and their life in Christ. As such, the Corinthian church is commendation enough for the Pauline team and should be sufficient for the Corinthian church. They should recognize this and reject Paul's critics.

My interest in this study is primarily found in what then follows. The false teachers' letters of commendation were undoubtedly written by early

---

good they should do but failing to live up to it. See earlier in this chapter, "Liberated from Bondage to the Law."

64. While some witnesses prefer "your" (*hymōn*, ℵ, 33, 1175, 1881), "our" (*hēmōn*) has far superior external attestation and fits the argument better.

Christian figures, perhaps from Jerusalem. However, the Pauline letter is "from Christ." The genitive *Christou* conveys the image of Jesus as the writer of the letter of commendation.[65] In other words, he authored the Corinthian church (Acts 18:1–17; 1 Cor. 2:1–5; 3:5–11).

While the work was done by Paul's team, in that it was done "in Christ," it was achieved by Christ's power—his Spirit. Paul and his team are pictured as the letter's couriers; the Corinthians penned by Christ are then "delivered by us." The church came into existence through their hard work of preaching in the city, people converting to the faith and receiving the Spirit, and the teaching ministry of Paul's team. This letter, the Corinthian church, is now publicly available for the world to observe.[66] As such, no human letters are required for Paul and his team. The Corinthians are sufficient.

The letter Christ wrote, however, was not with the usual ink used to pen letters nor the ink of the apostolic team. The inscription was made "with the Spirit of the living God." "Living God" is used of God in the biblical narrative,[67] in contrast with dead idols. The descriptor is used in Hebrews 9:14, a verse that mentions the role of "the eternal Spirit." Elsewhere, Paul mentions Gentiles who become "children of the living God" (Rom. 9:26 NIV; cf. Hos. 1:10), "the church of the living God" (1 Tim. 3:15), and believers who "have [their] hope set on the living God" (1 Tim. 4:10). Later, in 2 Corinthians 6:16, he describes the Corinthians as "the temple of the living God," implying God dwelling in them by his Spirit (cf. 1 Cor. 3:16; Eph. 2:22).[68]

However, this is the only explicit mention of "the Spirit of the living God" in the biblical material.[69] In this regard, the Spirit who emanates from God exhibits his livingness, brings his life to others, and forms them into a Spirit-community. The Spirit, here, is also the conduit of God's mission in Christ, empowering the apostolic team to establish the Corinthian church. Not only is the church here to be seen by the world, but it is also etched onto the hearts of the apostolic team. The contrast is between "tablets of stone" and "tablets of human [fleshly] hearts."

The image recalls God inscribing the original stones on Mount Sinai at the establishment of the Mosaic covenant. Having been invited up Mount Sinai to

---

65. Similarly, Fee, *GEP*, 302.
66. Here I disagree with the view of W. Paul Bowers. He argues that there is no missionary dimension to 2 Corinthians 3:2, as Paul's issue is to deal with the false teachers and it is not missional in any sense. W. Paul Bowers, "Church and Mission in Paul," *JSNT* 44 (1991): 89–111. However, while he is strictly correct in context, this is a reductionist perspective as the logic of a Jesus-written, Spirit-inked letter "to be read by all" carries out into the world.
67. In Jewish literature see Deut. 5:26; Josh. 3:10; 1 Sam. 17:26, 36; 2 Kings 19:4, 16; Ps. 42:2; 84:2; Isa. 37:4, 17; Jer. 10:10; 23:26; Dan. 6:20, 26; Hos. 1:10 (cf. Rom. 9:26); Add Esth. 6:13; Jub. 1:25; 21:4; 4 Macc. 5:24; Jos. Asen. 8:5–6; 11:10; 19:8; 21:10; Treat. Shem. 8:3; 12:9; Apoc. Adam 8:9; T. Ab. (A) 17:11; T. Isaac 2:5; 1. Adam 4:7. In the non-Pauline NT, see Matt. 16:16; 26:63; Acts 14:1; Heb. 9:14; 10:31; 12:22; Rev. 7:2
68. Similarly, Fee, *GEP*, 337.
69. Fee finds OT connections in Exod. 34:1; Ezek. 11:19; 36:26.

THE IMMEDIATE IMPACT OF THE SPIRIT

receive the tablets of stone with God's law and commandments (Exod. 24:12), Moses spoke with God, and God gave him the two stones "written with the finger of God" (Exod. 31:18) bearing "the writing of God, engraved on the tablets" (Exod. 32:16). However, seeing the golden calf and Israel's idolatry, Moses threw them to the ground, and they were shattered. Paul's words here liken the writing of the Corinthians on the hearts of the apostolic team to these tablets—God has inscribed them, and they are as solid as God's law. Letters of commendation are, at this point, rendered redundant. God has written, and it is so. If the Corinthians yield to the false teachers, they are in danger of shattering "the tablets" and worshipping false gods, as did Israel.

Paul's contrast of "tablets of stone" and "tablets of human hearts" invokes Israel's prophetic hope of the law inscribed on the hearts of God's people.[70] Paul draws on this motif in Romans 2:15 (above), where he considers righteous Gentiles who, despite being subject to sin, have traces of God's law inscribed on their hearts. Here in 2 Corinthians 3:3, Paul is using the idea differently—just as God wrote his law on the stone tablets and wrote his law on the hearts of believers by the Spirit, so also God etches the church that is established on the hearts of the church planters by his Spirit. The gospel worker and church are forever bound. Hence, where the work is genuine, the church should not require a letter of recommendation to accept their apostles. They are united in the Spirit, and such a requirement is preposterous.

As with Romans 2:14–15, 2 Corinthians 3:3 does not directly speak of the Spirit inscribing God's law on the heart. But the analogy and contrast refer to the same dynamics noted in the prior discussion. By his Spirit, God, in Christ, has inscribed his work on the hearts of believers. They are forever changed, knowing God's law inwardly, and are empowered to increasingly live to please God through the power of the Spirit. Christians are also bound together by the Spirit. The church planters have the planted church inscribed on their hearts. No doubt Paul would agree that the apostolic team is also written on the hearts of the Corinthians. By analogy, we can see that all Christians who come together to participate in God's work in missional teams and within churches, denominations, and in whatever capacity one can imagine are so inscribed on each other by God.[71]

The Spirit Who Participates in Rebirth

GALATIANS 4:19

In Galatians 4, Paul reminds the Galatians that they are God's adopted children and heirs, having been redeemed from the law (Gal. 4:1–7). Because of their faith in the man Jesus, who fulfilled the law, they were adopted as

---

70. Jer. 31:33; cf. Pss. 37:31; 40:8; Isa. 51:7.
71. As I write, I reflect on the churches in which I have worshipped and ministered over the years. I can feel the bond with these churches. It is spiritual and beautiful.

children. At that moment of faith, the Spirit of God's Son filled them crying out in and through them to God, "Abba! Father! (v. 6).

Recalling that they have been set free from captivity to false gods, the elemental powers of the world, Paul queries how they can return to such forces at the behest of the Judaizers (Gal. 4:8–10). He expresses his fear that his labor was in vain (Gal. 4:11). In Galatians 4:12–15, he urges them to emulate his example and their own when they initially welcomed Paul and the gospel. He ponders whether he is now their enemy and warns that the Judaizers will shut them out (Gal. 4:16–18).

In v. 19, he directly addresses them as "my children,"[72] which at one level sounds endearing but may be mocking their immaturity.[73] Paul implies that their conversion can be likened to childbirth, with Paul picturing himself as their again-pregnant mother having to go through the pains of giving birth to them again on God's behalf. As will be discussed further in the next chapter, because the Galatian believers are flirting with the Judaizers' heresy, he is thrust back into that state of a mother in the pains of childbirth until Christ is formed in them.

GALATIANS 4:29

Paul's "allegory" of Hagar/Ishmael and Sarah/Isaac creatively draws on the law to challenge the agitators demanding that the Gentile Galatians submit to the Torah, particularly the boundary markers for salvation and inclusion in God's people. Space precludes a complete analysis of the contrasts Paul creates from the stories of Hagar/Ishmael and Sarah/Isaac.[74] Suffice it to say they represent two contrasting systems. In Galatians 3–4, Hagar represents enslavement to the law, natural (fleshly) birth, Sinai, present-day Jerusalem bound under the law, and the production of more slaves. Sarah represents freedom from the law, birth according to a promise, the Jerusalem above, and the production of free children who are believers.[75]

After appropriating Isaiah 54:1 to speak of the joy because of the many children Sarah will produce (which is being fulfilled in the new covenant people), Paul tells the Galatians, Jews and Gentiles alike, that, as was Isaac, they are "children of promise" (v. 28). In v. 28, Paul returns to Isaac and Ishmael, alluding to Genesis 21:10 but introducing the Spirit into the passage. As in v. 23, Ishmael was born "according to the flesh." He persecuted Isaac, implying Paul identifies the Judaizers with Ishmael and his mocking of Isaac. As Ishmael and Hagar were excluded from the covenant, so the Judaizers must be cast out (cf. 5:13). Isaac is not named directly but described as "him who was born according to the Spirit." "Born of the promise" elides into "according to

---

72.   The reading τέκνα is to be preferred to τεκνία. See Longenecker, *Galatians*, 195.
73.   See Keown, *Galatians*, 472–78.
74.   For my full analysis of the passage, see Keown, *Galatians*, 481–516.
75.   On such things, see Fee, *GEP*, 413–14.

the Spirit." The giving of the Spirit is the first installment of the full realization of God's promises to Abraham (see 3:6–14).

Paul here implies the work of the Spirit in Sarah's giving birth to Isaac even though she was beyond the age of possible conception (cf. Rom. 4:19). By bringing in the Spirit here, Paul implies that the Galatians, too, are "born according to the Spirit," not in a biological sense as in the case of Isaac, but in a spiritual, new creation sense. This spiritual status is further implied in v. 31, where believers ("we" equals Jew and Gentile) are "not children of the slave but of the free woman." Whatever other complexities this passage involves, it implies the work of the Spirit in enabling a barren woman to fall pregnant and produce children of God.

TITUS 3:5

In this verse, Paul connects two ideas concerning the beginning of the Christian life: rebirth and renewal. Having discussed $\dot{\alpha}\nu\alpha\kappa\alpha\iota\nu\dot{\omega}\sigma\epsilon\omega\varsigma$ previously, here I consider ($\pi\alpha\lambda\iota\gamma\gamma\epsilon\nu\epsilon\sigma\dot{\iota}\alpha$) The noun compounds $\pi\dot{\alpha}\lambda\iota\nu$ ("again") and $\gamma\epsilon\nu\dot{\epsilon}\sigma\iota\alpha$, a term derived from the idea of birth, and so implies the notion of "rebirth." The compound is rare, used by Plutarch of gods regenerating in different forms (*E Delph.* 9), the regeneration of life (*De esu* 1.7), reincarnation (*Is. Os.* 72), and of thoughts being born again (*Quaest. conv.* 8.3.5). Intriguingly, Lucian employs it of the resurrection of a fly (*Musc. laud.* 7). Josephus's one use is of the rebuilding of a city (*Ant.* 11.66). Philo utilizes it for creation (*Mos.* 2:65), resurrection (*Cher.* 114; *Post.* 124; *Legat.* 325), a plant born of a seed (*Aet.* 103), and the Greek notion of the regeneration of the cosmos (*Aet.* 9, 47, 76, 85, 93, 99, 107). Each of these uses suggests regeneration from destruction or death.

The only other NT use is Matthew 19:28, which refers to the regeneration of all things at the consummation. For Titus, it describes being born anew by God in Christ. "Washing" here can indicate water baptism; however, more likely it speaks of Spirit baptism whereby believers are "washed" clean with the Spirit at the instance of Spirit reception at conversion. Still, water baptism enacts this and symbolizes what happens spiritually. Pneumaformation is the renewal of believers by the first installment of the Spirit at conversion, culminating in their full completion by God through the Spirit at the eschaton.

The Spirit Who Gives Life

ROMANS 8:2

Reference has already been made to Romans 8:2, where Paul describes God's Spirit as "the Spirit of life." As discussed, the genitive $\tau\hat{\eta}\varsigma$ $\zeta\omega\hat{\eta}\varsigma$ is a genitive of production: "the Spirit who produces life." The life produced is the life of the Spirit downloaded into the inner being of the believer. The life generated is the life of God, and those who yield to the nudging of the

Spirit are inwardly transformed to be increasingly conformed to God and his
Son. Ultimately, at the consummation, this Spirit-generated life will "swal-
low" death, and fully embodying and radiating life, believers will live forever
(1 Cor. 15:54).

ROMANS 8:10–11

Paul tells the Romans that "if Christ is in you, on the one hand, the body
is dead because of sin,[76] but on the other hand, the Spirit generates life because
of righteousness" (my translation).[77] Paul here uses a first-class conditional
sentence that denotes something true for the sake of argument. His statement
is true in this case, where the Roman believers are concerned.[78] By using this
form, Paul assures the Romans (whom he has already said are believers),[79]
as they all believe Christ is in them.[80] As the previous verse indicates, the
agency of Christ's presence in the believer is the Spirit of God and Christ.[81]
The believer's body "is dead." This death speaks of the problem all "flesh"
experiences in this ruptured world: bondage to decay and death introduced
through the sin of Adam (Rom. 5:12; 8:19–23). Until the last enemy of God,
death, is vanquished by Christ and the world is liberated from its bondage
to death and decay, all flesh is mortal, decays, and eventually gives up the
breath of life (1 Cor. 15:26). However, when the consummation comes the life
produced by the fullness of the Spirit will see the believer's body transformed,
free of decay and death.

Romans 8:11 is another first-class conditional sentence that can be
assumed true for the sake of argument. In the if-protasis, Paul sets up the
then-apodosis with the condition that "the Spirit [τὸ πνεῦμα] who raised
Jesus from death dwells in you [the Romans]." Again, Paul is not questioning
their possession of the Spirit but is preparing to state the consequence of this
reality in their lives. Notably, the Spirit is a life-giving Spirit in the protasis, the
very Spirit by whom God resurrected Jesus.

The apodosis draws out the consequence: "then he who raised Christ
Jesus from the dead will also give life to your mortal bodies through [διά]
the Spirit of him [αὐτοῦ πνεύματος] who dwells in you" (my translation).[82]

---

76. On the ludicrous notions that Christ's indwelling presence is the actual cause of the body being
dead because of sin and it is the spirit that is destined for eternal life not the body, see Fee's counter
arguments. Fee, *GEP*, 550.

77. The sentence lacks verbs. As such, I have added the verb "to be" to v. 10a and to v. 10b. Because of
Paul's understanding of the life-generating power of the Spirit, I have added "produces" in v. 10c as
the Spirit is life, and that life transforms. This is pneumaform power.

78. On the first-class condition, see Wallace, *Greek Grammar*, 690.

79. See Rom. 1:7–8.

80. I agree with Fee that here "righteousness" means the conferral of righteousness rather than righteous
living. However, by the Spirit, the former leads to the latter. Fee, *GEP*, 551–52.

81. Fee, *GEP*, 548: "Everything about the argument and the context suggests that 'Christ in you' is simply
Pauline shorthand for 'the Spirit of Christ in you,' or perhaps better in this case, 'Christ in you by his Spirit.'"

82. While the decision between διά + gen. (διὰ τοῦ ἐνοικοῦντος αὐτοῦ πνεύματος) and διά + acc.

The future tense suggests that Paul has the final resurrection state in view. The διά plus genitive (which is to be preferred) speaks of the agent by which God raised Jesus and will raise believers—the Spirit.[83] Still, this Spirit of life is in them already, and their future eternal life has begun spiritually. As such, they must live according to the Spirit, putting to death the misdeeds of the flesh, which are not congruent with the life of the Spirit (vv. 12–13). Living like this is the pneumaformed life.

1 CORINTHIANS 15:45

In 1 Corinthians 15, Paul responds to those in Corinth who are influenced by Greek ideas and reject the resurrection, considering that believers have a spiritual, non-bodily afterlife.[84] In vv. 42–44, Paul contrasts the "seed" of the perishable, dishonorable, weak, and natural Adamic body with the imperishable, glorious, powerful, and *spirit*ual body. The Adamic body is subject to decay and death through Adam's failure and because of the universal problem of sin (Rom. 5:12). The spirit gives it life up to 120 years (Gen. 6:3). The spiritual body is one where death is overwhelmed by the power of the Spirit and eternal life is gifted and generated.

To demonstrate the contrast, in v. 45, Paul draws on Genesis 2:7. He adapts the text by adding ὁ πρῶτος ("the first") and Ἀδάμ ("Adam") to ἄνθρωπος. The LXX originally translated אָדָם to ἄνθρωπος. In using both terms, Paul emphasizes his Adamic nature alongside his humanness. He retains the final

---

(διὰ τὸ ἐνοικοῦν αὐτοῦ πνεῦμα) is well balanced, the genitive is to be preferred on the basis of the combination of text types and early church preference for the genitive. See James D. G. Dunn, *Romans 1–8*, WBC 38A (Dallas: Word, 1988), 414; Richard N. Longenecker, *The Epistle to the Romans: A Commentary on the Greek Text*, NIGTC (Grand Rapids: Eerdmans, 2016), 677–78; Metzger, *TCGNT*, 456; Moo, *Romans*, 494n883. For the converse position, see Fee, *GEP*, 145–46; Eduard Schweizer, "Πνεῦμα," *TDNT* 6:422. As such, while Fee is correct to stress God's agency in the resurrection of Jesus, here διά + gen. indicates agency rather than cause (which would expect accusative).

83. I disagree with Fee, *GEP*, 553, who does not agree with the common view that the Spirit is the agent of Christ's (and believers') resurrection on the basis of the preferred reading of διά + gen. and other Pauline texts that point in this direction (Rom. 1:4; 1 Cor. 6:14; Eph. 1:19–21; Phil. 3:21; 1 Tim. 3:16; see also "the spiritual body" in 1 Cor. 15:44 [further below]). Romans 6:4 also speaks of Christ being raised from the dead through the glory of the Father. "Glory" here may indicate the agency of the Spirit. See N. Q. Hamilton, *The Holy Spirit and Eschatology in Paul*, SJTOP 6 (Edinburgh: Oliver & Boyd, 1957), 14. He writes, "Glory suggests the state to which Christ attained at His exaltation, and behind that state lies the Spirit. Then we may conclude that that same Spirit is the agent at work behind the glory which raised up Christ." Fee finds this speculative and doubtful (*GEP*, 502). With the link between glory and Spirit in Paul, I find it strengthens the case for the Spirit as God's agent of Christ's resurrection. See also Habets, *Anointed Son*, 172–73. He writes, "[Jesus] endured the sufferings and death through the power of the Spirit and was born again to eternal life by the Spirit (Rom. 8:11; 14:9; 1 Cor. 15:45; 2 Cor. 13:4); hence, the pneumatological-Trinitarian paradigm" (p. 173).

84. I briefly explain the background to 1 Corinthians 15 and especially v. 12 later in chapter 11, "1 Corinthians 15:35–58." My comments in the later section also bear on this one.

phrase from the LXX, εἰς ψυχὴν ζῶσαν, "became a living person" (NET).[85] As God breathed on Adam, the Spirit transformed the clay from which he was fashioned into a human. He became a living person animated by God's Spirit. However, this was only for a period—until death—because he was excluded from the source of eternal life.

With his adaptation of Genesis 2:7, Paul sets up the contrast with Jesus, the second "Adam." The "last Adam became a life-giving spirit." Here, Paul is not saying Jesus rose from the dead into a non-bodily spiritual existence. Instead, Jesus rose into a fully and eternally alive body in the Spirit. Now, through him, the Father sends the Spirit of Jesus into believers at their conversion. Then, by his Spirit, Jesus is in believers with the power to animate their bodies spiritually in the present (even while physically decaying) and completely and eternally in the life to come.

This verse is one where the line between Jesus and the Spirit is narrowed to the point that Paul identifies Jesus as the Spirit (cf. 2 Cor. 3:18). This should not cause us to repudiate the Trinity; instead, it shows that Jesus (and God) is in the believer by the Spirit. The two ideas are coterminous.

The verb ζῳοποιέω compounds ζωός and ποιέω, meaning "make alive." The term is unique to the LXX and NT.[86] John uses it for the final resurrection life (John 5:21), and for him, it is "the Spirit who gives life" (John 6:63). Peter employs it for the resurrection (1 Peter 3:18), and all of Paul's uses relate to resurrection life. It is God who gives life to the dead (Rom. 4:17). Just as God raised Christ from the dead, through his Spirit dwelling in them, God gives life to the mortal bodies of believers (Rom. 8:11). For Paul, the law has no power to generate resurrection life (Gal. 3:21); instead, "the Spirit gives life" (2 Cor. 3:6). He uses ζῳοποιέω thrice in 1 Corinthians 15. In v. 36, Paul states the agricultural axiom that a seed must die to come to life. Echoing Romans 8:11, in v. 22, "as in Adam all die, so also in Christ shall all be made alive." The upshot is that at the eschaton, the Spirit who raised Christ will raise believers into an immortal and imperishable existence.

2 CORINTHIANS 3:6

Paul crisply and clearly states what I am trying to say in this verse: "The Spirit gives life." The contrast is with the "letter" that kills. Here, Paul refers to the law (that opponents are trying to impose).[87] As his broader teaching indicates (e.g., 1 Cor. 15:56), the law cannot impart life; it merely makes people

---

85. The preposition εἰς has the sense "into" and is short for "turned into" or "became." Fee notes Paul adds "first" and "Adam" to help lead into the second line. Fee, *GEP*, 265.

86. In the LXX, it is used on the lips of Israel's king asking whether he is God who has the power to make alive (4 Kgdms. 5:7), of God's power to bring life at creation (2 Esdr. 19:6 [Neh. 9:6 EVV]), of God reviving the psalmist (Ps. 70:20 [71:20 EVV]), of the power of wisdom to give life (Eccl. 7:12), and of God not bringing alive the ungodly (Job 36:6).

87. In the background may be the "letters of recommendation," which, as Fee puts it, "in reality amount to nothing." Fee, *GEP*, 305.

aware of right and wrong and their inability to live up to it.[88] It serves to lead them to Christ. However, the Spirit of the living God (2 Cor. 3:3), imparted at the moment of believing, generates life within the believer. First, this life is experienced in mortal bodies subject to decay and death and is mainly spiritually experienced as God sustains the believer amid suffering, physical decline, and death.[89] Ultimately, the Spirit's power will be fully unleashed, and believers will experience complete pneumaformation, living eternally in bodies freed of sin and its consequences—eternal life.[90]

Associated with the Spirit is the language of "the new covenant." This new covenant is "the covenant of the Spirit," combining ideas from Ezekiel 36:26–27 and Jeremiah 31:31–34 (LXX 38:31–34).[91] In this age of the Spirit, God is enacting the vision Ezekiel saw of dead bones reanimated (Ezek. 37).[92]

GALATIANS 2:19–20

Here, Paul states that he has died to the law and its requirements (hence, there is no need to submit to it nor to those who seek to impose it) so that he might live to God. He has been crucified with Christ; in this sense, Paul is dead and buried. The Spirit is also involved in this experience of co-crucifixion.[93] However, Paul also experiences resurrection because Christ now lives in him by the Spirit (see chapter 2, "The Spirit Leads to Conversion"). Hence, he lives on through the power of the Spirit of Jesus in him. His ongoing fleshly existence is lived by faith in the Son of God, who loved him and gave himself for him (in his redemptive death on the cross). In Galatians 3:2, 5, Paul will link hearing the gospel with faith and the receipt of the Spirit, making explicit what is implied here—the Spirit is Christ in him, sustaining him in his fleshly life and empowering him to live the life of Christ in the world. This life of the Spirit is expressed in his ongoing faith, virtuous life (not through Torah observance), and mission to preach Christ to the nations.

---

88. On this, see Fee, *GEP*, 306. He cogently writes, "It is in this sense that 'the letter kills,' because it can arouse sin but is powerless to overcome it; the Torah lacks the one essential ingredient for life, the Spirit."

89. However, there is a bodily element as the Spirit brings succour, healing, and works through the mind in different ways to enable bodily life that pleases God as the believer lives out their existence in the body.

90. While Fee is right to see "life" in this verse as "eternal life" (Fee, *GEP*, 307), here, it also speaks of the sealing and down payment of the Spirit (2 Cor. 1:22) making believers alive inwardly.

91. Fee, *GEP*, 304.

92. See also Habets, *Progressive Mystery*, 82–83. He avers, "The essence of the New Covenant for Paul was that God would place his Spirit in men and women and create in them a new heart and a new obedience" (p. 82).

93. "What justification by co-crucifixion will imply, however, and not surprisingly, is that a theological rift between justification and sanctification is impossible, because the same Spirit effects both initial and ongoing co-crucifixion with Christ among believers, a lifelong experience of cruciformity or, in light of chapter one, theoformity—theosis." Gorman, *ITCG*, 40.

TRANSFORMATION

The Spirit Who Creates Anew

As one would expect from a Second Temple Jewish Pharisee, Paul considered God to be the creator (Rom. 1:25; 1 Cor. 8:5; Eph. 3:9). As Genesis 1–2 describes, God created all things (Rom. 1:20; cf. 1 Tim. 4:3–4). He also formed Israel (Rom. 4:17). This creation is subjected to futility by God (Rom. 8:20)[94] and, like a woman in the pains of labor, yearns for its release from its bondage to decay (Rom. 8:19, 21–23). Like a potter forming clay vessels,[95] God formed humankind from the dust of the earth (Rom. 9:20 [cf. Gen. 2:7]; 1 Cor. 11:9; 1 Tim. 2:13) and formed the first woman from man (1 Cor. 11:8, 12; 1 Tim. 2:13; cf. 2 Cor. 11:3). Corrupted by sin and death, creation is now a dangerous place in which mortal humankind faces innumerable threats that can cause death (Rom. 8:39). Unlike most Jews, Paul came to believe that Christ is God's Son, his image, the new Adam. As a Christian, he believes that God created this world through Christ (1 Cor. 8:6; Col. 1:16) and that it is Christ who sustains the universe (Col. 1:17). He also uses creation language and ideas to describe Christians, and these images speak of the work of the Spirit in forming Christians and the church.

2 Corinthians 5:17

As Paul defends himself against his detractors and seeks to bring the Corinthians into line, he restates his faith in Christ's death and resurrection (2 Cor. 5:14–15). As such, believers no longer view Christ in a purely fleshly way (κατὰ σάρκα), for he is raised from the dead and is, in a sense, a new creation. Similarly, people in Christ are no longer to be regarded in a purely fleshly manner (κατὰ σάρκα). Instead, if anyone is in Christ, that person is a new creation. For them, their old lives and perspectives have passed away, and the new has come. The Spirit is not mentioned, but the contrast between "new creation" and "flesh" (σάρξ) indicates Paul is thinking in his usual flesh-Spirit binary.[96] As such, it is implied that Christian life is a work of the Spirit renewing the believers.[97] They are a part of God's new creation inaugurated at Christ's resurrection.

---

94. See Moo, *Romans*, 538–39. It is surely God who subjects creation rather than Adam or Satan.
95. God as potter is a common prophetic motif (Isa. 29:16; 41:25; Jer. 18:4, 6).
96. "We know from a variety of passages that Paul's natural contrast to life κατὰ σάρκα is life κατὰ πνεῦμα, life that has undergone death and resurrection and is now lived from the perspective of, and in the power of, the Spirit." Fee, *GEP*, 331.
97. Fee approximates my view without explicitly seeing this as a Spirit-text. "In making this point, even though he does not directly use Spirit language, Paul characterizes the present age, which continues but which has come to an end for those who have been raised to new life in Christ, as κατὰ σάρκα (lit. 'according to the flesh,' = 'from the perspective of the old age that is passé in Christ') . . . the old order has gone, the new 'creation' has come in its place—not just in the life of the individual, but in the total sense of what God is doing in the world through Christ and the Spirit." Fee, *GEP*, 330–31. I affirm his further comments on this section.

EPHESIANS 2:10

After stating salvation is by grace through faith rather than works, Paul tells the Ephesians that they are God's workmanship. Only Paul uses ποίημα, and its only other use is of created things that give witness to God's existence (Rom. 1:20). New Christians saved by grace through faith are God's workmanship. They are created (aor. pass. κτίζω) in Christ Jesus. The aorist passive of the verb speaks of God's action at the moment of conversion when they believed, were included in Christ, and received the Spirit (Eph. 1:13–14). They were created for good works prepared beforehand by God so that they walk in them. Here, we see conversion and what should flow from it—good works God has prepared for believers to do. The initial new creation launches the pneumaformed life, and this flows outward to identifying and doing the works God has prepared for believers.[98]

EPHESIANS 4:24

In the following section, I will discuss the summons to the renewal of the mind in Ephesians 4:23. Here, in v. 24, Paul continues the theme of creation in Ephesians with the nuance that believers are "created (κτίζω) in accordance with God in righteousness and true holiness" (my translation). This new creation forms the basis for ethical life whereby they take off the former patterns of their old lives being destroyed by deceitful desires, are renewed in the spirit of their minds, and put on "the new person" they are created to be (pneumaformation). Here, Paul likens the beginning of the Christian life to the creation of humankind in God's image. In Ephesians 5:1–2, Paul urges them to be imitators of God as his loved children and walk in the pattern of Christ's self-giving and love for humanity.

GALATIANS 6:15

The Galatians are not to be enticed to circumcision and yield to the works of the law proposed by the Judaizers. Instead, they are to realize that they are now new creations in Christ by faith. Like Paul, the world has been crucified to them and them to the world.[99]

The Spirit Who Brings Renewal

Paul uses renewal language at times to speak of God's new creation work in believers. This self is being renewed in knowledge after the image of God. I will now consider these texts.

---

98. Here, we see God at work by his Spirit shaping history and inwardly in the believer so that the Spirit's work intersects as the believer does what God has gone ahead of them to prepare.

99. See the excellent discussion in Buchanan, "Spirit," 199–206. He notes that it points to the renewal of believers, the cosmos, and the church as "new creation." He also develops well the new creation motif as a pneumatological concept.

TITUS 3:5

The association of the Spirit and renewal is most apparent in Titus 3:5. In this verse, Paul connects two ideas concerning the beginning of the Christian life: rebirth (discussed in the next section) and renewal. These notions line up nicely with John's idea of being born from above (John 3:3, 5) and Peter's notion of being "born again" through the imperishable Word of God (1 Peter 1:23).

In Titus 3:1–2,[100] Paul urges his coworker to remind the Cretan Christians of a range of essential Christian virtues, and in v. 3, he reminds them of their past lives of sin and discord. In vv. 4–7, he recalls their salvation and its effect on their lives. First, he calls to mind Christ's appearance as the manifestation of God the Savior's goodness and loving-kindness. God saved believers (us) not because of works generated by human righteousness but in accordance with his mercy. He did this "by the washing of regeneration (παλιγγενεσία)[101] and renewal (ἀνακαίνωσις)[102] of the Holy Spirit" (Titus 3:5).[103] This Spirit had been lavishly poured out on believers through Jesus Christ their Savior (Titus 3:6).[104]

The first term Titus uses, παλιγγενεσία will be discussed in the next section. The second term he uses, ἀνακαίνωσις, speaks of being "new" (καινός), "again" (ἀνά), or "renewed." The compound is a Pauline neologism used only once elsewhere in his writings of the renewal of the mind at conversion (Rom. 12:2). The only other ancient use is a later Christian use of the renewal of people's spirits (Herm. Vis. 3.4.9). It thus speaks of something being renewed or rejuvenated. The genitive πνεύματος ἁγίου can be one of source, origin, or production—the latter is preferable. The agent of rebirth and renewal here is explicitly the Holy Spirit, pointing to the beginning of pneumaformation that continues through the Christian life. The ultimate outcome for those justified by grace and reborn and renewed in the Spirit is their inheritance according to the hope of eternal life. As will be discussed, these ideas lead to discussions of growth, spiritual formation, and participation in God's new creation.

---

100. See Fee, *GEP*, 778, for a structural analysis.

101. On the matter of whether this refers to baptism or the washing away of sins, I concur with Fee's argument and conclusion that this "is metaphorical and should be translated 'washing'" (p. 780). Still, baptism is a wonderful visual demonstration of this purification experienced in Christ through the Spirit.

102. Fee is also correct to argue that παλιγγενεσίας καὶ ἀνακαινώσεως represents one event rather than two. As he puts it, "Finally, those who see two separate events and consider the second to be confirmation, sanctification, or Spirit baptism, build their whole case on internal aspects of the phrase. But that will not do. The entire phrase is soteriological, pure and simple, modifying the main verb in the sentence, the aorist ἔσωσεν ('he *saved* us'). This διά phrase can thus refer only to the *means of salvation*. To force it to refer to something more is to read into the text what is not there." Fee, *GEP*, 782.

103. Fee notes we have here another Trinitarian formulation. Fee, *GEP*, 779.

104. Fee states concerning this verse, "The subject of the verb 'poured out' in v. 6 again is God. As in most places in Paul, the Spirit is understood to have been given by God, not by Christ (whatever else, *filioque* is not a Pauline point of view)." Fee, *GEP*, 783, emphasis original.

ROMANS 12:2

After his exposition of the mercies of God in Romans 1–11, Paul turns to paraenesis in Romans 12. In light of God's mercies, believers are to present their bodies as living sacrifices, which is the logical (λογικός) worship response to what God has done and which is pleasing to God.[105] In v. 2, they are no longer to conform to the current age's religious, philosophical, and ethical patterns.[106] Instead, they are to be "transformed by the renewal (ἀνακαίνωσις) of your mind." The Spirit is not mentioned, but it is implied that God's Spirit (or God, in Christ, by the Spirit) brings the renewal of thinking that Paul has in view.[107] In that it is premised on no longer being conformed to patterns of the age, renewal of the mind suggests thinking shaped by God's thoughts and ways that will be fully experienced in the eschaton. The Spirit impels such thinking and consequent actions. Such renewal enables believers to discern God's good, acceptable, and perfect will. The discernment process suggests internal communication of the Spirit to the believer's mind. Believers are to yield to these impulses and promptings.

Fee suggests that this transformation moves people in service that springs from a mind renewed by the Spirit. For him, this takes them in two directions: (1) Believers "no longer live in 'conformity' to the present age, from which the death and resurrection of Christ has delivered them." They do not do so because they are being conformed "into the likeness of Christ himself." Paul's thinking, then, is eschatological, whereby believers filled with the Spirit view everything differently "by the Holy Spirit."[108] (2) The renewal of the mind is the key to "all the community relationships that will be urged in the imperatives and their supporting argumentation that follow."[109]

2 CORINTHIANS 4:16

Paul uses the verb cognate to ἀνακαίνωσις, ἀνακαινόω, in this verse. It is not attested in wider Greek sources, with its only other use being in Colossians 3:10 (discussed below)—another Pauline neologism. It refers to the process of renewal.

As Paul juxtaposes suffering with God's comfort, he announces that despite all their anguish, he and his coworkers do not lose heart. He then

---

105. See further on Rom. 12:1, chapter 5, "Worship in and by the Spirit."

106. Romans 12:2 is discussed more fully in chapter 6, "Transformation Language."

107. Fee writes, "What is surprisingly missing, in light of the argument of chapter 8, is any direct reference to the Holy Spirit. Nonetheless, the Spirit is presupposed everywhere and lies close to the surface in the imperative 'be transformed by the renewing of the mind.'" Fee, *GEP*, 598. Fee also notes that "having the mind of Christ" and "having the Spirit of God" are nearly interchangeable (see 1 Cor. 2:16; 7:40), the verb ἀνακαινόω, "make new again," is linked to the Spirit in Titus 3:5, and there are verbal connections to 2 Corinthians 3:18 where the Spirit transforms believers into God's likeness (see p. 602).

108. Fee, *GEP*, 602–3.

109. Fee, *GEP*, 603.

speaks of the human problem of decay and decline, which he describes with the verb διαφθείρω. The language is also used of humans and animals in their mortal state (φθαρτός) as contrasted with the immortal (ἄφθαρτος) God (Rom. 1:23; cf. 1 Tim. 1:17) and the incorruptible state of believers in the eschaton (Rom. 2:7).[110] In Romans 8:21, Paul says the creation is enslaved to corruption (φθορά).

Here, φθαρτός refers to people aging and physically declining because of sin's impacts. Paul and his team are no different from others—they are also subject to decay and death. The pain of persecution amplifies their suffering. Yet, "inwardly [they] are being renewed day by day" (NIV). Paul here is pointing to the renewal of their inner beings by the Spirit.[111] The imperishable Spirit strengthens them in their perishability every day so they do not lose heart. The Spirit's role in suffering is a profound aspect of pneumaformation discussed more fully in chapter 8.

EPHESIANS 4:23

Ephesians 4:17 makes clear that most readers were formerly Gentiles who walked in a darkened, ignorant, and futile mental state and were alienated from God. With hardened hearts, they were given over to sensuality, greed, and impurity. However, now that they are Christians, they must put off these old, corrupted, and deceived selves. They are "to be renewed (ἀνανεόω) in the spirit of [their] minds" (Eph. 4:23).

The term ἀνανεόω means "renew" and is rarely found. It occurs in the Maccabees of the restoration of relationships[112] and the renewal of law-observance (4 Macc. 18:4).[113] Ephesians 4:23 is the only NT use, and here the Ephesians are to be renewed "in the spirit of your minds." Πνεῦμα here is not the Holy Spirit but the inward spirit of a person, and the whole phrase is an emphatic way of saying "the inner human being."[114] As such, this is similar

---

110. See also 1 Cor. 9:25; 15:42, 50, 52–54; Gal. 6:8; 2 Tim. 1:10; 2 Peter 2:12. The term is used in Luke 12:33 of the destruction to fabric things caused by moths. Luke uses it of the rotting of the deceased body that David experienced, but which did not occur after the death of Jesus and, as he is raised, will never occur to him (Acts 2:27, 31; 13:35–37). It is used in 1 Corinthians 3:17 of those who destroy (φθείρω) God's temple being destroyed (φθείρω) by God; moral or theological corruption (1 Cor. 15:33; 2 Cor. 7:2; 11:3; Eph. 4:22; 1 Tim. 6:5; 2 Tim. 3:8; 2 Peter 2:10; Jude 10, 12); worldly corruption (2 Peter 1:4; Rev. 19:2); things that perish (Col. 2:22; 1 Peter 1:18); incorruptible love (Eph. 6:24) and impeccable teaching (Titus 2:7); an imperishable inheritance (1 Peter 1:4); perishable and imperishable seed (1 Peter 1:23); imperishable beauty (1 Peter 3:4); and death (Rev. 8:9; 11:18).

111. Fee approaches this view. He states: "Thus, even though the Spirit again is not mentioned, this sentence is very much in keeping with vv. 10–12 above, where the body, full of the frailty of a clay vessel, is constantly being handed over to death. But the 'inner person,' who has been given life by the Spirit, is also constantly being renewed by that same Spirit." Fee, GEP, 324.

112. 1 Macc. 12:1, 3, 10, 16; 14:18, 22; 15:17.

113. In Job 33:24, it is used of restoring a deceased body.

114. Frank Thielman, Ephesians, BECNT (Grand Rapids: Baker Academic, 2010), 305–6. See also the detailed discussion in Fee, GEP, 710–11, where he weighs the options and concludes, "The net result

to Romans 12:2. Still, the Spirit is implied here, for it is by the Spirit of God (in giving life) that the mind (animated by the Spirit) is renewed.[115] This verse does not speak of conversion but is an encouragement to live up to the renewal God is doing in believers through the Spirit—pneumaformation.

COLOSSIANS 3:10

The verb ἀνακαινόω is used here to describe the transformation of conversion.[116] It is, as Fee says, a divine passive "where God is the unexpressed subject." He adds, "Therefore, since this language in Paul belongs to the activity of the Spirit, it is altogether likely that lying behind this 'renewing' activity is God the Holy Spirit."[117] Like all unbelievers in Paul's eyes, the Lycus Valley readers previously lived earthly lives replete with the many vices mentioned in Colossians 3:5–7. Having been raised and exalted with and in Christ (3:1), they have put on their new identities in him. This new self is being "renewed in knowledge after the image of its creator." The use of "image" and "creator" calls to mind Colossians 1:15–16, where Christ is the image of the invisible God and the conduit for the creation of the cosmos. The renewal in view in Colossians 3:10 is individual conversion and the impartation of the Spirit into believers. As such, the passage summons them to live out this renewal by seeking the things of God above by killing off these old attitudes and habits and putting on the virtues Paul will outline in Colossians 3:12–4:1.

The Spirit Who Sanctifies

Paul uses holiness language in a range of ways.[118] Of interest here is the connection between the Spirit and holiness or sanctification. For Paul, the *Holy* Spirit enters the believer, and that person is immediately declared holy (Rom. 15:16; 1 Cor. 6:11b–c; 2 Thess. 2:13). This event in the person's life is the first step in the process of the Spirit sanctifying the believer. This

---

is that one seems to be left with a highly peculiar way of speaking about the interior life of the human person" (p. 711).

115. Similarly, Fee writes, "But, since the original recipients cannot be expected to have been alert to fine points of usage, it seems most likely to me that they would have heard this phrase in terms of the Spirit, either directly or indirectly, as lying very close to whatever renewing work takes place in their own spirits. Probably, therefore, this is yet another instance where we should recognize the human spirit as the first referent, but be prepared also to recognize the Holy Spirit as hovering nearby, since in Paul's own theology, such renewal is indeed the work of the Spirit." Fee, *GEP*, 711–12.

116. Fee includes this in his discussion for the same reason—Paul's use of ἀνακαινόω. He also rightfully notes its resonances with Ephesians 3:16. Fee, *GEP*, 647.

117. Fee, *GEP*, 647. He suggests the "putting off" and "putting on" is baptismal language. I do not consider this the case. Baptism is immersion or sprinkling and speaks of death and resurrection. It is, then, the language of clothing oneself. Still, he correctly goes on to say, "The concern itself lies at the heart of Paul's gospel and has to do not with baptism but with the work of the Spirit: those who are Christ's must bear his likeness in their behavior." He also correctly cross-references this to Galatians 5:13–26.

118. Holiness language is also used of the holy Scriptures (Rom. 1:2), the holy law (Rom. 7:12), and a holy kiss (Rom. 16:16; 1 Cor. 16:20; 2 Cor. 13:12; 1 Thess. 5:26).

beginning is confirmed in the earlier discussion of the giving of the Spirit mentioned in 1 Thessalonians 4:8. The giving of the Holy Spirit is mentioned in conjunction with Paul's injunctions toward holiness, particularly sexual sanctity.

Seventeen times, Paul calls the Spirit "the Holy Spirit" or "the Spirit of holiness."[119] In using this adjective, NT writers state that the character of the Spirit is absolute holiness, which includes such ideas as otherness, being set apart, and moral and ethical purity and cleanness. One of the primary functions of the Spirit is to sanctify those in whom he dwells.[120] The common descriptor indicates that sanctification is a critical aspect of pneumaformation.

Believers, having been set apart by the Spirit, are thus labeled ἅγιοι, "saints, holy people."[121] This status remains even when acting in unholy ways, as evidenced in Paul's first letter to the Corinthians. The term implicitly calls believers to become what they are: holy.

ROMANS 11:16

As Paul explains the place of Israel in the purposes of God now that salvation has come to the Gentiles in Christ, he addresses the Gentiles in the Roman church. He reminds them of his apostolic calling to the Gentiles and states his hope that this will make Jewish unbelievers jealous, leading to some being saved. In v. 16, he draws on two analogies for the church that speak of the believers' shared status of holiness. The first image features Numbers 15:18–21, where Israel is told to set apart and present the first loaf to God (Neh. 10:37; Ezek. 44:30). Doing this ensures that the whole loaf is holy. He then uses a second analogy of a tree. If a root is holy, the branches are holy, as the tree receives sustenance from the root. As he develops his argument, the branches are Jews who believed in God, as did Abraham (4:12). However, some are broken off for rejecting Christ. At the same time, wild olive branches are grafted into the tree. These are the Gentile believers (like the Romans). Aside from the complexities of this verse, it states that those who believe in God and his Son are declared holy through the root, which is surely Christ, who is rooted in God. As such, believers are holy people sustained by the root. The feeding and nurturing of the tree speak of the work of the Spirit akin to nutrients flowing through plants as if by osmosis.

---

119. "Spirit of holiness" (Rom. 1:4); "Holy Spirit" (Rom. 5:5; 9:1; 14:17; 15:13, 16; 1 Cor. 6:19; 12:3; 2 Cor. 6:6; 13:14; Eph. 1:13; 4:30; 1 Thess. 1:5, 6; 4:8; 2 Tim. 1:14; Titus 3:5. This compares with seventy-five uses of "the Spirit." It is also used sixty-six times in the Gospels and Acts; five times in Hebrews; three times in the General Epistles; and none in Revelation.

120. Gorman puts it simply—"the Spirit effects holiness." Gorman, *Inhabiting the Cruciform God*, 109.

121. Forty times in Paul: Rom. 1:7; 8:27; 12:13; 15:25, 26, 31; 16:2, 15; 1 Cor. 1:2; 6:1, 2; 14:33; 16:1, 15; 2 Cor. 1:1; 8:4; 9:1, 12; 13:13; Eph. 1:1, 15, 18; 2:19; 3:8, 18; 4:12; 5:3; 6:18; Phil. 1:1; 4:21, 22; Col. 1:2, 4, 12, 26; 1 Thess. 3:13; 2 Thess. 1:10; 1 Tim. 5:10; Philem. 5, 7. In the LXX, it is rarely used of Israel's people (Ps. 73:3; Wis 5:5; Isa. 41:16; Dan. 7:22, 27).

ROMANS 15:16

In this verse, Paul narrates aspects of his mission to the Gentiles. Though never calling himself a "priest," he describes his mission as a "priestly service of the gospel of God." He designates the Gentiles as an offering that he hopes is acceptable to God. This description can refer to the collection, but it transcends what will come later in the passage and speaks of the Gentiles themselves as his offering to God.[122] They are "sanctified (ἁγιάζω) by the Holy Spirit." The verb is used all over Jewish Greek literature for the conveying of holiness, consecrating or setting something or someone apart consecration (or setting something or someone apart), and purification.[123] The notion was fundamental, with God considered holy and Israel's laws and elaborate rituals designed to purify people so they could be God's people in worship and life. "Sanctify" is used for sacrifices (Exod. 29:27), gifts (Exod. 28:38; Lev. 27:14), and offerings (Num. 5:9; 18:9; 2 Esd. 3:5 [Ezra 3:5 EVV]). When worshipers eat portions of the sacrifices rightly presented, they are sanctified (Lev. 6:11, 20). Psalms of Solomon 17:26 and 43 foresee the Messiah gathering a holy people from Israel free of aliens and foreigners. In Ezekiel 37:28, the nations will one day know that God sanctifies them.

For Paul and other NT writers, the hope of the sanctification of the nations and being brought to God is coming to pass. In the wider NT, this sanctification is by God,[124] through Jesus's atoning death,[125] and received by people based on faith (Acts 26:18). Similarly, Paul writes that believers are "sanctified in Christ Jesus" (1 Cor. 1:2), and Jesus sanctifies the church (Eph. 5:26). Here in Romans 15:16, the Spirit is the subject of the verb. So we can reason that God, through his Son, by the Holy Spirit, sanctifies the Gentiles, making them

---

122. On the offering being the people as the gift, see Keown, *Romans and the Mission of God*, 75n57. Alternatively, both people and gift are in view. See Peter T. O'Brien, *Gospel and Mission in the Writings of Paul: An Exegetical and Theological Analysis* (Grand Rapids: Baker, 1995), 31, 50–51. I prefer to see it as the Gentile converts, but if both the Gentiles and gifts are in view, the financial gifts are secondary.

123. Here are some examples. The verb is used of God being sanctified (Exod. 29:43; cf. Isa. 8:13; 29:23; Ezek. 28:22, 25; 36:23; 38:16, 23; 39:27; Philo, *Fug.* 59). It is also used of setting apart of special days for sacred purposes like the Sabbath (Gen. 2:3; Exod. 20:8, 11; Deut. 5:12, 15; 1 Esdr. 5:51; Jer. 17:22; Philo, *Leg.* 1:17–18) and Sabbath and Jubilee years (Lev. 25:10); the firstborn (Exod. 13:2, 12; Num. 3:13; Deut. 5:19; Philo, *Sacr.* 118); of God sanctifying people (Exod. 28:41; Lev. 6:11; 22:9; 1 Kgdms. 16:5; 3 Macc. 6:3; Zeph. 1:7; Ezek. 46:20; Dan. 4:22; Jub. 2:19); priests (Exod. 19:22; Lev. 8:12; Ezek. 48:11); Levites (2 Chron. 35:3); Nazarites (Judg. 13:5); prophets (Jer. 1:5); and women after menstruation (2 Kgdms. 11:4). It is also used of places like Sinai (Exod. 19:23; 1 Kgdms. 7:16); the tabernacle and other worship objects like altars (Exod. 29:36–37, 44; 40:8; Lev. 8:11; Num. 7:1); the temple and its objects (3 Kgdms. 9:3, 7; 2 Chron. 2:3; Tob. 1:4; Jdt. 4:3; 3 Macc. 2:16; Ps. 45:5 [46:4 EVV]); a field (Lev. 27:16); sanctifying clothing (Lev. 16:4); tithes (Sir. 35:8); a fast (Joel 1:14); assemblies (Joel 2:16); a battle (Joel 4:9); the Servant of the Lord (Isa. 49:7); and nations for war with Israel (Jer. 28:27).

124. See John 17:17, 19; Acts 20:32; Heb. 2:11.

125. See esp. Heb. 10:10, 14, 29; 13:12.

acceptable to God.[126] We can apply this to mission—by the Spirit, an evangelist presents converts to God as holy and pleasing in his sight.

The perfect passive of the verb ἁγιάζω speaks of the external agency of God through Christ by the Spirit. It indicates the holy status of those being offered to God. They are declared holy by God through the inward work of the Holy Spirit. The Spirit sanctifies new believers, setting them apart, consecrating them, and purifying them of all unholiness. Despite ongoing sin, where there is sincere faith, the Spirit maintains this status for every believer.

1 Corinthians 1:2

Paul begins his first extant letter to his wayward church in Corinth by asserting their status as sanctified people. Reminding them of their position as God's holy people is vital, as while his letter will address their lack of holiness in many ways, he wants them to know that he still recognizes them as God's people.[127] However, as holy people, they must yield to the πνεῦμα of God, who will enable them in their sanctification. They are "those sanctified [perf. pass. part. ἁγιάζω] in Christ Jesus." The participle ἡγιασμένοις connects back to those addressed as "the church of God in Corinth" (1 Cor. 1:1). It is passive, indicating God's agency in declaring them holy. The perfect tense indicates a state of being holy and remaining so. Being "in Christ" speaks of their participation in Christ's cosmic spiritual being by imbibing his Spirit and sharing in his anointing. As such, along with every person who calls on the name of the Lord Christ Jesus and so is saved (Rom. 10:12; cf. Joel 2:32; Acts 2:21), they are called "saints" or "holy people" (κλητοῖς ἁγίοις).

Paul may here be simply reasserting their status as holy people. For Paul, God's call speaks of their conversion whereby God called the Corinthians through the gospel, *and* they yielded to the message with faith.[128] However,

---

126. Cf. 1 Cor. 6:11; 1 Thess. 5:23; 1 Tim. 4:5; 2 Tim. 2:21. The language is also used in the NT of God's name being sanctified (Matt. 6:9; Luke 11:2); of the temple (Matt. 23:17, 19); of Jesus as sanctified by the Father (John 10:36); of an unbelieving spouse and children sanctified through the believing spouse (not salvation, but the influence of the Spirit on them, 1 Cor. 7:14); of being sanctified through a heifer under the Mosaic covenant (Heb. 9:13); to set apart Christ as Lord (1 Peter 3:15); and of being holy (Rev. 22:11).

127. This contrasts with other passages where Paul is dealing with seeming Christians who for Paul are not so (e.g., 2 Cor. 11:4; Gal. 1:6–9; Phil. 3:2).

128. Paul emphasizes call language in 1 Corinthians of the call of the Corinthians. They were "called into the fellowship of Jesus" (1 Cor. 1:9); are "the called" (1 Cor. 1:24); have received "your calling" (1 Cor. 1:26); "called to peace" (1 Cor. 7:15); called by God but to remain in the same life situation they were in prior to their conversion (1 Cor. 7:17–24); and invited to a meal (1 Cor. 10:27). He also employs it of his own conversion and missionary commissioning (1 Cor. 1:1; 15:9) and calling on the Lord (1 Cor. 1:2). See also the use of ἀνέγκλητος, "blameless," in 1 Cor. 1:8; παρακαλέω, "call alongside, appeal, urge" (1 Cor. 1:10; 4:13, 16; 16:12, 15), or "encouraged" (1 Cor. 14:31); παράκλησις, "encouragement, consolation" (1 Cor. 14:3). See also ἐκ-κλησία, "called out" (1 Cor. 4:17; 6:4; 10:32; 11:16, 18, 22; 12:28; 14:4, 5, 12, 19, 23, 28; 14:33–35; 15:9; 16:1, 19).

lacking a verb, κλητοῖς ἁγίοις is hortatory; they are "called *to be* saints."[129] If so, Paul is drawing out the implication of their status as God's sanctified people, the "called out ones" (ἐκ-κλησία),[130] effectively saying, "Be holy, because you are holy."[131] By the Spirit, God has called the Corinthians out of unholiness into holiness in Christ and given them the Spirit of God and his Son. Led by the Spirit, they are to yield to him and be increasingly holy in their lives. This holiness is moral, as they leave behind worldly sins, and relational, as they love God and others, both believers and unbelievers.

1 Corinthians 1:30

This text is critical for understanding the source of sanctification. Paul declares that Christ Jesus, who has become for believers (us) the incarnate wisdom of God, is God's "righteousness and sanctification (ἁγιασμὸς) and redemption." This statement is bold, declaring Christ the incarnation of these aspects of God's being and that on God's behalf, he is the basis of a believer's status as righteous, sanctified, and redeemed. The experience of receiving the Holy Spirit cannot be disconnected from Christ; instead, the Spirit's role is to convey Christ's righteousness, sanctification, and redemption to the believer. They are "in Christ" and participate in these things by the Spirit.

1 Corinthians 6:11b–d

Mention has been made of the lead-in to 1 Corinthians 6:11, and I have discussed the Spirit's role in the justification of the Corinthians. Now, I will consider the first and second aspects of conversion that Paul highlights; the first of these is "but you were washed (ἀπολούω)." The verb compounds ἀπό (away from) and λούω (bathe, cleanse) meaning to "wash something away from oneself, wash oneself."[132] In Greek Jewish writings, ἀπολούω is often used for ritual washing, something fundamental to maintain ritual purity.[133]

---

129. Gardner, *1 Corinthians*, 57.
130. "The noun ἐκκλησία, attested no later than the 5th century B.C., is evidently derived from the compound verb ἐκκαλέω, which means in the first instance 'to call out, call forth, summon.'" See *NIDNTTE* 2:134. See also *GGNTLHR* 174.
131. More fully: "Be holy, because you are holy, because I am holy, and I have sanctified you, by my Holy Spirit to be holy." See Lev. 11:44–45; 19:2; 20:7, 26; 21:8, 22:3, 32; 1 Peter 1:16.
132. BDAG, s.v. "ἀπολούω," 117.
133. Of washing oneself with snow (Job 9:30). In Christian-influenced literature it was used of Jesus washed in the Jordan at baptism (Sib. Or. 6:4) and believers having washed off vices in the waters of an immortal spring (the Spirit) (Sib. Or. 8:315). In Josephus it was used of Nehemiah purifying himself (*Ant.* 11:163); of a husband and wife by law bathing after sexual relations (*Ag.Ap.* 2:204); and of Essene ritual purification (*J.W.* 2:129) and cleansing after interaction with a Gentile (*J.W.* 2:149). Philo uses it of cleansing oneself from all ethical and other uncleanness (Philo, *Leg.* 3:141; *Det.* 170; *Her.* 113; *Mut.* 229; *Somn.* 1:148; 2:25); of washing off vain opinion to be pure (*Somn.* 1:82); the washing of the world by waterways (*Mos.* 2:64); the washing of the feet of a sacrifice (*Spec.* 1:207); cleansing oneself before entering the temple (*Spec.* 3:89); and washing after touching a dead body (*Spec.* 3:205, 206).

The only other NT use is Acts 22:16, where Paul is told to be baptized and to "*wash* away [his] sins." Hence, washing is placed first, perhaps because it "most naturally follows the 'filth' of the vice catalogue."[134] It also lends itself nicely to the ritual of baptism as a moment of cleansing. Yet, I would argue that while water baptism visibly enacts this cleansing and marks entry into the community of God's people, it is preceded by, or is coterminous with, the expiatory work of the Spirit in the human heart washing away all trace of sin (Spirit-baptism).[135]

Paul then adds, ἀλλ᾽ ἡγιάσθητε, "but you were sanctified" (v. 11c LEB). The verb here is ἁγιάζω, used in Romans 15:16, and discussed above. Here the verb is aorist passive; the passive indicates God's agency, and the aorist refers to the moment of faith in the crucified Jesus Christ when the Spirit floods the hearts of the crucified and spiritually resurrected Corinthians, cleansing and sanctifying them (cf. 1 Cor. 1:1).[136]

Notably, Paul tells the Corinthians that they were washed, sanctified, and justified "in the name of the Lord Jesus Christ and by the Spirit of our God." The "in the name" formula is found across the OT[137] and the NT.[138] Here, "the name" of Jesus is a metonymy for his being and person. This formula could relate to baptism, which in Paul and Acts is in the name of Jesus (1 Cor. 1:13).[139]

---

134. Fee, *GEP*, 129.

135. I commend Fee's excellent comments on baptism and washing here. He rightly recognizes the natural link but points out that Paul could have said "were baptized" here. As he rightly says, "The three metaphors emphasize the aspects of Christian conversion found in the theological terms 'regeneration, sanctification, and justification'; and for Paul these are the work of the Spirit in the believer's life, not the result of baptism." Fee, *GEP*, 131.

136. "The Spirit is that power which transforms a man [person] from the inside out, so that metaphors of cleansing and consecration become matters of actual experience in daily living." Dunn, *Jesus and the Spirit*, 201.

137. Speaking of acting in the name of another deity (Deut. 18:20; Mic. 4:5) or person (1 Sam. 25:9; Esther 2:22; 3:12; 8:8, 10); priests, Levites, prophets, kings, and others acting in the name of Yahweh (Deut. 18:5, 7, 22; 21:5; 1 Sam. 17:45; 20:42; 1 Chron. 21:9; 2 Chron. 33:18; Ezra 5:1; Neh. 13:25; Jer. 11:21; 26:9, 16, 20; 44:16; Zech. 13:3; James 5:7); blessing or cursing in the name of the LORD (2 Sam. 6:12; 2 Kings 2:24; 1 Chron. 16:2; Ps. 129:8); building an altar in the name of the LORD (1 Kings 18:32); speaking truth in the name of the LORD (1 Kings 22:16; 2 Chron. 18:15); setting up banners in the name of God (Ps. 20:5); trust in the name of the Lord our God (Ps. 20:7); God cutting off nations in the name of the LORD (Ps. 118:10–12); the Messiah coming in the name of the LORD and being blessed (Ps. 118:26); helping in the name of the LORD (Ps. 124:8); trust in the name of the LORD (Isa. 50:10); walking in the name of the LORD (Mic. 4:5); and refuge in the name of the LORD (Zeph. 3:12).

138. Believe in the name of Jesus or of the Lord (John 3:18; 1 John 3:23; 5:13); speak or preach in the name of Jesus (Acts 4:18; 5:40; 9:27, 28); give thanks to God in the name of Christ (Eph. 5:20); do everything in the name of Jesus (Matt. 21:9; 23:29; Mark 11:9; Luke 13:35; 19:38; John 12:13; Col. 3:17); command in the name of the Lord (2 Thess. 3:6).

139. See also Acts 2:38; 8:16; 10:48; 19:5. Matthew 28:19 prefers the threefold formula (the Father, Son, and Spirit). Also, to deliver a demon in the name of Jesus Christ (Acts 16:18); to anoint someone for healing in the name of the Lord (James 5:14); to assemble in the name of the Lord Jesus (1 Cor. 5:4).

However, as Paul clearly teaches, God's declaration of purity, sanctification, and justification comes immediately when the gospel is believed. Water baptism is ratification of that earlier moment. As such, this speaks of the instant that the person believed in Jesus and was included in Christ the Lord. At that moment, on the basis that "Christ died for our sins" (1 Cor. 15:3), the person is declared utterly pure, sanctified, and justified through the power of Jesus and the work of the Spirit.

The Corinthians, having been so cleansed, *must* not return to the vile behaviors of their past. The pneumaform person renounces and resists the vices listed in 1 Corinthians 6:9–11 and others (see chapter 5). They seek to live by the Spirit (Gal. 5:18).

2 THESSALONIANS 2:13

The work of the Spirit in declaring believers holy is crystal clear in this verse. Paul, on behalf of his team (ἡμεῖς), for the second time in the letter (fourth time in the Thessalonian letters), constantly expresses his gratitude to God for the Thessalonians (ὑμῶν).[140]

In contrast to those in vv. 10–11,[141] Paul describes them as "brothers and sisters loved by the Lord" (NIV). The causal ὅτι gives the reason for his gratitude, "*because* God chose you from the beginning as the firstfruits[142] for salvation by (ἐν) the sanctification of the Spirit (ἁγιασμῷ πνεύματος) and faith in the truth" (my translation). The preposition ἐν here is instrumental—God's choice of the Thessalonians for salvation was by means of or through the sanctification of the Spirit.[143] The genitive construction ἁγιασμῷ πνεύματος can be a subjective genitive, "the Spirit's sanctification power for us," of source or origin, "the sanctification sourced in the Spirit," or as is to be preferred, a genitive of production, "the sanctification produced by the Spirit."[144] "Faith in the truth" refers to people hearing and believing the gospel. As such, as evidenced by their believing the gospel Paul and his team preach, God chose the Thessalonians by pouring into their beings his Spirit. As receptacles of God's utterly pure Spirit, they are declared holy, sanctified, and no longer defiled.[145] This status should lead believers to conclude that they should live holy lives (cf. 1 Thess. 4:1–8).

---

140. The passage involves the three persons of the Godhead who are involved in salvation, so Fee, *GEP*, 78.

141. Fee, *GEP*, 78.

142. While the reading ἀπ᾽ ἀρχῆς, "from the beginning" has good support (א D K L Ψ 104. 630. 1175. 1241 𝔐 it vgᵐˢ syᵖ sa; Ambst), Paul does not use it elsewhere, whereas ἀπαρχή is a favored Pauline term (Rom. 8:23; 11:16; 16:15). For these and further reasons see Metzger, *TCGNT*, 568.

143. Jeffrey A. D. Weima, *1–2 Thessalonians*, BECNT (Grand Rapids: Baker Academic, 2014), 552.

144. Seeing an objective genitive here, "the holiness the [human] spirit receives," is hardly likely in light of the role of God's Spirit in election and conversion (1 Thess. 1:4–6) and, as here, sanctification (1 Thess. 4:8).

145. Salvation is described as sanctification. This is not a second work of grace. Sanctification is not purely something that happens after conversion. This is the work of the Spirit (cf. 1 Thess. 4:8). See Fee, *GEP*, 78.

One Spirit with the Lord

In 1 Corinthians 6:17, Paul writes that "the one joined [pres. pass. part. κολλάω][146] to the Lord is one spirit *with him*" (my translation).[147] First Corinthians 6:9–20 focuses on the matter of sin and especially sexual immorality. In the latter regard, it is the second frame in a chiasm. It parallels 1 Corinthians 5:1–13, a passage focused on incest and flagrantly unrepentant sin in the Christian life. The matter at hand in 1 Corinthians 6:9–20 seems to be Corinthian Christians continuing to engage in sexual relations with prostitutes (v. 16).

Before v. 17, Paul reminds the Corinthians that the unrighteous will not inherit God's eschatological kingdom. He lists a range of the sinful behaviors typical of such people and the Corinthians themselves in their pre-Christian lives (vv. 9–10). Some in the church were doing such things. Paul's purpose is to remind them that this is incompatible with the life God wants from those who have been cleansed and been declared holy and righteous in Christ's name by God's Spirit (v. 11). He challenges any notion that those who are cleansed, holy, and righteous are free to do anything they want, sexual or otherwise (v. 12). He repudiates the idea that they would allow themselves to be dominated by such sin and warns them of God's destruction (v. 13).

They are believers and should know that their bodies are not worthless shells to be discarded at death, that they are not free to debauch them. Instead, they are to be set apart for Christ the Lord. Conversely, Christ is "for the body," perhaps implying the importance of the body and his indwelling of the believer that enables them to live a life that honors God (v. 13). The value of the body is seen in God raising Christ from the dead. He will do the same for Christians, showing the importance of bodily life in the present (v. 14; cf. 15:20–23). In addition, the believer's body is a member of Christ—suggesting that the spiritual bond with Christ is threatened by a Christian being physically bound to someone other than their legal spouse.

Using the first person, in v. 15 Paul then asks whether he should take the Christian bodies and join them with prostitutes. As elsewhere, his use of μὴ γένοιτο indicates that such an idea is preposterous—"may it never be! No way!"[148] Using another rhetorical question and the axiomatic verse concerning marriage in Scripture (Gen. 2:24), in v. 16 and using the same

---

146. The verb κολλάω is used of sins reaching heaven (Rev. 18:5). Otherwise, in the NT, it speaks of very close association or connection. Uses include dust clinging to feet (Luke 10:11), joining a business for work (Luke 15:15), coming alongside a chariot (Acts 8:29), Jews associating with non-Jews (Acts 10:28), attaching oneself to good not evil (Rom. 12:9), joining in the church (Acts 5:13; 9:26; 17:34), and the joining of husband and wife in marriage (Matt. 19:5). Paul uses it in the previous verse (1 Cor. 6:16) of a person joining themselves in sexual relationship with a prostitute, which he considers the same as marriage (cf. Gen. 2:24).

147. Literally it says "is one spirit." Part one of the verse indicates the joining of the believer with Christ, and so "with him" makes sense of the joining of the believer with Christ.

148. See Rom. 3:4, 6, 32; 6:2, 15; 7:7, 13; 9:14; 11:11; 12:16; 1 Cor. 6:15; 7:23; 2 Cor. 6:14; Gal. 2:17; 3:21; 5:26; 6:14; Eph. 5:17.

verb, κολλάω, Paul tells the Corinthians that when a person engages in sexual intercourse with a prostitute, he becomes one flesh and body with her. They are, in effect, married (cf. Gen. 2:24).

In v. 17, Paul tells the Corinthians that those who are joined to Christ are now one spirit with him.[149] At the moment of conversion, when the Spirit of God is poured into the believer, the believer's spirit and body are fused together forever in Christ by the Spirit. As noted above, this cannot be limited to merely a Spirit-to-spirit bond but is affected by and impacts what the believer does with the body.

This deep bond is violated by sexual relationships outside of the marriage, something endorsed at creation for the filling of the earth (Gen. 1:27–28; 2:24).[150] For Paul, other sexual relationships are adulterous and contravene the oneness of the believer and Christ. As such, believers should flee from all manner of sexual immorality. It violates the oneness of the believer and Christ and threatens the eternal hope of the resurrection of the body. It jeopardizes the believer inwardly and eschatologically. It is thus a sin against one's own body.

In v. 19, Paul further explains the spiritual bond between the believer and Christ. The body is a temple of the Holy Spirit, who is within the believer. It is gifted from God. The believer's body is fused into the body of Christ and is no longer purely one's own possession. Bound to God in Christ and filled with the Spirit, the body is, in a sense, the possession of God, Christ, the Spirit, one's spouse, and the collective body of Christ. This ownership is because God bought them for a substantial price through the death of his Son. The conclusion is that all believers must glorify God in their bodies.

Two marvelous things are asserted here concerning the conversion of the believer.[151] First, new Christians become one in spirit with Christ the Lord.[152] Second, they are now receptacles for God's Spirit. These things must now shape how they live with their whole being, including their bodies.

The Spirit Who Brings Enlightenment

In 2 Corinthians 4:4,[153] Paul explains that those who do not yet believe but have heard the gospel have had their spiritual eyes blinded by the god

---

149. "In light of vv. 19–20, Paul's primary referent is to the work of the Holy Spirit, whereby through the 'one Spirit' the believer's 'spirit' has been joined indissolubly with Christ." Fee, *GEP*, 132.

150. Mark J. Keown, "A Biblical View of Marriage," *Candour* (2013): 10–12.

151. "What the text does affirm is what is plainly said in scores of other places, namely, that the Spirit is responsible for our being 'in Christ.' And here that is most likely understood as having happened at conversion." Fee, *GEP*, 134.

152. Fee, *GEP*, 133: "Thus, by the Spirit the believer is united to the Lord and thereby has become one S/spirit with him."

153. "Although there is no direct reference to the Spirit here, this paragraph is so closely tied to the preceding argument that a few items need to be noted as to the implied work of the Spirit that lies just below the surface. Indeed, this is the kind of passage which offers clear evidence that Paul does

of this age. Some argue that the "god of this age" is God. However, far more likely is the dominant view that this refers to Satan.[154] "This age" (τοῦ αἰῶνος τούτου), as in other uses, refers to this fallen world that is presently characterized by evil (Gal. 1:4) and incomprehension of God's wisdom by ignorant rulers who are perishing (1 Cor. 2:6, 8; cf. 1 Cor. 1:20; 3:18), and in which unbelievers are trapped (Eph. 2:2; 1 Tim. 6:17; 2 Tim. 4:10). This darkness is ruled by the spiritual forces of evil (Eph. 6:12). Satan disguises himself as an angel of light, seeking to deceive the faithful (2 Cor. 11:14).

Among these unbelievers are Judaizers and unbelieving Jews whose minds are veiled because they are still bound to the law and old covenant (2 Cor. 3:14–16). Such people believe themselves to be capable of shining light in the darkness through the law but are, in fact, trapped in a world darkened by sin (Rom. 2:19). They, like all unbelievers, have minds blinded by Satan and are perishing (2 Cor. 4:3). Such people exist in the "night" and are characterized by deeds of darkness (Rom. 13:12; also 2 Cor. 6:14). They are "darkened in understanding, alienated from the life of God because of the ignorance that is in them, because of the hardness of their heart" (Eph. 4:18 LEB).

When many unbelievers hear the gospel, they cannot "see the light of the gospel of the glory of Christ, who is the image of God" (2 Cor. 4:4 LEB). For Paul, God exists in inapproachable light (1 Tim. 6:16). Jesus brought to light life and immortality through the gospel (2 Tim. 1:10). When the gospel is preached, it is a new creation event. Similarly, the light of the gospel radiates into the darkness of the human heart "for the enlightenment of the knowledge of the glory of God in the face of Jesus Christ" (Eph. 1:17, my translation).

Therefore, when the gospel is proclaimed, those who hear and believe it have their darkened hearts flooded with God's light and experience illumination or enlightenment. They are declared to be God's holy people in the light, having been rescued from the dominion of darkness and transferred into God's kingdom (Col. 1:13). Believers are then like the Ephesians who have experienced God enlighten the eyes of their hearts (Eph. 1:18). Formerly darkness, they are now light in the Lord (Eph. 5:8). And now that they are children of light, they must live good, righteous, and truthful lives (Eph. 5:8–9). They exist in the light rather than darkness or night and must clothe themselves with the armor of light, including faith, love, and hope (1 Thess. 5:4–5). Similarly, believers must "cast off the works of darkness and put on the armor of light" and live decently as in the day, renouncing debauched sin (Rom. 13:12–13). They are

---

not always need to mention the Spirit by name in order for us to recognize his implied presence in an argument." Fee, *GEP*, 320–21.

154. Murray J. Harris, *The Second Epistle to the Corinthians: A Commentary on the Greek Text*, NIGTC (Grand Rapids: Eerdmans, 2005), 327–28: "ὁ θεὸς τοῦ αἰῶνος is a unique biblical expression and refers not to God the Father (as [ὁ] θεός generally does in the NT), but to Satan." For the alternative, see F. Young and D. F. Ford, *Meaning and Truth in 2 Corinthians* (Grand Rapids: Eerdmans, 1987), 115–17.

to leave behind such deeds of darkness and expose them (Eph. 5:11), for "what fellowship has light with darkness?" (2 Cor. 6:14). They are to shine as lights of the world in a crooked and depraved generation (Phil. 2:15).

This enlightening is the work of the Spirit.[155] The radiation of light inhabiting and illuminating the darkness calls to the mind the movement of the Spirit into the human heart. The Spirit can be likened to light invading darkness, beginning the formation of children of light. By the Spirit, believers will be further transformed as they yield. Ultimately, when their pneumaformation is completed at the eschaton, they will fully be light in the Lord. What a day that will be!

The Spirit Who Reveals

I here discuss 1 Corinthians 2:10, where Paul states, "These things God has revealed to us through the Spirit."[156] Leading up to this verse, Paul has explained that the rulers of the age who crucified Jesus did not grasp the "secret and hidden wisdom of God." The secret wisdom, in context, is the unanticipated truth of a crucified Messiah as the basis of God's salvation in the world. Aside from glimpses from Israel's prophets,[157] which were not understood in Second Temple Israel, no one saw this coming, including the rulers of the time. If they had, they would not have killed him (v. 8). In v. 9, Paul cites Isaiah 64:4, which lies in Isaiah's prayer for mercy. In both Hebrew and Greek, it speaks of the inability of humankind to hear or perceive any God other than Yahweh and speaks of his works in descending onto Mount Sinai in cloud and fire.[158]

On the face of it, Paul's wording of the passage speaks of the eternal destiny God has prepared for his people. However, as a whole, Paul appropriates it primarily of the unexpected action of God in and through the unforeseen event of a *crucified* Messiah.[159] The Spirit brings an understanding of the "logic" or "wisdom" of what appears oxymoronic to Jews and Gentiles alike— a crucified Messiah. Believers by the Spirit "understand the things freely given us by God" (1 Cor. 2:12). Christ's death solves the problem of human sin by his standing as humankind's substitute and representative, fulfilling the law,

---

155. "Again, the Spirit lies close at hand in the language of 'shining' and 'enlightening.'" Fee, *GEP*, 321.
156. What God has revealed is not expressly stated in the verse; however, this is supplied by the double ἅ, "things," in 2:9, which cites Isaiah 64:4. Furthermore, rather than 2:9 being the conclusion to vv. 6–8 (Fee, *GEP*, 99), v. 9 continues on from the citation explaining that it is by the Spirit that the deep things of God (including the mystery of Christ and the cross) have been revealed. As Taylor rightly asserts, "The context, however, supplies that Paul is speaking of God's plan of salvation in Christ crucified." Mark Taylor, *1 Corinthians*, NAC 28 (Nashville: B&H, 2014), 98.
157. For example, Psalm 22; Isaiah 53.
158. Gary Smith, *Isaiah 40–66*, NAC 15B (Nashville: Broadman & Holman, 2009), 687.
159. Certainly Paul did not, as evidenced by his persecution of the church. While Jesus was believed to be Messiah by his disciples, they did not understand his passion predictions. Arguably, the only people who understood that Jesus was a crucified Messiah were the thief on the right hand of Jesus who acknowledged his kingship in Luke 23:42 and the Roman soldier who stated his cosmic sonship in Mark 15:39 and Matthew 27:43 (but see Luke 23:47).

taking on himself the punishment for sin, and rising to new life. The Spirit brings what a person without the Spirit's influence cannot grasp—that in Jesus's death is the deep wisdom of God. A similar idea is in Colossians 1:26, where Paul speaks of the gospel as a mystery hidden for ages and generations now revealed to his holy people (see also Rom. 16:25–26).

First Corinthians 2:10 is a significant verse in this study. The sacrificial service of Jesus and his willingness to die for humankind becomes a pattern for a Christian's life. A deep understanding of his sacrifice and its meaning is essential for this. The Spirit brings this awareness. By the Spirit, God generates the Christoform life into which believers are called. This pneumaformity is living by the Christ pattern to the point of death (cruciformity), the life of the eschaton lived in the present (resurrectiformity). Moreover, this revealed understanding is passed on by the Spirit to others who interpret spiritual truths for those who are spiritual (2:13). By the Spirit, the mind of Christ is imparted to believers (2:16).

The power of the Spirit to reveal is also shown in Paul's prayer for the recipients of Ephesians in 1:17. Paul asks that God give his audience the Spirit of wisdom and revelation in the knowledge of Christ. This petition is especially interesting as Paul has already noted that the readers have *already* received the Spirit (1:14). As such, this speaks of a fresh and deepened revelation of God and his Son in Christ by the Spirit.[160]

It should also be noted that "revelation" is also a gift of the Spirit referred to by Paul in 1 Corinthians 14:6, 26, and 30. This gift seems to be fresh knowledge gifted by God in certain circumstances to believers (see further in chapter 9). Paul also speaks of his receiving the revelation of the gospel not through the medium of other people but through a revelation of Jesus Christ (Gal. 1:12, 16; Eph. 3:3). Other apostles and prophets experience such revelation by the Spirit (Eph. 3:5). Such a revelation experience is linked to their roles in the Gentile gospel mission and involves the Spirit. The Spirit reveals, as God wills, missions and other purposes to individual believers (see further chapter 3). Paul also speaks of receiving other revelation experiences, including one that caused him to travel to Jerusalem, which was perhaps Agabus's prophetic anticipation of famines in Judea (Acts 11:28; Gal. 2:1). He anticipates God revealing the truth at points of disagreement (Phil. 3:5).

The Spirit Who Guides

On several occasions, Paul speaks of people being "led by the Spirit."[161] So, in Romans 8:14, he tells the Romans that those who are led (ἄγω) by the Spirit of God are children (sons) of God. The verb ἄγω here is simple, meaning "to

---

160. In my view, this helps interpret the present "be filled with the Spirit" in 5:18. Although believers have received the Spirit, they can pray for a deepened experience of the Spirit strengthening them in various ways.

161. The only instance in the wider Bible of being "led by the Spirit" is Jesus being led into temptation by the Spirit after his baptism (Matt. 4:1; Mark 1:12; Luke 4:1).

lead/guide."[162] Again, in Galatians 5:18, Paul tells the Galatians that if they are led (ἄγω) by the Spirit, they are not under the law. Both uses are present passive, indicate external agency (God, in Christ, by the Spirit), and speak of ongoing, habitual responses.

Being led by the Spirit relates primarily to ethical living in both these instances and contexts. Hence, from spiritual rebirth, believers are guided by the Spirit concerning the appropriate attitudes, actions, and words for any given situation. As God's children, they are not living under the guidance of an external code, like the Torah, but are led by God's Spirit into a life of love. However, there is no need to limit Paul's thought to mere ethics here. While he does not emphasize the Spirit's role in mission as Luke does, it is implied that the Spirit guides all of life for the believer (see further chapter 10). The believer's role is to respond to the Spirit's promptings.

Paul speaks of the same sort of thing when he tells the Galatians that "if we live by the Spirit, let us also keep in step (στοιχέω) with the Spirit" (Gal. 5:25). The verb στοιχέω has military origins and so speaks of walking in rank behind the military commander who leads them into "battle," although the term has the more general sense of "follow, keep in step with, be in harmony with."[163] In Galatians 5:25, the verb is a hortatory subjunctive bringing into play every believer (let us . . .) and is present tense, again speaking of a continual, habitual practice of following the Spirit's lead. Notably, these metaphors link nicely to Paul's favorite way of describing the Christian life as a walk. Believers are to "walk by the Spirit" (Gal. 5:16).[164] This is not aimless but obedient to the summons of the Spirit.[165] They must keep in step with the Spirit in every aspect of their Christian lives.[166]

The Spirit Through Whom God Does Miracles

According to Galatians 3:5, not only does God continually supply (pres. ἐπιχορηγέω) the Spirit to believers,[167] but he performs miracles among

162. BDAG, s.v. "ἄγω," 16. Echoing Moo (*Galatians*, 356–57), Buchanan rightly observes the verb ἄγεσθε "suggests the idea of being continually *influenced by and directed by* the Spirit" (emphasis original). Buchanan, "Spirit," 173.

163. Gerhard Delling, "Στοιχέω, Συστοιχέω, Στοιχεῖον," *TDNT* 7:687–89.

164. See Dunn, *Jesus and the Spirit*, 222.

165. See further chapter 9.

166. See also the use of the verb group in Romans 4:14 (walking in the footsteps of the faith of our father Abraham which he had while uncircumcised); Galatians 6:16 (follow the rule [neither circumcision nor uncircumcision]); and Philippians 3:16 (walk in line with what we have already attained through the gospel; see also the call for imitation in 3:17).

167. See also Fee, *GEP*, 388. He writes, "The clear implication is that even though they have already received the Spirit, there is another sense in which God 'supplies' the Spirit again and again." He also rightly rejects there is anything here indicating the laying on of hands as the instrument of God's supply of the Spirit. See also Buchanan, "Spirit," 104. Contra J. K. Parratt, "Romans 1:11 and Galatians 3:5—Pauline Evidence for the Laying On of Hands?" *ExpT* 79 (1968): 151–52.

them,[168] based on faith, not works of the law. The pairing of "supply of the Spirit" and "miracles" with God as an agent (ὁ) suggests that it is by this Spirit that God exerts power. The miracles are unspecified but could include some things mentioned in Acts 13–14, including healings, exorcisms, resurrection from the dead, release from prison (below), and any range of ways in which God can act to bring relief in a believer's life (see further chapter 9).[169] Notably, Paul experienced healing at his conversion (Acts 9:18). This suggests healing may be experienced at the moment faith blossoms in a believer's inner being.

The Spirit's Strength to Proclaim

As discussed, Philippians 1:19 can either be rendered "the help provided by the Spirit" or "the supply of the Spirit." Either way, Paul is confident that the prayers of the Philippians and the ἐπιχορηγία of the Spirit will turn out for his σωτηρία. Here, σωτηρία has the double meaning of release from prison and, if not, eternal salvation.[170] No matter how his situation turns out, he is confident that by the Spirit and in response to the Philippians' prayers, God will give him the courage to proclaim Christ boldly and without shame before the authorities (v. 20). This suggests that the Spirit enables bold proclamation, strengthens in suffering, sometimes causes release from incarceration, and enables believers to persevere to the end.[171] New converts may then experience a desire to share their newfound faith with unbelievers boldly.[172]

The Spirit Who Begins Growth

Reference has already been made to the notions of rebirth and renewal by the Spirit used by Paul, especially in Titus 3:5. This rebirth is the beginning of a process of formation and growth that the Spirit continues in the life of the believer.

---

168. Fee argues the close link of the participles implies the supply of the Spirit and his working of miracles are connected. He suggests that "the fresh supply of the Spirit finds expression in miraculous deeds of various kinds." The two participles are not as linked as he argues. The first clause ὁ οὖν ἐπιχορηγῶν ὑμῖν τὸ πνεῦμα is followed by καί and then ἐνεργῶν δυνάμεις ἐν ὑμῖν. They are two separate things done to and among the Galatians by God. However, because of Paul's wider theology, I agree with Fee that it is by the Spirit God does miracles among the faithful. Still, the grammar does not demand this. He is right to see here and in 1 Thessalonians 5:19–22 "the genuinely 'charismatic' nature of the Pauline churches." He cogently adds, "The evidence in this case seems incontrovertible: the Spirit lay near the center of Pauline theology precisely because the experience of the Spirit in the life of the believer and the church was such a central feature of their experience and existence as believers" (p. 389).
169. See Acts 14:3, 8–10, 19–20.
170. See Fee, GEP, 738; Keown, Philippians, vol. 2, 227–30.
171. The association of the Spirit with missional speech is found in Jesus's teaching (Matt. 10:20; Mark 13:11; Luke 12:12; Acts 4:31; 1 Cor. 2:13; 12:8; 1 Thess. 1:5).
172. This was my experience as I instantly began evangelizing my friends at my conversion. They did not all appreciate it, but some came to the Lord. Hallelujah!

GALATIANS 3:3

Galatians 3:3 is nestled in Paul's direct address to the Galatians in which, for the second time, he laments their foolishness (cf. 3:1) for listening to the heretical ideas of the Judaizers by asking a series of five rhetorical questions, challenging them to remember their conversion experience and receipt of the Spirit.[173] In the previous verse (discussed later in this chapter), his question led them to acknowledge that they received the Spirit through believing the message of Christ and him crucified (vv. 1–2). Now he asks if they are foolish enough to seek pneumaformity through obedience to the law, that is, through their own efforts and cultural conformity. The LEB catches the sense nicely: "Having begun by the Spirit, are you now trying to be made complete by the flesh?" To yield to the Judaizers' demand to submit to the law is now antithetical to the Spirit life for Paul. Paul could then have answered his question with μὴ γένοιτο, for the journey of pneumaformation begins with the Spirit received by faith and is completed by the Spirit in the life of the faithful (and not by fleshly works).[174] Completion comes through the Spirit's work and is accelerated by believers' yielding to the Spirit's impulses, as Paul will stress in Galatians 5:16–6:10.[175]

1 CORINTHIANS 3:6

As Paul deals with those in Corinth who prefer the preaching of one person over another (1 Cor. 1:12; 3:4), he reminds the Corinthians of their conversion experiences using agricultural imagery. He likens himself to the farmer who went out and sowed the field with seed. As in Jesus's teaching and elsewhere, the gospel is like a seed, and mission work is like farming.[176] The missional work of Apollos (and presumably Peter and others) "waters" this seed, which causes more growth through new converts and the maturation of believers. The image is one of creation and life, with seeds planted by God at creation and growing into mature plants filling the earth (Gen. 1:11–12). Where the gospel is concerned, new life is generated when the word is received by faith, and this seed grows spiritually even though the body decays. It will mature into eternal life when a person is faithful to God. The ministry of Apollos and others includes further missional and edificatory ministries depending on whether they minister to believers or unbelievers. Either way, God brings the growth of

---

173. Fee, *GEP*, 380–81, suggests six rhetorical questions, including two in v. 3. With NA28 and USB5, I prefer to read v. 3 as one rhetorical question (with the participles epexegetical). However, the difference is minimal.

174. On the antithesis between flesh and Spirit here see Fee, *GEP*, 385. He writes, "Hence the ultimate contrasts in Paul are eschatological: life 'according to the flesh,' lived according to the present age that has been condemned through the cross and is passing away; or life 'according to the Spirit,' lived in keeping with the values and norms of the coming aeon inaugurated by Christ through his death and resurrection and empowered by the eschatological Spirit." See Buchanan, "Spirit," 98.

175. See further Buchanan, "Spirit," 97–108. He notes the chiasms in v. 3 with the correlates "having begun-are you ending," "with the Spirit-with the flesh," and "now" in its center.

176. Mark 4:3–9 and parallels; 1 Peter 1:23.

spiritual life. While πνεῦμα is not used, this act implies the work of the Spirit to cause the growth of the gospel seeds already planted by Paul, Timothy, and Silas in the people of Corinth (2 Cor. 1:19). We see here that at conversion, a person begins a growth journey. Preachers faithful to the gospel help sustain that growth. However, the growth is purely attributable to God.

ROMANS 11:17

This verse was discussed briefly regarding holiness earlier in this chapter. Here, I draw attention to the use of growth and creational imagery to describe the Christian life. After likening the church to a holy lump of dough, Paul shifts metaphors to the image of a tree with roots. The root (Jesus) is holy; hence, the branches, which derive their nutrition from the root, are holy. This movement of nutrients and water from root to branches vividly invokes ideas of the Spirit giving life and nurturing it as the Spirit, like water, carries nutrients for growth. In what follows, branches can be broken off from the source of life and so no longer experience the life of God derived from the nourishing root. Conversely, branches can be grafted in and share in this nourishment (v. 18). The root supports them, so they must not be arrogant regarding themselves or one another.

The Spirit Who Imparts Love

In the previous discussions of receiving the Spirit, I examined Romans 5:3–5. Paul makes clear in v. 5 that through the Spirit given to believers, God pours love into the hearts of believers.[177] This love brings assurance of God's acceptance and confidence that the believer will not experience shame at the hands of God and will always have hope. Nothing in creation can separate a believer from the love of God in Christ Jesus (Rom. 8:35–39). While we cannot determine that the receipt of the Spirit is the same for everyone, this verse implies many will experience the love of God as they believe. Receiving the Spirit can be experienced in tears, joy, hope, relational or physical healing, inclusion, warmth, laughter, tongues, or a desire to worship their Abba, Father (cf. Rom. 8:15; 4:6).[178]

The Spirit Who Blesses

ROMANS 4:7–12

As Paul draws on Abraham to defend his perspective that justification is premised on the response of faith and not works of the law, he also cites

---

177. Clearly, Paul's interest in love flows from his experience of love via the Spirit. As Gorman puts it, "Paul was nothing if not someone overwhelmed by the love of God. He experienced this divine love, according to his letters, in Christ and by the working of the Spirit." Gorman, *CPNSC*, 155.

178. I experienced some of these things and have observed some in others. We must not make any one experience determinative and absolute, for example one's experience of speaking in tongues. When God encounters a person, their experience will vary, for God meets us as who we are.

David in Psalm 31:1–2b (LXX, 32:1–2 EVV). He pronounces "blessed" by God those he declares righteous apart from works. They are blessed in that in this declaration of righteousness, their lawless deeds are forgiven, their sins are covered, and the Lord no longer holds their sin against them.

Here, the forgiveness of sin is the blessing experienced at conversion. This blessing is not merely for the circumcised, those who yield to the law's regulations; it is also for the uncircumcised. Paul defends this by arguing that Abraham's faith (Gen. 15:6) preceded his circumcision (Gen. 17:24), indicating that it was his faith response to God (grace) that caused God to declare him righteous and not his circumcision, which instead functioned as a seal of the righteousness *already* declared (Rom. 4:9–12). Later in Romans, Paul speaks of the spiritual blessing that converted Gentiles experience, no doubt including the gift of the Spirit and forgiveness (15:27). Similarly, in 1 Corinthians 9:23, he tells his readers that he renounces his right to receive money from preaching the gospel so that he may share with Jews and Gentiles alike in its multiple blessings.

GALATIANS 3:8, 14

In Galatians 3:8, Paul recalls Genesis 12:3 and the promise to Abraham that in him "shall all the nations be blessed." He then states that it is those who share Abraham whom God blesses. In Galatians 3:14, through Christ the promised seed, the blessing has come to the Gentiles who have received the promised Spirit through this faith.[179] However, this blessedness is threatened by their dalliance with the Judaizers, who want them to come under the law in addition to the faith (Gal. 4:15).

EPHESIANS 1:3–14

The most profound expression of blessedness from God at conversion in Paul is found in Ephesians 1:3–14, where Paul blesses God in response to his blessing of believers in Christ "with every spiritual blessing in the heavenly places" (v. 3).[180] With dense theological language, Paul speaks of the multiple blessings experienced at conversion, including pre-creational election, sanctification, love, predestination, adoption, grace in Christ, redemption, forgiveness, knowledge of his will and purpose to bring all things together in Christ, an inheritance, and the Spirit who seals believers and guarantees them eternal life.[181] All these and more are experienced first as the Spirit floods the soul. They are further unpacked and experienced as life is lived in Christ.

---

179. "The giving of the Holy Spirit is a climactic point in God's dealings with humanity, nothing less than the fulfilment of the promise that, in Abraham, all the nations would receive blessing." DeSilva, *Transformation*, 59.

180. Comparable, although not as theologically loaded, is 1 Peter 1:3–12.

181. For a fuller, detailed discussion, see Fee, *GEP*, 654–72. He notes rightfully that "the Spirit is implied" (669) and directly mentioned in v. 13. I also discuss Ephesians 1:13–14 in "Hearing and Believing," chapter 2, and "The Spirit Sealing and Guaranteeing Salvation" earlier in this chapter.

CONCLUSION

The Spirit affects many things in the believers' lives—they experience love, miracles, strength to share the message, enlightenment, and revelation. They are justified, and their hearts are circumcised and inscribed by Christ. They are sanctified, blessed, sealed, and guaranteed ultimate redemption. Their pneumaformation begins, and they receive the firstfruits of eternal life in the Spirit. They grow in Christ and are re-created, renewed, and reborn. The Spirit leads them in all aspects of life, character formation, church inclusion, and missional engagement. All these things are wondrous and can only be understood by those who have received the Spirit (1 Cor. 2:13–15). Yet, the things discussed in these last two chapters are focused on the individual and merely mark the beginning of the individual person's Christian life. As the next chapter will explore, the Spirit draws the person into the fellowship of the Spirit with others in Christ.

CHAPTER 4

THE SPIRIT AND THE CHRISTIAN COMMUNITY

The previous chapters focused on the role of the Spirit in personal salvation. When people believe in God and his Son, they receive the Spirit from God. This faith sometimes comes through direct theophany or christophany[1] and always involves a spiritual experience, a pneumaphany. Usually, belief is born at hearing the message when the hearer believes and yields to God and to Jesus Christ as Lord, and believes in him for salvation. The Spirit instantly baptizes the believer as God pours out the Spirit and the believer "drinks." The Spirit moves past any attempt by Satan to block and hinder through veiling the gospel and blinding the minds of unbelievers. The Spirit anoints the believer, circumcises the believing heart, seals the believer, and guarantees eternal redemption.

This chapter will focus on passages that speak of inclusion in the people of God, a people that itself is a product of the Spirit. The Spirit's work may start at an individual level, but that is just the beginning. The individual is incorporated into God's family and community, and it is in their relationship with God and others that their identity is found. The Spirit fuses people with God, Father, Son, Spirit, and other believers. A new community of faith is formed that should exhibit no elitism, even if the Spirit sets apart leaders to enable the spiritual growth of individuals and the community of God. This corporate oneness is expressed in local gatherings of Christians, namely, "churches"—people "called out of the world" and "into God's people and family." The community also transcends time and space, with all believers forming one great Christian body across time and space that will be so forever.[2]

---

1. When a person has an encounter with God (a theophany) or Christ (a christophany), I argue that these are also pneumaphany because, at the same time, the person has an experience of the Spirit.

2. See also Gregory J. Liston, *Kingdom Come: An Eschatological Third Article Ecclesiology* (London: T&T Clark, 2022), 146–50, of "the pneumatologically enabled community."

THE SPIRIT WHO RECONCILES PEOPLE TO GOD AND EACH OTHER

People are reconciled to God and receive the Spirit when they believe. Out of their belief, they are called to reconcile with one another; they are to live in peace with Jew and Gentile and let their relationships be shaped by God's virtues. They join in reconciling all things to Christ.

Romans 5:10–11

Having laid out his thesis that people are justified by faith and not works of the law, in Romans 5:1, Paul shifts to reconciliation.[3] He expresses this by saying believers "have peace with God through our Lord Jesus Christ." Their status is further expounded in terms of the access believers have to the grace of God's acceptance and the hope of participating fully in God's glory (5:2). As people are justified and reconciled to God, believers now boast in their sufferings, knowing the educative power of pain to produce endurance, character, and hope (5:3–5). The hope they have is not shame before God but honor, because "God's love has been poured into [their] hearts through the Holy Spirit who has been given to [them]" (v. 5). This hope recognizes the link between faith, justification, reconciliation, and the receipt of the Spirit. Believers experience God's love and hope through the Spirit.

In vv. 6–8, Paul expands on the last clause of v. 5, emphasizing the love of God demonstrated in Christ's sacrificial death for unworthy humankind. In v. 9, this justification effected by Christ's shed blood results in salvation from God's wrath. In v. 10, Paul describes sinful humankind as "enemies" (plur. ἐχθρός). The term is used in the NT of human opponents,[4] Satan in enmity with God,[5] generally all God's enemies,[6] and people in enmity with God and righteousness.[7] This hostility is due to sin and ungodliness, placing people before the wrath of a holy God (vv. 6, 8–9). However, now, rather than being crushed under the feet of the Lord (Ps. 110:1), people can yield to the Lord and be "reconciled to God by the death of his Son" (Rom. 5:10). The verb καταλλάσσω is Pauline, used of a wife being reconciled with her husband after separation (1 Cor. 7:11) and of Christ reconciling people to himself and God (2 Cor. 5:18–20). The focus here is the reconciliation of people *to* God.

In v. 11, believers have now received reconciliation (Rom. 5:11). The noun καταλλαγή is used for the reconciliation of the world to God (Rom. 11:25;

---

3. "Paul understands the event of becoming a Christian as one in which we receive the Spirit of God in reconciliation and justification." Habets, *Anointed Son*, 261.
4. See Matt. 5:43, 44; 10:36; 13:25 (parabolic of God), 28 (parabolic of God), 39; Luke 1:71, 74; 6:27, 35; 19:27 (parabolic of God's enemies), 44; Rom. 12:20; Gal. 4:16; 2 Thess. 3:15; Rev. 11:5 (of the witnesses and so God), 12 (see previous reference).
5. See Matt. 5:39; 13:39; Luke 10:19.
6. See Matt. 22:44; Mark 12:36; Luke 20:43; Acts 2:35; Rom. 11:28; 1 Cor. 15:25, 26 (death); Phil. 3:18; Col. 1:21; Heb. 1:13; 10:13; James 4:4.
7. Acts 13:10; Rom. 5:10.

2 Cor. 5:18–19). As a reconciled people, they shall be saved and now boast in God through the one by whom they were reconciled, Jesus. This reconciliation reverses the effect of sin and death caused by Adam and humanity. Thankfully, the grace of God and the new Adam has spread to many, bringing justification and eternal life (Rom. 5:12–21). The work of the Spirit is to reconcile believers to God, in Christ, and, obviously, in the Spirit. They are also reconciled to one another, although this is not the focus of Paul's ideas here.

Romans 11:15

In his discussion on the place of Israel in God's purposes, Paul again mentions reconciliation. He does so in a conditional sentence leading into a question. The parallel structure of ἡ ἀποβολὴ αὐτῶν, "their rejection," and τὸ παράπτωμα αὐτῶν, "their trespass," in v. 12 suggests this is a subjective genitive speaking of unbelieving Israel's rejection of the gospel, and hence, of Christ and God.[8] Israel's rejection of Christ and the gospel has resulted in "the reconciliation of the world." κόσμος is not universalistic, as the rejection of some is explicit.[9] The term can imply the world itself, as in Colossians 1:20; however, more likely, Paul here means the "people of the world" who respond to the gospel with faith.[10] The reconciliation here recalls reconciliation with God in Romans 5:9–10, but in a context discussing racial relations to God and one another, it hints at the consequent reconciliation of the people of the world in Christ to one another.

2 Corinthians 5:18–20

In his *apologia* and appeal to the Corinthians to reject the false teachers, Paul again mentions reconciliation.[11] "All these things" (πάντα) in 2 Corinthians 5:18 is vague but likely speaks of the benefits of the gospel referenced in the preceding section.[12] Such things are from God, who reconciles all believers (us) to himself. He also gave to Paul, his team, and others "the ministry of reconciliation."[13] The Spirit is not mentioned, but the ministry in view is participation in the new creation in the Spirit and not the flesh (v. 17).

---

8. While ἀποβολή can mean "loss," here it carries the meaning "rejection" (BDAG, s.v. "ἀποβολή," 108).

9. See vv. 11–12, 15, 20, 22–24.

10. The reconciliation of the actual earth is implied in Rom. 8:19–22; 1 Cor. 15:26.

11. This passage does not feature in Fee's exegetical analysis in *GEP*. However, I believe it flows out of the contrast of "new creation" and "flesh" in vv. 16–17, and so the Spirit is in view implicitly at least.

12. These include, potentially, God's power experienced in suffering (2 Cor. 4:7–18), the hope of resurrection (2 Cor. 5:1–5), the Spirit (2 Cor. 5:5), Christ's love (2 Cor. 5:14), Christ's redemptive death and resurrection (2 Cor. 5:14–15), and being a new creation in Christ (2 Cor. 5:17).

13. The genitive is effectively short for "the ministry of proclaiming the gospel of reconciliation" to reconcile people to God and one another in Christ. As such, it is a genitive of apposition (epexegetical). It could be one of product (the ministry that produces the reconciliation of people to God and each other).

This passage then speaks of the missional commission Paul, his team, and other similarly called believers have received of proclaiming God's reconciliation of the world to himself and each other. God no longer holds sin against all believers, and with that in mind, Paul and his coworkers are commissioned to proclaim the gospel of reconciliation to the world. Premised on this, Paul appeals to the Corinthians on behalf of Christ to turn from the poison of his enemies and "be reconciled to God" (2 Cor. 5:20). While this focuses on their reconciliation to God, it also speaks of their reconciliation with Paul and his team and, together with the whole body of Christ, reconciliation to God. The work of the Spirit is to shift people from enmity to God to a state of reconciliation. They are reconciled together in Christ.

Ephesians 2:16

Ephesians 2:1–10 stresses the basis of individual salvation—the people of God are saved by grace, through faith, and not by works. As new creations, they are set apart for works God prepares for them in advance. Ephesians 2:11–21 builds on this foundation,[14] emphasizing the coming together of Jews and Gentiles as one people in Christ.[15] Whereas before Gentiles were alienated from God and Israel, now, through Christ's blood, they have been made one with Jewish believers. The wall separating Jew and Gentile has been broken down so that, living in peace and not hostility, they form one cosmic "man." Jew and Gentile have been reconciled together in one body through the cross [v. 16]. Through Christ, faithful Jews and Gentiles equally "have access in [and by[16]] one Spirit to the Father" (v. 18). They are no longer strangers and aliens but are fellow citizens with other believers who form the household and temple of God. The Ephesian recipients are also a part of this community, being built together into a dwelling place for God by the Spirit. The Spirit, then, brings about the reconciliation of people not only to God and Christ but to one another in Christ.

Colossians 1:20–22

To thwart the diminishing of Christ in the Colossian heresy, Paul begins the body of the letter with a glorious hymn celebrating Christ's supremacy and deity (Col. 1:15–20). He is God's image, preeminent over his creation, which he sustains and holds together, and over his body, the church. Filled with God's being and fullness, Christ is pleased to reconcile to God all things in earth and heaven. This reconciliation has been achieved by making peace through Christ's blood shed on the cross.

---

14. Fee notes the use of "flesh" in Ephesians 2:11 and that the Spirit is implied in the background. Fee, *GEP*, 680–81. I agree. The Gentiles, then, formerly "in the flesh," are now "in Christ" and "in the Spirit." The fleshly identity of people remains (ethnicity, gender, social status), but in Christ and by the Spirit, people are united together in God.
15. See also Fee's discussion of 2:11–22, *GEP*, 681–90.
16. See the discussion "Baptized in the Spirit," in chapter 2.

In v. 21, Paul speaks of the former state of the Colossians as those alienated or estranged (ἀπαλλοτριόω) and "hostile in mind, doing evil deeds." This alienation is separation from God caused by sin. However, now that these Colossians are believers, God has reconciled them in Christ's body of flesh by his death (v. 22). They may stand firm in the faith, being holy, blameless, and above reproach before God. These attributes are not merely moral but social; their relationships are to be shaped by God's virtues (which Paul will outline in Colossians 3).

While the Spirit is not explicitly referenced in Paul's use of reconciliation language, it is apparent from other mentions of the Spirit and his broader theology that the Spirit brings people into a state of reconciliation with God. Furthermore, standing firm in the gospel, they are reconciled and are to love each other without falling into enmity and brokenness. Empowered by the Spirit, pneumaform people have received a ministry of reconciliation. They are to take the message of reconciliation to a world in enmity to God and divided from one another.

THE SPIRIT WHO WELCOMES AND ACCEPTS

In Romans 15:7, likely encouraging Christians across ethnic and cultural lines, Paul urges the Romans to "welcome (προσλαμβάνω) one another." They are to do so as "Christ has welcomed (προσλαμβάνω) you," speaking of Christ's open welcome to people from any ethnic or cultural background on the same basis: faith. On the face of it, this has nothing to do with the Spirit. But, more closely considered, it is by the Spirit that believers are welcomed by Christ (who sits at the right hand of God reigning [Rom. 8:34] and is present by his Spirit [Rom. 8:9–10]).

In Romans 14:17, Paul emphasizes the role of the Spirit in generating righteousness, peace, and joy. "Peace" in particular, in context, implies that welcome and acceptance are experienced in the Spirit. Believers, then, are to welcome (προσλαμβάνω) others who have differing opinions over trivial matters like food preference and holy days (Rom. 14:1, 3). Similarly, the Romans are to welcome (προσδέχομαι) Phoebe "in the Lord in a way worthy of the saints" (Rom. 16:2), the Philippians are to welcome (προσδέχομαι) Epaphroditus home "in the Lord with all joy" (Phil. 2:29), and the Colossians are to welcome Mark (Col. 4:10). The Corinthians are commended for receiving (δέχομαι) Titus "with fear and trembling" (2 Cor. 7:15). Similarly, Paul recalls the Galatians welcoming (δέχομαι) him as if he were an angel or the Lord himself, even though his suffering tested them (Gal. 4:14). Likewise, in 1 Corinthians 16:17, Paul embodies such an attitude as he rejoices at the coming of the three Corinthians to refresh his spirit.

The Spirit welcomes people into God's community of faith, and by the Spirit, believers are to welcome one another across social boundaries. In Pauline theology, this work of God is exercised through Christ and in and by the Spirit.

THE SPIRIT AND THE ADOPTION OF THE BELIEVER

Paul uses adoption (υἱοθεσία) language five times. The first of these refers to God's adoption of Israel in the OT (Rom. 9:4). The other four uses are important for the discussion of the role of the Spirit in integrating believers into God's people. The metaphor is discussed here because it is an inclusion metaphor, a collective idea whereby an individual is not adopted alone but instantly becomes a family member with all rights and obligations.

Ephesians 1:5

Ephesians begins with a stunning sentence that blesses God and Christ for the wonderful blessings they have bestowed upon believers (Eph. 1:3–14). Believers are spiritually blessed (v. 3) and chosen in Christ before creation to be holy (v. 4). In love, God predestined believers "for adoption (υἱοθεσία) through Jesus Christ for himself" (translation mine). Paul here reasserts, in a very general sense for all believers, what he writes about in Romans and Galatians. The basis for God's adoption of his people is love. This adoption is predestined. In what follows, Paul adds that this is an outworking of God's will and purpose and results in praise of his grace. This grace has been bestowed upon believers in "the Beloved," Christ. Although the Spirit is not mentioned here, the role of the Spirit features elsewhere in Ephesians, indicating that the fusing of believers into God's family is done in Christ by the Spirit (esp. Eph. 1:13; 2:22). It also parallels "the household of God" further defined as "the church of the living God" in 1 Timothy 3:15.

Romans 8:15

Amid Paul's discussion of new life in the Spirit for believers freed from the law, Paul assures the Romans that, as believers, they have not received "the spirit of slavery to fall back into fear." While some have argued this is the Spirit or the human spirit, more likely he uses the word rhetorically, as a hypothetical antithesis to the "Spirit of adoption:" "the Spirit that you have received is not a 'spirit of bondage' but a Spirit of adoption."[17] This motif speaks then of being bonded to law and the fear generated when one lives enslaved to gaining justification and inclusion through law observance, which, for Paul, is an impossibility. Instead, they have received a Spirit of adoption.

The alternative, "a Spirit of adoption," does speak of the Holy Spirit. Adoption has roots in the Roman legal practice of adopting a child with full inheritance rights. It also has antecedents in Jewish thought.[18] Where faith is found and the Spirit outpoured, God adopts a believer into his family.

---

17.   Moo, *Romans*, 523.
18.   See James M. Scott, "Adoption, Sonship," in *DPL* 15–18. He notes the Greco-Roman and OT-Jewish background of the idea.

Those who believe and are adopted by God are also led by the Spirit (Rom. 8:14).[19] Whereas in Galatians 4:6 it is the Spirit who cries out "Abba! Father!" when entering the believer's heart, in Romans 8:15, believers themselves cry out the same. In v. 16, this awareness of being children of God comes from the Spirit, who bears witness by "speaking" assurance of the believers' new identity to their spirit. The Spirit then leads believers, provokes deep worship in them, and gives an awareness of who God is and who they are in relation to him. These children are also heirs who experience freedom and glorification, provided they endure suffering with Christ (Rom. 8:17, 21).

Who God's children are will be revealed at the consummation (Rom. 8:19). As with other Pauline conversion motifs, "adoption" is realized in the present as the first installment of the Spirit fuses believers together as God's family, his church. Ultimately, at the consummation after judgment, believers will experience their full adoption into God's personal presence as his children and the liberation of their bodies from sin and death (Rom. 8:23). So, God and his people will forever be one family in the new creation.

Romans 8:23

The previous section considered the role of the Spirit in fusing people into God's people. They are freed from the fear of sin's consequences and the forces opposing God. Even though genuine terrors will afflict them, they know God is with them and will bring them through it by his deliverance or eternal salvation. Worship flows to God the Father as the Spirit enters and adopts people into God's family. In v. 16, the Spirit gives inward witness to the God-given spirit in believers, assuring them that they are indeed children of God. As children, they are full heirs of God along with Christ. However, the path to the inheritance of glorification with Christ is suffering, as it was for Jesus (v. 17). In the present, they suffer and lament together upheld by the Spirit. In the future, they will rejoice together eternally in the new creation.

In vv. 19–22, Paul personifies creation, which longs for those adopted, the children (lit. "sons") of God, to be revealed. In the meantime, the creation is subjugated by God to futility but has the hope of being set free from its slavery to corruption. The creation will experience the same liberation from the corruptive effects of sin that God's adopted children will know.

Meanwhile, believers have received the firstfruits of the Spirit, by whom God has adopted them. Like creation, as these believers to whom the Spirit has been imparted suffer with Christ, they inwardly groan as they wait for their adoption as children (lit. "sons"). Whereas Romans 8:16 focuses on adoption as a present spiritual reality, in Romans 8:23, it is future-oriented and focused on the body. Presently, believers are adopted but remain living in bodies of clay that are subject to φθορά and will die. In the eschaton, these

---

19. They are also children of Abraham (Rom. 9:7–9). These children are from the nations, fulfilling Hosea 1:10; 2:9 (Rom. 9:26–27).

mortal and perishable "lowly" bodies of "flesh and blood" will be transformed in the twinkling of an eye into "glorious" bodies, and believers' adoption will not merely be spiritual while in decaying bodies but be fully real and actual, as they are part of God's family forever. This climax is the redemption of our bodies, when the body becomes a fully "spiritual body," no longer an Adamic body of flesh subject to death (1 Cor. 15:44). It will be an immortal and imperishable body overflowing with life and free of sin and death. This future hope sustains them.

Galatians 4:6

In his argument that new Gentile converts do not need to yield to the demands of the Judaizers, Paul distinguishes a young son and a slave in the Roman household.[20] Before coming of age, the son is basically in the same place as a slave. While he is the heir, he has people appointed to manage him until the taking up of the toga at the date appointed by his father (Gal. 4:1–2).[21] Paul then applies this slave-son distinction to Israel's status before Christ—they were effectively children enslaved to "the elemental powers" of the world.[22] Verse 4 is the turning point, what God has done in sending Christ and the Spirit. When the time was right, God sent his Son, born of a woman and under law, to redeem those under the law (Israel) "so that we might receive adoption as children [lit. "sons"]." As with Romans 8:15, this speaks of the present status gifted to believers. They are already adopted into God's family as his children (see also Gal. 3:26).[23]

Verse 6 continues with Paul telling the Galatians that because they are children (lit. "sons"), "God has sent the Spirit of his Son into [their] hearts." Paul here is referring to the moment they believed the message, began their Christian lives, and received Spirit. This is the same Spirit God continues to supply to them (Gal. 3:2–5; cf. Phil. 1:19).

Whereas in Romans 8:15, the believer cries "Abba! Father," in Galatians 4:6, the subject of κράζω is the Spirit who cries, "Abba! Father!" as he is poured into believers.[24] This cry could be God-directed but could also be shouted in the hearing of the inward ears of believers, who then realize that they are chil-

---

20. See also the earlier discussion of Galatians 4:4 in chapter 2, "The Spirit Sent into the Human Heart."

21. See the discussion in Longenecker, *Galatians*, 162–64.

22. See on the στοιχεῖα, Keown, *Galatians*, 542–46. The "*stoicheia* are the religious and philosophical ideologies, ideas, and legal requirements from the religious of Israel and found throughout all cultures of the world and manifest in different ways" (p. 546). I also argue that as the ancient world did not separate the spiritual and material as we do today, that in this use "the spiritual dimension is there at least in the conceptual background." In Galatians 4:9, the spiritual power aspect is more prominent.

23. As in Romans, they are also children of Abraham (Gal. 3:7) and Sarah the free woman (Gal. 4:31), and so children of promise (Gal. 4:28). Those "birthed" by Paul on behalf of God are also Paul's children (Gal. 4:19).

24. See further on "Abba, Father!" chap. 4, "The Spirit and the Adoption of the Believer" and chapter 5, "Prayer and the Spirit."

dren of God (cf. Rom. 8:16). This cry may be heard by others, who join with them in rejoicing. Because the Spirit has come into the Galatians, they are no longer slaves or even young children still under managers and guardians. They are children (lit. "a son") and so heirs through God (cf. Rom. 8:17). The Spirit's role is critical to the inclusion of people into God's family both onti-cally and experientially.

In Galatians 6:10, Paul describes the community of believers as "the household (οἰκεῖος) of faith." Here, οἰκεῖος carries the sense of a "family."[25] "The faith" is a "locution for the Christian movement."[26] It emphasizes those who have responded to God by faith, as in the case of Abraham and believ-ers in Jesus. They are integrated into the family of God and Abraham. In Galatians, the receipt of the Spirit coincides with hearing with faith (Gal. 3:2, 5). Galatians 6:10 also follows Paul's warning to sow to please the Spirit, not the flesh, in vv. 7–9. Hence, the "household of faith" is synonymous with the "household of those who have received the Spirit," aligning Paul's thought here with the notion of the "temple of the Spirit" in 1 Corinthians 3 and 6 and Ephesians 2 (esp. Eph. 2:19).

THE SPIRIT WHO FORMS THE PEOPLE OF GOD

The notion of God's people is closely related and sometimes crosses over with adoption. When individuals believe and are justified by faith and adopted into God's family, they become part of God's λαός. Although καλέω language can be used in the sense of "invitation" in other contexts,[27] Paul uses the language of those not only summoned by God but who have also yielded to God's summons—God's effectual call.[28] The language is used for the call to a particular Christian vocation, such as Paul's apostleship (Rom. 1:1; 1 Cor. 1:1; 15:9; Gal. 1:15), but more often of all believers who are "the called"—they have been summoned and have believed. As such, they are "called to belong to Jesus Christ" (Rom. 1:6); "called to be saints" (Rom. 1:7; 1 Cor. 1:2); "called according to his purpose" (Rom. 8:28); "called 'sons and daughters of the living God'" (my translation); "called into one body" (Col. 3:15, my translation);[29] and God "calls [them] into

---

25. *BrillDAG* notes a range of options, all related mostly to the family.
26. Longenecker, *Galatians*, 283.
27. For example, Matt. 22:3, 4, 8, 9; Luke 14:9, 10, 12, 13, 16, 17. 24.
28. See N. T. Wright, *Pauline Perspectives: Essays on Paul, 1978–2013* (Minneapolis: Fortress, 2013), 290.
29. On this passage, see Fee, *GEP*, 647. Fee rightly notes the connection to Ephesians 4:3–4 and 1 Corinthians 12:13 and the role of the Spirit in God's calling people into one body (cf. Col. 3:16). He adds, "But as with the preceding passages, the Spirit is not mentioned in this text because that is merely the presupposition for Paul: his emphasis and concern in this passage lies elsewhere—with the fact that they were all called into the one body, the concluding word which ties together the whole of the preceding paraenesis."

his own kingdom and glory" (1 Thess. 2:12).[30] Such a call is experienced through and by the Spirit.

Here, Paul cites two passages from Hosea that are being fulfilled in Christ. First, Paul cites Hosea 2:23, where the prophet foresaw a day when God would declare others beyond Israel his people. Paul takes and adapts this text for the Christian movement, which includes Gentile believers. They are now God's people and his beloved. Second, in Romans 9:26, he takes a portion of Hosea 1:10 where the prophet looks to the day when people who were not God's people will be called "children [lit. 'sons'] of the living God."

Those who are adopted as God's children are incorporated into his people in continuity with the people of faith in human history (cf. 1 Cor. 14:21). God accepts such people of faith despite shifts in the salvation story, such as the coming of Christ and the reception of the Spirit (Rom. 11:1–2). Those from Israel who have historically been identified as God's people but are in rejection of Christ are also not rejected, for "God has the power to graft them in again," as the "natural branches" can "be grafted back into their own olive tree" (11:23–24), and "all day long [God has] held out [his] hands to a disobedient and contrary people." As such, if unbelieving Israelites yield to the gospel with faith, they too will be included in the people of God in Christ (Rom. 10:21//Isa. 65:2).

A SPIRIT-INDWELT TEMPLE

The temple was a symbol of God's presence until the New Covenant. Paul uses this metaphor to explain the Spirit's presence in God's people, both as a whole and individually.

1 Corinthians 3:16–17

In his challenge to the Corinthians' factionalism, their penchant for preferring one preacher over another (1 Cor. 1:12), Paul reminds the Corinthians of their origins. He picks up the OT idea of the Jerusalem temple to describe the church.

Notably, Paul uses ναός rather than ἱερόν, indicating that the Corinthians are the place of God's dwelling.[31] The notion recalls Israel's tabernacle and temple where God dwelt: "God is now present among his people in Corinth by his Spirit."[32] As discussed in chapter 1,[33] a range of OT passages point to God's presence in these structures (e.g., Hab. 2:20) and his glory filling the

---

30. See also Rom. 8:30; 1 Cor. 1:24, 26; 7:15, 17–18, 20–22, 24; Gal. 1:6; 5:8, 13; Eph. 1:18; 4:1, 4; Phil. 3:14; 1 Thess. 4:7; 5:24; 2 Thess. 1:11; 2:14; 1 Tim. 6:12; 2 Tim. 1:9); and the language of election (ἐκλέγομαι language: Rom. 8:33; 9:11; 11:5, 7, 28–29; 16:13; 1 Cor. 1:9, 27–28; Gal. 5:13; Eph. 1:4; Col. 3:12; 1 Thess. 1:4; 2 Thess. 2:13; 2 Tim. 2:10; Titus 1:1).

31. ναός refers to the inner aspects of the temple, whereas ἱερόν includes whole temple area. See Fee, *GEP*, 114; O. Michel, "ναός," *TDNT* 4:880–90.

32. Fee, *GEP*, 114.

33. See chapter 1, "The Spirit in the Tabernacle and Temple."

temple (e.g., 1 Kings 8:11; 2 Chron. 5:14). No such filling had come to Ezra's temple, and now Israel hopes for it (Ezek. 40–48; Hag. 2:7). For Paul, this is being fulfilled in the coming of the Spirit to his people. God's spiritual glory now dwells in a people, not a building.[34] With their city full of temples, the Corinthians would recognize the imagery and shift from worship in multiple temples and shrines to God's "one temple in pagan Corinth, and they are it."[35]

According to the grace given to him in his apostolic calling, as a master builder and through his preaching, Paul laid the foundation of Jesus—the only foundation of a church of God. Others, like Apollos, Peter, and anyone else who has ministered in Christ's gospel in the city, have built on the initial work.

In v. 16, Paul asks a question introduced with οὐκ and expects the answer "yes."[36] He asks whether the Corinthians know they are God's temple with God's Spirit dwelling in them, which they should. Here, unlike 1 Corinthians 6:19, Paul thinks corporately and not individually, as he speaks of the Corinthian church as one temple. This temple is likely a community of Christians broken up into multiple house churches but still seen as one "church of God that is in Corinth" (1 Cor. 1:1; 2 Cor. 1:1).[37] Thus, the Spirit fuses individuals as one people, one temple of God, in a given locale.

As discussed, the infilling of this group calls to mind God's glory filling the tabernacle and temple in Israel's story (Exod. 40:34–35; 1 Kings 8:11). Now, the Spirit indwells the people of God. This indwelling leads to a warning in v. 17 against anyone who destroys God's temple: they face the danger of God's destroying them.[38] Paul warns them because God's temple of his people, including the Corinthians sanctified in Christ, is holy (1 Cor. 1:1; 6:11). The broader implications of the passage call for the people of God to live in unity, holiness, and love. They are πνεῦμα-formed into a people of God and are to pneumaform in their attitudes, actions, and words together and in witness to the world.

1 Corinthians 6:19

In 1 Corinthians 6:12–21, Paul deals with the problem of sexual immorality in Corinth (vv. 13, 18), particularly believers engaging in sexual relationships with prostitutes (vv. 15–16). Clearly, some in Corinth misunderstand the freedom they have in Christ, considering it gives them license to do what they want with their bodies, such as to engage in sexual immorality and other

---

34. For Paul's transfer of images, see Fee, *GEP*, 115.
35. Fee, *GEP*, 114.
36. L&N 1:664.
37. Also 1 Cor. 11:18; 14:4, 5, 12, 23, 28, 35.
38. Fee, *GEP*, 117: "One can scarcely circumvent the awful nature of the warning. God obviously takes the local church far more seriously than did the Corinthians—and most contemporary Christians. The church is the apple of his eye; his holy people set apart by his Spirit for his holy purposes in Corinth. Those who are responsible for dismantling the church may therefore expect judgment in kind."

non-gospel behavior (v. 12). In his response, among a range of other arguments, Paul asks whether they know that the body is a temple of the Holy
Spirit who dwells within them.

Earlier in the passage, he argues that their bodies are members of Christ
and that having sexual relations with prostitutes violates a believer's unique
relationship with Christ (vv. 15–16).[39] In v. 17, the one who is joined to Christ
becomes one spirit with him. πνεῦμα here refers to the Holy Spirit, which
is the Spirit of Jesus (cf. Rom. 8:9; 2 Cor. 3:17–18; Phil. 1:19). As the Spirit
of Jesus enters the human life, the believer is bound to Christ by that Spirit.
Consequently, just as Joseph fled Potiphar's wife (Gen. 39:11–12), the believer
must flee from sexual immorality because it violates the unique relationship a
believer has with God, in Christ, by the Spirit.[40]

In v. 19, Paul picks up the same idea used in 1 Corinthians 3:16, where
the church is the temple of the Spirit but applies it to each Christian.[41] When
a person becomes a believer, their body becomes a temple of God's presence.
This inclusion and indwelling is a gift from God.[42] As a result, Christians
should glorify God with their body, for God inhabits them.[43]

So, just as the church is the temple of the Spirit, each Christian is a temple
of the Spirit. However, the same Spirit binds them together in Christ, the
Father, and with each other. Knowing this should lead them away from vices
of the body as they live by the Spirit who sanctifies them. Furthermore, such
an awareness should lead them away from destructive relationships with other
Christians, as these destroy the unity of the body. Indeed, Paul is adamant
God will respond to those who so destroy the church with judgment (1 Cor.
3:17; cf. 1 Thess. 4:6).

2 Corinthians 6:14–18

This passage confirms the link between the status of believers as God's
temple, their adoption into God's family, and their inclusion in his people. In

---

39. The only permissible sexual relation for a person in Christ is consensual intimate relations with one's
     spouse (Rom. 7:2–3; 1 Cor. 7:11–13).
40. Sexual relations within marriage are permitted for a believer because the married couple is bound
     together as one flesh and share a common spiritual bond (Eph. 5:31. see also Gen. 2:24; Matt. 19:6;
     Mark 10:8).
41. Fee, *GEP*, 135. Contra R. Kempthorne, "Incest and the Body of Christ: A Study of I Corinthians
     VI.12–20," *NTS* 14 (1967–68): 568–74, who considers the church here as the body of Christ. Still
     relevant is the refutation by Robert H. Gundry, *SOMA in Biblical Theology with Emphasis on Pauline
     Anthropology*, SNTSMS 29 (Cambridge: Cambridge University Press, 1976), 76.
42. "Paul now images the body as the *Spirit's* temple, underscoring that it is the 'place' of the Spirit's
     dwelling in the individual believers' lives. In the same way that the temple in Jerusalem 'housed' the
     presence of the living God, so the body of the believer 'houses' the presence of the living God by his
     Spirit." Fee, *GEP*, 136 (emphasis original).
43. This passage is a death knell to Hellenistic dualism of body and soul. "According to the Christian view
     there is no dichotomy between body and spirit that either indulges the body because it is irrelevant or
     punishes it so as to purify the spirit." Fee, *GEP*, 137.

context, while this has general application, this text is a summons away from the snares of the false teachers with their false gospel.[44]

With four questions signaled with τίς and all expecting the answer "none," Paul stresses the importance of not being drawn to corruption through relationships with false teachers (and generally, those engaged in graphic sin).[45] The final question rhetorically asks whether believers "are the temple of the living God." Paul then adds a catena of OT citations that stress God's dwelling and walking with his people (2 Cor. 6:16//Lev. 26:11); that he will be their God and they shall be his people (2 Cor. 6:17a–c//Isa. 52:11); God's appeal to them to separate themselves from that which is unclean (2 Cor. 6:17d//Ezek. 20:34); and that God is father to his people (including the Corinthians) and their status as children (2 Cor. 6:18//2 Sam. 7:8). While the Spirit is not directly mentioned, by cross-referencing to other Pauline texts concerning believers as the temple, adoption, and inclusion, the Spirit's role is implied.[46]

Ephesians 2:20–22

In Ephesians 2:1–10, Paul begins by describing the horrendous condition and consequences of being an unbeliever (Eph. 2:1–3). He then shifts to describe salvation by grace through faith, initiated by God's mercy and love (2:4–10). Ephesians 2:11–22 is concerned with this salvation's corporate effects, particularly breaking down the barriers between Jews and Gentiles in Christ. Now, through the death of Jesus, the formerly divided groups are one, reconciled together to God. Through Jesus, both Jews and Gentiles have access in and by one Spirit to the Father (v. 18).[47] They are fellow citizens with other Christians.[48] They and other believers are all saints, or holy ones. Moreover, all believers are members of God's family (οἰκεῖος).[49]

---

44. Keown, *Discovering: The Pauline Letters*, 189.

45. See also 1 Corinthians 10:7, where the Corinthians are warned away from idolatry, not unlike the people of Israel (ὁ λαὸς), who worshipped the golden calf and engaged in revelry (Exodus 32, citing v. 6). See also Titus 2:14, where Christ gave himself for believers to redeem them from all lawlessness "and to purify for himself a people [λαός] for his own possession who are zealous for good works."

46. "Thus, to bring items 2 and 3 together, if Paul does not use explicit Spirit language, it is because he is using OT sacral language, but language that is full of new covenant promises, that God would dwell among, walk with, be a father to his people. This is exactly the role of the Spirit in Paul's theology." Fee, *GEP*, 337.

47. See earlier chapter 2, "Baptized in the Spirit."

48. See Lincoln, *Ephesians*, 150–51; Thielman, *Ephesians*, 179. The term ἅγιοι (saints) here does not mean Israel (Markus Barth), Jewish Christians (E. Scott), the first Christians (Houlden), or angels (Schlier). As in all Paul's uses, it means "saints" or "holy ones," and as such "they form one citizenry with all other believers" (Thielman, *Ephesians*, 179).

49. Aside from Numbers 25:5, where οἰκεῖος is used of Israel as a people, and 2 Maccabees 15:12, where it is used of something belonging to virtue, all uses of the term refer to relatives (Lev. 18:6, 12, 13, 17; 21:2; 25:49; Num. 27:11; 1 Kgdms. 10:14–16; 14:50 [1 Sam. EVV]; 3 Macc. 6:8; Prov. 17:9 [LXX]; Amos 6:9; Isa. 3:6 [LXX]; 31:9 [LXX]; 58:7 [LXX]). Otherwise, only Paul uses it elsewhere in the NT of blood relatives (1 Tim. 5:8) and similarly to here of "the household of faith" (Gal. 6:10).

This household has been built on a foundation of Christ (the keystone),[50] apostles, and prophets.[51] Significantly, τῶν ἀποστόλων καὶ προφητῶν represent two groups equiped by the Spirit in their roles,[52] and, as such, the Spirit's work in and through people is critical to the formation of the building and family of God.

In v. 21, ἐν ᾧ is balanced with ἐν κυρίῳ, creating a possible chiasm. The two dative clauses emphasize that it is in Christ that the church is held together and grown. πᾶσα οἰκοδομὴ refers to the church as a whole.[53] In Christ, the church has been joined together (συναρμολογέω). In Ephesians 4:16, the verb speaks of Christ joining the church's people as one body. Here, they are joined together in one building. As such, this building grows into a holy temple in the Lord.[54]

Verse 22, like the previous verse, is flanked by two dative expressions, ἐν ᾧ . . . ἐν πνεύματι. The first dative phrase refers again to Christ. The final clause indicates that Christ is enacting his purposes for the church. As with all other believers in Christ and by the Spirit, the Ephesians (ὑμεῖς) also (καί) "are being built together (συνοικοδομέω) into a dwelling place (κατοικητήριον) for God." The Spirit is the agency of fusing God's people in Christ. By the Spirit, Christ grows the church. A fundamental means by which he is doing this is by gifts granted to Spirit-imbued believers who both do the work of ministry and equip others for the same (Eph. 4:11–16).[55]

THE BODY OF CHRIST

The "body of Christ" is an essential descriptor of the church for Paul. The integration of believers into Christ's body is linked to the Spirit in 1 Corinthians. I discussed 1 Corinthians 12:13 regarding receiving the Spirit in chapter 2. First Corinthians 12:12 uses the analogy of the one fleshly body comprised of many parts to describe the one body of Christ with many members and gifts. In and by the one Spirit, believers are baptized into the one body of Christ.

---

50. Whether Christ here is the cornerstone (first stone laid, so Fee, *GEP*, 687), the capstone (the top finishing stone), or the keystone (central stone at the head of an arch) is incidental to this discussion. In my view, Christ is all of the above, and ἀκρογωνιαῖος should not be excessively literalized any more than the prophets and apostles literally make up the foundation of a church. For Paul, Christ is the first stone laid and foundation (1 Cor. 3:11), and he is the head of the church, above all things, and holds all things together (Eph. 1:22; 5:23; Col. 1:17–18).

51. The apostles and prophets are discussed in chapter 9. Here, they are active NT-era prophets. These are not "offices" but charismatic functions. They do not supersede Christ (similarly, Fee, *GEP*, 687).

52. Ephesians 4:11 and the motif of the church as a present entity built on Christ and his people strongly indicates that "the prophets" here are contemporary figures rather than the prophets of the OT. See, e.g., Stephen E. Fowl, *Ephesians: A Commentary*, eds. C. Clifton Black, M. Eugene Boring, and John T. Carroll, NTL (Louisville: Westminster John Knox, 2012), 98.

53. Not multiple buildings (Lightfoot), but πᾶσα is adjectival (the whole building). See Thielman, *Ephesians*, 183.

54. On this verse, see also Fee, *GEP*, 688–89. He notes that the passage is Trinitarian (p. 690).

55. See also on this verse, Fee, *GEP* 689–90.

This body is made up of people from all manner of social groupings, whether Jews or Greeks or slaves or citizens. God gives all believers the one Spirit to quench their spiritual thirst. As such, it is in and by the Spirit that God incorporates people into his Son's being and community. People are included in Christ through the baptism of the Spirit.

In 1 Corinthians 12, Paul deals with questions of spirituality raised in the letter from the Corinthian church. Believers are imbued with the Spirit of God by whom they say "Jesus is Lord," whom they would never violate by cursing Jesus (12:3), and through whom God distributed to believers a wide array of gifts (1 Cor. 12:4–11). In 1 Corinthians 12:12, Paul observes that the body of Christ is analogous to one living body that is made of many parts.

In 1 Corinthians 12:13, using a chiasm, Paul recalls the moment of inclusion in Christ's body.

A1   καὶ γὰρ ἐν ἑνὶ πνεύματι ἡμεῖς πάντες εἰς ἓν σῶμα ἐβαπτίσθημεν,
      and in (and by) one Spirit we were all baptized into one body
  B   εἴτε Ἰουδαῖοι εἴτε Ἕλληνες εἴτε δοῦλοι εἴτε ἐλεύθεροι,
          Jews or Greeks, slaves or free
A2   καὶ πάντες ἓν πνεῦμα ἐποτίσθημεν.
      and all were made to drink of one Spirit

Parts A1 and A2 describe the receipt of the Spirit using two images related to water: baptism and drinking. Baptism in part A1 can be water baptism[56] or Spirit baptism.[57] If the former, Paul is speaking of believers being formed into one body at the moment of their water baptism. If the latter, Paul speaks of the moment of faith when they receive the Spirit.[58] The parallel with part A2 of the chiasm suggests that Spirit baptism is in view.[59] Spirit baptism also aligns with Paul's broader theology in which the Spirit is received at the moment of faith[60] and not tied to water baptism.

The dative ἐν ἑνὶ πνεύματι, as throughout Paul's letters, can be translated "by one Spirit" or "in one Spirit." Undoubtedly, the instrumental use of the dative, "by one Spirit," is included in the phrase.[61] Nevertheless, Paul is likely thinking more broadly of the sphere in which Christians now live in this eon—the sphere of the Spirit. Indeed, God in Christ baptizes them,

56. George R. Beasley-Murray, *Baptism in the New Testament* (Grand Rapids: Eerdmans, 1962), 167–71.
57. Fee, *GEP*, 181–82.
58. Similarly, Fee says, "Paul is referring to their common experience of conversion, and he does so in terms of its most crucial element, the receiving of the Spirit." Fee, *GEP*, 181.
59. Similarly, see Fee, *GEP*, 179.
60. The drinking of the Spirit is not a second experience, but Fee is right to say, "The lack of such usage elsewhere in Christian literature militates against it. Rather, as indicated above, this is most likely a piece of Semitic parallelism, where both clauses argue essentially the same point." Fee, *GEP*, 180. It is, then, the same experience described in two ways.
61. See earlier chapter 2, "Baptized in the Spirit."

indicating that here, sphere dominates agency. However, the phrase "in one Spirit" always includes agency and instrumentality but is much more. So, God uses the Spirit to exercise his agency by integrating believers into Christ's body with other Christians. They become one with other believers in Christ.

As I have demonstrated elsewhere, with other ancient writers, Paul uses εἴτε . . . εἴτε strings with an axiomatic statement integral to his thought that he then applies to the context.[62] The axiom here is formed from parts A1 and A2, "for in (and by) one Spirit we were all baptized into one body . . . and all were made to drink of one Spirit." The εἴτε . . . εἴτε string emphasizes the diversity of those in the church. "Whether Jews or Greeks" highlights the bringing together of people of diverse ethnicities and cultures. "Whether slave or free" draws attention to the inclusion of citizens and noncitizens into one group of believers without status discrimination. We know from Paul's other letters that such a diversity includes men and women and people of other ethnicities and cultures (Rom. 1:14; Gal. 3:28; Col. 3:11).[63] All of these groups of people who believe in Jesus and are baptized into his name are "made to drink of one Spirit." This imbibing speaks of the same event referred to in part A1—their Spirit baptism into the body of Christ.

In whatever ways we view baptism and the dative in this passage, what is clear is that the Spirit is the instrument by which people are included in the body of Christ. The Spirit generates charisms in and through them that serve the common good and grow the church.

THE FELLOWSHIP OF THE HOLY SPIRIT

One temple and one body, believers are bonded into one community—they share the root and anointing of Christ. They should encourage, have compassion and mercy, and give to one another, recognizing the sacredness of the body.

2 Corinthians 13:13 (13:14 EVV)

Second Corinthians ends with the memorable Trinitarian prayer-blessing:[64] "The grace of the Lord Jesus Christ and the love of God and the fellowship of the Holy Spirit [ἡ κοινωνία τοῦ ἁγίου πνεύματος] be with all of you" (LEB).[65] The genitive ἁγίου πνεύματος can be an objective genitive meaning "participation in the Holy Spirit" or "communion with the

---

62. Mark J. Keown, "Paul's Use of εἴτε . . . εἴτε Constructions and the Proclamation of the Gospel (Phil. 1:18a)," *Colloq* 48, no. 2 (2016): 195–208.

63. My research into the εἴτε . . . εἴτε constructions suggests Paul could have added a whole range of other relevant binaries. These might include "old or young," "rich or poor," "disabled or abled," and so on.

64. Fee, *GEP*, 362, rightly speaks of this as a "remarkable grace-benediction" that is "the only one of its kind in the extant Pauline corpus." He also highlights its Trinitarian form.

65. Fee may well be right to suggest that this is not merely a liturgical formula but that the order Lord-God-Spirit is ad hoc and attributable to Paul developing his more usual christological grace blessing. Fee, *GEP*, 363.

Holy Spirit."[66] Alternatively, the genitive can be subjective, giving a range of possible senses: "'the fellowship with one another that is engendered by the Spirit' or 'the participation granted by the Spirit in himself' or 'the sense of community created by the Spirit.'"[67] Strictly speaking, the latter is preferred, as the preceding two genitives are subjective, and one would expect consistency here.

However, the genitive could also be plenary, with the subjective sense producing the objective.[68] If so, the believers' fellowship in and with the Spirit generates the ideal of community fellowship. The plenary option fits with the previous two genitives, which may also be plenary. The grace and love experienced in Christ and God generate grace and love in the Corinthian community. This text and the one that follows in Philippians speak of the fellowship believers experience with the Spirit and the close communion generated by the Spirit. At conversion, believers are swept up into God's being and joined together in Christ as they are filled with the Spirit. They experience a deep intimate bond with God in and by the Spirit[69] and are immediately linked to every other Christian in the world. This intimate relationship binds them together as one people.[70] It also, as Fee says, "causes us to participate in all the benefits of that grace and salvation, indwelling us in the present by his own presence, guaranteeing our final eschatological glory."[71]

1 Corinthians 1:9

While this verse does not explicitly mention πνεῦμα, it refers to the bond between people and Christ through the Spirit. Paul culminates his thanksgiving for the Corinthians by assuring them of the faithfulness of God to sustain them to the end, blameless for the day of the Lord Jesus Christ (v. 8). Here, "through [God, the Corinthians] were called into the fellowship (κοινωνία) of his Son, Jesus Christ our Lord." This fellowship speaks of the intimate connection believers have with Christ, in whom they now have their beings. This closeness is the work of the Spirit, as the previous two verses make explicit.

---

66. Harris, *Second Epistle*, 939.
67. Harris, *Second Epistle*, 939.
68. In genitives that may be plenary, this is usually the case. See Wallace, *Greek Grammar*, 119.
69. See earlier chapter 2, "Baptized in the Spirit."
70. Gorman, *BGPPM*, 30, writes of this verse and Philippians 2:1, "In 2 Corinthians and Philippians Paul speaks of a *koinōnia* in the Spirit, which clearly in context means intimate communion, life-sharing, with God and with one another."
71. Fee, *GEP*, 364. Fee does not discuss the genitive but his analysis concurs with my plenary position. He notes that "the 'fellowship of the Holy Spirit' conveys the ongoing appropriation of [God's] love and [Jesus'] grace in the life of the believing community (3:6–18)." He asserts that God's *ḥesed* or "covenant love . . . has found its singularly concrete historical expression in the death and resurrection of Christ." The Spirit is characterized by κοινωνία, "participation in," or "fellowship with." Believers are brought into intimate and abiding relationship with God in the Spirit. We can extend this to relationship together with, in, and by the Spirit.

Romans 11:17

The image of Gentiles as wild olive shoots grafted in with believing Jews to the olive tree of God's faithful people invokes ideas of the Spirit. Those grafted in, both believing Jews and Gentiles, "became a partaker (συγκοινωνός) of the root of the richness of the olive tree." The hapax legomenon πιότης speaks literally of "fattiness," so it refers to the rich sap of the olive tree. Metaphorically, it implies wealth and prosperity, hence "richness."[72] The image of sap invoked by this creative expression includes thoughts of the Spirit in all its fullness and of spiritual riches flowing from the root to the ingrafted branch, generating life. The parts of the tree are bound together to the root and live by the nourishment carried in the sap. Olive oil is also an important economic product used for the anointing process. This significance is seen in Zechariah 4:14, where Joshua the priest and Zerubbabel are "the sons of the oil" (οἱ δύο υἱοὶ τῆς πιότητος), or "anointed ones" (LES). As such, the image of olive oil in the tree of God's people invokes thoughts of God's anointing of Christ with the Spirit[73] and believers sharing in that anointing (2 Cor. 1:21).

Philippians 2:1

A similar genitive construct to Romans 11:17 is used in Philippians 2:1 (κοινωνία πνεύματος). Here, it falls in the fourth part of a four-part "if any . . ." protasis that leads to the apodosis "complete my joy." The string of εἴ and τις poetically enunciates five things that believers experience as a result of their conversion to God, inclusion in Christ, and infilling of the Spirit.[74] The construct is also hortatory, summoning believers to live out what is experienced, and express these characteristics in their attitudes toward others in the church, toward other Christians in the world they are engaged with, and toward unbelievers.[75] They experience encouragement (παράκλησις) in Christ, comfort (παραμύθιον) from love, intimate familial relationship (κοινωνία), compassion (σπλάγχνον), and mercy (οἰκτιρμός). Each of these is to flow over into their community, healing the nascent rift between Euodia and Syntyche.[76] They must be seen in their broader Christian relationships beyond the church; for example, in further support for the likes of Paul,

---

72. BDAG, s.v. "πιότης," 814; LSJ, s.v. "πιότης," 1406. In the LXX, metaphorically of abundance or wealth (Gen. 27:28, 39; Job 36:16; Ps. 35:9 [36:8 EVV]), of oil (Judg. 9:9), fatness on the altar (1 Kings 13:3, 5), fattiness (Pss. 62:6 [63:5 EVV]; 64:12 [65:11 EVV]; Ezek. 25:4).
73. As the very title "Christ" implies, *messiah* means "anointed one."
74. See Fee, *GEP*, 747, for a structural analysis.
75. Paul has already prayed for the Philippians to overflow with more love without stressing an object, indicating it is inclusive of unbelievers (1:9–10). Such love motivates the Roman Christians sharing Christ (1:16). As Gorman says, "Such love for those outside will be consistent with the love of God revealed in the cross of Jesus, embodied imaginatively in Paul's own missional activity, and taught now by the Spirit." Gorman, *BGPPM*, 97.
76. "The Spirit who operates in the Church produces *koinōnia*, fellowship expressed in affection and compassion." Gorman, *CPNSC*, 255.

toward Timothy when he returns, as they welcome back Epaphroditus, as they give to needs such as they did formerly in the Jerusalem collection (cf. 2 Cor. 8:1–5), and toward the Christians of Thessalonica (cf. 1 Thess. 1:6–7). It must also be exhibited as they contend for the faith of the gospel and hold forth the word of life[77] toward unbelievers, including their enemies (Phil. 1:27–28; 2:15–16; 4:5a). Such attitudes have shaped them in their past, and Paul's joy will be complete when they do so again.[78]

Romans 15:9–12

Paul here cites a catena of four OT passages that are now being fulfilled as Gentiles praise and sing to God's name,[79] rejoice with God's people Israel (Rom. 15:10//Deut. 32:43), and yield allegiance to, and hope in, the descendent of Jesse (Rom. 15:12//Isa. 11:10). This further justifies Paul's call to bear with, please, build up, and welcome one another, and to glorify God in unity in 15:1–7.

Romans 15:27

In telling the Romans of his missional plans, Paul recounts how he is going to Jerusalem with a material expression of his service to the believers (Rom. 15:25). He recounts how the churches of Macedonia and Achaia were pleased to participate in the collection for the poor among the Jerusalem holy people (saints) (v. 26). Then Paul refers to the Gentiles having "shared [aor. κοινωνέω] in their [the Jewish saints] spiritual things [plur. πνευματικός]."[80] Paul does

---

77. Keown, *Congregational*, 125–47; Keown, "Holding Forth the Word of Life," in *Holding Forth the Word of Life: Essays in Honor of Tim Meadowcroft*, eds. John de Jong and Csila Saysell (Eugene, OR: Wipf & Stock, 2020), 98–117; Keown, *Philippians*, 1:486–502; Fee, *Philippians*, 248–50; G. W. Murray, "Paul's Corporate Witness in Philippians," *BSac* 155 (1998): 322–23; James P. Ware, *The Mission of the Church in Paul's Letter to the Philippians in the Context of Ancient Judaism*, NovTSup 120 (Leiden: Brill, 2005), 269–70.

78. I find Fee's discussion of this passage frustrating. He is unsure whether the "if" clauses focus on the work of Christ and the Spirit, the Philippians' common life together in Christ and by the Spirit, or their relationship with Paul. Fee, *GEP*, 749. To me, this is a redundant discussion as all are working together as my analysis above demonstrates. There is no need to decide between the three. Furthermore, it neglects the fourth missional dimension—these things are for the world and so become motivation for mission.

79. Rom. 15:9//2 Sam. 22:50; Ps. 18:49; Rom. 15:11//Ps. 117:1.

80. On πνευματικός, see the discussion in Fee, *GEP*, 28–31. He correctly writes, "There is not a single instance in Paul where this word refers to the human 'spirit' and has to do with 'spiritual life,' as this word is most often understood in modern English. For Paul it is an adjective that primarily refers to the Spirit of God, even when the contrasts are to 'earthly' bodies and 'material support'" (p. 32). My research suggests that πνευματικός is not used in the LXX and is used by Paul of spiritual gifts (Rom. 1:11; 1 Cor. 12:1; 14:1), the law being spiritual (Rom. 7:14), spiritual blessings (Rom. 15:27; Eph. 1:3), spiritual truths (1 Cor. 2:13), spiritual people (people imbued with the Spirit, 1 Cor. 2:13, 15; 3:1; 14:37; Gal. 6:1), spiritual things (1 Cor. 9:11), spiritual food (provided by Christ, 1 Cor. 10:3), a spiritual (resurrection) body (1 Cor. 15:44, 46), spiritual songs (Eph. 5:19; Col. 3:16), and negatively of the spiritual forces of evil (Eph. 6:12). See also Dunn, *Jesus and the Spirit*, 208, who recognizes a similar range.

not specify what he means by this, but at the heart of this must be Jesus himself and his Father. Other things he also has in view include the Spirit and the multiple blessings received by faith that he has expounded throughout Romans. As such, he believes the nations should respond to what they have received spiritually with material generosity (κοινωνία) to the Jewish believers. The "spiritual blessings," as the word πνευματικός implies, are received through the πνεῦμα of God and Christ.[81]

1 Corinthians 9:23

As Paul defends his apostolicity and his choice to be self-supporting in his mission rather than burden his converts and allow them to use him in their political games, he speaks of his missional strategy of adapting his behavior in different cultural settings to win as many people as possible to Christ. In this verse, he culminates the section by stating, "I do all this because of the gospel, so that I may share (συγκοινωνός) in it." Paul here has in view sharing in the many blessings of the gospel including being a part of God's people in Christ.

1 Corinthians 10:16

While Paul accepts the legitimacy of a Christian eating food sacrificed to idols (1 Cor. 8:1–8), he repudiates the idea of their attendance at idolatrous meals, urging them, in this case, to "flee from idolatry" (1 Cor. 10:14). In his refutation, he compares dining at these feasts with communion. Wanting them to judge for themselves (v. 15), in v. 16, Paul rhetorically asks, "The cup of blessing that we bless, is it not a participation [κοινωνία] in the blood of Christ?" Similarly, the bread that is broken is "a participation [κοινωνία] in the body of Christ." Paul here clearly refers to a cup of wine and bread shared at the Lord's Supper, which he will discuss again in more depth in 11:17–34.

Whether one takes the blood and body in a literal sense (transubstantiation), in coexistence in union (consubstantiation), spiritually, or symbolically, the participation Paul envisages implies the work of the Spirit connecting the believer to Christ and the redemptive benefits of his death. The many believers who make up the body of Christ all partake or share of the one loaf (v. 17). The uniqueness and sacredness of the Christian meal of blessing means believers must not partake in idol feasts celebrating the deity of and eating sacrifices made to demons (vv. 19–21). The mention of demons demonstrates the spiritual nature of such religious feasts for Paul, and Christians are exclusively set

---

81. While it can be argued that 1 Corinthians 9:23 refers to Paul sharing in the blessings of the gospel and, hence, the spiritual blessings it conveys (cf. ESV, NIV; C. K. Barrett, *The First Epistle to the Corinthians*, BNTC [New York: Harper & Row, 1968], 216), this is foreign to the context and theologically unlikely. Rather, Paul is likely meaning "for the sake of the *progress* of the gospel." Gordon D. Fee, *The First Epistle to the Corinthians*, rev. ed., NICNT (Grand Rapids: Eerdmans, 2014), 477.

aside by the Spirit for Christ.[82] As in 1 Corinthians 6:15–17, this relationship is sacrosanct and must not be adulterated.

FELLOW CITIZENS OF HEAVEN AND GOD'S KINGDOM

Citizenship was a critical notion in the Roman world. The status of Roman citizenship was much sought after and used in Rome to afford honor. The converse status, slavery, was not prized, with emancipation a hope for most, if not all, slaves. While Paul does not use citizenship language often or mention his own Roman citizenship, he makes it clear that at the moment of conversion, the convert is moved from a state of slavery to a fully-fledged citizen of God's kingdom and heaven. By the Spirit, believers are to grow in terms of living in a manner worthy of this status, in terms of their worship and ethics, and engage in the mission of declaring the lordship of Christ to the world.

Ephesians 2:19

In Ephesians 2:11–21, Paul speaks of the inclusion of faithful Gentiles into God's people alongside faithful Jews. In their pre-conversion, sinful states, they were "alienated from the citizenship (πολιτεία) of Israel." The term has a range of nuances, all related to being a citizen of a particular sociopolitical entity.[83] Here, the entity is Israel. Previously, Gentiles were not included in Israel's people and had no understanding of the covenants, Israel's eschatological hopes, or allegiance to God (2:12). Now, due to the work of Christ, both Jews and Gentiles are "fellow citizens (συμπολίτης) with the saints and members of the household of God." "Saints" here speaks of other Christians,[84] as does "members of God's household."[85] Christians then have full status in the new sociopolitical entity formed in Christ. They are being formed into a temple of God.

1 Corinthians 7:22

In 1 Corinthians 7:17–24, consistent with a rule he applies to all his churches, Paul urges the Corinthians to remain in the life station they held when they became believers. His view on this may be derived from his understanding of God, by the Spirit, shaping a person's life from conception, including their vocational station. They should leave their life stations only when guided by God circumstantially (indicating the Spirit's guidance in life) or through divine call and guidance.

---

82. It is possible Philippians 1:6 refers to the Philippians' participation in the grace that indicates the blessing of the gospel. However, in context, it likely refers to their participation with the grace of Paul's mission. See Keown, *Congregational*, 216–23.

83. See Hermann Strathmann, "Πόλις, Πολίτης, Πολιτεύομαι, Πολιτεία, Πολίτευμα," *TDNT* 6:519.

84. Thielman, *Ephesians*, 179.

85. Fee notes this shift from citizenship to household is typical (both are political ideas). He also observes the rapid-fire shifts of metaphor here: citizens-household members-building-temple. Fee, *GEP*, 686.

As having a foreskin means little, the circumcised should not seek epispasm, nor should the uncircumcised be circumcised (cf. Gal. 5:6; 6:15). Slaves need not be concerned about their status, although if freedom is offered them, they should take it. Their citizen/noncitizen status is of little consequence to Paul, as the slave called by the Lord is a freedman (ἀπελεύθερος) of the Lord. For Paul, a called person has not only heard the gospel but also believed its message. Hence, all Christians are declared citizens of Christ. They are citizens of the kingdom. They are free—not to sin, but to serve in love (Gal. 5:13).

Elsewhere, Paul speaks of believers in their former states as slaves to sin (Rom. 6:6, 16–17, 20), immorality and lawlessness (Rom. 6:19), the law (Rom. 7:25; cf. Gal. 2:4; 4:24–25; 5:1), fear (Rom. 8:15), decay (Rom. 8:21), their stomachs (Rom. 16:18),[86] the elemental powers (Gal. 4:3), false gods (Gal. 4:8–9), excessive wine (Titus 2:3), and various desires and pleasures (Titus 3:3). Now, due to the death of Jesus, who took the form of a slave and became obedient to death on a cross (Phil. 2:8), they have a new master, Jesus Christ the κύριος.[87] He sets them free from these things, and they should not return to slavery.

Here, in 1 Corinthians 7:22, Paul goes on to add that those who are free at the time of conversion are slaves of Christ, to remind the Corinthians of the essence of their commitment as citizens of the Lord—service of their "political" master. In v. 23, he reminds them they were bought with a price, referring to the redemption achieved through the death of Christ. He urges them not to become slaves of people. This instruction could be literal, telling Corinthian citizens not to sell themselves into slavery. More likely, consistent with the many appeals to restrain from engagement in the vices of their society, it is an appeal not to enslave themselves to the sinful habits of their world.[88] He concludes by restating the essential principle that converts should remain in their life station at their conversion.

Philippians 1:27

The first direct appeal of the letter to the Philippians urges the readers to live as citizens (πολιτεύομαι) worthy of the gospel of Christ. As Philippi was a proud Roman colony, the citizenship language was provocative. By using the verb πολιτεύομαι, Paul is tacitly encouraging the Philippians that whether they are slave or free, they have the same citizen status in God's kingdom. Their names have been inscribed in the book listing those with membership

---

86. The stomach here is metonymy for the desire for satiation of the body.
87. κύριος is used fifteen times in Philippians, perhaps emphasizing this shift of status (Phil. 1:2, 14; 2:11, 19, 24, 29; 3:1, 8, 20; 4:1, 2, 4, 5, 10, 23).
88. Fee, *The First Epistle*, 561. Alternatively, it is a double entendre involving both physical and spiritual slavery. See S. S. Bartchy, Μᾶλλον χρῆσαι: *First-Century Slavery and the Interpretation of 1 Cor. 7:21*, SBLDS 11 (Missoula, MT: Scholars Press, 1973), 121–25.

in God's *polis* and *politeuma*, the "book of life" (Phil. 4:3). This occurred at their conversion.

As citizens of God, they are to stand firm in one πνεῦμα. While this idea of one spirit can speak of the unified corporate spirit of the church, the parallel στήκετε ἐν κυρίῳ in Philippians 4:1 and the κοινωνία πνεύματος in Philippians 2:1 suggest Paul has the Holy Spirit in mind.[89] As such, as citizens, through the work of the Spirit, they are to stand firm together as one. The verb στήκω is a military term evoking images of the Macedonians and Romans defending and advancing their great empires in phalanx formations, the maniples, cohorts, and legions. Citizens gained status in war. Paul, then, is summoning the Philippians to recognize their status as citizens, live in a manner worthy of their calling, and in and by the Spirit,[90] stand firm as they defend and advance the gospel.

He then shifts the metaphor to athletics, another essential aspect of Greco-Roman society and another vehicle for gaining status. The Philippians are to be united as one (lit. "one-souled," μιᾷ ψυχῇ) and athletically contend "together" (συναθλέω) for the faith of the gospel. The phrase μιᾷ ψυχῇ implies the same unity in the Spirit in the chiastically balancing ἑνὶ πνεύματι.[91] Similarly, συναθλοῦντες τῇ πίστει τοῦ εὐαγγελίου chiastically balances στήκετε. The Philippian citizens of heaven are to stand firm like faithful soldiers. However, they do so with the mindset of athletes, together defending and advancing the gospel.

Philippians 1:27–2:4 is chiastically balanced with 2:12–18a, the Christ-hymn nestled in its center. Implicitly, Philippians 2:13 emphasizes the work of the Spirit in enabling the Philippians to work out their own salvation with fear and trembling. The Spirit enables them to cease grumbling and arguing, shine as lights of the world in fallen Macedonia, and hold forth the word of life.[92] The Spirit summons believers into heavenly citizenship, empowers them to live righteously and blamelessly, and energizes them for the mission.

Philippians 3:20

There are some indications that Philippians 3:20–4:3 is intentionally balanced with 1:27–30.[93] In Philippians 3:17, Paul restates his desire that the Philippians imitate his attitude of self-renunciation, form a deeper relationship with and reliance on Christ, participate in Christ's suffering and death, and press on to receive eternal life. The Philippians are together to imitate Paul and set their focus on others who emulate the Christ pattern—Timothy

---

89. Similarly, see Fee, *GEP*, 744–46, for other arguments.
90. See chapter 2, "Baptized in the Spirit."
91. On whether this is the corporate spirit of the church or the Spirit, see Fee, *GEP*, 744–46; Keown, *Philippians*, 1:290–93.
92. On "hold forth," see "The Fellowship of the Holy Spirit," earlier in this chapter.
93. These include the repetition of the language of citizenship, standing in (and by) one Spirit/in the Lord (see "Baptized in the Spirit," chapter 2), contending, opponents, and unity.

and Epaphroditus at the forefront, both of whom are exemplary heavenly citizens (Phil. 2:19–30).

Paul then refers to the enemies of the cross of Christ, those who are not citizens of heaven but are enslaved to living to satisfy their bodily desires, who delight in their shameful living, who are not focused on the things of heaven but on material things, and whose destinies are destruction.[94] Refusing to confess Jesus is Lord and bend their knee to him, they oppose the idea of a crucified Messiah. Consequently, their names are not inscribed on the scroll of life.

Conversely, having believed in Jesus, confessed him as Lord, and bowed in allegiance to God the Son, Savior, and Lord, the Philippians, and indeed all Christians, have their citizenship (πολίτευμα) in heaven. While πολίτευμα is slippery with a range of possible translations, it clearly implies that they are citizens of heaven (indicating this is what Paul means in Phil. 1:27).[95] From there, believers—remaining on earth, standing and contending for the faith of the gospel, united in the Spirit—await Jesus the Christ, their Lord, and, now that he has died for the sins of the world, their Savior. This passage speaks of Christ's return, at which time, by his immense power enabling him to subjugate every enemy to himself, the believers' bodies beset with the humiliation of suffering, decay, and destined for death will be transformed to be like his glorious body.

Accordingly, the Philippians, whom Paul dotes and glories over, are to stand firm in their heavenly citizenship. They are to "stand firm in the Lord," which re-expresses "stand firm in one Spirit" (1:27).[96] Euodia and Syntyche must end their vying for honor and be united in the Lord and engage with Clement, Epaphroditus, and other coworkers in the mission of the gospel, as they have done in former times. True pneumaformity results in unity and mission. Like all heavenly citizens, these coworkers have their names inscribed in the scroll of those promised eternal life.

The injunctions that follow in Philippians 4:4–9 are not disconnected from Paul's desire for unity in 4:2–3.[97] As heavenly citizens, whose names are in God's book of the eternally living, they are to embody aspects of life that the Spirit will generate in them. By his power, they will work out their salvation and shine like lights in a dark world by together rejoicing in the Lord always (2:15–16), letting their reasonableness be evident to believers and

---

94. In Keown, *Congregational Evangelism*, 61–62, I argued this is a general term for all who oppose the gospel. In more recent publications, I argue that these are Gentile licentious opponents. See Mark J. Keown, "Paul's Answer to the Threats of Jerusalem and Rome," in *The Gospel in the Land of Promise: Christian Approaches to the Land of Promise*, 2:248-66, eds. Philip Church, Peter Walker, Tim Bulkeley, and Tim Meadowcroft (Eugene, OR: Pickwick, 2011), 28–45; Keown, *Philippians*, 248–66.

95. On possibilities see Keown, *Philippians*, 1:268–70.

96. That this is the Spirit of God and not the human Spirit is clear from 2:1 (fellowship in the Spirit), and the parallel 4:1, "stand firm in the Lord." See Fee, *GEP*, 743–46; Keown, *Philippians*, 1:290–93.

97. See my discussion in Keown, *Philippians*, 2:330.

unbelievers alike (4:4), and praying to the Lord, who is near, and experiencing God's peace and protection (4:5b–7). Unlike the enemies, whose minds are on earthly things, they are to ponder the good and beautiful things of God, his Son, his Spirit, and his world, and to emulate Paul's example in their lives while experiencing God's peace (4:8–9). Such Spirit-generated fruit are marks of those made heavenly citizens by God, in Christ, and by the Spirit. Their concern for reconciliation will spill over into a concern to see creation itself coming into the fullness of reconciliation (societal transformation and ecomission).[98]

MUTUAL PRESENCE BY THE SPIRIT

Much could be written about 1 Corinthians 5 concerning Paul's response to the man engaging in incestuous sexual relations with his father's wife and the arrogance of the church. In the chapter, Paul calls for the Corinthians to remove the man from the church so that he may turn from fleshly living to the way of the Spirit and be saved.

My interest here, however, is Paul's first use of πνεῦμα in 1 Corinthians 5:3–5 and its implications for how God's people are bound together in the Spirit. After stating the nature of the issue in vv. 1–2, Paul makes his judgment. He writes,

> For I—on the one hand, though absent in body, on the other hand, am present in the Spirit [τῷ πνεύματι]—have already made judgment as present having accomplished this in this way, in the name of our Lord Jesus, when you and my spirit [τοῦ ἐμοῦ πνεύματος] gather with the power of our Lord Jesus, hand this man over to Satan for the destruction of the flesh [τῆς σαρκός], so that the spirit [τὸ πνεῦμα] might be saved on the day of our Lord. (translation mine)

Πνεῦμα is used three times. The first and second uses are clearly references to Paul's spirit, as the pronoun ἐμοῦ indicates. The third use is fascinating. The handing over of the man to Satan indicates his excommunication from the temple of God's Spirit into the pagan world that remains under the power of the evil one.[99] While τὸ πνεῦμα can be God's Spirit, Paul can hardly want to see God's spirit saved when Jesus returns in judgment. Neither is it likely that Paul is hoping for a purely spiritual salvation of the man in question, as Paul argues against such ideas in 1 Corinthians 15. Most likely, then, Paul is using σαρκός and πνεῦμα in antithesis, wanting the effect of his

---

98. For a short account of my views on the ecological implications of Paul's theology, see Mark J. Keown, "The Apostolic Green Imperative," in *Living on the Planet Earth: Faith Communities and Ecology*, ed. Neil Darragh (Auckland: Accent, 2016), 33–39. See also Keown, *Romans and the Mission of God*, 259–68.
99. Fee, *GEP*, 126: "to turn him back out into Satan's sphere."

expulsion to see him turn away from the work of the flesh (incest) to the life of the Spirit and, ultimately, his complete salvation.[100]

Returning to the first use of πνεῦμα here, with Paul writing from Ephesus, this may refer to Paul's presence in Corinth through his emissaries or letter. Alternatively, he is present "with them in spirit" or "you are in my thoughts,"[101] so to speak. However, because Paul carefully avoids the personal pronoun ἐμοῦ here, he likely means he is present with them "in" or "by the Spirit [of God]."[102] Paul is saying that he is present with them in and by God's Spirit, that he is together with them. Also present is the "power of our Lord Jesus" (v. 4), which is another way of expressing the presence of the Spirit.[103]

The idea of Christians fused together by the Spirit across distances[104] is another aspect of the omnipresent Spirit binding believers together. This bonding is also, of course, an intimation of the "body of Christ" metaphor. Further, the intimate spiritual bond of believers to Jesus is stated in 1 Corinthians 6:17.[105] Additionally, in that both individuals (6:19) and all believers in a church are collectively the "temple of the Spirit," and in that the Spirit is omnipresent, one can surmise such an interconnectedness. However, what is implied in such things is explicit here. Paul and the Corinthians being bound by the Spirit so that Paul's spirit can be present with them in such a way indicates that all living Christians in the world at any one time are bound together as one in the ubiquitous Spirit of Jesus. Believers are not merely saved into individual salvation or even just into a local body of Christ; they are fused with other believers in and by the Spirit. Such an insight reinforces the point this chapter is making. When we receive the

---

100. Fee, *GEP*, 126–27: "In this case, 'flesh' and 'spirit' each 'designates' the whole person as viewed from different angles. 'Spirit' means the whole person as oriented towards God. 'Flesh' means the whole person as oriented away from God. The 'destruction' of one's 'flesh' would thus belong to the same kind of imagery as in 'crucifying' it (Gal. 5:24; cf. Rom. 7:5–6); the salvation of 'his spirit' is therefore a basically anthropological expression, very much as in 2 Cor. 7:13: 'his spirit was refreshed,' meaning 'he' was refreshed. So also here, Paul simply means that 'he' will be saved; he expresses it in this more unusual way because of the preceding language 'flesh.'" He adds, "Paul does not intend that he must wait until the final Day to be saved. Rather this is one of Paul's ordinary ways of expressing salvation. Salvation is primarily an eschatological reality, experienced in the present to be sure, but to be realized fully at the day of the Lord" (p. 127).

101. Fee, *GEP*, 123. Fee is right to reject this, as it is anachronistic to place a contemporary idiom into this text.

102. Similarly, Fee, *GEP*, 123–24. While his first two reasons given are weak, he rightfully notes that ὡς παρών, "as present," speaks of his actual presence with them and that Paul states "when you and my spirit gather" in v. 4.

103. Fee, *GEP*, 126. "The term 'power' in a context like this is almost certainly a further reference to the Spirit, who is dynamically present among them when they are assembled together."

104. Ancient Ephesus was about 500 kilometers by sea and land from ancient Corinth.

105. See earlier, chapter 3, "One Spirit with the Lord." Fee writes, "In light of vv. 19–20, Paul's primary referent is to the work of the Holy Spirit, whereby through the 'one Spirit' the believer's 'spirit' has been joined indissolubly with Christ. Thus, by the Spirit the believer is united to the Lord and thereby has become one S/spirit with him." Fee, *GEP*, 133.

Spirit of God, we become one people not just because we share the same belief system but because we're entwined and fused (umbilically, one might say) in Christ and God by the Spirit.

CONCLUSION

The Spirit brings people into God's kingdom. Its king is Jesus Christ, their Lord and their Savior. Its capital is heaven, from where Jesus reigns. When they hear the gospel and confess Jesus is Lord and bend their knee in allegiance to him, people are reconciled to God and one another. They welcome and accept each other because they have been adopted as God's children. With the faithful of salvation history, they form one multicultural people of God. In and by the Spirit, individually and collectively, locally and internationally, with other believers they are God's tabernacle and temple in which God and Christ dwell by the Spirit.

Although unique in their identities and mix of gifts, they are incorporated into Christ's body as members, intertwined with other believers. As God's people, they experience familial fellowship with God, Jesus, and other believers. With these siblings in Christ, they are citizens of God's kingdom. There is no status inequality amongst them, even if some are set apart as leaders. The church's shared vocation is to serve, emulating the example of Christ in his service, suffering, and sacrifice to the point of death. As citizens, their code of living is the gospel, which shapes their worship, relationships, and mission. Their initiation as Christians is merely the beginning of their pneumaformation, whereby the Spirit shapes them to be more and more like Jesus in their individuality and, arguably more importantly, in Spirit-impelled partnership with others.

CHAPTER 5

THE SPIRIT AND WORSHIP

Thus far, it has been established that the Spirit is active in the world, summoning people to become believers. Sovereignly, through the creation and his work in history, and as believers share the gospel with others, people are invited into a saving relationship with him by faith. Some believe and are "the called" or "the elect." At the instant of conversion, the Spirit of God, in and through his Son, enters believers, filling them and baptizing them. The Spirit participates in their justification as they are declared righteous. They receive this Spirit, drinking of God's being. The Spirit unites them with God the Father and his Son. Believers are liberated from bondage to the powers of the age, from sin, and from its consequences. The Spirit is a guarantee by whom they are sealed for redemption. Their hearts are circumcised. They are declared holy saints of the most high God. They are truly alive for the first time, with the resurrection power of God in their beings. They are born again as new creations to live forever in the renewed cosmos. The law is inscribed on their hearts.

In the last chapter, we saw how the Spirit integrates people into God's people. They are reconciled to God and welcomed into his presence by the Spirit. God adopts them as his children, promising them a shared inheritance with Christ after their suffering and service. They are part of God's people from all history with a faith like Abraham's. Together they become part of the body of Christ. They experience fellowship with the Spirit and are integrated into the temple of God, built on the foundation of apostles and prophets. Having yielded to Jesus Christ the Lord, they are declared citizens of God's kingdom.

However, all this is just the beginning. Their pneumaformation continues as the Spirit works in them to transform them from the inside out. As they yield daily to God and his Son, the Spirit works to transform their characters. The Spirit is the agent of Christoformity, as believers are transformed to be more and more like Jesus. They are increasingly cruciform, as they take on his attributes of love, humility, service, sacrifice, and suffering until death. They become resurrectiform as their lives increasingly conform to the worship and ethics of the eschaton in this present age. God changes those in Christ by the power of the Spirit so that they are increasingly theoform. One dimension of this is pneumatologically enabled worship,[1] which I will now consider.

WORSHIP IN AND BY THE SPIRIT

Worship responds to God's gospel and the Spirit's work. God's one people and temple give themselves up in service, present a pleasing odor to the Lord, and approach God's throne.

Philippians 3:3b–c

The central parts of Philippians 3:3 are important concerning the Spirit's role in worship. It refers to οἱ πνεύματι θεοῦ λατρεύοντες καὶ καυχώμενοι ἐν Χριστῷ Ἰησοῦ, "the ones who worship God in [and by] the Spirit and boast in Christ Jesus." In context, Paul is asserting that neither Jews in disbelief of Christ nor Judaizers who demand law allegiance are those who "worship in Spirit and in truth" (as John might put it, John 4:24).[2] Instead, it is Christians, including Paul's team and all others who yield to Jesus as Lord. Christians, whether Jews or Gentiles, are able to worship God because of the Spirit. It is those whose hearts are circumcised by the Spirit, not those merely circumcised outwardly, who are the true worshipers. The dative πνεύματι can be a marker of sphere (condition or state, "in the Spirit") or instrument or means ("by/with the Spirit"). Deciding between these two here is problematic.

Paul uses ἐν πνεύματι seventeen times. In Romans 8:9, it is clearly a marker of a state or condition whereby believers live "in the Spirit" rather than "in the flesh." Similarly, in Colossians 1:8, Epaphras has told Paul and his team of the Colossians' love "in the Spirit."[3] Romans 14:17 is also locative, with believers living in the sphere of God's righteousness, peace, and joy. Still, it is also "by the Spirit" that they experience these things. It also possibly includes the sense of Ephesians 2:22, where believers in Christ are being "built up together into a dwelling place of God in the Spirit" (LEB). However, they could be being built up "by the Spirit."[4]

However, the majority of Paul's uses of ἐν πνεύματι are instrumental or speak of agency, "by the Spirit" or "with the Spirit."[5] Christ was vindicated

---

1.   Liston, *Kingdom Come*, 150–54.

2.   On πνεῦμα as the Holy Spirit in John 4:24, see Andreas J. Köstenberger, *John*, BECNT (Grand Rapids: Baker Academic, 2004), 157.

3.   Fee discusses the object of their love. Possibilities include all the saints (v. 4), Paul himself (which Fee favors, *GEP*, 639), and others beyond the orb of the church (also acknowledged by Fee). Likely, Paul does not state the object as all are in view—they are a loving church. Their love is generated by the Spirit in which they now exist.

4.   The two ideas are bound together, and sometimes Paul emphasizes the instrumental but mostly uses the sphere which incorporates the instrumental. See chapter 2, "Baptized in the Spirit."

5.   Based on τὸ πνεῦμά μου in 1 Corinthians 14:14, the uses of [ἐν] πνεύματι and the datives πνεύματι in 1 Corinthians 14:15–16 probably refer to the spirits of people rather than the Holy Spirit (similarly

by the Spirit (who raised him, 1 Tim. 3:16).[6] In 2 Corinthians 3:3, the phrase connotes the means by which the Corinthian church is a letter inscribed with the [ink of] the Spirit. People are circumcised in heart "by the Spirit" (Rom. 2:29); are washed, sanctified, and justified by the Spirit (Rom. 15:16; 1 Cor. 6:11); and their Christian lives and pneumaformation is begun by the Spirit (Gal. 3:3). They are filled by the Spirit (Eph. 5:18), live by the Spirit (Gal. 5:16, 25), and led by the Spirit (Rom. 8:14; Gal. 5:18). As they live in Christ, by the Spirit they put to death the misdeeds of the body (Rom. 8:13), their consciences bear witness to the truth in (and by) the Spirit (Rom. 9:1), they are taught in words by the Spirit (1 Cor. 2:13), they speak by the Spirit (1 Cor. 12:3; 14:2; 1 Thess. 1:5), they minister by the Spirit (2 Cor. 6:6), and things are revealed to them by the Spirit (Eph. 3:5).[7]

Here, in Philippians 3:3 (and Ephesians 6:18), both senses work equally well, and we should probably not decide between them. Believers "in (and by) the Spirit" worship God. Yet, equally, they worship God "by the Spirit." As such, at least in this instance, the two are closely related, for believers are "in the Spirit" and "the Spirit is in them"; hence, both are realities. In and by the Spirit, believers worship God.[8] The verb λατρεύω has a semantic range from "serve" to "offer worship to God."[9] Here, it may be the latter in view, as Paul next talks about "boasting in Christ Jesus" (LEB). Still, serving God as an act of worship is in view.[10] As Dunn puts it, "Worship was no longer a matter of obligation and requirement, but a *spontaneous* urge to praise God."[11]

The object of worship is not specified. Still, the Spirit of God is God-facing (Rom. 8:26–27), so God must be in view. Yet, that does not exhaust the context; those who worship by and in the Spirit of God are also "boasting in Christ Jesus." While "in Christ Jesus" can be locative, and it most likely is, here it also speaks of Jesus as the object of Christian boasting. In the Spirit, believ-

---

the use of νοῦς μου in v. 14, which means we should translate the two datives τῷ νοΐ τῷ νοΐ as "the minds of people"). Similarly, ἐν πνεύματι πραΰτητος may indicate a "with a gentle spirit." See also Fee, *GEP*, 229; Keown, *Galatians*, 696–99.

6. On 1 Timothy 3:16, see Fee, *GEP*, 762–68. Against Fee, the most natural interpretation of ἐδικαιώθη ἐν πνεύματι ("vindicated in the Spirit") refers to the Spirit raising Jesus from the dead. Fee prefers that this refers to Christ's earthly ministry. However, the previous clause speaks of his life in the flesh. I find Fee's attempt to explain the clause as "the supernatural realm of existence" strange. If I am correct, against Fee, the emphasis of ἐν πνεύματι is instrumental and δικαιόω is used in the sense, "to render a favorable verdict, vindicate" (BDAG, s.v. "δικαιόω," 249).

7. See chapter 2, "Baptized in the Spirit."

8. Fee prefers the instrumental view. *GEP*, 753.

9. BDAG, s.v. "λατρεύω," 587; Keown, *Philippians*, 2:151.

10. Fee, *GEP*, 752, rightly warns that "worship" can be misleading. He avers that it was used particularly for cultic religious duty. Further, in Romans 1:9 and 12:1, service is more clearly in view. He also notes that the service of circumcision is now redundant, and it is believers who perform appropriate "ritual service . . . in the realm of the Spirit." I would respond by agreeing but argue by analogy that this extends to all forms of service and worship (gathered or otherwise). Where there is faith, those people are God's people, and worship and serve him in and by the Spirit.

11. Dunn, *Jesus and the Spirit*, 223.

ers worship God and boast in and about Jesus Christ. For Paul, to authentically boast is to boast in the Lord.[12] As such, believers worship God and his Son by the power of the Spirit.

Romans 12:1

Romans 12:2 will be discussed in the next chapter concerning God's forming people into the image of his Son with renewed minds that have renounced conformity to this present age. Romans 12:1 is a critical verse, providing the beginning of Paul's paraenetic section that describes what it looks like to be so conformed. The οὖν (therefore) and διὰ τῶν οἰκτιρμῶν τοῦ θεοῦ (because of the mercies of God) indicate that Paul is drawing out inferences from his glorious exposition of the gospel and God's mercies up to this point in the letter.

He urges the Roman brothers and sisters (παρακαλῶ . . . ὑμᾶς, ἀδελφοί) to "present [their] bodies as a living sacrifice, holy and pleasing to God" (LEB). This appeal summons them to give themselves entirely to God's service. The use of "bodies" may be intentional, to link them to the One who gave his "body" in service, suffering, and death to save them.[13] They are to be conformed in a manner holy and pleasing (or acceptable) to God. In their use of their bodies and whole beings, they are to serve God under his will. Doing so is the Romans' τὴν λογικὴν λατρείαν.

Aside from this use,[14] Paul uses λατρε - language fourteen times. Nine times he uses the language in his repudiations of idolatry and idolaters, who will not inherit the kingdom of God.[15] Aside from λατρεία here, Paul uses it in passages that will be discussed below. It carries the dual notion of worship and service.

The choice of λογικός is intriguing. The term is absent from the LXX but was used widely among Greek philosophers and Philo and indicates careful thought, and so, "thoughtful."[16] In Testament of Levi 3:3, archangels "serve and offer propitiatory sacrifices to God for the sins of ignorance of the righteous ones. They present to the Lord a pleasing odor, a rational (λογικὴν) and bloodless oblation."[17] Philo uses the term 163 times, always with the sense of reason and rationality.[18] The only other NT mention is 1 Peter 2:2, where it

---

12. 1 Sam. 2:10 LXX; Jer. 9:24; 1 Cor. 1:31; 2 Cor. 10:17; Gal. 6:14.

13. While Fee does note the sacrificial connection, he does not explicitly mention Christ's sacrifice in terms of this view. Fee, *GEP*, 588–89. To me the link is obvious—we are being conformed to the image of the one who gave himself as a living sacrifice for the world.

14. Outside of Paul: worship or service to God (Matt. 4:10; Luke 1:74; 2:37; 4:8; 16:2; Acts 7:7; 24:14; 26:7; 27:23; Heb. 9:1, 6, 9, 14; 10:2; 12:28; 13:10; Rev. 21:8; 22:3), false worship and idolatry (Acts 7:42; 1 Pet. 4:3; Rev. 22:15), service of the law (Heb. 8:5).

15. See Rom. 1:9; 1 Cor. 5:10–11; 6:9; 10:7, 14; Gal. 5:20; Eph. 5:5; Col. 3:5. He also uses it of temple service in Israel's religious tradition (Rom. 9:4).

16. BDAG, s.v. "λογικός," 598.

17. Translation James H. Charlesworth, *The Old Testament Pseudepigrapha*, 2 vols. (New Haven, CT: Yale University Press, 1983).

18. For example, reason (*Opif.* 77, 153; *Leg.* 2.22) and reasoning (*Leg.* 1.57, 71; 2.45), rational life (*Opif.* 119), a rational soul (*Opif.* 137; cf. *Leg.* 1.41) or the rational part of the soul (*Leg.* 1.70–72; 2.2),

refers to pure rational milk. While the term is regularly translated as "spiritual," and its use in Paul and Peter is not divorced from spiritual matters (in a world where the sacred and secular are fused), "spiritual" does not capture its meaning.[19] Instead, it has the sense of "thoughtful,"[20] or as I propose, "*reasoned worship*." It goes without saying that for Paul, this worship is Christ-informed. Just as Christ gave himself for the world, believers do the same. This response is the gospel-informed (*logos*-informed) and Spirit-informed worship of God. Romans 12:2 indicates that this worship involves worldly minds renewed by the gospel by the Spirit. Paul here is speaking of renewal by the wisdom of God centered on Jesus and him crucified. This wisdom defies that of the world referred to frequently in 1 Corinthians 1–4.[21] In a sense, what follows speaks of the Spirit of wisdom that imbues the Messiah (cf. Isa. 11:2; 1 Cor. 1:30) and in which believers share.[22]

Romans 1:9 and 2 Timothy 1:3

In Romans 1:9, Paul uses λατρεύω in its broader sense of "service" concerning his mission. Paul is no idolator.[23] Instead, he worships God through his service. His service is "in my spirit" (ἐν τῷ πνεύματί μου), which is clearly not the Holy Spirit, but his inner being, which is linked to God's Spirit. The sphere of his service is "in the gospel of his Son"; hence, Paul is speaking of his intense commitment to serving God by preaching the gospel throughout the world. By stating that "God is my witness," Paul indicates that God knows of this wholehearted service, indicating the Spirit's work in connecting his inner being to God; hence, God knows Paul and his inner unction on his behalf. The implication is that the Spirit is in him, connected to his spirit, and communicating with the Father.

---

rational divine natures (*Opif.* 144), rational nature in a human (*Opif.* 149, 150), humans as reasoning beings (*Leg.* 1.10), reasoning power (*Leg.* 2.23), rational creatures or beings (*Leg.* 2.23, 75), rational parts of an animal (*Leg.* 2.58), a rational disposition (*Leg.* 3.210), a rational mind (*Det.* 22), God the archetype of the rational nature (*Det.* 83), a rational life (*Post.* 68). It is often contrasted with ἄλογος, "irrational" (*NIDNTTE* 3:128).

19. *BrillDAG*, s.v. "λογικός," suggests "spiritual," even though the vast majority of cross-references relate to reason and rationality. However, *NIDNTTE* 3:158, while defending the link to the spiritual, note that such translations "fail to bring out the cognitive element." They also consider "reasonable service" an option; however, "reasonable" for a modern does not bring out the rational aspect of the term particularly. See also Fee on λογικήν (*GEP*, 599–602). He rightly notes that "the word has nothing at all to do with the Spirit" (p. 599) and should not be translated as "spiritual" (p. 601). He opts for "reasonable," but there are a range of other options like "thoughtful, logical, intellectual, rational, reasoned."

20. BDAG, s.v. "λογικός," 598.

21. 1 Cor. 1:21, 24, 31; 2:6, 7; cf. 12:8.

22. See the link of Spirit and wisdom in Exod. 31:3; 35:31; Acts 6:3, 10; 1 Cor. 2:4, 13; 12:8.

23. Rom. 1:25; 1 Cor. 5:10, 11; 6:9; 10:7, 14; Gal. 5:20; Eph. 5:5; Col. 3:5. It is also used of those who serve in temple worship (Rom. 9:4). Important here is 1 Corinthians 10:14, where participating in idolatry is not to participate in the life of the Holy Spirit, but wrong spirits and demons. See also 1 Cor. 10:20–22.

In 2 Timothy 1:3, Paul mentions his service that he conducted with a clean conscience, as did his ancestors—the faithful among the Jewish people (cf. Rom. 9:4). An aspect of this worship is prayer (further below), which Paul constantly does for Timothy.

Ephesians 2:18

This verse sits in the context of Paul drawing out the corporate implications of salvation for Gentiles—they are now formed as one people and temple with Jewish believers in Christ. Indeed, the consequence of Jesus's mission to preach peace and reconciliation is that (ὅτι) "through him, [believers][24] have access [προσαγωγή] in [and by, ἐν] one Spirit to the Father." The noun προσαγωγή has a range of nuances, including gaining an audience with someone, bringing a sacrifice, and approaching to attack a place.[25]

Here, it speaks of gaining an audience or access to God the Father. Claiming open access to God is astonishing, considering Israel's understanding of God's holiness. For Israel, God was enthroned in the veiled inner sanctum of the tabernacle, Solomon's temple, and will be again in Ezekiel's eschatological temple, all in the "Holy of Holies."[26] Containing the ark of the covenant and mercy seat and guarded by the gold-plated cherubim, it was the meeting place of heaven and earth.[27]

Only one Israelite was permitted entry, the high priest, once a year on the Day of Atonement, and only following the strictest of protocols, or the result could be death (Lev. 16). Entry required a bull as a sin offering and a ram as a burnt offering (Lev. 16:3, 6, 11), a male goat as a scapegoat (Lev. 16:7–10), another male goat (Lev. 16:3, 7–10), and correct clothing and bathing (Lev. 16:4). The priest then sacrificed the bull as a sin offering for himself and the ram as a burnt offering for the people. Next, he took coals of fire and incense inside the veil and burned it so that the cloud covered the mercy seat to ensure he did not die and sprinkled the blood of the bull on the mercy seat as per requirements (Lev. 16:11–14). After sacrificing the goat, he then sprinkled the blood over the mercy seat in the same way (Lev. 16:15–16). This blood atoned for the sins of Israel (Lev. 16:16). After this, he released the scapegoat, symbolizing the sending of the people's sins into the wilderness (Lev. 16:20–22). Because the Babylonians stripped it, the Holy of Holies was

---

24. Fee, *GEP*, 683, argues this should be "we both together have access," drawing on "both" is used twice in the preceding sentence. While in a broad ethnic sense I agree, I prefer to not add "together" here as it is not in this sentence and approach to God can come at any time, whether together or alone.

25. For example, Arrian, *Anab.* 1.20.8; Diodorus Siculus, *Hist.* 13.46.1; Herodotus, *Hist.* 2.58; *Let. Aris.* 42; Plutarch, *Aem.* 13.3; Plutarch, *Luc.* 15.4; Polybius, *Hist.* 9.41.1; Polybius, *Hist.* 21.27.3; Xenophon, *Cyr.* 7.5.45. See further nuances *BrillDAG*, s.v. "προσᾰγωγή."

26. Of the tabernacle, see Exod. 26:33–34; on Solomon's temple, see 1 Kings 6:16; 8:6; and on Ezekiel's temple, see Ezek. 41:4; 42:13; 45:3.

27. Phillip J. Long, "Holy of Holies," *LBD*. On the Holy of Holies, see Exod. 26:31–37; 1 Kings 6:16; 7:50; 8:6; 1 Chron. 6:49; 2 Chron. 3:8–14; 4:22; 5:7; Ezek. 41:4; 45:3; Heb. 9:3–5.

empty in the Second Temple Period.[28] The Roman general Pompey entered it but did not touch anything.[29] To suggest anyone, Jew or Gentile, can approach God freely and legitimately is nigh on blasphemous in a Jewish setting.

Here, in Ephesians 2:18, believers, Jew and Gentile alike, have access to the Father in (and by) one Spirit (ἐν ἑνὶ πνεύματι).[30] It is implied that Christ's love motivates self-giving, "for us, a fragrant offering and sacrifice to God" (Eph. 5:2), and satisfies the requirements of atonement. In addition, the Spirit given to those sanctified in Christ becomes almost an entry ticket to God's presence. All believers can now approach God without the formerly required sacrifices because they are holy. Both Ephesians 3:12 and Romans 5:2 use προσαγωγή of people being allowed to do so because of their faith.

The idea of "one Spirit" is consistent with 1 Corinthians 12:13, where believers (we) are all baptized in one Spirit and given one Spirit to drink, whether Jews or Greeks, slaves or freedpeople.[31] In Ephesians and 1 Corinthians, this is undoubtedly the Holy Spirit. As with other dative constructs, this can be locative or instrumental. As discussed, while it may well be locative with believers entering the realm of the Spirit, the instrumental is implied (in and by the Spirit).[32] In what follows in Ephesians 2:19–22, Jewish and Gentile believers are being formed into one temple in which God dwells by his Spirit.

Ephesians 2:18 is critical as it shows that not only did the death of Jesus satisfy the requirements for full access to God's presence, but the Spirit is instrumental in this process. Believers are declared holy by faith and filled with God's Holy Spirit, who sanctifies them. Their status as those filled with the Spirit means that although they remain sinners and people of the flesh, God accepts them into his presence. This knowledge should give believers immense confidence to approach God in prayer (Eph. 3:12).

Ephesians 5:18–20

These verses fall in the paraenetic section of Ephesians 4:1 to 6:20, where Paul gives instructions for Christian living.[33] As the readers are now children

---

28. Josephus, *J.W.* 5.219. However, see 2 Baruch 6:7, which suggests the holy implements were taken to heaven until their restoration.
29. Josephus, *J.W.* 1.152–53.
30. See earlier, "Baptized in the Spirit," in chapter 2. Fee, *GEP*, 683, sees the stress here as locative, and he is correct in this. However, by the Spirit is still implied in that the instrument of our entering is not merely our own effort—the Spirit takes us there (spiritually).
31. Fee, *GEP*, 685, also notes connections to 1 Cor. 12:8; Eph. 4:4; and Phil. 1:27. He writes, "For Paul it is the common experience of the one Spirit, by Jew and Gentile alike, that attests that God has created something new in the body of Christ (cf. v. 15). Thus, the one Spirit who has formed them into the one body, also brings them together as that one body into the presence of the Father. It is as they live together in the common sphere of the Spirit that they have entrée with God. Two matters of the immediate context further support this view."
32. Clinton E. Arnold, *Ephesians*, ZECNT (Grand Rapids: Zondervan, 2010), 167–68; Fee, *GEP*, 682n80. Fee rightly notes the Trinitarian aspects of the passage.
33. See also Fee's extensive discussion, *GEP*, 648–57.

of the light, they must carefully live as people characterized by God's wisdom, making the most of their time to do good in an evil world. They are not to be ignorant but know the will of the Lord (Eph. 5:17). This passage addresses the community rather than individuals.

In v. 18, Paul contrasts being drunk on wine, which leads to debauched living, with being filled with the Spirit (πληροῦσθε ἐν πνεύματι).[34] The Ephesians are to do the latter and not the former. The idea of being filled with the Spirit is found in the OT description of Bezalel, who was consequently equipped with skills of craftmanship used to build the tabernacle (Exod. 31:3; 35:31). The prophet Micah declares that he is filled with the Spirit to proclaim God's judgment on Israel (Mic. 3:8). In the NT, Luke employs the notion regarding Elizabeth, Zechariah, and their son John being filled with the Spirit (Luke 1:15, 41, 67). He commonly refers to believers being filled with the Spirit in Acts.[35] These examples may indicate that the faithful people of Israel experienced the full receipt of the Spirit prior to Pentecost. However, as is commonly agreed, these experiences were likely transitory rather than the Spirit's full, permanent residing in a believer after Pentecost. This text is the only use of the idea of being filled with the Spirit in Paul.

Elsewhere, Paul likens the Spirit to a liquid into which one is baptized (1 Cor. 12:13a[36]), that is imbibed (cf. 1 Cor. 12:13b), and by which people are washed and renewed (Titus 3:5). The contrast of wine and the Spirit arguably speaks of the best wine in the cosmos, to be drunk liberally, and which has the opposite effect to debauchery—love and the other fruit of the Spirit mentioned through Ephesians 4:1–6:20.

As with Ephesians 1:17–18 (above), this can be taken in one of two ways. It could mean that Paul imagines people repeatedly filled with the Spirit because, to put it colloquially, "they leak" (as I have heard it said). Alternatively, it is not that people require repeated filling, for they have received the Spirit, but that they repeatedly yield to the Spirit they received and so experience that empowerment. That is, they "let the Spirit in you fill you," which leads to the possibility of fresh experiences. The latter may be more consistent with Paul's understanding of receiving the Spirit at conversion. As shown

---

34. See also Fee, GEP, 720, who discusses the possibility that the contrast relates to two types of ecstatic behavior. See also C. Rogers, "The Dionysian Background of Ephesians 5:18," BSac 136 (1979): 249–57. He posits a background in the Dionysus cult leading to worshipers exhibiting "ecstatic" activity. The noun ἀσωτία is derived from σῴζω, "save," and so has the converse sense to ideas like salvation, preservation, deliverance, and so indicates things like "wastefulness . . . reckless abandon, debauchery, dissipation, profligacy." BDAG, s.v. "ἀσωτία," 148. Considering that Paul's use of σῴζω always relates to salvation, ἀσωτία speaks of destructive behavior that leads to destruction. Alcohol is also an important component of first-century (and present-day) debauchery, so Paul may have in view the notion "leads to debauchery" (NIV). Conversely, "the Spirit is life" (Rom. 8:6, 10).

35. Acts 2:4; 4:8, 31; 9:17; 13:9, 52.

36. And arguably many of the other references to baptism in Paul's letters (e.g., Rom. 6:3–4; Gal. 3:27; Col. 2:12).

in the previous section, it is foolhardy to think believers cannot have new encounters with the same Spirit.[37] Indeed, throughout Ephesians, as will be explored further following this discussion, Paul has prayed as much for them (Eph. 1:17–18; 3:16–19). Fee correctly draws out the corporate and communal dimensions of this idea—they are to be filled with the Spirit together as they worship, relate to one another, and share the gospel.[38]

WORSHIP CONCEPTS AND THE SPIRIT

When the Spirit enables believers, who are made new but still sin, to approach God, they respond by terminating idolatry. They rejoice, glorify and honor, boast in God's work rather than their own, love God, and so on.

Idolatry

The polar opposite of worshipping "in the Spirit" and "by the Spirit" is idolatry. In Romans, this is the central universal human problem catalyzing the wrath of God against all ungodliness (Rom. 1:18–25). While Paul considers idols to be nothing, God and his Son are to be exclusively worshipped (1 Cor. 8:4–6). Believers must flee from idolatry (1 Cor. 10:14) and avoid participation in temple feasts. Only participation in the Lord's Supper is acceptable, as it is participation in the blood and body of Christ (1 Cor. 10:15–17).

For Paul, participation in pagan feasts opens the possibility of participation with demons (1 Cor. 10:18–22). Paul employs a wide range of language to describe the forces inimical to God.[39] While there is an ongoing discussion of these beings' ontology, they are undoubtedly spiritual beings for Paul. Their reality is seen in Ephesians 2:2, where Satan is "the *spirit* [πνεῦμα] that is now at work in the sons of disobedience."[40] Again, in Ephesians 6:12, the opponents are not "flesh and blood" but are "*spiritual* beings [πνευματικός] of evil in the heavenly places" (my translation). The connection of hostile spiritual beings with pagan temple worship suggests that for Paul, idolatry is not worship by the Spirit but is worship by false spirits that enslave the idolatrous (Gal. 4:8). The Corinthians themselves were in this place led astray before their conversions (1 Cor. 12:2).

At conversion, Paul anticipates believers turning from idolatry to serving the living and true God, as the Thessalonians did when they converted

---

37. Examples of fresh experiences are found in Acts, such as the group in Acts 4.
38. Fee, *GEP*, 722.
39. These include ἄγγελος (Rom. 8:38; 1 Cor. 6:3; 2 Cor. 11:14; Gal. 1:8; Col. 2:18), ἀρχή (Rom. 8:38; Eph. 6:12), δύναμις (Rom. 8:38), δαιμόνιον (1 Cor. 10:20–21; 1 Tim. 4:1), Βελιάρ (2 Cor. 6:15), Σατανᾶς (2 Cor. 11:14; 2 Thess. 2:9), στοιχεῖον (Gal. 4:3, 9; Col. 2:8, 20), ἄρχοντα τῆς ἐξουσίας τοῦ ἀέρος (Eph. 2:2), διάβολος (Eph. 4:27; 6:11; 1 Tim. 3:6, 7; 2 Tim. 2:26), ἐξουσία (Eph. 6:12), κοσμοκράτορας τοῦ σκότους τούτου, τὰ πνευματικὰ τῆς πονηρίας ἐν τοῖς ἐπουρανίοις (Eph. 6:12), τοῦ πονηροῦ (Eph. 6:16; 2 Thess. 3:3).
40. On this verse, see Fee, *GEP*, 679–80. He astutely notes this is the only place Satan is designated a spirit. He considers this a parody. Jesus rules his realm in the heavenlies (Eph. 1:20–23). Believers are no longer under Satan's dominion as they are now seated with Christ (Eph. 2:4–6).

(1 Thess. 1:9). As such, believers must not associate with idolatry (2 Cor. 6:16). Idolatry is a work of the flesh to be repudiated (Gal. 5:20). In contrast, believers are to be led by the Spirit and filled with Spirit fruit (Gal. 5:20). They are to put idolatry to death (Col. 3:5). They are to worship in and by the Spirit. They must "flee idolatry" (1 Cor. 10:14).

Fear of God

For Israel, "the fear of the Lord," in an exclusive manner and with a sense of reverence and awe, is essential to being faithful to the God of the covenant.[41] The notion is found outside of Paul across the NT, as in the churches of Israel and Palestine "living in the fear of the Lord and the encouragement of the Holy Spirit" (Acts 9:31 LEB) and in Peter commanding his readers to "fear God" (1 Peter 2:17).[42]

In Paul, sinful humanity has no fear of God (Rom. 3:18). In 2 Corinthians 5:11, the fear of the Lord is one of the motivations for Paul and his team's determination to persuade people to believe in Christ. He encourages the Corinthians to accomplish holiness with the fear of God (2 Cor. 7:1). He urges the Colossian slaves to obey their masters with the same motivation (Col. 3:22). The Ephesians are to submit to one another out of the fear of Christ (Eph. 5:21). Paul likely has a fear of the Lord in mind in his references to "fear and trembling" (1 Cor. 2:3; 2 Cor. 7:15; Eph. 6:5; Phil. 2:13).[43]

Overall, believers are to live their lives and engage in mission knowing who God is and revering him for his supremacy in every sense. Although the Spirit is not mentioned in any of these passages other than in the Lukan Acts 9:31, the Spirit is intertwined in mission, obedience, holiness, mutual submission, and the whole Christian life. One of the transformations the Spirit does is increasing believers' awareness of who God is and who they are in light of his greatness. They had no fear of God before conversion, but now they live in the assurance of God's grace. Led by the Spirit, they develop an increasing sense of awe and reverence for God, the king and judge, and his Son.

Reverence of God

Terms related to σεβω, "to show reverence to, worship," are used across the NT of the worship of God.[44] In the Pastoral Epistles, the language is used

---

41. For example, Lev. 19:14, 32; 25:7; Deut. 6:2, 13, 24; 10:12, 20; 13:4; 17:19; 31:12–13; Josh. 4:24; 1 Sam. 12:14, 24; 2 Chron. 19:9; 26:5; Job 28:28; Pss. 2:11; 15:4; 19:9; 22:23; 25:12, 14; 33:8, 18; 34:7, 9, 11; 102:15; 103:13, 17; 111:10; 112:1; 115:11, 13; 118:14; 135:20; 147:11; Prov. 1:7, 29; 2:5; 3:7; 8:13; 9:10; 10:27; 14:2, 26, 27; 15:16, 33; 16:6; 19:23; 22:4; 23:7; 24:21; Isa. 11:2–3; 33:6; 59:19; Jer. 2:19; Hos. 10:3; Mic. 6:9; 7:17; Mal. 3:5.

42. Luke 18:2, 4; 23:40; Acts 10:2, 4, 22; 10:35; 13:16, 26; Rev. 14:7; 15:4; 19:5.

43. Keown, *Philippians*, 1:457–59.

44. Outside Paul: of worship (Matt. 15:9; Mark 7:7; Acts 18:13; 19:27); worshiper (John 9:31); worshipfulness, reverence, or godliness (Acts 3:12; 2 Peter 1:3, 6, 7; 3:11); Gentiles who worship the Jewish God but are not proselytes (Acts 10:2, 7; 13:43, 50; 16:14; 17:4, 17; 18:7); objects of

frequently for being reverent and holy.[45] Such a worshipful life is profitable for everything (1 Tim. 4:8). This godliness is grounded in Christ's teaching (1 Tim. 6:3) and the Scriptures (2 Tim. 3:16) and is contrasted with the words of the false teachers whom the Spirit repudiates (1 Tim. 4:10). This godliness is to be pursued by the "man of God" (1 Tim 6:11), and so the one in whom the Spirit dwells (2 Tim. 1:14; Tit. 3:5). Such a godly life "in Christ Jesus," and so, "in the Spirit," also leads to persecution (2 Tim. 3:12). Believers are devoted to God and filled with the Spirit—a worshipful life.

Glorification and Honor of God

For Paul, God is the glorious father (Eph. 1:17),[46] replete with the riches of his glory (Eph. 3:16; Phil. 4:19) and glorious might (Col. 1:11).[47] Christ is "the Lord of glory" (1 Cor. 2:8) and the Christian message is "the gospel of the glory of Christ" in whose face is the glory of God (2 Cor. 4:4, 6; cf. 3:18). The riches of God's glory are found "in Christ Jesus" (Phil. 4:19). The glorious wealth of the mystery is experienced in Christ, the hope of glory (Col. 1:27). It is into the glory of the Father and Son that people are called (1 Thess. 2:12; 2 Thess. 2:14). On the contrary, unbelievers are shut out from the glory of his strength (2 Thess. 1:9).

Sadly, sinful humanity, trapped in its idolatry, fails to glorify the entirely glorious God as they should (Rom. 1:21), exchanging his glory for empty images of created beings (Rom. 1:23). Conversely, Abraham is commended not only for his faith but for giving glory to God (Rom. 4:20). Consequently, Paul frequently cries out in his letters, ascribing eternal glory to God.[48] Generous giving causes people to give thanks, and this abounds to the glory of God (2 Cor. 4:15) and Christ (2 Cor. 8:19, 23).[49] His glorious grace shown in Jesus, his purpose of bringing all of creation together under Christ, and the Ephesians' salvation and Spirit-sealing lead to the praise of the glory of his grace (Eph. 1:6, 12, 14). Believers, then, are to do all things, including eating and drinking, for the glory of God (1 Cor. 10:31).

---

worship (Acts 17:23); people who worship God unknowingly (Acts 17:23); Augustan Cohort (Acts 27:1); ungodly (1 Peter 4:18; 2 Peter 2:5, 6, 9; 3:7; Jude 4, 15, 18). Otherwise, Paul uses the language negatively of ungodly behavior (Rom. 1:18; Titus 2:12), idolatrous worship (Rom. 1:25), ungodly people (Rom. 4:5; 2 Tim. 1:9) for whom Christ died (Rom. 5:6), ungodliness (Rom. 11:26), a fake powerless godliness (2 Tim. 3:5). Otherwise, he uses it positively of sacred things (Phil. 4:8), objects of worship (2 Thess. 2:4), and the mystery of godliness found in Christ (1 Tim. 3:16).

45. 1 Tim. 2:2, 10; 3:4, 8, 11; 4:7; 5:4; 6:5, 6; Titus 1:1; 2:2, 7, 12.

46. The genitive ὁ πατὴρ τῆς δόξης is likely attributive.

47. See also 1 Thess. 2:12.

48. See Rom. 11:36; Gal. 1:5; Eph. 3:21 (more fully, "glory in the church and in Christ Jesus"); Phil. 4:20; 1 Tim. 1:17; 6:16; 2 Tim. 4:18; cf. Rom. 16:27.

49. "Lord" in 2 Corinthians 8:18 is ambiguous, possibly God or Jesus. In light of 8:23, Christ is probably in view. While "the glory of Christ" can be the churches in 2 Corinthiasn 8:23, it is more likely the apostles. See Harris, *Second Epistle*, 612.

Those who yield fully to Christ's lordship bring glory to God (Phil. 2:11). When these believers, overflowing with a discerning love, are filled with the fruit of righteousness generated by the Spirit (Gal. 5:22–24), they bring glory and praise of God (Phil. 1:11). Believers should glorify God with their bodies with sexual fidelity (1 Cor. 6:20). Evangelism leads to the word of the Lord being glorified so that God and Christ are glorified (2 Thess. 3:1). Those being formed by the Spirit increasingly glorify God and his Son.[50]

Love for God

While Paul frequently uses love language (esp. ἀγάπ- language), he uses it sparingly for believers loving God. This scarcity is interesting because, no doubt, Paul had prayed the Shema twice or more daily for his whole life up to his conversion and probably beyond.[51] Still, the concept is not absent from his letters. It is for those who love God and who are called according to his purpose that God (or the Spirit)[52] works all things together for good (Rom. 8:28). Similarly, no person can conceive what God has prepared for those who love him (1 Cor. 2:9). The person who loves God is known by God (1 Cor. 8:3). While not a strong emphasis of Paul's, believers are to respond to God with love and adoration.

Boasting

Paul's understanding of boasting is complex due to the Roman penchant for self-exaltation through boasting and that of Paul's opponents.[53] As such, while Paul engages in ironic boasting to repudiate their claims,[54] he rejects bragging about one's achievements.[55] Neither should believers boast about other believers over and against one another, such as when comparing them as preachers (1 Cor. 3:21). Paul wants people to boast about God and his Son above all else, including in the hope of the glory of God (Rom. 5:2). They are even to boast in their afflictions, not for their own sake, but because God uses them to strengthen them in perseverance, character, and hope (Rom. 5:3–5).

---

50. As McKnight says, "Any ministry or leadership that does not lead through the Spirit to Christ to the glory of the Father subverts the gospel." McKnight, *PPNCCC*, 167.
51. See Jacob Neusner, "The Shema," in "Liturgy of Judaism," *EJ* 2:816–19.
52. See this chapter, "Prayer and the Spirit."
53. In Corinth, and in wider Roman culture, "Public boasting and self-promotion had become an art form." Ben Witherington III, *Conflict and Community in Corinth: A Socio-Rhetorical Commentary on 1 and 2 Corinthians* (Grand Rapids: Eerdmans, 1995), 8.
54. 1 Cor. 9:15–16; 15:31; 2 Cor. 1:12; 10:8, 15, 16; 11:10, 12, 16, 17, 18, 30; 12:1, 5, 6, 9.
55. No one can boast as if their righteous achievements gain them merit before God (Rom. 3:27; 4:2; 1 Cor. 1:29; Eph. 2:9). Some boast in God but do not acknowledge Jesus as Christ and Lord (Rom. 2:17), and some boast in the law (Rom. 2:23). Gentile believers must not boast against the Jews (Rom. 11:18). Believers must not boast in their giftedness, for it is from God (1 Cor. 4:7), nor in their sinfulness (1 Cor. 5:6). It is not love to boast in giving oneself over to self-giving (1 Cor. 13:3). Judaizers want to boast in the flesh of the Galatians (Gal. 6:13). See also Gal. 6:4.

Supremely, believers boast in God through Christ for his reconciliation (Rom. 5:11), and in Christ Jesus (Rom. 15:17).

To this end, Paul cites Jeremiah 9:24 twice, "Let the one who boasts, boast in the Lord" (1 Cor. 1:31; 2 Cor. 10:17). While κύριος in Jeremiah is undoubtedly God, in Paul, Jesus fills this space as the one being the form of God to whom every person yields (Phil. 2:6, 9–10). To boast ἐν κυρίῳ can refer to the sphere of boasting, that is, only doing so where it elevates Christ. While this is possibly the case, Jesus is also the object of boasting. Jesus as the object makes sense considering Jeremiah 9:24, where the object is not to be a person's wisdom, might, or wealth, but that he knows Yahweh, who shows love, justice, and righteousness. Similarly, 1 Kingdoms 2:10 LXX (1 Sam. 2:10 EVV) says much the same thing, urging the wise, strong, and wealthy not to boast in their wisdom, strength, and wealth but to understand and know God.

In Galatians 6:14, Paul boasts about the cross of Christ, which is ironic in light of the public shame associated with the cross. Paul's desire for people to boast in Christ is seen in Philippians 1:26, where he hopes that by coming to Philippi, the Philippians will abound in boasting in Christ Jesus. Such boasting is possible because believers "boast in Christ Jesus" and not in the flesh and its achievements (Phil. 3:3).[56] As such, pneumaformed believers are to boast in Christ Jesus and God the Father.

Blessing

Another aspect of pneumaform worship is blessing God. The Greek εὐλογητός literally means to speak good words, and in the NT, it is most often used for doing so toward God. In a spontaneous but intentional outburst against the idolatry he is condemning, Paul uses it in Romans 1:25, stating, "[God] is blessed forever! Amen." As such, God is the "blessed God" (1 Tim. 1:11) and "the blessed and only ruler" (1 Tim. 6:15). In Romans 9:5, Paul declares either God or, as is likely, Messiah Jesus blessed forever (as he does in 2 Cor. 11:31).[57] For Paul, it is inconceivable that a believer imbued with the Spirit would curse Jesus; instead, that person confesses his lordship (1 Cor. 12:3).

Moreover, as Paul does, believers bless God and his Son. Twice Paul breaks from his habit of beginning letters with thanksgiving and prayer[58] and starts letters by blessing God. In 2 Corinthians 1:3, he launches into a blessing, praising God the Father and Christ for their mercies and comfort in affliction. Again, in Ephesians 1:3–14, in a stunning passage laden with theological grist, Paul blesses God for blessing believers with the many benefits of salvation.

---

56. Paul is also comfortable in believers boasting over others but not over some against others (2 Cor. 1:14; 5:12; 7:4, 14; 8:24; 9:2, 3; 10:13; Phil. 2:16; 1 Thess. 2:9; 2 Thess. 1:4).

57. See Moo, *Romans*, 586–88.

58. Aside from 2 Corinthians and Ephesians discussed here, Paul begins with thanksgiving in all letters aside from Galatians—as though indicating he has little to be thankful for.

Praise

Using αἰν- terms,[59] Paul summons Spirit-filled believers to praise God. Concerning Gentiles coming to faith in God, he cites Psalm 117:1, where the Gentiles and all humankind praise God while filled with the Spirit of hope. Cosmic worship is coming to pass in the world as the gospel advances through the efforts of Paul and others (Rom. 15:11). In Ephesians 1:6, Paul praises God's glorious, unmerited favor (grace). Three times in Ephesians, he uses the formula "the praise of his glory," which is something that springs from God's grace, that believers exist for, and that is from the giving of the Spirit (Eph. 1:6, 12, 14). Similarly, the Philippians, filled with the fruit of righteousness, bring glory to God (Phil. 1:11). Praise of God is not merely expressed when believers gather. Still, gathering to praise him with spiritual songs and in other ways is essential to pneumaform life.

In Ephesians 5, the participle λαλοῦντες connects v. 19 to v. 18. Wallace rightly argues this participle indicates result, "with the result of."[60] The dative pronoun ἑαυτοῖς is commonly translated as "to one another." However, this translation is unlikely here for a few reasons. First, neither Paul nor any other part of the NT mentions believers singing praise *to one another*. Second, the object of the singing is given at the end of the 19 and 20: τῷ κυρίῳ, "to the Lord," and τῷ θεῷ καὶ πατρί, "to the God and Father." Third, a dative does not have to be translated "to" but can equally be "with." Hence, it is better to translate the dative in terms of corporate singing "*with* one another," that is, "together." This translation indicates Paul is calling readers to corporate worship.[61]

The categories of song, "psalms, hymns, and spiritual songs," may indicate different understandings of worship songs in the early church. Certainly, psalms could refer to the Psalter. However, the distinction between hymns and spiritual songs is uncertain.[62] It is better to see the three as a way of describing "all manner of Christian worship songs" that are to be shared in worship services (cf. 1 Cor. 14:26).[63] These would include the OT psalms, songs written for Christian worship, and spontaneous songs sung under the unction of the Spirit (cf. 1 Cor. 14:15).

---

59. Sometimes the language is used of people praising others (Luke 16:8; 1 Peter 2:14), advising or urging another person (Acts 27:9, 22), or of God praising people (1 Peter 1:7). Outside of Paul, those praising God include infants (Matt. 21:16), angels (Luke 2:13), shepherds (Luke 2:20), crowds (Luke 18:43; 19:37), Christians (Acts 2:47; Heb. 13:15; Rev. 19:5), and a healed man (Acts 3:8, 9). Paul also uses the language of people being praised (Rom. 2:29; Rom. 13:3; 1 Cor. 4:5; 1 Cor. 11:2, 17, 22; 2 Cor. 8:18), or something praiseworthy (Phil. 4:8).

60. Wallace, *Greek Grammar*, 639.

61. Here I completely disagree with Fee, *GEP*, 652, who considers the dative to mean "to one another." However, the parallel in Colossians 3:16 argues against this point. See also Mark J. Keown, "How Much Should We Sing?" *Colloq* 19, no. 3 (2012): 5–13.

62. Keown, "How Much Should We Sing?" 5–13.

63. Similarly Fee, *GEP*, 654.

Still, the third category, ᾠδαῖς πνευματικαῖς, "spiritual songs,"[64] indicates the Spirit's role in generating worship music for the gathered community. It speaks not only of music created in and by the Spirit by believers but
sung together in the Spirit (with feeling, emotion, thought, harmony, and so
on).[65]

The dative τῇ καρδίᾳ does not indicate silent song but rather songs "from
the heart." This source of worship speaks of a wholehearted, mental affection
for God, as expected in the first great commandment (Deut. 6:4). Such praise
should always be done with an attitude of gratitude in everything in life (cf.
1 Thess. 5:18), directed to God the Father in the name of their Lord Jesus
Christ. Hence, pneumaformed believers are to be constantly filled with God's
Spirit, who abides in them and leads them in worship, and join with others to
sing songs of heartfelt worship to God, through Christ in whom they abide.
This passage and Colossians 3:16 indicate that, as Fee puts it, "where the Spirit
of God is there is also singing."[66]

Rejoice

Another aspect of pneumaform worship is rejoicing and joy that, at times,
the worshiper experiences. Romans 14:17 indicates that the experience of joy is
"in the Holy Spirit." God is the source of joy and fills believers with joy, peace,
and hope by the power of the Holy Spirit (Rom. 15:13). Joy is a fruit of the
Spirit (Gal. 5:22) and leads to thanksgiving (Col. 1:11–12). The Thessalonians
received the gospel despite affliction "with the joy of the Holy Spirit" (1 Thess.
1:6). The genitive here is one of production, indicating that the Spirit generates
joy in the believer.[67] As such, Paul frequently encourages his converts to yield to
the Spirit's promptings to rejoice.

The Romans are to rejoice in hope (Rom. 12:12). In close proximity is
Paul's injunction to "be fervent in the Spirit" (v. 11b), and it may be that
Paul sees rejoicing in hope as an expression of appropriate spiritual fervor.

---

64. While the adjective πνευματικαῖς can modify all three categories, it is better to take it with
the third. Fee, GEP, 653. Fee translates it "charismatic hymnody," which I reject as a label as the
term "charismatic" is now loaded with theological baggage related to Pentecostal and charismatic
extremes, and "hymnody" is loaded with the liturgical baggage of "hymns" referring to old songs and
"contemporary" to new ones. "Spiritual songs" is more appropriate. "Odes" is now outdated.

65. Dunn, Jesus and the Spirit, 239, suggests the hymnic pieces in the NT may represent such songs. He
notes Rom. 7:25a; 11:33–36; 1 Cor. 15:57; 2 Cor. 1:3–8; Gal. 1:5; Eph. 1:3–14; 3:21; 5:14; Phil. 2:6–11;
4:20; Col. 1:15–20; 1 Tim. 1:17; 3:16; 6:15–16. However, it is debatable whether they are songs of any
sort, and if so, whether they could equally be "hymns." Aside from "psalms," which are obvious, we
are left uncertain of what hymns and spiritual songs connote.

66. See further Fee, GEP, 656.

67. Fee, GEP, 46–47, notes that this tells us about the drudgery of paganism compared with being "filled
with such an untrammeled joy . . . even in the midst of genuine hardships related to their having
become believers." Further, "this is the one characteristic of their life in the Spirit that Paul recalls for
them as evidence of their conversion. This suggests in the strongest possible way that for Paul joy is
one of the certain hallmarks of genuine spirituality" (Spirit-uality?).

Whether this is the case, believers are to rejoice in the hope they have in God that speaks of the present experience of God in the Spirit, in community, and in their future eschatological glory.

There are certainly times to celebrate and rejoice, such as when Paul at last goes to Rome (Rom. 15:32), when Paul hears the good news of other Christians' faithfulness and obedience (Rom. 16:19; Col. 2:5), when another Christian is honored (1 Cor. 12:26). We rejoice at the truth (1 Cor. 13:6), when Christians are reunited (1 Cor. 16:17; 2 Cor. 7:13; 2 Tim. 1:4), when other Christians love others and repent (2 Cor. 7:7, 9), due to confidence in those to whom we minister (2 Cor. 7:16; Phil. 1:4), when others preach the gospel of Christ (Phil. 1:18), at one's salvation (Phil. 1:18), at the sacrifice and service of others (Phil. 2:18), and at the material generosity of Christians to others (Phil. 4:10).

However, the call to rejoice in hope is not mindless rejoicing in terrible circumstances. There is also a time to lament, as when other believers are grieving (Rom. 12:15; 1 Cor. 12:26), and the genuinely loving Christian does not rejoice at unrighteousness (1 Cor. 13:6). At times, a person's joy is incomplete due to other Christians failing to live fully worthy of the gospel (Phil. 2:2).

Yet, through it all, at a deeper level, believers still have a reason to rejoice—"in the Lord" (see 2 Thessalonians 3:1–4). Because of the Christian hope, pneumaform believers can rejoice differently than unbelievers who lack the hope of eternal life and the presence of the Spirit (1 Cor. 7:30). Paul can work for the joy of the Corinthians, even though they cause him sorrow and not joy (2 Cor. 1:24; 2:7). Hence, he tells the Corinthians he is "always rejoicing" regardless of grief (2 Cor. 6:10) and overflows with joy despite affliction (2 Cor. 7:4). He commends the Macedonians for their abundance of joy despite poverty and affliction (2 Cor. 8:2). He and his team rejoice in the face of their weakness (2 Cor. 13:9). The Corinthians should rejoice notwithstanding his challenging letter to them (2 Cor. 13:11). He wants the Philippians to advance in joy despite their sufferings (Phil. 1:25), to join him in rejoicing even with their difficult mutual circumstances (Phil. 2:17–18), and to receive the long-suffering Epaphroditus home with joy (Phil. 2:28–29). The Philippians remain "my joy" for Paul regardless of their nascent conflict (Phil. 4:1; also 1 Thess. 2:19–20; 3:9). Paul, too, can rejoice in his sufferings on behalf of the Colossians, because he knows that he suffers in and for Christ and his mission (Col. 1:24). Philemon generates joy in Paul, despite Philemon's falling-out with Onesimus (Philem. 7). Paul's attitude toward joy is summed up in the statement "rejoice in the Lord" (Phil. 3:1; 4:4; also 1 Thess. 5:16).[68]

---

68. See also Fee, *GEP*, 53–55. He rightly notes that the imperatives of 1 Thessalonians 5:16–18 are "Spirit texts," despite it not being obvious, especially noting the linking of Spirit and joy in 1 Thessalonians 1:6 and Galatians 5:22. He avers, "Life in Christ, and therefore life in the Spirit, is a life of joy, prayer, and praise—in any and all circumstances."

So, while there is a time to grieve, weep, and empathize, for Paul, at a deeper level, a pneumaformed person can find that deep joy in Christ even in lament.

Thanksgiving

Throughout the previous section, I have regularly mentioned Paul's repeated use of thanksgiving language. This emphasis is because thankfulness to God is essential to a pneumaform existence. After his initial prayer blessing for his converts that concludes his prescripts, Paul invariably turns to thanksgiving, or less often, to blessing God.[69] There are various indicators that these thanksgivings are Spirit-led. First, he sometimes prays prayers "through Christ Jesus" (διὰ Ἰησοῦ Χριστοῦ), with Christ Jesus present with believers by and in the Spirit (Rom. 1:8). At other points in his letters, Paul highlights thanksgiving. Regularly he uses the formula "grace be to God" (χάρις τῷ θεῷ), which is usually translated as "thanks be to God." At times, this thanksgiving is "through Jesus," indicating the spiritual connection of God, Christ, the Spirit, and the believer.[70] A characteristic of idolatrous humankind is that they do not give such thanks to God (Rom. 1:21). In that the source of grace is God, in Christ, by the Spirit in Paul, this is grace poured into people which, in turn, led by Christ's and the Spirit's intercession (Rom. 8:26–27, 34), is poured back to God (grace responding to grace). Thanksgiving is an integral part of gathered worship that edifies others where the words are understood (1 Cor. 14:16–18). It is a positive outcome of prayer for others (2 Cor. 1:11), expanding grace (2 Cor. 4:15) and generous giving (2 Cor. 9:11, 12). Paul also asserts that believers should use their mouths for thanksgiving rather than gross speech (Eph. 5:4).

Believers should be "giving thanks always and for everything to God the Father in the name of our Lord Jesus Christ" (Eph. 5:18, 20). Two things suggest the Spirit's involvement in perpetual gratitude here. First, "in the name of our Lord Jesus Christ" implies that this name evokes the power to connect the believer's speech with God through Christ Jesus by the Spirit. Second, the participle εὐχαριστοῦντες is dependent on the main verb πληροῦσθε in πληροῦσθε ἐν πνεύματι, indicating that giving thanks for everything is an outworking of being filled with the Spirit (v. 18). Philippians 4:6 also indicates that all prayer given to God is to be conducted "with thanksgiving."

Again, in Colossians 1:12, believers are those "with joy" (a fruit of the Spirit, Gal. 5:22) who "are giving thanks to the Father." Doing this is due to their having been "strengthened with all power, according to his glorious might, for all endurance and patience" (v. 11). Thus, having been firmly established in Christ and the faith, they are "overflowing with thankfulness" (Col. 2:7 NIV). "Overflow" suggests the abundance of the Spirit's work in a Christian's life. With the word of Christ dwelling in them richly by the Spirit, they

---

69.   Initial thanksgivings (Rom. 1:8; 1 Cor. 1:4; Eph. 1:16; Phil. 1:3; Col. 1:3; 1 Thess. 1:2 [also 1 Thess. 2:13]; 2 Thess. 1:3 [also 2 Thess. 2:13]; 1 Tim. 1:12; 2 Tim. 1:3; Philem. 4).

70.   Rom. 6:17; 7:25 (includes "through our Lord Jesus Christ"); 1 Cor. 15:57; 2 Cor. 2:14; 2 Cor. 8:16; 9:15.

should sing all manner of Christian songs "with thankfulness in [their] hearts to God" (Col. 3:16), give "thanks for all things in the name of the Lord Jesus to God the Father through him" (Col. 3:17 LEB), and be devoted and alert in prayer "with thanksgiving" (Col. 4:2). The pneumaformed person cannot help but thank God, even in dark times.

In 1 Thessalonians 5:18, it is God's will for the Thessalonians that they "give thanks in all things." This injunction is immediately followed by an appeal not to quench the Spirit. While the concern for quenching the fire of the Spirit may relate more to what follows,[71] it could be that a failure to express gratitude is linked to this, that is, one quenches the Spirit when one is not thankful.[72]

God is the ultimate object of thanksgiving; he is thanked in Christ via the Spirit. Believers are to thank God for all manner of things. These include faith (Rom. 1:8); missional endeavors (Rom. 1:8; 16:4; 2 Cor. 8:16); that people are saved and transformed from their former lives (Rom. 6:17); food and drink (1 Cor. 10:30; 11:24; 1 Tim. 4:3–4); the Lord's Supper (1 Cor. 11:24); the grace given others (1 Cor. 1:4); God's victory in Christ given to believers (1 Cor. 15:57);[73] deliverance from danger (2 Cor. 1:11); God's leading of his people in triumphal procession spreading the fragrance of Christ (2 Cor. 2:14); people's material generosity (2 Cor. 4:15; 9:11–12); those to whom we minister (Eph. 1:16); such things as people's fellowship in the gospel (Phil. 1:3–5); their love, faith, hope, and extension of the gospel (Col. 1:3); their ministry effort premised on faith, hope, and love, and the reception of the gospel (1 Thess. 1:2–4; 2:13; 3:9; 2 Thess. 1:3; cf. Philem. 4); his glorious salvation and its benefits (Col. 1:12); God's call and sanctification (2 Thess. 2:13); our own conversion and empowerment by God in Christ (1 Tim. 2:12–14); and all people (1 Tim. 2:1). Indeed, believers should give thanks for everything, the good or the bad, for this is God's will for those being formed by the Spirit (1 Thess. 5:18, also Eph. 5:20).[74]

PRAYER AND THE SPIRIT

A critical aspect of pneumaformation is the prayer life of believers. Speaking to God implies he can hear our prayers and will respond. This connectedness suggests a spiritual bond between God and people due to his omnipresence, our participation in Christ, and his Spirit. Praying is an activity done "in the Spirit" and "by the Spirit."[75] Praying enhances the connection between the

---

71. Fee, *GEP*, 57.

72. Paul employs asyndeton through the passage, and while it is probably correct to link the quenching of the Spirit with prophecy, relating it to what precedes (or both ways) cannot be ruled out. See also εὐχαριστία in 1 Cor. 1:14; 14:18; 1 Thess. 3:9; 1 Tim. 2:1.

73. See on the Spirit and victory over sin, deSilva, *Transformation*, 58.

74. Paul also somewhat ironically gives thanks that he baptized only a few of the Corinthians (1 Cor. 1:14); sometimes it is general (1 Cor. 14:16–18; Eph. 5:4; Phil. 4:6; Col. 2:7; 3:15–17; 4:2).

75. See also Dunn, *Jesus and the Spirit*, 239–42. He considers it surprising that "Paul never designates

person praying and God; God's Spirit is released or experienced differently through prayer.

Intercession

The start of any discussion of the Spirit's role in worship is the intercessory ministry of the Spirit on behalf of believers. The Spirit helps believers in their weaknesses and illnesses, whatever they are. Believers are often unsure of the will of God. This uncertainty is especially the case when they mature and realize that when bad things happen, it is not necessarily God's judgment. Indeed, God is working all things together for those he loves and has called for his purpose (Rom. 8:28).

Nonetheless, when believers do not know what to pray, "the Spirit helps [them] in [their] weakness" and "the Spirit himself intercedes (ὑπερεντυγχάνω) for [them] through wordless groans" (Rom. 8:26 NIV). God knows people fully, inhabiting them and having full access to every thought, feeling, and inclination (cf. 1 Cor. 2:10–11). God also fully knows the mindset (φρόνημα) of the Spirit (cf. 1 Cor. 2:12). This is "because [ὅτι] he intercedes [ἐντυγχάνω] on behalf of the saints in accordance with God" (my translation). The verb ἐντυγχάνω in broader biblical and pseudepigraphal texts can be used in a range of senses relating to appealing, accusing, or charging on behalf of another (Acts 25:24).[76] Paul uses it here of prayer or appeal to God (Rom. 11:2; Heb. 7:25).[77]

The compound term ὑπερεντυγχάνω ("to intercede on behalf of another") is a Pauline creation, here indicating "intercedes on behalf of" and, based on the context, implies believers (saints). Paul then shifts to the synonym, ἐντυγχάνω, as he specifies those for whom the Spirit intercedes: ἁγίων, "saints, holy ones."[78] The clause στεναγμοῖς ἀλαλήτοις speaks of wordless sounds gushing forth to God from the Spirit.[79]

---

prayer as a charisma" (p. 239). However, this is because prayer is integral to every believer's very existence and our joining Christ and the Spirit entails raising our prayers to God.

76. See also 1 Macc. 8:32; 10:61, 63, 64; 11:25; 4:36; 3 Macc. 6:37; Wis. 8:21; 16:28; Dan. 6:13; T. Job 17.5; Let. Aris. 174.

77. Also, of the earth bringing accusations to God (1 En. 7:6) and the souls of the dead appealing to God (1 En. 9:3, 10; 22:5–7, 12). It can also be used of reading something (2 Macc. 2:25; 6:12; 15:39; Sib. Or. Prol. 7, 60). The cognate noun ἔντευξις, "petition," is used in 1 Tim. 2:1; 4:5.

78. Here I disagree with Dunn, who considers that Jesus alone fills the role of heavenly intercessor (Rom. 8:34) and limits this intercession to the Spirit within the believer. Dunn, Jesus and the Spirit, 241. However, that is not clear in the passage or necessary. Christ is in the believer interceding by the Spirit and the Spirit is in Christ interceding to the Father on behalf of the saints. There is distinction between their persons and intercessory roles, but there is also a divine harmony in their prayer. Believers join this beautiful chorus of inspired prayer to "Abba, Father!" Habets rightly states, "When we pray, we do so with confidence that the Spirit will intercede on our behalf (Rom. 8:26), and that Jesus will represent us to the Father." Habets, Anointed Son, 292.

79. See Dunn, Jesus and the Spirit, 241–42. He rightly rejects tongues as "wordless stammering of ecstasy," or "unutterable" words, but something like "sighs too deep for words" (RSV) or "inarticulate groaning."

While the Spirit is generating life in the believer, he is also God-the-Father-facing, praying for those who welcome him into their being by faith. This indwelling and intercession is marvelous and indicates that any act of worship we seem to have initiated is merely joining the prayers of the Spirit on our behalf. Wonderfully, the Spirit searches our hearts and intercedes for God's holy people in accordance with God's will. The believer joins the Spirit in "charismatic prayer."[80]

It is possible Romans 8:28 should be read as a continuation of the discussion of the Spirit's work in Romans 8:26–27. Romans 8:28a can be read traditionally as, "And we know that for those who love God all things work together for good . . .". However, the accusative πάντα suggests a direct object of some personal agency. Hence, as in P[46], A, B, and 81, all of which supply ο θεος, it can read, "And we know that for those who love God, *God* works all things together for good . . .". Alternatively, it can be translated, "And we know that for those who love God, [the Spirit] works all things for good."

Fee discusses this possibility and opts for the latter.[81] He suggests that context supports the Spirit reading, as the Spirit dominates 8:1–27. However, others note that God dominates what follows in v. 29, and the ὅτι connection with 8:28 favors God's agency (if there is one).[82] Still, even if God is the subject of even "all things," I argue that the work of the Spirit is implied here. God, *by his Spirit*, who with Christ intercedes for his faithful, shapes history toward what is best for those who love him and have been called to his purpose. Knowing this is immensely reassuring for believers struggling in a fallen world. Those who believe have the Spirit in their beings at all times, crying out to Abba, Father, with prayers, petitions, supplications, confession, cries of desperation, praise, thanksgiving, and any other prayer category they can imagine. As they tune into the Spirit's intercession, they experience the flood of God's love and strength.

Of course, mention must be made here of Christ's intercession for believers in Romans 8:34 (cf. Heb. 7:25). The picture Paul paints is of the crucified, raised, and now ascended and exalted Messiah, sitting at the right hand of God, interceding for believers (us). Christ and the Spirit send a continuous flow of prayer for God's people to the Father. This truth gloriously assures believers that God will redeem his creation and his people and that all things work together for the good of those he loves, predestined, called, justified, and will glorify. As God is for them, even if horrors come to pass, as they do in a shattered and sin-ridden world, nothing can separate them from his love or bring charges against them and condemn them. Such gospel truths are reason

---

80. Dunn, *Jesus and the Spirit*, 241.
81. Fee, *GEP*, 588–90. He also argues that the Spirit reading is supported by the use of a *syn* compound in v. 28 as earlier (vv. 16, 26), the parallel with Testament of Gad 4:7; and "we know that" responds to "we do not know" what to pray for in v. 26.
82. Moo, *Romans*, 550.

enough to join the Son and Spirit in worship. And they are pneumaformed to be more and more like Jesus as they do.

Prayer Life

Ephesians 6:18 culminates the section devoted to believers clothing themselves in God's armor. It is unclear whether prayer constitutes the final piece of Christian armory in this section,[83] or whether there is a shift from the armor to the prayer that undergirds the armor and sustains the Christian clothed in God's armor. Either way, Paul says to the readers, they should "[pray] at all times in [and by] the Spirit, with all prayer and supplication."

The phrase ἐν πνεύματι has been discussed earlier. Here, its sense is similar to Philippians 3:3 –believers are in the Spirit and are to pray by the Spirit. In the context of prayer, as believers are always "in the Spirit," it leans toward the idea of being led *by* the Spirit in prayer.[84] The two terms for prayer, προσευχῆς and δέησις, do not speak of two distinct types of prayer but together mean "all kinds of prayer."[85] Believers must consciously focus on the Spirit's unction as they pray.

The clause ἐν παντὶ καιρῷ indicates that this prayer should be happening at all times. It echoes Ephesians 5:17 where readers are to know God's will and be filled with the Spirit rather than drunk on alcohol. Furthermore, they are to speak to God by singing songs from the heart and *always* giving thanks to God for *everything* in Christ's name. Paul's injunction here also aligns with his many references to his constant prayer for others[86] and those of Epaphras (Col. 4:12).

Paul goes on in 6:18 to urge the Ephesians to always be alert and pray persistently for all the saints, that is, all other believers. This appeal suggests Christians praying for other Christians in various locations throughout the world, as Paul is in Rome and asking the Ephesians. He asks them to pray that God would give him the appropriate message when he speaks and that he would boldly make the gospel known to his hearers at his point of incarceration. Prayer is the starting point of our involvement in evangelism.

Prayer Blessings

Paul's letters feature many prayer blessings that speak of the Spirit's work in conveying God's grace, peace, and love to believers. Eight times in his letters, after naming the sender(s) and recipients, Paul pronounces the same blessing

---

83.   Fee, *GEP*, 730.
84.   See chapter 2, "Baptized in the Spirit." Fee rightly rejects this being limited to tongues. Fee, *GEP*, 730–31.
85.   "They are employed together here primarily for the sake of intensification, but usually the former term has a more general and comprehensive reference, while the latter indicates more specifically the request or petition aspect of prayer." Lincoln, *Ephesians*, 452. See also my discussion of these terms in Keown, *Philippians*, 2:343–45.
86.   Often signaled with πάντοτε, "always" (Rom. 1:10; 1 Cor. 1:4; Eph. 5:20; Phil. 1:4; 4:4; Col. 1:3; 1 Thess. 1:2; 5:16; 2 Thess. 1:3, 11; 2:13; Philem. 4) or less often, ἀδιαλείπτως, "unceasingly" (Rom. 1:9; 1 Thess. 1:2; 2:23; 5:17).

on the Christian recipients: "Grace to you and peace from God our Father and the Lord Jesus Christ."[87] Two other letters include abbreviated versions of the same,[88] while Titus 1:4 replaces "Lord" with "Savior" concerning Jesus and the letters to Timothy add mercy (1 Tim. 1:2; 2 Tim. 1:2). God through his Son is the source of grace and peace, and prayer intensifies the experience of them.

Additionally, Paul ends his letters with prayer blessings, creating an inclusio of blessings in each letter[89] The fullest is 2 Corinthians 13:13 (13:14 EVV), where Paul prays for grace, love, and unity to be with the Corinthians. These three blessings are assigned to one or another member of the Godhead but are all experienced through the Spirit. Two letters end with a prayer for the grace of the (or our) Lord Jesus Christ to be with the collective spirit of the recipients (Phil. 4:23; Philem. 25).[90] Galatians expands this by adding ἀδελφοί·ἀμήν (Gal. 6:18). Colossians 4:18 and 1 Timothy 6:21 end with the simple "grace be with you." First Corinthians 16:23 expands this slightly, adding "of the Lord Jesus." First Thessalonians 5:28 slightly extends this to "the grace of our Lord Jesus Christ be with you," and 2 Thessalonians 3:18 adds "all." Second Timothy 4:22 prays for the Lord to be with Timothy's spirit, adding, "grace be with you." Finally, Ephesians 6:24 adapts the simple "grace be with you," replacing "you" with "all who love our Lord Jesus Christ in incorruptibility." These blessings come from Paul's desire to see his converts experience the fullness of God's grace, shalom, and love and be formed into vessels of these things toward others. Such prayers for grace and peace for others should punctuate the pneumaform life.

Relevant Prayer Texts

ROMANS 1:8–12

Having prayed for the Romans to experience more grace and peace from God and Jesus, as is his custom, Paul thanks God through Jesus Christ for all the Romans. His gratitude is "because" (ὅτι) their "faith is being proclaimed in the whole world." Then, Paul does not so much pray for the Romans but tells them of his regular prayers for them (v. 9). His prayer forms an essential aspect of his wholehearted ministry of preaching the gospel of Christ, as it should for any Spirit-shaped Christian. Paul calls God to testify on his behalf that he constantly (ἀδιαλείπτως) remembers the Romans. Summoning God

---

87. Rom. 1:7; 1 Cor. 1:3; 2 Cor. 1:2; Gal. 1:3; Eph. 1:2; Phil. 1:2; 2 Thess. 1:2; Philem. 3.
88. 1 Thess. 1:1 and Col. 1:2 include a shorter version of the same.
89. The ending of Romans is uncertain. Least likely in my view is: η χαρις του κυριου ημων Ιησου Χριστου (– Ιησου Χριστου F G 629) μετα παντων υμων (μεθ υμων 630). αμην (– 630) D F G L Ψ 629. 630. 1175. 1241. 1505. 1881 𝔐 ar vg^cl sy^h (p. [25–27] 33. 104. 365 sy^p bo^ms; Ambst; *sed* – ημων P)—because it repeats v. 20 and is itself full of variants. If it is not original, then there is no blessing, which is unusual. The doxology may be original, but it is uncertain. See Metzger, *TCGNT*, 476–77.
90. Walter G. Hansen, *The Letter to the Philippians*, PNTC (Grand Rapids: Eerdmans, 2009), 332.

as a witness is, of course, figurative; however, as Paul's words are read, the Spirit likely confirmed Paul's fidelity to the hearts of the Romans (v. 9).

Paul then zeroes in on one aspect of his constant prayer: he always (πάντοτε) asks in his prayers that he may at last go to Rome as God wills (v. 10). Mention of the will of God speaks of Paul having his own plan but being sensitive to the leading of the Spirit in his mission, as it is the Spirit's mission. Knowing this in his heart, he plans his course knowing that the Lord by his Spirit will determine his steps (Prov. 16:9). This deference to God's will is reflected in Luke's account of Paul's second major Antiochian mission as he is directed by the Spirit away from Bithynia and Asia Minor to Macedonia (Acts 16:6–10).

ROMANS 8:15 AND GALATIANS 4:6

In these two texts, the cry "Abba, Father" comes from believers who have received the Spirit of God and have experienced their adoption as God's children.[91] The Romans verse is set in the context of Paul's exposition of his flesh-Spirit antithetical appeal to the readers to live by the Spirit. The Spirit-filled Christian is not to live according to the flesh, moving toward death, but by the Spirit, leading to eternal life (vv. 12–13). This is because all the people the Spirit leads are children (lit. "sons") of God (v. 14), a stunning statement of the believer's identity as a member of God's family.

Verse 15 further explains their inclusion in God's family. When they believed in God's Son, they did not receive a spirit of slavery again for fear.[92] Instead (ἀλλ '), they received the Spirit of adoption as children (lit. "sons"). By the Spirit, believers cry out "Abba, Father." Here, the believer, filled with the Spirit, cries out. Like newborn babies crying out at birth, they cry out to God as their Father.[93] The cry echoes Christ's address to God in Gethsemane and speaks of deep intimacy with God the Father, welcome into his family, and adoption to the full status of "sons" and heirs.

The Galatians text says much the same thing. Believers in Christ are no longer under the law (vv. 1–3). They are free because God sent forth his Son into the world, born of a woman and under the law, to redeem those under the law. He did this so that they would receive adoption into God's family (v. 4). They are no longer under the tutelage of the law but are God's children in Christ. Because (ὅτι) we (all Christians) are children (lit. "sons"), God sent forth his Spirit into our hearts crying, "Abba, Father" (v. 6).

Significantly, the Spirit is the one who cries out through the believer as they are welcomed into God's family. Believers are no longer slaves to the law or the elemental principles and spirits of their pagan pasts. They are God's

---

91. See also Dunn, *Jesus and the Spirit*, 240.
92. The adverb πάλιν can go with πνεῦμα δουλείας (spirit of slavery again) or with εἰς φόβον (again). The former seems appropriate in terms of the context. See the discussion in Fee, *GEP*, 565.
93. See also the discussion in chapter 2, "Receiving the Spirit."

children. They cannot help praying to God as Father with intimate love. As Dunn says of these verses, "In both Rom. 8.15f and Gal. 4.6 therefore it is clear that Paul is speaking of prayer as inspired utterance."[94] Such a familial cry, led by the interceding Spirit, sees believers join a chorus of human prayer, acknowledging God's cosmic fatherhood and gratefully receiving their status as children.

Romans 9:3 and 10:1

In Romans 9:3, Paul prays for unbelieving Israel. In vv. 1–2, he emphatically asserts that he is speaking the truth in what follows—he speaks the truth in Christ, he is not lying, and his conscience bears witness in the Holy Spirit. This confidence indicates his inward self-searching to see if God is exposing any duplicity in him. He has found none. In mentioning himself, Jesus, and the Spirit, Paul presents three witnesses as required in Jewish law.[95] The reference to the Spirit indicates the power of the Spirit to convict and approve a Christian's inward thoughts. Furthermore, his mention of the Spirit here implies the role of the Spirit in his prayer for Israel that he describes in what follows.

Verse 3 begins with εὔχομαι, which means to pray or to wish.[96] While this is often translated as "wish" here, there is no reason not to translate this as "pray," as all other NT uses refer to prayer to God.[97] Paul's prayer is that he himself be accursed from Christ on behalf of his people according to the flesh, Israel. His prayer to be accursed speaks of being cut off from Christ and facing destruction if that saves his people. There is some irony here, as in Paul's theology, Christ became accursed to save humankind from the curse of sin and law (Gal. 3:10–14). As such, Paul prays this, knowing that it will not come to pass, as he has no power to take the sins of unbelieving Israel on himself. Christ has done this.[98] It is implied that he prays in line with the Spirit—pneumaform prayer.

In Romans 10:1, Paul again mentions prayer for Israel in unbelief. He tells the Roman Christians (Ἀδελφοί) that the desire of his heart (εὐδοκία τῆς ἐμῆς καρδίας) and his prayer to God (δέησις πρὸς τὸν θεὸν) on behalf of Israel (ὑπὲρ αὐτῶν) is for their salvation (εἰς σωτηρίαν). These two references to Paul's passionate desire for Israel's salvation summon believers to pray for the lost, including their own people in unbelief. God calls as he wills. Led by the Spirit, we pray for all people from the depths of our beings. The pneumaformed believer wants others to experience the same thing, which begins with believing in Christ—hence we pray for this.

---

94. Dunn, *Jesus and the Spirit*, 241.
95. Deut. 17:6; 19:15; Matt. 18:16; 2 Cor. 13:1; 1 Tim. 5:19; Heb. 10:28.
96. BDAG, s.v. "εὔχομαι," 417.
97. Acts 26:29; 27:29; 2 Cor. 13:7, 9; James 5:16; 3 John 2. See similarly Cranfield, *Romans*, 2:454. See my perspective in Keown, *Romans and the Mission of God*, 315–17.
98. Keown, *Romans and the Mission of God*, 316.

ROMANS 15:5–6

Other prayer wishes dot Paul's letter to the Romans, showing his confidence in God to respond to his prayers and generate life in his converts by the Spirit. In Romans 15:5–6, a passage that forms a frame with Romans 15:13 around what follows, Paul prays that the "God of endurance and encouragement" will give to the Romans (ὑμῖν) the same mindset (φρονέω) in one another according to Christ Jesus, "so that with one common passion,[99] with one voice [the Romans] might glorify the God and Father of our Lord Jesus Christ." Here, Paul prays explicitly for a common phronesis among the Romans that aligns with Christ.

Before this prayer, Paul appeals for the strong in the church to bear with the weak rather than please themselves (Rom. 15:1). The readers must live for the good and edification of their neighbor (Rom. 15:2). In Romans 15:3, Christ is given as an example of living for the good of others and not his pleasure. He did this by taking on himself human sin and shame, taking the insults of humankind on himself, and in so doing, fulfilling Psalm 69:9.

This prayer for a shared mindset is a petition for their cruciformity and resurrectiformity, or Christoformity. The genitive τῆς ὑπομονῆς καὶ τῆς παρακλήσεως is one of source or production, whereby God produces endurance and encouragement (or consolation) in his people. He does this by his Spirit (cf. v. 13), forming the Romans into a harmonious group of worshipping believers who emulate Christ's example of self-giving and sacrifice.

ROMANS 15:13

In Romans 15:7, Paul draws the logical inference from his prayer-wish in vv. 5–6. The Romans should accept one another despite cultural and social differences, just as Christ accepted them. Such acceptance brings glory to God. Paul then commends Christ as the servant of the Jewish people to confirm the Abrahamic promises on behalf of God's truth (vv. 7–8). These promises include the blessing of the nations seen in the Gentiles glorifying God for his mercy (v. 9). Paul then strings together a catena of OT texts that foresee the Gentiles praising God with song, rejoicing, and placing their hope in the Davidic Messiah, who is Christ (vv. 9–12).[100]

Romans 15:13 is another prayer-wish, chiastically framing vv. 7–12 with vv. 5–6. Paul prays, "Now, may the God of hope fill you with all joy and peace in believing so that you may overflow in the hope with the power of the Holy Spirit" (my translation). His prayer describes God as the God who fills you with joy and peace, again a genitive of source or production, indicating that

---

99. The adverb ὁμοθυμαδόν compounds ὁμός, "one and the same, common," and θυμός, which relates to fire and can be negative (anger, wrath) but positively speaks of "an intense expression of the inner self . . . strong desire, *passion, passionate longing*." Hence, "with one common passion."

100. Citing Deut. 32:43; Pss. 18:49; 117:1; Isa. 11:10.

God produces peace. This peace includes reconciliation with his rebellious image bearers who do not know the way of peace (Rom. 3:17; 5:1, 10),[101] in their Christian relationships (Rom. 14:17, 19; Eph. 4:3; 1 Thess. 5:13), with unbelievers (Rom. 12:17), between parties and nations, within themselves (Rom. 8:6; Col. 3:15), in families (1 Cor. 7:11), and in the creation itself (Rom. 16:20; Col. 1:20), and includes eternal peace in the fullest sense in the eschaton (Rom. 2:10)—shalom!

The purpose of the prayer is signaled by the infinitive πληρῶσαι: "so that God would fill [the Romans, ὑμᾶς] with all joy and peace in believing, so as to cause you to abound in hope by the power of the Holy Spirit." Here, the Spirit is explicitly the agent by which God fills up the faithful Romans with all joy, peace, and overflowing hope. Such virtues characterize the pneumaformed.

ROMANS 15:30–33

In Romans 1:8–10, the emphasis is Paul's prayers for the Romans. Here, in chapter 15, he requests prayer for his ministry. In such requests, we see that partnership in prayer is a critical aspect of a pneumaformed life and community. In what precedes the prayer, Paul outlines his plans to travel to Jerusalem with the collection, come to Rome, and then travel to Spain to preach the gospel (Rom. 15:22–29).

Using his regular verb of pastoral encouragement, παρακαλῶ, "I exhort, urge, appeal," Paul next exhorts the Roman brothers and sisters to struggle together (συναγωνίσασθαί) with him in praying to God on his behalf. They are to do this "through our Lord Jesus Christ and through the love of the Spirit." The two διά + genitive clauses indicate agency, "through [the agency of], by."[102] First, "our Lord Jesus Christ" is the agent through whom the prayers reach God. "The love of the Spirit" is the second agent.[103] The genitive τοῦ πνεύματος can be subjective (the love the Spirit has for believers).[104] However, more likely, it is a genitive of source, origin, or production, whereby the Spirit bestows love into the hearts of believers. This love becomes their primary motivator for praying for other Christians.[105] Hence, we have a crucial aspect of pneumaformity: being motivated by love to pray with and for others.[106]

---

101. Also, 2 Cor. 5:18–20; Eph. 2:16; Col. 1:22.
102. BDAG, s.v. "διά," 225. Fee, *GEP*, 632 suggests these are genitives of "efficient cause"; however, I consider they speak of agency.
103. Fee notes correctly that here we see "how Trinitarian Paul's basic assumptions about God actually are." Fee, *GEP*, 633.
104. John Murray, *The Epistle to the Romans: The English Text with Introduction, Exposition, and Notes*, NICNT (Grand Rapids: Eerdmans, 1965), 2:221.
105. Thomas R. Schreiner, *Romans*, BECNT (Grand Rapids: Baker Academic, 1998), 781.
106. I diverge from Fee here who prefers to see this as a reference to the "the love for all the saints . . . that the Spirit engenders." Fee, *GEP*, 632. However, his discussion is too binary. It is the love that God poured into their hearts by the Spirit that generates their love for one another.

The purpose of the prayer (ἵνα) is twofold. First, Paul prays that he will be delivered from the unbelievers in Judea and that the Jerusalem collection will be well received by the saints there (v. 31). Second, that through the will of God, he will come to the Romans with joy and to be refreshed by them. The "will of God" recalls 1:10 in which Paul's travel plans are subject to God's desires. Paul hopes the combined effects of his prayers and theirs will move God to open a way to Rome. The wider NT indicates that this prayer was answered affirmatively through God's sovereign power to shape events to his purposes by his Spirit. Paul ends by praying that the God of peace will be with all the Romans. His prayer speaks of God's presence by the Spirit.

Romans 15:33 reads like the final verse in the letter. However, even though it creates an inclusio with Romans 1:7, generally Paul prefers to conclude his letters with a prayer for grace. This text marks the end of the section on his travel plans before commending the letter courier Phoebe and beginning his greetings. By using "God of peace," Paul prays again (as in 1:7) that God will be with the Romans so that they experience peace and reconciliation in every aspect of their lives. Notably, he wants that peace for all the Romans, not a select few. Peace is sourced in God and Christ in Romans 1:7 and 15:13, and elsewhere it is a fruit of the Spirit (Gal. 5:22). As such, Paul wants the Spirit fruit peace of God and Christ by the Spirit to flow through the church.[107] Shalom is the climax of pneumaformity for believers and the cosmos.

1 Corinthians 7:5

Dunn observes in this verse that "devotion to prayer is the other side of the charisma of voluntary celibacy."[108] Indeed, this text suggests that Paul considered that, at times, it is appropriate for married couples to abstain from sexual relations and instead focus on prayer. However, this is not to be a permanent state to ensure neither party lapses into sexual immorality. Paul's guidance implies prayer is an essential part of a Spirit-led marriage.

1 Corinthians 11:4, 13

As Dunn rightly observes, these verses indicate that Paul expected men and women to pray in the church, albeit appropriately dressed. As prayer is paired with prophesying, Dunn considers this verse speaks of spontaneous, inspired utterances.[109] However, while the pairing of activities may indicate they are both momentary, there seems no reason to limit prayer to the spontaneous. It could include prayers prepared at home or joining in with others in corporate

---

107. Also 1 Cor. 7:15; 14:33; 16:11; 2 Cor. 13:11; Gal. 6:16; Eph. 2:14–15, 17; 6:15; Phil. 4:7; 1 Thess. 5:3; 2 Thess. 3:16; 2 Tim. 2:22.
108. Dunn, *Jesus and the Spirit*, 239.
109. Dunn, *Jesus and the Spirit*, 239.

prayers.[110] Either way, men and women expressing the spiritual gift of prophesying in the gathered church community is an aspect of Spirit-led worship.

1 CORINTHIANS 14:14–17

This passage sits in Paul's discussion of using tongues in the Corinthian church. In the first person, Paul states, "I will pray with my spirit, but I will pray with my mind also." He adds other aspects of prayer life—praise, singing, and giving thanks. As noted when discussing Philippians 3:3 earlier in the chapter, while a case can be made for this being the Spirit of God in v. 14, it is more likely the inner being (as evidenced by the use of μου). The Holy Spirit is still in view, as praying with his spirit includes exercising the spiritual gift of tongues. However, as he has stressed in the passage, tongues without interpretation in the church are meaningless to hearers. As such, in the church, he will also pray with his mind, speaking of comprehensible and edifying prayers. These could include tongues with interpretation and prayer in the lingua franca of those in the church.[111]

EPHESIANS 1:15–23

I am discussing this pericope here because it suggests that Paul believes that prayer, for people who have received the Spirit, can lead to a fresh encounter with the Spirit of God.[112] The passage follows Paul's long blessing to God for the many spiritual blessings bestowed on believers. Paul then reminds the Ephesians of their conversion experience (Eph. 1:1–13). In v. 14, a critical aspect is receiving the Spirit and being "sealed with the Spirit."

In v. 15, Paul turns to prayer for these Spirit-imbued Christians. Because he knows of their faith in Christ and love for others, he prays for them ceaselessly, remembering them in prayer (v. 16). The ἵνα in v. 17 launches the purpose and content of his prayer, namely, that God "may give you the Spirit (πνεῦμα) of wisdom and revelation in the knowledge of him."[113] πνεῦμα may not mean the Spirit of God here, and if so, Paul is speaking of "a spirit of wisdom and revelation" (LEB, NASB, NRSV) or "spiritual wisdom and revelation" (NET). However, several factors suggest "Spirit of wisdom and revelation" is justified. First, in all three LXX uses, similar constructs speak of God's wisdom (Exod. 35:31; Wis. 7:7; Isa. 11:2).[114] Second, what follows in v. 18 further defines the activity of this

---

110. Especially when we consider that the point in the passage is not the activity of praying itself, but that men and women have their hair and head arranged in a culturally appropriate manner.

111. See also Dunn, *Jesus and the Spirit*, 239. Dunn also discusses how tongues functions as another aspect of prayer: "The other reason Paul values glossolalia is because it is for him primarily a prayer language" (p. 245). See 1 Cor. 14:2, 14–17.

112. See also Fee, *GEP*, 672–73, for his short analysis.

113. Similarly, see Fee, *GEP*, 673.

114. In Exodus 35:31 in the MT, it is "the Spirit of God" (רוּחַ אֱלֹהִים). In Wisdom 7:7, the Spirit is implied as the author calls out to God and what is received is from him. In Isaiah 11:2, the phrase further defines "God's Spirit" who will rest on the one imbued.

πνεῦμα, which is more suggestive of the Spirit of God than an inner mood. As such, I am confident Paul means the Spirit here.[115]

The participle πεφωτισμένους in v. 18 may be causal, "since, because," showing the cause or reason God might give them the Spirit in this way (NET).[116] However, it is more likely purposive (telic)—"so that the eyes of your hearts may be enlightened . . ." (similarly, NRSV). Paul hopes his prayer will lead to the Ephesians experiencing a more profound spiritual insight into the hope of salvation and eternal life, a fuller understanding of their status as God's heirs, and an experience of the greatness of God's power exercised toward those who believe (the same power that raised Christ and seated him at God's right hand). This power is the Spirit in Romans 1:4 and 8:11. As such, Paul wants God, by his Spirit, to give the readers a deeper understanding of all that God has given them.

As the Ephesians have received the Spirit, Paul is not praying for a first reception of the Spirit. Instead, he asks for a fresh impartation of (or from) the Spirit of God. This replenishment could mean another outpouring of the Spirit or a fresh experience of the same Spirit to deepen their wisdom and give them fresh and more profound revelations of the God they have come to know. Whichever way you spin it, believers can have fresh experiences of the Holy Spirit. Arguably, we see this in Acts, where people who were filled with the Spirit at Pentecost had fresh experiences.[117] In this instance, the fresh experience Paul is praying for will cause them to know God and who they are in him more deeply. Mature Christians formed in and by the Spirit should be praying for such experiences for others. We should delight in hearing others are praying for us to have such experiences of the Spirit. They are clearly crucial to ongoing pneumaformation.

Ephesians 3:14–21

As with the previous two references, these verses again indicate Paul wanted his converts to have new encounters with the Spirit.[118] In Ephesians 3:1–11, Paul reminds the Ephesians of his apostolic commission to preach

---

115. Fee concurs, adding other arguments. First, the absence of the article "has nothing at all to do with whether Paul is here referring to the divine Spirit or the human spirit." Second, the language concurs with Colossians 1:9, where the Spirit is implied in συνέσει πνευματικῇ. Third, the key to gaining wisdom and revelation is the Spirit. Fourth, the ideas of wisdom and revelation are linked in other Spirit passages (1 Cor. 2:10–13; 12:8; Eph. 3:5). Fifth, to suggest "a spirit of revelation" is "near nonsense." Fee, *GEP*, 675–76. His other comments on the passage are salutary.

116. Wallace notes that most perfect participles function in this way. However, he goes on to say, "But the perfect anarthrous participle often belongs to another category (especially periphrastic or predicate adjective), even though it may appear at first glance to be adverbial." Wallace, *Greek Grammar*, 631.

117. After the initial Pentecost experience (Acts 2:1–4), Luke writes of other "fillings" for Peter (Acts 4:8) and the whole church (Acts 4:31). Similarly, after Paul's initial receipt of the Spirit (Acts 9:17), he appears to have had a fresh experience of being filled with the Spirit in Pisidian Antioch (Acts 13:9). See Keown, *Discovering: The Gospels and Acts*, 342–47.

118. See also Fee's discussion of this passage, *GEP*, 693–97.

God's mystery now revealed to the Gentiles. Now, in Christ, believers have confident boldness to approach God (v. 12). He urges them not to be discouraged because of what he is going through in Rome for them but to see his sufferings as their glory (v. 13), and then he turns to prayer.

Τούτου χάριν can look back to the promises of the gospel and the open access believers have to God, or as seems preferable, looks forward to what he will pray for. The posture of bending the knee is found in Isaiah 45:23, where every knee will bend to God and every tongue swear by God. It speaks of kneeling on the knee before someone seen as superior, such as a royal figure, in homage and humility.

The broader literature uses the idea of bending the knee in homage to God.[119] In the NT, it is unique to Paul, used three other times in his letters, twice as he uses Isaiah 45:23 of universal homage to Jesus as Lord (Rom. 14:11; Phil. 2:10). The other use is of the faithful kneeling to God at the time of Elijah (Rom. 11:4). Here, as Paul prays, he bends his knee before God, who is described as the one who has put in place and named every family of beings in heaven and earth.

The purpose of the prayer is given in v. 16: "that [ἵνα] according to the riches of his glory he may grant you to be strengthened with power[120] through his Spirit in your inner being." This rich verse confirms the link between prayer and the release of God's power in believers. Paul here does not pray for any fresh impartation of the Spirit but the release of power through (διά) God's (αὐτοῦ) Spirit.[121] The final phrase εἰς τὸν ἔσω ἄνθρωπον, likely speaks of the inner beings of the individual Ephesians.[122]

The infinitive κατοικῆσαι in v. 17 speaks of the purpose of this strengthening through the Spirit: "so that Christ might dwell (κατοικέω) through faith in your hearts, rooted and established in love" (my translation).[123] The verb

---

119. Odes Sol. 8:11; Sib. Or. 3:616; 4:106; Pr. Man. 1:11.

120. On "power through his Spirit," and "be strengthened," see Fee, *GEP*, 695. "Be strengthened" elaborates on or gives content to the previous. He notes that the use of power, Spirit, and strengthened derives from the OT and is common with Luke. The link of power and Spirit indicates 1:19 and 3:20 has the Spirit in view as well. He adds, "This passage [with Rom. 15:13] shows that for Paul the 'power of the Spirit' is not only for more visible and extraordinary manifestations of God's presence, but also (especially) for the empowering necessary to be his people in the world, so as to be true reflections of his own glory." See also Habets, *Anointed Son*, 292.

121. Verse 14 shows that God the Father is clearly the antecedent of the pronoun.

122. See on "inner person" Fee, *GEP*, 695–96. It is uniquely Pauline. It is both "the seat of personal consciousness, [and] the seat of our moral being." He suggests it gives "objective expression to concepts which occur elsewhere in terms of 'indwelling' or 'in the heart'"; however, for me, the ideas of indwelling and in the heart explicate the inner being and the inner being is not "concrete." He correctly notes that God indwelling people occurs in this "inner person," which is another way of saying "our hearts" (cf. 2 Cor. 1:22). It incorporates the cognitive and experiential aspects of being human. He rightly stresses that while this is individualistic, it is set in the context of the united community of Jew and Gentile.

123. Alternatively, as Fee suggests, it is epexegetical so that "this is what it means for them to be strengthened by the Spirit in the inner person, namely, that Christ himself thus dwells in their hearts; all of this

κατοικέω, in the NT, speaks of living in a particular place, including God dwelling in the temple (Matt. 23:21), and in Acts, of God not dwelling in human-made dwellings (Acts 7:48; 17:24).[124] In Colossians, the fullness of God dwells in Christ's body (Col. 1:9; 2:9). Here, Christ dwells in believers through their believing in him. His doing so recalls Ephesians 1:13–14, where Paul confirmed the Ephesians' belief and reception of the Spirit. This verse confirms that Christ dwells in them by his Spirit. In that they have already received Christ by the Spirit, Paul is praying for a fresh experience of his power in them to know that Christ resides in them. They are the body of Christ, the temple of the Spirit.

Their prior receipt of the Spirit is confirmed in the two perfect passive participles that follow, ἐρριζωμένοι and τεθεμελιωμένοι. The verb ῥιζόω is agricultural, speaking of something taking root.[125] Paul also uses it in Colossians 2:6 of the Colossians being rooted in Christ. The second verb, θεμελιόω, speaks of something set on a foundation.[126] Two LXX ideas flow into the term. First, it is used repeatedly of God laying the earth's foundations, implying an organic idea.[127] Hence, both verbs are suggestive of a new creation. Second, θεμελιόω is commonly used for establishing the temple.[128] Believers are a living temple of

---

transpires by faith." Fee, *GEP*, 596. He chooses this to avoid consequential views that suggest they must be strengthened by the Spirit so Christ can dwell in their hearts. However, his solution does not resolve the problem, as Christ dwells in their hearts whether they are strengthened or not. Rather, I think it is a purpose infinitive, not that the purpose of their strengthening will cause Christ to dwell in their hearts, but that they will experience his dwelling there in a fresh way. It is thus a prayer for a fresh experience of Christ's indwelling by the Spirit.

124. κατοικέω is used of where people dwell (Matt. 2:23; 4:13; Luke 13:4; Acts 1:19, 20; 2:5, 9, 14; 4:16; 7:2, 4; 9:22, 32, 35; 11:29; 13:27; 17:26; 19:10, 17; 22:12; Heb. 11:9; Rev. 2:13; 3:10; 6:10; 8:13; 11:10; 13:8, 12, 14 [2x]; 17:2, 8). Also of an evil spirit residing in a person (Matt. 12:45; Luke 11:26) and righteousness dwelling in the new heavens and new earth (2 Peter 3:13).

125. See *BrillDAG*, s.v. "ῥιζόω." Josephus uses it literally of plants taking root (*J.W.* 4.471). LXX uses include Israel being rooted in God (Pss. Sol. 14:4), rulers being established (Isa. 40:24), evil people taking root (Jer. 12:2), and ethically of evil (Sir. 3:28) and wisdom (Sir. 24:12) taking root. Philo also uses it literally of rooted plants (*Plant.* 11), God planting the middle mind in paradise (*Plant.* 45), of the earth and water rooted on earth (*Plant.* 4), rooted plants (*Plant.* 74), ethically of God rooting people in virtues (*Alleg. Interp.* 1.45), virtues taking root (*Alleg. Interp.* 1.89), God planting virtues in people (*Plant.* 46), and wickedness rooted on earth (Moses 2.285).

126. *BrillDAG*, s.v. "θεμελιόω."

127. The establishment of the heavens and astral bodies (Ps. 8:4 [8:3 EEV], also T. Sol. 20:17; Jos. Asen. 12:3), the earth (Pss. 23:2 [24:2 EVV]; 88:12 [89:11 EVV]; 101:26 [102:25 EVV]; 103:5 [104:5 EVV]; Prov. 8:23; Job 38:4, also Jos. Asen. 12:3), mountains and plains (Ps. 103:8 [104:8 EVV]; Zech. 12:1; Isa. 48:13; 51:13, 16; also 1 En. 18:12; 21:2), and God's vault on the earth (Amos 9:6).

128. Of the foundations of Zion (Ps. 86:5 [87:5 EVV]; Isa. 14:32), of Jerusalem (Ps. 47:9 [48:8 EVV]), and of the temple (3 Kgdms. 6:1; 7:47; 2 Chron. 8:16; 1 Esdr. 5:55; 6:10; 2 Esdr. 3:6, 10; Ps. 77:69 [78:69 EVV]; Hag. 2:18; Zech. 4:9; 8:9; Isa. 44:28). The verb is also used of the foundations of a city (Josh. 6:26; 2 Kgdms. 16:34). The foundations of piles of offerings (2 Chron. 31:7), the beginnings of a journey (2 Esdr. 7:9), the foundations of walls (Jdt. 1:3; Sir. 50:2), the foundations of faithfulness on earth (Ps. 118:90 [119:90 EVV]), the foundations of God's decrees (Ps. 118:152 [119:152 EVV]), and the foundations of a palace (Prov. 18:19) or columns (like legs) (Song 5:15). Also, the foundations of the number ten (*Opif.* 102) and wisdom (Ebr. 31).

the Spirit in a corporate and an individual sense (1 Cor. 3:16; 6:19). The verb is also used for the Colossians being founded in faith (Col. 1:23) and by Peter of Christ's power to establish his suffering readers (1 Peter 5:10).[129] The participles are probably causal; by God's power, the Ephesians will experience afresh Christ in them because they have been rooted and established in love.

"Love" again draws our thoughts to the Spirit as, by the Spirit, love has been poured into believers' hearts (Rom. 5:5). Love is also the head fruit of the Spirit (Gal. 5:22). Love is the most excellent way (1 Cor. 12:31). The Ephesians, in love, were predestined to be adopted into God's family through Christ (Eph. 1:4) and are his beloved children (Eph. 5:1). Because of God's love for them, he has saved them (Eph. 2:4). They are now Christ's beloved (Eph. 5:2), for whom he gave himself up (Eph. 5:25). God is the source of love (Eph. 6:23). The Ephesians, saved by grace, are rooted and established in love. This love will flow through them, confirm their status as God's children, and flow from them to Christ (Eph. 6:24), to one another,[130] and to the lost.

The following ἵνα clause can indicate the purpose of their being rooted and established in love or is a second indicator of what Paul prays. The former seems more likely, although the difference is minimal, and what follows is part of the content of Paul's prayer. His purpose in praying is that they "may grasp together with all the saints what is the breadth, and length, and height, and depth, and to know the love of Christ that surpasses knowledge, in order that [they] may be filled up to all the fullness of God." Just what they are to grasp in this complete way is not completely clear, leading to a wide range of ideas.[131] Arnold notes seven options, of which five are reasonable:[132] (1) the vastness of God's power, (2) the love of Christ, (3) the "mystery" of God's plan, (4) the manifold wisdom of God, and (5) the new temple.

I consider (3), (4), and (5) less likely than (1) and (2). Where (5), the temple, is concerned, the temple God is forming with Jewish and Gentile believers, which is built on the apostles and prophets with Christ as the capstone/cornerstone and is a dwelling place for God by his Spirit, certainly features in Ephesians 2:19–22. Paul also refers to the building up of the body of Christ and building each other up with gospel-worthy speech (Eph. 4:12, 16, 29). Furthermore, θεμελιόω in the previous verse hints at the temple. However, it is unlikely Paul would pray that his converts know more of the temple; other ideas are more likely in the context, and the basis on which the temple is formed (Christ) is a better idea here.

---

129. Also in the NT, the founding of the earth (Heb. 1:10) and a house founded on a rock (Jesus's teaching; Matt. 7:25).
130. Eph. 1:15; 4:2, 15, 16; 5:2, 25, 28, 33; 6:21, 24.
131. See the summaries in Arnold, *Ephesians*, 215–16; Lincoln, *Ephesians*, 207–13. Some speculative options include "the four arms of the cross, the Gnostic man, the heavenly Jerusalem (Rev. 21:16; cf. Ezek. 48:16; Herm. Vis. 3.2.5)."
132. Arnold, *Ephesians*, 215–16.

Concerning (3), "mystery" (μυστήριον) is a core idea in Ephesians. Paul mentions the mystery of God's will (Eph. 1:9), the mystery of Christ and the church (5:32), and the "the mystery of the gospel" (6:19), and uses the term three times in chapter 3, including "the mystery of Christ" (3:4) and "the mystery hidden from the ages by God" (3:9). This idea has merit. However, a better answer is what the mystery is—Jesus.

An even better possibility than (3) is (4), with "wisdom" (σοφία) an idea that features in the letter and immediate context. God has caused the believers to abound in wisdom (Eph. 1:8), and Paul has prayed for God to give the Ephesians the Spirit of wisdom (1:17). In the previous passage, Paul's ministry is to preach Christ and bring to light the plan of the *mystery* hidden for ages in God so that "the many-sided wisdom of God might be made known now to the rulers and the authorities in the heavenly places through the church" (3:10 LEB). It could be that Paul, having prayed earlier for the Ephesians to have the Spirit of wisdom, is now praying that they understand its full extent. The four aspects (breadth, length, height, and depth) could correlate loosely with πολυποίκιλος, "many-sided." Still, while this idea has merit here, it is what, or better who, God's wisdom comprises that is the focus of Paul's prayer here—Christ.

Whether or not there is a link to be made here to magical papyri, option (1), the power of God, is a realistic option. In vv. 16–17, Paul prays explicitly that the Ephesians may be inwardly strengthened with God's power (δυνάμει) by his Spirit so that Christ may dwell in their hearts through faith. Again, in v. 20, Paul prays to God as the one who is able (δυναμένῳ) to do immeasurably more than believers can contemplate. Furthermore, δύναμ-language features in the letter. In 1:19, Paul prays for the Ephesians to know the greatness of God's power toward believers exercised in Christ, whom God has raised above every power. Power language features five times in chapter 3 and three times in this prayer (above). In 3:7, God's power generates Paul's apostolic gift of grace.[133] Another four uses are found in 6:10–16 for believers' capacity to withstand evil forces (vv. 10, 11, 13, 16). However, while a persuasive case can be made for God's power here, it would be strange for Paul to pray, as he does in v. 18, that God would empower the Ephesians and all other believers, to grasp the full dimensions of God's power. Instead, they are being empowered by God to grasp something other than power. A better answer is the source or conduit of power—Jesus.

---

133. See also Ephesians 3:4, where it refers to the Ephesians' ability to understand Paul's insight into the mystery of Christ. See also Fee, *GEP*, 693, who briefly comments on this verse noting, its resonances with Colossians 1:29. The term δύναμις, "power," is almost interchangeable with "Spirit." He sees three things here of Paul: "(a) he himself is a servant [of Christ or the gospel, is to be understood], (b) as a direct result of grace that as been given to him, which (c) is made effective by the empowering of the Holy Spirit."

We are left with two other possibilities. The first is the favorite idea, the *love* of Christ. If so, the sentence that follows is epexegetical, drawing out that Paul wants them to know the fullness of Christ's love that surpasses knowledge. As outlined above, love is a crucial idea in Ephesians, whether it be God's love that motivates his action to save and father believers;[134] the ground on which the Ephesians are planted in God and Christ (Eph. 3:17); the love Christ has for his people;[135] or the Ephesians' love for others,[136] for Christ (6:24), for their own bodies (5:28b), and for the beloved Tychicus (6:21). Without doubt, Paul may be praying that the Ephesians come to more deeply understand the love of Christ. Still, I believe there is a better option.

The best possibility hinted at through the analysis thus far is the person who stands behind all ideas previously broached: that the Ephesians know the full extent of *who Christ is*. And they will know this "by the Spirit." Not only does Christ regularly feature in the letter,[137] but Paul has stressed the Ephesians' relationship with Christ in many ways up to this point in the letter. God has blessed them *in Christ* with every spiritual blessing (1:3), bestowed grace on them *in him* (v. 6). New believers are created *in Christ Jesus* (2:10). In the prayer, *Christ* dwells in their hearts (3:17); he prays they know the knowledge-surpassing love of *Christ* so that they are filled up to all the fullness of God (3:19); and God receives glory *in* the church and *Christ Jesus* forever (3:21).

It is the *body of Christ* that is built up as these gifts are exercised until it reaches maturity and the fullness of the head, *Christ* (4:12–13, 15). It is *Christ* and the truth *in him* who is the content of the Ephesians' learning, and *he* is their teacher (4:20–21). They are to learn what is pleasing to *him* (5:10) and that learning is utterly christocentric, Christ-focused, christological, and christotelic in every sense.

As such, I conclude that Paul wants the Ephesians to know the breadth, length, height, and depth *of Christ*. By this, they know the dimensions of God, whose fullness is in Christ. They will know God's power, wisdom, knowledge, and love in Christ completely, *in and by the Spirit*.

Whether I am right that Paul wants them to know the full dimensions of Christ, he makes it explicit in v. 19 that he wants them to know "the love of Christ." The infinitive is purposive. He wants them to know the fullness of Christ "*so that* they may know the love of Christ that surpasses knowledge." He wants them to do this "*so that* [ἵνα] [they] might be filled up with[138] all the fullness of God." Knowing the fullness of who Christ is and his love for them is so that they are filled up with God. This filling refers to

---

134. Eph. 1:4; 2:4; 5:1; 6:23.

135. Eph. 3:19; 5:2b, 25c; 6:23.

136. Eph. 1:15; 4:2, 15, 18; 5:2a, 25a–b, 28, 33.

137. Jesus, 20x; Christ, 46x; "Christ Jesus," 11x; "Jesus Christ," 1x (without Lord); Lord, 23x; "Lord Jesus Christ," 6x; Savior, 1x; "Lord Jesus," 7x; "him/his/whom," 27x.

138. The εἰς here indicates "being filled up to" in the sense of the wholeness of God.

those in Christ whom God fills with his fullness by the Spirit. Indeed, as Paul writes to Colossians, God has filled Christ with his fullness (Col. 1:19; 2:9). So, to know Christ more is to know God! Paul wants readers to experience all that the Triune God brings in his amazing salvation. If the prayer is fulfilled, they will live up to this in the world, worship God fully, love and build one another up, and give Christ-centered witness to the world. This prayer is a petition for complete pneumaformity whereby God, in Christ and by the Spirit, forms his people into the image of God's Son—that they are fully Christoform.

The penultimate part of the prayer is the prayer-wish in Ephesians 3:20, in which Paul restates God's omnipotence. Being infinitely powerful, God can do more than anything they might pray or think.[139] The power at work in them is God's presence in Christ by the Spirit. He finishes in 3:21, praying that God's infinite glory would be recognized and demonstrated in the church and in Christ Jesus forever.

Ephesians 5:14

I include a brief comment on this passage for different reasons than Fee. He notes the lack of mention of the Spirit but that some early Fathers (e.g., Theodoret) read this as an example of "each one of you has a hymn" from 1 Corinthians 14:26. This leads him to posit that we have evidence of how early Christians understood "spiritual songs" (Eph. 5:19; Col. 3:16). He claims the introductory formula "Therefore it says" (also 4:8)[140] indicates Spirit inspiration as in the Psalms. I find all this conjecture. However, the words of the hymn imply the work of the Spirit.[141]

First, the sleeper (the spiritually dead, cf. Eph. 2:1–3) is to awake and rise from the dead. These states imagine the Christian's death and resurrection in those of Christ neatly reenacted in water baptism. Although Fee rejects the notion, I have argued that the Spirit is the agent by which God raised Christ and will raise believers.[142] Second, the motif of Christ shining as light upon the believer speaks of the work of the Spirit emanating from the Father through the Son. It implies baptism in, and the ongoing filling with, the Spirit that believers experience (cf. 5:18).

---

139. Fee notes that the power is the same as in vv. 16–17, *GEP*, 697.
140. In Ephesians 4:8 the formula introduces Psalm 68:18. However, this usage is not a known OT text. Arnold notes that it has resonances to Isaiah 26:19 and 60:1–2 LXX. He contends Paul is citing an early Christian hymn, perhaps influenced by these OT texts. He also discusses life settings posited by scholars, and while it is speculative as Arnold concludes, to me, baptism seems the best option (see, e.g., Lincoln, *Ephesians*, 331). See Arnold, *Ephesians*, 334.
141. Arnold concludes, and I agree: "It may well be another way of referring to the presence of the Holy Spirit, who is grieved when believers sin (4:30) but powerfully enables them when they are willing to turn from sin and pursue a life of holiness." Arnold, *Ephesians*, 336.
142. See chapter 3, "The Spirit Who Gives Life." See Rom. 1:4; 1 Cor. 6:14; 15:44; Eph. 1:19–21; Phil. 3:21; 1 Tim. 3:16.

PHILIPPIANS 1:9–11

After his prescript, as he often does, Paul begins Philippians with thanksgiving and shifts to intercession. On its face, these verses do not mention the Spirit. However, the outcome of the prayer is all about the Spirit. He prays that the love of the Philippians will overflow more and more in knowledge and insight. In that love is poured into believers' hearts by the Spirit (Rom. 5:5) and heads the fruit of the Spirit (Gal. 5:22), this is effectively a prayer for them to yield to the Spirit of love in all situations. If they do, they will be able to discern what is excellent so that they are pure and blameless at Christ's coming and judgment.

Verse 11 draws explicitly on the "fruit" analogy also used in Galatians 5:22: "filled with the fruit of righteousness that comes through Jesus Christ." The fruit in mind here could be God's declaration of righteousness over them.[143] However, it more likely speaks of "the fruit of righteous activity and attitude."[144] The fruit comes *through Jesus Christ*, linking the production to Jesus. This fruit is expressed in lives that are cruciform. The Spirit works in believers, growing them in this so that they bear the fruit of the Spirit that conforms to the attitude of Christ.

PHILIPPIANS 1:19

The clear link between praying and the Spirit in Ephesians 5:18 draws other Pauline passages into view when thinking of the Spirit and prayer. One of these is Philippians 1:19. Having expressed his joy that the gospel is advancing in his city of incarceration (likely Rome), Paul shifts in 1:18e to talking about his situation, hopes, and plans. He begins boldly declaring that he knows his situation in imprisonment will turn out for his σωτηρία. The term may be used here regarding deliverance from prison or eternal salvation. As Paul only uses σωτηρία in terms of the latter,[145] this should be supposed here. However, Paul may be using it more subtly, meaning that while he is very confident his situation will turn out for his release (v. 25), even if it does not and he dies, it will end with his salvation.[146]

The διά can indicate causality, or, as is more likely, it is instrumental, indicating how this salvation "is accomplished or effected."[147] The instrument by which Paul will be saved (and/or released) is τῆς ὑμῶν δεήσεως καὶ ἐπιχορηγίας τοῦ πνεύματος Ἰησοῦ Χριστοῦ, "your prayers and the help (or supply) of the Spirit of Jesus Christ."

The first instrument is "your prayers" (τῆς ὑμῶν δεήσεως), clearly indicating the Philippians' intercession for Paul. The second instrument, καὶ ἐπιχορηγίας τοῦ πνεύματος Ἰησοῦ Χριστοῦ, can mean either "the

---

143. Fee, *Philippians*, 103–4.
144. Keown, *Philippians*, 1:166.
145. See Keown, *Philippians*, 1:463.
146. Keown, *Philippians*, 1:227–30.
147. See for this meaning BDAG, s.v. "διά," 224.

supply of the Spirit of Jesus Christ"[148] or "the help given by the Spirit of Jesus Christ." The noun ἐπιχορηγία is a compound formed from ἐπί, "on, upon," and χορηγέω, "provide, supply." As I have discussed elsewhere, the language is used of God supplying a range of things, including "seed and bread [2 Cor. 9:10], the Spirit [Gal. 3:5], and eternal reward [2 Pet. 1:11]."[149] In Ephesians 4:16, ἐπιχορηγία is used of every "ligament that serves for support."[150] The associated verb, ἐπιχορηγέω, is used in the NT of God providing seed and bread for food (2 Cor. 9:10), entrance into the kingdom (2 Peter 1:11), and, importantly for this verse, the Spirit (Gal. 3:5). All in all, it could mean either supply or help. Yet, even if supply is in view, the lavishing of the Spirit on Paul brings him help. So, either way, the supply or help of the Spirit combined with the prayers of the Philippians will turn out for Paul's salvation.

The genitive Ἰησοῦ Χριστοῦ, "of Jesus Christ," can be objective genitive, meaning "the supply that is the Spirit of Jesus Christ" or "the help that is the Spirit of Jesus Christ."[151] However, because Paul is already a full recipient of the Spirit, it is better to understand it here as "the help that the Spirit of Jesus Christ affords."[152] The genitive "demonstrates perichoretic unity of Christ and the Spirit."[153] It also implies that Christ is with Paul via the Spirit. The blend of the prayers of the Philippians and the Spirit's help will see him delivered from prison and, if not, sustain him to salvation. Here, the Spirit's help in suffering is linked to prayer—prayer enhances the power of the Spirit to help a person in suffering.

The καί that links the prayer and Spirit here is interesting. It is not one or the other that brings about Paul's release or salvation, but the combination of prayer and the Spirit. While, without doubt, the primary agency for Paul is the Spirit, who prompts prayer in the first place, people's prayers prayed in and by the Spirit change and affect situations.[154] Notably, it is the Spirit of Jesus Christ,[155] indicating that Christ is the agent who works through the Spirit[156] and with the prayers of the saints, who, via the Spirit's prompts, brings to pass Paul's deliverance/salvation. We have here a text where the unity of Christ and the Spirit in outworking God's purposes is expressed (cf. Rom. 8:9; 2 Cor.

---

148. Fee, *GEP*, 740–41.

149. Keown, *Philippians*, 1:231.

150. BDAG, s.v. "ἐπιχορηγία," 387.

151. As in Galatians 3:5 ("the supply of the Spirit of Jesus Christ" with God as the implied subject; see, e.g., Markus Bockmuehl, *The Epistle to the Philippians*, BNTC [London: Continuum, 1997], 84; Hansen, *The Letter*, 79–80).

152. Gerald F. Hawthorne, *Philippians*, rev. ed., WBC (Dallas: Word, 2004), 49; Keown, *Philippians*, 1:232.

153. Keown, *Philippians*, 1:232. See also Rom. 8:9; 2 Cor. 3:17–18.

154. See also Romans 1:10, where Paul's prayers will eventually see him in Rome. His subjection of this to the will of God demonstrates his desire for prayer that aligns with the Spirit's promptings and desires.

155. It can be subjective, "the Spirit sent by Christ" (also source or production), or identification or relationship, "the Spirit who belongs to Christ." Fee, *GEP*, 742.

156. "The Spirit of Christ is the Spirit that now proceeds from Christ, as from the Father in the Old Testament." Habets, *Anointed Son*, 136.

3:18). A critical aspect of pneumaformity is prayer impelled by the Spirit of Jesus, and so, cruciformity.

PHILIPPIANS 4:5–7

After directly appealing to Euodia and Syntyche to resolve their differences, Paul emphatically summons the Philippians to rejoice. He then urges them to let their gentleness (or clemency, tolerance, or reasonableness) be evident to all people.[157] The preceding statement, "the Lord is near" (ὁ κύριος ἐγγύς), can look forward to the imminent coming of Christ. However, as I have established previously, the phrase is used in the psalms to indicate the nearness of the Lord to minister to his people.[158] "The Lord" can be Yahweh, as it is in the Hebrew from which the LXX was translated in verses that utilize the two Greek terms as here (Pss. 34:18; 145:16). However, in Philippians, κύριος is almost certainly Christ in every instance.[159] As such, we have another example of Paul seeing Christ as the fulfillment of eschatological hopes associated with Yahweh (cf. Isa. 45:23; Phil. 2:10). God, then, is present with the Philippians, in Christ—God the Son. God and Christ, in turn, are near to the Philippians by the Spirit. He is near "to all who call on him, to all who call on him in truth" (Ps. 145:18), and hears the prayers of the Philippians and all who believe. As God and Christ are near to hear the prayers of the Philippians by the Spirit, they are not to be anxious about anything but are to present their requests to God. With thanksgiving, they should do so with the full range of prayers (Phil. 4:6).[160]

Verse 7 indicates what results from their prayers: "the peace of God that surpasses all understanding will guard [their] hearts and [their] minds in Christ Jesus" (LEB). For Paul, the Spirit is life and peace (Rom. 8:6). The kingdom of God is not about what people eat or drink or other incidental matters, but righteousness, peace, and joy in the Holy Spirit (Rom. 14:17). Believers are filled with peace through the power of the Spirit (Rom. 15:13). Peace is another fruit generated by the Holy Spirit in the lives of God's people (Gal. 5:22). Unity and the bond of peace are maintained in the church by the power of the Spirit (Eph. 4:3).[161] As such, Paul is speaking of the peace from

---

157. Mark J. Keown, "The Use of the OT in Philippians," in *All the Prophets Have Declared*, ed. Matthew R. Malcolm (Milton Keynes: Paternoster, 2015), 139–65.

158. ἐγγὺς Κύριος (Ps. 33:19 [34:18 MT, EVV]); ἐγγὺς εἶ, Κύριε (Ps. 118:151 [119:151 MT, EVV]); ἐγγὺς Κύριος (Ps. 144:18 [145:18 MT, EVV]).

159. Explicitly in Phil. 1:2; 2:11, 19; 3:8, 20; 4:23. While we cannot be absolute about other uses, the emphatic use especially in Philippians 2:11 and 3:20 would suggest Christ is in view in all uses. Furthermore, the phrase ἐν κυρίῳ always implies Christ (Phil. 1:14; 2:24, 29; 3:1; 4:1, 2, 4; 4:10). Additionally, the five uses in Philippians 4:1–10 are likely Christ in light of 3:20 (and 3:1, which parallels 4:4).

160. See the discussion of these categories, Keown, *Philippians*, 2:343–47.

161. See also Liston, *Kingdom Come*, 142–45, where based on 1 Corinthians 3–4, he discusses a pneumatologically enabled unity.

God enveloping the inner worlds of those praying, reducing their anxiety. The Lord is present by the Spirit, and his power to settle hearts and minds is released as people raise their prayers to God. Hence, the pneumaform person knows God is near in Christ, approaches him constantly in prayer, and, even in turmoil and grief, is guarded by his peace by his Spirit.

COLOSSIANS 1:9

As with some of the previous verses discussed, Paul here prays for a fresh experience of the Spirit for the Colossians. Paul begins Colossians with his usual prescript, a thanksgiving for their faith, love, and hope, and a reminder of their hearing the gospel from Epaphras (Col. 1:1–8). In v. 9, as is his custom, he turns from thanksgiving to prayer. Since they heard of the Colossians' conversions from his coworker, Paul and his team have not ceased praying for them. The conjunction ἵνα (so that) introduces the purpose of the prayer. His prayer is that they "may be filled [πληρωθῆτε] with the knowledge of his will in all wisdom and spiritual [πνευματικῇ] insight" (LEB). This prayer is not unlike Ephesians 3 discussed earlier.

"Filled" is passive (aorist) and alerts us to an external agent. The context of prayer makes God the obvious source of the filling. Elsewhere Paul uses the verb of God's action in filling people with various things and in differing ways (Rom. 15:13–14;[162] 2 Cor. 7:9;[163] Eph. 3:19; Phil. 1:11), and in Ephesians, Christ fills all things (Eph. 1:23; 4:10). Significantly, as will soon be discussed, he fills people with the Spirit (Eph. 5:18). Even more important, in Colossians 2:10, it is God who has filled the Colossians in Christ (in him). Clearly, God fills the Colossians with this knowledge, or more correctly, God, in Christ, by his Spirit.

What he fills them with is the knowledge of God's will in all spiritual wisdom and understanding.[164] This statement can be restated as developing cruciform, Christoform, or, as I am describing it, pneumaform minds. The adjective πνευματικός does not merely imply "spiritual" in a generic sense, but "holy spiritual,"[165] a mind conformed to that of the Spirit, who transforms people from the things of this age to the mind of Christ, who embodies the mind of the Father.[166] This, then, is a prayer for pneumaform minds.

---

162. In Romans 15:13, Paul prays God will fill the Romans with all joy (cf. 2 Tim. 1:4), peace in believing, and explicitly refers to the Spirit's power that leads to their having hope. In the following verse, God by the Spirit is the implied agent of filling the Romans with "all knowledge" and an ability to instruct one another.

163. The primary agent of filling Paul with comfort is not specified in 2 Corinthians 7:4 but is clearly God, based on 2 Corinthians 1:3–7, although the Corinthians are a secondary agent or means by which God comforts, as indicated by v. 5 that follows.

164. Alternatively, it is a compound reality: "all Spiritual wisdom and understanding." Fee, *GEP*, 642.

165. On πνευματικός see Fee, *GEP*, 28–31.

166. In the context of the false teaching, it is not fleshly or earthly. Fee, *GEP*, 641.

In vv. 12–14, the result of this is that "with joy,"[167] the Colossians "give thanks to the Father." God is then defined as the one who qualified the Colossians for the inheritance of the saints and who has rescued all believers (us) from the dominion of darkness and transferred them into the kingdom of Christ, their beloved redeemer and forgiver (1:13–14). Pneumaformed minds are increasingly filled with knowledge and insight, resulting in their living in a way that is pleasing to and worthy of Christ, reflected in their fruitfulness and growth in good works and a deepening knowledge of God. He enables them to persevere, be patient, and with joy to give thanks to their heavenly Father.[168]

COLOSSIANS 3:16–17

Colossians 3:16–17 sits in an ethical section that begins in Colossians 3:1.[169] Paul draws out the implications of their being in Christ and raised with him—they must set their minds on the things of God above and not the sinful things of this world. They are to put to death a range of vices that characterized their pre-Christian lives, things that invoke God's wrath. As a unified multicultural community of God's chosen people being renewed in knowledge after the image of God, they are to put on the virtues of God and let Christ's peace (in them by the Spirit) rule their hearts. They are to be thankful, again showing the importance of thanksgiving for Paul.

The idea of them letting the word of Christ[170] dwell in [them] (cf. Col. 1:15–23)[171] richly[172] and continually[173] surely speaks of the Spirit inscribing God's Word in Christ on their hearts, as the prophets had hoped (Jer. 31:33). Paul now believes this is happening in the new covenant (2 Cor. 3:1–3). With this word in them, in and by the Spirit, they are, with all wisdom, to teach and admonish one another.[174] As they allow the word to richly indwell them, they

---

167. While μετὰ χαρᾶς can be placed with what precedes in v. 11 (as the verse markers suggest), it more naturally fits with what follows, indicating the joyous gratitude that flows from the Colossians to God. Paul associates joy and thanksgiving in Philippians 1:2–4.
168. Mention should be made here of Colossians 2:1–3. Paul's struggle (ἀγῶνα) could indicate prayer here (cf. Col. 4:12). If so, he prays that their hearts are encouraged, they are unified together in love, and they understand the full assurance and wealth of knowledge and mystery of God that are in Christ. This is so that they are not deceived by persuasive false teaching, and Paul would have joy knowing of their perseverance.
169. See also the translation of Fee, *GEP*, 647, and what follows concerning this verse and Ephesians 5:18–19 in 648–57.
170. While "the word of Christ" is unusual, it is strongly supported in witnesses, and so is preferable to "word of God" or "word of the Lord." See Metzger, *TCGNT*, 558. Fee also argues that "word of Christ" is supported by his being the key focus of the letter (Fee, GEP, 650).
171. Fee, *GEP*, 649. As he says, ἐν ὑμῖν here indicates "in your midst."
172. Fee rightfully agrees ἐν πάσῃ σοφίᾳ should be placed with what follows. See *GEP*, 652.
173. The verb ἐνοικείτω is present and so speaks of an ongoing practice.
174. Fee accurately states, "As the parallel passage in Ephesians makes explicit, Paul considers all of this activity to be the result of their being filled with the Spirit." Fee, *GEP*, 650.

are to pour forth songs of praise by the Spirit. This hymnody includes psalms, hymns, and spiritual songs[175] with grace in their hearts to God.[176] As noted when discussing Ephesians 5:18–20, the third category, ᾠδαῖς πνευματικαῖς, indicates the *Pneuma's* role in generating Spirit-inspired worship music for the gathered community that is sung in the Spirit.

The mention of grace in their hearts[177] speaks of the Spirit lavishing God's favor on believers (1:2, 6; 4:18), their responding with grace (thanks, gratitude) toward God, and their sharing God's grace with unbelievers flavorsomely (4:6).[178] In v. 17, they are instructed that whatever they do or say, they must do so in the name of the Lord Jesus. They are to give thanks to God the Father through Jesus. Again, the Spirit who implants the peace of Christ, the word of Christ, and grace in them generates in them a desire to sing, do good works, speak the words of the gospel to each other and unbelievers, and give thanks to God.[179]

COLOSSIANS 4:2–4

Moving on from his household code (3:18–4:1), Paul urges the Colossians to be devoted to and alert in prayer with thanksgiving. As is typical, he asks them to pray for him and his team (us). And as is frequent in Paul's prayer advice, the ἵνα signals the purpose for which they are to pray.

First, Paul hopes God will open doors to speak the mystery of Christ. God does this through his Spirit. Often indicating a door, gate, or entrance,[180] θύρα is at times used figuratively for the opening of a way to accomplish something.[181] Paul uses it thrice of gospel opportunities. First, in Corinth, "a great and effective *door* has opened" (LEB, empasis mine) for him. This clause speaks of an excellent opportunity to advance the gospel there (1 Cor. 16:9). No agency is mentioned, but God, in Christ, by his Spirit, is in view. Then, in 2 Corinthians 2:12, Paul came to Troas "for the gospel of Christ and a *door*

---

175. I agree with Fee that the three song types form a unit. See Fee, *GEP*, 652–53.

176. Here θεῷ has superior external attestation to κυρίῳ. See Metzger, *TCGNT*, 558.

177. I agree with Fee that "in your hearts" goes with "singing." However, he is concerned that this may suggest singing in the heart only and prefers "singing with your whole heart." Fee, *GEP*, 655. I prefer "singing in and from your heart." This speaks of singing impelled from the Spirit bursting from the chest, so to speak.

178. Here, I concur with Fee, who rejects the common translation "with gratitude" for ἐν [τῇ] χάριτι, strongly preferring here "the grace of God." Fee, *GEP*, 655. The article is likely original due to better external attestation. Fee, *GEP*, 648n51.

179. As Fee agrees, τῷ θεῷ speaks of God as object of worship. Fee, *GEP*, 655–56. When we add the Spirit into the mix, this is Trinitarian—they dwell on the word of Christ, and by the Spirit, pour forth praise to God.

180. Matt. 6:6; 24:33; 25:10; 27:10, 60; Mark 1:22; 2:2; 11:4, 7; 13:24–25 (figuratively of the kingdom), 29; 15:46; 16:3; John 10:1, 2, 7, 9 (figuratively of the way to enter God's pen); 18:6; 20:19, 26; Acts 3:2; 5:9, 19, 23; 12:6, 13; 16:26–27; 21:30; Rev. 4:1.

181. See Acts 14:27 (a door of faith is opened to the Gentiles); James 5:9 (God standing at the door to enter and judge); Rev. 3:8 (Jesus opening a door for the Philadelphians); Rev. 3:20 (Jesus standing at the door of the Laodiceans knocking so as to enter).

was opened for [him] by the Lord" (LEB). The final clause suggests Christ's agency, which of course, speaks of his action in and by the Spirit. Here, in Colossians 4:3, Paul asks for prayer that God might open such a door for himself and his team (ἡμῖν) for the word so that he would "speak [λαλῆσα[182]] the mystery of Christ."

After an aside—"for whom I am also bound"—referring to his imprisonment, Paul adds a second purpose for their prayer: "so that (ἵνα) I may make it known, as it is necessary for me to speak" (my translation). Paul believes that prayer can open opportunities to share the gospel and enable the evangelizer to speak the gospel with clarity. While not all of those formed by the Spirit are evangelists with a vocational call to preach and equip others, all carry the responsibility to share their faith when given the opportunity (Col. 4:5–6). God opens such opportunities and enables believers to speak. Pneumaformed people discern the doors by the Spirit, follow him into them, and share Christ with Spirit-impelled warmth, attitudes, actions, and words.

2 THESSALONIANS 1:11–12

As he commonly does, Paul begins 2 Thessalonians with thanksgiving. This one develops into an assurance that God will punish his readers' opponents with eternal separation from God (2 Thess. 1:3–10).[183] In v. 11, he tells them of his team's (our) constant (πάντοτε) prayer for them. His first prayer purpose[184] is that the Thessalonians may be "worthy of the calling of our God," implying God's work in them, by the Spirit, to enable them to live up to the virtues of the gospel.

The second purpose is "that [ἵνα] God, with power [ἐν δυνάμει], may fulfill every desire for goodness and [every][185] work of faith."[186] Fee rightfully asserts, "With this phrase [ἐν δυνάμει], Paul probably intends 'by the power of his Holy Spirit.'"[187] Hence, this is a direct prayer for God, by his Spirit, to observe the Thessalonians' prayers, plans, and efforts and, by his Spirit-power, bring them to pass. By praying this, Paul indicates that the blend of his team's prayers, those of the Thessalonians, their Spirit-impelled plans, and their actions to bring the plans to pass can be empowered by God. God inhabits his people's good desires and works, amplifying their effect. Understanding this liberates present-day believers to submit their plans and intentions to God and ask him to empower them.

---

182. This is likely a naked infinitive, indicating purpose.
183. For the options and a conclusion, I lean toward Gary Steven Shogren, *1 & 2 Thessalonians*, ZECNT (Grand Rapids: Zondervan, 2012), 259–63.
184. BDAG, s.v. "εἰς," 290. εἰς ὅ here denotes "for which purpose."
185. The feminine πᾶσαν likely governs both feminine clauses that follow. Both genitives are subjective. BDAG, s.v. "πᾶσαν," 290.
186. Fee, *GEP*, 69, states this prayer picks up the two concerns of love and faith from v. 3; however, this is questionable.
187. See Fee, *GEP*, 69, and his supporting arguments.

Paul's ultimate purpose is "so that" (ὅπως) Christ's name is glorified in and through the Thessalonians, "according to the grace of our God and the Lord Jesus Christ." "Grace" here again speaks of God's action by his Spirit toward the Thessalonians. The Spirit enabling people to live righteously and do good works for God enhances the glorious name of Jesus. As Christ's glory is infinite, it cannot be multiplied in an ontic sense. However, glorifying his name speaks of more and more people acknowledging him as Lord as the gospel spreads (cf. 2 Thess. 3:1 below).

2 THESSALONIANS 2:16

After refuting the idea that the day of the Lord has come or is imminent by reminding the Thessalonians that a rebellion and rising of the man of lawlessness must happen first (2 Thess. 2:1–12), Paul gives thanks for the Thessalonians (v. 13a). As he does this, he reminds them of Christ's love, their election for salvation, their sanctification by the Spirit, their belief in the truth, God's call through the gospel, and the hope of the glory of Christ (v. 13b–14). In v. 15, he appeals to them to stand firm and hold resolutely to the traditions Paul and his team taught them through word or letter.

Using the full threefold name of Christ, he next prays for a blessing from Jesus and God. He reminds them that God has loved his people (us) and has granted them "eternal comfort and good hope through grace" (v. 16). The aorist ὁ ἀγαπήσας does not merely speak of their past love but speaks gnomically of a timeless, general fact.[188] Conveyed into their beings by the Spirit, the love of the Father and Son has brought them to the present, is with them now, and will be with them through death and into the new creation.

The infinitive παρακαλέσαι signals the purpose of his prayer-blessing. He wants God to bless the Thessalonians by comforting or encouraging their hearts and strengthening them in every good work and good word. This encouragement and strengthening is from God and his Son but experienced through the Spirit sent into believers' hearts. As Paul does here, pneumaformed believers ask God to bless the good work and words of other Christians. God responds and empowers the efforts of the pneumaformed by his Spirit.

2 THESSALONIANS 3:1–5

We have already seen that Paul requested prayer for his mission and believed in the power of the Spirit to open doors for the message and provide the words for those sharing it. Here, having asked for the Thessalonians' prayers for his team in 1 Thessalonians 5:25, he again requests they pray for them.

His first purpose in doing so is "so that [ἵνα] the word of the Lord may run [pres. subjn. τρέχω] and be glorified [pres. subjn. δοξάζω] just as also with you" (v. 1, my translation). The word "run" alludes to Psalm 147:15 where God sends

---

188. On the gnomic aorist, see Wallace, *Greek Grammar*, 562.

his command to the earth and "his word runs swiftly."[189] In the psalm, God is the agent by whom the word speeds out. So in 2 Thessalonians, God is the agent. The message is the "word of the Lord," indicating that God acts in and through the word of Christ.[190] The genitive "word of the Lord" likely speaks broadly of Christ (empowered by God) as the source, producer, and content of the message Paul and others preach.[191] Paul also hopes the word will be glorified among the Thessalonians, indicating fruit born by Christians and people as they yield to his lordship to the praise and glory of God the Father (cf. Phil. 2:11).

The second purpose (καὶ ἵνα) is that his team might be delivered from evil and wicked people, recognizing that not all have faith (v. 2). This recognition suggests these are Jewish and Gentile opponents. Because he is writing from Corinth, this could be related to rejection by the Jews of Corinth (Acts 18:6) and the Gallio incident (Acts 18:12–17). Paul may simply be thinking generally in light of his own persecution of the Christians and his suffering since his conversion from Jews and Gentiles alike.[192]

Whatever opponents he has in mind, Paul believes Christ (the Lord), by his Spirit, has the power to rescue his group from danger as he wills. Indeed, Paul goes on to say, "the Lord is faithful" (v. 3a).[193] As such, Jesus also has the power to strengthen the Thessalonians and guard them from the evil one (τοῦ πονηροῦ, v. 3).[194] Reference to Satan here implies the adversary's involvement in the persecution Paul is experiencing through evil and wicked (πονηρῶν)

---

189. LXX: ἕως τάχους δραμεῖται ὁ λόγος αὐτοῦ.

190. "Lord" in the Thessalonian letters is Christ as in 2:16 (see also 1 Thess. 1:1, 3; 2:16, 19; 3:11, 13; 4:1, 2, 15, 16, 17; 5:2, 9, 23, 28; 2 Thess. 1:1, 2, 7, 8, 12; 2:1, 2, 8, 14; 3:6, 12, 18).

191. It is not likely to be subjective ("Jesus's word") but broad, encompassing source or origin (Leon Morris, *1 and 2 Thessalonians*, TNTC [Downers Grove, IL: InterVarsity Press, 209], 51n45: "the word sourced in Jesus"), content (I. Howard Marshall, *1 and 2 Thessalonians*, NCB [Grand Rapids: Eerdmans, 1983], 55), production (the message produced by Jesus), and objective ("message about Jesus [the Lord]," Gordon D. Fee, *The First and Second Letters to the Thessalonians*, NICNT [Grand Rapids: Eerdmans, 2009], 43). Jesus is the message; it is from God through him; he is the basic content; he produces it by the Spirit; and so on.

192. By this stage, Paul has been smuggled out of Damascus (Acts 9:23–25; 2 Cor. 11:32), left other cities due to persecution (Acts 13:50–51; 14:5–7; 16:35–40; 17:10–15; 1 Thess. 2:1–2), was stoned in Lystra (Acts 14:19–20; 2 Cor. 11:24), and experienced other things found in his catalog in 2 Corinthians 11:23–29.

193. In other similar texts, it is God who is faithful (1 Cor. 1:9; 10:13; 2 Cor. 1:8; 1 Thess. 5:24 [in Paul, the one who calls is God]). Jesus shares God's attributes as his Son. Father and Son express their faithfulness to believers by the Spirit.

194. τοῦ πονηροῦ is somewhat ambiguous. The arthrous masculine noun can refer to "evil" or "the evil one" (Matt. 5:37; John 17:15); "the evildoer(s)" (Matt. 5:39; 12:35; 13:49; Luke 6:35, 45); either "the evildoer," "evil," or "the evil one" (Matt. 6:13). Often, it clearly refers to Satan (Matt. 13:19, 38; 1 John 2:13, 14; 3:12; 5:18, 19), rather than "evil" as an abstract concept. The arthrous neuter noun is also used of evil spirits (Luke 7:21; 8:2; Acts 19:12, 13, 15, 16; cf. Luke 11:26). Paul uses the neuter τὸ πονηρόν to describe "what is evil" and to be avoided (Rom. 12:9), and the arthrous masculine of an evil person (1 Cor. 5:13, citing Deut. 17:7 LXX). However, in Ephesians 6:16, it is clearly Satan, as this figure fires flaming arrows. The previous verse of the plural of πονηρός is of "wicked and evil people" (τῶν governs both nouns) and the singular here suggests not an evil person, but Satan.

people in v. 2. This is the spiritual warfare we read of in Ephesians 6:16 where the evil one fires flaming arrows to defeat the believer.

In the Lord, Paul is also confident that the Thessalonians will remain obedient. "In the Lord" speaks again of Christ's agency by his Spirit (v. 4)— because they are "in the Lord," as are Paul and his team, Paul is confident.

Paul prays that "the Lord will direct the hearts of [the Thessalonians] to the love of God and to the perseverance of Christ" (my translation). The verb is κατευθύνω, formed from κατά and εὐθύνω, which itself is formed from εὖ, "good," and θύνω, meaning "to throw," hence, "good throw." With κατά, it yields something like "along a good throw" or "direct or guide accurately." Paul, then, is praying that God will guide or direct the Thessalonians accurately. Where he wants them guided is "to the love of God," which can speak of them loving God (obj. gen.), God's love for them (subj. gen), or of their loving other people (gen. of production, source). Paul's use of love language in the letter would suggest love for one another (2 Thess. 1:3, also, 1 Thess. 3:12), God's love for them (2 Thess. 2:13, also, 1 Thess. 1:4), and perhaps love for the truth (2 Thess. 2:10). Furthermore, in 1 Thessalonians Paul has also mentioned love in terms of their labor motivated by love (1 Thess. 1:3), love for all people (3:6; 5:8), unbelievers (3:12), and leaders (5:13). With such a versatile use of love language, Paul's prayer is probably best interpreted in the broadest sense: that they are directed to the love of God in him and for them and that it flows from them to the Triune God, believers, others, and the gospel itself. This love is experienced and lived out in and by the Spirit.

2 Thessalonians 3:16

In 2 Thessalonians 3:6–15, Paul has strongly addressed the problem of disorderliness in the church, commanding that the lazy or disorderly among them work to provide for themselves with their hands. Second Thessalonians 3:16 begins the end of the letter, which is in the form of a chiasm.

A1 Blessing
   B Greeting
A2 Blessing

The first blessing is a prayer for peace. "The Lord of peace" in 2 Thessalonians is Jesus. The genitive is likely one of source or production—Christ generates peace. Indeed, in Ephesians 2:14, Christ "is our peace," having reconciled Jew and Gentile together in him by his Spirit. In 1 Thessalonians 5:23 and times elsewhere,[195] Paul describes God as "the God of peace," showing that while Christ bestows peace, it is God's doing in, through, and by Jesus. Moreover, peace is a fruit of the Spirit (Gal. 5:22); hence, the Thessalonians can experience this gift from the Lord by the Spirit.

---

195. Rom. 15:33; 16:20; Phil. 4:9.

Paul wants the Thessalonians to experience peace through everything in every way (διὰ παντὸς ἐν παντὶ τρόπῳ). His desire includes every aspect of the Christian life, including their inner worlds; their relationships with each other and those beyond the church; and their relationships with God, Father, Son, and Spirit. The final clause can either be a statement, "The Lord is with you all," or another aspect of the prayer, "May the Lord be with you all." The second option fits the context of prayer—that the Thessalonians would more fully experience the presence of Christ in their lives. These things are *all* the work of the Spirit, for Jesus is at God's right hand and communes with his people through the Spirit. Again, we see the Spirit bringing blessings—here, peace. We also see again the power of prayer to enhance believers' experiences of God's presence and peace.

2 TIMOTHY 1:16

This verse is a prayer for a particular Christian, Onesiphorus, and his family. Paul asks the Lord to grant mercy to Onesiphorus's household because he had often (πολλάκις) provided Paul with refreshment and was not ashamed of Paul's chains. Plainly, Onesiphorus had often provided hospitality,[196] potentially meaning he housed Paul and provided for him on his Ephesus visits. Onesiphorus had also served others in Ephesus (v. 18). Unashamed to be associated with the prisoner Paul, he had traveled approximately 1,670 kilometers (1,040 mi) from Ephesus, across the Adriatic, and to Rome and had found him. Twice (vv. 16, 18), Paul prays that "the Lord" may grant him mercy. "The Lord" may here be Jesus or God.[197] Whoever is in view, if Paul is thinking of present-day mercy, the Spirit is also in view. The second prayer for mercy points to the day of judgment (that day)[198] and it is not the Spirit in that context: God and Christ together judge in 2 Timothy 4:1.

These prayer blessings asking that God and Jesus would pour out grace and peace on the readers demonstrate that Paul was confident that God, through Jesus, is the source of grace and peace for believers and that prayer will see that experienced more lavishly. The prayers for grace appeal for God's and Jesus's beneficence and favor to abound to them: the grace of salvation, receiving God's gifts, gracious speech and behavior, generous giving, and grace responding to God's grace. Similarly, the prayers for peace ask for the fullness of God's shalom to be experienced in every aspect of life: peace with God, concord within church and family relationships, and as far as it depends on the readers, peace with others, and the peace of the new heavens and earth to be experienced now.

---

196. The Greek is ἀναψύχω, compounding ἀνά ("again") and ψύχω ("make cool, cold"). As such, it means to refresh as if with cool air or water (in the Middle Eastern hot climate). See "ἀναψύχω," *NIDNTTE* 4:734.

197. In favor of Jesus is the ascription "Lord Jesus Christ" in 2 Timothy 1:2. Second Timothy 1:8 is likely Jesus as Paul refers to God in the same verse. However, some texts are ambiguous (2 Tim. 2:7, 22; 3:11; 4:8 [cf. 4:1], where both God and Christ judge; 4:14, 17, 18, 21). Second Timothy 2:20 is likely God. Of course, the difference is minimal, for God supplies through Christ by the Spirit in any case.

198. The use of "that day" pointing to the Lord's day of judgment is also found in 2 Timothy 1:12, 18; 4:8.

"Mercy" in Titus 1:4 and the description of Jesus as Savior highlight God's salvation bestowed on undeserving sinful humankind in Christ. Although not explicitly stated, it is by the Spirit that God and his Son bestow this grace, peace, and mercy on believers. Again, prayer enhances the believers' experience of God's lavish blessings.

PHILEMON 4–6, 22

As in all his letters, Paul introduces himself (with Timothy, the co-sender) and then prays. As in eight of his letters, he prays that the audience experiences grace and peace from God and his Son (Philem. 3). Paul next gives thanks, as in all letters but Galatians. He tells Philemon of his frequent (πάντοτε) prayers of thanksgiving to God and his remembrance of him (v. 4).

The participle ἀκούων in v. 5 is causal, "because." It is also present, indicating that Paul heard regularly of Philemon's love and faith toward both Jesus and other Christians across the empire (πάντας τοὺς ἁγίους). Somewhat unusually, instead of ἵνα Paul uses ὅπως to indicate the purpose of his prayer; the effect is the same. The purpose is that "the fellowship of your faith may become effective in the knowledge of every good thing that is in us for Christ" (LEB).

With what follows in the letter, Paul implicitly begins his appeal to Philemon. Probably converted by Paul in Ephesus (Acts 19:1–10),[199] Philemon was a commendable pneumaformed Christian leader in Paul's network of churches with a history of generosity toward Paul and other Christians (Philem. 5, 7, 22–23). The κοινωνία of faith Paul wants Philemon to experience in v. 7 is not further evangelization[200] but the idea that he will receive Onesimus back as a Christian brother as if he were welcoming Paul himself (vv. 16–17). Paul here reminds Philemon of the bountiful blessings of God that he and other believers have received to serve Christ.

This prayer shows that Paul believed that the Spirit has the power to enhance Christian relationships; enable forgiveness, reconciliation, and restorative justice;[201] and break down social barriers etched into the fabric of the Roman world. He also believed that prayer enables this to happen. By his Spirit, in Christ, God will enable Philemon to receive his newly converted runaway slave not merely as a slave, or even just as a Christian, but as if he were the apostle Paul himself.

In v. 22, Paul tacitly asks Philemon, Apphia, Archippus, and the others in their house church (plur. ὑμῶν) to pray for him to be restored to them (plur. ὑμῖν). Again, we see Paul's belief in the power of prayer and the Spirit's capacity to see Paul released from prison to come to Colossae. The mutual prayers

---

199. Colossians 1:7 indicates Epaphras planted the Colossian church. It is not impossible that Philemon was led to Christ by Epaphras, and Paul takes credit as Epaphras's sender. More likely, Paul was God's agent in his conversion.

200. As the NIV1984 indicates in its poor translation of the verse as "sharing your faith."

201. Mark J. Keown, "Philemon and Restorative Justice," *Stimulus* 25, no. 1 (2018): 12–19.

of the Pauline team and the Colossians testify to the κοινωνία πνεύματος experienced by believers in Christ.

The importance of prayer is seen all over Paul's letters as he prays for his converts and others[202] and Christians pray for other Christians,[203] for others (1 Tim. 2:1–2), and to consecrate food (1 Tim. 4:5),[204] hence his injunctions to be devoted to prayer.[205] Similarly, he regularly asks his converts to pray for him.[206] Interestingly, his appeal to the Romans that they contend in prayer with him for his deliverance from unbelievers in Judea, for a warm reception for the collection in Romans 15:30, and for his coming to Rome is all given "through [διά] our Lord Jesus Christ and through [διά] the love of the Spirit." The genitive τοῦ πνεύματος indicates source or production, "the love sourced in/or produced by the Spirit."

Several things are of note here. First, the close connection of Jesus and the Spirit as instruments by which Paul appeals shows their oneness in acting together for God's purposes. So, cruciformity is pneumaformity. Second, the love produced in Paul by the Spirit and Christ leads to his own prayers and his appeal for theirs. Third, although strictly speaking, the love of the Spirit prompts Paul's appeal here, there is a sense in which the love generated by the Spirit envelops the whole process of appealing for prayer and the prayer itself.

CONCLUSION

Those transformed by the Spirit to be more and more like Jesus are people of worship. The Son of God leads this worship, the Spirit enables it, and people do it in a Christ-informed and Spirit-informed way. They worship and serve by the Spirit, revering, glorifying God, loving, boasting of Christ, blessing God, praising him, rejoicing, and thanking. They are people of prayer, in Christ, and led by the Spirit. While the Spirit intercedes for them, believers pray for all manner of things at all times, including for blessings of grace and peace and for their own Christoformity. Worship and prayer, then, are hallmarks of the pneumaformed believer. Yet, these are merely one part of transformation by the Spirit. As such, the next chapter focuses on the profound way in which the Spirit forms believers to be increasingly like Jesus Christ, the Son of God.

---

202. See 2 Cor. 13:7, 9; 1 Thess. 1:2; 3:10; 2 Tim. 1:3–7.

203. See 2 Cor. 9:14; Phil. 1:4; Col. 1:3; 4:12.

204. See also 1 Cor. 7:5, 8; 11:4–5; 1 Tim. 5:5.

205. See Rom. 12:12. Notably, proximate to his injunction to pray in Romans 12:12c is the injunction to "burn in the Spirit" in Romans 12:11b, bringing spiritual fervor into close connection with prayer (and other things in the context including love, goodness, honoring others, zeal, service to Christ, joy, patience, generosity, and hospitality).

206. See also 2 Cor. 1:11; Col. 4:2; 1 Thess. 5:17; 2 Thess. 3:1–2.

CHAPTER 6

THE SPIRIT AND CHRISTOFORMITY

In a sense, this chapter cuts to the heart of the purposes of this book. Here, I consider passages that speak of the inner transformation worked by God for those "in Christ"—the work of the Spirit. I will demonstrate that the work of the Spirit is to transform believers into the image of God's Son—generating in them cruciformity, resurrectiformity, and Christoformity. There is no dichotomy between Christ and the Spirit—the Spirit who transforms them *is* the Spirit of Jesus.[1] Jesus takes sinful people, broken by the world, and where they willingly yield to him, miraculously remakes them into God's children walking in the pattern of their big brother and Lord.

TRANSFORMATION LANGUAGE

Central to this chapter is μορφ-terminology, from which we get μορφ terms used in English (e.g. metamorphosis). As such, I begin with passages that speak of transformation using this language. The μορφ-terms are used sparingly in the wider NT. Μεταμορφόω is used for Jesus's stunning transfiguration (Matt. 17:2; Mark 9:2). In the second longest endings of Mark, μορφή is used to describe the different form of Jesus's appearance to two walking in the country (Mark 16:12). Paul employs μόρφωσις of the law as the embodiment of knowledge and truth (Rom. 2:20).

Romans 8:29

Romans 8:29 is critical to this study.[2] It is placed in a passage in which Paul draws on a wide range of theological ideas to give the Romans hope as

---

1. Dunn rightly speaks of "Jesus as the definition of the Spirit." Dunn, *Jesus and the Spirit*, 319.
2. In his discussion of Romans 8:28–30 (see *GEP*, 586–91), Fee acknowledges that as believers, "we are being conformed by that same Spirit into the image of the Son of God" (p. 590). However, he does not link this to the Spirit. This is a shame, because he considers the Spirit the subject of the verb συνεργεῖ in v. 28, and it is natural to consider that the Spirit is implied in the pneumaformation of believers in v. 29.

they suffer for and in Christ and wait for the glory of the consummation.[3] Romans 8:26–27 focuses on the Spirit's role in helping people in their weakness and suffering. The Spirit assists by interceding for them according to God's will (see below). Romans 8:28 confirms God is active in the world by the Spirit, shaping history for good for his loved and called people.

The causal conjunction ὅτι that launches Romans 8:29 indicates continuity with the previous verse. Believers know that all things work for good for God's people because whatever transpires in a world under spiritual powers and corrupted by sin, decay, and death, they are known, predestined, called, justified, and ultimately glorified by God.

My primary interest in this verse is the clause συμμόρφους τῆς εἰκόνος τοῦ υἱοῦ αὐτοῦ, "conformed to the image of his Son." God predestined them for this transformation. The renewal comes as a result of his call and justification (v. 30). The clause likely points to the result of God's work in the believer's life—their final conformity to the image of the new Adam who has saved them. However, it also implies the present work of God in believers by his Spirit as they are conformed.[4]

"His son" is obviously Jesus. Elsewhere in Paul, Jesus is the very image of God (2 Cor. 4:4; Col. 1:15; 3:10), the new Adam (Rom. 5:14–21; 15:45–49). While all have sinned (Rom. 3:23), people remain made in the image of God (1 Cor. 11:7). However, due to Adam's sin and their participation in it (Rom. 5:12), bearing the image of Adam, they are subject to death (1 Cor. 15:49).

Here, the purpose of their predestination is that they may be transformed into conformity with the image of God's Son, Christ, the new Adam. This transformation process is not described in this passage; it is simply stated. As will be shown in the ensuing discussion, it is by the Spirit that God transforms people to Christ's image—progressively when they yield in this age and entirely so in the age to come (chapter 11).

The purpose of this conformity (εἰς + inf.) is that Jesus would be the firstborn among many brothers and sisters. The brothers and sisters are those adopted into God's family (Rom. 8:14–15, 23). Such a transformation is pneumaformity, whereby flawed, corrupted image bearers become the children of God that God created them to be—if they will heed the gospel and yield daily to the Spirit in line with Paul's ethical instructions in Romans 14–15 and other passages.

Romans 12:2a

Paul uses μορφ- language in this verse as well.[5] Having expounded God's salvation and the place of Israel in God's purposes, Paul appeals to the Romans to

3. See Mark J. Keown, "Notes of Hope in the Face of Suffering (Rom. 8:18–39)," *Stimulus* (2020), https://hail.to/laidlaw-college/publication/1tI5uq8/article/YeNLe05.
4. "The Spirit is also the author of eschatological transformation." Habets, *Progressive Mystery*, 86.
5. See also the earlier discussion on Romans 12:1, chapter 5, "Worship in and by the Spirit."

respond to God's mercies by presenting themselves as holy and acceptable living sacrifices in reasonable worship to God. The language of "bodies" (τὰ σώματα) calls to mind Christ's self-giving, suggesting Paul is summoning the Romans, as the body of Christ, to together and individually emulate Christ's sacrifice and service in their whole beings, even to the point of death (cf. Phil. 2:8).

In v. 2, they are not to be conformed (συσχηματίζω) to this age. The verb's only other use in the NT is 1 Peter 1:14, where Peter urges his readers not to be *conformed* to "the passions of your former ignorance."[6] Peter may well have had Romans 12:2 in mind as he wrote this from Rome, as he venerated some of Paul's letters as Scripture (2 Peter 3:15–16).[7]

Here, in Romans 12:2, "this age" (τῷ αἰῶνι τούτῳ) speaks of the present world in its fallenness. It is an evil age (Gal. 1:4), blinded under Satan, the god of this age (2 Cor. 4:4), and characterized by false wisdom (1 Cor. 2:6; cf. 1 Cor. 1:20; 3:18). Its people and its nations, to a large extent, are ruled by people of this age who do not understand God's wisdom, who crucified Christ, and so who are perishing (1 Cor. 2:6, 8). Like the Ephesians in their former lives, the Romans, too, lived according to the patterns of this age (Eph. 2:2) but have now been saved from it (Eph. 2:4–9; cf. Gal. 1:4; Col. 1:13). They are not to be conformed to its ungodliness, wickedness, and idolatry. They are not to go the way of the hoarding rich (1 Tim. 6:17) or of Demas, who loved this present age and deserted Paul (2 Tim. 4:10). As Paul says to Titus of the Cretans, they are to renounce ungodliness and worldly passions, and live self-controlled, righteous, and godly lives in the present age (Titus 2:11–12).[8]

Rather than being conformed to the false patterns of this age, believers are to be transformed (μεταμορφοῦσθε) by the renewal (ἀνακαινώσει) of the mind so that they may approve what the will of God is. The use of μορφη-language calls to mind σύμμορφος in Romans 8:29 and suggests that Paul is speaking further of the process of the predestined being transformed into the image of Christ. This verb is also used for transformation in 2 Corinthians 3:18.

As discussed regarding Titus 3:5 in chapter 3,[9] the verb ἀνακαίνωσις is a Pauline creation that means "to be made new again" and so refers to the renewal of the mind. The use of the present μεταμορφοῦσθε suggests this is a process begun at conversion and continued in the life of the believer. The passive voice implies the agency of God by the Spirit. In Romans 12 (aside from v. 11 where believers are to be fervent in the Spirit) Paul does not mention the Spirit in terms of this transformation, so it can seem that this is discon-

---

6.   *BrillDAG*, s.v. "συσχηματίζω σύν, σχηματίζω."

7.   Of the possible Pauline letters in view, Romans is the leading possibility, as Peter writes from Rome just eight to ten years after the epistle to the Romans arrived in the city.

8.   DeSilva sees the work of the Spirit in Titus 2:11–14—the Spirit empowers people to "just say no" to the things of the world that are not of the Spirit. DeSilva, *Transformation*, 51.

9.   See "The Spirit Who Participates in Rebirth" and "The Spirit Who Brings Renewal." Romans 12:2b (εἰς τὸ δοκιμάζειν ὑμᾶς τί τὸ θέλημα τοῦ θεοῦ, τὸ ἀγαθὸν καὶ εὐάρεστον καὶ τέλειον) will be discussed under the heading "The Spirit Who Gives Discernment" later in this chapter.

nected from pneumatology. However, Romans 12 builds on his earlier teaching whereby believers have had love poured into them by the Spirit (Rom. 5:5), are to serve in the newness of the Spirit (Rom. 7:6), live according to the Spirit (Rom. 8:4), have their minds on the Spirit (Rom. 8:5–6), put to death sinful bodily deeds by the Spirit (Rom. 8:13), be led by the Spirit (Rom. 8:14), and pray by the Spirit (Rom. 8:26–27). Unquestionably, the present power of transformation is the Spirit. The Spirit transforms believers' minds so that they can discern the will of God. The implication here is that those who have such minds *will* have the capacity to discern that which is good, acceptable, and perfect (τὸ ἀγαθὸν καὶ εὐάρεστον καὶ τέλειον).

Without exhausting what Paul means by this but focusing on what he has heard about the Roman church, what follows in Romans 12:3–15:7 further explains what it looks like to be a person conformed to the image of the crucified Christ; people no longer conformed to the patterns of the age but transformed with renewed minds.

2 Corinthians 3:18

Second Corinthians continues Paul's *apologia* designed to draw the Corinthians back from the false teachers and critics to the Pauline pattern of thinking, his gospel, and participation in God's work.[10] The Corinthians are a letter from Christ, written with the Spirit, that is inscribed on his team's hearts. He then contrasts ministry under the Mosaic covenant with the superior glory of the ministry of righteousness and reconciliation under the new covenant. Israelites who reject Christ have their minds hardened and hearts veiled when Moses is read. However, "when one turns to the Lord [κύριος], the veil is removed." While κύριος can be God here, 2 Corinthians 4:5 indicates that Jesus is in view.[11]

---

10. On 2 Corinthians see my introduction in Keown, *Discovering: The Pauline Letters*, 171–202.

11. Fee, *GEP*, 311, argues that κυρίου here is not God or Christ but the Spirit. For Fee, Paul is applying κύριος twice in Exodus 34:34 to the Spirit. I disagree with Fee here. As I have argued concerning 2 Corinthians 4:5, κύριος in the letter normally means Christ. Verse 16 also suggests "the Lord" is Christ, for it is to Christ Jewish believers turn. Further, up to this point in the letter, κύριος has primarily referred to Christ (2 Cor. 1:2, 3, 14; 2:12 [possibly]). Most that follow the passage are Christ (2 Cor. 5:6 and 8 [probably], 11 [probably]; 8:5 [probably], 9, 19 and 21 [probably]; 10:8 [probably], 17, 18; 11:17 [probably], 31; 12:1 [probably]; 13:10, 13). Those that are likely God are 2 Cor. 6:17, 18 (although Paul may have Christ in view, despite the OT texts referring to God; cf. 10:17); 12:8 (possibly). However, Paul is not identifying Christ and the Spirit since throughout his letters they are individual (but connected) entities. Instead, he is saying that the Lord is present among believers by the Spirit, and by the Spirit, he brings freedom from sin, condemnation, and death. Notably Harris, *The Second Letter*, 310, notes identifying Jesus with the Lord here is the dominant view (although he prefers to identify this as God, as confusingly as that is [considering he thinks the Lord is the Spirit here], as does Fee, *GEP*, 312). As such, Paul is speaking, as Harris puts it, "Functional equivalence or dynamic unity or 'economic identity' rather than 'personal identification.'" In the end, it makes little difference as God, in Christ, and by the Spirit, brings the freedom of which Paul speaks. As Fee rightly says, "The Spirit is, as always, the Spirit *of the Lord*" (emphasis his).

The sentence ὁ δὲ κύριος τὸ πνεῦμά ἐστιν, "this comes from the Lord who is the Spirit," is the closest Paul comes to drawing together the identities of Christ and the Spirit. The unity of Christ and the Spirit is also seen where Paul speaks of the "Spirit of Christ" (Rom. 8:9), "the Spirit of Jesus Christ" (Phil. 1:19), "the Spirit of his Son" (Gal. 4:6), and "the last Adam became a life-giving Spirit" (1 Cor. 15:45).[12]

More often, he draws God and the Spirit similarly close to the "Spirit of God."[13] Both God and Jesus are tightly associated with the consecutive use of "the Spirit of God" and "the Spirit of Christ" in Romans 8:9. Several passages also indicate that the Spirit knows God's mind and will (Rom. 8:27; 1 Cor. 2:10–11). First Corinthians 12:4–6 testifies to the coordinated work of the three persons of the Godhead in equipping Christians with spiritual gifts. The point I am making is that while Paul distinguishes most often the Father, Son, and Spirit, he sees them working in perfect harmony. Hence, for him to say "the Lord is the Spirit" is to speak of Christ and the Spirit being one in unity and purpose at work in the world.[14] Hence, pneumaformity is Christoformity and theoformity, whereby believers are transformed to be more and more like their God and their Lord and Savior, Christ the Son (cf. Eph. 5:1–2).

Paul goes on to state that where the presence of the Spirit of the Lord is, there is freedom. The Spirit of the law is present in people's lives when they believe. By the work of the Spirit, believers experience freedom. In the context of 2 Corinthians 3, freedom is not a Roman or contemporary "everything is legally permissible" freedom to do as one wants (cf. 1 Cor. 6:12; 10:23). Instead, it is freedom from the law of Moses that kills, and freedom from death[15]—for the Spirit brings life (v. 6, also Rom. 7:3). From Paul's other letters, we know that this freedom is also freedom from sin,[16] for it is a sin that brings death. The law excites sin, and so brings death. This freedom is thus freedom from death into eternal life (Rom. 6:22–23).[17] Based on Christ's completion of the law (Rom. 10:3) and his redemptive

---

12. See also Romans 8:10, where Christ is in the believer, and the Spirit brings life, suggesting it is by the Spirit that Christ is in and works in the believer.

13. See Rom. 8:9, 14; 15:19; 1 Cor. 2:11, 14; 7:40; 12:4; Eph. 4:30; Phil. 3:3. Perhaps 2 Corinthians 3:17 indicates this as well (see the discussion above).

14. Fee rightly states that it is unlikely Paul is identifying the Spirit with Christ. He suggests context indicates that the Spirit validates the ministry as one that has come in glory and is "a literary moment, pure and simple." He adds, "The Spirit, we are now reminded, is the key to our experience of the presence of God." Fee, *GEP*, 318–19. I would add, "and in and through his Son." Sadly, Fee does not draw out the cruciform and pneumaform aspects of this passage. A double nominative construct (ὁ δὲ κύριος τὸ πνεῦμά) connected with the present verb ἐστιν should *not* be translated "the Lord *of* the Spirit," contra Habets, *Anointed Son*, 180.

15. See also Rom. 8:2; Gal. 2:4; 5:1.

16. See Rom. 6:7, 18, 20, 22.

17. Ultimately, it will be the freedom of the creation from its slavery of decay, into the freedom of the glory of the children of God (Rom. 8:21).

death for sins (1 Cor. 15:3), this freedom is due to the work of the Spirit, as indicated in this passage and elsewhere (Rom. 8:2).

In v. 18, those with the unveiled faces are all believers in Christ, including Jews and Gentiles.[18] Throughout 2 Corinthians 3, Paul has drawn on Exodus 34:29–35, where Moses descended from Mount Sinai with the tablets with a face so radiant from God's presence that the people were afraid, causing Moses to veil his face. He would remove the veil when speaking to God, convey what God said to the people, and then don the veil again.

Paul recalls this, speaking of Israel's failure to gaze on Moses's face due to its glory (v. 7). This "ministry of death" under the old covenant has now ended. It now has no glory at all (v. 10). The "ministry of the Spirit" has more glory (v. 8), has surpassed it (v. 10), and is permanent (v. 11). The veil on Israel remains in place where there is no faith in Christ and is removed when one turns to the Lord. So, whereas the present middle participle of the verb κατοπτρίζω can mean "reflect," here it means "contemplating," as it does in its only other use in comparative literature[19]

Believers with unveiled faces can contemplate the glory of the Lord. Like Moses, they have access to God's glorious presence due to Christ's sacrifice that opened the way to him. As such, they are "being transformed [μεταμορφόω] into the same image [εἰκών] from glory to glory, as from the Lord, the Spirit" (LEB).

Again, Paul uses μεταμορφόω, speaking of their transformation. The image here is vague but clarified in 2 Corinthians 4:4: it is Christ (cf. Rom. 8:29).[20] Believers are being changed to conform to the image of God's Son and God's very image. "From glory to glory" speaks of the present experience of glory, the Spirit's presence in them, which culminates at the consummation, when believers experience the fullness of God's glory. The final clauses state the source of this—the Lord is the Spirit. That is, through Christ in whom believers participate, the glory of God is mediated to and into believers from the Spirit of God, who is Christ in the believer.

---

18. Fee notes two views here. Some link this to the contrast between Moses, "who had to *veil* his face so that the glory could not be seen by others and who therefore was not allowed to 'reflect' the glory of his face," and Paul and others, "whose faces are *unveiled* precisely so that through the Spirit they might *reflect* the glory of the Lord" (emphasis his, *GEP*, 315). However, he rightfully endorses the alternative, where the emphasis is on the contrasts between the glory of Christian ministry and the glory of Mosaic service. Others see the contrast between the effect on the recipients of the two ministries. While those in the Mosaic era have veiled hearts (v. 15) that Christ can remove, Christians have turned to the Lord, the veil is taken away, and they experience freedom in the Spirit. Fee, *GEP*, 315–19.

19. *Alleg. Interp.* 3.101

20. Similarly Dunn, *Jesus and the Spirit*, 320. He adds, "That is to say, the distinctive mark of the eschatological Spirit is an immediacy of relationship with God which makes the believer more like Jesus."

Galatians 4:19

Mention has been made of Galatians 4:19 concerning the Spirit's role in the rebirth of believers. In the verse, Paul seeks to draw his children in the faith away from the bewitching of the Judaizers, and he speaks of again being in the anguish of childbirth until Christ is formed (μορφόω) in them. This verse not only alludes to their new birth using the image of Paul as their mother, but it also speaks of their deficient Christ formation. When speaking of the Christian relationship with Christ, Paul most often speaks of people being "in Christ." Here, he reverses the idea: Christ is being formed within the Galatians. While the image is awkward, it suggests the growth of Christ in the believer, shaping them to be like Jesus. As they are fashioned increasingly into the image of God's Son, they will move away from false ideas, such as the Judaizers' demand for circumcision, Jewish holy days and times, and kosher food.

This passage then states their deficient pneumaformation and Christoformation. They began their Christian lives by hearing the gospel, believing, and receiving the Spirit (Gal. 3:2, 5). They now seek to continue their Christian lives through law observance, no longer relying on grace, faith, and living by the Spirit. They are thus attempting to be completed (ἐπιτελέω) by the flesh (3:3). They are regressing from the kind of maturity Paul expects from brothers and sisters yielding to the Spirit; hence, his address τέκνα μου, "my children," is a possibly a challenge to their maturity and Christian growth. Paul wants his converts to mature through being led by the Spirit and not the flesh. He will stress this in Galatians 5–6, where his converts are to renounce the Judaizers' non-gospel and the works of the flesh and be led by the Spirit in their lives. Therefore, we can unhesitantly say the essence of Christian discipleship is yielding to the Spirit who forms Christ in believers.

Philippians 2:6–7

As is well known, Philippians 2:5–11 lies at the heart of any discussion about cruciformity or Christoformity. Having written extensively on the passage, I will assume that Paul uses it ethically, or more accurately, socio- and missio-ethically.[21] He describes the example of Christ inviting the Philippians, divided by a degree of contention, to cement their unity. Doing so will strengthen them as a church and in their mission.

Preceding the passage, Paul thanks God for the Philippians' participation in the gospel mission (Phil. 1:3–8), prays for them to exhibit love more and more (Phil. 1:9–11), expresses his joy at the gospel advancing at his point of incarceration (Phil. 1:12–18a), describes his dilemma as he faces potential death as he goes to trial (Phil. 1:18b–26), and begins his appeal to the Philippians in 1:27–2:4. His appeal is that they live as heavenly citizens worthy of the gospel of Christ (1:27a). They are to do this standing firm in the unity the

---

21. See Keown, *Philippians*, 1:378. See also, Mark J. Keown, "A Missional and Liturgical Reading of the Christ-Hymn," unpublished paper presented at Tyndale New Testament Study Group, 2021.

Spirit generates and by contending for the gospel without being intimidated by their opponents (1:27b–28). They are to renounce selfish ambition and empty self-glorification and make his joy complete by living with the attitudes of God and Christ that they experience in Christ and the Spirit as they walk in fellowship and share their faith: encouragement, comfort, partnership, compassion, affection, humility, esteeming others, and selflessness (2:1–4).

Following the passage, Philippians 2:12–18 provides the second frame of the thematic chiasm around the Christ-hymn.[22] Paul restates what he wants from the Philippians, summoning them to continue in obedience, work out their own salvation with fear and trembling, desist grumbling and arguing, live blamelessly in their social relationships so that they will give exemplary ethical witness to Christ, hold forth the word of life,[23] and partner with Paul in joy.

The Christ-hymn is not merely a magnificent declaration of who Jesus is, as some scholars argue. Chiastically framed as it is by the two exhortation sections, it urges believers to emulate the phronesis of Christ during his earthly mission. The missio-ethical intent is also evident in Philippians 2:5, which urges them to do this very thing. The Philippians are to take on the attitude Christ demonstrated in his earthly life and death. Obeying this will assure them of unity in their social lives and mission.

The hymn traces the movement of Christ. He exists in the form of God and has an equal status with him (2:6a, c). However, as he was born into human history as a human man, he did not exploit his divine power and equality with God the Father for self-aggrandizement or his own purposes (2:6b).[24] Rather than seek empty self-glory (cf. 2:3), he emptied *himself* out for the world.[25] In so doing, Jesus stands in direct contrast to despotic, autocratic imperial leaders like the Macedonian Alexander the Great, the Caesars, the many such despots from history, spiritual powers including Satan, the man of lawlessness in 2 Thessalonians 2, and of course, Adam.[26] Jesus did this by assuming the form of a slave, despite being the one in the form of God, equal to him with eternal divine glory and power.

This description of the form of a slave is further explicated in his being born in human likeness and being discovered in human form. It is most graphically demonstrated in his voluntary self-humbling, "by becoming obedient to the point of death, even death on a cross" (v. 8). Death on the cross was the most shameful way to die in the Roman world.[27] As such, Christ's movement from

---

22. Keown, *Philippians*, 1:282.
23. On "hold forth," see chapter 4, "The Fellowship of the Holy Spirit."
24. On Philippians 2:6, see Keown, *Philippians*, 1:383–401.
25. He did not empty himself of any attributes; instead, he (subject) emptied (verb) himself (object)—he poured himself out in service and death for the world. Keown, *Philippians*, 1:401–6.
26. See my discussion of the background of the Christ hymn: Keown, *Philippians*, 1:354–65.
27. See Fee, *Philippians*, 217; Joseph H. Hellerman, "The Humiliation of Christ in the Social World of Roman Philippi, Part 2," *BSac* 160, no. 640 (2003): 427–30; Martin Hengel, *Crucifixion* (Philadelphia: Fortress, 1977), 62–63; Keown, *Philippians*, 1:419–20.

the very highest place as God to the most humiliating death possible demonstrates what it means to be the God who loves the world. It also shows readers what it means to be truly human.

Paul includes the hymn so that the Philippians will soak in the Christ story and live with the same kind of mindset (v. 5). They are to be cruciform, Christoform, or, as I put it elsewhere, live out the Christ pattern.[28] Philippians is full of language explaining how such living should and should not look. It is *not* envy or rivalry (1:15), selfish ambition (1:17), self-glorification (2:3), grumbling, arguing (2:14), and the like.

Instead, it is exhibiting virtues such as voluntary enslavement (1:1), grace, peacefulness (1:2), joy (1:4), unity in the gospel (1:5), "love" (1:9), blamelessness (1:10), "humility" (2:3), esteeming others (2:3), pursuing the interests of Christ and others (2:4, 20), gentleness (4:4), and other "fruit of righteousness" (1:11). If they live like this, their strained social relationships will be restored and their witness enhanced (2:14–16a).

Philippians oscillates between passages of exhortation and example.[29] In the exhortatory passages, Paul urges them to live as citizens worthy of the gospel of Christ, stand firm in one Spirit, contend as one soul for the faith of the gospel (1:27), embody a range of godly attitudes (2:1–4), work out their own salvation (2:12), desist from complaint and argument (2:14), and be united in the Lord (2:2; 4:2). While conveying reports of his situation and his travel plans, he gives positive examples of what it looks like to be formed into the pattern of Christ. They are to be like the well-motivated Romans who preach Christ out of goodwill, love, and a correct understanding of Paul's God-sent mission (1:16); Timothy (2:19–23); Epaphroditus (1:1; 2:25–30); Paul (throughout but esp. 3:4–17; 4:9); and themselves in their earlier history (4:2). They are not to emulate those motivated by envy, rivalry, and selfish ambition in Rome (1:15, 17), nor the Judaizers and enemies of the cross (3:2, 18–19).

Throughout the letter, Paul is careful to himself embody the attitudes he hopes will form in the Philippians. He describes himself and Timothy as slaves (1:1). He expresses his gratitude and affection for the Philippians (1:3–8). His primary concern is the gospel rather than his dire personal circumstances (1:12–18a). Faced with potential death, he wants to live on to continue to partner in God's mission (1:19–26). He is prepared to send two coworkers to Philippi, even though his situation is uncertain (2:19–30). In 3:4–11, he exalts himself as a Jew par excellence and then writes his credentials off as nothing compared to knowing Christ. He states his determination to press on to the end and calls the Philippians to emulate his example (3:12–17).

---

28. Mark J. Keown, "The Christ Pattern for Social Relationships in Philippians and Beyond," in *Paul and His Social Relations*, eds. Stanley E. Porter and Christopher D. Land, Pauline Studies 7 (Leiden: Brill, 2012), 301–31.

29. Keown, *Philippians*, 1:80–83.

Paul yearns for the Philippians to be fully mature in Christ, Christo-formed. While he does not mention the Spirit often, the power for this is "he who began a good work in you" and who "will bring it to completion at the day of Jesus Christ" (Phil. 1:6); Christ, the source of encouragement (2:1) and one who has the "power that enables him even to subject all things to himself" (3:21); God, in Christ, by the Spirit—the one working in them "both to will and to act for his good pleasure" (2:13); "the power of his resurrection" (3:10); and the one in whom Paul can do all things whatever his material state (4:13).

More explicitly, the prayers of the Philippians and "the help [or supply] of the Spirit of Jesus Christ" will enable him to live the Christ life well (Phil. 1:19). The same Spirit who has forged the unity of the Philippians (1:27b; 2:1) will enable them to stand firm together as they contend for the faith of the gospel unintimidated by their opponents or thwarted by their suffering (Phil. 1:27; 4:1 [the Lord]). In and by this Spirit, they worship God (3:3).

Philippians 3:10

We must pause and consider Philippians 3:10, which utilizes μορφ-language and so speaks of Christian formation. In Philippians 2:6–7, Paul writes of Christ, the one in the form of God, taking on the form of a slave. Here, Paul expresses his desire to know this theoform One who has become *doulos-* and *anthrōpos*-formed, the crucified, risen, and exalted Christ. Knowing Christ, whom he formerly persecuted, is now the most crucial thing in his life (v. 7). All else is loss and excrement[30] besides gaining Christ and being declared righteous by faith in him (vv. 8–9). He desires to know Christ and the power of his resurrection, the Spirit (Rom. 1:4, 8:11).

However, his passion for knowing this power does not lead him to trium-phalism; instead, he wants to share in Christ's sufferings, being conformed to his death. Such a desire is not literal, for Christ has already died and risen. Instead, Paul yearns to embrace the pattern of Christ's self-giving for the world by suffering in his service and, if need be, dying for him. He identi-fies with the Christ who humbled himself to the point of death, even death on a cross (2:8). It is in and by the Spirit (the power of the resurrection), and bound together in and with Christ, that he will do this.

In a way, Philippians 3:10 is arguably the most explicit statement of pneumaformation in Paul's letters. Joined to God in Christ, energized by the Spirit that raised Jesus and empowered him, he wants to live his life wholly given over to Jesus, even to the point of participating in his suffering as he engages in mission. By this power, Paul will persevere to his last breath for Jesus and experience his resurrection out of the dead.

Paul's determination to live the Christ life is expressed in Philippians 3:12–14: having been taken hold of by Christ and not resting on the laurels of his remarkable career as a Pharisee and Christian, he wants to press on to win

---

30.   Keown, *Philippians*, 2:146–48.

the prize of eternal life with Christ. He twice expressly urges the Philippians to emulate his example in doing this (Phil. 3:15, 17). He is confident that if any in the church have other ideas, God will reveal the truth to them—by the Spirit implied (3:16). The outcome will be their final transformation, as we see in the next verse discussed.

Philippians 3:21

Framing Paul's testimony and appeal in Philippians 3 are warnings of false teachers. Philippians 3:2 speaks of the Judaizers[31] and sets up Paul's self-elevation and denigration in emulation of Christ (Phil. 3:4–7), his desire to know Christ (Phil. 3:8–11), his determination to press on (Phil. 3:12–14), and his appeal to the Philippians to imitate him (Phil. 3:15–17). Philippians 3:18–19 refers again to enemies. These may be Judaizers, licentious, so-called Christians, or unbelievers who corrupt the gospel in the direction of Greco-Roman licentiousness.[32] Whoever is in view, their end is destruction.

In 3:20, Paul assures the Philippians of the outcome of their pneumaformation—their final transformation. First, he reminds them that their real homeland is heaven, where their citizenship is rooted (v. 20). Second, he speaks of the believers' yearning for the return of the Lord Jesus Christ, the Savior, what he has called thus far in the letter "the day of [Jesus] Christ" (1:6, 10; 2:16).

At his return from heaven, Jesus will transform (μετασχηματίζω) the believers' lowly bodies (lit. "bodies of humiliation") so that they are conformed (σύμμορφος) to his glorious body, according to the working of God's powerful ability in Christ to subject to himself all things. Explicated more fully in 1 Corinthians 15:50–55 (also 2 Cor. 5:1–5; 1 Thess. 4:13–5:11), this moment is the instant of the final transformation of believers, the result and consummation of their pneumaformation (chapter 11). Those who, by the Spirit, seek to live in conformity to the theoformed one who took the form of a human slave dying on a cross, will hear the upward call of God and know this transformation. This change will be achieved by Christ's power by which he is subjugating all God's enemies, fulfilling the hopes of Psalm 110:1. This power is his Spirit.

THE SPIRIT WHO BUILDS PEOPLE UP

The Christian life begins in and by the Spirit, but people are to grow as they are formed to be more and more like Jesus. Paul uses a range of language to describe the growth. One of these is the *oiko-* terms that punctuate his letters.

Growth from God

Using language of growth from God, Paul likens the church to God's building (θεοῦ οἰκοδομή, 1 Cor. 3:9). The Spirit works through missional leaders like Paul to establish these churches with Christ as the foundation (Rom. 15:20;

---

31. Keown, *Philippians*, 2:98–105.
32. Keown, *Philippians*, 2:248–54.

1 Cor. 3:10; 2 Cor. 10:8). Or, as in Ephesians, the church is formed on the foundation of the apostles and prophets, with Jesus as the capstone and/or cornerstone (Eph. 2:19–21).[33] God continues this growth through the ministries of those who follow Christ—as with Apollos and Peter in Corinth (1 Cor. 3:10)—and through founding missionaries like Paul and his team. All such leaders must lead well, pneumaformed to the gospel and character of Christ. God will judge them for their work (1 Cor. 3:11–15). Their task is faithfulness, and it is God who gives the growth (1 Cor. 3:6). He builds his building or temple by his Spirit (1 Cor. 3:16; Eph. 2:22)—the household of faith (Gal. 6:10) or the household of God (1 Tim. 3:15).

Gifts

The gifts of the Spirit are for building up the church and its people. First Corinthians 14 encourages the Corinthians, when they gather as a church, to focus on gifts like prophecy that build others up (1 Cor. 14:3–5, 12, 17). A full range of spiritual gifts is to be expressed in their meetings to ensure that believers continue to grow (1 Cor. 14:26). The leadership gifts are given to leaders to equip the rest of God's people for works of ministry so that its church in love grows in maturity, resists false teaching, and is extended through missional engagement (Eph. 4:12–16).

Building One Another Up

Christians are to build one another up (1 Thess. 5:11). People are built up by one another through inclusivity and warm acceptance (Rom. 14:19). Again, this is the work of the Spirit (Rom. 14:17). Similarly, believers are to emulate the example of Christ in seeking the best for their neighbors, especially the "weak" (Rom. 15:1; cf. 1 Cor. 8:10). This is because love, the supreme fruit of the Spirit, builds others up (1 Cor. 8:1). Not everything has this edifying effect; therefore, believers should be considerate when gathered with unbelievers or others who are vulnerable to ensure what they do builds the others up (1 Cor. 10:23). They encourage one another with edifying speech (Eph. 4:29). Paul's letters themselves embody his desire to build up his readers (2 Cor. 12:19; 13:10). Believers, then, are to walk in Christ, rooted and built up in him, and established in the faith (Col. 2:7). The pneumaformed believers are also devoted to seeing others formed similarly.

THE SPIRIT WHO BRINGS PEOPLE TO MATURITY

Paul also uses *telei*- language of Christian growth. The term τέλειος is used for maturity, and this maturation is the work of the Spirit. As he told the Galatians, people receive the Spirit as they hear the gospel and believe it (Gal. 3:3). They do not do so through works in any sense, whether works of the law (as the Judaizers demand) or any other works. Having been established in Christ,

---

33.   See the earlier discussion of Ephesians 2:20–22 in chapter 4, "A Spirit-Indwelt Temple."

believers must continue to walk in faith, by the Spirit, and not by resorting to a works-based Christian life. The Galatians are being diverted from faith and the Spirit to this very thing, a law-based, Judaizing faith. Such a "gospel" urges believers to seek righteous standing before God through their capacity to fulfill the required works, with the flesh's power.[34] For Paul, this is implausible, as the flesh has insufficient power to enable complete resistance to sin. Paul's response is to challenge them with a rhetorical question: "Are you so foolish; having begun by the Spirit, are you now being completed by the flesh?" (3:3). The maturation process, for Paul, involves continuing to believe in God and his Son and being led by the Spirit toward completion.

In 1 Corinthians 14:20, set in a passage critiquing the Corinthian obsession with tongues,[35] Paul uses a chiasm to urge the Corinthians not to be childlike but mature in their thinking (while being infants concerning evil things).[36] As such, τέλειος describes someone who is "grown up" in the faith. Paul's ministry goal is to proclaim Christ through warning and teaching so that all his converts are presented mature in Christ (Col. 1:28). The function of leaders is to ensure the maturity of the whole church "to the measure of the stature of the fullness of Christ" (Eph. 4:13). Epaphras's intercession ministry focuses on the Colossian Christians standing mature and fully assured in God's will (Col. 4:12). Being mature indicates being advanced in pneumaformity, for it is by the Spirit that God through Christ transforms believers.

Philippians 3:12, 15

Having referred to his hope of resurrection, in Philippians 3:12, Paul tells the Philippians that he has not yet been made complete (τελειόω); consequently, he presses on in his life and mission to the day he hears God's call home. Paul then urges those who are mature among the Philippians to emulate his attitude (Phil. 3:15). Paul states his confidence that if any disagree with this in any way, God will reveal to them what is right. Implicitly, this speaks of the work of the Spirit.

2 Corinthians 12:9

Second Corinthians 12:9 does not directly speak of the maturation process, but the use of τέλειος has some importance to this discussion. The context is Paul's thorn in the flesh. Whatever the issue, and despite his threefold prayer, Paul lives with something malevolent (ἄγγελος

---

34.   See also Galatians 5:16, where Paul urges the Galatians to walk by the Spirit and not by completing (τελέσητε) the desires of the flesh.

35.   Fee observes of 1 Corinthians 12–14, "The correctives are *all* aimed at the abuse of tongues in the assembly, which seems to be both singular in its emphasis and disorderly in its expression." Fee, *GEP*, 148 (emphasis original).

36.   A1 μὴ παιδία γίνεσθε ταῖς φρεσὶν, "do not be children in your thinking"
        B ἀλλὰ τῇ κακίᾳ νηπιάζετε, "but in evil be infants"
        A2 ταῖς δὲ φρεσὶν τέλειοι γίνεσθε, "and in thinking be mature" (my translation)
        Similarly, see Fee, *The First Epistle*, 752.

THE SPIRIT AND CHRISTOFORMITY

σατανᾶ) that causes him great suffering.[37] Rather than deliver Paul from this piercing problem, Christ (the Lord) has spoken to him. As a result of his encounter with Christ, Paul has come to believe that the thorn was given to him to torment him (κολαφίζω)[38] and to stop him from becoming self-exalted (ὑπεραίρω, 2 Cor. 12:7).[39] Paul then records Christ saying to him that "my grace is sufficient for you, the power is being *perfected* [τέλειος] in weakness" (my translation).

This encounter suggests several things relevant to this discussion. First, Christ speaking to Paul suggests the work of the Spirit, for it is by the Spirit Jesus speaks (other than in a vision or direct Christophany—although I would argue these, too, are pneumaphanies). Similarly, the idea of God's grace being sufficient for him speaks of God's reaching out to Paul in Christ by the Spirit, bringing his beneficence to bear in Paul's suffering. Similarly, "the power" here would be experienced in and by the Spirit.

Second, the setting is prayer, indicating the Spirit is encountered in the context of speaking and listening to God. Third, Paul credits a messenger of Satan (ἄγγελος σατανᾶ) with being God's vehicle for the delivery of this torment. There is, thus, a spiritual element to his problem.

Fourth, there is a relationship between Paul's suffering and Christ's power reaching its zenith in him. The effect of this perfecting (τελέω, v. 9) is τέλειος, deeper maturity, in Paul. Specifically, the Spirit of God and his Son actes in Paul to ensure he does not become arrogant and lofty due to the fantastic revelations he has experienced. This juxtaposition of revelation and suffering becomes a criticism of the Judaizing pneumatic opponents who are making theological claims based on their spiritual experiences. As such, we see the importance of prayer for maturation and the role of the Spirit speaking to people's needs and assisting their maturation. Such texts also point to the importance of suffering for maturation, something expounded in Romans 5:3–5 (see chapter 8).

The outcome of the process of full maturation in the believer is also mentioned in Paul. Paul speaks of this several times using the associated term ἐπιτελέω, most often denoting "to complete."[40] The Spirit achieves this completion (Gal. 3:3, above). The τέλος of sanctification is eternal life (Rom. 6:22). Believers are to participate with God in their sanctification through cleansing themselves so that holiness is *completed* in fear of God (2 Cor. 7:1). Paul affirms their ability to do this: Christ will sustain them to the end

---

37. See further chapter 8, "Formation Through Suffering."
38. Used five times in the NT of being struck with fists (Matt. 26:67; Mark 14:65; 1 Cor. 4:11; 2 Cor. 12:7; 1 Peter 2:20).
39. BDAG gives ὑπεραίρω the meaning "to have an undue sense of one's self-importance, rise up, exalt oneself, be elated." The term is used of the self-exaltation of that man of lawlessness (2 Thess. 2:4). Paul uses it twice in the verse to give emphasis to this.
40. *BrillDAG*, s.v. "ἐπιτελέω."

(τέλος),[41] blameless for the day of Christ (1 Cor. 1:8). Similarly, God will bring to completion (ἐπιτελέω) the good work begun in the Philippians (Phil. 1:6). He will sanctify the Thessalonians *entirely*, so they are blameless at Christ's coming (1 Thess. 5:23).

In these texts, Paul refers to the role of Christ's Spirit in this maturation process. Believers must cooperate with the Spirit's work. At that time, the perfect (τέλειος) will come, and the partial, including ongoing human frailty and sin, will be no more (1 Cor. 13:10). Paul himself has achieved this goal, completing the race he was running (2 Tim. 4:7; cf. Phil. 3:12–14).

τέλειος is also used ironically for the seemingly mature Corinthians (1 Cor. 2:6)[42] and of God's perfect will, which is more easily discerned with transformed and renewed minds (Rom. 12:2), and the eschatological perfection that is to come and transcends present experience (1 Cor. 13:10).

THE SPIRIT WHO GROWS PEOPLE

At times, Paul prefers αὐξ- language when speaking of the process of growth. Such language is used for biological growth and is symbolic of growth in other senses. Paul employs the language for the growth of the church.

Corinthians

While the spiritually endowed ministers of the gospel labor to establish God's church and minister to it, God causes it to grow (1 Cor. 3:6–7). This growth implies both new converts and the maturation of the believers in the church. God does this via the Spirit, as is seen throughout 1 Corinthians, especially in 1 Corinthians 12 and 14. Similarly, he causes the harvest of Corinthian righteousness to grow (2 Cor. 9:10). In context, this speaks of increasing their capacity to give to the Jerusalem collection and produce the fruit of meeting the material needs of the saints of Jerusalem (and to exhibit such generosity at other times). The Spirit, then, impels giving to those in need. By the Spirit, God grows the faith of the Corinthians, extending Paul's influence in and through those in the church he planted (2 Cor. 10:15).

Ephesians

In Ephesians 2:21, Paul uses the growth metaphor of the building that is God's one people growing into a holy temple in the Lord, in which God dwells by his Spirit (Eph. 2:21). In Ephesians 4:15–16, the church leaders who are gifted with the Spirit equip the church members for works of service.[43] As a result, believers and the church speak "truth in love" and grow up into Christ, the head of the church. The body of the church is then built up in love.

---

41. See also Paul's use of τέλος of the end (1 Cor. 15:24).
42. See also Fee, *The First Epistle*, 110.
43. Thielman, *Ephesians*, 277–79.

Colossians and Thessalonians

In Colossians, the gospel itself is bearing fruit and growing as people come to Christ (Col. 1:6). So, Paul prays that the Colossians will bear fruit in every good deed and grow in the knowledge of God (Col. 1:10). As in Ephesians, the church, sustained by Christ the head of the church, like a body held together with ligaments and sinews (LEB), "grows with the growth of God" (Col. 2:19). By his Spirit, in and through his spiritually endowed people, God is growing his people and his church in Christ. In 2 Thessalonians 1:3, the faith of the Thessalonians is growing to an exceeding degree (ὑπεραυξάνω),[44] which causes Paul to give thanks (2 Thess. 1:3).

Paul sometimes uses the verb πλεονάζω for the development of Christians and the church.[45] The verb carries the nuances of "to be more, grow, or increase."[46] He prays that the Lord may cause the Thessalonians to increase and abound in love for others (1 Thess. 3:12). Then in 2 Thessalonians 1:3 (mentioned in the previous section), the Pauline group thank God continually for the increasing (πλεονάζει) love of the Colossians. These two references show that God is the source of this increase, implying his work in Christ by the Spirit. They also show that the prayers of the Pauline team were answered in abundance. As elsewhere, the link between prayer and the power of the Spirit is seen.

THE SPIRIT WHO BRINGS ABUNDANCE

One of Paul's favorite language groups is the *periss-* nexus of terms that connote abundance. The Spirit is the source of this overflow that goes in various directions.

Romans 15:13

The Spirit's role in generating the abundance experienced in Christ is seen in Romans 15:13. Paul prays that God will fill the Romans with all joy and peace in believing so that by the power of the Holy Spirit they may abound (περισσεύω) in hope. The God of hope's filling of the Romans is enacted through the Spirit. God generates Spirit fruit: joy, peace, and hope. The context is prayer, revealing the close connection between believers' prayers and the experience of the Spirit. The Spirit forms the believer toward joy, peace, and hope.

2 Corinthians 1–7

For Paul and his team, participating in Christ also means sharing abundantly in his sufferings, as they live cruciformly in a hostile world (2 Cor. 1:5).

---

44. The use of the prefix ὑπερ speaks not only of growth, but to "grow wonderfully, increase abundantly." See BDAG, s.v. "ὑπερ," 1032.
45. Paul also uses πλεονάζω of the increase of grace (Rom. 5:20; 6:1; 2 Cor. 4:15), of sin (Rom. 5:20), of not gathering too much (2 Cor. 8:15), and of profit in the Philippians' accounts (Phil. 4:17).
46. Silva, "πλεονάζω," *NIDNTTE* 3:77.

Yet, even more, God, who is the Father of mercies and God of all comfort, comforts believers in affliction (2 Cor. 1:3–4). Further, through Christ, "our comfort overflows also" (2 Cor. 1:5 LEB). While the Spirit is not directly referenced, it is implied that God comforts in Christ by his Spirit (see further chapter 8). The Spirit, then, comforts and encourages believers in their suffering. However, it does not stop there, for in and by the Spirit, working in Paul and his team, relief overflows to the letter's recipients (v. 6). The Corinthians share in suffering, and Paul hopes that they will also share in the comfort given by God through his Spirit (2 Cor. 1:7).

In 2 Corinthians 2:4, Paul expresses the abundant love that he has for the Corinthians (cf. 2 Cor. 12:15). While the Spirit is not mentioned, love is a fruit of the Spirit for Paul, so we can imply his work here (Gal. 5:22). Similarly, Titus's affection (σπλάγχνον) for the Corinthians overflows as he remembers the Corinthian obedience (2 Cor. 7:15).

Elsewhere, Paul expresses his longing for the Philippians with the affections of Christ Jesus (Phil. 1:8). The genitive Χριστοῦ Ἰησοῦ is likely a genitive of source or production: the affections generated by Christ in believers.[47] Such longing is the Spirit's work in Paul and, presumably, in Titus. Despite Paul and his team's afflictions, he overflows with joy (2 Cor. 7:4; cf. 7:13). This recalls 2 Corinthians 1:3–7, where God is the source of comfort by his Spirit (as proposed), suggesting we should assume the Spirit is also in view here. We know from the aforementioned Romans 15:13 that the source of this joy is the Spirit. The joy then overflows into abundant generosity.

2 Corinthians 8–9

In his extensive appeal to the Corinthians to give to the Jerusalem collection in 2 Corinthians 8–9, Paul uses περισσεύω ten times. While he doesn't always mention God as the source of the superfluity, several factors indicate that Paul considered the Spirit the source of this abundance. And, as has been argued throughout this book, it is by his Spirit that God exerts his power into the world to produce the abundance experienced by God's new covenant people.

God's power is evident from 2 Corinthians 9:8–14, where, as Paul wraps up his appeal, the source of abundance is God in every sense. God can cause all grace to abound to the Corinthians so that they are well provisioned and can "overflow in every good work" (2 Cor. 9:8 LEB). Paul cites Psalm 111:9 LXX (112:9 EVV) of God giving lavishly to the needy (2 Cor. 9:9). God supplies seed and bread, multiplies the Corinthian seed, and causes their harvest of righteousness to grow (2 Cor. 9:10). He has made them rich in every way to be radically generous to the needs of the saints, resulting in overflowing thanksgiving to God (2 Cor. 9:11–12). The Jerusalem saints will glorify God and pray longingly for the Corinthians "because of the surpassing grace of God upon [them]" (2 Cor. 9:13–14). Paul finishes expressing thanks to God

---

47. Keown, *Philippians*, 1:154.

for his indescribable gift. Undeniably, God is the source of all the abundant giving represented in the chapters. God's action in generating generosity can be assumed to be achieved through his exertion of power by the Spirit.

The Jerusalem collection is an aspect of Paul's ministry. He then explains that the "ministry of the Spirit" and "ministry of righteousness" overflows (περισσεύω) much more (πολλῷ μᾶλλον) than ministry under the Mosaic covenant.

Paul remembers the Macedonian's overflowing joy in giving to the Jerusalem collection despite affliction and poverty. Consequently, we can be confident that the abundance of joy expressed by the Macedonians, despite severe persecution, is generated by God (see Rom. 15:13 above). Despite their extreme poverty, their overflowing generosity is due to "the grace of God that has been given among the churches of Macedonia." God is the source of the grace that overflows among the Macedonian churches. Their philanthropy is evidence of the Spirit generating the Macedonian response because it is Spirit-impelled grace (2 Cor. 8:2). The Spirit is intimately involved in every aspect of the Pauline team's ministry, including the Jerusalem collection. The Spirit moved Paul to take it up, and he moves God's people to give.

The overflow of the Corinthians in faith, speech, knowledge, and eagerness is clearly from God (2 Cor. 8:7).[48] Indeed, as Paul wrote earlier to them, they are rich in all speech and all knowledge and lack no spiritual gift (1 Cor. 1:5, 7).[49] God will generate their capacity to excel in grace toward the Jerusalem Christians (2 Cor. 8:7). He has given them material abundance in the present so that they can help the needy Jerusalem Christians. The same should come to pass when the boot is on the other foot (8:14). God is able to make all grace abound to the Corinthians so that they have all sufficiency in all things at all times and so can abound in every good work (9:8). He does this through Christ, in and by the Spirit.

Focus on 2 Corinthians 8:9

Mention must also be made of 2 Corinthians 8:9. Paul anchors his appeal in God's giving, exemplified in the grace of Christ's self giving. He, his team, and the Corinthians know (we know) what Christ has done. In fact, Paul, Timothy, and Silas, followed by a range of other preachers, have preached this Christ among them.[50] Paul describes this as "the grace of our Lord Jesus Christ," linking Christ's self-giving to people giving to others in need.

Paul uses the term χάρις ten times in the passage.[51] Twice he mentions God's grace as the source of giving; first, for the Macedonians (2 Cor. 8:1), and second, for the Corinthians (9:14). In 8:9, it is the grace of Christ expressed in

---

48.   On this passage, see Fee, *GEP*, 339. I will discuss this in relation to spiritual gifts.

49.   See also Fee, *GEP*, 85.

50.   Acts 18:1–16; 1 Cor. 2:1–5; 3:4–9; 2 Cor. 1:19.

51.   2 Cor. 8:1, 4, 6, 7, 9, 16, 19; 9:8, 14, 15.

his self-giving from riches to poverty to save humankind in its poverty. Believers participating in giving is a grace that reflects the giving of God and his Son (8:4). Giving through the Jerusalem collection, then, is a particular expression of this grace (8:7, 19). God can cause this grace of giving to abound so that believers overflow in giving (9:8). Twice the term is used for giving thanks back to God for his grace (8:16; 9:15). At the heart of Paul's use of "grace" is giving, whether it be gifts from God, Christ, or material gifts toward the Jerusalem collection.

Christ's grace, then, is seen in him giving himself for the world. Paul clarifies this with an explanatory ὅτι that explains this grace.[52] It signals that Christ gave himself "for the sake of" (διά + acc.) the Corinthians (ὑμᾶς). In Paul's broader theology, this is Jesus's self-giving to save them. In his self-giving, Jesus, although rich (ὤν),[53] made himself poor (ἐπτώχευσεν). The riches Paul has in mind are the unlimited spiritual and material wealth of his being in the form of God in his preexistent state as God's Son. His poverty at least includes full participation in the human condition. It might include Jesus's material poverty if Paul knew that aspect of Christ's life.[54]

The purpose (ἵνα) is so that the Corinthians (ὑμεῖς), by Jesus's poverty, might become rich. We know that Corinth was a city of "new money."[55] There are also indications that the Corinthian church had some wealthy members.[56] As such, the emphasis here is the spiritual riches experienced in their life in Christ, which includes the Spirit and all that God through Christ does in them by his Spirit. Still, Paul believes that in the present age, God supplies every need of believers according to his riches in glory in Christ Jesus (Phil. 4:19). At times, Paul has experienced abundant (περισσεύω) provision (Phil. 4:12), including in his present situation in Rome due to the Philippians' gift (Phil. 4:18). At other times, he and other Christians face poverty and struggle. In any such situation, God strengthens Paul and others (Phil. 4:13). As such, Paul mainly has in mind the Corinthians, ultimately enjoying the riches of the eternal inheritance that awaits them.

Paul's placement of 2 Corinthians 8:9 has several significant spinoffs for this study. First, the passage sits alongside Philippians 2:6–11 as a Pauline text indicating the essence of the life Paul is summoning his converts to live.[57] As

52. BDAG, s.v. "ὅτι" 2a, 732.
53. The participle here may be concessive, "although."
54. Christ's material poverty is seen in his family taking the "cheap" option of sacrificing birds at his circumcision (Luke 2:24; cf. Lev. 12:8). He also died destitute, with nothing after his cloak was taken by the soldiers (Mark 15:24). As I accept that Mark and Luke traveled and worked with Paul in the gospel, I find it highly likely Paul was aware of Jesus's actual poverty.
55. Keown, *Discovering: The Pauline Letters*, 459; Witherington, *Conflict*, 34.
56. G. Theissen, *The Social Setting of Pauline Christianity: Essays on Corinth*, trans. J. H. Schütz (Philadelphia: Fortress, 1982), 69–120, 145–74.
57. To a lesser extent, Romans 15:3, where Jesus took on the reproaches of those who reproached others (a citation of Psalm 69:9). However, this has nothing like the downward movement of 2 Corinthians 8:9 and Philippians 2:6–8.

cruciform or Christoform people, they are to emulate Christ's self-giving for the world. Second, material giving is somewhat visible in Philippians, where the Philippians' sacrificial giving to Paul is a crucial aspect of the letter. Here, Paul explicitly shows that material giving is a critical aspect of Christoformity. Second Corinthians 8:9 is nestled in a passage urging the Corinthians to give to the collection. They are to do so by emulating the sacrificial attitude of Christ. Key to doing this is their being led by Spirit in giving to the needs of the Jerusalem saints as Jesus was led by God as he divested himself of heavenly riches to alleviate the spiritual needs of sinful humanity.

2 Corinthians 10

In 2 Corinthians 10, Paul begins boasting ironically against his adversaries. Unlike his opponents, who appear to boast of their ministry achievements in churches Paul established, he specifies that he will only boast concerning his own ministry sphere. Obviously, the Corinthians fall sphere of influence. Hence, as he boasts concerning them, he is not boasting of the work of others. In the complicated text 2 Corinthians 10:15, Paul expresses his and his team's hopes that as their faith continues to grow, the team's sphere of activity among the Corinthians will greatly expand (εἰς περισσείαν). This expansion is the work of the Spirit building faith and enlarging the influence of the gospel in Corinth and the environs where Paul and his team have worked.[58]

Ephesians 1:3–14

I have already discussed the wonderful blessing of Ephesians 1:3–14, a passage that speaks of the blessings conveyed upon believers at their conversion.[59] The incredible array of blessings through the passage are aspects of the riches of God's grace lavished (περισσευω) on believers (ἡμᾶς), experienced in Christ, including redemption and forgiveness. All these things are the work of the Spirit (Eph. 1:13).

Philippians 1:9–11

In his prayer for the Philippians, Paul prays that the Philippians' love will overflow (περισσεύῃ) yet more and more in knowledge and all insight (Phil. 1:9). Considering the connection between the Spirit and prayer in Paul and the association of love and Spirit, this love will be the work of the Spirit. Paul's purpose is that through their knowledgeable and discerning love, they will approve what is excellent so that they may be pure and blameless when Christ comes as judge (Phil. 1:10).

Paul explains this purity and blamelessness as their having been "filled with the fruit of righteousness that comes through [διὰ] Jesus Christ." While the "fruit of righteousness" here can be a way of expressing their status of

---

58. Fee, *GEP*, does not mention this verse in regard to the Spirit's work.
59. See chapter 3, "The Spirit Who Blesses."

being righteous, it more likely refers to the fruit of righteousness that issues forth from those who are justified by faith.[60] It is another way of speaking of the "fruit of the Spirit" in Galatians 5:22–23, where "love" leads the list. Paul wants them to be filled with such fruit, virtues expressed in their lives sourced in the indwelling Spirit. Notably, it "comes through Jesus Christ," indicating that this Spirit fruit is received *through* Jesus Christ for those *in* him. The love he wants for them is God's love experienced in Christ (Phil. 2:1). It is inclusive of their love for God and his Son, love for all humankind, love for Paul (Phil. 1:16), and particularly their love for one another that will make Paul's joy complete (Phil. 2:2). Such love will heal their fracturing relationships (Phil. 4:2–3).

Philippians 1:26 and 3:3

Another aspect of abundance generated by the Spirit in the believer's life is worship. Paul hopes that his release and coming to Philippi will enable the Philippians to boast more in Christ Jesus (Phil. 1:26). While ἐν Χριστῷ Ἰησοῦ can speak locatively of the sphere of being "in Christ," here it speaks of Christ Jesus as the object of their boasting.[61] This text fits with other passages where believers are to boast in the Lord.[62] It also aligns with Philippians 3:3, where it is believers (ἡμεῖς) who "worship by the Spirit of God and boast in Christ Jesus" (LEB). The Spirit generates lavish worship and glorying or boasting in the one who saved them, Christ Jesus.

1 Thessalonians 3:9–10

Another aspect of the abundance the Spirit generates in believers is gratitude. In Colossians 2:6–7, the Colossians, having received Jesus, are rooted, built up, and established in the faith, and are to walk in him as they have been taught, "abounding [περισσεύω] in thanksgiving." First Thessalonians 3:9–10 refers to Paul and his team's thanksgiving due to their delight at the Thessalonians. The Pauline team prays superabundantly (ὑπερεκπερισσοῦ) night and day that they may come to the city and supply what is lacking in the Thessalonians' faith.[63] In the context of "spiritual warfare," Ephesians 6:18

---

60. Keown, *Philippians*, 1:166. Moisés Silva, *Philippians*, 2nd ed., BECNT (Grand Rapids: Baker Academic, 2005), 52, rightly notes that if we take "righteousness" forensically, it still implies the ethical reading.

61. Bockmuehl, *Philippians*, 95; Keown, *Philippians*, 1:271. Others take it of the sphere of boasting, e.g., Joseph Barber Lightfoot, *Saint Paul's Epistle to the Philippians*, CCGNT (London: Macmillan, 1913), 94. Hansen considers it is sphere leading to Christ as object. See Hansen, *The Letter*, 92.

62. 1 Cor. 1:31; 2 Cor. 10:17; Gal. 6:14; cf. 1 Sam. 2:10 LXX; Jer. 9:24; Rom. 5:11.

63. Περισσ- language is also used of an advantage (Rom. 3:1; 1 Cor. 8:8); God's truth abounding (Rom. 3:7); Christ's grace abounding for many (Rom. 5:15); believers receiving the abundance of grace (Rom. 5:17); grace abounding more (Rom. 5:20); greater honor to body parts and so "weaker" believers (1 Cor. 12:23–24); to excel (1 Cor. 14:12); work harder (1 Cor. 15:10, 58); especially (2 Cor. 1:12); excessive sorrow (2 Cor. 2:7); overflowing in glory (2 Cor. 3:9); something superfluous (2 Cor. 9:1); excessive boasting (2 Cor. 10:8); far more labors and imprisonments (2 Cor. 11:23); excessive

speaks of believers praying "at all times in [and by] the Spirit," suggesting that we can not only assume the influence of the Spirit on the Pauline team's intercessory prayer ministry but know that Paul wants this for all his converts.

First Thessalonians 3:12 is like Philippians 1:9–10 as Paul prays that the Lord, who in this book references is Christ, will "cause [the Thessalonians] to increase and abound/overflow [opt. περισσεύω] in love for one another and for everyone" (my translation). This love, then, is to shape the inner relationships of the Thessalonian Christians. Such love emulates that which the Pauline team has for the Thessalonians. The purpose of the prayer indicates that abounding love for others will ensure their relational purity at the consummation.

This emphasis on love is restated in 1 Thessalonians 4:9–10. So confident is Paul that the Thessalonians love one another (φιλαδελφία), that he has no need to say anything about it, for the Thessalonians have been "taught by God to love one another," and their love extends to all the Christians of Macedonia. Yet, in 3:12, Paul wants them to abound even more (πλεονάσαι καὶ περισσεύσαι τῇ ἀγάπῃ). Considering 1 Thessalonians 3:12 and 4:9–10 together, the real issue in the prayer is not that they have deficiencies in their love for one another. So it may be love for "everyone else" (εἰς πάντας) that Paul is emphasizing in 3:12.[64] The phrase suggests love for non-Christians and so putting love of unbelievers at the center of their mission. We know the Thessalonians were proactive in evangelism in Macedonia, Achaia, and beyond (1 Thess. 1:8).[65] Perhaps Paul is concerned that they remember that love for those they evangelize is central to being God's emissaries (cf. 2 Cor. 5:14; Phil. 1:16).

Finally, Paul applies the notion of growing abundance in 1 Thessalonians 5:13. Here, Paul asks the Thessalonians to really know[66] those who labor among them, lead them in the Lord, and admonish them. They are to esteem them superabundantly (ὑπερεκπερισσοῦ) in love because of their work. The clear connection of Spirit and love in Paul ensures that Paul has in view the Spirit shaping the way believers know and love their leaders. In 1 Thesslonians 4:1, Paul also uses *perisseuo* (GK) of the Thessalonians increasingly pleasing God. This verse will be discussed further in the next section, "The Spirit Who Sanctifies."

---

zealousness (Gal. 1:14); God's ability to do beyond all measure (ὑπερεκπερισσοῦ) more than people can ask or imagine, abundant eagerness (1 Thess. 2:17).

64. There is no basis for reducing "for all" to "pagans who were present in the Christian assemblies." Abraham J. Malherbe, *The Letters to the Thessalonians: A New Translation with Introduction and Commentary*, AYB 32B (New Haven, CT: Yale University Press, 2008), 213. As Bruce says, the phrase means "all mankind. The love of God poured into the believers' hearts *by the Holy Spirit* could not be reserved for members of their own fellowship; it must overflow to others without restriction." F. F. Bruce, *1 and 2 Thessalonians*, WBC 45 (Dallas: Word, 1982), 72.

65. Keown, *Congregational*, 257–60; James P. Ware, "The Thessalonians as a Missionary Congregation: 1 Thessalonians 1, 5–8," *ZNW* 83 (1992): 126–31.

66. The Greek is εἰδέναι, hence the best translation is "to know." Bruce, *1 and 2 Thessalonians*, 118. It is dubious if it means "respect," although some defend this position. See H. Seesemann, "οἶδα," *TDNT* 5:117; cf. Ign. *Smyrn.* 9.1.

THE SPIRIT WHO SANCTIFIES

In chapter 3, I discussed a range of texts that indicate that Paul considers that a person is declared holy or sanctified at the moment of their call and conversion. In Christ, the Holy Spirit enters, they partake in Christ's holiness, and are declared holy (2 Thess. 2:13). As "saints" or "holy people" rooted in God and his Son who is incarnate holiness (Rom. 11:16; 1 Cor. 1:30), Christians who have been washed and sanctified by the Spirit are "called to be holy."[67] Paul develops this idea at different points in his letters.

Holy Scriptures

By declaring the Scriptures "holy" in Romans 1:2, Paul implicitly indicates that the Scriptures are a means by which a believer can progress in holiness and pneumaformation.[68] Here, γραφαῖς speaks of the Jewish Scriptures that include the writings of the prophets. Such writings not only point toward God's redemption in Christ but are for the instruction, endurance, encouragement, and hope of present believers (Rom. 15:4).[69] Similarly, the application of a range of situations of God's judgment in Israel's history can be applied to the Corinthian church.[70] These things are written as examples for contemporary believers, "that we might not desire evil as they did" (1 Cor. 10:6). Paul then links the present sinfulness of the Corinthians to OT examples: idolatry (Exod. 32), sexual immorality (Num. 25), testing God and Christ (Num. 21), and grumbling (Num. 21). For Paul, these things that happened were recorded for the instruction of present believers.

His belief in the importance of reading Scripture as part of the believer's pneumaformation is seen in his many instances of citing, alluding to, and echoing the Old Testament (e.g., Rom. 1:17). However, these Scriptures can be misunderstood and even become a means by which a person can be led astray from Christ, as in the case of the Judaizers or gospel-peddlers (2 Cor. 2:17). So they must be read "in Christ" and "by the Spirit." Readers must "not go beyond what is written" (1 Cor. 4:6).[71] So then, unlike the false teachers Hymenaeus and Philetus, Timothy must cut the word of truth along a straight path (2 Tim. 2:15).[72]

---

67.   Rom. 15:16; 1 Cor. 1:2; 6:11b–c; 2 Thess. 2:13.

68.   On Romans 1:2, also see Fee, *GEP*, 477. He notes that for Paul, "Prophets, whether in ancient Israel or in the contemporary church, speak by the Spirit." He also notes the phrase "sacred Scriptures" implies the doctrine of inspiration is a Pauline supposition.

69.   See also 1 Corinthians 9:9–10, where Deuteronomy 25:4 is written "for our sake"—instructing the Corinthians concerning payment for labor for God (also 1 Tim. 5:18).

70.   God's presence by cloud in the wilderness, exodus, God's judgment (Num. 14:29, 37; 26:64, 65; Ps. 106:26).

71.   On this verse, see Mark J. Keown, "'Do Not Go Beyond What Is Written' (1 Cor. 4:6)," *Stimulus* (2015): 45–47.

72.   The Greek ὀρθοτομέω compounds ὀρθός, "straight," and τέμνω, "cut"; here it means to "cut a straight path for the word of truth," and so figuratively to "guide the word of truth along a straight path." BDAG, s.v. "ὀρθοτομέω," 722. See further Marshall and Towner, *A Critical and Exegetical*

Believers must be people of the word because Scripture is sacred (τὰ ἱερὰ γράμματα) and God-breathed (πᾶσα γραφὴ θεόπνευστος, 2 Tim. 3:16).[73] The noun ἱερός indicates something of "transcendent purity" or "holiness."[74] It is used in 2 Maccabees 8:23 of the public reading of "the sacred book."[75] The construct is synonymous with "holy writings" in Romans 1:2 and speaks of Israel's Scriptures.[76] As these were learned from childhood, it is unlikely they include Christian writings such as Paul's letters, which Peter elsewhere describes as "scripture" (2 Peter 3:16). Timothy is to continue in what he has learned and believed, remembering those who taught him. These holy writings are "able to make [Timothy] wise for salvation through faith in Christ Jesus."

Paul defines all the Scriptures as "God-breathed." The actual term, Θεόπνευστος, compounds θεός and πνευστός, "exhaled."[77] It is rare, used of divinely inspired streams in Cyme, God-given breath giving life to people, divinely breathed ointment, and the divine inspiration of Revelation.[78] As was discussed in chapter 1, God's breath is synonymous with God's Spirit. By his breath (Spirit), God imparted life and created Adam (Gen. 2:7; 6:17; Job 12:10; 33:4; Eccl. 12:7), parted the sea at Exodus (Exod. 15:8, 10; 2 Sam. 22:16), brings judgment (Job. 4:9; cf. 2 Thess. 2:8), cleared the heavens (Job 26:13), causes ice (Job 37:10) and causes it to melt and waters to flow (Ps. 147:18), and created the hosts of heaven (Ps. 33:6). Here, the Scriptures are God-breathed—God, by his Spirit, breathed them into existence through human writers. Such God-breathed writings are profitable for teaching, reproaching, correction, and discipline in righteousness. They are alive, and so elsewhere Paul can describe the gospel as the "word of life" (Phil. 2:16; 1 John 1:1). Other NT writers speak of them as "living and active" (Heb. 4:12) and the "living and abiding word of God" (1 Peter 1:23).[79] They exist "so that the man or woman of God may be complete, equipped for every good work."

Commentary, 748–49. I would add that this metaphor fits with the word as the "sword of the Spirit," so that perhaps it is the Spirit who cuts this path as the word of truth is authentically proclaimed.

73.   On this verse, see Fee, GEP, 793–94. The descriptor indicates the Scriptures are "completely of divine origin." This indicates for Paul the "sacred scriptures were given by divine in-'spiration,' that is, by the 'breath' of God, the Holy Spirit."

74.   BDAG, s.v. "ἱερός," 470.

75.   The noun is also used in the LXX of holy aspects and things associated with Israel's worship (Josh. 6:8; 1 Esdr. 1:39, 43, 51; 2:7; 6:17, 25; 7:2, 3; 8:17, 55; 2 Macc. 4:48; 5:16; 9:16; 3 Macc. 3:21; 4 Macc. 13:8; Ezek. 27:6; Dan. 1:2); sacred clothing (1 Esdr. 8:68, 70); sacred places like temples, gates, or temple enclosures (Jdt. 4:1; 2 Macc. 6:4; 8:33; 3 Macc. 2:28; 3:16; 4 Macc. 4:3; Ezek. 28:18; Dan. 9:27); a sacred oath (4 Macc. 5:29); a holy people (4 Macc. 6:30; 14:6; 16:12); a holy life (4 Macc. 7:4); holy teeth (4 Macc. 7:6); a holy battle (4 Macc. 9:24); holy music (4 Macc. 14:3); a holy nature (4 Macc. 15:13).

76.   Similarly, Fee, GEP, 478.

77.   BrillDAG, s.v. "πνευστός."

78.   Sib. Or. 5:308; 5:406; T. Ab (A) 20:11; Fragments of Papias 10.1.

79.   See also Pss. 118:116; 119:50; Matt. 4:4.

The Scriptures are pneumaformed. When people believe, they receive the same Spirit who acts on and in them as they read or hear the Scriptures.[80] The Spirit forms these people through the words he has inspired. They are essential to pneumaformation whereby the Scripture-formed believer becomes equipped to effectively pass the word on to others in pastoral leadership and mission. As such, as Paul says to Titus, a church overseer must reject false teaching, be full of the virtues of God, and "must hold fast according to the teaching of the trustworthy word, so that he [or she] may be able both to encourage with sound teaching and to reprove those who speak against it" (Titus 1:9).

Still, they must be read well, and the power required to live according to the Scriptures comes from the Spirit. If this is not understood, Christians can become legalistic and driven by their own efforts as they live under Scripture. Instead, by the Spirit, the Scriptures shape and renew minds when read with faith, and the Spirit empowers the life to which the Scriptures summon believers. Indeed, as deSilva sagely comments,

> As we pray and examine ourselves before God, practicing openness, vulnerability, and silence before God, his Spirit brings the Word to bear on us as we are in that moment, sometimes convicting, sometimes affirming. As we band together with other Christians similarly committed to transformation, we share insights into one another and help one another see the blind spots, see from outside our own perspective on ourselves.[81]

Romans 6:19, 22

In Romans 6, Paul draws out more implications of believers being justified by faith. They are baptized into Christ's death so that they will live a new way of life (Rom. 6:1–4). Their old selves are crucified with Christ, so they are no longer enslaved to sin (Rom. 6:5–7). Knowing they have died with Christ should lead believers to recognize that they are dead to sin (Rom. 6:8–10). Therefore, those under grace, by the new way of the Spirit (Rom. 7:6), must not yield to sin's desires but present themselves to God as instruments of righteousness (Rom. 6:12–14). Being under grace should not lead to further sin. Instead of presenting themselves as slaves of immorality and lawlessness (which begets yet more lawlessness), believers are to present themselves as "slaves to righteousness leading to sanctification" (Rom. 6:15–19). The declaration of a righteous status sees the believer shift allegiance from sinful desires of the flesh to serving righteousness. This results in deepening sanctification. In that Christ is "sanctification" (1 Cor. 1:30), this is effectively stating believ-

---

80. See also Ephesians 5:26, where Christ gave himself for the church to cleanse the church "with the washing of water by the word," so that the church is "without spot or wrinkle or any such thing" and that it will "be holy and without blemish" (LEB).

81. DeSilva, *Transformation*, 57.

ers give their allegiance to Christ. The Spirit is not yet brought strongly into the discussion, although hints are given in Romans 7:6. In Romans 8, Paul will explain how it is by the Spirit that this sanctification grows.

2 Corinthians 7:1

In this verse, Paul draws out implications from the promises outlined in vv. 16–18: believers are the temple of God; he will dwell with them and walk with them; he will be their God, and they will be his people; and he is their father, and they are his children. As they have such promises, his beloved Corinthians must "cleanse [themselves] from every defilement of the flesh and spirit, completing *holiness* in the fear of God (my translation). The Corinthian correspondence suggests Paul may have in view here sexual and other sins highlighted in 1 Corinthians (esp. 1 Cor. 6:9–10). Here in 2 Corinthians, it carries the edge of repudiating the teaching of the false teachers. Still, it also summons them to cleanse themselves of all manner of idolatrous sinful behavior, including such things as impurity, sexual immorality, and sensuality (2 Cor. 12:21).[82] Doing so enables them to complete their holiness, that is, grow in their sanctification. "In the fear of God" picks up a characteristic OT theme whereby God is to be honored with awe and reverence, being utterly supreme and the judge of the world who acts in history to bring to pass his purposes (cf. 2 Cor. 5:11).[83] The agency for this is the Holy Spirit.

1 Thessalonians 4:1–8

As discussed in chapter 3, God has chosen the Thessalonians through the sanctification by the Spirit and belief in the truth (2 Thess. 2:13). Ongoing sanctification is expected of these holy people. In the licentious Roman world, it is little surprise, then, that sanctification, particularly sexual holiness, features strongly in 1 Thessalonians 4:1–8.

In 1 Thessalonians 4:1, Paul appeals to the Thessalonians to increasingly abound (περισσεύω) in bringing pleasure to God by their obedience. He then focuses on sanctification and sexuality. The clear implication is that some in the community were becoming sexually immoral, violating what Paul and his team had taught them in their earlier days with them there. Paul reminds them that

---

82. Fee, *GEP*, 338, rightly notes the importance of idolatry in 2 Corinthians 6:16–7:1 and connects idolatry and fleshly sin here. He writes, "Since the old has gone, including walking in the 'flesh' and therefore making judgments about idolatry from the perspective of fallenness, and the new has come, they are to 'cleanse themselves from every kind of pollution that has to do with flesh.'" He notes, too, that idolatry is linked to the demonic in Paul (1 Cor. 10:20–22). Hence, he correctly adds, "Not only must the 'flesh' be gone, but also the 'spirit' must be the place of the Spirit's habitation (1 Cor. 6:17), not a place where one is open to 'spirits.'"

83. See, for example, Gen. 20:11; 2 Sam. 23:3; 2 Chron. 20:29; Neh. 5:15; Job 28:28; Ps. 36:1 (Rom. 3:18).

the will of God for them is their sanctification and, specifically in their context, that they abstain from sexual immorality (πορνεία, 1 Thess. 4:1–3).[84]

Verse 4 can be understood to refer to each man in the community acquiring a wife or learning to live with a wife in sanctification and honor (thereby avoiding sexual immorality). More likely σκεῦος here has the sense of "vessel," indicating the sexual organs.[85] The sanctification of the Thessalonians includes their gaining control over their bodies in holiness and honor. Verse 5 tells them what they should not do—live out the passion of desires as seen among the godless Gentiles.

Verse 6 specifies that the Thessalonians should not transgress or wrong a fellow Christian (τὸν ἀδελφὸν αὐτοῦ) in this matter. This verse suggests that some in the church had engaged in sexual relations outside marriage.[86] Paul warns them in no uncertain terms that Christ, "the avenger," will deal with them if they do. This warning calls to mind 1 Corinthians 5, where the incestuous believer is to be excommunicated. It may also imply the work of the Spirit in the discipline.

Verse 7 restates v. 3—God has called believers (us) into holiness, not impurity. Verse 8 warns the Thessalonians, and contemporary Christians for that matter, that those who disregard his teaching here disregard God's instruction, not merely human teaching. Critically for our study, Paul reminds them that God is the one "who gives his Holy Spirit to [the Thessalonians]." This final clause suggests that to reject Paul's injunctions here is to reject not only God and Christ the Lord but also the Spirit.[87] Paul draws the Holy Spirit into the discussion as the agent of sanctification.[88] The Thessalonians are to be sanctified through yielding to the impulses of the Spirit, drawing them away from sexual immorality and other sinful desires so that they grow in sanctification.[89] Little wonder Paul ends the letter praying that the God of peace would sanctify the Thessalonians entirely and that their whole beings would be kept blameless for the coming of Christ (1 Thess. 5:23). This prayer supposes the work of the Spirit strengthening believers to live according to those things Paul has taught them.

---

84. There is no evidence Paul preached sexual ethics in his evangelism. However, texts like 1 Thessalonians 4:1–8 indicate that sexual holiness must have been a part of Paul's initial discipleship. Mark J. Keown, "Initial Discipleship and Sexual Holiness," paper presented at the Evangelical Theological Society, Denver, 2022.

85. The main options for σκεῦος are "wife" (Malherbe, *The Letters to the Thessalonians*, 226–28), "body" (Shogren, *1 & 2 Thessalonians*, 161–64), or as I prefer, "genitals" (also BDAG, s.v. "σκεῦος," 927). It may be metonymy for the body. See Keown, "Initial Discipleship."

86. Keown, "Initial Discipleship."

87. Fee, *GEP*, 51.

88. Fee, *GEP*, 51. "God himself, who is holy . . . gives his Holy Spirit to them, so that they, too, might be holy."

89. Fee, *GEP*, 53, rightly states, "the 'presentness' and 'indwelling' nature of the Spirit as gift point to *effectual power* in the struggle against sin. This does not mean that the Spirit guarantees perfection— hardly so—but it does mean that one is left without argument for helplessness" (emphasis original).

The Pastorals

Purity and sanctification are key themes through the Pastorals. Christ gave himself for humankind to purify for himself a people who will be eager to do good works (Titus 2:14). The aim of Paul's instruction is that Timothy will exhibit love that flows from a pure heart (1 Tim. 1:5). Women in the Ephesian church are not to teach or dominate but are to continue in faith, love, and holiness with self-control (1 Tim. 2:11–15). Believers are set apart as holy, ready for every good work (2 Tim. 2:21). Elders are to be holy (Titus 1:8), and older women are to train young women to be pure (Titus 2:5). Timothy must keep himself holy (1 Tim. 5:22) and join with others who call on the Lord with a pure heart (2 Tim. 2:22).[90]

The passages discussed concerning holiness in Paul's letters indicate that the *Holy* Spirit is the agent of God's sanctification of believers. Essential to pneumaformation is the Spirit enabling believers declared righteous and holy at conversion to be increasingly conformed to the holiness of Christ and God.

THE SPIRIT WHO SUSTAINS

Dunn has rightly shown that Paul's doctrine of grace speaks of the sustaining power of the Spirit in the believer's life. Believers continue to experience the Spirit and are sustained by God's power (Rom. 5:5).[91] In 1 Corinthians 10, Paul creatively draws on OT examples to reinforce his instruction to the Corinthians. Using a disclosure formula, in v. 1 he states his desire for the Corinthians to be aware of Israel's story (as they are now participants in the same ongoing salvation story of God). He reminds them of being under the cloud of God's glory and passing through the Red Sea (v. 2). He interprets this experience as their baptism "into Moses in the cloud and in the sea" (v. 3). He continues, stating that all Israel ate the same spiritual food and drank the same spiritual drink (vv. 3–4).

At one level, this speaks of the supply of manna and quail (Exod. 16; Num. 11:6–9; Deut. 8:3, 16) and the provision of water (Exod. 17:6; Num. 20:8–9). At a more profound level, as Paul continues, it speaks of their spiritual sustenance in the wilderness. In one of the most daring identifications of Christ in the OT, he states that they drank from the spiritual rock (πνευματικῆς . . . πέτρας) of Christ, who followed them as they were led by the cloud of God's presence. Aside from the question of how Paul comes to this conclusion and its legitimacy, Christ is the source of spiritual food for Israel in his wandering. While this is pre-Pentecost, the glory of God leads them, and Christ follows them, speaking of God's protection of the nation. He has also come on Israel's leaders by the Spirit through whom he guides. He provides for them spiritually and materially.

---

90.   See also 1 Timothy 4:5, where food is sanctified by the Word of God and prayer; Titus 1:15, where to the pure, all things are pure, and to the defiled and unbelieving, nothing is pure.

91.   Dunn, *Jesus and the Spirit*, 203.

It is implied here that Christ is at least as much with the Corinthians as he was in the desert—and much more, as they have received the Spirit. He supplies spiritual food (πνευματικὸν βρῶμα ἔφαγον) and spiritual drink (πνευματικὸν ἔπιον πόμα) through the Spirit gifted to them. Paul here intimates that, just as God was with Israel in the wilderness, believers experience even more support from Christ and his Spirit as they go about their lives. It also points forward to the Lord's Supper later in the chapter and in the next. Fee makes this connection to the Supper and rightly doubts that this refers to the actual "sacramental character of the food, or that in some way it *conveyed* the Spirit."[92] Instead, it speaks of the Spirit applying to believers "the benefits of the cross, as represented in the food, to the life of the believer."[93] Yet, the spiritual sustenance God provides by the Spirit in Christ for believers, now that the promised Spirit has come, is in all of life. Now God in Christ by the Spirit is not only following the Corinthians and leading them but is within them, sustaining them and prompting them toward the life God has for them. This result should be a determination not to partake in sin, particularly those he emphasizes in this section and letter.

THE SPIRIT WHO EQUIPS

Believers are those God has prepared beforehand for glory (Rom. 9:23). God is preparing them for bodily resurrection life, and the Spirit guarantees this (2 Cor. 5:5). The Spirit equips and prepares people for the work God has for them. In Ephesians 2:10, believers filled with the Spirit are God's creation, formed in Christ Jesus for good works, which God prepared beforehand so that his people would walk in them. We see here the work of God, by the omnipresent Spirit, going ahead of believers and creating opportunities for them that they are to make the most of (cf. Eph. 5:16). Their feet are to be clad with the readiness of the gospel of peace, prepared to advance or defend the word of life, the sword of the Spirit (Eph. 6:15, 17).[94] Similarly, having been cleansed for God's use, believers are "ready for every good work" (2 Tim. 2:21; Titus 3:1).

Believers praying for other believers is another key to this equipping and strengthening. Hence, Epaphras struggles for his beloved fellow Colossians in prayer so that they may "stand mature and fully assured in all the will of God" (Col. 4:12). Also crucial in this equipping are the God-breathed Scriptures by which the Spirit prepares believers for ministry.

God raises spiritually gifted leaders in the church—apostles, prophets, evangelists, teachers, and pastors.[95] Aside from doing such ministries (i.e.,

---

92. Fee, *GEP*, 143 (emphasis original).
93. Fee, *GEP*, 144.
94. Keown, *Congregational*, 308–18.
95. I take it as five offices rather than four (pastors who teach). See Keown, *Congregational*, 177; also Arnold, *Ephesians*, 260–61. Fee, *GEP*, 708, thinks the offices are paired with one article because they

prophesying, evangelizing), their task is to equip the saints for the work of ministry to build up the church (Eph. 4:11–12, 16).[96] Through these leaders, the Spirit thrusts people into ministry, equips believers, and builds God's church (Christ's body, the temple of the Spirit through them). God enables them to stand firm in one Spirit,[97] contending together as a military unit for the faith of the gospel (Phil. 1:27, also 4:1).

Paul prays for restoration in 2 Corinthians 13:9, again showing it is the Lord who draws believers together in unity (by the Spirit). Thus, he appeals to them to "aim for restoration" (2 Cor. 13:11). Restoration comes from believers who are "spiritual" (πνευματικοί)—the Spirit-formed. Such pneumaform Christians humbly restore a fellow Christian who falls prey to temptation (Gal. 6:1). Paul and his team yearn to see the Thessalonians face-to-face to restore or complete what is lacking in their faith (1 Thess. 3:10).

THE SPIRIT WHO GIVES DISCERNMENT

Dunn observes that Paul's use of δοκιμάζω is often ethical and Spirit-connected. The verb means "to make a critical examination of something to determine genuineness."[98] Where ethics is concerned, it relates to ethical decision-making.[99] Paul uses it in Romans 2:18 of Jewish discernment through the law. He also employs it for ethical discernment in terms of Christian virtue.

Romans 12:2b

In Romans 12:1, with God's marvelous mercies in view, believers are to worship God by devoting their lives sacrificially to him. Then, in v. 2, they are instructed to be cognitively transformed—no longer formed by their former pagan and Jewish worldviews but in line with God's will. As discussed elsewhere,[100] this is the work of the Spirit even when not mentioned. They are to be spiritually reformed "so they may approve [or discern, δοκιμάζω] what is the will of God." The verb means to test, to approve something, and to "discern."[101] What they are to discern is God's will. The implication is that the mind renewed by the Spirit *can* discern God's will. Paul then describes

---

refer to local church ministries and the same people tended to perform both functions. I believe this is unnecessary.

96. Their role is not merely performance of "works of ministry," but also equipping others for the task. See the discussion on 4:11–12 in chapter 10, "Spiritual Gifts and Mission."

97. While this can be "one spirit" as in the unified corporate inner life of the church, the parallel with 4:2 (stand firm in the Lord) and the proximate "the help given by the Spirit of God" (1:19) and "fellowship in the Spirit" (2:1) suggest this is the Holy Spirit that is in view. The Spirit binds believers together.

98. BDAG, s.v. "δοκιμάζω," 255.

99. Dunn, *Jesus and the Spirit*, 223.

100. See chapter 5, "Worship in and by the Spirit."

101. See further my analysis of the verb in Keown, *Philippians*, vol. 1, 159–61.

the nature of God's will with three adjectives—it is "good and acceptable and perfect." The Spirit-formed believer can discern and approve the will of God.[102]

Ephesians 5:10

In Ephesians 5:7–9, as he summons Asian readers to live in a manner worthy of their calling (4:1), Paul draws on the light-darkness image. They are not to share in the vices of their Gentile contexts as previously (cf. Eph. 2:1–3; 4:17–19; 5:3–6). Instead, they are now participants in the light of God shining in and through Christ (by the Spirit). They are God's children and are to live as "children of light," bearing the fruit of goodness, righteousness, and truth. Verse 10 begins with δοκιμάζοντες, giving the participle prominence. The participle is one of means—they bear such fruit by "testing and approving" or "discerning" what is well pleasing to the Lord.[103] This discernment is made through the Spirit, which is implied but not stated. It is arguably an aspect of being filled with the Spirit (v. 18).

Philippians 1:10

Paul's prayer is that God would enable the Philippians to abound in love more and more.[104] In that love is a fruit of the Spirit (Gal. 5:22), the agency of God acting in Christ by the Spirit is implied.[105] This prayer is not merely for love but for a knowledgeable and discerning love—implying the leading of the Spirit in their application of love in any given circumstance. While Paul would no doubt agree this applies to love for God, for other Christians, and for the yet-to-be-saved, in particular, he has in view the mending of relationships in the church (cf. 4:2–3). The preposition εἰς in v. 10 here is purposive. Paul's purpose in their overflow of love is that they may discern "what is excellent," indicating "the best course of action in any and every situation."[106] They will also be filled with righteousness that comes through Jesus Christ (via the Spirit) that will lead to more glory and praise for God as they worship by the Spirit of God (3:3). Ethics then, for Paul, are generated by the Spirit who

---

102. "By this last phrase [τῇ ἀνακαινώσει τοῦ νοὸς] Paul evidently has in mind that fundamental reshaping and transformation of inner motivations and moral consciousness (νοῦς) which he elsewhere thinks of as the writing of the law in the heart, and as the work of the eschatological Spirit (II Cor. 3.3)." Dunn, *Jesus and the Spirit*, 222.

103. The dative can be "in the Lord," speaking of the sphere of experience. However, more likely here it implies "to the Lord." "The Lord" here is Christ, but in Paul's theology, this is what is good to the Triune God.

104. For more detailed analysis see my work in Keown, *Philippians*, 1:154–64.

105. "For the overflow of love in the heart is but another way of talking about the experience grace/ Spirit . . . it is the inner compulsion of love (or Spirit) which expresses itself in acts of love (or walking κατὰ πνεῦμα)." Dunn, *Jesus and the Spirit*, 224.

106. Keown, *Philippians*, 1:161.

enables believers to abound in love and as they do, discern the right and most loving course of action in any given situation.[107]

THE SPIRIT WHO GENERATES SOCIAL ONENESS

At times, the Spirit restores the church to unity. Mention has been made of Philippians 1:27, where the Philippians are to stand "firm in one Spirit." In 1 Corinthians 1:10, Paul urges the Corinthians toward the same thing so that there be no divisions among them and that they are restored (καταρτίζω) to the same mind and purpose.[108] The Corinthians have been called into fellowship with Christ and are to be restored in their relationships.

Multiple texts in Paul emphasize social oneness.[109] In 1 Corinthians 12:13b, Paul uses an εἴτε . . . εἴτε string. As I have examined elsewhere, consistent with the frequent use of εἴτε . . . εἴτε strings in wider Greek literature, Paul uses them to apply an axiomatic statement to a specific statement.[110] The theological statement that stands as an axiom of his theology here is "For in one Spirit[111] we were all baptized into one body . . . and all were made to drink of one Spirit." The εἴτε . . . εἴτε clause is selective, pertinent to what Paul is stressing in terms of this axiom for his readers' particular situation. (He could add more clauses that explicate the axiom if necessary.) Here, he focuses on ethnic and social unity that flows from receiving the Spirit of God.

The first pair focuses on ethnicity. The plural of Ἰουδαῖος indicates the Jewish people of God, including those born into Judaism and proselytes. The plural Ἕλληνες does not refer just to natives of Greece but is synonymous with ἔθνη, signifying all non-Jewish people (the Gentiles).[112] While Gentiles may have dominated the Corinthian church, the church was multicultural. It included Jews like Sosthenes (Acts 18:17; 1 Cor. 1:1) and Crispus (Acts

---

107. Paul uses δοκιμάζω on other occasions in relevant ways. In Romans 2:28, the unbelievers in rejection of God cannot discern God with knowledge (as they do not have the Spirit). Then, in Romans 14:22, believers are to make ethical judgments based on their Spirit-led discernment. However, they may differ in what they think best, but where nonessential matters are concerned (like holy days, food and drink), they should not judge others in their ethical decisions. This shows a fallibility in terms of ethical decision-making as we see the will of God by the Spirit. Believers are to examine themselves and their faith rather than others, including at the Lord's Table (1 Cor. 11:28; 2 Cor. 13:5; Gal. 6:4). Every action and idea is also to be tested for its goodness (1 Thess. 5:21). God tests and approves people (1 Thess. 2:4) and will test the decisions made by believers at judgment (1 Cor. 3:13). Still, there are times to examine others to see if they are worthy of a task, such as carrying the Jerusalem collection (1 Cor. 16:3; 2 Cor. 8:8, 22; 1 Tim. 3:10).

108. The Greek verb καταρτίζω has the sense of being restored to a former condition, put right. BDAG, s.v. "καταρτίζω," 526.

109. For example, Rom. 15:5–6; 1 Cor. 1:10–12; Gal. 3:28; Eph. 4:1–6; Phil. 2:2; Col. 3:10–11). Unity within the body of Christ is the work of the Spirit. The Spirit's work in bringing social unity is evident in 1 Corinthians 12:13.

110. Keown, "Paul's Use of εἴτε . . . εἴτε," 195–208.

111. See earlier "Baptized in the Spirit," chapter 2.

112. "Paul actually says 'Jews or Greeks,' but he almost certainly intends by this our common English parlance 'Jews or Gentiles.'" Fee, First Epistle, 672n202.

18:8; 1 Cor. 1:14); and Gentiles like Titius Justus (Acts 18:17); Gaius (Rom. 16:3); Tertius (Rom. 16:22); Erastus (Acts 19:22; Rom. 16:23; 2 Tim. 4:20); and Stephanas, Fortunatus, and Achaicus (1 Cor. 1:16; 16:15, 17).[113]

The second pair focuses on social status, something important in status-hungry Corinth.[114] At this time, one is born into slavery (εἴτε δοῦλοι) or the freedom of citizenship (εἴτε ἐλεύθεροι). The Corinthian church included slaves (1 Cor. 7:21; cf. 1:26–27) and citizens (1 Cor. 7:22–23). Unlike the broader society in which such things cut people out of community, people of all ethnicities and social statuses are included in Christ and his church. They are all recipients of the Spirit on the same basis—faith.

By including this εἴτε string in the center of the chiasm, Paul highlights ethnic and social oneness in the people of God, who are in Christ, bound together by the one Spirit. Such unity is stressed elsewhere in Paul's letters (esp. Gal. 3:28; Col. 3:12). Paul may omit εἴτε ἄρσενες εἴτε θήλειαι (whether men or women) because the Corinthian women were misappropriating Paul's teaching on gender relationships.[115] Whether or not this is the case, while Paul delighted in human diversity, he had no room for status divisions within the body of Christ. The receipt of the Spirit means the breaking down of such divisions.

CONCLUSION

The Spirit of God and his Son is the power that transforms people who are *sarx*-formed into the pneumaform. Jesus is the image of God, and the Spirit in believers forms them into the image of God's Son. The Spirit works internally, refocusing the inner being toward God's will and purposes. This formation includes full participation in the life of Christ—his suffering, death, and resurrection—bringing growth and maturity. The Spirit increases and can provide an abundance of Christ's characteristics into the lives of believers, including love, joy, and generosity. Core to reshaping the saints is the sanctification empowered by the Spirit. The God-breathed Scriptures are essential to this transformation; the Spirit reshapes believers as God encounters them through his Word. People so pneumaformed increasingly conform to God's will in their lives. Christ sustains them as they do so, and his body is built up as believers do the work God prepared for them. And as the next chapter will stress, they are ethically renewed by the Spirit.

---

113. I am assuming that at least some of them are Gentiles on the basis of their names being Greek (Gaius, Tertius, Erastus, Stephanas, Achaicus) or Latin (Titius Justus, Fortunatus).

114. Witherington, *Conflict*, 22–24.

115. For example, B. J. Oropeza, *1 Corinthians: A New Covenant Commentary*, NCCS (Eugene, OR: Cascade, 2017), 166n144.

CHAPTER 7

THE SPIRIT, ETHICS, AND VIRTUE

One of the critical things that the Spirit does in the life of believers is transform them ethically.[1] There is a shift from living under law to living by grace, whereby the life God wants for his people is generated within them by the Spirit. the life God wants for his people are attributes of God and his Son. As they grow in these attributes, they are conformed to the image of his Son, the image of the invisible God. I will explore this in passages linking the Spirit and ethics.

SPIRIT FRUIT

The pressing background issue in Galatians is whether newly converted Gentile Christians need to yield to the Mosaic law for salvation and inclusion in God's people. Claiming Christians are not under the law leads to the question of ethics—are Christian ethical ideals no longer defined by the Mosaic law? Are they based on something else?

In Galatians 1:1–4:31, using a range of strategies, Paul tells the Galatians unreservedly that the declaration of righteous status before God is granted based on faith and not works of the law. Believers in Christ are not under the law; they are released from it. If so, what is the basis for Christian ethics?

Paul hints at the answer throughout the letter and lands it in Galatians 5–6.[2] In 5:5–6, we get the first direct reference to ethical living: Believers by the Spirit wait eagerly for the hope of righteousness. Paul goes on to say that the state of a man's circumcision is neither here nor there; what matters is

---

1. "The term 'ethics' refers to the moral principles and values that govern the conduct of an individual and/or a group. It also embraces the virtues to be cultivated and the vices to be avoided, as well as the good and bad actions that flow from them." Daniel S. J. Harrington, "Ethics," *EDEJ* 605.

2. These hints include Paul living by faith in the Son of God (Gal. 2:20), the receipt of the Spirit by faith and completion by the Spirit (Gal. 3:2–3; 4:6), adoption as children of God hinting at emulation of him (Gal. 4:5), and Christ being formed in the Galatians (Gal. 4:19).

their "faith working through love." Here, the Spirit is in believers, giving them eschatological hope. The person is "in Christ," and what matters for a person imbued with the Spirit is that they believe and that this faith is worked out through love.

In Galatians 5:13–14,[3] Paul digs further into ethics. Believers in Christ are set free from the law and demands of the Mosaic covenant, as these are powerless to enable the life in God.[4] They are no longer slaves but children. However, this freedom is not given so that they can live out the desires of the flesh. Instead, they must "through love serve one another." Neither is this freedom antinomian, for the law itself states the supreme ethic they must live by: "You shall love your neighbor as yourself" (v. 14; Lev. 19:18).

In Galatians 5:16–25, Paul explains how they are to do this. They are not to live up to this standard through their own will and determination but by the Spirit. Paul states this in different ways: "walk[5] [in and] by[6] the Spirit" (v. 16; cf. 2 Cor. 12:18[7]), be "led by the Spirit" (v. 18),[8] "live by the Spirit" (v. 25), and "keep in step with the Spirit" (v. 25). In Galatians 6:8, they are to "sow to the Spirit." These are different ways of saying the same thing: live a life yielding to the impulses of the Spirit. If believers do this, they will never carry out the desires of the flesh (v. 16)[9] and they are not under the law (v. 18). Those who belong to Christ have crucified the flesh with its passions and desires (v. 24).

---

3.   See on this passage Fee, *GEP*, 425.

4.   Similarly Fee, *GEP*, 422.

5.   As is well known, περιπατέω is Paul's usual term for ethical living (Rom. 6:4; 8:4; 13:13; 14:15; 1 Cor. 3:3; 7:17; 2 Cor. 4:2; 5:7; 10:2, 3; 12:18; Gal. 5:16; Eph. 2:2, 10; 4:1, 17; 5:8, 15; Phil. 3:17, 18; Col. 1:10; 2:6; 3:7; 4:5; 1 Thess. 2:12; 4:1, 12; 2 Thess. 3:6, 11). The verb is active, so "go on walking by the Spirit" is implied. Fee, *GEP*, 430.

6.   As throughout this book, πνεύματι is a dative of sphere but implies the Spirit's agency (hence, in and by the Spirit). As Fee says, "I would argue for more of an overlap in Pauline usage than for rigid grammatical categories. That is, even though one is to walk by means of the Spirit, one does so because one is also to walk in the sphere of the Spirit, that is, in the arena of the Spirit's present life and activity." Fee, *GEP*, 430.

7.   In 2 Corinthians 12:18, Paul asks the Corinthians whether Titus defrauded them when among them, expecting the answer, "No!" He then asks whether he and his team walk in the same Spirit and in the same footsteps. See Fee, *GEP*, 357, for a cogent defense that the Holy Spirit is in view. This supposes that Paul and his other team members, like Titus, would not countenance defrauding them through the taking up of the collection (see also chapter 10, "Spirit and Mission"). This is because they walk in the Spirit, are led by the Spirit, and keep in step with the Spirit. This is the language of Christoformity, whereby people are led by the Spirit and walk in the same footsteps as Jesus and those who walk in accordance with him.

8.   As Fee puts it, "Having begun by the Spirit, one comes to completion by the Spirit. The key to ethical life, including everyday behavior in its every form, resides in the fundamental Pauline imperative: 'Walk by/in the Spirit, and you will not fulfill the desire of the flesh.' The Spirit is the empowering for life that is both against the flesh (so that one may not do whatever one wishes, v. 17) and in conformity to the character of God (here as the 'fruit of the Spirit')." Fee, *GEP*, 422.

9.   Capturing the force of οὐ μή, see Fee, *GEP*, 432.

Galatians 5:19–23

In vv. 19–23, Paul gives two contrasting lists, the first comprised of fifteen vices that characterize those who live by the flesh. Undoubtedly, they are chosen because they are relevant to Galatia and the Galatians in their former lives. For Paul, these are obvious (φανερὰ). The first three relate to sexual immorality (πορνεία, "sexual immorality," ἀκαθαρσία, "impurity," ἀσέλγεια, "sensuality");[10] the next two false religion (εἰδωλολατρία, "idolatry," φαρμακεία, "sorcery");[11] eight contribute to shattered relationships (ἔχθραι, "enmities," ἔρις, "rivalry," ζῆλος, "jealousy," θυμοί, "fits of rage," ἐριθεῖαι, "selfish ambitions," διχοστασίαι, "dissensions," αἱρέσεις, "factions," φθόνοι, "envies"); and the final two debauched living (μέθαι, "drunkenness," κῶμοι, "debauchery"). The clause καὶ τὰ ὅμοια τούτοις (and things like this) indicates that this list is not exhaustive. Paul finishes by reminding the Galatians again (ἃ προλέγω ὑμῖν, καθὼς προεῖπον) that those who practice these things (present, πράσσοντες) will not inherit (future, κληρονομήσουσιν) the kingdom of God.[12]

Several of these vices are the antithesis of love in 1 Corinthians 13:4–8. So, "love is not jealous" (οὐ ζηλοῖ, v. 4) and "love does not rejoice in unrighteousness" (οὐ χαίρει ἐπὶ τῇ ἀδικίᾳ, v. 6). At a conceptual level, a couple of others touch on the list. So, "love does not act dishonorably" (οὐκ ἀσχημονεῖ, v. 4) indicates that the first three and arguably the final vice in the Galatians' list are antithetical to love. Similarly, "love is not provoked to anger" (οὐ παροξύνεται) contrasts with θυμοί, "fits of rage."

More broadly, a few concepts are associated with love in Paul's letters. After Paul tells the Ephesians to live a life of love in Ephesians 5:2, πορνεία heads the list of things they should not do in v. 3, and the sexually immoral (πόρνος) and impure (ἀκάθαρτος) will not inherit the kingdom in v. 5.[13] This is immediately followed by ἀκαθαρσία. Love is critical to the life of the Ephesians (Eph. 4:2, 15–16). In contrast, the Gentiles are given over to all manner of uncleanness (Eph. 4:19). The opposite of ἀκαθαρσία, καθαρός, is used concerning love and a *pure* heart in 1 Timothy 1:5 and 2 Timothy 2:2. In 1 Thessalonians 4, Paul tells the Thessalonians God's will for them is to abstain from πορνεία (v. 3) and ἀκαθαρσία (v. 7). In v. 9, he urges instead that they love one another with sexual purity and in a holistic sense. In Colossians 3, πορνείαν and ἀκαθαρσίαν are paired in v. 5 as things to be rejected and contrasted with love (v. 14), which is in line with what Paul says in 1 Timothy 1:10. Contrastingly, the goal of Paul's instruction is "love [ἀγαθῆς] from a pure [καθαρός] heart" (1 Tim. 1:5).

---

10. Similarly, Fee, *GEP*, 441.

11. Similarly, Fee. *GEP*, 441.

12. Further, see Keown, *Galatians*, 646–52; Keown, "Initial Discipleship."

13. Also seen as antithetical to a life of love is αἰσχρότης, "obscenity," and εὐτραπελία, "coarse jesting."

Paul uses the term for "jealousy" (ζῆλος) and the associated verb ζηλόω elsewhere positively of zeal for God (Rom. 10:2), for other believers,[14] and gifts including prophecy.[15] That is, love leads to ardor for the good things of God, whereas the flesh delights in false zeal (cf. Gal. 4:18). In Colossians 3:8, Paul mentions ὀργήν, "anger," and θυμόν, "fit of rage," as things to be put to death in favor of love (Col. 3:14). The motivations, "envy" (φθόνος) and "selfish ambition" (ἐριθεία), in Philippians 1:17 and 2:3 directly contrast the commendable attribute of love in Philippians 1:16 and 2:1–2 (cf. 1:9–10). "Envy" (φθόνος) is also contrasted with love in 1 Timothy 6:4 and 10 and in Romans 13:10 and 13. "Drunkenness" (plur. μέθη), "debaucheries" (plur. κῶμος), and "strife" (plur. ἔρις) also feature the vice list that follows Paul's endorsement of love as the supreme virtue (Rom. 13:8–10).[16] As such, we can describe all of these as anti-love attributes, and so anti-God, anti-Christ, and anti-Spirit. The Spirit impels people away from these and toward love and consequent virtues.

Galatians 5:22–23

Paul gives a list of nine virtues that he labels "the fruit of the Spirit.'" (ὁ δὲ καρπὸς τοῦ πνεύματός). Without a doubt, here the genitive of πνεῦμα refers to the Holy Spirit rather than the human spirit. In using καρπός, Paul employs an agricultural notion that suggests growth. The genitive πνεύματός is one of source, origin, or better, production. Hence, the image is of a person as a fruit tree with the Spirit causing fruit to bud and ripen in the believer's life rather than something that the believer does alone. The fruit is the virtue generated in those formed by the Spirit.

The five ways of describing a believer who submits to the Spirit in Galatians 5–6 build on the picture of the Spirit growing virtue—these grow and ripen as the believer walks by the Spirit, is led by the Spirit, lives by the Spirit, follows the Spirit, and sows to please the Spirit. As with the vices, the list is not exhaustive but representative[17] and specifically chosen to challenge the areas of weakness among the Galatians.[18]

The fruit includes ἀγάπη, "love," χαρὰ, "joy," εἰρήνη, "peace," μακροθυμία, "patience," χρηστότης, "kindness," ἀγαθωσύνη, "goodness," πίστις, "faith/faithfulness," πραΰτης, "gentleness," and ἐγκράτεια,

---

14.   2 Cor. 7:7, 11; 11:2; Gal. 4:17, 18 (even if their motives are not good).

15.   1 Cor. 12:31 (taken as an imperative, in line with 14:1) and 14:39.

16.   Fee discusses this and rightly argues that while πνεῦμα is not used, this passage presupposes the Spirit. He defends this with logical and appropriate connections to Romans 8:4; 12:9; 14:15; Galatians 5:22, where love is a "fruit of the Spirit," and Romans 15:30. As he says, "Paul does not need to mention the Spirit in order for the Spirit to be the theological presupposition of such a passage." Fee, *GEP*, 614.

17.   Similarly Fee, *GEP*, 444.

18.   The list eludes categorization. Fee, *GEP*, 444.

"self-control." It is no surprise that "love" heads the list, with Paul having already signaled twice that it is the supreme Christian virtue (vv. 6, 14).[19]

In 1 Corinthians 13:4–7, several of the virtues in this list define love. These include "patience" (μακροθυμεῖ), "kindness" (χρηστεύεται), "joy" (συγχαίρει δὲ τῇ ἀληθείᾳ),[20] and "faith/faithfulness" (πάντα πιστεύει). Peaceful relationships (εἰρήνη) are, of course, a consequence of love. It is no surprise that the ideas in the list are linked regularly in Paul's letters.[21] Patience[22] and gentleness (πραΰτης) are expressed "in love" in Ephesians 4:2. Patience, kindness, the Holy Spirit, and "love without hypocrisy" (LEB) are all bound together in 2 Corinthians 6:6.[23] God's love (Eph. 2:4) is expressed in kindness (χρηστότης) toward humankind in Christ Jesus (Eph. 2:7).

Again, in Ephesians 4:32, Paul's appeal to be kind toward one another is followed by an appeal to imitate God by emulating the love Christ has for humankind (Eph. 5:2). Believers are also to put on love over all the many virtues he wants for them in Colossians 3:12–14, including kindness (χρηστότης), gentleness (πραΰτης), and patience (μακροθυμία).

In Titus 3:4, albeit with a different Greek word (φιλανθρωπία, "love for humankind"), love is linked with God's kindness (χρηστότης). The love of God and Christ head Ephesians 5:1–2, and a fruit of light that flows from those who imitate God and his Son is goodness (ἀγαθωσύνη). Love and gentleness (πραΰτης) are also associated in Paul.[24] Of course, faith and love are constantly linked in Paul. For Paul, faith brings a person into a saving relationship with God, and love is the supreme ethic worked out from faith (Gal. 5:6).

The point of the above discussion is that love is the supreme ethical attribute or virtue God wants in his children. All other fruit, while supremely important in their own right, are, in a sense, consequential. The Spirit then is working in believers to urge them away from works of the flesh that are antithetical to love and moving them toward love and its outworking. The believers' role is to yield to or cooperate with the Spirit and express their faith with "Spirit-directed practices."[25] Pneumaformity is moving toward love.

A few other things are worthy of note concerning Galatians 5:16–6:9. Galatians 5:17 indicates that ethical pneumaformity is not easy. The flesh and the Spirit are in opposition, as they have different desires for a person. This hostility suggests that yielding to the Spirit is sometimes a struggle.[26] Indeed,

---

19. Similarly, Fee, *GEP*, 446–47. For a more detailed discussion on each virtue, see Fee, *GEP*, 446–53.
20. See other texts where joy and love are linked: 2 Cor. 13:11; Phil. 2:2; 4:1; Philem. 7.
21. See Rom. 1:7; 2 Cor. 13:11; Eph. 6:23; 1 Thess. 5:13; 2 Tim. 1:2; 2 Tim. 2:22.
22. Patience and love are also linked in 2 Cor. 6:6; 2 Tim. 3:10.
23. In Greek: ἐν μακροθυμίᾳ, ἐν χρηστότητι, ἐν πνεύματι ἁγίῳ, ἐν ἀγάπῃ ἀνυποκρίτῳ.
24. See 1 Cor. 4:21; Eph. 4:2; Col. 3:12; 2 Tim. 2:22, 25; Titus 3:2, 4.
25. DeSilva, *Transformation*, 48.
26. I cannot here fully agree with Fee, who in an overly triumphalist manner sees here no hint of any internal struggle that leaves a believer in a state of helplessness. He himself concedes the point,

the believer is in a "warfare between Spirit and flesh," and "the warfare does not end when the Spirit comes, that is when it really begins."[27]

Second, those led by the Spirit are not under the law—the Christian is not obligated to live out the demands of the Mosaic law but is to be led by the Spirit. As the Spirit always directs a person toward love, and love is the supreme virtue of the law, believers move in the direction of the demands of the law anyway. The movement is from the inside out, Spirit-impelled, and not from determination to live up to an external code. It is from yielding to the Spirit, not a Spirit-coerced response.

Third, Paul is not saying that a believer who strays into the works of the flesh, which all people do from time to time, will not inherit God's kingdom. Paul is adamant that a person is saved and justified by grace through faith. As such, when Paul states a person who does these things does not inherit the kingdom, he is talking about someone who is an unbeliever without the Spirit. Possibly it is someone who claims to be a Christian but whose life is utterly and habitually characterized by these vices.[28] Such situations lead to pastoral complexities, as only God knows when a person is in this space. Those lending support to such people can only warn the person of the consequences rather than judge another person's salvation.

Fourth, by saying that there is no law against such things as the fruit of the Spirit (v. 23), Paul effectively states that the fruit are above the law and never wrong. They are utter goodness. Fifth, by living according to the Spirit, believers are living out their status as those whose flesh, with its passions and desires, has been crucified in Christ. Believers no longer live, but Christ lives within them. They no longer live in the flesh but by faith in the Son of God (Gal. 2:20). The world has been crucified to them, and they to the world (Gal. 6:14). As such, in living by the Spirit, they are living the new life for which they have died and been raised to live.

Sixth, this Spirit-led living is not purely individual; it is lived in community. Each Spirit fruit generates the kind of *agapē koinōnia* God wants for his people. In Galatians 6, believers have a role in helping other Christians live by

---

saying, "The 'sphere' of the flesh is obviously still about, and by implication the believer could fall prey to its perspective. In that sense there is always 'tension' for the Spirit person. But this is also where the Spirit comes in—as the intractable foe of the flesh." Fee, *GEP*, 435. The reality for believers is that we oscillate in our capacity to yield to the Spirit or the flesh and at times, we fall. Paul instructs believers to support one another in such situations (6:1–2). I prefer the analysis of Dunn, *Jesus and the Spirit*, 312–16. He speaks of the believer as "a divided man [person]," whereby "[he] lives in the overlap of the ages and belongs to both of them *at the same time*. So long as this age lasts he [she] has a foot in both camps—both sinner and justified *at the same time*" (emphasis original). I disagree with him that Romans 7:14–25 speaks of the general human experience before conversion; I side with those who see it as referring to Paul's post-Christian reflection on his pre-Christian Jewish life. However, it becomes the experience of the Christian who lapses into legalism, whether Judaizing or other legalistic works theologies.

27. Dunn, *Jesus and the Spirit*, 312, 315.
28. Fee, *GEP*, 443.

the Spirit. With the Spirit of gentleness and humility, the spiritual should support and restore those who are tempted (Gal. 6:1).[29] Paul exhibits such restoration to Corinthians as he desires to come not with a rod but with love and the Spirit of gentleness (1 Cor. 4:21).[30] Christians are to bear one another's burdens. Doing this fulfills the law of Christ, the law of love (Gal. 6:2).[31] At the same time, believers are not to fall prey to comparing themselves with others but must test themselves as they will stand before God in judgment (Gal. 6:3–5). Finally, believers must be Spirit-led in doing good to all people, especially other Christians (Gal. 6:9–10).

LED BY THE SPIRIT

Romans 8:1–17 has some threads of thought in common with Galatians 5–6. However, it is worth looking at as it builds on the ethical picture. Romans 1–7 focuses on human sin and God's solution to the problem: one is justified by faith. Unlike in Galatians, Paul is less assertive and draws on a much more comprehensive range of ideas to ensure the Romans know full well that all humankind is unrighteous and that it is by faith in Christ that a person is justified before him.

As in Galatians, Paul hints at ethics throughout the letter.[32] In Romans 1:18–3:20, Paul clearly outlines humanity's ethical failure due to its rejection of God. Next, in 3:21–4:25, Paul makes clear that justification is by faith and always has been (as seen in Abraham).[33] In Romans 5, Paul adds to the picture of justification by explaining its coordinating consequence—reconciliation (5:1–11). He next explains how Jesus is the new Adam (the image of God implied, cf. 8:29), who resolves the problem of death (5:12–21). He hints at what is to come in Romans 5:5, telling the Romans that God has poured love into their hearts by the Spirit. The Spirit implants this love and moves believers to live it out, loving God, other Christians, and unbelievers.[34]

In Romans 6–7, Paul lays more important theological spadework for ethics, hinting again at the solution of the Spirit, which he will expound on in Romans 8. They are dead to sin, as demonstrated in baptism (Rom. 6:1–3).

---

29. On this being the Spirit of God, see Fee, *GEP*, 27.

30. Fee, *GEP*, 26, 121.

31. Fee writes, "God's glory is their *purpose*, the Spirit is their *power*, love is the *principle*, and Christ is the *pattern*. . . . Christ serves as the pattern for the principle, love itself. Thus, 'the law of Christ' is first of all an appeal not to some new set of laws or even to some ethical standards that the gospel imposes on believers, but to Christ himself, who in this letter has been deliberately described as the one 'who gave himself for our sins' (1:4) and who 'loved me and gave himself for me' (2:20)." Fee, *GEP*, 463.

32. See my analysis *Romans and the Mission of God*, 148–58.

33. See also Hab. 2:4 (Rom. 1:17) and Ps. 32:1–2 (Rom. 4:7).

34. On this passage, see Fee, *GEP*, 493–98. See also Dunn, who writes, "The Spirit is the source of that wave of love and upsurge of joy which overwhelms the forces that oppose from without." Dunn also notes that the Spirit is understood "as something whose reception may be verified." Dunn, *Jesus and the Spirit*, 202.

They have been spiritually raised to "live a new way of life" (Rom. 6:4 LEB).[35] Having been crucified with Christ, they are freed from sin and dead to it (Rom. 6:6–7), alive to God in Christ Jesus (Rom. 6:8–11).

Next, Paul draws out the behavioral consequences. Believers must not yield to the desires of the body and must live righteously (Rom. 6:12). They are under grace (Rom. 6:14), but this is not license to sin (Rom. 6:15). They are now slaves of righteousness who are to obey God and grow in sanctification (Rom. 6:16–23). They are released from the law. Now they are to "serve as slaves in newness of the Spirit and not in the oldness of the letter of the law" (Rom. 7:6, my translation). The law, which is good, functions to bring awareness of sin but does nothing to liberate a person from it—the law is a powerless code that informs the mind as to what sin entails (Rom. 7:7–11). The dissonance caused by knowing the law but not being able to live it is resolved by Christ (Rom. 7:12–25).

Having told the Romans that God has poured his love in the hearts of believers through the Spirit and that they must serve as slaves in the newness of the Spirit (Rom. 5:5; 7:6), Paul now explains to the Romans how they are to live. Put simply, as in Galatians 5, they are to live by the Spirit.

Because Christ has condemned sin in his flesh, the law of the Spirit of life in Christ Jesus has set them free from the law of sin and death (Rom. 8:1–3).[36] Now the requirements of the law are fulfilled in those who live by the Spirit and not the flesh (Rom. 8:4). Those who live by the Spirit are intent on the things of the Spirit (Rom. 8:5), assuming the mindset of the Spirit, who generates life and peace and, unlike the flesh, brings pleasure to God (Rom. 8:6–8).

In Romans 8:12–13, the Romans are to put to death the deeds of the body by the Spirit, which leads to life. As in Galatians 5:18, believers who are God's children are to be led by the Spirit (Rom. 8:14). The foundation of Paul's ethics is the Spirit. The responsibility of all believers is to yield to the Spirit's impulses, away from sinful desires and toward righteous behavior.

While the Spirit is rarely mentioned substantively in terms of ethics in the paraenetic section Romans 12:1–15:13,[37] Romans 8 indicates that readers should assume that the Spirit generates the behaviors and attitudes Paul seeks. They must yield to the Spirit's impulses.

RENEWED MINDS

Romans 12:1 and 2 have both been discussed previously.[38] In these verses, Paul urges the Romans to emulate the attitude of Christ by presenting their bodies

35. On different translation options see Fee, GEP, 502n78.
36. I heartily recommend Fee's full analysis of Romans 8:1–17 in GEP, 515–70.
37. Only Rom. 12:11 (debated); 14:17; 15:13. Also Rom. 15:16, 19, 30.
38. See on Rom. 12:1, chapter 5, "Worship in and by the Spirit." See on Rom. 12:2, chapter 3, "The Spirit Who Brings Renewal"; chapter 6, "Transformation Language"; "The Spirit Who Gives Discernment."

as a living sacrifice of reasoned worship and taking on the mindset of Christ rather than that of this age. I have argued that the notion of renewal implies the work of the Spirit that Paul speaks of in Romans 8. Hence, the following appeal for specific ways of living refers to the outcome of the work of the Spirit in a person's life. The level to which believers are changed will be determined by their capacity to yield to the impulses of the Spirit, taking them away from the thinking of this age to the mind of God and Jesus. In what follows, Paul expounds what living by the Spirit looks like for the Roman readers.

Romans 12:3–8

Some terms in this passage indicate Paul has the Spirit in view: "grace given" (vv. 3, 6),[39] "the measure of faith that God has assigned" (v. 3), and "gifts that differ" (v. 6). What Paul speaks of is the work of the Spirit. Before speaking of the diverse gifts, Paul urges the Romans to be humble and yet realistic about what God has equipped them to be and do. They are to avoid self-adulation in terms of who they are. They are unified as one body but consist of different people with different gifts, so they must use what they have been given. Implied is that they are to use their gifts in God's service, build the church, and bring his salvation to the world. They are to yield to the Spirit in this regard.

Romans 12:9–15:14

Paul next outlines a range of Christian attitudes and behaviors that will strengthen the church and shape its relationships with unbelievers. These include worship and service notions, such as not losing their passion, being spiritually fervent,[40] serving Christ (the Lord), rejoicing in hope, and being devoted to prayer (12:11–12).

Although having a potentially broader scope, many of the injunctions appear to focus on Christian *koinōnia*, including familial love for one another (12:10a), in honor esteeming one another highly (12:10b), and sharing with saints in need (12:13a). The instructions also include being hospitable to one another,[41] empathetically rejoicing with the joyful and weeping with the grieving (12:15a), being united in their thinking (12:16a), avoiding arrogant thoughts (12:16b), associating with those who are in a lowly position in life (12:16c), and not thinking of themselves as wise (12:16d).

Some injunctions focus on relationships with unbelievers, including blessing persecutors (12:14), not retaliating against evil (12:17), not taking revenge but leaving that to God, showing hospitality to enemies (12:19–20),

---

39. On this passage, see further chapter 9, "Romans 12:3–8."

40. I see no need to follow the majority position that τῷ πνεύματι ζέοντες should be translated "fervent in spirit."

41. The love of strangers (φιλοξενία) may indicate welcoming other Christians with hospitality, whether travelers or other Christians in the church. It may encompass showing hospitality to unbelievers. Keown, *Romans and the Mission of God*, 286–88.

submitting to the government authorities (13:1–7), and dispensing with sins common in the Roman world (13:12–13).

Some aspects of the passage are global, involving the Romans' response to all people, believer or not. These include the appeal for genuine love, abhorrence of evil, and attachment to goodness (12:9), pursuing the love of strangers (12:13), seeking peace with all people (12:18), overcoming evil with good (12:21), and loving one's neighbor (13:8–10). The final injunction draws on Leviticus 19:18, which focuses on love for one's fellow Israelite. However, according to Leviticus 19:34, the same love is to be shown to the stranger who dwells in the land because Israel's people were strangers in Egypt.

The command then is universal; the Romans are obligated to love *all* people (but especially those in the family of faith, cf. Gal. 6:10). The four laws mentioned in 12:9 all refer to gross violations of human relationships and are loveless behaviors. However, rather than assert decalogue "do not" relational laws, Paul prefers the positive statement that sums up the intent of all relational decalogue commands. Paul does imply the fulfillment of these laws when the Romans love one another. Those who love others will, of course, love their spouses rather than engage in adulterous relationships. They will be pro-life and value other image bearers to the degree that they would never contemplate murder. They respect the property of others and honor them to such a degree that they would not contemplate theft. Finally, they will value other people to the point that they have no desire for their things. The Levitical love command is again cited as the summative law. Love does not contemplate committing evil against another person. To love is to fulfill the law.

With the link of Spirit and love made in Romans 5:5 and at other points in Paul's letters, Paul is here speaking of the work of the Spirit. To clothe oneself in Christ is to yield to him and allow his Spirit to shape one's existence, particularly in the direction of love.

MINDS ON THINGS ABOVE

Colossians 1–2 focuses on laying a theological foundation that refutes the nascent heresy afflicting the church. In these chapters, Paul assures the Colossians of the hope they have in heaven (1:4). He prays for them to be filled with the knowledge of God's will so that they might be empowered to live in a manner worthy of the Lord and bear fruit in good deeds, increased knowledge of God, and gratitude for redemption (1:9–14). Likely because the false teachers are diminishing Christ's status, he poetically declares Christ's divine nature and complete supremacy over everything, including the church (1:15–20).[42] Paul affirms their reconciliation to God despite their former lives

---

42. Pao notes that there are two views on the reason for the hymn's use: (1) The hymn is from the rivals and gives common ground for debate; (2) Paul downplays Jesus's exaltation in favor of his death against the false teachers. See David W. Pao, *Colossians and Philemon*, ZECNT (Grand Rapids: Zondervan, 2012), 85. However, I disagree profoundly with both views. The false teachers are diminishing Christ

of alienation and evil (Col. 1:21–23). Implicitly, he summons them to greater maturity and knowledge of Christ, for which he works with all his being (Col. 1:23–2:5).

He urges the believers to be firmly rooted and built up in the divine Savior Christ, rejecting the false ideas of the heretics (Col. 2:6–23). As he does, Paul reminds them of their burial with Christ in baptism and their resurrection from the dead with him (Col. 2:11–15). We perceive from Colossians 2:16–23 that these false teachers are likely Jewish and demanding that the Colossians follow food regulations and Jewish calendric expectations.

In Colossians 3, Paul turns from the faulty ethical expectations of the teachers to the eschatological ethics of those in Christ. Colossians 3:1 begins with the postpositive οὖν, signaling that Paul is drawing inferences from the preceding for readers (cf. Rom. 12:1; Eph. 4:1). The verse is a conditional sentence positing what should follow if they have been raised together with Christ—something he has already asserted in Colossians 2:12. If so, they should "seek the things that are above, where Christ is, seated at the right hand of God."

Verse 2 restates how they are to live more emphatically. They must develop a heavenly *phronēsis* by setting their minds on the things above and not the things of earth. He will outline what sorts of things he has in mind in vv. 5–15. Verse 3 draws a consequence of being in Christ—having died and been risen in and with Christ, their lives are now hidden with Christ in God. However, when Christ is made known (speaking of the return of Christ), the fullness of who the Colossians are will be made known with him in glory (v. 4).

In that they are "in Christ" and their lives are hidden in him, Paul draws out the inference (οὖν) for ethics in 3:15–17. They must put to death their earthliness. Paul explains this with a vice list, including many of the same things rejected in Ephesians 4–5. He begins with five characteristic sins of the Greco-Roman world: sexual activities outside of monogamous and heterosexual marriage (πορνεία), uncleanness (ἀκαθαρσία), lust (πάθος ἐπιθυμίαν), evil desire (ἐπιθυμίαν κακήν), and greed, which, again, is idolatry (see above, Eph. 5:5). Such things are the characteristics of the "children of disobedience" (who the Colossians were) and incur God's wrath (vv. 6–7; cf. Eph. 5:6).

Paul shifts to six socially destructive sins expressed with speech and violence, the first four of which were discussed in the previous section concerning Ephesians 4:31: "anger" (ὀργή), "fits of rage" (θυμός), "wickedness" (κακία), and "slander" (βλασφημία). The fifth, αἰσχρολογία, is a hapax legomenon, found only here and in Jewish Greek sources, and refers to "shameful" or "obscene speech."[43] Such rotten speech should not come

---

and so Paul begins by exalting him to counter their diminution of him. See Keown, *Discovering: The Pauline Letters*, 283–86.

43.   It compounds αἰσχρός, "shameful," and λόγιον, "saying." *BrillDAG*, s.v. "αἰσχρολογία," notes that it is used in this way by Aristotle, *Eth. nic.* 1128a.23; Plutarch, *Def. orac.* 417c; Xenophon, *Lac.* 5.6.

from the Colossians' mouths. The final vice is also found in Ephesians, albeit with different language (4:25): "do not lie to one another" (μὴ ψεύδεσθε εἰς ἀλλήλους). The participle ἀπεκδυσάμενοι is causal: "*because* you have taken off the old person with its deeds."

As in Ephesians 4:22, the Colossians are no longer people characterized by earthly things because they have removed these vices. Instead, in v. 10, "they have put on the new [person] that is being renewed [τὸν ἀνακαινούμενον] in knowledge according to the image of its creator." Earlier in Colossians 1:15, Christ is the image of the invisible God, and all things were created in him. Hence, this renewal is their transformation into the image of Christ. The use of renewal and creation language invokes thoughts of the Spirit by whom Christ is in the believer bringing this transformation.

Significantly, in v. 11, God's transformation transcends all ethnic divisions. As in Galatians 3:28 and 1 Corinthians 12:13, in Christ, there is neither Greek (used in the sense of Gentile) nor Jew, circumcised nor uncircumcised. The dividing wall of hostility has been shattered in Christ, and Greeks and Jews are being formed into one body. Other ethnic divisions are also shattered. Greeks are united in this new people along with barbarians from the wider world and Scythians from the Russian steppes (cf. Rom. 1:14). The social divisions of slave and free are shattered (Gal. 3:28). Rather, Christ is all things, and in all people.[44]

In Colossians 3:12–15, as he often does, Paul turns from vice to virtue, enunciating ethical attributes that should characterize the Colossians. Stressing their status in Christ as God's chosen people who are holy and beloved, they should put on these things: First, he identifies six core attributes, including compassion (σπλάγχνον),[45] mercy (οἰκτιρμός),[46] kindness (χρηστότης),[47] humility (ταπεινοφροσύνη),[48] gentleness (πραΰτης),[49] and patience (μακροθυμία). Then, in v. 13, he focuses on bearing with one another and forgiving each other if anyone has a complaint against them, just as the Lord (Christ) forgave them. The Spirit shapes believers to emulate Christ, including the forgiveness at the heart of salvation.

Verse 14 again shows the supremacy of ἀγάπη love—they must put love on over all these things (the attributes already listed). Such love is "the bond of perfection," "the bond that produces perfection,"[50] or, as an attributive genitive, "the perfect bond."[51] BDAG rightly states, "Love is σύνδεσμος τῆς

44. Mark J. Keown, "The Vision for Intercultural Church in Ephesians 2 and Colossians 3" (paper presented at the Annual Meeting of the Society of Biblical Literature, Denver, 2022).
45. See 2 Cor. 6:12; 7:15; Phil. 1:8; 2:1; Philem. 7.
46. See Rom. 12:1; 2 Cor. 1:3; Phil. 2:1.
47. See Rom. 2:4; 3:12; 11:22; 2 Cor. 8:6; Gal. 5:22; Eph. 2:7; Titus 3:4.
48. See also Phil. 2:3; Col. 2:18, 23.
49. See Eph. 4:2
50. BDF §163, 90: a genitive of production.
51. Stanley E. Porter, *Idioms of the Greek New Testament* (Sheffield: JSOT, 1999), 94.

τελειότητος the *bond that unites* all the virtues (which otherwise have no unity) *in perfect harmony* or *the bond of perfect unity* for the church."[52] All other virtues named are to be clothed in love.

Verse 15 appeals for the Colossians to let the peace of Christ rule (βραβεύω) in their hearts. The verb βραβεύω is a hapax legomenon meaning "judge, decide," or as here, "control, rule."[53] "Hearts" speaks of the whole inner person, including the mind. Paul reminds them that they were called into this in the one body (formed of the diversity noted in v. 12). They are also to "be thankful" (v. 14c).

Colossians 3:16–17 was discussed earlier in chapter 5, "Prayer and the Spirit." Suffice it to say the readers are to allow Christ's word to dwell in them richly as they instruct one another in wisdom and sing all manner of songs together to God with grateful hearts. Whatever they do in word or deed, they are to thank God for it through Christ.

As in Ephesians 5:22–6:9, Paul turns to the family in Colossians 3:18, albeit with an abbreviated version of the Ephesians text. It is likely that Ephesians was delivered on the same trip as Colossians and may have been designed as a general letter for the Asian churches, not just Ephesus. If so, Paul may have included this section in an intentionally brief form, knowing that the Colossians would ultimately read Ephesians.

Whether or not this is the case, the code has the same basic three-section, two-part structure as Ephesians. It lacks the general imperative to submit to one another. Wives are to submit (imperative ὑποτάσσω) to their husbands (Col. 3:18). This is proper or fitting (ἀνήκω) in the Lord.[54] Husbands are to love their wives and not to embitter (πικραίνω) them (v. 19).[55] Children are to obey their parents, which is pleasing to the Lord (v. 20). Again, mothers are not mentioned in terms of the children; instead, fathers are not to provoke (ἐρεθίζω) their children,[56] or they will be discouraged (ἀθυμέω, v. 21).[57] Slaves are also to obey their masters fully, whether being watched or not, with sincerity of heart and

---

52. BDAG, s.v. "σύνδεσμος," 966 (emphasis original).

53. BDAG, s.v. "βραβεύω," 183. It is found once in the LXX of wisdom ruling in favor of the righteous and in Sibylline Oracles 2.64 of adjudicating justly. It can be used of crowning someone (Sib. Or. 2:45). It is at times used of governing including God's governance (e.g., Josephus, *Ant.* 4.47; Philo, *Prov.* 2.2).

54. The verb ἀνήκω is used two other times by Paul: of obscene talk, which is not fitting (Eph. 5:4), and of Paul's confidence in Philemon to do what is proper or fitting concerning Onesimus (Philem. 8).

55. Aside from this use, the verb πικραίνω is only used in Revelation of bitter water that kills (Rev. 8:11), or a scroll that is bitter in the stomach (Rev. 10:9–10).

56. Ἐρεθίζω is used once else in the NT, in 2 Corinthians 9:2, of the Achaians stirring up the Macedonians to give to the Jerusalem collection.

57. Ἀθυμέω is a hapax legomenon meaning "to be discouraged, lose heart, become dispirited" (BDAG, s.v. "ἀθυμέω," 24). A discouraged heart is one of the covenantal curses (Deut. 28:65). Hannah experienced this when she was barren (1 Kgdms. 1:6–7), Samuel felt it when Saul disobeyed God (1 Kgdms. 15:11), David felt this when Uzzah died touching the ark (2 Kgdms. 6:8; 1 Chron. 13:11). See also Jdt. 7:22; 1 Macc. 4:27; Isa. 25:4.

out of the fear of the Lord. They are to work in service of the Lord (Christ) from their souls, knowing God will reward them. On the other hand, God will pay back those who do wrong without partiality (vv. 22–25). Masters are to treat the slaves with justice and fairness, as they also have a master (κύριος) in heaven—Christ their κύριος. Again, the Christoform life shaped by the Spirit should profoundly affect the way Christians engage in families, workplaces, and other points of social interaction.

Colossians 4:2–3 was discussed in the previous chapter.[58] Suffice to say here that as he does commonly, Paul stresses that they are to devote themselves (προσκαρτερέω) to prayer (Rom. 12:12)[59] and to do so with thanksgiving.[60] Then, he asks them to pray for him and for God-opened opportunities for evangelism shared with clarity (vv. 3–4). Colossians 4:5–6 will be discussed more fully in chapter 10.[61] In the verses, the focus turns from Paul's mission to the readers' missional engagement—they should act wisely among outsiders, redeem every opportunity, and speak the word with grace and seasoned speech, so that they may know how to answer inquiries. The pneumaform believer aspires to share their faith with godly speech and attitudes.

THE GREATEST OF THESE IS LOVE

The Spirit is not mentioned in 1 Corinthians 12:31–13:13. Yet, without doubt, Paul's exposition of love as "the most excellent way" speaks of the Spirit's role in the Corinthians, individually and collectively. The pressing issue is οἱ πνευματικοὶ, which may refer more broadly to "spiritual gifts," "spiritual people," or "spiritual things," including both spiritual gifts and people.[62] The latter is preferred, as the term is used for spiritual things, gifts, and people elsewhere in the letter and for both gifts and people in 1 Corinthians 12–14.[63] Concerning "matters of the Spirit," then, Paul wants them to move from ignorance to understanding (1 Cor. 12:1).

In 1 Corinthians 12, Paul reminds them of the false spirituality of their former idolatrous pagan life (vv. 1–2). Rather than the gift of tongues, the mark of receiving the Spirit is a person's refusal to curse Christ and the courage to acknowledge that he is Lord (v. 3). Paul then instructs the Corinthians concerning the gifts of the Spirit. (1 Cor. 12:4–11). Then, reminding them of their experience of receiving the Spirit, Paul stresses that the church is one body, one unit (1 Cor. 12:12–13). He emphasizes the importance of

---

58. Chapter 5, "Relevant Prayer Texts."
59. Also Acts 1:14; 2:42; 6:4.
60. Col. 1:3, 12; 2:7; 3:17; 2:7; Phil. 4:6; 1 Tim. 2:1.
61. Chapter 10, "Prayer and the Spirit in Mission."
62. Gifts dominate the first part of 1 Corinthians 12. However, later Paul shifts to move between gifts and people in 1 Corinthians 12:12–31 (members with different gifts who are to be included and encouraged to use their gifts by all).
63. Spiritual gifts (1 Cor. 14:1); spiritual people (1 Cor. 2:15; 3:1; 14:37); other spiritual things (1 Cor. 2:13; 9:11; 10:3–4; 15:44, 46).

every gift for the functioning of the church, including the seemingly less important gifts, which are, in fact, to be cherished with even more care and value (1 Cor. 12:14–24).

As such, there must be no division in the body, each part should have equal concern for the others, and the church should be united in suffering and joy (1 Cor. 12:25–26). After again reminding them that they are each a part of the one body of Christ, Paul speaks of those God appointed to various leadership roles, helping, and tongues. Then he explains that not all people have these gifts. He urges the Corinthians to desire the greater gifts (1 Cor. 12:27–30). In v. 31b, he turns to our point of interest, love. He leads into his exposition of ἀγάπη by describing it as "a far better way"[64] that he will show the Corinthians. This descriptor of love assumes its superiority over other approaches to life.

First Corinthians 13 breaks into three neat sections. In part one (vv. 1–3), Paul tells them that unless the gifts God gives are exercised with love, the person exercising them is nothing, and they provide that person no benefit. In part two (vv. 4–7), Paul defines love with fifteen verbs. Seven of these are virtues that are expressed as verbs indicating how love is to be exercised. The other eight are vices that, when negated, also define love.

Positively, love *is* showing patience, being kind, and rejoicing in the truth. It always endures, trusts, hopes, and perseveres. Conversely, love *is not* being jealous, boasting, puffing up, behaving dishonorably, seeking one's own things, becoming enraged, contemplating evil, or rejoicing in unrighteousness. As the other virtues define love, love is the supreme attribute the Spirit cultivates in a believer, and other desired virtues are expressions of love. The negated vices indicate the sorts of things the Spirit is prompting the believer away from.

The third part of the passage (vv. 8–13) emphasizes that while other gifts and some virtues are temporary, love is a permanent virtue that endures in this age and into eternity. Unlike love, prophecy and tongues will no longer be required in eternity, as believers will be fully complete, they will know God and his purposes fully, and the scrambling of human languages at Babel will be undone. Similarly, faith and hope are critical in the present, as the future is always uncertain. Consequently, trust in God and hope for his promises are essential virtues to sustain us. Faith will become full knowledge in the eschaton, and hope will be realized. However, as love continues into eternity, it is the greatest virtue.[65] The Spirit enables believers in this age to endure and grow in faith and hope to hold firm until the end. Even more, the Spirit leads believers to love now and into their eternal futures. This love will be expressed through a raft of accompanying virtues.

---

64. BDAG, s.v. "ὑπερβολή," 1032.

65. "Along with its companions, faith and hope, [love] abides in the present. But it is greater, at least as the point of this argument, because it abides into eternity." Fee, *GEP*, 213–14.

In 1 Corinthians 14, Paul applies love to the problems in the Corinthian worship gatherings. He urges them to pursue love and seek the spiritual gifts that build others up, especially prophecy (v. 1). In vv. 2–25, with a range of arguments, Paul argues for the superiority of prophecy over untranslated tongues that are incomprehensible and have no edifying effect on hearers. Pneumaformed believers know that they must express their gifts with love to edify others.[66]

Verses 26 to 40 include injunctions for gathered worship, including the bringing of expressions of their gifts to share for their mutual edification (v. 26), instructions for the orderly use of tongues and prophecy (vv. 27–33), the women of Corinth stopping their involvement in chaotic worship (vv. 34–36),[67] and Paul's challenge to the πνευματικοί of Corinth to acknowledge his authority and heed what he has said in the passage (vv. 37–40).

LIFE WORTHY OF GOD'S CALLING

Paul calls his audience to define their lives by love. The two vice and virtue lists in Ephesians 4–6 show the believers how to live this life of love, of Christoformity, in their cultural situations.

Ephesians 4:1–6

Paul turns from expounding the blessings of God in salvation (Eph. 1:3–14; 2:1–22), his mission (1–13), and his prayers for the saints (1:15–23; 3:14–21) to the paraenetic exhortation in Ephesians 4:1–6:20. As in Romans 12:1, the postpositive οὖν looks back on the sweep of the letter thus far and draws the logical inference for the Ephesians.[68] In light of God's goodness in the gospel, they must live in a manner worthy of their call (vv. 1, 4).[69] Paul outlines what this looks like in vv. 2–6 with a profound emphasis on unity in the body of Christ, in which Jew and Gentile are fused into one (cf. 2:11–21). The life required must be lived "with all humility and gentleness, with patience, bearing with one another in love" (v. 2).

These are virtues generated by the Spirit.[70] Fee comments pertinently, "The point to make, of course, is that the unity that is theirs by virtue of

---

66. For a full discussion of 1 Corinthians 14:1–25, see Fee, *GEP*, 214–46. He rightly notes that the key question is intelligibility, and especially in vv. 6–19, the matter of the edificatory power of intelligible speech.

67. See further Ben Witherington III, *Women in the Earliest Churches* (Cambridge: Cambridge University Press, 1988), 103.

68. Paul loves to use οὖν, an inferential particle usually denoting a result of inference from what has gone before (BDAG, s.v. "οὖν," 736). He uses it 110 times. It at times leads into a paraenetic passage as here in Ephesians 4:1 (also Rom. 12:1; Gal. 5:1; Col. 3:1; 1 Thess. 4:1). He will use it again inferentially as his teaching develops through the passage (Eph. 4:17; 5:1, 7, 15).

69. The *inclusio* of the genitive of κλῆσις creates a frame for the passage (vv. 1, 4).

70. These four are listed as fruit of the Spirit in Galatians 5:22–23: "Gentleness" (πραΰτης); "patience" (μακροθυμία), "love" (ἀγάπη), and "peace" (εἰρήνη). Similarly Fee, *GEP*, 700. While ταπειν language is not directly associated with the Spirit, by extension, it almost certainly is seen as a Spirit

their common experience of the Spirit will be maintained only as the Spirit also produces the virtues necessary for it."[71] The role of the Spirit is emphasized in v. 3. The readers are to be consistently and constantly zealous (pres. part. σπουδάζω) to "maintain the unity of the Spirit" (τὴν ἑνότητα τοῦ πνεύματος).[72] The present participle σπουδάζοντες gives the purpose of doing the things listed thus far "with constant eagerness keeping the unity of the Spirit."[73] The noun ἑνότης is related to εἷς and one of its forms, ἑνός, denoting "oneness, unity."[74] The genitive is one of source, origin, or production, as in the expression "fellowship of the Spirit" (2 Cor. 13:14; Phil. 2:1). The Spirit generates humility, gentleness, patience, and love, and readers are to be eager to express these to maintain the desired unity. They are to do so "in the bond [δεσμός] of peace."

The δεσμός was a bond or fetter used to restrain people as in the case of the demoniac (Luke 8:29; also Phil. 1:7).[75] Σύνδεσμος means "that which binds together" in a range of senses, including the joining of tendons; hence, this imagery fits with the church as a body in vv. 4, 12, and 16.[76] The genitive is descriptive (the bond characterized by peace)[77] or epexegetical (the bond which is peace).[78] Peace is another fruit of the Spirit (Gal. 5:22), and so the passage speaks of the readers yielding to the impulses of the Spirit toward love and associated virtue. This unity is in Christ, for he is our peace (Eph. 2:14).[79]

Verse 4 lacks a connective, so its relationship with the previous verse in a strict sense is unclear. The passage is very poetic and could be a creed or hymn.[80] Obviously, considering the passage repeats "one" eight times, oneness is the theme. It also picks up ἑνότης, confirming the unity and oneness of the Christian faith.

The first aspect of oneness (σῶμα) is undoubtedly the "body of Christ," the church—there is one church of God.[81] The second (πνεῦμα) speaks of the

---

fruit by Paul. Also, the use of the language in Philippians 2:3 is arguably an aspect of the "fellowship of the Spirit" (κοινωνία πνεύματος) Paul mentions in Philippians 2:1.

71.   Fee, *GEP*, 700.

72.   Fee links this to 2:18, where Gentiles and Jews are unified in one body and Spirit. This is correct, but Paul's point transcends this and can be applied to all believers unified in Christ (a point Fee also notes as secondary).

73.   See the discussion of this kind of participle in Wallace, *Greek Grammar*, 622–27.

74.   BDAG, s.v. "ἑνότης," 338.

75.   See also Acts 16:26; 20:23; 26:29; Phil. 1:13, 14, 17; Col. 4:18; 2 Tim. 2:9; Philem. 10, 13; Jude 6). Δεσμός could be used of an imprisonment (Acts 23:29, 31), being mute (tongue bound, Mark 7:35), the bond of a disability (Luke 13:16), and eternal bonds (Jude 6).

76.   *Pseud. Tim.* 218.26. Also Eph. 1:23; 2:16; 3:6; 5:23, 30.

77.   On the descriptive genitive, see Wallace, *Greek Grammar*, 78–79.

78.   On the epexegetical (apposition, definition), see Wallace, *Greek Grammar*, 95–100.

79.   Fee, *GEP*, 701.

80.   Barth, *Ephesians*, 2:429. See also Lincoln, *Ephesians*, 228–29, who sees here traditional, creedal material adapted by the writer.

81.   Fee, *GEP*, 703, is likely right that Paul started here as it is the primary concern in the passage.

one Spirit of God, the Holy Spirit, the central theme of this book, received by faith.[82] The third points to the multivalent hope to which believers are called, expounded on in Ephesians 1:3–14.[83] The fourth, κύριος, is Christ rather than God. The fifth is πίστις, speaking of the faith that sees the grace of salvation granted to believers (Eph. 2:8–9).[84] The βάπτισμα can refer to either Spirit or water baptism. The choice is difficult in some instances, but water baptism is in view here because the Spirit is already mentioned in the list.[85]

The sequence climaxes with "one God," who is brilliantly described as "Father of all, who is over all and through all and in all" (v. 6). It is unclear whether the three uses of πᾶς should be read as "all people" (masculine) or "all things" (neuter). If the former, the three adjectives can refer to people in general or only Christians.[86] However, it is better to read these as neuter; hence, the sentence poetically expounds God's cosmic fatherhood of all creation, sovereignty over all things, and presence in all things. This reading is likely because of Ephesians 1:10, where in the fullness of time, all things in the heavens and on earth, inclusive of the non-human creation, are brought together in Christ.[87]

Ephesians 4:7–16

Verse 7 shifts to the impartation of gifts (ἡ χάρις) to believers per the measure to which Christ allows them to share in his giftedness. As Arnold says, "This fits well with the overall context of Ephesians which stresses God exalting Christ to supremacy over everything (1:22), his intent to bring all things together under one head (1:9–10), and his filling all things through his people (1:23; 4:10)."[88]

Attention turns more specifically to Christ in v. 7. Using Psalm 67:19 (68:18 EVV) with minor variations, Paul alludes to Christ's exaltation (ascended on high). As Jesus was exalted, he led believers (those caught in captivity) with

---

82. Fee, *GEP*, 703, again may be correct that the Spirit comes second as the oneness of the body stems from baptism in the Spirit (1 Cor. 12:13).

83. Fee, *GEP*, 703, considers Paul's mention of the calling here in light of the Spirit's role. That is possible, but the call comes from God, as always in Paul.

84. Fee, *GEP*, 704, rightly comments that faith and baptism both represent "entry" experiences. Obviously πίστις here is not "faithfulness."

85. Similarly Fee, *GEP*, 703.

86. John Eadie, *A Commentary on the Greek Text of the Epistle of Paul to the Ephesians*, ed. W. Young (Edinburgh: T & T Clark, 1883), 276; Harold W. Hoehner, *Ephesians: An Exegetical Commentary* (Grand Rapids: Baker, 2002), 519–20; Rudolf Schnackenburg, *Ephesians: A Commentary* (Edinburgh: T&T Clark, 1991), 167. See also the textual variants ημιν (D F G K L Ψ 0278. 365. 630. 1175. 1505 𝔐 lat sy; Ir) and υμιν (1739c).

87. Lincoln, *Ephesians*, 32–34.

88. Arnold, *Ephesians*, 236–37. He notes it is consistent with 1 Corinthians 8:6 and Romans 11:36. Although uniquely expressed, Arnold notes, too, that similar expressions are found in Stoicism (although Paul avoids pantheism [and panentheism]) and Philo's statements concerning the one true God, who is "the ruler of all things (πάντων) (*Creation* 1.75), near to us in all things (ἐν πᾶσιν; *Migration* 1.56), and penetrating all things (διὰ πάντων διελήλυθεν; *Alleg. Interp.* 3.4), although he never says God is 'over' (ἐπί) all things" (p. 237).

him,[89] and they are now spiritually seated with him in the heavenly realm (Eph. 2:6). In line with the military image from the OT context and Ephesians 6:10–17, Paul pictures Christ's ministry as a conquest with believers as prisoners of war paraded behind him to demonstrate his supremacy (cf. 2 Cor. 2:14). This same Christ "gave gifts to men" (v. 8b), clearly referring to spiritual gifts like those listed in v. 11. Verses 9 and 10 are clarificatory, explaining that his ascension implies his descent to earth (incarnation) and that now Christ (the one who ascended) is ascended and exalted in the heavens. The final ἵνα clause speaks of both the result of his exaltation in that he already fills all things (Eph. 1:22–23) and his missional purpose that climaxes him filling all things and people by his Spirit (cf. Eph. 1:11, 14; 3:19).

While it is Christ who is the imparter of gifts through this passage, there are hints of the Spirit's role in 4:3 and 4, the fruit of the Spirit in 4:1–4,[90] and the language of grace (v. 7), giving (vv. 6–7), gifts (v. 7), and filling (v. 10). Similarly, God's presence "in all," where believers are concerned, points to the work of his Spirit. However, unlike 1 Corinthians 12:4–8, where the Spirit's role is dominant,[91] this passage emphasizes Christ's role in distributing gifts by the Spirit. Further, it is a measure of Christ's gift that believers receive, indicating that they participate in Christ's giftedness imparted to them.

In v. 11, Christ is the giver of five (or four) ministry gifts, which Paul will discuss in chapters 5 and 6. The focus is on people with specific functions, not offices, gifts, or ministries (although they are implied).[92] As Fee appropriately says, "Also as with all such enumerations, they are ad hoc and probably representative, not exhaustive or definitive."[93] The actual roles themselves will not be discussed here, but in chapter 9, regarding Ephesians 4:7–16.[94]

In what follows, vv. 12–16, these charismatic "appointments of God" are given to equip believers (the saints)[95] for the work of ministry. They are to build up the body of Christ so that the church may attain unity and maturity regarding Christ's fullness and be inoculated against false teaching. While

---

89. Paul masterfully uses two cognates (an example of epanalepsis) to state this: ἠχμαλώτευσεν αἰχμαλωσίαν. The verb αἰχμαλωτεύω refers to capturing people in war and the accusative of αἰχμαλωσία to a captured military force. BDAG, s.v. "αἰχμαλωσία, αἰχμαλωτεύω," 31.

90. Including gentleness, patience, love, and peace. By analogy, humility and hope should be seen as Spirit fruit as well.

91. In 1 Corinthians 12, God is agent in vv. 6, 18, 24, 28; Christ in v. 5, 12; and the Spirit in vv. 4, 7, 8 (2x), 9 (2x), 11, 13.

92. Similarly, Fee, *GEP*, 706–7.

93. Fee, *GEP*, 707.

94. A couple of comments are appropriate. Fee suggests the first three are probably itinerant ministries. Fee, *GEP*, 707–8. This is definitely true of apostles; however, it is not clear whether prophets functioned within churches or traveled. Agabus's presence in Antioch and later Caesarea could indicate so (Acts 11:28; 21:10). If Philip is paradigmatic (Acts 21:8), then it may be true of evangelists. Fee maintains the latter two are local ministries; however, as we will discuss in chapter 9, this is not clear for teachers. It is likely correct for pastors or shepherds.

95. So also Fee, *GEP*, 707.

the emphasis here is intensive growth (the building of the church itself), the mention of apostles and evangelists and the earlier expressed notion of Christ filling all things indicates the growth is also extensive—people becoming Christians.[96] They then must be equipped for maturity and mission.

The ministry gifts of apostle, prophet, and teacher are aspects of the πνευματικῶν and χάρισμα from the Spirit in 1 Corinthians 12 (vv. 28, 29).[97] Also, the metaphors of building and growing the body are explicitly linked to the agency of the Spirit (Eph. 3:12; 4:12, 15, 16). Moreover, the church as a body speaks of its organic nature and growth.

Also, the knowledge of the Son of God is connected to the Spirit in Ephesians (Eph. 1:17). In v. 14, the tossing of the waves speaks of chaos sourced in darkness.[98] The "wind" (ἄνεμος) contrasts with πνεῦμα, which can imply evil "winds" or "spirits."[99] Further, pejorative concepts like "trickery" (κυβεία),[100] "craftiness" (πανουργία), and "scheming of deceit" (μεθοδείαν τῆς πλάνης) are suggestive of demonic influence through human agency, and the contrast with "truthing" (ἀληθεύω, v. 15) is indicative of the role of the Spirit rather than these corrupt spirits (cf. Eph. 6:10–17). Assuming the Spirit is in view implicitly, and since their role is equipping others for works of service, spiritually endowed leaders are critical to building the church in unity and maturity.

As the Spirit works in the ministry of the leaders, God mobilizes, equips, and empowers people for these ministries, and the body of Christ is increasingly pneumaformed. Love, the lead fruit of the Spirit, is also mentioned twice, indicating that character formation by the Spirit in these believers is pivotal to the upbuilding of the church (vv. 15, 16). The Spirit forms the posture of the saints' ministries. There is also an interplay between the individual and collective pneumaformation in the passage. Individuals set apart by God and equipped with his Spirit equip others for love-motivated ministry. Yet, the context for this is the church, and the outcome is not merely the building up of individuals but the whole body of Christ, bound together with this love, each part working in harmony with the other as in a healthy human body.

---

96. See my arguments that Ephesians 4:12–16 includes growth through evangelism and converts: Keown, *Congregational*, 181–83.

97. Although God is the agent of appointment in v. 28, clearly, in light of vv. 1, 4, 7–11, and 13, the Spirit is the means by which God has done this in Christ.

98. The verb κλυδωνίζομαι is used in Isaiah 57:20 of the wicked. See also Sib. Or. 1:289; Josephus, *Ant.* 9.239.

99. The term is used in Testament of Solomon 22:2 of a spirit.

100. Even though it is the "trickery of people," it does not rule out demonic influence, which Paul associates with false teaching (e.g., 2 Cor. 11:12–15; Gal. 4:8–10; Col. 2:8; 1 Tim. 4:1). Arnold touches on this idea, noting that Alexandrinus adds "of the devil" (τοῦ διαβόλου), which leads him to say, "Although this reading is too poorly attested to be regarded as original, it does reflect an early Christian interpretation of this passage as having demonic overtones. This interpretation fits well with Paul's view of false teaching. Paul often sees the powers of darkness as actively inspiring various forms of dangerous teaching. . . . He will return to this theme in Eph. 6:10–20." Arnold, *Ephesians*, 268.

Ephesians 4:17–32

Paul urges the Ephesians to take off their ignorant, corrupted, and godless patterns of thinking and licentious living that characterized them as τὰ ἔθνη.[101] Instead, in v. 20, they must live out their Christian education: they have learned Christ, heard him, and have been taught by him, as the truth is in Jesus. Paul does not say here that the Ephesians have been taught about Christ—they have been taught Christ (acc. τὸν Χριστόν) and have heard him (accusative αὐτός), indicating Christ's agency through their teachers of the gospel. Learning here concerning the exalted Christ is mediated through his Spirit.

While ἐν αὐτῷ ἐδιδάχθητε in v. 21 can be translated as "taught by him," here it should instead be translated "taught in him," speaking of participation in Christ as the context in which they heard Jesus and continue to do so. Confirmation for this idea comes in what follows, where the truth is *in* Jesus (v. 21c). Believers then participate in Christ and his truth; in this context, they hear Christ and are taught by him. Hearing the exalted Christ suggests the role of the Spirit as the means by which Christ is learned and heard. Dwelling in Christ and filled with his Spirit, they hear the voice of Christ through the Spirit.

As people instructed in Christ, the Ephesians are to take off their former sinful lives and ἀνανεοῦσθαι δὲ τῷ πνεύματι τοῦ νοὸς ὑμῶν, "but take off the spirit/Spirit of your mind" (v. 22, my translation). While πνεῦμα here can be the human spirit and the genitive of place (the mind is the place being renewed),[102] it is far more likely that Paul is speaking of the Holy Spirit here. First, aside from Ephesians 2:2, where it speaks of Satan, πνεῦμα in Ephesians consistently means the Holy Spirit.[103] Second, the dative πνεύματι, in every instance, speaks of the sphere and/or agency of the Spirit.[104] Third, there appears to be an intentional contrast here between "the Spirit of your mind" and "the futility of the mind" (ματαιότητι τοῦ νοὸς αὐτῶν) in which the Gentiles and Ephesians, in their former lives, walked (v. 18). Fourth, the genitive τοῦ νοὸς ὑμῶν can form the subject of ἀνανεοῦσθαι, "be renewed of your mind." Then τῷ πνεύματι becomes the sphere and agency in which the mind is renewed.

Fifth, seeing πνεῦμα as the Spirit brings the passage in line with the previously mentioned use of the dative of πνεῦμα and also with other texts involving renewal through God's πνεῦμα in Ephesians. First, in Ephesians 1:17, Paul prays that God will give the Ephesians the "Spirit" of wisdom and

---

101. As in Ephesians 4:1 and 5:1, 7, 15, Paul uses οὖν, drawing an inference from the church growing through the Spirit's gifting and empowering leaders who equip the church to grow in unity and maturity in love.

102. Hoehner, *Ephesians*, 608.

103. Eph. 1:13, 17; 2:18, 22; 3:5, 16; 4:3, 4, 30; 5:18; 6:17, 18.

104. Eph. 1:13; 2:18, 22; 3:5; 5:18; 6:18.

revelation as they come to know Christ so that their hearts (synonymous to minds) are enlightened (by the Spirit) to know fully the hope to which God has called them. Second, in Ephesians 3:16, he prays that God's power will strengthen the Ephesians through his "Spirit" in their inner person (including the mind). Arnold neatly sums up Paul's intent:

> The mind ($\dot{o}$ νοῦς), then, is the focus of the Spirit's renewing work. Technically, since the infinitive is in the passive voice, the genitive case of "the mind" should be understood as a subjective genitive; that is, it serves as the subject of the passive verb with the Spirit being understood as the agent of the renewing work: "the mind is being renewed by the Spirit."[105]

Finally, reading this verse as an appeal for the renewal of the mind by the Spirit aligns it neatly with Romans 12:2 which refers to turning from the mindset of this age to that of God. Whereas in Romans 12, it is implicitly the work of the Spirit (no agency is supplied), here it is explicitly the Spirit's work.

Not only are they to have their minds renewed in (and by) the Spirit, in v. 24, they must "put on the new person in accordance with God, created in the righteousness and holiness of the truth" (my translation). The previous clause indicates this is the Spirit's work. Moreover, the passive of the verb κτίζω implies both God's agency and creational growth by the Spirit, so we see the interchangeability of God and Spirit in terms of human formation. This renewal is in the direction of righteousness and holiness that align with the truth in Christ and the gospel.

In Ephesians 4:25–32, Paul expounds what this new person with a renewed mind looks like in negative and positive terms. Through these verses, there is a clear pattern of Paul stating the negative that they must put aside and then the positive that they must put on.

Lying is put aside; they must speak truthfully to other believers, as they are mutually dependent on each other (v. 25). In v. 26, Paul draws on Psalm 4:4 to tell the Ephesians not to allow their anger, righteous or otherwise, to flower into sin. What he means is likely the extremes of anger repudiated in v. 31 and even the violence that can then follow. Instead, believers must deal with it before darkness comes. Verse 27 indicates that failure to do this could give a place for the devil to accuse them. The Ephesians must not steal but earn their living with their own honest effort with the purpose (ἵνα) that they may be able to share with others in need (v. 28). The pneumaformed person works to provide for themselves and their family and to be generous to others.

Verses 29–30 are awkwardly expressed but with a simple intent—to challenge the Ephesians to renounce λόγος σαπρὸς. The substantive σαπρὸς can mean "rotten." In the Testament of Abraham (B) 13:15, the

---

105. Arnold, *Ephesians*, 289.

angel Death declares, "There is no other more full of *decay* (σαπρός) than I."[106] Hence, it carries a sense of decay and death. Jesus employed it figuratively of bad or rotten (σαπρός) trees that produce bad fruit, in contrast to the good trees (people),[107] or bad (rotten) fish that must be thrown out, signifying the wicked who will go to eternal destruction (Matt. 13:48). Here it is rotten or evil speech, speech that is so vile and destructive that it increses the rot and death of others and God's creation. No such words must issue from the mouth of the pneumaformed believer.[108] In contrast, believers' speech must edify others at their point of need so that it may give grace to those listening.[109]

Verse 30 (see also chapter 3) should be read with the previous verse, as it is linked with the conjunction καί. In contrast, there is no conjunction in v. 31.[110] Paul adds to his encouragement to speak grace-fully, "do not grieve [λυπέω] the Holy Spirit of God, by whom you were sealed for the day of redemption." The verb λυπέω is a strong word meaning "to pain, sadden, afflict" someone. No other NT writer uses it of people grieving God, and this is Paul's only use in this sense.[111] Isaiah speaks of Israel grieving God's Spirit when they rebelled against him (Isa. 63:10).[112] Here, it is destructive rotten speech that grieves the Spirit. Such speech brings death.

Conversely, we can deduce that speech that builds up people in need and brings life and grace to hearers pleases the Spirit. Like other passages in the NT (especially James 3:1–12), the Spirit is within believers, urging them to speech that edifies and gives grace. Our task is to pause and yield to that impulse in every situation.[113]

---

106. Translation Charlesworth. Philo uses it of an aged woman (*Agr.* 153).

107. Matt. 7:17–18; 12:33; Luke 6:43.

108. Literally, "Every rotten word from your mouth must not go out."

109. This is in the form of a conditional sentence. Literally, "But if any good for the edification of need, so that it may give grace to the hearers."

110. Arnold notes there is debate concerning how this links as there is no conjunction. After surveying the options, he concludes, "The best explanation is that it applies directly to the evil speech *in the previous verse* by providing a motivation to eliminate this practice. In other words, rotten talk is not only harmful to the health of the Christian community; it grieves the Spirit of God." Arnold, *Ephesians*, 305–6 (emphasis mine).

111. Paul elsewhere uses λυπέω of a Christian being grieved by what another Christian eats (Rom. 14:15), of Paul causing the Corinthians sorrow and vice versa (2 Cor. 2:2, 4, 5; 7:8–9, 11), grieving in his ministry (2 Cor. 6:10), and believers' grieving at death unlike unbelievers (1 Thess. 4:13). Outside of Paul in the NT, λυπέω speaks of Antipas's grief at killing John (Matt. 14:9), the distress of the disciples at Jesus predicting his death (Matt. 17:23), the extreme sadness of slaves at the maltreatment of a debtor (Matt. 18:31), the rich man having been told to sell all and follow Jesus (Mark 10:22), the disciples when Jesus stated one would betray him (Mark 14:19), Jesus praying in Gethsemane (Matt. 26:37), the coming sorrow of the disciples (John 16:20), Simon Peter's distress at Jesus asking him if he loves him (John 21:17), and Christians in Asia Minor suffering (1 Peter 1:6).

112. See Fee, *GEP*, 713, for more detail. See also Isaiah 54:6, where Israel is like a wife grieved of spirit.

113. See further Fee, *GEP*, 712–17. He rightly notes that the material in this section is focused on maintaining the unity mentioned in vv. 1–16 (p. 713) and represents two ways of walking that either

Verses 31–32 support the previous injunction. The Ephesians must remove from themselves five false attitudes that spill forth in Spirit-grieving, death-creating speech. First, bitterness is rejected. Bitterness is a feature of sinful humanity in Romans 3:14, where Paul cites Psalm 9:28 LXX [10:7 EVV]). The author of Hebrews similarly warns against "the root of bitterness" springing up (Heb. 12:15).[114] The second and third false attitudes are synonyms that refer to intensely angry attitudes and speech. The noun θυμός can refer to God's wrath[115] but here refers to blazing anger and is in Paul's vice lists (2 Cor. 12:20; Gal. 5:20; Col. 3:8). Similarly, ὀργὴ is commonly used of God's righteous anger (Eph. 2:3; 5:6), and sometimes human rage.[116] Christians are to renounce their wrath, for God will judge as he wills (Rom. 12:19), and the governments are his servants in exercising wrath against wrongdoers (Rom. 13:4–5). James, likewise, urges his readers to be "slow to *orgē*" (James 2:19–20). As noted, such sinful extremes of anger are in view in 4:26. These cause death, physical and spiritual.

The fourth thing to be renounced is κραυγή, which means "a loud cry or call, shout."[117] Here, it is associated with anger and indicates yelling in rage at others, as in Acts 23:9, where Sadducees and Pharisees argued over Paul's perspectives. The fifth vice, βλασφημία, can have the sense of slandering God,[118] but here likely includes all "speech that denigrates or defames"—reviling, disrespectful, or slandering speech (also Col. 3:8).[119] All such speech is to be removed or lifted off (αἴρω). John employs αἴρω of the sinless Jesus taking away sins (1 John 3:5).[120] Paul employs it of Jesus

---

enhance or destroy unity (p. 713). Lurking in the background is the temple motif (2:22). He notes the full ascription "The Holy Spirit of God," which is "not just a form of solemn speech, calling special attention to the role of the Spirit in ethical life, but also an emphatic declaration that the *Holy* Spirit is none other than the Spirit *of God*."

114. See also Job 7:11; Sir. 4:6; 31:39; Amos 6:12; Isa. 37:29. The term is used of bitter plant (Heb. 12:15), bitter water (Exod. 15:23), and bitter grapes (Exod. 32:32). It is also used of a bitter spirit (3 Macc. 4:4; Sir. 7:11) or soul (Job 3:20).

115. Romans 2:8 and regularly in Revelation.

116. God's wrath (Matt. 3:7; Luke 3:7; John 3:36; Rom. 1:18; 2:5, 8; 3:5; 4:15; 5:9; 9:22; Col. 3:6; 1 Thess. 1:10; 2:16; 5:9; Heb. 3:11; 4:3; Rev. 6:17; 11:18; 14:10; 16:19; 19:15); Christ's anger (Mark 3:5; Rev. 6:16).

117. BDAG, s.v. "κραυγή," 585. The shout can be positive and celebratory (Matt. 25:6; Luke 1:42, also 2 Kgdms. 6:15; 2 Macc. 15:26), or it can be cries of anguish in prayer, as at Gethsemane (Heb. 5:7), or at suffering (Rev. 21:4). It is commonly used in the LXX of Israel's cries of anguish under persecution (e.g., Exod. 3:7, 9; Esther 4:3; Ps. 5:2).

118. Although it is used of Jesus's claims before the high priest (Mark 14:64), to forgive sin (Luke 5:21), and of oneness with God (John 10:33). In Revelation 13:1, the beast has a slanderous name and speaks blasphemies against God (Rev. 13:5–6), and the scarlet beast of Revelation 17:3 is full of such names. In Jude 9 it is used of not slandering the devil.

119. BDAG, s.v. "βλασφημία," 178. Also 1 Tim. 6:4. Jesus repudiates such speech (Matt. 15:19; Mark 7:22). Such speech uttered against the Spirit is unforgivable (Mark 3:28). See also Rev. 2:9.

120. The verb is very common and usually carries the sense of picking up, or lifting off, as with the healed paralytic, "pick up your stretcher" (Mark 2:11–12), or "take up your cross" (Mark 8:34). It is used of removing a sinful person from the church (1 Cor. 5:2). Paul's other use is of taking a member of the church and joining them to a prostitute (1 Cor. 6:15).

removing the certificate of indebtedness for sin in believers (Col. 2:14). Here, believers are to remove false speech patterns from their lives along with everything evil.

In place of such destructive speech, believers are to become kind (χρηστός), compassionate (εὔσπλαγχνοι), and forgiving to one another (χαριζόμενοι ἑαυτοῖς). Χρηστός speaks of being "morally good and benevolent."[121] Frequently in Jewish literature and once in Paul, it is an attribute of God that leads people to repentance (Rom. 2:4; cf. Luke 6:35).[122] Paul's only other use is in a maxim warning the Corinthians that "bad company corrupts *goodness*" (1 Cor. 15:33, my translation). Paul may have in view Psalm 111:5–6 in the LXX, which speaks of the goodness of the person who is compassionate and lends to others; such a person will never be shaken and will be remembered eternally (112:5 EVV; similarly Prov. 2:21).

The second term is εὔσπλαγχνος, which compounds εὖ (good, well) with σπλάγχνον. Σπλάγχνον literally denotes the viscera and entrails (Acts 1:18), and, in the NT, conveys compassion and affection that derives from the depths of one's being.[123] Luke and James attribute such gut compassion to God (Luke 1:78; James 5:11), and the verb is repeatedly used for Jesus's attitude to the needy people of Israel.[124] The compound indicates "to be merciful"[125] or to have "tender feelings for someone, tenderhearted, compassionate."[126] Peter urges his readers to embody the same attitude (1 Peter 3:8).

The third attribute uses χαρίζομαι. The verb means to "give," a sense Paul usually uses for God's gifts to people.[127] So this can mean Paul wants them to adopt a giving spirit toward one another. However, it is also used for the forgiveness of sins.[128] This sense is clearly in view in the final clause: "just as God in Christ forgave [aor. χαρίζομαι] you" (also Col. 3:13). The Ephesians are to forgive others their wrongs, for they have experienced redemption and forgiveness of sins through Christ's blood (Eph. 1:7).

---

121. BDAG, s.v. "χρηστός," 1090.
122. See also Matthew 11:30 of the easy yoke that Jesus places on his people, and the goodness of old wine (Luke 5:39); 1 Peter 2:32, citing Ps. 33:9 (34:8 EVV). In the OT, see 2 Macc. 1:24; Pss. 24:8 (25:8 EVV); 51:11 (52:9 EVV); 68:17 (69:16 EVV); 85:5 (86:5 EVV); 99:5 (100:5 EVV); 105:1 (106:1 EVV); 106:1 (107:1 EVV); 108:21 (109:21 EVV); 118:39 (119:39 EVV); 68 (119:68 EVV); 135:1 (136:1 EVV); 144:9; Wis. 15:1; Pss. Sol. 2:36; 5:2, 12; 8:32; 10:2, 7; Nah. 1:7; Jer. 40:11; Dan. 3:89 (LXX).
123. Used by Paul in 2 Cor. 6:12; 7:15; Phil. 1:8; 2:1; Col. 3:12; Philem. 7, 12, 20. See also 1 John 3:17.
124. Matt. 9:36; 14:14; 15:32; 20:34; Mark 1:41; 6:34; 8:2; 9:22; Luke 7:13. Also Matt. 18:27; Mark 9:22; Luke 10:33; 15:20.
125. *BrillDAG*, s.v. "εὔσπλαγχνος." They note it is also used of a good intestine.
126. BDAG, s.v. "σπλάγχνον," 413.
127. Rom. 8:32; 1 Cor. 2:12; Gal. 3:18; Phil. 1:29; 2:9; Philem. 22. The verb is used of a gift in Luke 7:21; Acts 27:24.
128. See Luke 7:42–43; 2 Cor. 2:7, 10, 13; Col. 2:13.

Ephesians 5:1–2

Using his characteristic μιμητ- language uniquely in terms of emulating God,[129] Paul now steps out of ethical teaching to its foundation.[130] The Ephesians are to "become imitators of God as beloved children." Formerly, the Ephesians were "[children] of disobedience" and "children of wrath" (Eph. 2:2, 3). Now they are described as God's children, indicating that they are to grow up into the image of God gifted to them by their Father and Creator. At its core, as with Jewish ethics,[131] Christian ethics is the imitation of God.[132] Believers are to "walk in love," bringing ἀγάπη to the forefront as God's imitation-worthy attribute.[133] Rather than further extrapolate what aspects of God they are to imitate, Paul switches attention instantly to Jesus, who incarnated love. Then, to unpack love, Paul tells them they must love "as Christ loved us and gave himself up for us, a fragrant offering and sacrifice to God" (v. 2). Elsewhere, in Romans 5:8, Christ's death for people is a demonstration of God's love. God's inseparable love is "in Christ Jesus" (Rom. 8:39).[134] Indeed, love in the Christian faith is defined by Christ's self-giving to save the world.

Paul's choice of the verb here, παραδίδωμι (rather than just δίδωμι), is intended as it is used of Jesus being handed over by people—to be arrested, tried, and put to death. The same construct, παραδόντος ἑαυτὸν, in Ephesians 5:25, is used of Christ giving himself over for his bride, the church (also Gal. 2:20). Jesus gave himself "as an offering and sacrifice to God" (or a "sacrificial offering"). For the NT writers, Christ is the fulfillment and completion of Israel's sacrificial system to ensure holiness before God. As an offering, he was "a sweet fragrance," invoking the ancient notion of the smell from the offering rising to God (or the gods) to bring pleasure to the deity. Jesus's death opened God's infinite favor to humankind.

Overall, this is an appeal for the Ephesians to live cruciformly. They are to give themselves as living sacrifices (cf. Rom. 12:1). As they act in love, giving themselves in service of God and others, they bring pleasure to God. The Spirit is not mentioned, but, as elsewhere, it is by the Spirit that they will live cruciform lives. The pneumaformed live out of a self-sacrificial love for the betterment of others. Such actions emit a fragrance that pleases God and spreads to others (2 Cor. 2:15).

---

129. Again introduced with οὖν as in 4:1, 17; 5:7, 15.
130. See imitation of Christ (1 Cor. 11:1; 1 Thess. 1:6), imitation of Paul (1 Cor. 4:16; Eph. 3:17; 6:12; 1 Thess. 1:6; 2:1; 2 Thess. 3:7, 9); outside of Paul, imitation of the former faithful saint (Heb. 6:12; 13:7) and imitating goodness and not evil (3 John 11).
131. See Menachem Kellner, "Ethics of Judaism," *EJ* 1:152.
132. E.g., Matt. 5:48; Luke 6:36; 1 Peter 1:16.
133. See 2 Cor. 13:14 (13:13 EVV).
134. Also 1 Cor. 16:24; 2 Cor. 5:20 (subj. gen.); Eph. 6:23; 1 Tim. 1:14; 2 Tim. 1:13.

Ephesians 5:3–20

Paul again shifts to the life the children of God will live. First, they will renounce another set of vices. Recalling that ἀσέλγεια, ἀκαθαρσία, and πλεονεξία characterize nonbelievers' behavior in Ephesians 4:19, children of God who emulate God and Christ are to reject these things: sexual immorality (πορνεία),[135] uncleanness (ἀκαθαρσία), and greediness (πλεονεξία). Such things must not be mentioned amongst them as God's holy people. Reinforcing the rejection of "rotten words" in Ephesians 4:29, God's children also reject improper obscenity (αἰσχρότης) and foolish talk (μωρολογία), or coarse jesting (εὐτραπελία, 5:4). Rather, God's children express thanksgiving (εὐχαριστία).[136]

Ephesians 5:5 reinforces Paul's prohibition as he warns them that people who are characterized by sexual immorality (πόρνος), uncleanness (ἀκάθαρτος), or greed (πλεονέκτης) have no inheritance in God's kingdom. For Paul, greed is idolatry.[137] The vices are seen in this way because they focus on bodily affections and desires of the flesh—sexual gratification, consumption, and self-satiation—rather than God.

Paul has already made plain to the Ephesians that they are saved by grace through faith and have received the Spirit as a seal and deposit guaranteeing their inheritance (Eph. 1:14; 4:30). Consequently, Paul is not saying that a person who fails in these areas is cut out of the kingdom of God. Instead, he is speaking of those who are unbelievers who do this and people who claim the name of "brother" or "sister" but are perpetually defined by these things and not the works of the Spirit.[138]

In v. 6, as he does in association with a similar warning in 1 Corinthians 6:10 (also Gal. 6:7),[139] he tells them not to let anyone deceive them with "empty words" (κενοῖς λόγοις). Paul has implicitly warned of false teaching from "human trickery" (τῇ κυβείᾳ τῶν ἀνθρώπων) in Ephesians 4:14–15.[140] There, the Spirit-empowered leaders are tasked with equipping the church to

---

135. As defined by BGD, s.v. "πορνεία," 693, "every kind of unlawful sexual intercourse." Paul endorses Genesis 1:28 and 2:28, and hence it refers to anything outside a heterosexual, monogamous, marital relationship. He uses the language twenty-one times, always negatively (1 Cor. 5:1, 9, 10, 11; 6:9, 13, 15, 16, 18; 7:2; 10:8; 2 Cor. 12:21; Gal. 5:19; Eph. 5:5; Col. 3:5; 1 Thess. 4:3; 1 Tim. 1:10). Here in Ephesians 5:3, it is prominently placed for emphasis.

136. As does Paul in Ephesians 1:15 and as he will stress again to the Ephesians in 5:20 (both εὐχαριστέω).

137. Alternatively, Best may be right to argue that all three vices are in view and not just greed. This is probable because, as he demonstrates, sexual immorality, impure behavior, and greed are all associated with idolatry. Furthermore, the singular neuter ὅ rather than the masculine πλεονέκτης may point in this direction. Best, *A Critical and Exegetical Commentary*, 480. However, the singular ὅ ἐστιν leaves open the possibility Paul only means greed here. Thielman, *Ephesians*, 332–33.

138. Keown, "Initial Discipleship."

139. See also 1 Cor. 15:33; Gal. 6:7; Col. 2:24; 2 Thess. 2:3.

140. The substantive κυβεία is a *hapax* and not found elsewhere in Jewish Greek literature. It is used of a "game of dice" (Aristotle, *Rhet.* 1371a.3; Plato, *Phaedr.* 274d; Xenophon, *Mem.* 1.3.2). Here, it means "cunning, trickery."

ensure church members are not swept away. Here, the Ephesians are to take responsibility for themselves.

Ephesians 5:7–16 focuses on the duality of light and darkness, a motif common across all religious literature, ancient or otherwise.[141] Light represents good, and darkness evil, which for Paul are two mutually exclusive spheres (2 Cor. 6:14). The children of God are "children of light" (v. 8; 1 Thess. 5:5). Again, marking the transition with οὖν, v. 7 directly tells the Ephesians they must not be fellow sharers (plur. συμμέτοχος) with the idolaters. Here, Paul has in mind those things mentioned in vv. 3–6, including the rampantly sinful and deceivers, "the children of disobedience." The Ephesians were formerly such people (Eph. 2:1–3; 4:22) whom he already characterized in Ephesians 4:17–20. Paul again reminds them of this, "for at one time you were darkness." Paul uses the light motif earlier as he prays for the eyes of his readers' hearts to be enlightened and for his own ministry of enlightening people through the preaching of the gospel (Eph. 1:18; 3:9). Darkness is also associated with inimical spiritual forces in Ephesians 6:12, indicating that unbelievers are held captive by such forces (cf. Eph. 2:3).[142] Light invokes thoughts of the Spirit—it radiates from a source, as does the Spirit from God through his Son.[143]

Now, the Ephesians are light in the Lord and thus must live as children of light (Eph. 4:8). Such children of light bear the fruit in all goodness, righteousness, and truth—summative terms for living lives worthy of their calling that feature the many virtues found in the passage thus far. Such people test what is pleasing to Christ, the Lord (Eph. 4:10). They do not participate in unfruitful deeds of darkness; instead, they expose them. In context, this is to bring them into the light and convict (ἐλέγχω) them for what they are—evil, unrighteous, and false.[144]

Verse 12 confirms that this exposure is not positive but negative, for "it is shameful even to speak of the things that they do in secret." So, they are not to be talked about positively; they are to be exposed to the light, shown for what they are, and repudiated. Verses 13 and 14 repeat the use of ἐλέγχω and

---

141. See also in Paul: Rom. 2:19; 13:12–13; 1 Cor. 3:13; 4:5; 5:4–5, 7–8; 2 Cor. 4:4–6; 11:14; Phil. 2:15; Col. 1:12–13. In the wider NT, see Matt. 4:16; 5:14–16; 6:22–23; 8:12; 13:43; 24:49; 25:1–13; Mark 4:22; Luke 1:79; 2:32; 11:33–36; 12:35; 16:8; John 1:5–5, 7–9; 3:19, 21; 5:35; 8:12; 9:5; 11:9–10; 12:35–36, 46; Acts 13:47; 26:18, 23; Heb. 6:4; 10:32; 1 Peter 2:9; 2 Peter 1:19; 1 John 1:5–7; 2:8–11.

142. On Ephesians 2:3, see Fee, GEP, 680–81. While he agrees it is not a Spirit text, he notes the double use of σάρξ hints in the direction of the Spirit and shows how presuppositional the Spirit is for Paul.

143. Fee, GEP, 717, suggests that this text "adds nothing to our understanding of the Spirit in this letter." However, the motif of light suggests otherwise. Significantly, although the original reading is likely φωτός (text-types 𝔓49 ℵ A B D* G P 33 81 1739* it vg syrp, pal copsa, bo goth arm eth Origen), some later texts changed it to πνεύματος (𝔓46 Dc K Ψ 88 104 614 1739mg al.). This shows that early interpreters considered "the Spirit" to fit the context, even if it is a recollection of Galatians 5:22. See further Metzger, TCGNT, 539–40.

144. BDAG, s.v. "ἐλέγχω," 315. The darkness-light motif here implies exposing them with the implication of censure.

affirm Paul's previous point—"all things exposed by the light are made visible, for everything made visible is light" (LEB).

Verse 14b–e is a credal and perhaps baptismal saying or song.[145] It likely draws on a range of OT texts.[146] While some versions translate γάρ as "therefore" (e.g., ESV, LEB),[147] it is better translated as "for"—a marker of clarification. It does not so much explain why or make an inference concerning the exposure but explains what happens when one becomes a believer—Christ's light shines on and into the saved person exposing deeds of darkness. This exposing power evokes thoughts of the Spirit penetrating the believer, exposing and conviction of sin, and restoring from sinfulness to goodness.

The short statement urges the sleeper to rise or wake up (ἐγείρω). The metaphor of a sleeper speaks of one in darkness, one spiritually dead and so asleep to God's goodness.[148] Such a person arises. The second line restates this with the imperative "arise from the dead," which occurs at conversion (Eph. 2:5–6). The final line states what then occurs: "Christ will shine on you." Christ, then, is the source of the light that beams onto and into the new convert.

The metaphor of light for Paul is not static but speaks of God's power in Christ to "invade" what is evil (dark) with his goodness. For Paul, God's power comes as the gospel is proclaimed. Just as God commands the light to shine in the primordial darkness (Gen. 1:3), the "light of the gospel of the glory of Christ" shines into the once darkened and blinded hearts of unbelievers "to give the light of the knowledge of the glory of God in the face of Jesus Christ" (2 Cor. 4:4–6). This light keeps shining. The readers, who have been enlightened by Christ at salvation, must walk in God's light, symbolized by baptism. Christ's action in this regard is via the Spirit. When the Ephesians believed, the Spirit shone powerfully into their hearts and minds, saving them from darkness and sealing them for redemption.

In vv. 15 and 16, Paul appears to shift metaphors from light/darkness to wise/unwise living. However, wisdom is associated with hearts and minds enlightened by God (Eph. 1:17; 3:10; cf. 1:8). Believers are to live wisely in the light, not foolishly in darkness. They are to do this, making the most of (redeeming) their time, living by Christ's will, because the days are evil (dark). Such living includes repudiating drunkenness and being filled with the Spirit,

---

145. On the potential origin, see Lincoln, *Ephesians*, 318–19. He suggests three options: (1) an OT text, perhaps Isaiah 60:1 with Isaiah 26:19 (cf. 4:8). An OT source is unlikely as the language is quite different; (2) an apocryphal text, e.g., Apoc. El. 3:3, which is again unlikely; (3) an early Christian hymn with a baptismal setting.

146. Possibly Isa. 26:19; 51:17; 52:1; and 60:1.

147. Or causal, as with "for this reason" (NET); "this is why" (NIV).

148. See Rom. 13:11–12; 1 Thess. 5:5–7, 10. Sleep as a metaphor for death: 1 Cor. 15:6, 18, 20–21; 1 Thess. 4:13–15; also Acts 7:60; 13:36; 2 Peter 3:4. Jesus used the motif of those ready or not for his return (Matt. 24:43; 25:5). See also the disciples asleep in the garden (Mark 14:34, 37–38).

by whom the light of Christ shines on them (something discussed earlier). This enlightened living spills over into worship and thanksgiving (vv. 18–20).

Ephesians 5:21–6:9

The participle ὑποτασσόμενοι that launches v. 21 is transitional. As in all its Pauline uses, the verb indicates submission or subjection (Eph. 1:22; Col. 3:18).[149] It is linked to what follows, as it governs the verbless v. 22. Yet, by using the participle rather than the imperative,[150] Paul indicates that the verb expresses another aspect of being filled with the Spirit in v. 19. Still, while it is disputed, the participle is clearly imperatival to some extent, in that Paul expects them to do what is required, "submit."[151] Being filled with the Spirit should flow over into their relationships in the family.

The verse states that all believers must submit to one another, pushing against the carefully structured first-century society with its apparent class structures and expectations. All are to be in submission to all. The final phrase, "out of reverence for Christ," continues the focus on worship in the preceding verses. Mutual submission is an act of worship. Verse 21, then, is the summative command that sets up the whole passage.

As I have explored elsewhere, Ephesians 5:22–6:9 works out what Spirit-led mutual servanthood and submission look like for all Christians, especially men.[152] The passage is a three-section unit, with each section broken into two distinct halves. The first half of each section focuses on the socially "inferior" party in the family structure (wives, children, and slaves),[153] and the second half on the paterfamilias's role in the family unit regarding the social inferiors.

---

149. Literally connoting "stand under," it is used in the NT of things or people in subjection to something else. Paul uses it of the flesh not being in submission to God's law (Rom. 8:7); creation in subjection to decay by God (Rom. 8:20); Jewish unbelievers not submitting to God's righteousness (Rom. 10:3); people in submission to governing authorities (Rom. 13:1, 5; Titus 3:1); the spirits of prophets subject to prophets (1 Cor. 14:32); women in submission (1 Cor. 14:34); all creation subject to Christ and God (1 Cor. 15:27–28; Eph. 1:22; Phil. 3:21; Heb. 2:8; 1 Peter 2:13); the Corinthians in submission to leaders (1 Cor. 16:16); the church in submission to Christ (Eph. 5:24); wives in submission to husbands (Eph. 5:21, 24; Col. 3:18; Titus 2:5; 1 Peter 3:1, 5); slaves subject to masters (Titus 2:9; 1 Peter 2:18); believers subject to God (Heb. 12:9; James 4:7); all spiritual powers subject to Christ (1 Peter 3:22); young men subject to elders (1 Peter 5:5). See also Jesus submitting to his parents (Luke 2:51); demons submitting to disciples (Luke 10:17, 20); the world to come not subject to angels (Heb. 2:5).

150. Paul prefers the imperative in Rom. 13:1; 14:34; Col. 3:18.

151. Wallace questions this. He rightly notes that the main verb is πληροῦσθε in v. 18 and suggests other options, including the means by which they are filled, the manner in which they are filled, attendant circumstances (that sit alongside being filled), result (a result from being filled), and imperatival. While it may be a result, there is clearly still an imperative to submit to one another here and not merely an assumption that they will. Wallace, *Greek Grammar*, 639.

152. Mark J. Keown, "Paul's Vision of a New Masculinity," *Colloq* 47, no. 1 (2016): 47–60.

153. Of course, this is from the commonly agreed social structure of the first-century Roman world. It was clearly a given that wives were universally recognized as submissive to their husbands, children obedient to their parents, and slaves obedient to their masters.

In that the paterfamilias is the focus of all three sections, the emphasis falls on the transformation of men by the Spirit who fills them.

The first section focuses on the relationship between wives and husbands. As was expected culturally, wives were to submit to their husbands. They were to do so as unto "the Lord" (v. 22). While headship can be read as " source," there is a clear aspect of authority in Christ's headship of the church, which parallels the headship of the husband. In the first half, Paul affirms the ancient stereotype—husbands are the heads of wives, and wives are to be subject to their husbands.

However, v. 21 has already conditioned this headship, and the whole church has already been informed they are to be subject to one another. Verses 25 to 33 show how the husband is to do this regarding his wife. He is to love his wife as Christ loved the church and sacrificed himself for her to sanctify her (vv. 25–27). This command is exceptional in the ancient world. Overall, husbands were not expected to love their wives. However, for Paul, love is the chief fruit of the Spirit, and being filled with the Spirit empowers husbands to love their wives with sacrificial service. Christ's self-giving has already been mentioned as the basis of the Ephesian believer's imitation of God (Eph. 5:1–2). Such an absolute sacrifice of himself reshapes any notion of leadership in κεφαλή away from authority and dominance. The husband leads by sacrificing himself for his wife so that she becomes who she is created to be in holiness. Authority and roles are subsumed in something greater: love and mutual service (cf. Gal. 5:13). The seeming authority of the husband and submission of the wife is transformed into servanthood and mutual submission. Being filled with the Spirit leads to marriages in which the wives are submissive to their husbands and husbands are self-sacrificially loving. Pneumaform marriages involve both spouses serving humbly and sacrificially.

The second section is short and to the point. Yet, it is even more provocative than the injunctions to husbands toward their wives. Children are to obey their parents (Eph. 6:1). This has been the case in all ancient cultures since at least the giving of the Ten Commandments (Exod. 20:12; Deut. 5:16). Whereas the promise in the original command is that Israel will live long in the promised land, Paul adapts it to the promise of long life on the earth. Children who obey their parents will be blessed with a long life.

In v. 4, Paul shifts focus to both parents but particularly the paterfamilias—the same person addressed as the husband in the previous section. The father is instructed not to cause his children to be harshly angry but to "bring them up in the discipline and instruction of the Lord." In that women in the ancient world were charged with the responsibility of raising children, this is an even more astounding statement than the previous injunction pertaining to their wives. Spirit-filled fathers are not to leave the raising of children to wives and other women but are themselves responsible for the nurture of children in the Lord.

The third section addresses slaves and masters, with the paterfamilias again primarily in view (having authority over the household slaves). Slaves are charged with obeying their masters sincerely, as if serving Christ himself (Eph. 6:4–7). They do this because they will receive their reward for doing so (6:8). Counterculturally, v. 9 urges masters to do the *same things* to them (τὰ αὐτὰ ποιεῖτε πρὸς αὐτούς). This command is nonspecific, and it is then debatable what they are to do. Certainly, it includes what follows—they are not to threaten them. Yet, Paul adds, "there is no partiality with him." Here, "him" is "the Lord," so Christ is in view. Taking this all at face value, Paul envisages the end of the domination of masters over slaves. Masters are to treat slaves gently and equitably, as if they were not slaves. I believe this hints at the end of slavery, even if Paul does not go there.

Philemon 15–17, which envisages Philemon welcoming back Onesimus as a beloved brother, and as if he were Paul himself, without any punishment for wrongdoing, insinuates the same thing. The Spirit-filled man in the first-century world treated his slaves with gentleness and impartiality, as he should any employee. Pneumaformity transforms the home. It can be argued that the Spirit, hinting in this direction in Paul, enabled believers to see that slavery was wrong and work to ban it.

Ephesians 6:10–20

Paul ends his ethical exhortation in Ephesians 6:10–17 with the military metaphor. He acknowledges the existence of demonic forces against which believers struggle.[154] Readers, male and female, are to be strong in the Lord and his power (v. 10). The appeal is another way of saying "by the empowerment of Christ's Spirit." They are to put on God's armor that will enable them to stand and resist the stratagems of these spiritual powers.

The six elements of the armor are metaphors that summon the Ephesians to live lives worthy of God's call (Eph. 4:1), as fully equipped and mature believers (Eph. 4:12–16), as renewed people (Eph. 4:23–24), as God's children who imitate God and his Son (Eph. 5:1–2), as children of the light (Eph. 5:7), as wise people (Eph. 5:15), and as those filled with the Spirit (Eph. 5:18).

The first two elements of the armor are summative, calling readers to live in line with the truth and live fully righteous and just lives (v. 14). The third speaks of feet ready to take a stand and defend against false teaching,

---

154. See on this the work Clinton E. Arnold, "The Exorcism of Ephesians 6:12 in Recent Research," *JSNT* 30 (1987): 71–87, and *Ephesians: Power and Magic; The Concept of Power in Ephesians in Light of Its Historical Setting*, SNTSMS 63 (Cambridge: Cambridge University Press, 1989). See Fee, *GEP*, 725, for a discussion on "the spiritual forces of evil" (τὰ πνευματικὰ τῆς πονηρίας). He rightly states that they are not a fourth category but a "comprehensive term that embraces all the former ones." His comments on the section are excellent. See also the monograph by Kabiro wa Gatumu, *The Pauline Concept of Supernatural Powers: A Reading from the African Worldview*, PBM (Milton Keynes: Paternoster, 2008), especially 93–208.

and, where able, to advance the gospel (Eph. 6:15).[155] The fourth and fifth focus on being strong in the faith and confident in their status as God's saved people (cf. Eph. 2:8–9). The sixth element speaks of their capacity to know God's Word and defend themselves from false teaching and, when the opportunity arises, to advance it.[156] While some consider prayer as another element of the armor,[157] the absence of any military language in v. 18 suggests that Paul is not speaking of another "weapon" but is highlighting that consistent prayer in and by the Spirit should underlie every aspect of this perceived Spirit-filled life.

Ephesians 4:1–6:20 is a magnificent exposition of the pneumaformed life. It envisages believers filled with God's Spirit and being utterly renewed into the image of God and his Son. The Spirit does not need to be continually mentioned, but Paul moves interchangeably between God, Christ, and the Spirit to draw the Ephesians away from lives of fleshly living to those characterized by God's virtues, supremely, but not limited to, love.

CONCLUSION

Paul was a brilliant ethicist. At the heart of his ethics is the Spirit. The Spirit works in believers, transforming them from conformity to the world to conformity to God and his Son. From the moment of faith, the Spirit runs through a believer's inner being, generating life and leading them to live in the light. Most supremely, the love that flows into a believer at conversion overflows toward others. Countless other virtues that outwork love flow with it. Believers are conformed to the degree that they can obey the Spirit's promptings away from living by the flesh and toward the will of God. The Spirit renews mind and heart, reshaping a believer's thinking, emoting, and living. All this work is relational, as the believer participates in the Godhead shaped by love, united to God in Christ by the Spirit, and held together as one people. The recurring patterns of the world's elitism are brought into submission to the gospel that has no prejudice, and families, societies, and the world are transformed.

---

155. Keown, *Congregational*, 288–92.

156. "Clad with the gospel of their salvation, they must not only withstand the enemy's fiery missiles, but they must take the offensive as well." Fee strangely suggests the only piece of armor to be used is the sword; however, surely the shield is to be used as well to parry flaming arrows. Fee, *GEP*, 728. Keown, *Congregational*, 292–96.

157. Fee, *GEP*, 730.

CHAPTER 8

THE SPIRIT AND SUFFERING

I n this chapter, I examine the relationship of the Spirit to suffering.[1] This discussion is complex, as suffering language is used frequently by Paul and he links all figures of the Godhead to suffering. As consistently argued, such a study cannot be limited to explicit references to the Spirit. Paul moves interchangeably between God, Christ, and Spirit language as he writes, all the while aware that it is always "by the Spirit" that God's purposes are fulfilled in Christ. A complete perspective is gained by considering all of Paul's suffering ideas that connect with God, Christ, or the Spirit at work in believers.

As such, I have arranged the material in this chapter around seven subheadings exploring the universal experience of human suffering, the suffering the Spirit "causes" for believers seeking to please God and engage in ministry, suffering "in Christ," how God by the Spirit forms believers in and through suffering, the Spirit's present support to believers who are suffering, and the ultimate alleviation of suffering for the people of the Spirit.

THE HUMAN CONDITION OF SUFFERING

It is evident that Paul sees suffering as a universal condition. This distress results from Adam and Eve's failure in the garden.[2] Death came to all human-kind due to Adam's sin and their own participation in it (Rom. 5:12). The effect was cosmic, with the whole of creation subjected to futility and enslaved to decay so that it groans and travails for its liberation (Rom. 8:19–22). All living beings and things are subjugated to God's final enemy, death (1 Cor. 15:26).

Christians are not immune, as seen in Christ's death (Rom. 5:6) and in passages like 1 Corinthians 12:26, where Paul acknowledges that there will

---

1. "For Paul, as we saw in chapter 3 and as Galatians makes clear, suffering and the experience of the Spirit are not antithetical experiences. Indeed, they can be closely connected." Gorman, *CPNSC*, 151.
2. Esp. Rom. 5:12–21; 1 Cor. 15:22, 43–49; 2 Cor. 11:3; 1 Tim. 2:13–14.

be members of the Corinthian church who suffer. In 1 Thessalonians 4:13, written a short period after Paul had left the city,[3] members of the church had died (fallen asleep).[4] Although Paul urges the Thessalonians not to grieve as others do because of the hope they have in Christ, such grief at human death is the norm, and Christians participate in it, even if differently (Rom. 12:15; 1 Cor. 12:26). Indeed, Paul indicated that he would have experienced "sorrow upon sorrow" if not for Epaphroditus's recovery.

Sin is universal and causes great suffering with the relationship between God and creation violated by people's atheism, agnosticism, and idolatry. A wide array of sins of self-determination and self-gratification mar human relationships at every level. This damage is seen at a marriage level, even among believers (1 Cor. 7:28).[5] All people decay and die as they age. Sickness is a real issue, even experienced by Christians such as Epaphroditus (Phil. 2:27), Timothy frequently (1 Tim. 5:23), the Thessalonians (1 Thess. 5:14), and Paul himself in his missions (Gal. 4:13–15). Paul also suffered from a permanent problem (2 Cor. 12:7). The idolatry of humankind also comes through God's handing them over to deeper sinfulness and consequent brokenness (Rom. 1:24, 26, 28). Paul's vice lists catalog a wide array of sins whereby people's relationships with one another are shattered and worsened.[6]

While Paul emphasizes human sin rather than spiritual forces, he holds an apocalyptic spiritual worldview recognizing that evil spirits hold unbelieving people in bondage and cause them great suffering.[7] Suffering and death are unavoidable for the world, including believers.[8] The requirements of love explained to the Corinthians indicate that Christians need patience, kindness, and endurance and are vulnerable to things like jealousy, conceit, crudeness, selfishness, anger, resentment, and unrighteousness (1 Cor. 13:4–7).[9] Paul's letters are also full of evidence that he understood that believers remain vulnerable to feelings of pain and alienation, such as being discouraged

---

3. The Thessalonian letters were likely written within three to six months of Paul leaving. Keown, *Congregational*, 257–60; Keown, *Discovering: The Pauline Letters*, 289–90.
4. Clearly, "fallen asleep" is a euphemism for death (also 1 Cor. 15:6, 18, 51; 1 Thess. 4:14, 15; 5:10). Other references to believer's dying include Rom. 8:36 (possibly), 38; 1 Cor. 4:9 (possibly); 11:30.
5. The tone of Paul's household codes also challenge the paterfamiliases to love their wives sacrificially (Eph. 5:25–33; Col. 3:19), raise their children with gentleness (Eph. 6:4; Col. 3:21), and treat their slaves with justice and fairness (Eph. 6:9; Col. 4:1). Similarly, the appeal to wives to be submissive and children and slaves to be obedient is also designed to ensure good family relationships (Eph. 5:22–23; 6:1–2, 5–8; Col. 3:18, 20, 22–25). See also 1 Tim. 3:2, 4–5, 12; Titus 1:6.
6. See in Paul, Rom. 1:29–31; 13:13; 1 Cor. 5:10–11; 6:9–10; 2 Cor. 6:9–10; 12:20–21; Gal. 5:19–21; Eph. 4:31; 5:3–5; Col. 3:5, 8; 1 Tim. 1:9–10; 2 Tim. 3:2–5; Titus 3:3. J. Daryl Charles, "Vice and Virtue Lists," *DNTB* 1255.
7. Rom. 16:20; 1 Cor. 5:5; 7:5; 10:20–21; 2 Cor. 2:11; 11:14; 12:7; Gal. 4:3, 9; Eph. 2:2; 4:27; 6:11; Col. 1:13; 2:8, 20; 1 Thess. 2:18; 3:5; 2 Thess. 2:9; 1 Tim. 1:20; 3:6–7; 4:1; 5:15; 2 Tim. 2:26.
8. See, e.g., "the discouraged" (παραμυθέομαι, lit. "small-souled"), in 1 Thess. 5:14.
9. See also the catalogs in the vice lists of Paul.

(1 Thess. 5:14), taking offense,[10] vulnerability to shame,[11] groaning (Rom. 8:22), weakness,[12] anxiety and worry,[13] distress (Rom. 9:2; 2 Cor. 2:4; Phil. 2:26), feeling pressure (2 Cor. 11:28), anguish (2 Cor. 2:4), being disturbed or unsettled (Gal. 1:7; 5:10; 2 Thess. 2:2), fear (2 Cor. 7:5; 10:9; Phil. 1:28), and weeping.[14]

THE SUFFERING "CAUSED" BY THE SPIRIT

One might expect me first to discuss how the Spirit supports believers in suffering. Indeed, as will be shown, receiving the Spirit brings an amazing array of God's resources into the life of the suffering believer, alleviating suffering on occasion and strengthening Christians in their suffering. These resources cannot be downplayed. Yet, there is another layer in Paul's understanding whereby the experience of suffering is somehow heightened by becoming God's children by faith, being included in Christ, and receiving the Spirit.[15]

Suffering and Conversion

First, there is suffering at conversion. Paul's descriptions of the life of the ungodly indicate that before conversion, people are locked into cultures and societies beset with sin.[16] They are under the influence of demonic spiritual forces (Eph. 2:2). They live by the flesh and its desires, not the Spirit. Leaving behind one's lusts, desires, and addictions can be a painful process.

As discussed in chapter 2, at conversion, the "sword of the Spirit" (Eph. 6:17) pierces the inner being, and faith is born. Likewise, the image of circumcision of the heart also conveys the notion of pain as God severs sin from one's inner being (Rom. 2:29).

While God's new life enters a believer through the Spirit at conversion, the image of the crucifixion is suggestive of some degree of pain, even if not anything like that physical pain Jesus went through on the cross. There is a crucifixion of the self whereby one dies in Christ, and the "old man or woman" is put to death. Further, the world is crucified to the believer and the believer to the world, speaking of a rupture of relationship with the sin of the world. This sin is embedded in its structures, so there is a painful ripping away from

---

10.   See Rom. 14:21; 1 Cor. 8:13; 10:32; 2 Cor. 6:3.
11.   See Rom. 1:16; 6:21; 1 Cor. 4:14; 2 Thess. 3:14; 2 Tim. 1:8, 12, 16; 2:15; Titus 2:8.
12.   See Rom. 6:19; 8:26; 1 Cor. 2:3; 2 Cor. 11:30; 12:5, 9, 10; 13:4.
13.   See 1 Cor. 7:21, 32, 33, 34; 11:28; 12:25; Phil. 2:20; 4:6.
14.   See Rom. 12:15; 2 Cor. 2:3; Phil. 3:18; 2 Tim. 1:4.
15.   Paul is not alone with this view. Many NT writers speak of persecution and suffering that comes from being Christian. E.g., see Matt. 5:10; 24:9; Mark 4:17; Luke 11:49; 21:12; John 15:20; Acts 8:1 (inflicted by Paul); 13:50; Heb. 10:33; James 1:2; 1 Peter 4:19; 2 Peter 2:9; Rev. 1:9; 2:10.
16.   See especially Rom. 1:18–2:24; 3:9–20; 13:13; 1 Cor. 5:10–11; 6:9–10; 2 Cor. 12:20–21; Gal. 5:19–21; Eph. 4:17–19; 5:3–6; Col. 3:5–9; 1 Thess. 4:5; 1 Tim. 1:8–10; 2 Tim. 3:1–5.

one's former loves, allegiances, and institutions at conversion (Rom. 6:6; Gal. 2:20; 5:24; 6:14).

In Paul's case, this was a moment of God revealing his Son *into* him, suggesting a profound experience (Gal. 1:16). Luke's account includes Paul's blinding—God causes him to be disabled at his conversion, even if only for a brief time.[17] Paul's sevenfold résumé in Philippians 3:4–7 indicates a degree of "loss" and rubbishing of his special status in Judaism through conversion. While Paul delights in his new pursuit of Christ and his ministry, he has not forgotten his former glory as a Pharisee.[18] There has been a graphic loss of vocation and status and a reasonable degree of shame as Paul and others have converted to Christianity. Similarly, in Galatians 1:13–14, Paul was not only persecuting God's church but was "extremely zealous for the traditions of [his] fathers." While we do not have much to go on in Paul's letters, it's clear the moment of conversion can be a disruptive event in the convert's life.

Similarly, often people who convert face immediate persecution. The Thessalonians receive "the word in much affliction" (θλῖψις, 1 Thess. 1:6). Then, in 1 Thessalonians 2:14, Paul gives thanks again for their imitation of the Judean churches who have suffered persecution (Acts 4–8) "because [they] suffered the same things from [their] own countrymen." No doubt, in turning from idols to God (1 Thess. 1:9), they have experienced rejection and ostracization.

Acts 17:1–10 details some of this, with the conversions of a few God-fearing Gentiles and prominent women through Paul's synagogue ministry. His success provokes an immediate violent response from the Jews of the city, who form a mob with some from the agora and attack the home of Jason, who is undoubtedly one of the first converts. He and others are dragged before the city officials, charged with subversion of Caesar's absolute power and Roman law, and required to pay fines to be released. The frequent references to suffering in 1 Thessalonians indicate this persecution went on after Paul leaves.[19]

First Thessalonians 2:1–2 also confirms the account of the persecution of Paul and Silas in Acts 16. Philippians 1:30 indicates persecution from the local authorities continues in Philippi after Paul leaves. First Thessalonians 2:14–15 also verifies that the Judean Christians are persecuted by fellow Jews (Acts 4–8), which continues the pattern of killing the prophets, Christ, and persecuting Paul and his team.

As the gospel of a crucified Messiah is a stumbling block to Jews and foolishness to Gentiles (1 Cor. 1:23) and there are many "enemies of the cross" (Phil. 3:18), Paul and his converts frequently experience such persecution.

---

17. Acts 9:8–9, 12, 17; 22:11, 13.
18. As I have argued, Philippians 3:14 does not indicate Paul has forgotten his past (indeed he can still recite his résumé, 3:5–6), but he no longer pays attention to it. It is behind him. Keown, *Philippians*, 2:203–4.
19. 1 Thess. 1:6; 2:14; 3:3, 7; 2 Thess. 1:4–6.

Indeed, for Paul, it is axiomatic that "all those who desire to live a godly life in Christ Jesus will be persecuted" (2 Tim. 3:12; also 2 Thess. 3:4). First Timothy 3:6 suggests new converts are vulnerable to the devil's condemnation, especially if they are elevated into church leadership too quickly. This injunction suggests that Paul believes that believers in the early stages of the faith are more vulnerable to demonic threat (see further in the next section).

Suffering Through Pneumaformation

At conversion, the believer's allegiance shifts from other gods and powers to God and his Son, who rules the cosmos. The Spirit floods the believer, and the pneumaformation of the person begins. The Spirit then begins to lead the believer away from flawed selfish desires of the flesh toward love and humble service. This process is not easy. Indeed, Paul speaks of the Christian life as a battle, for "the desires of the flesh are against the Spirit, and the Spirit is against the flesh, for these things are in opposition, so that you do not do what you want to do" (Gal. 5:17). While Romans 7:7–24 is likely Paul's reflection on life under the law now that he is converted (rather than his actual experience before conversion),[20] the passage testifies to the cognitive dissonance all humans experience when they know what God wants but struggle to live up to it.[21] In particular, the war that seeks to take him captive, waged by the law in his members with the law of his mind, speaks of a profound inner struggle to please God that all believers feel on occasion (Rom. 7:23).

Other passages indicate such a struggle for believers as the Spirit seeks to lead them away from their former lives of sin to the life of God. It is often difficult to shift one's mindset from the flesh to the Spirit (Rom. 8:5–8), as is putting to death the misdeeds of the body even with the Spirit's help (Rom. 8:13). The image of following the Spirit suggests walking *away* from former objects of desire (Rom. 8:14). Showing love to challenging believers, submitting to the state, being loving and forgiving and offering hospitality to one's enemies, and refusing to yield to temptations are all challenging (Rom. 12:9–13:13). Romans 14:1–15:7 and 1 Corinthians 8:1–13 testify to disagreements within churches over nonessentials, such as holy days and what foods Christians eat. The resolution of these things requires Paul's intervention, showing the local Christians' struggle to resolve them.

Many of Paul's converts, like the Corinthians, were formerly involved in sexual immorality, idolatry, adultery, same-sex relationships, theft, greed, alcohol abuse, abusiveness, and rapacious behavior, and they struggled with the summons to God's virtues (1 Cor. 6:9–11, 18). The reference to the conflict

---

20. See earlier, chapter 3, "Liberated from Bondage to the Law."
21. Paul may be both reflecting on his life as a Jew now that he is saved and looking forward to life any Christian will experience if they submit to Judaizers and Torah. By analogy, the passage also explains the experience of anyone under oppressive ideologies, including any Christian legalism. The either-or debate about the passage may miss that Paul has all such things in view.

of Spirit and flesh in Galatians 5:17 is closely followed by the vice list of the deeds of the flesh and the virtue list of the fruit of the Spirit. Movement from one way of being to the other is not always easy.

Suffering in Prayer

Another sphere of Spirit-induced struggle is that of prayer. The Romans are exhorted through Christ and the love of the Spirit to contend together (συναγωνίζομαι) with Paul in prayer (Rom. 15:30). Epaphras is commended for struggling in prayer for the Colossians (Col. 4:12). The terms used of struggle in prayer are (συναγωνίζομαι, "struggle together," and ἀγωνίζομαι, "struggle, wrestle"), are athletic terms indicating "strenuous and consistent intervention with the Lord on behalf" of others.[22] Such verses indicate that prayer itself can be a real source of struggle in the Christian life.

SUFFERING AND EVIL SPIRITUAL FORCES

While Paul's apocalyptic dualism is somewhat muted compared to some pseudepigraphal apocalyptic works and Revelation, he does acknowledge the danger of spiritual forces challenging Christians. Clearly, the suffering caused by demonic forces is not the direct agency of the Spirit. However, turning to Christ and following the Spirit moves one into the apocalyptic battle between God and the forces of darkness. Moreover, God uses evil forces in dealing with Christians, as in Paul's thorn in the flesh (further below).

The danger of evil spirits is acknowledged throughout Paul's letters, even if limited. Such spiritual forces can generate slavery to fear (Rom. 8:15);[23] cause spiritual blindness (Rom. 11:8; 2 Cor. 4:4); bring about the destruction of the flesh (1 Cor. 5:5);[24] cause sexual temptation (1 Cor. 7:5; 10:8); entice the desire of evil things, idolatry, and associated revelry; and cause testing Christ, and grumbling (1 Cor. 10:6–13).[25] These beings can negatively influence believers who participate in idolatrous feasts (1 Cor. 10:20–21), can mislead Christians through deception (1 Cor. 12:10; Gal. 3:1),[26] and disguise themselves as messengers of the gospel causing the propagation of a false gospel (2 Cor. 11:4, 14;

---

22. Douglas J Moo, *The Letters to the Colossians and to Philemon*, PNTC (Grand Rapids: Eerdmans, 2008), 344.

23. In that the Spirit is concrete in this passage, Paul may have in view spiritual forces that bind people into fear, akin to the στοιχεῖα (cf. Gal. 4:3, 9).

24. Fee, *GEP*, 126–27.

25. The implication of the general ἐπιθυμητὰς κακῶν, "desires of evil things," is broader than the issues in this passage and would potentially encompass temptation to do any manner of things that are opposed to God's goodness (e.g., the vice lists of 1 Cor. 5:11; 6:9–10). However, 1 Corinthians 10:13 indicates God's limitation of this and his provision of a way out of this.

26. The gift of discerning spirits in 1 Corinthians 12:10 may be associated with recognizing a demonic false utterance. The bewitching of Galatians 3:1 likely indicates demonic deception. See Hans Dieter Betz, *Galatians: A Commentary on Paul's Letter to the Churches in Galatia*, Hermeneia (Philadelphia: Fortress, 1979), 131n31; Fee, *GEP*, 381. For my analysis see Keown, *Galatians*, 408–12.

2 Thess. 2:2; 1 Tim. 4:1).[27] They can cause fleshly torment (2 Cor. 12:7), bring believers back into slavery to elemental spiritual powers and ideas (Gal. 4:9; Col. 2:8), attack those with extreme anger issues (Eph. 4:26),[28] hinder missional travel plans (1 Thess. 2:18), and tempt believers in general (1 Thess. 3:5). The spiritual forces of darkness work against believers through evil and wicked people (2 Thess. 3:2–3),[29] teach excommunicated believers not to blaspheme with false teaching (1 Tim. 1:20), bring condemnation on a conceited convert, especially a new one (1 Tim. 3:6), trap those disgraced through bad relationships outside the church (1 Tim. 3:7), lead believers totally astray to following Satan (1 Tim. 5:15), and set a snare for believers from which they must escape (2 Tim. 2:26).

The most developed discussion of the struggle with spiritual forces is Ephesians 6:10–20, which envisages the Christian as a soldier at war with invisible spiritual powers that strategize against God's people (Eph. 6:12; also 2 Cor. 2:11) and must be resisted (Eph. 6:13), and as fighting against fiery, flaming arrows that must be blocked and extinguished by the shield of faith (Eph. 6:16). To resist Satan, believers must wear God's complete armor of righteous faith, virtue, fidelity to the truth, and prayer in and by the Spirit (v. 18). This all suggests a real struggle that is painful at times.

Suffering in Service

In Romans 7:6, Paul tells his readers that they have been released from bondage to the law and are released "so that we serve in the new way of the Spirit and not in the old way of the written code." Indeed, it is a beautiful thing to be filled with God's Spirit and to receive gifts, something Paul believes is the experience of all Christians (1 Cor. 12:7). However, his letters indicate that obeying the summons of the Spirit and using these gifts in his service inevitably leads to suffering. This inescapability is particularly so for Paul, who regularly refers to his tremendous suffering in his Spirit-led mission (Rom. 15:19).[30] Others in his team were participants in this suffering, as implied by the frequent use of "we," especially in the Corinthian letters. He also mentions the explicit missional suffering of Timothy (2 Tim. 1:8; 4:5). This kind of experience is the same for all believers who dare to share the gospel in a fallen world. Indeed, for Paul, the road on which the Spirit leads believers to glorification is necessarily paved with suffering (Rom. 8:17).[31]

---

27. Also 1 Tim. 5:15; 2 Tim. 2:26.
28. This could apply more broadly in the passage and generally to flagrant sin along the lines of the vices listed in Ephesians 4:17–31.
29. The strengthening and guarding of believers against the evil one immediately follows reference to evil and wicked unbelievers who are challenging Paul.
30. Examples of Paul's missional suffering include 1 Cor. 4:9–13; 15:30–32; 2 Cor. 1:5–10; 2:4; 4:7–18; 6:4–10; 11:23–33; 12:7–10; 16:9; Gal. 5:11; 6:12, 17; Eph. 3:13; Phil. 1:14–24, 29; 2:17; 3:8; 4:12; Col. 1:24; 2:1–2; 1 Thess. 2:2, 9, 15, 17; 3:4, 7; 1 Tim. 4:10; 2 Tim. 1:8, 12; 2:9; 4:6–8, 15.
31. More generally of missional suffering: Rom. 8:35; 12:12, 14–21; 1 Cor. 12:26; Gal. 3:4 (contra Fee, GEP, 386–87, who sees this as the experience of the Spirit). See for my reasoning Keown,

Another aspect of struggle in service is self-provision, something Paul was committed to because the Corinthians treat him as a client (1 Cor. 9:1–15)[32]; this is to ensure the gospel is offered free of charge (1 Cor. 9:18), to ensure he is not a financial burden,[33] to avoid being seen as a peddler of the gospel like others (2 Cor. 2:17), and to set an example to his converts of work and faith (2 Thess. 3:8–15). He is prepared to accept financial support when he leaves a city and where it is offered without the constraints of the patron-client relationship (Phil. 2:25–30; 4:10–19). While Paul believes that providing for himself enhances his mission, it also causes him to suffer through the night-and-day labor involved in tentmaking (Acts 18:3) and preaching the gospel (1 Thess. 2:9; 2 Thess. 3:8). He also has periods of poverty in his ministry, indicating that Christian missionaries are not immune to financial privation (1 Cor. 4:13; 2 Cor. 11:27; Phil. 4:12).

Strong opposition to Paul is mentioned at times in 1 Corinthians (1 Cor. 15:32;[34] 16:9). Second Corinthians is full of intense descriptions of his team's suffering during their mission to Asia Minor (2 Cor. 1:8–11), more generally (2 Cor. 4:7–18; 5:4; 6:3–10), and in Macedonia (2 Cor. 7:5). Paul's ironic boast of his sufferings in 2 Corinthians 11:22–33 speaks of a life racked with imprisonment, violence, near drownings and death (cf. Rom. 16:4; Phil. 2:27), danger, hard work, hardship, and multiple pressures of church leadership. His "thorn in the flesh" could relate to torment caused by others (2 Cor. 12:7). Whatever it was, Paul knew weakness, insults, calamities, persecutions, and difficulties (2 Cor. 12:10). Death was a real possibility (Phil. 1:20–23), and it is imminent in 2 Timothy 4:6–8. Paul's appeal to the Galatians to not become weary in doing good hints at the danger of compassion fatigue (Gal. 6:10).

The employment of military, athletic, labor, work, and farming metaphors used of mission also point to struggle and suffering for the cause of the kingdom.[35] A good example is Philippians 1:27–30, where the Philippians

---

Galatians, 306–10. I note that the term πάσχω is used exclusively by Paul of Christ's sufferings and/or a believer's participation in them (Phil. 1:29–30; 2:17; 3:18; 1 Thess. 2:14; 2 Thess. 1:5). See also Cosgrove, Cross, 185.

32. Garland writes, "He did not want to become a client of the donors. Gifts brought obligations to reciprocate in some way. . . . Friendship in the ancient world was built around a system of unwritten accounts and debits. One had to respond in kind to gifts or benefits . . . Paul would not have been 'free to preach the gospel with boldness if he is having to run around kissing men's hands, sending them gifts, groveling before them, and slavishly flattering them.' . . . 'He must be free to rebuke, and his praise must be above the suspicion of being bought.' He did not want to get trapped in the sticky web of social obligations that would hinder his freedom to preach and admonish. . . . He refused to become anyone's 'kept apostle' (cf. 2 Cor. 12:14) or 'house apostle.'" Garland, 1 Corinthians, 419.

33. See 2 Cor. 11:9; 12:13–16; 1 Thess. 2:9; 2 Thess. 3:8.

34. On this as metaphorical, see Abraham J. Malherbe, "The Beasts at Ephesus," JBL 87, no. 1 (1968):71–80.

35. Military (Rom. 13:12; 1 Cor. 14:8; 2 Cor. 6:7; 10:3–6; Eph. 6:10–17; Phil. 1:12, 27–28; 2:25; 1 Thess. 5:8; 1 Tim. 1:18; 6:12; 2 Tim. 4:7; Philem. 2); athletic (1 Cor. 9:24–27; Gal. 2:2; Phil. 1:27; 2:16; 3:12–14; 4:3; 2 Thess. 3:1); labor (1 Cor. 3:8; 4:12; 15:10, 58; 16:16; 2 Cor. 11:27; Gal. 4:11 [childbirth and

are to be observed standing firm in one Spirit (στήκετε ἐν ἑνὶ πνεύματι), contending as one soul for the faith of the gospel (μιᾷ ψυχῇ συναθλοῦντες τῇ πίστει τοῦ εὐαγγελίου) without being intimidated by the opposition that is inflicting the same kind of suffering on them that Paul has experienced in Philippi (Acts 16:11–40) and Rome (1:12–26). Paul's description of their sacrifice and service in Philippians 2:17 confirms this suffering.

Epaphroditus is to be honored for falling ill and nearly dying while delivering the Philippian gift to Paul in prison (Phil. 2:25–30). Paul testifies to Epaphras's hard work on behalf of the Christians of the Lycus Valley (Col. 4:13). Ephesians 6:15 and 17 focus on a Christian's readiness to stand and move with the gospel of peace and use the sword of the Spirit, the Word of God, for defending and advancing the gospel. The use of military language indicates struggle and contention.

The Thessalonians are very active in gospel work, with the word of the Lord resounding from them into the world (1 Thess. 1:8; cf. 1:3).[36] This active evangelization may have been a reason for the persecution they experienced.[37] Paul's challenge to Timothy to join him in suffering for the gospel also indicates Paul expected it (2 Tim. 1:8; 2:3).

A range of other challenges comes from following the Spirit into mission. These challenges include demonic interference in Paul's mission plans (1 Thess. 2:18), the immense amount of travel many early Christians engaged in to share the faith (e.g., Rom. 15:19, 22–32; 1 Cor. 16:5–9), uncertainty over travel plans (Rom. 1:10–13; 2 Cor. 1:15–17), anguish from kith and kin who have not accepted the gospel (Rom. 9:1–4; 10:1). And there are risks taken to save others (Rom. 16:4), hospitality and making one's home available for church gatherings (Rom. 16:5, 13, 23), secretarial work (Rom. 16:22), and concern over coworkers (2 Cor. 2:13).[38] Engaging in mission brings suffering for the pneumaformed believer.

Suffering from Others Who Claim to Be Christians

Much of the suffering Paul endures comes from those he perceives as false teachers. In Romans, Paul quotes opponents who distort his theology with

---

mothering]; Eph. 4:28; Phil. 2:16; Col. 1:29; 1 Thess. 1:3; 2:9; 3:5; 5:12; 2 Thess. 3:8; 4:10; 5:17); work (Rom. 2:7; 16:6, 12, 21; 1 Cor. 3:13–15; 4:12; 9:1; 15:58; 16:16; 2 Cor. 9:8; Gal. 6:4; Eph. 2:10; 4:12, 16, 28; Phil. 1:22; 2:12, 30; Col. 1:28; 4:13; 1 Thess. 1:3; 2:9; 4:11; 5:12; 2 Thess. 1:11; 2:17; 3:8–12; 1 Tim. 3:1; 5:10, 18, 25; 6:18; 2 Tim. 2:15, 21; 3:17; 4:5; Titus 3:1; also coworkers—Rom. 16:3, 9, 21; 1 Cor. 3:9; 2 Cor. 1:24; 6:1; 8:23; Phil. 2:25; 4:3; Col. 4:11; Philem. 1, 24); farming (Rom. 1:13; 1 Cor. 3:6; 9:7; 2 Cor. 9:10; 2 Tim. 2:6).

36. On 1 Thessalonians 1:8 as indicative of active evangelization, see Keown, *Congregational*, 257–60; Ware, "The Thessalonians as a Missionary Congregation," 126–31.

37. First Thess. 1:6; 2:15; 3:3; 2 Thess. 1:4, 6.

38. I concur with Fee that this is the human spirit (contra Robert Jewett, *Paul's Anthropological Terms: A Study of Their Use in Conflict Settings*, AGJU 10 [Leiden: Brill, 1971], 192–94). Fee, *GEP*, 297. However, I would aver that it is with the internal spirit of Paul that God, in Christ, by the Spirit, "spoke" to Paul, generating in him deep concern for Titus as he did not find him in Troas.

outrageous conclusions (Rom. 3:8; 6:1, 14). Such people are likely those who cause dissensions and temptations contrary to sound doctrine, who gluttonously serve their own stomachs, and who use smooth speech and flattery to deceive the hearts of the unsuspecting (Rom. 16:18).

In Paul's elaborate defense against false teachers in 2 Corinthians 10–12, he notes many who are peddlers of the word (2:17). In the final chapters, he defends himself against teachers attacking the Corinthians. They are Jewish (11:21–22) critics who demean his ministry (10:10); commend themselves (10:12); preach another Jesus and gospel (11:4); and are super-apostles (11:5; 12:11), false apostles, and deceitful workers who disguise themselves as apostles of Christ (11:14).

The letter of Galatians is occasioned by advocates of Jewish laws of circumcision (2:3, 12; 5:3; 6:12–13), eating (2:11–14), and the calendar (4:10) who are bewitching (3:1) the Galatians with a false gospel.[39] Galatians 2:17 suggests that these teachers argued Paul's doctrine of justification makes Christ an agent of sin and accused him of inconsistency concerning circumcision (5:11). Paul is astonished at the Galatians' entertaining these ideas (1:6), shocked enough to call them foolish and bewitched (3:1, 3). They have made him afraid that his work among them is fruitless (4:11) and that he has become their enemy (4:16). Adopting the posture of a profoundly concerned mother, he is perplexed with them in their limited christoformation (4:19–20).

Paul responds to the same types of people in Philippians 3:2–11 and with other Greco-Roman licentious enemies in 3:18–21.[40] Colossians 2 alludes to a Jewish philosophical gospel advocating adherence to the Jewish calendar and a diminution of Christ to the status of an angel (vv. 2:8–23).

There are indications that Paul is dealing with opponents, Christian or otherwise, in his apologia in 1 Thessalonians 2:1–12 (also 1:5).[41] The backdrop of 1 Timothy is people teaching other doctrines, including an interest in myths, genealogies, and speculations (1:3–4). They misunderstand the law (1:7–10). They likely include Hymenaeus and Alexander, who have been excommunicated (1 1:20), and some women (2:9–15). These teachers are demonically deceived, forbid marriage, restrict certain foods (4:1–5), and preach to make money (6:3–10). Second Timothy likely refers to the same group, including Hymenaeus and Philetus, who preach that the final resurrection has occurred (1:17–18). They are characterized by a range of vices, including loving money and pleasure, denying the power of God (the Spirit), manipulating vulnerable women (3:1–9), and creating a gospel of myths aligned with their desires (4:3–4).

---

39. Gal. 1:6–8; 2:4–5; 4:17; 5:7–12.

40. Keown, *Philippians*, 2:253–65.

41. These may be Christian critics of his approach. However, considering the early date of 1 Thessalonians (ca. AD 50), these may be Judaizers. Paul is likely defending himself against charges of using deception, flattery, and greed.

Titus gives evidence of divisive false Jewish teachers in Crete who seek dishonest gain and focus on Jewish myths, laws, and genealogies (1:10–14; 3:9–11). Such false teachers undoubtedly caused immense suffering as Paul and his churches sought to follow the Spirit's lead.

Suffering from Christians

At other times, Paul suffers at the hands of genuine Christians with questionable motivations. The letters to the Corinthians are addressed to τοῖς ἁγίοις in Corinth, Achaia, and beyond, and so are written to people Paul still considers Christians (1 Cor. 1:2; 2 Cor. 1:1).[42] Yet, 1 Corinthians is replete with evidence of Christians causing Paul no end of anguish through their preference for other preachers, divisions, and broken relationships destroying the unity of the temple of the Spirit (1 Cor. 1:10–12; 3:16–17, 22; 11:18). They have also preferred to continue in sexual immorality (5:1–13; 6:12–21) and public lawsuits (6:1–11), falling back into other old vices (5:11; 6:9–11; also 2 Cor. 12:21). False understandings of marriage (chapter 7), disagreements over idol food (8:1–13; 10:23–11:1), anti-Paulinism (chapter 9), idolatry (10:1–22), dishonorable dress and treatment of the Lord's Supper (11:2–34), misunderstandings of spiritual gift use in worship, particularly tongues (chaps. 12, 14), loveless treatment of one another (12:31–13:13), and false understandings of resurrection (chapter 15) have also prevented true unity. The letter itself speaks of Paul's need to censure them and even excommunicate one from their midst (5:5), and to do so again if need be (5:13; cf. 1 Tim. 1:20; Titus 3:10–11). Such decisions create suffering and pain for those making the decisions, the person involved, and the church.

Several passages indicate suffering due to money matters. One aspect of the Corinthian problem was Paul's refusal to accept their patronage while accepting the benefaction of others (1 Cor. 9:1–15; 11:8–9; 12:14–17). Paul also had issues getting the Corinthians to contribute to the Jerusalem collection (esp. 2 Corinthians 8–9).

Second Corinthians speaks of a member of the Corinthian church who was causing Paul great anguish. Paul acknowledges that the member has done the same to the Corinthians, and that the Corinthians have punished that person (2 Cor. 2:1–6). Paul's letters have also caused the Corinthians grief (7:8), and he determines not to travel again to the city to avoid further grief (2:1–11; 7:12). He also mentions the "godly" grief that leads to sorrow and repentance (7:10). This speaks of the convicting work of the Spirit.

While the problem in Galatia is false teachers, the letter indicates struggle among Christians. Notable is the public clash between Paul and Peter over Jews and Gentiles eating together (Gal. 2:11–14). Galatians 5:13, 25, and the

---

42. Also notable is the use of ἀδελφοί twenty-one times as a term of address through the two letters. See also "my beloved children" (1 Cor. 4:14, 17); "my beloved" (1 Cor. 10:14; 2 Cor. 7:1; 12:19); "my beloved brothers [and sisters]" (1 Cor. 15:58).

vice list of vv. 19–21 indicate a range of divisive and destructive behaviors that have beset the Galatians as some flirted with false teaching.

An example of Christians causing Paul suffering is Philippians 1:14–18. Paul is in Roman custody, and his presence has catalyzed other believers to preach the gospel. The description "preach Christ" indicates that they are not false teachers, as opposed to those mentioned in Philippians 3:2 and 18.[43] Among those actively engaging in evangelism in the city are those motivated by envy, rivalry, selfish ambition, and a desire to cause Paul suffering. Philippi's contending parties are also falling prey to similar attitudes and are in danger of serious rupture (Phil. 4:2–3).[44] Little wonder Paul refers to "the daily pressure on me of my anxiety for all the churches" (2 Cor. 11:28).

Suffering in the Lead-Up to Christ's Return

Paul does not speculate too much on the events leading to the return of Christ and the end of the age. However, although heavily disputed, I consider that 2 Thessalonians 2:1–10 stands in parallel to the abomination in Mark 13:14 and the beasts of Revelation 13 and presages a period of magnified suffering on earth before the consummation.[45] These passages stand in continuity with Jewish messianic woe texts.[46] Other Pauline texts potentially hint at this.[47]

In 2 Thessalonians, Paul speaks of a rebellion, the revelation of the "man of lawlessness," or "the son of destruction" who opposes every aspect of religion and declares himself God and establishes himself in God's throne room (2:3–4). Paul here seems to be referring to a period of intense suffering prior to Christ's return.[48] This period of suffering seems to be an extreme escalation of the persecution Christians experience at the hands of a world hostile to God and his people. God restrains this amplification in some way until he is revealed at the time of God's choosing. It will climax with Jesus's return and his destruction of the lawless one. The period will involve the mass deception of many through false but powerful signs and wonders and the deception of those who are deluded and perishing and do not accept the gospel. Those so

---

43. Whereas these preachers "preach Christ," those in 3:2 are "dogs, evil workers, mutilators," and in 3:18 they are "enemies of the cross of Christ." Clearly, the former are not in the same category as those in chapter 3.

44. The rhetorical power of earlier parts of Philippians suggests Paul has an eye on the contention between Euodia and Syntyche, supposing that some of the issues they were dealing with included envy, rivalry (Phil. 1:15), selfish ambition (Phil. 1:17; 2:3), a pursuit of personal glory (Phil. 2:3), and grumbling and arguing (Phil. 2:14).

45. Similarly, see Bruce, *1 & 2 Thessalonians*, 166–69.

46. See Stanley E. Porter, "Tribulation, Messianic Woes," *DLNTD* 1180–81.

47. See especially 1 Thessalonians 5:3. Rather than contradict 2 Thessalonians 2 as some argue, this passage simply speaks of the sudden onset of the period of destruction including the events of the chapter. See also Romans 8:22, if Paul has in view a woman's pains in childbearing that grow stronger near birth.

48. See F. F. Bruce's analysis mentioned above.

deceived will be condemned to eternal destruction. There is no evidence of a secret rapture in Christ, but a climactic, publicly visible return of Christ (1 Thess. 4:13–5:10).[49]

Suffering as a Gift

In Philippians 1:28–30, Paul says that suffering is a gift from God. The passage gives clear indications of what is going on for the Philippians. First, the Philippians are being challenged by adversaries (ἀντίκειμαι). The word ἀντίκειμαι is the antonym of κεῖμαι which Paul uses in Philippians 1:16 of his own "appointment" to defend the gospel. These adversaries are "appointed" to oppose Christians.[50] This description may imply demonic interference under God's sovereignty.

Second, the Philippians are having the same "agony" that Paul has in Philippi earlier and now in his imprisonment. His earlier visit would have been either the evangelization of the city (Acts 16:11–40) or his two visits on his Jerusalem collection trip.[51] On the first trip to Philippi, he is flogged by the Roman authorities and imprisoned. He suffers severe persecution on his second visit (2 Cor. 7:5), and we know nothing of persecution in his third (which appears to have been brief).[52] Presently, Paul is in Rome, where there is contention among Christians concerning him (Phil. 1:15–18a), and he is facing trial and perhaps death (Phil. 1:19–24). Some consider that false teachers are causing the suffering. However, these are not mentioned until Philippians 3:2 and appear to be an external threat more than anything within Philippi. Hence, it is likely that in 1:29–30, Paul is referring to the threat of Roman authorities who punished and imprisoned him. They could also be part of the problem of 2 Corinthians 7:5. As such, it is likely that the local town leaders are persecuting the Philippians at the time Paul writes.

Whatever the exact problem, the Philippians' unwavering commitment to defending and advancing the gospel functions as a sign of their salvation and the destruction of their enemies (Phil. 1:28). Furthermore, Paul considers the sign to function in this way "for it has been granted to you that for the sake of Christ you should not only believe in him but also suffer for his sake."[53] As

---

49. While 1 Thessalonians 4:17 might refer to a rapture of the dead in Christ, there is nothing secret about it, and the event appears to be the end of the age. At this point, believers go with Christ to heaven (e.g. Charles A. Wanamaker, *The Epistles to the Thessalonians: A Commentary on the Greek Text*, NIGTC [Grand Rapids: Eerdmans, 1990], 169–70); or they accompany Christ to earth (Shogren, *1 & 2 Thessalonians*, 189–90), as I prefer (Keown, *Discovering: The Pauline Letters*, 299–303).

50. Keown, *Philippians*, 1:303.

51. Paul's original intent was to travel through Macedonia to Achaia and then to Jerusalem. However, he changed his plans and went through Macedonia to Achaia and back and then on to Jerusalem (see Acts 20:1, 3; Rom. 15:26; 1 Cor. 16:5; 2 Cor. 1:16; 2:13; 7:5; 8:1).

52. See Acts 20:3, where ὑποστρέφειν διὰ Μακεδονίας speaks merely of passing through.

53. Translation mine; see Keown, *Philippians*, 1:283.

I have explored elsewhere in some depth,[54] both the faith in Christ exercised by the Philippians and their suffering at the hands of the Roman authorities in Philippi are seen as gifts from God.

This perspective is consistent with Paul's view of suffering elsewhere in Philippians. His imprisonment is "in Christ" (1:12); his suffering at the hands of opponents is causing the gospel to advance and Paul to rejoice (1:12, 15, 17, 18a). His chains may end in death, but Paul rejoices because he knows it will turn out for his deliverance (if released) and, if not, his salvation (1:19). Moreover, he will have the opportunity to give bold witness before the authorities so that Christ is exalted in his body, whatever the outcome (1:20).

Participation in suffering is to live out of the phronesis of Christ, who died on the cross (2:5, 8). Wonderfully, due to his self-emptying, voluntary enslavement and his humble obedience to death to save the world, God then gifted (same Greek, χαρίζομαι) Jesus the name above every name. This points to believers being transformed to have a body of glory like his at their own resurrection (3:20–21). The Philippians' suffering is a sacrifice and service coming from their faith, being poured out as a libation (2:17), as is Paul's. Epaphroditus's service in becoming ill and nearly dying to bring the Philippians' gifts to Paul emulates Christ's sacrifice (esp. 2:30). They are urged to follow Paul's single focus of pressing on in his faith and mission despite enemies of the cross (3:12–19).

Through all this, they will grow in their knowledge of Christ and "the power of his resurrection, and the partnership in his sufferings, being conformed into the likeness of his death" (3:10, my translation).[55] Like Paul, in poverty, they will learn the secret of God's strengthening to enable them to survive all situations (4:12–13) and of his provision, often through other Christians (4:14–19).

While God is not the direct agent of the suffering people experience, this suffering is, for Paul, a gift. In and through it, believers grow in their relationship with God and are pneumaformed as the Spirit transforms them through their suffering and ministers to them in their pain. Furthermore, while the suffering itself is repulsive, God works through it to bring redemption to others, as the power of his message is amplified for those with ears to hear. As such, suffering is a redemptive gift for believers and for unbelievers.

SUFFERING IN CHRIST

While Paul recognizes that Christ's suffering and death is a unique salvific event, he understands Christian suffering to be participation in the sufferings of Christ. A believer's suffering is a gift from Christ and on his behalf (Phil. 1:29). Yet, at times, Paul goes further than merely saying Christian suffering

---

54. Keown, *Philippians*, 1:311–15.
55. Translation mine; see Keown, *Philippians*, 2:164.

is for Christ's sake; he links Christian suffering to Christ himself and sees it as participation in and an extension of Christ's suffering.[56]

In Romans 8:17, those who have received the Spirit of adoption and are led by this Spirit are God's children. As children, they are heirs of God and joint heirs with Christ (συγκληρονόμος). However, the full receipt of this glorious inheritance is for those who "suffer *with* him" (συμπάσχω). The Spirit leads people on the journey to glory along the path of suffering with Christ as they serve him and his purposes in the world. Again, while God's comfort is assured for believers, the "sufferings of Christ *overflow* to us" (2 Cor. 1:5 LEB). This suggests that Christian suffering is an extension of Christ's suffering. The link between Christ and the believer in this regard is the Spirit.

Philippians 3:10 confirms both that Christian suffering is participation in Christ's suffering and that the Spirit is intimately involved. Paul wants to know Christ and the power of his resurrection. Here, the "power of his resurrection" is the Spirit who raised Christ from the dead.[57] Yet, Paul does not stop there—he does not simply yearn to know this power in terms of miracles and signs and wonders (important though this is to him). He wants to know this power in the context of partnership in Christ's sufferings. And this is not a trifling desire; he wants to be conformed to his death. That is, Paul wants to give his whole life to service and suffering for Christ and his mission, even to death. This mindset is his focus in Philippians 2:5–8. He wants the Philippians to join him in it (Phil. 3:15–17).

In Colossians 1:24, Paul speaks of Christians partnering with Christ in a different way again. Believers "fill up in [their] flesh what is lacking of the afflictions of Christ" (LEB). The suffering of believers is seen in some way as a continuation and completion of Christ's life of suffering. It is by the Spirit that this comes to pass, as Christ participates in the believer's life by his Spirit. This toil includes Paul's great struggle for the Colossians and Laodiceans, which is on their behalf (Col. 2:1).

FORMATION THROUGH SUFFERING

Romans 5:3–5

I will focus here on Romans 5:3–5, discussed at different points in this book, as I bring out different aspects of the Spirit's work in believers. In Romans 5, having argued for justification by faith and not works of the law, Paul turns to other consequences of Christ's work for those justified by faith.

---

56. Paul's boasting in 2 Corinthians 11:21–33 is also premised on his understanding that suffering in the service of Christ is evidence of the depth of his service as compared to his opponents.

57. Keown, *Philippians*, 2:166–70.

In Romans 5:1–2, Paul tells the Romans that their former enmity with God due to sin is dealt with in Christ. They now have "peace with God," achieved through Jesus's propitiatory death (v. 1).[58] Moreover, through Christ, they have access to God's grace by believing in him. In this grace, they now stand firm (v. 2). Having received these blessings, all believers (we) now boast in the hope of the glory of God. Hope suggests this is a future eschatological hope of the day they inherit eternal life in all its glory.

Not only do they boast in their future experience of the fullness of glory, but believers boast in sufferings. These sufferings include all things that blight people due to sin and the consequent corruption of the cosmos—relational discord, injustices, oppression, war, illness, abuse, demonic oppression, decay, death, and so on. They also include the suffering the Spirit "causes" in believers seeking to live in a manner worthy of the Lord—ethical struggle, relational challenges, and persecution.

Oxymoronically, believers boast in these hideous things that inflict so much pain. Paul then explains why with the causal εἰδότες, "because we know that . . .". Suffering produces the ethical transformation of the believer. He demonstrates this with a chain (*litotes*) of consequences produced in the believer, beginning with suffering and climaxing with hope.

First, suffering produces or works (κατεργάζομαι) perseverance or endurance (ὑπομονή).[59] While the subject of the verb is the nominative θλῖψις, suffering is not an entity that has the power to do anything. It is impotent in and of itself. As such, while he is personifying suffering and other virtues in this section, Paul is implying that it is not the suffering itself that is the subject of this working, but God, working in and through the negative experience of the person in Christ, by his Spirit. Indeed, the role of the Spirit becomes explicit in v. 5. By his Spirit, as believers experience suffering following the Spirit, the same Spirit generates endurance, perseverance, resilience, and hope in them.

In the second element, ὑπομονή is the subject, and the same verb κατεργάζομαι is implied. Again, the agency of the Spirit is intimated as the presence of God to empower the Christian toward δοκιμή. Δοκιμή is translated "character," but as the term is used for a testing process or ordeal (2 Cor. 8:2),[60] it carries the idea of proven character, reliability under fire, and resilience.[61] The Spirit of God, then, uses suffering to produce perseverance and character in his people.

---

58.   See further chapter 4, "The Spirit Who Reconciles People to God and Each Other."
59.   On ὑπομονή see further in this chapter, "Perseverance in Suffering."
60.   BDAG, s.v. "δοκιμή," 256.
61.   The term is used to describe Timothy in Philippians 2:22. He is proven and reliable through his unfailing service to Christ in the gospel with Paul.

In the third element of the litotes, the subject becomes "proven character" (δοκιμή), again the verb is implied, and what is produced is ἐλπίς, "hope."[62] Hope is a confident expectation for the future, despite present suffering. This hope includes the eschatological hope of the consummation when Christ returns and the world is liberated from its bondage to decay. This dimension of hope is the sense of v. 5, where the outcome of the suffering Christian's life is not shame, but its implied converse, honor (the glory of God, see v. 2). Yet, v. 5b indicates that hope is not just for the age to come. The basis for hope and honor, not shame, is the outpouring of God's love into believers' hearts through the Spirit given to believers by God. The love of God poured into the hearts of suffering Christians in the present comforts them and assures them of their status in Christ. The Spirit, the foretaste of the eschaton, works in the believers, not only forming them but also assuring them.

This passage alerts readers that suffering is an essential aspect of their pneumaformation.[63] Through the suffering caused by other people, fallen creation, and demonic forces, God works to shape his people and church to be more Christlike.[64] His opponents have no theology of suffering, believing life in Christ is prosperity and blessing. Paul knows better, and so must we as we face prosperity ideas today.

2 Corinthians 11:23–33

In 2 Corinthians 11:23–33, Paul "boasts" of his many missional sufferings that demonstrate his commitment to Christ compared to that of his opponents. Then, speaking of himself impersonally (I know a man), he recounts a remarkable heavenly visionary experience (likely to match or better such visionary claims from his opponents). Rejecting boasting of such things, he boasts about his weaknesses (2 Cor. 12:5, 7). He does so because they demonstrate his participation in Christ and his commitment to the gospel mission.

In 2 Corinthians 12:7, Paul shifts to a thorn in the flesh given to him. Many options concerning this thorn include opponents, a psychological issue, or a physical ailment.[65] Whatever Paul has in mind, this is "a messenger of Satan [ἄγγελος σατανᾶ]," indicating that the source of this is demonic. Yet, for Paul, God is sovereign over demons as well, and in that he allowed Paul to be afflicted in this way, God is the ultimate giver of the thorn. The purpose of his doing so is so that this spiritual being would buffet (κολαφίζω) him to ensure he does not become arrogant.

---

62.   On hope, see further later in the chapter, "Hope in Suffering."

63.   "Suffering therefore has redemptive value, as believers experience the presence of God's Spirit in prayerful anticipation of the future glory (Rom. 8:26–27) and suffer with Christ (8:17) as a continuation of the narrative of divine love." Gorman, *CPNSC*, 328–29.

64.   "Even Christ, on the human side, was made perfect through suffering, and though He were a son, yet learned He obedience through the things which He endured." Lewis Sperry Chafer, *Systematic Theology* (Grand Rapids: Kregel, 1993), 2:231. See Heb. 5:8.

65.   I consider a physical ailment most likely. See also Fee, *GEP*, 352; Harris, *2 Corinthians*, 857–59.

Verse 8 indicates that Paul thrice pleads (παρακαλέω) with Christ (τὸν κύριον) about this (ὑπὲρ τούτου). The content of his prayer is that (ἵνα) "it would depart from me" (ἀποστῇ ἀπ᾽ ἐμοῦ). Although the Spirit is not mentioned, implied is Paul's request that the Spirit drive away the demonic influence.

It is clear from v. 9a that God chooses not to do so. Instead, God answers that his grace is sufficient for Paul. Here, χάρις is a description of the work of the Spirit in Paul—God and his Son reaching out to Paul by the Spirit and providing help and support in his torment.

Verse 9b is launched by a causal γάρ indicating the reason God has chosen to leave Paul in his suffering with his grace (the Spirit) as support: "because my power [δύναμις] is made perfect in weakness." What Paul means by δύναμις being perfected is not clear. For Paul, undoubtedly, God's power is already perfect and absolute; hence, he does not here mean some enhancement of God's power. God is utterly omnipotent! Instead, it likely has two aspects. First, it refers to the power of God's influence within the sufferer as the love of the Spirit generates perseverance, character, and hope in the believer (cf. Rom. 5:3–5). In this regard, God's power generates the fruit of the Spirit in sufferers as they place their dependence on him and are transformed by God's grace and power.

Second, it speaks of the capacity to influence others as the power of God works through the suffering believer toward them. This impact is seen when believers suffer immensely yet display the character of the Spirit, and others observe in them such things as an ongoing commitment, faith, hope, resilience, missional engagement, and the fruit of the Spirit. Another dimension of this is where believers in genuine suffering engage in ministry. The power of the gospel is enhanced as people observe the resilient sufferer sharing their experience of God's grace without losing confidence in God and still proclaiming his excellencies.

This passion is evident in Paul. He suffered greatly as an apostle. Yet, by his Spirit, God worked in and through Paul, transforming him and converting others, including the Corinthians. As a result, despite God leaving him with an "angel of Satan" to torment him, Paul boasts most gladly (Ἥδιστα οὖν μᾶλλον καυχήσομαι, v. 10d) in his weaknesses. The content of his boast is that (ἵνα) the power of Christ may tabernacle (ἐπισκηνώσῃ) in him.

The term ἐπισκηνόω is derived from σκηνόω, meaning "to pitch a tent."[66] It thus invokes thoughts of the tabernacle (e.g., Exod. 25:9; 26:1), where God meets Moses (Exod. 29:42) and into which he descended as Israel moved through the wilderness and into the land (Exod. 33:9–11; 40:34–36). The verb invokes Paul's idea of the believer and church as "the temple of the Spirit." The power in view then is the Spirit. Of course, Paul already has the Spirit in him, having believed in him and received the Spirit at conversion. Hence, the

---

66.   BDAG, s.v. "ἐπισκηνόω," 278.

mention of the "power of Christ" speaks of an enhanced experience of that power due to his suffering.

As such, Paul not only boasts in his weaknesses, but because they lead to the enhancement of God's power in his person and ministry, he delights (εὐδοκέω) in them. His delight is like that of God for his Son[67] and his people (Luke 12:32); it is akin to the delight of God to fill Christ (Col. 1:19), save people (1 Cor. 1:21), and call Paul (Gal. 1:15).[68]

Paul next gives a short list of his other sufferings that he delights in because of how it enhances the power of God in his being and ministry: "insults" (ὕβρις), "hardships" (ἀνάγκη), "persecutions" (διωγμός), and "anguishes" (στενοχωρία) experienced for the sake of Christ. Signaled by γάρ, he concludes in the final clause of v. 10 with what may be a Pauline maxim: "for whenever I am weak, then I am strong."

We can surmise from this that Paul believes that sufferings experienced in the service of Christ are the Lord's means of advancing their character and ministry. The challenges actually enhance the experience of the Spirit inwardly, increasing the capacity of the believer to produce the fruit of the Spirit. Further, they empower a believer's ministry.

THE SPIRIT'S SUPPORT IN SUFFERING

Much has been discussed above concerning the Spirit as a "cause" of suffering for the good of the Christian, the church, and the mission. Yet, God does not leave his people as orphans in their suffering. Paul understands that the Spirit, God, and Christ are an endless resource of support to believers as they experience the miseries of life and the suffering that comes from being a Christian in a hostile world. While God calls his people to suffer, he equips them to endure and grow through their pain.

The Intercession of the Spirit and Son

The first aspect of this equipping is the ongoing intercession of the Spirit for believers in Romans 8:26–27, discussed more fully in chapter 5.[69] En route to glory, believers suffer with Christ (Rom. 8:17). As creation writhes and groans in travail in its suffering, so also believers groan inwardly and endure, patiently awaiting their final redemption (Rom. 8:19–23, 25). In Romans 8:26–27, the Spirit helps believers in their weakness and uncertainty concerning how to pray by interceding for believers with wordless groans and in accordance with God's will. Similarly, seated at the right hand of God, Christ intercedes for believers (Rom. 8:34).

---

67. See Matt. 12:28; 17:5; Mark 1:11; 2 Peter 1:17.
68. Or the delight of the Christians of Macedonia and Achaia to contribute to the Jerusalem collection (Rom. 15:26–27); or of Paul to preach to the Thessalonians (1 Thess. 2:8). Also 1 Cor. 10:5; 2 Thess. 2:12; Heb. 10:6, 8, 38.
69. Chapter 5, "Prayer and the Spirit."

God's Love in Suffering

Perhaps the most fundamental aspect of the Spirit's support is the ongoing experience of God's love in suffering. By the Spirit who resides in believers' hearts, God reaches out to his people bringing emotional support and strengthening that enables believers to persevere through the most horrible of times.

ROMANS 5:5–8

God's comfort through love is apparent in Romans 5:5, where Paul lists an inferential chain of afflictions, endurance, character, and hope. Hope does not disappoint or bring shame because God has demonstrated his love in Christ's death (Rom. 5:8) and poured his love into the hearts of believers. Love sustains believers in suffering.

ROMANS 8:35–40

Romans 8:18–39 picks up some of the same themes as Romans 5, but focuses more intently on God's help in suffering and the hope believers have in Christ.[70] The memorable Romans 8:35 and 37–40 restate this with more detail. Paul asks whether there is anyone or anything in creation that can separate a beloved believer (Rom. 1:7) from the love of God and Christ. Included in Romans 8:35 are general descriptions of affliction (θλῖψις ἢ στενοχωρία, "affliction or distress"), human violence that causes suffering (διωγμὸς, "persecution," κίνδυνος, "danger," and μάχαιρα, "violence by the sword"), and common problems associated with suffering (λιμὸς, "starvation," γυμνότης, "lack of clothing"). The implied answer is, "No, they cannot separate a believer from the love of Christ."[71]

The rationale is given in vv. 38–39—Paul is convinced nothing can separate a believer from the love of God in Christ Jesus. He gives another list of threats, including the future termination of earthly life that is inevitable (θάνατος, "death"), present experience (ζωή, "life," ἐνεστῶτα, "things present"), spiritual and political powers (ἄγγελοι, "angels," ἀρχαὶ, "rulers," δυνάμεις, "powers," ὕψωμα, "things above," βάθος, "the depth"),[72] or anything that can come (μέλλοντα). Finally, Paul generalizes his list into "any other created thing" (τις κτίσις ἑτέρα), emphatically indicating that nothing in the created order can separate a believer from God's love. Consequently, the love of God poured into believers by the Spirit sustains them as they suffer.

---

70. Keown, "Notes of Hope."

71. The genitive τῆς ἀγάπης τοῦ Χριστοῦ is clearly subjective.

72. The terms "height" and "depth" were used in astrology, while "powers" may refer to a magician's capacities. Leon Morris, *The Epistle to the Romans*, PNTC (Grand Rapids: Eerdmans, 1988), 341–42. See also Ernst Käsemann, *Commentary on Romans* (Grand Rapids: Eerdmans, 1994), 251–52. They are not merely spatial, as Moo claims. Moo, *Letter to the Romans*, 568. See also Keown, *Romans and the Mission of God*, 105–6.

PHILIPPIANS 1:28–2:1

Linked to the same thread, the Philippians experience consolation *from love* during persecution. This suffering is likened to that of Paul's in times past in Philippi and his present incarceration (1:28–2:1). Hence, it is unsurprising that Paul prays for the Thessalonians that God and Christ "who has loved [them] and given [them] eternal encouragement [παράκλησις] and good hope by grace, might encourage [παρακαλέω] [their] hearts and strengthen [them] in every good work and word" (2 Thess. 2:16–17 LEB). Similarly, he prays again that the Lord would "direct [their] hearts toward the love of God and toward the patient endurance of Christ"[73] (2 Thess. 3:5 LEB). Nothing can sever the umbilical connection between God's love experienced in Christ by the Spirit and believers.

The Help (or Supply) of the Spirit

I have already discussed Philippians 1:19, where, speaking out of his context of suffering in prison and facing a trial that could see him killed, Paul speaks of the ἐπιχορηγίας "of the Spirit of Christ Jesus."[74] The Greek can mean either the "supply" or "help" of the Spirit. Likely, Paul has in view the former, but the effect of God's supply is the latter—God, through Christ, lavishes the Spirit of Jesus on Paul, assisting him as he faces trial and hopes of deliverance and salvation. The Spirit's supply and help are critical to Paul's perseverance, release, and ultimate salvation despite severe persecution.

Strength and Power in Suffering

Another dimension of the Spirit's aid in suffering is the strengthening of believers to endure through God's power. I have discussed the Spirit's role in strengthening and upbuilding people earlier.[75] As such, I will focus on passages where suffering is explicitly mentioned.

2 CORINTHIANS 1:8

The Spirit's role in strengthening people to endure suffering is implied in 2 Corinthians 1:8, where Paul and his team suffered beyond their strength, and God brought them through with comfort and deliverance.

2 CORINTHIANS 4:7–20

Later, in 2 Corinthians 4:7, Paul speaks of believers having "this treasure in earthenware jars" (LEB). The treasure here can refer to the gospel (4:4); however, it is what belief in the gospel generates in believers that is in view.[76] Where the

---

73. See also Rom. 15:30; 2 Cor. 13:11, 13; Gal. 2:20; Eph. 2:4; 3:19; 5:1–2; 2 Thess. 2:13.
74. See chapter 5, "Relevant Prayer Texts."
75. Chapter 6, "The Spirit Who Builds People Up."
76. Fee takes it this way based on 4:4 and 6. However, 4:4 mentions "the light of the gospel," not the gospel itself. Furthermore, v. 6 does not mention the gospel but again mentions light (a metaphor for the Spirit's presence within—by which God is experienced in Christ). Fee, *GEP*, 322.

gospel is believed, just as God declared light into existence at creation, God's light shines into the heart of the newly created child of God. The believers' hearts are enlightened with the knowledge of the glory of God in the face of Christ. The treasure, then, is Christ within the believer by the Spirit.[77]

The role of the Spirit in Paul's thought here is likely, as the Spirit is mentioned seven times in the previous chapter. The term "glory" also features throughout 2 Corinthians 3, used eleven times. Paul finishes 2 Corinthians 3 speaking of the freedom that comes from the Spirit of the Lord (v. 17). Those who have received the Spirit reflect the glory of the Lord and are being transformed into the image of God's Son from glory to glory—just as from the Lord, who is the Spirit (v. 18)! Hence, the Spirit is the glory of God who descends and fills the temple of the Spirit—new believers and the church. This glory is the "power" from God and not from people Paul refers to in 4:7b.

After speaking of this power of God in the believer, in vv. 8 and 9 Paul discusses with vivid language his and his team's suffering and the power of Christ in them by the Spirit to sustain them in suffering. He does so with four initial participle statements about present suffering, to which he responds with four negated ἀλλά clauses stating how the suffering does not vanquish him and his group.

A1 ἐν παντὶ θλιβόμενοι, "in every way, afflicted"
    B1 ἀλλ᾽ οὐ στενοχωρούμενοι, "but not crushed"
A2 ἀπορούμενοι, "at a loss"
    B2 ἀλλ᾽ οὐκ ἐξαπορούμενοι, "but not in despair"
A3 διωκόμενοι, "persecuted"
    B3 ἀλλ᾽ οὐκ ἐγκαταλειπόμενοι, "but not forsaken"
A4 καταβαλλόμενοι, "thrown down"
    B4 ἀλλ᾽ οὐκ ἀπολλύμενοι, "but not destroyed"

In vv. 10–12, to make the same point that God, in Christ, by his Spirit, empowers believers to persevere in suffering, Paul three times contrasts the experience of suffering and decaying toward death with the life that Jesus generates in the believers' bodies. This renewal is the work of Jesus, by the Spirit, for it is by the same power referred to in v. 7. The first two contrasts focus on Paul and his team's experience, while v. 12a continues the focus on Paul and shifts to the life being generated in the Corinthians (you). The first two both include an initial statement leading into a ἵνα, purpose clause. The

---

77. As noted, Fee sees this treasure as the gospel. However, he goes close to my position, adding, "Nonetheless, in keeping with the argument of 3:1–18, despite the frailty of his person, his ministry was accompanied by the Spirit, with God's 'surpassing splendor of power.' As before, power has to do with the effectiveness of his ministry, with the Corinthians as Exhibit A, not with miracles and wonders as such, which for the Corinthians and the insurgents had apparently become a kind of end in itself leading to improper boasting. All of this to observe, then, that once more lying close to the surface in Paul's use of 'power' language *is the implicit ministry of the Holy Spirit in his life*." Fee, *GEP*, 322, emphasis mine.

third is a ὥστε clause drawing out the inference of the previous two (therefore . . .) for the Corinthians.

A1 πάντοτε τὴν νέκρωσιν τοῦ Ἰησοῦ ἐν τῷ σώματι περιφέροντες, "always, the death of Christ being carried around in our bodies,"
> B1 ἵνα καὶ ἡ ζωὴ τοῦ Ἰησοῦ ἐν τῷ σώματι ἡμῶν φανερωθῇ, "so that, also, the life of Jesus in our bodies may be made known"

A2 ἀεὶ γὰρ ἡμεῖς οἱ ζῶντες εἰς θάνατον παραδιδόμεθα διὰ Ἰησοῦν, "for, continually, we, the living ones, are being handed over to death because of Jesus"
> B2 ἵνα καὶ ἡ ζωὴ τοῦ Ἰησοῦ φανερωθῇ ἐν τῇ θνητῇ σαρκὶ ἡμῶν, "so that also, the life of Jesus is being made known in our mortal flesh"

A3 ὥστε ὁ θάνατος ἐν ἡμῖν ἐνεργεῖται, "therefore, death is working in us,"
> B3 ἡ δὲ ζωὴ ἐν ὑμῖν, "but life is working in you"

2 Corinthians 12:9

In 2 Corinthians 12:9, Christ's power does not heal Paul but dwells in him in his thorny travail. The power is perfected in his weakness[78] So, Paul can say in v. 10, "For when I am weak [ἀσθενέω], then I am strong [δυνατός]." Christ's presence by his Spirit in the weakened Paul strengthens him as he faces not merely the thorn but such things as "weakness" (ἀσθένεια), "insults" (ὕβρις), "pressure" (ἀνάγκη), "persecution" (διωγμός), and "distress" (στενοχωρία). The five ἐν clauses represent all the suffering he experiences as an apostle. In them, he even delights, despite the pain they bring. He does so because he is strengthened and sustained in them, and God's power shines through him and his ministry. This power is that which raised Christ from the dead, in which Paul and his coworkers live, and that is extended toward the Corinthians (2 Cor. 13:4).

Philippians 3:10–11

In Philippians 3:10, having been justified by faith and not through law observance, Paul yearns to know Christ and the power of his resurrection. The first clause could refer to future resurrection (as in v. 11) but more likely speaks of the power by which God raised Christ from the dead—the Spirit (Rom. 1:4; 8:11).[79] The context in which he wants to experience this power is "the fellowship of his sufferings, being conformed [συμμορφίζω] to his [Christ's] death" (LEB).

As in other passages considered, Paul understands the Christian life to be conformity to the pattern of Christ, seen in the movement described in the Christ-hymn—Christ in the form of God and equal to him, renouncing using his divine power to force people to yield to his cosmic lordship, emptying

---

78. See this chapter, "Formation Through Suffering."
79. See chapter 3, "The Spirit Who Gives Life."

himself, taking the form of a slave, becoming human, humbling himself, and being obedient to death on a cross. While Paul knows Christ's redemptive death was one-off and unique, he also knows he is in Christ and that Christ's Spirit is in him. Paul's own suffering is "in Christ," and he wants to experience this fully. He wants to know the Spirit as he does so. He is sustained and strengthened in his ministry despite suffering and death. He is also impelled by the hope of resurrection from the dead that will come (v. 11). At this time, the power that enables Christ to bring all creation under his authority will transform believers' bodies, subject to decay and death (of humiliation), to be like his glorious spiritual body (Phil. 3:21; cf. 1 Cor. 15:42–54).

EPHESIANS 3:14–16

In Ephesians, Paul prays for his readers to know the greatness of God's power toward believers, which is the same mighty strength that raised Christ and exalted him to cosmic Lord above all other powers (Eph. 1:19–21). This divine power also worked in Paul as he was graciously gifted his ministry of service to God's gospel (3:7).

In Ephesians 3:14–16,[80] Paul bends his knees in prayer to God, asking that, "according to the riches of his glory," the Ephesians would "be strengthened in the inner person, with power (dat. δύναμις), through his Spirit (διὰ τοῦ πνεύματος αὐτοῦ)" (my translation). The Spirit, then, is the agent by which God strengthens believers with power in all situations, including suffering. Paul goes on to explain what he hopes will come from this strengthening. The purpose (inf.) is "that Christ may dwell through faith in [their] hearts, having been rooted and established in love" (my translation).

The mention of love links his thought to the Spirit, for love is a fruit of the Spirit, and God poured his love into their hearts at their conversions (cf. Rom. 5:5; Gal. 5:22). Hence, he is praying here for a strengthening of faith to further establish them in Christ and his dwelling in them. Such an impartation speaks of the Spirit, for it is by the Spirit that Christ dwells in believers from the point of believing. Moreover, the prayer speaks of their having a fresh understanding of Christ, who is in them. Paul expresses a purpose that will flow from this: that they may be strong enough to grasp with other believers the fullness of Christ in them and to know his inestimable love, with the ultimate outcome that they are "filled with all the fullness of God." Then, in Ephesians 6:10, believers are likened to God's soldiers who are "to be strong in the Lord and in the strength of his might."

COLOSSIANS 1:9–11

The prayer summary of Colossians 1:9 pictures the Pauline team (us) gathered in prayer, asking God to fill the Colossians with spiritual knowledge, wisdom, and understanding. He prays this so they may live worthy of

---

80. See chapter 5, "Relevant Prayer Texts."

Christ, pleasing him, bearing fruit through good work, and increasing in that knowledge. Verse 11 speaks of God strengthening the Colossians with "all power" in accordance with his glorious might for (εἰς) all endurance (πᾶσαν ὑπομονὴν) and patience (μακροθυμία).[81] Again, Paul speaks of God's power being exercised without using πνεῦμα; however, as throughout his letters, it is via the Spirit (cf. 1:8) and in Christ that God strengthens believers to endure with patience as Paul prays. The link between prayer and the release of the Spirit is again seen: Pneumaformed communities pray and see the power of the Spirit strengthen believers to endure suffering patiently.

PHILIPPIANS 4:13

Here, Paul speaks of situations of financial prosperity and hardship. Whatever material situation he is in, Paul knows the secret of being content: the one who strengthens him.[82] The one in mind can be God, Christ, or the Spirit. Likely, it is all of the above, or more technically, God, in Christ, by the Spirit. The Spirit enables Paul to endure and be content in times of wealth and poverty (and analogous situations of suffering).

1 AND 2 TIMOTHY

Paul refers to the strengthening role of the Spirit in his final letters as he faces imminent trial and death. In 1 Timothy 1:12, he gives thanks to "the one who strengthens" (ἐνδυναμόω) him (LEB).[83] The aorist of the verb is not a marker of the past here but speaks of the action as a whole up to the point of Paul's career (and implied beyond).[84]

Paul's final letter urges Timothy to join Paul in suffering for the gospel "by the power of God" (2 Tim. 1:8). Implied here is that as Timothy engages in mission, he will experience suffering (see 2 Tim. 22:3, 9, 12; 4:5). However, he will be sustained by the power of the Spirit of God. By the Spirit, he will be "strengthened by the grace that is in Christ Jesus" (2:1).

Then, in 2 Timothy 4:17, "The Lord [κύριος][85] helped" and "strengthened" (ἐνδυναμόω) Paul for the fulfillment of his ministry of proclamation to the Gentiles; this, despite the many tribulations he suffered through his career.

---

81. Alternatively, "and patience with joy" (μετὰ χαρᾶς). In favor of the latter is the juxtaposition of suffering and joy in other places in Paul. However, the linking of thanksgiving and joy in 1 Thessalonians 3:9 and Paul's joyful prayers (Phil. 1:4) may suggest the paragraphing in both the NA28 and UBS5 (cf. 1 Thess. 3:9). The phrase ὑπομονὴν καὶ μακροθυμίαν could also be a hendiadys, "for all patient endurance."

82. Keown, *Philippians*, 2:412–13. See also Habets, *Anointed Son*, 292.

83. The verb ἐνδυναμόω compounds ἐν, "in," and δῠνᾰμόω, "strengthen." It has the meaning "strengthen, reinforce" (*BrillDAG*, s.v "ἐνδυναμόω"). See also Acts 9:22; Rom. 4:20; Eph. 6:10; Phil. 4:13; 2 Tim. 2:1; 4:17.

84. A constative aorist or perhaps a gnomic; see Wallace, *Greek Grammar*, 557, 562.

85. "The Lord" here can be Jesus or God. Explicitly, κύριος is Christ in 2 Timothy 1:2, and almost certainly in 1:8. Κύριος is used of God in a citation of Numbers 16:5 in 2:19 (and likely a second time as well [2:22]). As such, it is uncertain whether Christ or God is in view in other texts (1:16, 18; 2:7,

1 Corinthians 16:13–14

Believers are also urged to "be strong" by Paul. An example is 1 Corinthians 16:13, where the Corinthians are to be on the alert, stand firm in the faith, act courageously, and be strong. Yet, if this sounds militant, he follows it up by urging the Corinthians to do all things in love (v. 14). The Spirit is assumed but not stated. Another aspect of the Spirit's role in strengthening is whereby Christians who are made strong in the Lord by the Spirit bear with those who are less strong. Rather than merely live their lives as they want, they seek to help others (Rom. 15:1).

Perseverance in Suffering

The theme of perseverance or endurance (esp. ὑπομονή)[86] in suffering is important to Paul, as seen at many points in his letters.

Romans 5:3

Perseverance in Romans 5:3–5 is produced by suffering. This truism is grasped by the modern proverb "What doesn't kill you makes you stronger." Such endurance forms character. The Spirit pours love into the hearts of believers, fortifying them and increasing their ability to persevere (v. 5).

Romans 8:18–27

Romans 8:18–25 begins with Paul comparing present suffering with the eternal glory God's people anticipate. This suffering is real and deadly as the whole creation writhes in agony like a woman in childbirth, yearning for liberation from the bondage of decay. Believers also participate in the groaning of the cosmos but do so with real hope, eagerly awaiting their adoption and bodily redemption. The sufferings are not worth comparing to the glory. They hope for this unseen reality with patient endurance (v. 25).

The shift to the role of the Spirit that comes in vv. 26–27 is not surprising when we consider Paul's understanding of the Spirit's power in suffering. As believers await with eager expectation and endurance, the Spirit helps them in their weakness, interceding for them with wordless groans when they do not know how to pray in line with God's will. The presence and intercessory sighs of the Spirit enable perseverance when believers are being overcome with the weakness experienced in a fallen and hostile creation.

Romans 15:4

For Paul, the Scriptures are God-breathed or spirited (2 Tim. 3:16). God speaks through his word. In Romans 15:4, what was formerly written (in the

---

24; 3:11; 4:8, 14, 17, 18, 22). The effect is of course the same. God or his Son delivers Paul. The agent is the Spirit.

86. A term compounding ὑπό ("upon") and μονή ("stay, dwell") creating the meaning "stay upon," and hence, "endure, persevere."

Scriptures) was written for the instruction of believers (in the present). Such Spirit-inspired writings bring encouragement and, with patient endurance, generate hope. One way the God of perseverance enables endurance in suffering is through the Scriptures and prayer (v. 5).

1 CORINTHIANS 10:13

Another aspect of the Spirit's role in endurance is touched on in 1 Corinthians 10:13.[87] I will discuss this more fully in the final sections of this chapter. What interests me here is the final clause. Paul has been drawing on a string of Old Testament situations in which the people of Israel lapsed into sin and experienced God's judgment. Paul refers to these examples to warn his Corinthian readers, who were lapsing into a range of such sins, away from similar behaviors in the present (vv. 11–12).

In v. 13, he explains to them that their experience of temptation is not unusual—it is common to all people. He speaks of God's capacity to enable them to overcome such things. The work of the Spirit in such a situation is implied in two ways: he will limit the temptation according to the strength of the Christian involved, and he will supply a way out that the Christian can take. Pneumaformity relies on the Spirit to open paths of escape and on us to take those paths (as Paul says here). Believers are to trust God, who is faithful, and look for the exit from the situation that he, by his Spirit, allows them to face". Those pneumaformed see this opportunity, and like Joseph with Potiphar's wife, take it (Gen. 39:11–12).

2 CORINTHIANS 1:3–7

Endurance in suffering features in the suffering-focused passage 2 Corinthians 1:3–7.[88] In vv. 3–4, Paul blesses God because as the "Father of mercies and God of all comfort," he comforts Paul and his team in their severe troubles experienced in Asia (vv. 8–10).[89] As argued previously, this is the work of God in Christ by the Spirit. The comfort provided by God via Christ and the Spirit is so that Paul and his coworkers may be able to comfort others experiencing troubles (v. 4). For by the Spirit, the sufferings of Christ overflow to Paul and his group, and through the Pauline team, to the Corinthians (vv. 5).

In v. 6, the affliction experienced by the Pauline group is for the comfort and salvation of the Corinthians. The comfort received from God in Christ by the Spirit is "for your comfort which brings about your *endurance* [ὑπομονή] in the same sufferings which we also are suffering" (translation mine). The genitive παρακλήσεως τῆς ἐνεργουμένης is awkward if taken as a unit; however, the participle is more likely attached to what follows, creating a

---

87. A passage not touched on in Fee, *GEP*.
88. See earlier in this section, "Comfort and Peace in Suffering."
89. See also 2 Corinthians 6:4 where the Pauline group as servants of God show great endurance in afflictions, distresses, and difficulties.

relative clause, rather than to παρακλήσεως. The participle ἐνεργουμένης could be middle but is more likely passive with God as the agent behind receiving the comfort: "[your comfort] which God produces within you." The dative ἐν ὑπομονῇ might be instrumental, meaning that endurance (ὑπομονή) produces comfort (παράκλησις). However, this reverses the line of reasoning whereby God provides comfort in the context of their perseverance, not the other way around. Hence, the dative is likely locative, speaking of the comfort God produces in them as they endure. Also implied here is that the comfort of God produces endurance, even if Paul does not quite say that. The same sufferings are not identical to Paul's, but part of the big picture of participating in the sufferings of being human, specifically Christian sufferings such as rejection and persecution and their common sufferings in Christ. As with so many other Pauline passages, while God is the agent, it is evident in Paul's broader theology that this comfort experienced in their ongoing endurance of sufferings, which produces yet more endurance, is experienced in Christ and by the Spirit.

2 CORINTHIANS 6:4–7

Later in 2 Corinthians 6:4, in a catalog of another of his ironical apostolic self-commendations used to refute his accusers and to draw the Corinthians away from them to Paul and his team, he again mentions endurance. He and his apostolic team commend themselves in the face of their accusers and to his converts as servants of God in every way. Heading a series of nineteen statements employing ἐν is "in great endurance" (ἐν ὑπομονῇ πολλῇ). This phrase is likely a dative of manner. Its placement as first makes their "great endurance" prominent and the importance of perseverance as a core dimension of his understanding of his apostolic service.

The context in which the Pauline team perseveres is not merely in ministry itself but in experiencing the suffering described in the nine ἐν clauses that follow, all of which are datives of sphere. They give nine situations of suffering: (1) "in persecutions" (θλίψεσιν), (2) "in pressure situations" (ἀνάγκαις), (3) "in difficulties" (στενοχωρίαις), (4) "in beatings" (πληγαῖς), (5) "in imprisonments" (φυλακαῖς), (6) "in riots" (ἀκαταστασίαις), (7) "in labors" (κόποις), (8) "in times of sleeplessness" (ἀγρυπνίαις), and (9) "in times of hunger" (νηστείαις).

Then, in vv. 6–7, there are nine ἐν clauses, datives of manner or means, that balance the previous nine datives related to suffering. Some describe the manner with which the Pauline group conducts their commendable ministry: (1) "with sincerity" (ἁγνότητι), (2) "with knowledge" (γνώσει), (3) "with patience" (μακροθυμίᾳ), (4) "with kindness" (χρηστότητι), (5) "by the Holy Spirit" (πνεύματι ἁγίῳ), (6) "with genuine love" (ἀγάπῃ ἀνυποκρίτῳ), and (7) "with the word of truth" (λόγῳ ἀληθείας). The fifth and middle ἐν clause is not merely a dative of sphere, but also of agency: "by the Holy Spirit" (πνεύματι ἁγίῳ).

The final one, "by the power of God," is a dative of means followed by a genitive that speaks of possession, source, origin, and production: δυνάμει θεοῦ. These two datives indicate the source of the power in which the Pauline team endured suffering and conducted their exemplary ministry. The seven attributes in vv. 6–7 are the product of God's power generated in them by the Spirit in whom they dwell and who abides in them. Needless to say, this divine Spirit-power works through what follows in the bad times and good: "with the weapons of righteousness for the right hand and for the left; through honor and dishonor, through slander and praise. We are treated as impostors, and yet are true; as unknown, and yet well known; as dying, and behold, we live; as punished, and yet not killed; as sorrowful, yet always rejoicing; as poor, yet making many rich; as having nothing, yet possessing everything" (vv. 7–10).

2 Thessalonians 1:4

Paul links endurance (ὑπομονή) and suffering in 2 Thessalonians 1:4. He tells the Thessalonians how the Pauline team in Corinth boasts about them (ἐν ὑμῖν) among (ἐν) the other churches of God. The content of their boasting to the other churches is "[their] patient endurance and faith in all [their] persecutions and the afflictions that [they] are enduring" (LEB). This reference to endurance in suffering sits in the letter's first thanksgiving to God, in which Paul thanks God for their flourishing faith and increasing love for one another. Hence, Paul supposes that God is to be credited for their endurance and faith (v. 3).

2 Thessalonians 3:5

Confirming the impression that God is the source is 2 Thessalonians 3:5. Paul has asked for the Thessalonians to pray for his team's deliverance, stated his confidence in the faithfulness of "the Lord" (Christ) to strengthen and guard his team against Satan, and said he will ensure the obedience of the Thessalonians. Now, Paul asks Christ to "direct [their] hearts toward the love of God and toward the patient endurance of Christ" (τὴν ὑπομονὴν τοῦ Χριστοῦ). The genitive τοῦ Χριστοῦ can be subjective ("Christ's endurance"), objective ("endurance in Christ"), or a plenary whereby believers participate in the endurance that Christ demonstrated in his obedience to the point of death. Alternatively, it is a genitive of source, origin, or better, production, speaking of the endurance Christ pours into his brothers and sisters in him by the Spirit.

However we construe the genitive, it implies Christ's power via the Spirit, enabling the Thessalonians (and by extension, all believers) to endure persecution. Notably, this shows the vital link between prayer, receiving God's power, and endurance, even in the kind of suffering experienced in first-century Thessalonica.

1 Timothy 6:11 and 2 Timothy 3:10

It is the same Spirit-power Paul has in view when he urges Timothy to pursue ὑπομονή (1 Tim. 6:11, cf. Titus 2:2) and congratulates him in the second letter for doing so (2 Tim. 3:10). It is God's power that enables Paul to "endure [ὑπομονή] everything for the sake of the elect" (including his suffering and imminent death at the hands of Nero that the letter references), and so reign with him (2 Tim. 2:10, 12).

Joy in Suffering

In the previous section, I mentioned 1 Corinthians 12:26, where Paul urges members of the body of Christ to rejoice with other believers who are honored. Joy in the context of suffering is found in the initial reception of the gospel in Thessalonica. The Thessalonians responded to the gospel, emulating Paul's team and Christ, receiving the word, despite facing intense suffering due to persecution (ἐν θλίψει πολλῆ). They did so with "the joy of the Holy Spirit" (μετὰ χαρᾶς πνεύματος ἁγίου, 1 Thess. 1:6). How this joy manifested is undefined but could include any positive emotions.[90] Joy is sourced and produced by the Holy Spirit.[91]

2 Corinthians 7:4

The relationship between suffering and joy is also mentioned in 2 Corinthians 7:4. Despite referring to real life and death struggles in Asia Minor (1:8–11) and Macedonia (7:5), Paul states that he not only boasts about the Corinthians but is filled with comfort. Here we see Paul's capacity to experience joy despite extreme experiences of threat, danger, and affliction. This capacity is partly due to his theology whereby God is sovereign over all things, even the bad, and works out his purposes despite suffering (e.g., Rom. 8:28).

Subsequently, Paul is "always rejoicing" despite the ongoing grief of his ministry situations (2 Cor. 6:10) and can say he is absolutely "overflowing[92] with joy in all our affliction" (LEB).[93] He mentions the Macedonian churches who, although experiencing extreme persecution and poverty, abounded in joy and overflowing financial generosity to the collection (8:2).

Colossians 1:24

In Colossians 1:24, Paul goes as far as unconditionally rejoicing in his sufferings on behalf of the recipients of the letter (cf. Rom. 5:3). As he goes through suffering for God in Christ, he metaphorically continues Christ's sufferings, and so in a sense, Paul fills up in his own flesh what is lacking in the sufferings of Christ (Col. 1:24). By the Spirit, Christ's sufferings continue in the missional afflictions of his people.

---

90. This could include a feeling of happiness, laughter, tears of joy, inward warmth, the embrace of others, familial belonging, and the like. We should beware of speculation but ponder possibilities.

91. A genitive of production or source (see on theses genitives, Wallace, *Greek Grammar*, 104, 109).

92. The compound first-person present verb ὑπερπερισσεύω is surely intensive.

93. See 2 Cor. 7:4, also 7, 9, 13, 16.

PHILIPPIANS

Paul undoubtedly wants those in the churches he plants to show the same level of maturity and find joy in the Lord in their suffering. This desire is seen most intensely in Philippians. Both Paul and the Philippians are experiencing Roman persecution and threats from others who are Christians or claiming to be so. Paul's very life is under threat.[94] They share a deep mutual concern for Epaphroditus (2:25–30). The Philippians were facing times of poverty, as had Paul (2 Cor. 8:2; Phil. 4:10–12). Paul is also concerned with the unity and effective mission of the Philippians (4:2–3).

Yet, despite all this, Paul prays for them with joy (1:4), rejoices that the gospel is extending despite his suffering and the poor motives of some of the evangelizers (1:18), rejoices with the Philippians (2:17), describes them as his crown and joy (4:1), and rejoices in their financial gifts—despite their inability to send money in more recent times (4:10). Paul also expresses his desire for the Philippians to enhance his already overflowing joy by finding unity through emulation of God and his Son (2:2). He urges them to rejoice with him (2:18), always and in the Lord (3:1, 4:4), and he wants them to rejoice in the return of Epaphroditus and welcome him with joy (2:29). He expresses his confidence he will soon come to Philippi to help them grow in the joy of faith (1:25).

ROMANS 12:12

The juxtaposition of joy and suffering lies behind Romans 12:12, where, using an imperatival participle, Paul urges the Romans to "rejoice in hope, be patient in tribulation, be constant in prayer." For Paul, because of his immense confidence in God and his sovereignty, even extreme suffering never extinguishes hope. Consequently, believers can live out his imperatives even under challenging situations. The hope spoken of here is due to God's ongoing presence with believers by his Spirit, enabling them to endure all situations.

There is no accident that Paul then jumps to prayer, for by prayer, God's power is released to enable endurance, and at times, God directly intervenes by his Spirit to relieve pain. An aspect enabling this is the empathy referred to in the previous section—believers, bound together by the Spirit, rejoice together when experiencing the good times and weep together when tragedy strikes. The connection between joy and the Spirit indicates that joy in suffering is the work of the Spirit to which believers yield (cf. Rom. 14:17; 15:13; Gal. 5:22).

The Spirit and Restoration and Renewal

In Romans 15:32, Paul speaks of his desire to come to Rome after Jerusalem "with joy" and "by the will of God" so that he can rest together with the Romans. The verb συναναπαύομαι compounds σύν ("together, with") with

---

94.   Phil. 1:7, 12–26, 28–30; 3:2, 18.

ἀναπαύω, which at times means "cease, stop, rest." Ἀναπαύω is used of spiritual refreshment: Paul's by the Corinthian trio, Titus's by the Corinthians, and Paul and other Christians' by Philemon (1 Cor. 16:18; 2 Cor. 7:13; Philem. 7, 20).[95] The compound is found once in the LXX of the leopard lying down with a young goat in eschatological peace (Isa. 11:6).[96] This literary context yields the meaning here, "to rest together" or "to be refreshed together."[97]

Paul hopes to come to Rome and be refreshed with the church. Paul is looking for the mutual encouragement and sharing of spiritual gifts he writes about in Romans 1:11–12. The Spirit is not mentioned explicitly, but Paul's uses of ἀναπαύω in the Corinthian letters and Philemon speak of the inward renewal of the πνεῦμα (spirit) and σπλάγχνα (inner being, heart).[98] This inward renewal of the human spirit is the work of God's Spirit; hence, it is implied.

Paul speaks of the power of God enabling believers to persevere in suffering. Throughout the chapter, the Spirit is implied (further below). In 2 Corinthians 4:16–18, Paul speaks of the work of the Spirit in renewing believers. They do not lose heart despite being subject to death, decay, and suffering (see vv. 7–12). They are sustained because, even though the outer persons (the bodies) of believers are being destroyed (by God's final enemy, death), the "inner person is being renewed (ἀνακαινόω) day after day."[99] This revitalization is the work of the Spirit in believers and generates God's life, despite the human condition's inexorable decay. Verse 17 slightly shifts the focus to future eschatological hope. This suffering life produces eternal glory.

Hope in Suffering

Alongside love and faith, for Paul, hope is one of the core virtues of the Christian (1 Cor. 13:13; 1 Thess. 1:3). One aspect is the power of the Spirit to generate hope in suffering.[100]

ROMANS 5:2, 5

Paul precedes the litotes of Romans 5:3–5 in v. 2 by declaring that believers, having been justified by faith, and having access to grace, boast in the hope of the glory of God. The hope here is primarily future, whereby believers experience

---

95. See also Matt. 11:28; 26:45; Mark 6:31; 14:41; Luke 12:19; 1 Peter 4:14; Rev. 6:11; 14:13.

96. See also soldiers resting together (Appian, *Bell. civ.* 5.79), to sleep together with women (Plutarch, *Dion* 3.2; *Quaest. conv.* 3.4.3).

97. *BrillDAG*, s.v. "συναναπαύομαι."

98. Technically, σπλάγχνον means the innards, "inward parts, entrails" (BDAG, s.v. "σπλάγχνον," 938), but here functions as a synonym for the heart or spirit.

99. See also Col. 3:10 (LEB).

100. Hope is also a fundamental dimension of Paul's spirituality, "one of the primary blessings of the Spirit" for the apostle. Gorman, *CPNSC*, 304.

the fullness of salvation, their full new Adamic glory, the glory of eternal life, and glorification at the resurrection and judgment (cf. 2 Cor. 3:12; Col. 1:27).[101]

Then, in the chain that follows, Paul rejoices in suffering because, through it, God produces in believers endurance, which produces character, and character hope. Hope here is not so much the future eschatological hope mentioned so often in Paul; this is the present hope generated by the Spirit (the eschatological implantat of eternity in the believer's heart). The down payment of the Spirit guarantees future redemption (2 Cor. 5:5). The present dimension is apparent because Paul goes on to state that the hope generated through suffering and inward transformation in the believer does not bring shame, dishonor, or disappointment (Rom. 5:4). This is so because (ὅτι) God's love has been poured into the hearts of believers through the Spirit given to them (Rom. 5:5). It is, then, God's love generated in the believer by the Spirit that brings present hope.

ROMANS 15:13

In Romans 15:13, we see the Spirit's role in filling believers with hope again. God is described as "the God of hope." Paul prays, believing that, as such, God can and will fill the Romans with joy and peace in believing "so that" (εἰς + inf.) the Romans "may abound in hope by the power of the Holy Spirit." Whereas in Romans 5:4–5 hope comes at the reception of the Spirit at initial faith, this speaks of the ongoing work of the Spirit to generate fresh hope (also joy and peace) in challenging situations.

GALATIANS 5:5

The connection of the Spirit and hope is also found in Galatians 5:5. As Paul pleads with the Galatians to pull back from their flirtation with justification through works of the law in favor of faith, he tells them that "in [and by] the Spirit,[102] we [all believers] from faith wait for the hope of righteousness [ἐλπίδα δικαιοσύνης]" (my translation).[103] Here, hope is future,[104] yet

---

101. See 1 Thessalonians 4:13 for the converse.

102. The phrase πνεύματι ἐκ πίστεως is prominently placed first after ἡμεῖς γὰρ and with the pronoun is emphatic. Similarly Fee, *GEP*, 417. As throughout this book, I take the dative πνεύματι as one of sphere (in the Spirit), but that implies instrument or agency (by the Spirit).

103. Fee suggests the genitive can be "the righteousness for which we hope" or "the hope that our justification by faith in Christ and the Spirit has secured." He prefers the latter. Fee, *GEP*, 418. Paul's theology holds in tension assurance and conditionality. A binary solution is regrettable as the first option is premised on the second and vice versa, and Galatians affirms that the readers are justified by faith but must hold firm to that to receive the hope of righteousness. The genitive can be one of production too, "the hope produced by righteousness." Indeed, Fee kind of concedes this by adding that the realization of this hope is realized, "provided we continue in faith and the Spirit and do not return to slavery, which promises no eschatological reward, only death." He claims this is not Paul's point here. In fact, it is his very point, as vv. 2 and 4 make clear (p. 419).

104. See also Rom. 5:2; 8:20, 24–25; 1 Cor. 15:19; Eph. 1:18; Phil. 1:20; Col. 1:5; 1 Thess. 5:8; Titus 1:2; 2:13; 3:7. Buchanan rightly observes the consensus that "in 5:5, the Spirit and future righteousness/justification are closely related to each other but not equivalent." Buchanan, "Spirit," 162. He also

it is experienced in the present by those declared righteous by faith and who have received the Spirit. It is through the Spirit that they experience hope.[105] We can surmise that references to future hope in Paul's letters also refer to the inward work of the Spirit, enabling believers to look forward to eternal life and all that it entails with hope.[106] Indeed, at times, Paul uses ideas that conceptually overlap the Spirit in association with hope.[107]

This future hope involves more than mere individual salvation and the redemption of the body but includes the liberation of the cosmos from its bondage to decay and death. Creation does not yet see this, but it hopes and awaits it eagerly. It will ultimately see it come to pass (Rom. 8:20, 24–25). As such, by the Spirit, believers rejoice in hope (12:12a). They also love (1 Cor. 13:13) and pray as they endure affliction (Rom. 12:12c) and any other situations (1 Cor. 13:7). The Scriptures, breathed into existence by the Spirit of God, also bring ongoing encouragement as believers endure (Rom. 15:4; 2 Tim. 3:16).[108]

Comfort and Peace in Suffering

Believers have the mind of the Spirit, which leads to life and peace no matter what they are suffering. The Spirit provides comfort as well as this peace, and believers share in them and embody them to one another.

ROMANS 8:6

Paul links peace with the Spirit. In his characteristic antithesis of flesh and Spirit, whereas the "mind of the flesh" is death, the "mind of the Spirit is life and peace" (Rom. 8:6, my translation). The mind here is likely that of people, not the mind limited to fleshly impulse or that of the Holy Spirit. The genitive may be one of production—the mind produced by the flesh—or attributive—the fleshly mind as opposed to the Spirit-ual mind. The mind produced by focus on the flesh yields death. This death includes the process of decay to actual physical death and, ultimately, the eternal death that follows for the unbeliever. The contrast is life and peace—both in the sense of a present experience of God's life and, ultimately, eternal life. The "peace" includes present peace with God (Rom.

---

notes that if we overstress the present dimension here, we obscure that "it is only the Spirit's presence that guarantees the eschatological future—the hope of righteousness" (p. 164).

105. Gal. 3:1–3, 5, 14; 4:6.

106. Other Pauline passages linking hope and suffering include 2 Cor. 1:7 (Paul's hope for the Corinthians because they share in suffering and comfort from God); Eph. 4:4 ("one Spirit" immediately precedes reference to "one hope of your calling"); Phil. 1:19–20 (where the help or supply of the Spirit with prayer gives Paul hope he will not be ashamed but will boldly speak to exalt Christ).

107. These include hope "in Christ" by the Spirit (Eph. 1:12); similarly, "in the Lord" (Phil. 2:19), "in the Lord Jesus Christ" (1 Thess. 1:3); "Christ in you" by the Spirit (Col. 1:27); the eyes of the heart enlightened (by the Spirit) to know the hope of one's calling (Eph. 1:18). See also Eph. 4:4; Phil. 1:19–20 (previous note); God giving good hope by grace, that is, via the Spirit (2 Thess. 2:16); hope through your prayers, invoking the Spirit (Philem. 22).

108. See, for example, Isaiah's hope of the Gentiles being ruled by the Davidic king and worshiping God being fulfilled in the present (Rom. 15:12 fulfilling Isa. 11:10).

5:1), inward personal peace, peaceful relationships (ideally speaking), and, ultimately, the experience of eternal shalom. The Spirit generates peace in all situations, including suffering.

2 Corinthians 1:3–11

A more focused link between the Spirit and comfort in suffering is found in 2 Corinthians 1:3–11. Here, Paul writes of an intense experience of suffering in Asia Minor. He and his team, while taking up the Jerusalem collection, experienced θλῖψις in Asia. The term carries the idea of being crushed and pressured[109] and, across biblical literature and Greek Jewish writings, is regularly used for intense suffering.[110] It is used commonly in this way in Paul and the wider NT, sometimes in the sense of general suffering or persecution.[111]

This persecution occurred in Asia, likely the province of Asia Minor, which covered a substantial area of the western tip of modern Turkey on the Aegean Sea and would have happened during his mission in Ephesus, summarized by Luke in Acts 19 (ca. AD 53–55). While there is a reasonable degree of speculation concerning this period of travail, including imprisonment (from which he may have written some letters traditionally attributed to Rome), there seems no reason to dispute Luke's account. As such, the suffering refers to the riot in Ephesus inspired by Demetrius because of the threat to his business and worship of Artemis (Acts 19:23–27). Luke gives no account of imprisonment; however, the description in 2 Corinthians 1:8–11 suggests that the threat was not brief, was extreme, and may have caused Paul and his team to be killed.

Paul's blessing of God in 2 Corinthians 1:3–4 is set in the context of God's presence with him and his team during this intense persecution. God is the Father of Christ and beautifully described as ὁ πατὴρ τῶν οἰκτιρμῶν καὶ θεὸς πάσης παρακλήσεως, "the Father of mercies and the God of all comfort." The term οἰκτιρμός is not often used in wider Greek sources. Pindar uses it in the sense of "pity," stating envy is superior to οἰκτιρμοῦ. In the LXX, it almost always translates רַחֲמִים (raḥămîm),[112] usually in the plural, conveying

109. Heinrich Schlier, "Θλίβω, Θλῖψις," *TDNT* 3:139.
110. Such as Israel's anguish under Pharaoh in Egypt (Exod. 4:31); the suffering promised if they break the covenant (Deut. 28:53, 55, 57); and in warnings of suffering from the prophets of Israel (Hos. 5:15; Obad. 12; Nah. 1:9; Zeph. 1:15; Isa. 8:22; 10:3; 30:20; Jer. 6:24; 10:18).
111. Paul uses it of the affliction of eternal judgment (Rom. 2:9); general Christian suffering possibly including persecution (Rom. 5:3; 8:35; 12:12; 2 Cor. 1:4; 6:4; 7:4); suffering caused by marriage (1 Cor. 7:28); persecution (2 Cor. 1:8; 7:4; Eph. 3:13; Phil. 1:17; 4:14; Col. 1:24; 1 Thess. 1:6; 3:3, 7; 2 Thess. 1:4, 6); pastoral suffering (2 Cor. 2:4); suffering from poverty (2 Cor. 8:13). Outside of Paul, concerning Christian general suffering including persecution (Matt. 13:21; John 16:33; 2 Cor. 4:17; 8:2; Rev. 7:14); Christians being persecuted (Matt. 24:9; Mark 4:17; Acts 11:19; 14:22; 20:23; Heb. 10:33; Rev. 1:9; 2:9, 10); human suffering in general (Matt. 24:21, 29; Mark 13:19, 24); the affliction of childbirth (John 16:21); Joseph's afflictions before Egypt (Acts 7:10); the suffering of widows and orphans (James 1:27); the affliction of God's judgment (Rev. 2:22).
112. In Zechariah 12:10, οἰκτιρμός translates חֵן (ḥēn), "grace, favor."

intense compassion, especially when used of God.[113] Often, the term is qualified with adjectives emphasizing the greatness or abundance of God's mercy
toward his people. So, for example, the LXX of Psalm 118:156 (119:156 EVV)
reads, "Great is your mercy, O Lord, give me life according to your justice."[114]
Importantly, οἰκτιρμός is connected to the Spirit in Zechariah 12:10, where
God declares: "And I will pour out upon the house of David and upon those
living in Jerusalem a Spirit (πνεῦμα) of grace (χάριτος) and compassion
(οἰκτιρμοῦ), and when they look toward me, because of whom they danced
in triumph and they will mourn for him with a mourning as upon a beloved
one and they will be in pain with pain as for a firstborn son" (my translation).

In Johannine writings, this passage in Zechariah is cited concerning
Christ's death (John 19:37) and his return (Rev. 1:7). In Galatians 4:26, Paul
contrasts the Jerusalem below with the Jerusalem above, which is the mother
of the free people in Christ. It would not be unlikely if he, too, connected
Christ's piercing death and God's mercies with the work of the Spirit based on
Zechariah 12:10.

God is also the "God of all comfort (παράκλησις)." God as the source of
consolation or comfort features in the LXX (Ps. 93:19; Isa. 57:18; Jer. 38:9).[115]
The term παράκλησις often conveys the idea "encouragement" or "exhortation," but here, in the context of suffering, "comfort" or "consolation" is appropriate.[116] By saying God is the God of all comfort, Paul is stating that God is
the source of the comfort believers experience in all situations of suffering
(whatever the cause).

In 1 Corinthians 1:4, Paul has received such παράκλησις from God,
which "enables Paul and his team to comfort others," including the Corinthians. It is through Christ that this God-given comfort overflows to others
(v. 5). The severe suffering that he and his team have experienced is for the
Corinthians' comfort and salvation, as Paul and his team grapple in ministry for their maturation. So, also, the comfort he receives from God through
Christ is for the Corinthians (v. 6). The Corinthians share in the same sufferings and comfort (v. 7).

---

113. BDB, s.v. "רַחֲמִים," 933.

114. Similarly, see 2 Kgdms. 24:14; 1 Chron. 21:13; 2 Esdr. 19:19, 27, 31; Ps. 68:17; Sirach 5; 6; Hos. 2:21;
Zech. 1:16; 7:9; 12:10; Bar. 2:27. See also 3 Kgdms. 8:50; 2 Chron. 30:9; 2 Esdr. 11:11; 19:28; 1 Macc.
3:44; 3 Macc. 2:20; 6:2; 4 Macc. 6:24; Pss. 24:6; 39:12; 50:3; 76:10; 78:8; 102:4; 105:46; 118:77; 144:9;
Isa. 63:15; T. Jos. 2:3; T. Ab. (A) 14:10.

115. In Isaiah 66:11, Jerusalem is the source of comfort. Παράκλησις is used of people consoling one
another (Job 21:2); prophetic prediction of an absence of consolation (Hos. 13:14; Nah. 3:7; Jer. 16:7).
The term can also carry the meaning "encouragement" (see 1 Macc. 10:24; 15:11) or "appeal" (see
2 Macc. 7:24; Isa. 28:29; 30:7).

116. Encouragement (Acts 4:36; 15:31; 2 Cor. 7:4; Philem. 7; Heb. 6:18); exhortation (Acts 13:15; Rom.
12:8; 2 Cor. 8:4; 1 Thess. 2:3; 1 Tim. 4:13; Heb. 12:5; 13:22); appeal (2 Cor. 8:17). It has the sense of
consolation or comfort regularly (Luke 2:25; 6:24; 2 Cor. 7:4, 7, 13).

God is the source of παράκλησις elsewhere in Paul, as are the God-breathed Scriptures (Rom. 15:4–5 [cf. 2 Tim. 3:16]; Phil. 2:1; 2 Thess. 2:16).[117] For Paul, παράκλησις is a gift of the Spirit (Rom. 12:8). It is also a consequence of Spirit-inspired prophecy (1 Cor. 14:3). Hence, we can surmise that it is in and by the Spirit in Christ that Paul and the Corinthians experience God's comfort in suffering. They are bound together with God, Christ, and other believers in the shared experience of suffering and comfort from the Spirit.

Romans 14:17

Paul reasserts the centrality of peace and the Spirit's agency in Romans 14:17, where what matters is not petty things like food, drink, or holy days (which are dividing the Romans), but righteousness, peace, and joy in the Holy Spirit (ἐν πνεύματι ἁγίῳ). The dative, as in other such cases in Paul, speaks of the sphere of existing in the Spirit by faith and the agency of the Spirit in generating these attributes in believers. Hence, believers can differ over nonessential matters like what one eats and drinks and holy days but maintain an overall unity in the Lord based on the peace generated by the Spirit.[118]

2 Corinthians 7

The comfort received in Christ by the Spirit is shared between believers. Titus is comforted amongst the Corinthians, and Paul and his team are comforted in turn as Titus reports about their passion for the apostle. This news again leads to Paul's rejoicing, which flows as comfort and mercy are experienced (2 Cor. 7:7–8). In 2 Corinthians 7:13, Paul restates this, speaking again of his comfort received through Titus (παρακαλέω, παράκλησις), which leads to their rejoicing (χαίρω, χαρά). This comfort and joy flow from Titus's spirit (τὸ πνεῦμα αὐτοῦ) and is refreshed among the Corinthians. Πνεῦμα here speaks of Titus's human spirit,[119] but it is there that the Holy Spirit connects with people and generates peace, comfort, and joy in their person (cf. Rom. 8:16; Philem. 7).

Philippians 2:1

Another text that speaks of God's comfort is Philippians 2:1. Using a fourfold conditional protasis launched by εἰ plus τις, each part refers to an aspect of God's character and among the Philippians, which Paul urges them to imitate and embody. The first term, παράκλησις (discussed above), can be translated as "comfort," especially considering that the preceding verses speak of suffering due to opposition (1:28–30). Alternatively, it is slanted more to

---

117. Παράκλησις is associated with the work of the Spirit in Acts 9:31.
118. See also on this passage the excellent analysis of Fee, *GEP*, 617–21.
119. Fee rightly says that this use of πνεῦμα "is undoubtedly an anthropological term referring to the interior dimension of one's person." Fee, *GEP*, 339.

the notion of encouragement. Either way, this is experienced "in Christ," implying participation by the Spirit in the life of Jesus.

The second is παραμύθιον, a hapax legomenon with a similar range of encouragement to comfort to consolation.[120] The genitive ἀγάπης is one of source, origin, or production. Love, in Paul, is particularly associated with the Spirit, and so the Spirit is the source and producer of the love Paul has in mind here (esp. Rom. 5:5; 15:30; Gal. 5:1). The Spirit is the explicit producer of the third attribute, κοινωνία (unity, fellowship, partnership). The final two concepts, σπλάγχνα καὶ οἰκτιρμοί (affection and compassion), are also derived from God and experienced in Christ by the Spirit.

1 Thessalonians 4:18 and 5:11

The Thessalonian correspondence also mentions the power of the Spirit in believers comforting one another. In 1 Thessalonians 4:18, παρακαλεῖτε ἀλλήλους ἐν τοῖς λόγοις τούτοις can be rendered, "comfort one another with these words," which fits the context in which members of the church are grieving the dead (cf. v. 13). Also, in 5:11, παρακαλεῖτε ἀλλήλους καὶ οἰκοδομεῖτε εἰς τὸν ἕνα can similarly be translated, "comfort one another and build up each other." The injunctions παραμυθεῖσθε τοὺς ὀλιγοψύχους and ἀντέχεσθε τῶν ἀσθενῶν summon the Thessalonians to "console the discouraged (small-souled)" and "help the sick," speaking of them each comforting and supporting those facing discouragement and sickness. Such support is Spirit-impelled and should not be quenched (v. 19).

The Spirit in Others Bringing Relief

Another aspect of the Spirit's role in suffering is through the community of faith. Support in suffering is an aspect of the κοινωνία πνεύματος (fellowship of the Spirit) where the love of God and grace of Christ are experienced in the Christian community (2 Cor. 13:13 [v. 14 EVV]; Phil. 2:1). Paul speaks of such community in Ephesians 4, urging the recipients to walk in humility, gentleness, patience, and love and be eager to "maintain the unity of the Spirit in the bond of peace" (vv. 2–3).

One possible dimension of Christians helping each other is the role of physicians like Luke. He is described as a ἰατρός, indicating a "doctor, healer, physician."[121] The manner in which Paul identifies Luke as such suggests that he is known to the Colossians as "the beloved physician," indicating his ongoing medical work and the love people feel for him. Considering Paul's policy

---

120. See "παραμύθιον," in *BrillDAG*. These meanings are noted: "encouragement, exhortation, incitement"; "comfort, consolation"; and "lightening, alleviation, relief." They opt for the "comfort, consolation" in Philippians 2:1. Similarly, BDAG, s.v. "παραμύθιον," 769: "solace"; *NIDNTTE* 3:634, "comfort."

121. *BrillDAG*, s.v. "ἰατρός."

of those in his mission group working for a living,[122] Luke likely provided for himself through his medical work. He probably functions as the doctor for the Pauline team and among those to whom they minister.[123] Comfort through medical healing within the faith community is likely an aspect of the Spirit's work in the church. (This anticipates the critical role of medicine in future missions.)

Empathy is a critical aspect of the pneumaform Christian community. Paul says to the Corinthians at one point that those who weep and rejoice should live as if they do not weep and rejoice. This does not seem to be his overall view of communal lament and joy but seems to be related to the particular crisis they were experiencing at that moment (1 Cor. 7:30).[124] More broadly, believers empathize with one another in the good times and bad.

Such mutual concern is reflected in Romans 12:15, where the church members rejoice with those rejoicing. Conversely, the community laments when a member weeps because of life's tragedies in a broken, hostile world. They do so because if one member of the body of Christ suffers, all suffer together, as the Spirit has bound them together. Conversely, when a member is honored, all members rejoice together (1 Cor. 12:26, see further below). Paul here uses the indicative—the suffering or honoring of one member indicates the suffering and honor of all members. However, the verse also summons believers to participate actively in empathetic suffering and rejoicing as they support one another.

Earlier in this chapter, mention was made of mutual comfort in 2 Corinthians 1:3–8. Comfort is sourced in God and Christ—he comforts Paul and his team in affliction—so that they may comfort others with the same comfort received in Christ. In Christ, believers share in Christ's sufferings and his comfort. Paul and his team are afflicted as they serve God in the gospel, yet he hopes the Corinthians will share in the same comfort.

The mutuality of comfort in Christ is a distinguishing feature of faith—people are pneumaformed in relationships with others. Such comfort is experienced in the arrival of other Christians, such as when the Corinthian trio met Paul (1 Cor. 16:17). The work of the spiritually imbued is to enhance the Christian joy of those to whom they minister (2 Cor. 1:24; Phil. 1:25). The capacity of a faithful community to generate joy in its leaders is seen in

---

122. First Corinthians 9:2 indicates Barnabas and Paul provided for themselves (Garland, *1 Corinthians*, 406). The use of "we" in 1 Thessalonians 2:9 shows that Paul's group worked to provide for themselves (Green, *The Letters to the Thessalonians*, PNTC [Grand Rapids: Eerdmans, 2002], 129) as does 2 Thessalonians 3:7–9 (Bruce, *1 & 2 Thessalonians*, 205). Paul, Priscilla, and Aquila were tentmakers (Acts 18:3). Luke was likely a doctor, but what the others did is intriguing speculation.

123. Witherington, *Conflict*, 463, speculates Luke provided Paul support for his thorn and other problems.

124. See the excellent discussion in Garland, *1 Corinthians*, 322–25. He concludes it might be a famine, as Winter proposes. Bruce W. Winter, "'The Seasons' of This Life and Eschatology in 1 Corinthians 7:29–31," in *"The Reader Must Understand": Eschatology in Bible and Theology*, eds. K. E. Brower and M. W. Elliott (Leicester: Apollos, 1997), 323–34.

Colossians 2:5, where Paul is with them in the Spirit,[125] rejoicing at their discipline and perseverance of faith. The power of other Christians to generate joy is seen in Paul's description of the Thessalonians and the Philippians as his joy (Phil. 4:1; 1 Thess. 2:19–20). This creation of joy in Paul is restated with detail in 1 Thessalonians 3:9 and seen in statements of Timothy and Philemon generating joy in him (2 Tim. 1:4; Philem. 7).

Many other things could be said to indicate how the Spirit brings succor through believers to others. Paul's ethics is profoundly communal, with the fruit of the Spirit, such as love, patience, kindness, gentleness, and goodness, shaped in the direction of mutual upbuilding. Paul also speaks often of believers using ἀλλήλων, "one another." Believers are "members of one another" (Rom. 12:5, my translation; also Eph. 4:25). They are to support one another in many ways.[126]

Provision

Paul is not a prosperity teacher advocating that sufficient faith will make a believer immune from suffering, including poverty. Instead, his letters give evidence of the reality of material deprivation for Christians in famine-struck contexts and for himself and others called into ministry. Led by the Spirit, Paul is determined that he act to alleviate poverty. He invites others to participate in doing the same.

PHILIPPIANS 4:10–19

Here, Paul brings the letter body to a close, carefully acknowledging the Philippians' recent financial gifts sent through Epaphroditus and taking great care not to give the Philippians any sense of further obligation to Paul.[127] Throughout the passage, he acknowledges that God is the ultimate source of

---

125. See on Colossians 2:5, Fee, *GEP*, 645. Fee correctly argues that this is the Spirit, not Paul present in spirit or in their thoughts. While Fee suggests his use of σάρξ does not necessarily indicate Paul has the Spirit in view, in my view the choice of "in the flesh (σάρξ)" rather than "in the body" makes it clear to readers the divine Spirit is intended. Fee ends up in the same place: "Most likely, therefore, something very close to the sense of 1 Cor. 5:3 is in view, where Paul considers himself as truly present by the Spirit, as they gather in the presence and power of the Spirit for the reading of his letter."

126. Encouraging one another by each other's faith (Rom. 1:12); loving one another (Rom. 12:10; 1 Thess. 3:12; 4:9; 2 Thess. 1:3); outdoing one another in showing honor (Rom. 12:10); living in harmony with one another (Rom. 12:16; 15:5); loving one another (Rom. 13:8); not judging one another (Rom. 14:13); building up one another (Rom. 14:19; 1 Thess. 5:11); welcoming one another (Rom. 15:7); instructing one another (Rom. 15:14); greeting one another with a holy kiss (Rom. 16:16; 1 Cor. 16:20; 2 Cor. 13:12); waiting to eat with one another (1 Cor. 11:33); having the same care for one another (1 Cor. 12:25); serving one another (Gal. 5:13); bearing one another's burdens (Gal. 6:2); bearing with one another in love (Eph. 4:2; Col. 3:13); being kind to one another (Eph. 4:32); submiting to one another (Eph. 5:21); considering one another more significant than oneself (Phil. 2:3); encouraging one another (1 Thess. 4:18; 5:11); doing good to one another (1 Thess. 5:15). See also Gal. 5:15, 26; Col. 3:9; Titus 3:3.

127. See further Keown, *Philippians*, 2:289–92; G. W. Peterman, "'Thankless Thanks': The Epistolary Social Convention in Philippians 4:10–20," *TynBul* 42 (1991): 261–70.

this provision. First, he rejoices in the Lord (Christ) that they have renewed their concern for him (v. 10). This rejoicing indicates Paul's acknowledgment of Christ's involvement, by the Spirit, in their giving. Second, in v. 13, he speaks of his ability to "do all things through him who strengthens me." The "things" in context speak of his capacity to endure in times of relative prosperity *and* when facing poverty and need. The one who strengthens him can be God (vv. 19–20), the Lord Jesus Christ (v. 10), or the Spirit. As argued throughout this book, this is a flawed trichotomy—it is God, in Christ, and by the Spirit who is in view. God—Father, Son, and Spirit—empowers Paul to find contentment even when facing hunger, thirst, and other situations of deprivation. Third, God is the one who provides for needs (v. 19).

To stop at God's involvement would miss the vital role God's people have in provision. The Philippians had supported Paul throughout his earlier ministry and now again in Rome (or Ephesus). They had taken up a collection, emulating what Paul and others had done in the Jerusalem collections. Epaphroditus and others (who no doubt accompanied him) had delivered gifts to Paul in prison in his extreme need. It is often through people that God and Christ, by the Spirit, relieve those in poverty and need.

2 CORINTHIANS 8–9

In these chapters, we see the same pattern of God's provision through his people for those in need. Paul also adds the nuance of God providing for people through the natural world. There are many indications that Paul considers God the source of the provision of the Jerusalem collection. The means of doing this is by the Spirit. While acknowledging the painful reality of poverty, hunger, thirst, nakedness, and need, Paul believed in God's power to provide for his people. God's capacity is seen most clearly in Philippians 4:10–19 and 2 Corinthians 8–9.

First, Paul describes the Macedonians generously giving out of poverty and suffering with joy through the "*grace of God* that has been given" them (2 Cor. 8:1–2). The collection is described in terms of God's Spirit-given grace again as the passage unfolds (8:6, 8). Second, they served the saints after giving themselves *to the Lord*, then to Paul, by the will of God (8:5). Worship and communion with God are implied here. Third, central to his appeal is the example of the grace of the incarnate Christ who, despite his riches, gave himself for the sake of the Corinthians (all people implied), making himself poor (literally) so that, by his poverty, the Corinthians (and all people) may become rich (8:9).

Fourth, in v. 16, Paul thanks God that Titus has informed him that the Corinthians have welcomed his request that they give to the collection, indicating Paul credits God for their doing so. Fifth, in 9:6–8, God blesses and graces abundantly those who give cheerfully and without compulsion so that they will overflow in the good work of giving to others. These verses speak of God's material and spiritual provision as he provides for the believers' needs and generates a desire to bless others. Paul restates this in 9:10–12, where God supplies food and produces in believers a growing "harvest of righteousness," rich generosity, which results in grateful worship of God. This sequence is seen in the Jerusalem collection, whereby the Jerusalem believers will glorify God because of their yielding to Christ, and they will thank their *koinōnia* in giving to them and others, leading them to pray for the Corinthians (and others who give to the collection). Paul ends with his own eucharistic exclamation to God for his gifts to humankind in Christ and history (v. 15).

While the Spirit is not mentioned in the chapters, throughout the role of God's πνεῦμα is implied. The capacity to be radically generous in believers is a work of the Spirit who generates in the pneumaform an increasing desire to do so.

There are the Jerusalem collections of Paul.[128] There are indications that the collection was partially motivated by the Jerusalem Christians' poverty. Paul states in Romans 15:26 that he was taking up this collection "for the poor among the saints at Jerusalem." Second Corinthians 8:13 indicates that the collection will bring "relief" (ἄνεσις),[129] suggesting struggle in Jerusalem. Similarly, in v. 14, Paul contrasts the Corinthian abundance with "their need," and in 9:12, of "the needs of the saints." Moreover, the notions of sowing and reaping sparingly and not bountifully point to material privation in Judea (2 Cor. 9:6), as does the mention of the poor in the citation of Psalm 112:9 in 9:9.

There are also places where Paul mentions privation as a common aspect of life (Rom. 12:20). Indeed, he recognizes that the infinitely rich Lord Jesus Christ became poor that people living in spiritual and material poverty might become spiritually rich in the present age, and infinitely rich in the age to come (2 Cor. 8:9). This verse acknowledges the relative material poverty of Jesus in his life.[130]

There are other indicators that many other Christians in the churches associated with Paul faced material needs.[131] Indeed, "the poor" is an assumed category in Galatians 2:10. There is no indication that Paul thought the poverty experienced by these Christians was due to their failure through

---

128. In my read of Paul and Acts, there are two collections. The former is referenced in Acts 11 during Claudius's reign, when in the 40s there were a number of famines, including in Judea. Inspired by the revelation of Agabus, Barnabas and Paul delivered gifts from the Antiochian church to Jerusalem (Acts 11:26–30; also Gal. 2:2). Then, encouraged by the Jerusalem apostolic leaders, they agreed to "remember the poor" (Gal. 2:10). One aspect of this commitment was to embark on a major trip west to the churches Paul had planted in Anatolia, Macedonia, and Achaia. It is this collection mentioned in Rom. 15:25–31; 1 Cor. 16:1–4; and 2 Cor. 8–9.

129. Paul's desire that the Corinthian giving does not cause them θλῖψις, "affliction," also suggests that the Jerusalem Christians were experiencing this—Paul does not want the situation reversed.

130. The poor offering in Luke 2:23 (Lev. 12:8) indicates his family was poor at his birth. See also James R. Edwards, *The Gospel According to Luke*, PNTC (Grand Rapids: Eerdmans, 2015), 82. Further indications include Matthew 8:20.

131. Rom. 8:35; 12:13; 16:2; 1 Cor. 11:21, 34; 2 Cor. 8:2; Eph. 4:28; Phil. 4:19. While these passages refer to Christians in need, they are general in scope and do not imply suffering specifically due to their being Christians.

things like a lack of faith or sin. Nor is there evidence that it is God's direct judgment. Paul also recognized that Christian service often brought with it material hardship. Frequently, he mentions such suffering in his own experience and that of his coworkers.[132]

Protection and Paths out of Suffering

While Paul clearly expected Christians to experience suffering at times, Paul indicates that God, by the Spirit, intervenes to protect believers and provide paths out of suffering.

1 CORINTHIANS 10:13

First Corinthians 10:13 has been mentioned briefly above. It is the culmination of Paul's use of OT examples to warn the Corinthians to step away from evil (v. 6), idolatry (v. 7), sexual immorality (v. 8), testing Christ (v. 9), and grumbling (v. 10). We can surmise that these issues were present in the congregation. He warns them directly in v. 12 that those who arrogantly assume they can stand firm through such challenges must watch out (βλεπέτω), lest they fall prey to them (cf. Gal. 6:1).

In v. 13, Paul balances this warning. The temptations they are challenged by are common to all humankind. However, God is faithful as people experience the challenges of desire.[133] Along with the temptation (σὺν τῷ πειρασμῷ) God will also (καί) provide a way of out (ποιήσει ... ἔκβασιν). This promise suggests the presence of the Spirit in situations of extreme challenge. The pneumaform believers, as they yield to the Spirit, will become more astute in recognizing the path provided by their faithful God, in Christ, and by the Spirit, and will flee the sin.

In what follows, Paul applies his injunctions to idolatry. Believers must flee idolatry (v. 14) as they must sexual immorality (6:18). They are to sense the Spirit's path out of the situation and take it. One aspect of this is desisting from participation in idolatrous feasts where they become vulnerable to demons (vv. 20–22). So, one dimension of recognizing the Spirit's summons is not putting themselves in situations where they can become vulnerable and fall.

2 CORINTHIANS 1:10

Second Corinthians 1:3–7 is discussed earlier in this chapter concerning God's comfort in suffering. After his exposition on God's comfort, Paul explains to the Corinthians the extent of his team's suffering in Asia Minor—they were burdened beyond their capacity and despaired of life itself (v. 8). This happened during Paul's Ephesus mission and may relate to events associated with the riot of Acts 19:23–20:1. The seeming death sentence forced Paul and his team to rely on God, who has the power to raise the dead (v. 9). Their

---

132. 1 Cor. 4:11; 6:5, 10; 2 Cor. 11:9, 27; Phil. 2:25; 4:11–12, 16.
133. See also 1 Cor. 1:9; 2 Cor. 1:18; 1 Thess. 5:24; 2 Thess. 3:3.

prayers and hopes were answered and "he delivered [aor. mid. ῥύομαι][134] us from a massive threat[135] of death." The term ῥύομαι means "to rescue from danger, save, rescue, deliver, preserve."[136]

Paul ends v. 10 with καὶ ῥύσεται (fut.), "and he shall deliver us," alluding to his trust that God will deliver them from further danger from his context in Macedonia. Such danger is mentioned in 2 Corinthians 7:5, where Paul explains how they could not find bodily rest when they came to the region, as they were "afflicted in every way" (LEB). He further clarifies this as "conflicts on the outside, terrors on the inside" (my translation). Such a description refers to being caught in extreme intimidation from those outside the church (cf. 2 Cor. 8:2; Phil. 1:28–30) that generated genuine terror in Paul and his team. God is, thus, the one in whom Paul and his group have put their hope, namely, "that he will deliver us again." Verse 11 is both an appeal for prayer and an expression of confidence in the outcome—they will be rescued to deliver the gift, which will generate thanksgiving.

Throughout this passage, God is the agent of their deliverance. However, the passage implies his work in their situation by the Spirit protecting them and bringing about the circumstances for their escape from persecution in Asia, Macedonia, and travel to Jerusalem. When God occasions it, he acts, in time, by his Spirit, to deliver his people.

PHILIPPIANS 1:19–26

After expressing his joy that the gospel is advancing in Rome despite his imprisonment and the genuine danger he is in, Paul continues to rejoice because of his confidence in the future. He knows (οἶδα) that through the prayers and the help (or supply) of the Spirit of Jesus Christ, his situation will turn out for his salvation (σωτηρία). Paul here uses σωτηρία cleverly to indicate possible release from prison (deliverance) or, ultimately, eternal salvation (if he dies).[137] As the passage plays out, Paul expects to be courageous to honor Christ in his speech and body, whatever happens. While at one level, to die is better by far, he knows that remaining will enable him to continue his fruitful ministry. Although he is torn between these two options, somehow, he knows he will remain for the good of the Philippians. There is much that could be discussed in this passage.[138] What is important here is the role of the Spirit in Paul's situation. He knows he will be okay through the Spirit's help and the Philippians' prayers. If he is to die, the Spirit of Jesus Christ will sustain him to boldly glorify Christ in his defense of the gospel and to be

---

134. While this might be passive, it is likely emphasizing God's active agency specified by ὅς.

135. The phrase τηλικούτου θανάτου uses τηλικοῦτος ("so great") and the genitive θανάτου, and thus speaks of their deliverance from an extreme danger or threat of being killed.

136. BDAG, s.v. "ῥύομαι," 907.

137. Keown, *Philippians*, 2:227–30.

138. Mark J. Keown, "Did Paul Plan to Escape from Prison? (Philippians 1:19–26)," *JSPL* 5, no. 1 (2015): 89–108.

faithful up to and through death. If he is released, as he somehow believes he will be, the Spirit of Jesus Christ will empower him for further ministry bearing fruit, including the progress and joy of faith in the Philippians and their consequent boastful worship of God in Christ. By the Spirit, Jesus will act in Paul's situation. As consistently in Paul, we see the link between prayer and the Spirit—somehow, as people pray, history is pneumaformed into God's desired outcome. As such, prayer is essential to pneumaformity. The Spirit of Jesus Christ sometimes responds with deliverance, always with comfort and strength, and when our time has come, through death to salvation.

2 Thessalonians 3:1

In 2 Thessalonians 3:1–2, Paul prays that God's Word would speed ahead and be honored in other places, as in Thessalonica. He then prays that God will deliver him and his team from evil opponents who are unbelievers (v. 2).[139] While Paul knows suffering is to be expected and experienced, this knowledge does not hinder him from praying for God's rescue. In v. 3a, he declares Christ (the Lord) is faithful, indicating his confidence that Christ can be trusted whatever happens. Then, in v. 3b, he assures the Thessalonians that Christ will further establish them (στηρίξει) and protect them (φυλάξει) against the evil one. This assurance pictures the utterly trustworthy Christ enabling the Thessalonians to grow deeper in their faith and standing guard over them against Satan. This work Jesus does by the Spirit.

Paul's assurance of this protection leads him to state his confidence that the Thessalonians will respond to his letter with obedience and that Christ will lead (κατευθύνω) them to the love God has for them and their love for him (plenary genitive) and to perseverance sourced in Christ (ὑπομονὴν τοῦ Χριστοῦ, see earlier under "Perseverance in Suffering"). All this speaks of the Spirit's role in delivering people from opposition (where God wills this, v. 1), further establishing believers in their faith, guarding them against hostile spiritual forces, and leading them into perseverance and God's love.

2 Timothy 3:11

As Paul begins his final appeals to Timothy (2 Tim. 3:10–4:18), Paul reminds Timothy of his faithfulness in following Paul's ways of life.[140] Timothy did this during Paul's persecutions and sufferings in Pisidian Antioch,[141] Iconium, and Lystra.[142] Luke records that Timothy joined Paul in Lystra on his second major Antiochian mission, so this cannot refer to the persecutions Paul experienced on his first visit to the region (Acts 13–14). It may have been

---

139. As discussed in chapter 5, "Relevant Prayer Texts," this could be the Gallio incident of Acts 18:12–17.
140. Paul mentions teaching, conduct, purpose, faith, patience, love, and perseverance.
141. While this could be Syrian Antioch, the two other cities are Galatian, and so this is likely Pisidia.
142. The two datives leading v. 11 are likely durative rather than aspects of Paul's life Timothy followed (he followed Paul's ways during these times of persecution).

persecution experienced on this second trip as they passed through Phrygia and Galatia (Acts 16:7), during his third major Antiochian mission (Acts 18:23), or when he revisited this area during his possible post-Philippian trip. Whichever is in mind, Paul endured (aor. ὑποφέρω) these persecutions.[143]

Moreover, "the Lord" rescued (aor. ῥύομαι) him from all of them (see discussion on the verb in the above section on 2 Corinthians 1:10). This recollection infers Paul was able to get away safely from the persecutions he endured in the southern Galatians region (cf. 2 Cor. 1:10; 2 Thess. 3:2; 2 Tim. 4:17–18 [further below]).[144] At times, God and Christ, by the Spirit, act in history to deliver people from situations of suffering.

2 Timothy 4:17

While Paul expects his imminent death (2 Tim. 4:6–8), he mentions an earlier experience of God's deliverance. He writes that "the Lord stood by [παρίστημι][145] me and strengthened [ἐνδυναμόω] me,[146] so that through me the message might be fully proclaimed and all the Gentiles might hear it. So I was rescued [aor. pass. ῥύομαι] from the lion's mouth." This verse first refers to God or his Son's presence beside Paul, supporting and aiding him—the Spirit is implied. Second, God and Christ strengthen Paul—something that happened, no doubt, by the Spirit. The purpose and result (ἵνα)[147] of this is that through Paul, the message (κήρυγμα) has been fulfilled. This completion probably refers to Paul being able to boldly and fully announce the gospel before Nero's judiciary. "All the Gentiles" clearly does not mean the whole world, which was far from evangelized; this likely refers to all involved at the center of the empire.[148]

Third, the Lord delivered Paul from the lion's mouth,[149] almost certainly referring to Paul's previous deliverance from death at his earlier trial before Nero's courts. Paul then states confidently that the Lord will rescue him from

---

143. The term is ὑποφέρω means to "bear with" or endure (LSJ 1901) such things as temptation (1 Cor. 10:13), sorrows (1 Peter 2:19), or as here, persecutions.

144. Paul uses the verb of Christians being delivered from the domain of darkness into Christ's kingdom of light (Col. 1:13) or Christ delivering believers from coming wrath (1 Thess. 1:10). Paul asks the Romans to pray for him that he might be delivered from unbelievers in Judea (Rom. 15:31). Paul also employs it of being delivered from his body of death (Rom. 7:24), and Christ "the Deliverer" from Zion (Rom. 11:26; cf. Isa. 59:20). It is also used of deliverance from evil or the evil one (Matt. 6:13), Christ being rescued from the cross (Matt. 27:43), God's historical deliverance of Israel from enemies (Luke 1:74), and God rescuing Lot from Sodom (2 Peter 2:7) and the godly from trials (2 Peter 2:9).

145. The term compounds παρά, "beside," and ἵστημι, yielding "stand beside" with a range of nuances. Here, it has the sense of Christ supporting, helping, or aiding Paul.

146. See earlier in this chapter on Philippians 4:13.

147. Here, the purpose and outcome are expressed with ἵνα. Marshall and Towner, *A Critical and Exegetical Commentary*, 824.

148. Marshall and Towner, *A Critical and Exegetical Commentary*, 824: "'All the nations' is then obviously not literal but rather expresses the representative, cosmopolitan character of the audience."

149. This metaphorically speaks of Paul escaping the clutches of death at the hands of the emperor and his judiciary (see Josephus, *Ant.* 18:228, where Tiberius is labeled ὁ λέων). This calls to mind Daniel in the lion's den (Daniel 6).

"every evil deed and bring me safely into his heavenly kingdom"—this speaks of his confidence that whatever happens, God and his Son will bring him into eternal salvation. While Paul expected suffering and death, he maintained confidence that God could and, at times, would act to comfort and strengthen his people in suffering and deliver them. Such a balanced theology is critical to the pneumaform life.

Healings and Miracles

As discussed above, Paul has a rich theology of God using suffering as a means of pneumaformity. Further, the Spirit is pivotal in enabling believers to endure suffering. Still, the notion of God directly intervening in Christ by his Spirit in a situation to bring healing and perform miracles is not absent from his thinking and praxis. Signs and wonders are an integral aspect of Paul's ministry.

In his missional summary in Romans 15:18–19, Paul mentions preaching "by the power of signs and wonders, by the power of the Spirit of God." The structure of Greek could indicate two different aspects of his ministry:

ἐν δυνάμει σημείων καὶ τεράτων

ἐν δυνάμει πνεύματος [θεοῦ].[150]

More likely, the second ἐν clause indicates the power energizing his preaching ministry and signs and wonders.[151]

The first term, σημεῖον, speaks of a sign and is often used for miraculous events that point to God and his power. This usage is found in Paul[152] and other NT writings.[153] Τέρας is "something that astounds because of transcendent

150. I am working with the assumption (with Metzger) that the best reading here is πνεύματος θεοῦ, albeit recognizing that the better reading may be πνεύματος ἁγίου (but definitely not the conflated πνεύματος θεοῦ ἁγίου). It makes little difference to my argument here as the Spirit of God, which is the Holy Spirit, is clearly in view. For a discussion see Metzger, *TCGNT*, 478.

151. Fee, *GEP*, 473. He sees the second clause as explanatory: "'What I mean,' he says, 'is by the power of the Spirit of God.'"

152. Rom. 15:19; 2 Cor. 12:12; see also Acts 15:12. He also mentions the Jewish desire for such signs (1 Cor. 1:22), his signature as a sign of authenticity (2 Thess. 2:17), and fake signs (2 Thess. 2:9). Otherwise, Paul uses it of the sign of circumcision (Rom. 4:11) and tongues as a sign for believers (1 Cor. 14:22).

153. The term is used of a sign of the times (Matt. 16:3); signs of the fall of Jerusalem, Jesus's coming, and the end of the age (Matt. 24:3, 30; Mark 13:4; Luke 21:7, 11, 25); the sign of a kiss to betray Jesus (Matt. 26:48); the sign of the baby in the manger (Luke 2:12); Jesus as a sign to be opposed (Luke 2:34); and astral signs (Acts 2:19; Rev. 12:1, 3; 15:1; 19:20). It is used of miracles, including false miracles (Matt. 24:24; Mark 13:22; Rev. 13:14; 16:14); exodus miracles (Acts 7:36); and in requests for Jesus to do miracles to authenticate his ministry through miraculous signs and his response including the sign of Jonah—the resurrection (Matt. 12:38–39; 16:1, 4; Mark 8:11–12; Luke 11:16, 29, 30; John 6:30; also Luke 23:8); Jesus's miracles (Acts 2:22; Heb. 2:4); and Christian miracles (see also Mark 16:17, 20; Acts 2:43; 4:16, 22, 30; 5:12; 6:8; 8:6, 13; 14:3; 15:12). It is John's customary term for miracles (John 2:11, 18, 23; 3:2; 4:48, 54; 6:2, 14, 26; 7:31; 9:16; 10:41; 11:47; 12:18, 37; 20:30).

association, prodigy, portent, omen, wonder."[154] Aside from one use of apocalyptic astral signs (Acts 2:19), τέρας is paired with σημεῖον as a description
of miracles,[155] whether false[156] or authentic, including those performed by
Paul.[157] The combination does not indicate two types of miracles but summarizes the types of miracles found in Christ's ministry and Acts, and anything
else God may do.[158]

These signs and wonders are the miracles performed in Paul's ministry.
Paul hints at them three other times. First, in Romans 15:19, he speaks in a
general sense of miracles. Similarly, as he combats his pneumatic Jewish opponents in 2 Corinthians 12:12,[159] he acknowledges that he performed "signs and
wonders and mighty works." These he describes as "signs of a true apostle,"
signifying that they are understood to accompany the apostolic gift.[160] Notably,
these have been performed among the Corinthians (among you), so his readers
are witnesses to them, so they should not question his apostolic credentials.[161]
They were done so "with utmost patience," suggesting these miraculous works
were experienced in an ongoing way in his time among them.[162]

Critical here is the following clause, which explicitly indicates that the
Spirit of God is the means of these miracles. As noted above, the construct
qualifies what goes before Paul's proclamation and miracle ministry. The ἐν
is likely both locative ("in the realm of the Spirit of God") and instrumental
("by" or "through the power of the Spirit of God"), as the former implies the
latter. As such, the power of Paul's ministry of miracles is the Spirit. These
passages show that not only does the Spirit lead God's people into contexts of
suffering and support them as they endure it, but in Christ, by the Spirit, at
times, God chooses to intervene with miracles that bring relief from suffering.

---

154. BDAG, s.v. "τέρας," 999.

155. See also the pairing of the terms in the LXX of the exodus miracles (Exod. 7:3, 9; 11:9–10; Deut.
    4:34; 6:22; 7:19; 11:3; 26:8; 29:2; 34:11; Pss. 77:43; 104:27; 134:9; Jer. 39:20–21; Bar. 2:11); others that
    prophets perform (Deut. 13:2–3); curses of the covenant (Deut. 28:46); and others (Wis. 8:8; 10:16;
    Isa. 8:18; 20:3; Dan. 4:37).

156. See also Matt. 24:24; Mark 13:22; 2 Thess. 2:9.

157. See also of Paul's miracles in Acts 14:3; 15:12; 2 Cor. 12:12. See also those of Moses (Acts 7:36); Jewish
    demands for them (John 4:48); Jesus's miracles (Acts 2:22); and believers (Acts 2:43; 4:30; 5:12; 6:8;
    Heb. 2:4).

158. Here I slightly differ from Fee, who considers them to be the range "one finds in the large variety of
    narratives in Acts." Fee, GEP, 356. In my view, we can think more broadly than Acts to the range of
    miracles God performs through and on behalf of his people through the biblical narrative, as he wills,
    in Christ, and by his Spirit.

159. The origin of the idea of the marks of a true apostle could come from Paul's opponents, the
    Corinthians, or a Pauline idea as he defended his apostleship. Harris, Second Epistle, 874.

160. See Fee, GEP, 355.

161. Similarly, Fee, GEP, 356.

162. Fee ponders whether this indicates that the Corinthians struggled to hold miracles and endurance in
    affliction in tension. Fee, GEP, 356. To me, the phrase ἐν πάσῃ ὑπομονῇ modifies κατειργάσθη and
    speaks of the ongoing nature of their experience of miracles, not eschatological tension. See similarly
    Harris, Second Epistle, 874–75.

The second indicator that Paul believes that sometimes God intervenes in suffering to bring radical relief is seen in his churches. In Galatians 3:5, Paul mentions miracles performed by God among the letter recipients due not to their adherence to the Jewish Torah but because of their faith. The present tense ἐνεργῶν refers not to Paul's past miracles among them but their present experience of them.[163] The mention of the supply of the Spirit clearly indicates the Spirit's agency. God acted in this way by the Spirit, based on the faith of the Galatians.[164]

There are indications also that Timothy is frequently ill with stomach ailments, and he recovers. Paul's advice to take some wine appears medicinal (1 Tim. 5:23).[165] Paul also mentions Trophimus's illness in Miletus. Still, we do not know the outcome (2 Tim. 4:20). We also know that some Christians died from illness in Corinth, which Paul appears to interpret as God's judgment on those who abuse the Lord's Supper (1 Cor. 11:30).

At other times, Paul speaks of God's intervention to deliver him and his team from precarious situations.[166] His request that the Romans pray for his deliverance from unbelievers in Judea and his subsequent trip to Rome is fulfilled, albeit in precarious circumstances (Acts 21–28; Rom. 15:28–32). While it is disputed that Paul is released from the imprisonment referred to in Philippians, there are some indications his hope in Philippians 1:19–26 is fulfilled and he is released from prison.[167] His catalogs of sufferings in Second Corinthians imply his deliverance from many situations of danger (2 Cor. 4:8–11; 6:4–10; 11:23–29). God also provides for Paul in situations of material privation, especially through his tentmaking and the generosity of the Philippians (Phil. 4:10–19).

Paul believes that God, in Christ, by his Spirit, can intervene in human affairs to bring healing, deliverance, rescue, and provision. This aspect is seen in Luke's account of Paul's mission which mentions healings, exorcisms, and God's rescue from persecution.[168] Yet, Paul knows that ultimately all people will suffer in various ways, including the amplification of suffering from being a Christian in a hostile world. He knows that while Jesus has risen from the dead and, in a realized eschatological sense, death has been defeated, all people, including Christians, are subject to decay and physical death. Indeed, death is the

---

163. These would include the miracles on Paul's first mission into the region (Acts 14:3, 8–11, 19–20). See also Buchanan, "Spirit," 104.

164. On the question of the relationship of faith to miracles, see Keown, *Discovering: The Gospels and Acts*, 474–85.

165. "The beneficial effects of wine as a remedy against dyspeptic complaints, as a tonic, and as counteracting the effects of impure water were widely recognized in antiquity." See Prov. 31:6; Hippocrates, *Med.* 13; Plutarch, *Tu. san.* 14. See J. N. D. Kelly, *The Pastoral Epistles*, BNTC (London: Continuum, 1963), 129.

166. See 2 Cor. 1:10; Phil. 1:20, 24–26; 2 Thess. 3:2; 2 Tim. 3:11; 4:17, also 1 Thess. 2:1.

167. Keown, *Philippians*, 1:24–34.

168. E.g., Acts 13:4–12; 14:3–23; 15:12; 16:16–18, 25–34; 19:11–12; 27:23–25; 28:1–10.

final enemy to be ultimately defeated. The whole creation, believers included, is subjected to frustration and yearns for its liberation from decay.

Still, one aspect of pneumaformity is the sovereign choice of God to intervene and alleviate suffering. Linked to this is Paul's passion for prayer—he knows that prayers activate the power of God as God wills. Even where prayers are not answered as requested, as in his thorn in the flesh, the Holy Spirit responds to guide, comfort, and strengthen.

THE ULTIMATE ALLEVIATION OF SUFFERING

For Paul, the cosmos culminates in the return of Christ and the judgment, the resurrection of the dead—their transformation from humble bodies subject to sin and death into glorious Spirit bodies—and the liberation of the cosmos from its bondage to decay. This hope sustains Paul. As will be discussed in more detail, τὸ πνεῦμα τοῦ θεοῦ is intimately involved in these things. What is important here is that the Spirit will ultimately fill the created order, with all God's enemies spiritual or otherwise subjugated, evil vanquished, decay and death no more, and God's adopted, redeemed people free from suffering.

CONCLUSION

All people suffer because they are mortal beings in a world full of decay and danger. Christians are not immune. Not only do they face the vicissitudes of life, but being a Christian brings even more acute suffering. Anguish can come through the pain of conversion, giving up former lives, losing relationships, social marginalization, and other consequences of choosing Christ. Engaging in mission brings challenges from engaging with resistant unbelievers, false teachers, and even sincere Christians. Being a Christian is not always easy.

Yet Paul's letters give us immense encouragement that God is with those of us who are in Christ by his Spirit. We are in Christ, he participates in us, and we are "in him" as we suffer. Spirit and Son pray for us, and our hope in suffering relies on their love. The Spirit is supplied to us and brings us aid. This aid comes in the form of strength, endurance, joy, restoration, renewal, hope, comfort, peace, relief, protection, and provision. Sometimes we experience God's intervention as he opens a way through the trial or acts miraculously to alleviate suffering. The Spirit who guarantees our future redemption and release from suffering also implants the hope of righteousness in us. Ultimately, our suffering will end, and we will be with the Lord forever; in this we hope.

CHAPTER 9

THE SPIRIT AND PARTICIPATION IN CHURCH LIFE

F or Paul, the church is the temple of the Spirit. This image speaks of a people bound to God as his adopted family and who participate in the being and life of Christ by the Spirit. As such, the Spirit resides not only in individuals but between them, creating a beautiful unity of the Godhead and God's people as one. People are drawn into God's life together as the temple of the Spirit of God. Empowered by the Spirit, they worship God together (chapter 5); they are formed to be more and more like God's Son (chapter 6); they relate to one another clothed in the virtues of God (chapter 7); and they join together rejoicing, hoping, loving, comforting, refreshing, strengthening, building up, persevering, and so on, in the midst of suffering (chapter 8). They will also join together in continuing God's mission to the world (chapter 10). Together, they will inherit eternal life under God's reign (chapter 11). As these things are covered elsewhere, this chapter will focus on their participation together in church life as they not only bear the fruit of the Spirit (Gal. 5:22–24) but exercise their Spirit-given gifts for building up the church.

Before discussing the gift lists of Paul, it is critical to place them in the context of Paul's broader understanding of the pneumaform life. Such a life is characterized by living under, in, and out of the love of God and his Son (Eph. 5:1–2). It is the mutual presentation of bodies as living sacrifices and the renewal of the mind in the direction of God and Christ, not this fallen age (Rom. 12:1–2). It involves freedom from sin and all its enablers (e.g., the law) and consequences. However, this freedom is not expressed as "everything is permissible" (1 Cor. 6:12; 10:23) but as a Spirit-led life of "serving one another in love" (Gal. 5:13) and the posture imagined by the fruit of the Spirit (Gal. 5:22–24). It is not a life of individual faith and self-expression but one bound up in the desire for the betterment of others—that they may come to Christ (1 Cor. 10:23–31) and be strengthened in their faith (Rom. 14–15; 1 Cor. 8).

The overall picture of the gift lists is not merely of individuals exercising their gifts but of the whole body of Christ fulfilling the ministry of Christ together as a unit. It envisages God's people bound together by the Spirit moving together in unity, the oneness of faith, love, and hope, and the same goal—the growth of God's people, and the reconciliation of the nations and creation itself. Westerners struggle to grasp that the work of the individual within this body of Christ, by the Spirit, is merely a part of a whole church participating in Christ and doing his work throughout the world.

Each of the lists Paul gives at various points in his letters are contextually driven lists of gifts that he feels are worth mentioning because of their particular relevance to the given situation. They are then not comprehensive, so it is inadequate to gather a list from them to establish a comprehensive list of the gifts of the Spirit. Worse, it is reductionist to create church surveys to discern whether people have this or that gift in Paul's list. Instead, the gifts are representative, and while it is not without warrant to establish a carefully thought-out list from them, it is important to recognize God at work in people's lives in other ways not listed in his groupings.

When God's Spirit enters a person's being, God forms them. He enhances the giftedness his sovereign hand placed in them through nature and nurture (all by his Spirit). As I like to quip, "He takes what is natural and 'nurtural,' and makes these things supernatural and 'supernurtural.'" To this giftedness, he adds new Spirit-breathed abilities, new gifts—the sorts of things we read about in Paul's lists. Believers are to use all these gifts and everything they have and are in the service of God, his people, and his world. As such, to evaluate someone's spiritual giftedness, we should help them reflect on their whole being and life, who they are, their heritage, their vocations, their skills, and so on, along with anything that aligns with the gifts Paul lists. In this way, we discern who a person is in Christ. It is in such a spirit that I will now discuss the spiritual gift lists.[1]

Paul uses a few gifts in more than one list. In order to consolidate the discussions on these gifts, each gift will be analyzed once. Under Romans 12:3–8 will be prophecy, teaching, generosity, and leading. The section on 1 Corinthians 1:5 will host the discussions of speech and knowledge, and the one on 1 Corinthians

---

1. On the Greek, χάρισμα, see Fee, *GEP*, 32–35. He rightly notes that on its own, it has nothing to do with the Spirit, but is a "gracious bestowment" (p. 33) and that in half of the instances it refers to the Spirit. This leads him to remove Romans 12 and other passages from his study. However, as I am taking a broader view of the Spirit, including God and Christ's bestowal of gifts (by the Spirit), I will consider all references to the term in this analysis. I also disagree with him that it is implausible that the Romans would see this as a spiritual gift list. Fee, *GEP*, 606. This ignores that Phoebe is delivering the letter and will add explanation (16:1–2). Romans 16 indicates many of Paul's friends are in the church, including Priscilla and Aquila, who know him and his theology extremely well, having worked in him in Corinth (v. 2). Gifts of God are mentioned in two letters that may be linked to Rome: 1 Peter 4:10, which includes χάρισμα; and Hebrews 2:4. Finally, Paul's letters were circulating early (2 Peter 3:15–16). Fee also veers in my direction on p. 607.

12:4–11 faith, healings, workings of power (miracles), and tongues and their interpretation. Finally, with 1 Corinthians 12:27–31 we will study apostleship. All other gifts are considered with the passage they appear in.

ROMANS 12:3–8

Romans 12:3–8 follows Paul's appeal in vv. 1–2, first, for the Romans to follow in the footsteps of Christ and, as their rational worship, to present themselves to God as living sacrifices, and second, that their minds, previously conformed to the patterns of their society, be renewed by God's Spirit in conformity with his Son. In other words, Paul wants them to be increasingly cruciform or Christoform, giving themselves entirely in service as Christ did, with their minds transformed by the Spirit. What follows in 12:3–15:13[2] draws out a range of contextually relevant aspects of the emulation of Christ and the *pneuma*-renewal of minds.

The first aspect of this in Romans 12:3–8 is that they should recognize God's grace at work in them (by the Spirit) and the measure of faith they have received from God (again, by the Spirit), and live humbly within the context of the church (the body), confidently expressing their specific individual gifts.[3] The church is described as "one body," which is the "one body in Christ" in v. 5.[4] As each animal body has multiple parts, so does the church. Notably, "the members not all have the same function (πρᾶξις)" within the church.

What follows in vv. 6–8 is a fourfold εἴτε . . . εἴτε sequence plus three other clauses with the εἴτε implied.[5] Previously I have argued that such chains with multiple εἴτε's are always attached to a Pauline axiomatic statement revealing what is, for him, a Christian truism.[6] This pattern applies here. The truism is found in v. 6a, where Paul restates the principle articulated in v. 3b—God has graced each person in his church and each one differently. Each εἴτε clause mentions a gift and then urges the Romans to exercise the gift. The structure urges them to recognize the gifts in others and let them use them.

The first clause implies that believers with the gift of prophecy, and by implication all gifts, should express them in proportion to God's gift to them by the Spirit (the proportion of their faith).[7] The next three indicate that those

---

2.   The section can be broken into Romans 12:1–13:14 and 14:1–15:13—however, I maintain that the whole section extrapolates the pneumaform life conformed to that of Christ with renewed minds.

3.   I find myself here in disagreement with Fee on this passage. He considers that while the Romans would recognize these things as being from the Spirit, they are not "spiritual gifts." Fee, *GEP* 606. The list includes gifts mentioned elsewhere (prophecy and teaching) and as such, would appear to be another set of gifts.

4.   "The Spirit incorporates believers into the body of Christ, he himself is the unity of that body composed of the bearers of the gift of the Spirit." Habets, *Anointed Son*, 183.

5.   It is possible that these four should be grouped together and dependent on the third εἴτε. However, more likely, εἴτε is implied in the final three.

6.   Keown, "Paul's Use of εἴτε . . . εἴτε," 195–208.

7.   On this see Fee, *GEP*, 607. He rightly concludes that Paul has in view the measure of faith afforded each person, rather than seeing the measure of faith in v. 6 as "the faith."

gifted with these gifts (and others) should express them in the church. The final urge is for believers with these three gifts (and others) to do so lavishly, enthusiastically, willingly, and cheerfully.

εἴτε προφητείαν κατὰ τὴν ἀναλογίαν τῆς πίστεως, "if it is prophecy, [it is to be exercised] according to the proportion of her (or his) faith."

εἴτε διακονίαν ἐν τῇ διακονίᾳ, "if service, [it is to be exercised] by serving."[8]

εἴτε ὁ διδάσκων ἐν τῇ διδασκαλίᾳ, "if teaching, [it is to be exercised] by teaching."

εἴτε ὁ παρακαλῶν ἐν τῇ παρακλήσει, "if exhorting, [it is to be exercised] with exhortation."[9]

ὁ μεταδιδοὺς ἐν ἁπλότητι, "if giving, [it is to be exercised] with generosity."

ὁ προϊστάμενος ἐν σπουδῇ, "if leading, [it is to be exercised] with eagerness."

ὁ ἐλεῶν ἐν ἱλαρότητι, "if showing mercy, [it is to be exercised] with cheerfulness."

I will now briefly consider what Paul means by each gift.

Prophecy

Paul endorses the OT prophets as those who spoke from God by the Spirit.[10] On one occasion, he draws on a pagan prophet, Epimenides, in describing the Cretans (Titus 1:12).[11] He sees prophecy in the age of the church as a

---

8. Or "with service," or ministry.
9. Or encouraging, consoling.
10. See Rom. 1:2; 3:21; 11:3. He also cites a range of OT prophets including Moses (Pentateuch, e.g., Gen. 17:5 = Rom. 4:17), David (Psalms, e.g., 51:4 = Rom. 3:4), Malachi (1:2–3 = Rom. 9:13), Hosea (1:10 [2:1] = Rom. 9:26), Joel (2:32 [3:5] = Rom. 10:13), Isaiah (52:15 = Rom. 15:21), Habakkuk (2:4 = Rom. 1:17; Gal. 3:11), and Jeremiah (9:24 [23] = 1 Cor. 1:31). We can add any number of allusions and echoes. These are drawn from Moisés Silva, "Old Testament in Paul," DPL 631.
11. On this passage see Fee, GEP, 777. The citation is from Epimenides (ca. 600 BC). Fee notes this is the only use of the prophet word group not used of OT or Christian prophets. He notes possibilities here, including that Epimenides unconsciously spoke prophetically, that Paul is turning the tables on the false teachers of Crete who revered him, or that Paul simply reflected the common view of the revered Epimenides. Fee rightly argues that with these uncertainties, we can discern little of Paul's perspective on "charismatic phenomena outside the Christian faith." Fee rightly concludes,

gift.[12] The gift in the NT tradition suggests someone who receives from God messages for the church in accordance with the revelation of Christ and the gospel.[13] As in the case of Agabus, it may be a predictive message.[14] Equally, it may be a message to the community, calling for a particular response. Or both dimensions are fused—a summons to a response accompanied by something futuristic, for instance, that there will be famine, therefore, the church needs to raise funds for those who will be impoverished by it (Acts 11:28–30).[15] Indeed, any proclamation in the church can be prophetic if God has fused it with his Spirit and he speaks through the speaker into the situation.[16]

Paul has high regard for prophecy in the gathered community, urges people to seek it, and encourages men and women to do so (1 Cor. 11:4–5;[17] 14:1–40). He encourages the Thessalonians not to "despise prophecies." This injunction responds to one aspect of their refusal to "quench the Spirit."[18] However, they are to "test everything," suggesting the use of the prophecy in gathered worship but with the messages tested for authenticity (1 Thess. 5:19–21).[19] He also endorses the role of prophecy in 1 Timothy 1:18, as he appeals to Timothy to deal with the false teachers of Ephesus "in accordance with the prophecies previously made about you."[20]

"The result is powerful irony. A nonChristian 'prophet' speaks truly about some would-be Christian leaders, who because of their false teaching and behavior are true 'Cretans,' liars all."

12. On prophecy in the Roman non-Jewish world, see Dunn, *Jesus and the Spirit*, 228.

13. Dunn, *Jesus and the Spirit*, 228–29, rightly notes we cannot reduce prophecy to preaching. It is "a word of revelation," "inspired speech."

14. Acts 11:28; 21:10–12. So also Judas and Silas (Acts 15:32). See also Acts 11:27; 13:1; 1 Cor. 14:32, 37; Eph. 2:20; 3:5; Rev. 11:10; 16:6; 18:20, 24; 22:6, 9. There are also false prophets (Acts 13:6; 2 Peter 2:1; 1 John 4:1; Rev. 16:13; 19:20; 20:10).

15. See also Dunn, *Jesus and the Spirit*, 230. "It would include both fore-telling and forth-telling."

16. Concerning pastors, as McKnight says, "In nurturing Christoformity in a congregation sometimes the pastor teaches and sometimes preaches, and sometimes the pastor's communications are prompted by the Spirit in such a manner that we must say the words are prophetic." McKnight, *PPNCCC*, 18. We can also note that many of the gifts, like this one, relate to speaking. Dunn notes this and rightly says (citing Hendrikus Berkhof, *The Doctrine of the Holy Spirit* [London: Epworth, 1965], 36), "Spirit and speaking belong together." Dunn, *Jesus and the Spirit*, 226–27.

17. On this passage, see Fee, *GEP*, 144–45. He rightly recognizes this as applying to gathered church worship and agrees that "both men and women apparently shared equally in the praying and prophesying" in appropriate attire. See also Dunn, *Jesus and the Spirit*, 280.

18. I take "do not quench the Spirit" as relating to the whole section and not just what follows. See chapter 12, "Living by the Spirit." Here I differ from Fee, *GEP*, 57–62, who argues that this sits with what follows only with Paul addressing an issue like Corinth with too much emphasis on spiritual phenomena, or is preventative of this very thing. The passage lacks connectives, and in that so many of the aspects of it indicate fruit of the Spirit, or Spirit-impelled actions; the fire of the Spirit is not merely related to charismata mentioned but the fruit of the Spirit and aspects of worship held in the passage.

19. Similarly, see Fee, *GEP*, 60. However, I would argue vv. 21–22 are general rather than merely focused on good prophetic words versus evil ones.

20. See on this verse Fee, *GEP*, 758–59. This verse correlates with 1 Timothy 4:14 and 2 Timothy 1:6–8, 14, which together emphasize the importance of the Spirit, the giving of gifts, and prophetic encouragement in Timothy's life and ministry. Fee contends this experience goes back to the origins

Chapter 14 of 1 Corinthians is devoted to the use of prophecy in gathered worship, filling out the intent of 1 Thessalonians 5. Where speaking gifts are concerned, prophecy is to be sought above all else (1 Cor. 14:1, 39). It is to be exercised with love, the most excellent way (12:31–14:1a). Genuine prophecy builds up, encourages, and consoles believers and the church (14:3–5). Prophecy has the power to convert unbelievers visiting the church gathering (vv. 23–25). In orderly worship, while all can prophesy, two or three with the gift of prophecy are permitted to speak in turn so that the church's people can learn and be encouraged (vv. 29–31). Verse 32 likely refers to those with the gift of assessing the spiritual source and significance of the prophecy.[21]

"A prophet" (not something all believers are, 1 Cor. 12:28–29) is likely someone who prophesies commonly, accurately, and in accordance with the gospel of Christ.[22] It is also a crucial leadership role that, for Paul, follows the founding apostle's work (1 Cor. 12:28; Eph. 4:11). It differs from the gift of the teacher, evangelist, and pastor (see further below). As such, it likely speaks not so much of unpacking God's Word, converting the lost, caring for God's flock, or instructing others concerning the things of God, but bringing God's Word dynamically through word and Spirit with a prophetic edge. As such, the dynamic communication of God's Word is a priority in his churches.[23]

Not all have the charismatic function (1 Cor. 12:29); however, believers are right to seek it, all can at times prophesy, and it is a crucial gift with enormous power to build people up and even convert the lost (1 Cor. 14:1–25). No one in this age has complete prophetic knowledge, and if they did, without love, it is worthless (1 Cor. 13:2, 9). The prophets and leaders of the community have the responsibility of testing each prophecy to ensure it aligns with the kerygmatic tradition, it comes with love and expresses love, and it builds up the community.[24]

---

of his ministry; however, the verb προάγω merely means "prior or before." So, we cannot be sure at what point in his ministry they occurred, other than earlier. Fee is correct in saying that "it was *the Spirit himself* who expressly *singled Timothy out* for this ministry in which he had long been involved, and which is now being tested in Ephesus" (p. 759). Fee rightly rejects reading "ordination" into this, and we cannot be sure what the prophecies involved other than preparing him for the kind of ministry of mission and church leadership he was involved in with Paul. This ministry involved "warring" with false teachers. Fee's comments on the plural are speculative. The most we can say about the plural is that there was more than one prophecy (speculation about the context[s] is futile).

21. See also Dunn, who notes that the prophets had "authority to evaluate the oracle of another prophet, or indeed, no doubt, any other prophecy." Dunn, *Jesus and the Spirit*, 281.

22. Fee, *GEP*, 170: "some people are called 'prophet,' probably because they were frequent speakers of 'prophecies.'" Dunn, *Jesus and the Spirit*, 281: "The community did not install a man [or woman] into a prophetic 'office' and then allow him [or her] to prophesy; on the contrary, the community simply recognized a man [or woman] as a prophet because he [or she] already prophesied regularly . . . he [or she] was a prophet because he [or she] prophesied."

23. Paul gives prophecy the key role of "building up the community." Dunn, *Jesus and the Spirit*, 280.

24. See the excellent section Dunn, *Jesus and the Spirit*, 293–97.

Service

While διακονία can imply "ministry" or "deacon," here the second clause suggests Paul has in view the gift of service.[25] This gift is not otherwise mentioned in the Scriptures but perhaps speaks of those with an extraordinary capacity and skill in supporting leaders and/or showing hospitality. Notably, Paul shifts from an important leadership gift (prophecy) to something seemingly mundane.[26]

Teaching

Paul continues the oscillation between leadership gifts and the seemingly banal, mentioning "teaching," another crucial leadership gift. God is the ultimate teacher in Christ by the Spirit (1 Thess. 4:9; cf. 1 John 2:27). He sets people apart with a special gift of teaching others. The gift speaks of those with an exceptional ability to instruct others concerning the gospel.[27] It is distinct from prophecy and follows it in 1 Corinthians 12:28.[28] In Ephesians 4:11, it is listed last and is also distinct from evangelist and pastor.[29] It is not merely preaching the gospel or bringing a fresh prophetic word but the extraordinary capacity to discern and teach God's ways and will, especially from the Scriptures.[30]

This link between God's Word and teaching is seen in Colossians 3:16a–b, where the Colossians are to let "the word of Christ dwell in [them] richly, teaching and admonishing one another in all wisdom."[31] Similarly, 1 Timothy

---

25. See for a specific ministry (albeit retaining the notion of ministry as service), Acts 1:17, 25; 6:1, 4; 11:29; 12:25; 20:24; 21:19; Rom. 11:13; 15:31; 1 Cor. 12:5; 16:15; 2 Cor. 3:7, 8, 9; 4:1; 5:18; 6:3; 8:4; 9:1, 12, 13; 11:8; Eph. 4:12; Col. 4:17; 1 Tim. 1:12; 2 Tim. 4:5, 11; Heb.1:14. More generally of service, see Luke 10:40; Rev. 2:19. "It is best taken to mean a particular kind of service for which the same individual is regularly responsible, or regular acts of service of different kinds undertaken by the same person." Dunn, *Jesus and the Spirit*, 249.

26. Keown, *Romans and the Mission of God*, 232.

27. In the Gospels and Acts, Jewish teachers are mentioned (Luke 2:46; John 3:10; Acts 5:34); Jesus is often considered a teacher and his ministry teaching (e.g., Matt. 4:23; 5:2; 7:28–29; 8:19; Mark 1:21–22; 4:1–2, 38; Luke 4:15; 8:49; John 1:38; 7:16); teaching is essential to the Great Commission (Matt. 28:20); the Spirit teaches believers (John 14:26); the teaching of the apostles is foundational (Acts 2:42; 5:42); teachers were part of the Antiochian church (Acts 13:1); there were false teachers (Acts 15:1); and Paul and Barnabas taught (Acts 15:35; 20:20; 28:31). In Hebrews, maturity enables people to teach (5:12) the basics and more advanced things (6:2); in the new covenant, all can teach all (6:11), and false teaching is a threat (13:9; 2 Peter 2:1; 2 John 9, 10; Rev. 2:14, 15, 20, 24). James warns that teachers receive greater judgment (3:1). Teaching is an important aspect of Paul's understanding of ministry (Rom. 16:17; 1 Cor. 4:17; Col. 1:28; 2 Thess. 2:15; 1 Tim. 2:7; 2 Tim. 1:11; 3:10; Titus 2:1). See also 1 Cor. 14:6; Eph. 4:21; Col. 2:7; Titus 2:7, 10.

28. We see the distinction in Galatians 1:12, where Paul received the gospel by a revelation of Christ, and not through teaching (the passing on of the tradition).

29. On the question of whether it should be translated "pastors who teach," see the discussion of the passage later in the chapter on Ephesians 4:7–16.

30. Fee, *GEP*, 193. "There were some who regularly gave a 'teaching' in the communities, who thus came to be known as teachers."

31. The mention of the psalms later in the verse also shows that teaching through music is an aspect of church strengthening.

4:11–12 links the public reading of the Scriptures to Paul's twofold admonition to Timothy to teach (also v. 16), and the God-breathed Scriptures are helpful for teaching (2 Tim. 3:16).

A person with a teaching gift should express it.[32] Not all Christians are teachers in this way, but seminaries are full of such people, as are the cell groups of the world. People in the local church with the gift should share it with others (1 Cor. 14:6, 26). Unsurprisingly, there are many with the gift, as teaching fortifies believers from false ideas.[33] The task of all these charismatically equipped leaders is given in Ephesians 4:12. They are appointed "for the equipping of the saints for works of service" (my translation). It is disputed whether "for works of service" (εἰς ἔργον διακονίας) applies to the saints or the group of leaders ("for the work of ministry"). The latter view sees the three prepositional clauses in v. 12 as coordinate.

πρὸς τὸν καταρτισμὸν τῶν ἁγίων, "for the equipping of the saints"

εἰς ἔργον διακονίας, "for work of ministry"

εἰς οἰκοδομὴν τοῦ σώματος τοῦ Χριστοῦ, "for the upbuilding of the body of Christ"

This view is unpersuasive. First, there is the shift from πρός to εἰς, and the article is absent in the second and third clauses. Second, the focus in vv. 7–13 is "all" Christians in service and reaching maturity, not just leaders. Third, all believers are to speak the truth in love, not merely those with these gifts. Fourth, the passage culminates in *all* joined and held together in unity, building itself up. The movement from Christ to the leaders to all makes sense in the passage.[34]

The task of these charismatic functionaries is to equip others for apostolic, prophetic, evangelistic, pastoral, and didactic functions in the church and beyond. As the "specialists" do their work and "the others" are equipped, the church is built up in the unity of faith and a shared understanding of Christ, the Son of God. The church and its people grow to maturity and are guarded against false doctrines. Knowing the truth, they articulate it with love that the church may become more and more Christ-shaped. Like a body, held together by its every part, small and large, it works properly, grows through the acquisition of new converts and in maturity, and builds itself up in love. This passage describes the types of pneumaform churches desperately needed to defend and advance the gospel in an increasingly hostile world.

---

32. While Fee is technically correct to distinguish the "teacher" from "teaching" in Romans 12:7, to avoid repetition, I have discussed them together earlier. Fee, *GEP*, 192.
33. Eph. 4:14; Col. 1:28; 2:22; 1 Tim. 1:3, 7, 10; 4:1, 6; 6:1–3; 2 Tim. 4:2–4; Titus 1:9, 11.
34. Similarly, see Thielman, *Ephesians*, 277–79.

Women also receive the gift, although 1 Timothy 2:12 speaks of either a complete Pauline prohibition of women teaching men or, as I prefer, a limitation in Ephesus due to the perpetuation of false ideas through women in the church.[35] Either way, women with the gift at least teach other women in Paul's churches (Titus 2:3). Teaching is a specific requirement for elders (1 Tim. 3:2; cf. 2 Tim. 2:24) and some are to receive honor, "those who labor in preaching and teaching" (1 Tim. 5:17). Those with the gift are to find others and develop them for the next generation (2 Tim. 2:2).[36]

Exhortation

Due to the semantic breadth of the language, ὁ παρακαλῶν (one who is called to one's side) can be a person who comforts, encourages, or exhorts.[37] The language is used for preaching in a general sense (Acts 13:15) and of the ministries of John the Baptist (Luke 3:18), Peter (Acts 2:40), Paul,[38] and Judas and Silas (Acts 15:32). Paul's team exercised the gift despite being slandered (1 Cor. 4:13). In Romans 15:4, Paul speaks of the παρακλήσεως τῶν γραφῶν, which potentially links the gift to using God's word as a basis for exhortation and encouragement. It is also an outcome of authentic prophecy (1 Cor. 14:3, 31) and an aspect of the proclamation ministries of Paul, Timothy, and Titus.[39] Believers are to exhort one another.[40] Perhaps deciding between these meanings is not required, as it may indicate a person with the capacity to do all these things—one who goes alongside others and ministers to them, whatever their situation. This charism may be a leadership gift but may equally be something found among the wider church community. Whatever it connotes, believers are to exercise it by encouraging, consoling, and exhorting others.

Generosity

The term μεταδίδωμι is used for those who share with others: materially (Luke 3:11; Eph. 4:28), spiritual gifts (Rom 1:11), the gospel (1 Thess 2:8), and their lives (1 Thess. 2:8).[41] Here, then, it could indicate someone who

35. "Although, then, the prohibition may appear to be universally applicable to women, it is in fact meant for a specific group of women among the recipients of the letter." Marshall and Towner, *A Critical and Exegetical Commentary*, 455.
36. Dunn, *Jesus and the Spirit*, 237–38. He considers that for Paul, teaching "included both a recognition of traditional material as authoritative and an appreciation of the need for it to be interpreted and applied charismatically to the ever changing needs and situations of the believing communities" (p. 238).
37. On the range, see BDAG, s.v. "παρακαλέω," 764–65.
38. Acts 11:23; 14:22; 16:40; 20:1–2.
39. 2 Cor. 5:20; 1 Thess. 2:12; 3:2; 2 Thess. 3:12; 1 Tim. 4:13; 2 Tim. 4:2; Titus 1:9; 2:6, 15. Paul uses the plural of παρακαλέω frequently as a term of address in the sense of "urge, plead with, encourage" (e.g., Rom. 12:1; 15:30; 1 Cor. 1:10; 2 Cor. 2:8; Eph. 4:1; Phil. 4:2; 1 Thess. 4:1; 1 Tim. 2:1; Philem. 10).
40. 1 Thess. 4:18; 5:11; cf. Heb. 3:13; 10:25; 13:22.
41. See also Dunn, *Jesus and the Spirit*, 250–52. I do not concur with Dunn, who broadens this out to "giving and caring"; the Greek implies giving and it is primarily financial (although it should always be done with love, cf. 1 Cor. 13:3).

shares spiritually with others. Still, in the context of a letter written during Paul's Jerusalem collection mission, it may speak of the generous giving we see in Phoebe, Rufus's mother, and Gaius (Rom. 16:2, 13, 23). The phrase ἐν ἁπλότητι may indicate sincerity and genuineness;[42] however, in regard to material giving, it suggests "generosity" (2 Cor. 8:2; 9:11, 13). The one with the gift of giving should do so lavishly. The gift is mentioned again in 1 Corinthians 12:3, hyperbolically indicating that such giving should be motivated by love, or it avails nothing. It is also implied in 2 Corinthians 8:7 as Paul commends them for the abundance of their faith, speech, knowledge, and eagerness due to God's grace. Paul wants the Corinthians to abound in the gift of giving toward the struggling Jerusalem Christians.

Leadership

Ὁ προϊστάμενος speaks of the notion of standing out front and so "leading."[43] Paul uses it for church leaders (1 Thess. 5:12; 1 Tim. 5:17) and those who manage their homes well and so are suitable to be overseers or deacons (1 Tim. 3:4–5, 12) or elders (1 Tim. 5:17).[44] Here, then, it speaks of members of the Roman church leadership. Such people are to carry out their leadership roles with σπουδή, "eagerness, earnestness, diligence, willingness, [or] zeal" (cf. Rom. 12:11).[45]

While it is common to translate κυβέρνησις as "administration," in 1 Corinthians 12:27–31, it is parallel to ὁ προϊστάμενος, "leadership." "Administration" does not capture the leadership dynamic implied in the term.[46] Those equipped with this gift give leadership to the church. The language is used nautically of a helmsman on a ship (Acts 27:11; Rev. 18:17). It was used of government officials, deities including God, and Christ as the helmsman of the church.[47]

Merciful Acts

The final gift is ὁ ἐλεῶν, "showing mercy" or better, "doing acts of mercy"—in that true Christian mercy flows from attitude to action.[48] Again, Paul follows a leadership gift with something purportedly "ordinary."

---

42. BDAG, s.v. "ἁπλότης," 104. See also 2 Cor. 1:12; 11:3; Eph. 6:5; Col. 3:22.

43. *BrillDAG*, s.v. "προΐστημι."

44. Used of a chief servant (2 Kgdms. 13:17); political leadership (1 Macc. 5:19); the master of an eagle (Prov. 23:5); leaders of a home (Amos 6:10); priestly leaders (Bel. 8). See also Titus 3:8, 14.

45. BDAG, s.v. "σπουδή," 939. See also 2 Cor. 7:11–12; 8:7–8, 16; Heb. 6:11; 2 Peter 1:5. Dunn suggests "with zest." Dunn, *Jesus and the Spirit*, 251.

46. I see no reason to take this gift in the sense "one who gives aid" or "cares for others" or merely "giving guidance" as Dunn suggests. Someone who helms a boat is a key leader. Dunn, *Jesus and the Spirit*, 251–52. Neither does "administrative skills," as Fee prefers. Fee, *GEP*, 193.

47. Hermann Wolfgang Beyer, "Κυβέρνησις," *TDNT*, vol. 3, 1035–37. The verb κυβερνήτης is used in the LXX of a ship's helmsman (4 Macc. 7:1; Prov. 23:34; 24:6), someone skillful in navigation (Prov. 1:5), people without direction (Prov. 11:14), and people steering Tyre politically (Ezek. 27:8, 27, 28).

48. See also Dunn, *Jesus and the Spirit*, 250–52.

However, it is far from ordinary, as mercy is a characteristic of God, the "Father of mercies" (Rom. 12:1; 2 Cor. 1:3).[49] It is a trait Jesus showed and wanted in his disciples[50] and one that Jude wants his readers to show to others who doubt or waver in faith (Jude 22–23). The gift is in those who have a heightened capacity to respond to others with compassion, grace, and empathy despite their being difficult. Such people are to do so with cheerfulness.[51] The gift is "a reflection of God's unmerited generosity in Christ."[52]

Summary of Romans 12:3–8

We see from this passage that by God's Spirit, those in Christ receive various gifts as God decides. Those in the process of being pneumaformed (vv. 1–2) are to accept them, whether they are seemingly relational-support gifts or gifts of leadership and proclamation. They are to exercise them with humility, in unity, for fellow believers, and in God's mission as the church connects to the world. The gifts include, but are not exhausted by, prophecy, service, teaching, exhortation, giving, leadership, and mercy. The gifts are to be exercised generously, diligently, humbly, and cheerfully per a person's God-given capacities. By implication, believers should encourage others to exercise their gifts as Paul intends here.

1 CORINTHIANS 1:5

As Paul begins 1 Corinthians, he tells his readers how he perpetually gives thanks to God for them because of the grace (χάρις) given to them in Christ (1:4). His reason (ὅτι) is that they have been enriched in Christ ἐν παντὶ λόγῳ γνῶσις καὶ πάσῃ γνώσει. This clause includes a summarized list representing their remarkable giftedness as a church (v. 7). The misuse of these gifts lies at the heart of the Corinthians' problem.[53] But while it is tempting to see irony or flattery here because Paul will set about correcting aspects of their thinking concerning speech and their faulty knowledge, this can be ruled out because the verse refers to Paul's prayer life. He would hardly be ironic or flatter others as he prays (cf. 2 Cor. 4:2; 1 Thess. 2:3–5). Instead, he acknowledges their genuine giftedness as a church, even if they need correction.[54]

---

49. Also Luke 1:50, 54, 58, 72, 78; 6:36; Rom. 9:15–16, 18, 23; 11:30–32; 12:1; 15:9; 1 Cor. 7:25; 2 Cor. 4:1; Eph. 2:4; Phil. 2:27; 1 Tim. 1:2, 13, 16; 2 Tim. 1:2, 16, 18; Titus 3:5; Heb. 8:12; James 3:17; 5:11; 1 Peter 1:3; 2:10; 2 John 4; Jude 2. Also Christ (Heb. 2:17; 4:16; Jude 21).

50. See also Matt. 5:7; 9:13, 27; 12:7; 18:33; 23:23; Luke 6:36; 10:37; James 2:13.

51. In classical and later Greek, the term means "glad, merry, cheerful." Rudolf Bultmann, "Ἱλαρός, Ἱλαρότης," TDNT 3:297. See also Dunn, Jesus and the Spirit, 250, who notes that the term was common in Jewish and Christian wisdom (Prov. 22:8 LXX; Sir. 35:8; Lev. Rab. 34:9; 2 Cor. 9:7).

52. Dunn, Jesus and the Spirit, 250.

53. Fee, GEP, 87: "They are selected here because . . . they were both noticeably evident in this community and also highly prized among them."

54. As Fee puts it, "The problem after all lay not in the Corinthians' giftedness, but in their attitude toward such gifts." Fee, GEP, 85.

Verse 6 links their enrichment to their receipt of the gospel from Paul and his team (cf. Acts 18:3–11; 1 Cor. 2:1–5; 2 Cor. 1:19). Just as the testimony about Christ was established in them, so God imparted to them spiritual gifts. These came through the giving of the Spirit. Indeed, where spiritual gifts are concerned,[55] they are a church that lacks nothing (v. 7). However, as the epistle plays out, Paul exposes their deficient ethics based on their inadequate Christology and pneumatology, reflected in their immaturity. They are not fully pneumaformed.

Speech

Λόγος here is likely used in the broad sense of "speech," referring to gifted speaking inclusive of rhetorical ability (in a general sense) and special speaking gifts.[56] Corinth is renowned as a center of rhetoric.[57] As such, this could indicate that many in the church are excellent orators. However, their love of rhetoric is skewed in at least five ways, as Paul's response in the letter indicates.

First, their interest in rhetorical eloquence has caused them to factionalize around preferred orators—Paul, Apollos, and Cephas (1:12). They have failed to realize that all such preachers are merely servants of Jesus, and it is Christ they should be united in, by the Spirit. What matters is the clear articulation of the gospel appropriate to the context, not the speaker's style and complexity. Paul addresses this with a series of creative arguments in 1:12e– 4:21. Second, their interest in brilliant speaking has diverted them from the importance of clearly proclaiming Christ so that people are converted by the power of the gospel and not their rhetorical flamboyance (2:1–5). Third, their

---

55. Fee, *GEP*, 86, rightly observes 1 Corinthians 1:7 is the first use of χάρισμα in the Pauline corpus and suggests a translation "gracious endowments." This is technically correct, but I will persevere with the common understanding for simplicity.

56. See also 1 Cor. 1:17; 2:1, 4; 4:19, 20; 12:8; 14:9. A range of views exist. (1) Λόγος = lower knowledge; γνῶσις = higher knowledge. This has no credence as the two categories do not exist in Paul. (2) Λόγος = tongues; γνῶσις = prophecy. Again, implausible, as Paul never associates the Greek terms with these gifts. (3) Λόγος = the gospel received; γνῶσις = their acceptance. This is ludicrous as again, the terms do not carry that weight. (4) Λόγος = outward expression; γνῶσις = inward conviction and receipt of the gospel (the view of Lightfoot and O'Brien). See J. B. Lightfoot, *Notes on the Epistles of St Paul from Unpublished Commentaries* (London: Macmillan, 1895); Peter T. O'Brien, *Introductory Thanksgivings in the Letters of Paul*, NovTSup 49 (Leiden: Brill, 1977), 118. While this is reasonable for λόγος, γνῶσις does not fit the context and cannot be limited to just this (also Fee, *GEP*, 87). (5) Λόγος = rational gifts; γνῶσις = ecstatic gifts; Günther Zuntz, *The Text of the Epistles* (London: British Academy, 1953), 101. Again, these categories do not exist in Paul, nor does this fit context. (6) Λόγος = legalistic following of Jesus's teaching; γνῶσις = awareness of the gospel freeing us from "conventional rules." These are arbitrary intrusions into 1 Corinthians, as there is nothing in the letter to suppose these are at stake. See Fee, *GEP*, 87; K. Grayston, "Not with a Rod," *ExpT* 88 (1976): 13–16. (7) Λόγος = the spiritual gifts in chaps. 12–14 (knowledge, wisdom, tongues, prophecy, etc.); γνῶσις = special knowledge from prophetic revelation (12:8; 13:2; 14:6). Fee, *GEP*, 88. My view is similar but extends to speaking skills generally and knowledge generally (the gifts specified are subsets of the broader categories, not the other way around).

57. Witherington, *Conflict*, 100–101.

desire for oratorial gifts led them to value tongues disproportionately, something Paul addresses in chapters 12 and 14.

Fourth, in their zeal for speaking prowess, they have failed to realize the critical importance of love as a motivation for all speech. Paul deals with this in chapter 13. Fifth, as they seek to be great orators, they do not acknowledge the critical importance of prophecy as the supreme speaking gift, in that it brings God's Word dynamically to hearers, edifies believers, and converts unbelievers (chapter 14).

The two gifts, "word of wisdom" and "word of knowledge" (12:8 LEB), are likely two aspects of speaking that Paul recognizes, as are tongues and prophecy. The same gift is mentioned in 2 Corinthians 8:7, where Paul confirms that God is the source of the gift by his grace and that the Corinthians abound or overflow (περισσεύω) in the gift. They are a church with outstanding speakers; however, they are ethically challenged. They need to allow the fruit of the Spirit to shape their speech as they continue to serve God.[58] Further, they need to stop judging preachers based on their ability to titillate and entertain.

Knowledge

The second term, γνῶσις, speaks of the Corinthians' knowledge and, considering the theological deficiencies exposed in the letter, may reference their excellent capacity for philosophical thought expressed in their speech. Mention of such knowledge suggests that although not many of the Corinthians were elites (1 Cor. 1:26), the church had many articulate, intelligent people able to think theologically. However, the letter exposes their level of understanding.

First, they are divided in their thinking and need to be restored to unified knowledge of the gospel (1 Cor. 1:10–11).[59] Second, they do not fully understand the ethical implications of Christ's death—the need for cruciformity and Christoformity.[60] Third, and related, while they are hungry for things of the Spirit and especially speaking gifts, they fail to acknowledge the decisive role of the Spirit in forming them to be cruciform people with the mind of Christ, which is the mind of the Spirit (1 Cor. 2:1–16).[61]

---

58. Also of interest is 2 Corinthians 11:6, where Paul replies to his critics that he is untrained in speech (λόγος) and knowledge (γνῶσις). While this is not a spiritual gift list, it confirms their importance as general categories of God's gifts to his people, including the Corinthians. It is evident that his critics are arguing that Paul is untrained (ἰδιώτης) in rhetorical speech and knowledge. This is false of course, as Paul is an apostle and equipped by God to know the gospel and proclaim it. However, for the sake of argument, Paul concedes that he is not trained in rhetoric but refutes their claim that he has no knowledge. See also Fee, *GEP*, 345.

59. See especially 1:10: ἦτε δὲ κατηρτισμένοι ἐν τῷ αὐτῷ νοῒ καὶ ἐν τῇ αὐτῇ γνώμῃ, "to be restored into the same mindset and into the same understanding."

60. While unlike the world, which has false wisdom and complete ignorance of the cross (1:21; 2:8), the Corinthians believe in Christ and are believers (1:2 [sanctified saints], 12 [brothers and sisters]); their knowledge is inadequate as it does not lead to a reshaping of their ethics.

61. Creatively, Paul moves from Christ to the Spirit seamlessly in 2:10 and emphasizes the Spirit's role in his Christocentric proclamation, ending with believers having the mind of Christ—by the Spirit!

Fourth, those with great intellect and speech are arrogant. In the Corinthians' zeal for brilliance and acclaim, their messages lack the power generated when Christ is articulated simply, clearly, and understandably. Hence, Paul wants to come to Corinth in love to show them the difference by demonstrating the power of Christ by his Spirit to transform, as he did when he was first in Corinth (4:19–20; cf. 2:1–5).[62]

Fifth, they do not understand the importance of a bodily Christian existence shaped in its every aspect by God's love, whether relational or sexual. Thus, they veer from Christian sexual ethics and have distorted understandings of marriage, sexuality, and the resurrection of the body. Paul deals with all these matters throughout the letter (1 Cor. 5–7; 15).

Sixth, in their arrogance (e.g., 8:1–2) and seeming spiritualism, they have a defective understanding of the place of love in Christian life. Hence, while some know it is legitimate to eat food sacrificed to idols, they do not defer to their weaker brothers and sisters who do not fully realize this (1 Cor. 8; 10);[63] do not express their gifts, including knowledge with love, and so render their giftedness and knowledge void (13:1–3, esp. v. 2); do not understand what love is and its supreme importance (13:4–7); do not acknowledge the partiality of present knowledge (13:8–12);[64] and fail to exercise their gifts with love (chapter 13–14). Their understanding of spirituality and spiritual gifts is inadequate, something Paul addresses in 1 Corinthians 12.[65] Through the letter, Paul encourages them to grow in knowledge and share messages of knowledge (12:8; 14:6) but, out of love, to ensure others understand and grow in the faith (14:7, 9).

Seventh, their inflated view of their knowledge leads them to demean Paul, meaning he has to defend himself to win them over (e.g., 1 Cor. 1:12; 9:1–27; 14:37–38). Finally, and connected with their lack of understanding of the importance of the body, they have a flawed understanding of the resurrection, which Paul deals with in 1 Corinthians 15.[66]

(esp. 2:11, 14). See the excellent discussion of this passage in Fee, *GEP*, 93–112. He writes, "By 'mind' he probably means Christ's own understanding of his saving significance, as revealed to us by the Spirit. In fact, in the Greek Bible that Paul cites, the word 'mind' translates to the Hebrew *rûah*, which ordinarily means 'spirit' (Isa. 40:13)" (p. 109).

62. I read Paul's mention of power in 1 Corinthians 2:5 and 4:19 as referencing the power of the gospel to convert if it can be proclaimed clearly and understandably.

63. See the contrast in the use of knowledge language in 8:1–3 with 9:7, 10–11. This loveless, inflated knowledge has the effect of potentially destroying a brother or sister in Christ. Similarly, 10:1 begins a disclosure formula with Paul stating his desire that they do not remain ignorant and spells out the danger of their uncontrolled sinfulness and practice of eating at temple feasts.

64. See the use of γινωσκω language five times in vv. 8–12.

65. Note especially how Paul, again, begins in 12:1 with a disclosure formula—he does not want them ignorant about spiritual gifts and their use in the church. Again, in v. 3, he wants them to know what constitutes evidence of receipt of the Spirit—not tongues, but confessing Christ and repudiating cursing him.

66. Again, Paul begins with "I want you to know" in v. 1.

"Word of knowledge" as a gift could refer to either a general word that is knowledgeable or a momentary charismatic revelatory word of knowledge.[67] However, as discussed, knowledge permeates the letter and relates to a complete understanding of God, Christ, the Spirit, and God's work in the church and world. As such, it perhaps indicates a message that reflects this breadth, including the cross but much more.[68] Such a message should not puff the speaker up with arrogance (8:1) but should be a Spirit-given message showing understanding of the same gospel that enhances the knowledge of others (cf. 8:7, 10–11).

Paul considers such messages necessary in the gathered community (14:6). As with wisdom in the previous, 1 Corinthians 13:2 adds that if someone could understand and declare "all knowledge," it is futile without love. As all will be known, the need for the gift will pass away in the eschaton (13:8).[69]

While not exactly as God wants it, the giftedness of the Corinthians concerning knowledge is confirmed in 2 Corinthians 8:7 where they overflow with knowledge through God's grace.[70] Yet, as the content of 2 Corinthians indicates, their knowledge remains inadequate as they are being drawn away to false ideas. Paul writes to draw them back to the gospel of God.

1 CORINTHIANS 12:4–11

In 1 Corinthians 12–14, Paul deals with spiritual matters raised in the letter from the Corinthians (7:1).[71] The core issue appears to be their love of tongues, which they see as a decisive mark of receiving the Spirit.[72] In his response, Paul includes four spiritual gift lists and a chiasm emphasizing the importance of love in the exercise of spiritual gifts.[73]

---

67. E.g., Fee, *GEP*, 167, calls it a "'Spirit utterance' of some revelatory kind." Yet, that is undefined and could happen as preparing a sermon or in a church meeting. As such, I don't find this helpful—the phrase implies a message conveying God's knowledge, in whatever form. See Dunn's excellent analysis of wisdom in Paul (*Jesus and the Spirit*, 219–22). He states (p. 220) that "it probably means simply some charismatic utterance giving an insight into, some fresh understanding of God's plan of salvation or the benefits it brings to believers . . . an inspired proclamation with saving power." He goes on (p. 221) to suggest it fits "the charisma of a teacher"; however, to me, it fits the charisma of an apostle (e.g., Paul) or an evangelist.

68. Ultimately, Fee is correct that the difference between wisdom and knowledge Paul has in view is "perhaps forever lost to us." Fee, *GEP*, 167. See also the thoughts of Dunn, *Jesus and the Spirit*, 218–19.

69. Fee, *GEP*, 167.

70. See also the comments in the previous section (footnote 53) on 2 Corinthians 11:6.

71. Martin, *Spirit*, 7–8.

72. Fee writes, "The problem is an *abuse* of the gift of tongues." This is suggested especially in the "running contrast" between tongues and prophecy in 14:1–25, that "the correctives are *all* aimed at the abuse of tongues in the assembly," and "only tongues is included in every list of 'gifts' in these three chapters." Fee, *GEP*, 148–49 (emphasis original).

73. A1 1 Corinthians 12: The gifts.
     B 1 Corinthians 13: The most excellent way in which all gifts must be expressed—love.
     A2 1 Corinthians 14: Speaking gifts in the gathered community.

In vv. 1–3, Paul introduces the subject matter (things of the Spirit);[74] reminds the Corinthians of their being formerly misled into the worship of mute gods and meaningless, supposedly ecstatic and inspired speech;[75] and establishes that the evidence of the reception of the Spirit by a Christian is their utter refusal to curse Jesus and the fundamental declaration that "Jesus is Lord."[76] Paul then turns to the matter of spiritual gifts.

Verses 4 to 6 do not delineate the three different types of gifts (gifts, services, activities) as sourced from different members of the Trinity.[77] Instead, they indicate that the source of all the various gifts, including the ones listed and any others that are received, is the Triune God.[78] Here we have an excellent example of the claim made in the introduction of this book: God and Christ (or God through Christ) act in the world through the Spirit. Notably, the gifts are empowered in all believers. Verses 7–9 and 10 clearly indicate that the Spirit is the means by which God, in Christ, distributes gifts. As the source is one, and the gifts are diverse, Paul here emphasizes diversity within unity without uniformity.[79] Furthermore, as God is the source, all gifts are to be valued, as are all believers.

In v. 7, Paul emphasizes that each Christian is given a particular manifestation of the Spirit for what is profitable or advantageous (συμφέρον). This verse includes the third use of συμφέρω in the letter.[80] The gifts are to

---

74. Here I agree with Fee, who translates it this way because although gifts (χαρίσματα) are in view at points, to translate τῶν πνευματικῶν as "gifts" is too narrow.

75. Agreeing with Fee that here, Paul is not just contrasting their former pagan lives with their present one but is setting a contrast between truly Spirit-inspired speech and that of paganism. Fee, GEP, 153–54.

76. "To curse Jesus is proof in itself that one does not possess the Spirit; conversely, one can only acknowledge Christ in the power of the Spirit." Habets, Anointed Son, 136. It is not important whether the cursing of Jesus is hypothetical, actual in persecution contexts, synagogues, or pagan situations (see Fee, GEP, 156–57). A true believer would not countenance such a thing in any setting. While it is true that anyone can say "Jesus is Lord," it is the combination of the curse and confession that marks off a believer. Furthermore, the confession is the earliest Christian confession tied to his resurrection and lordship. See also Fee, GEP, 157.

77. Paul uses the Greek διαιρέσεις, which carries the nuance of something dividing up, so "apportionment, division," or "difference, variety" (BDAG, s.v. "διαιρέσεις," 229). Martin may be correct to suggest Paul uses it in 12:4 of legitimate division to contrast with αἱρέσεις of destructive divisions in Corinth in 11:19. Martin, Spirit, 12–13.

78. Similarly and in detail, Fee, GEP, 161–63.

79. Similarly, Fee, GEP, 159–60.

80. In response to the Corinthian claim that "all things are permissible," he twice responds that not all things are beneficial or helpful (1 Cor. 6:12; 10:23). BDAG, s.v. "συμφέρω," 960. The verb can have other meanings but in the NT often indicates something that betters or profits others. So, it is used of something better than something else—amputation is better than being thrown in hell (Matt. 5:29, 30); being drowned with a millstone around the neck is better than leading a "little" believer into sin (Matt. 18:6); singleness is better than marriage (Matt. 19:10); one man dying for the nation is better than the whole nation perishing (John 11:50; 18:7); it is better that Jesus goes away so the Spirit can come (John 16:7); teaching what is profitable is for the betterment of others (Acts 20:20); it is beneficial to the Corinthians to give to the collection (2 Cor. 8:10); there is no benefit from ongoing boasting (2 Cor. 12:1); being disciplined is for one's benefit (Heb. 12:10).

be used for betterment, that is, the benefit of God, the church, the mission, and others.[81]

Through the use of the dative ᾧ, "to whom," and then ἄλλῳ, "to another"…ἑτέρῳ, "to another"…ἄλλῳ…ἄλλῳ…ἄλλῳ…ἑτέρῳ…ἄλλῳ (used interchangeably)[82] in the nine-gift list of vv. 8–10, Paul emphasizes that the Spirit distributes the gifts across all the church's people—no one has them all (creating dependence), and all have at least one (creating a service opportunity). The gifts elude classification.[83] Tongues and interpretation are placed last to challenge the Corinthians' cherishing of them as most important.[84] The nine gifts are word of knowledge, prophecy, and the following.

Word of Wisdom

Λόγος indicates this is a speaking gift, one that forms part of the overall supreme rhetorical giftedness of the Corinthians (1:5).[85] The genitive of σοφία suggests a capacity to speak with wisdom. This wisdom could be general—the capacity to speak with insight. As some charismatic theology holds, it could be a momentary revelatory word of wisdom. However, these should be ruled out, as the σοφία nexus of terms in 1 Corinthians is otherwise used exclusively in the first three chapters in regard to God's wisdom contrasted with worldly wisdom (which is folly), and particularly, the cross as the wisdom of God.[86] Hence, it speaks of a Spirit-given message centered on the gospel of a

---

81. While I agree to an extent with Fee's assertion that in v. 7, "Paul proceeds to articulate how that diversity is worked out in the life of the church," this is too limiting. There is no mention of the body of Christ at this point; this comes later. The gifts are expressed in the context of the church and its subgroups. As Christians engage in the world—and so are missional and broader than the church—its people engage in church and in the world.

82. While in classical Greek ἄλλος indicated "another where there are many," and ὁ ἕτερος, "the other when there are two," this passage is a clear indication as to why "in the κοινή and the NT this kind of distinction becomes quite impossible." Friedrich Büchsel, "Ἄλλος," *TDNT* 1:264.

83. See Fee, *GEP*, 165. Some argue they descend in value, e.g., F. F. Bruce, *1 & 2 Corinthians*, NCB (Grand Rapids: Eerdmans, 1980), 119. However, this is unlikely as prophecy is the greatest gift in chapter 14. Others break it into three: (1) gifts of instruction; (2) gifts of supernatural power; and (3) gifts of inspired utterance. See, e.g., Martin, *Spirit*, 12. However, wisdom and knowledge are not instructive, necessarily, and prophecy arguably is (chapter 14). As Fee points out, discernment breaks the pattern.

84. Fee's perspective on the organization of the list is cogent. He rejects various ideas and rightly notes that wisdom and knowledge are important in Corinth, and then the others are "random" before landing on the issue at hand: tongues and interpretation. Fee, *GEP*, 164–65.

85. See Martin, *Spirit*, 13, who notes that Paul takes two Corinthian favorites and reframes them.

86. Wisdom language is used twenty-six times in 1:17–4:21 in these senses: (1) wisdom of words (rhetorical brilliance, 1:17; 2:1, 4); (2) worldly wisdom that Greeks seek and that God is destroying and will destroy (1:19, 20, 21 [2nd], 22, 26, 27; 2:5, 6 [2nd]; 2:13; 3:18 [1st], 19 [2x], 20); (3) God's predetermined, hidden wisdom of Christ crucified now revealed, that at its most "foolish" is wiser than worldly wisdom, which forms the basis of the church Paul planted (1:21 [1st], 24, 25, 30; 2:6, 7; 3:10, 18 [2nd]). See also Fee, *GEP*, 166–67. See also the contrast between fleshly wisdom and grace of God. Fee, *GEP*, 286. I also encourage readers to read Liston, *Kingdom Come*, 136–41, which speaks of a pneumatologically transformed imagination based on 1 Corinthians 1–2.

crucified Messiah.[87] Indeed, it is arguably parallel to the "message of the cross" in 1:18. Paul states in 1 Corinthians 13:2 that even if one could know and proclaim "all knowledge," without love, the knowledge gains nothing.

Faith

As all believers must have faith to believe, and so, such faith is assumed,[88] this likely refers to a heightened capacity in some believers to believe in and trust in God in situations others find difficult. It is spoken of hyperbolically as the faith that can move mountains.[89] Such faith must be exercised in love (13:2). "Faith" in 2 Corinthians 8:7, given as an act of grace in the believer's life, likely refers to the same gift.

Healings

This charism is the gift exercised by Jesus multiple times and through believers, especially in Acts.[90] The plural could indicate capacities to heal different diseases or in different ways.[91] Intriguingly, in his letters, Paul never mentions exorcism, although according to Luke, he exercises the gift in Acts.[92] It may be included in this gift or the one that follows.[93] He may include resurrection miracles here or below.[94] In his letters, he lumps all such things and perhaps those in the following category under the notion of "signs and wonders" (Rom. 15:19; 2 Cor. 12:12).

Paul mentions the spiritual gift of healing three times in 1 Corinthians 12 (vv. 9, 28, 30). In each, he uses the identical plural construct χαρίσματα ἰαμάτων, literally "gifts of healings." The use of the plural "gifts of healings" may be significant. Carson suggests it indicates diversity within the healing gift.[95] Thiselton concurs, stating that the plural "becomes a device for carrying the notion of *more than one kind* of what

---

87. See 1 Cor. 1:17, 19–22, 24, 30; 2:1, 4–7, 13; 3:19.

88. See 1 Cor. 2:5.

89. Similarly Dunn, *Jesus and the Spirit*, 211; Fee, *GEP*, 167. Carson suggests someone like George Müller would fall into the category in *Showing*, 38.

90. E.g., Luke 6:17–19; Acts 3:1–10; 5:16; 8:7. These include healings by Paul (Acts 14:8–10; 19:10–12; 28:8–9).

91. Fee is right to say that the gift is given to the healer and not the person healed, as is clear from v. 28, where the list speaks of people with the particular gifts, including this. However, while every healing is a gift, the plural says nothing about the permanence of the gift, contra Fee, *GEP*, 169. No gift is permanent; all are partial, and all are worked out in different ways in different people. Dunn suggests the gift is the healing, not the power. Dunn, *Jesus and the Spirit*, 211. However, this is binary as the power and healing are intertwined, and God is the source of both. Hence, the gift encompasses both dimensions. Carson, *Showing*, 39, suggests different kinds of healing.

92. Acts 16:18; 19:12. See also Luke 10:17; Acts 5:17; 8:7.

93. Fee, *GEP*, 169, includes it in miracles, as do others. Dunn, *Jesus and the Spirit*, 210, suggests it fits with ἐνεργήματα δυνάμεων; however, that is only one possibility.

94. Matt. 10:8; Acts 14:19. Paul also raised Eutychus (Acts 20:9–10).

95. Carson, *Showing*, 40.

the question conveys."[96] These may include exorcisms, supernatural healing events as often recorded in the Gospels and Acts, and, arguably, healing through medicine.[97]

Paul also mentions the spiritual gift δυνάμεις, "acts of power, miracles."[98] Some people are "miracle workers." What they do is undefined, but the gift may point to an ability to pray that people experience God's intervention other than healing and exorcism and that this sometimes comes to pass. These might include events beyond everyday experience, including deliverance from persecution, natural events (e.g., earthquakes), or privation (provision). The gift was a component of apostleship (2 Cor. 12:12).

There are also examples of healings and miracles in Paul's letters. Regarding healing, Paul is ill in Galatia, was cared for by the Galatians, and must have been restored either naturally, by a miracle, treatment from the likes of Luke (Col. 4:14), or a combination of all three (Gal. 4:13–16). Whatever way he has been healed, with his high view of God's sovereignty and his likely awareness of Sirach 38, Paul probably sees his recovery as the act of God.[99]

For example, Paul attributes Epaphroditus's recovery in Rome to God's mercy. His doing so indicates that whether he has been instantly healed through the laying on of hands or through medical intervention (or a combination of both), for Paul, God intervenes to restore him (Phil. 2:27).

Workings of Power (Miracles)

While in Galatians 3:5 miracles may include healing and exorcism, in light of the previous gift, this would refer to situations where God acts through believers in other ways, perhaps including resurrection from the dead; miracles affecting nature;[100] miracles of provision,[101] deliverance or survival,[102] or judgment;[103] and exorcisms.[104]

---

96. Anthony C. Thiselton, *The First Epistle to the Corinthians: A Commentary on the Greek Text*, NIGTC (Grand Rapids: Eerdmans, 2000), 946. He translates it "various kinds of healing."

97. See Justin Martyr: "For numberless demoniacs throughout the whole world, and in your city, many of our Christian men exorcising them in the name of Jesus Christ, who was crucified under Pontius Pilate, have healed and do heal, rendering helpless and driving the possessing devils out of the men, though they could not be cured by all the other exorcists, and those who used incantations and drugs." See Justin Martyr, *The Second Apology of Justin* 2.6 (ANF[1] 190).

98. Here I diverge from Dunn, who suggests that the miracle is the actual event disassociated from the person. However, while I agree miracles are events, here Paul's point is that not all do them—which can lead him to instruct the Corinthians that not all speak in tongues. Hence, here, "miracle worker" is in view. Compare Dunn, *Jesus and the Spirit*, 210.

99. "The mention of Luke the beloved physician (Col. 4:14) shows Paul's favorable attitude to the medical profession (cf. Sir 38:1–15)." Graham H. Twelftree, "Healing, Illness," *DPL* 378.

100. Such as calming the storm (Mark 4:35–41); walking on water (Mark 6:45–52); turning water to wine, which is also a provision miracle (John 2:1–10).

101. Such as the feeding miracles (Mark 6:30–44; 8:1–10). See also 2 Cor. 9:10; Phil. 4:19.

102. Such as 2 Cor. 1:10; 1 Tim. 3:11; see also Rom. 15:31; 2 Cor. 11:24–33; 1 Thess. 3:2; 4:17–18.

103. 1 Cor. 11:30; Acts 13:8–12.

104. Carson, *Showing*, 40, includes exorcisms here.

Discerning Spirits

Διάκρισις indicates, here, "the ability to distinguish and evaluate, distinguishing, differentiation."[105] For some, this is the capacity to weigh and discern what is said (1 Cor. 14:29). Fee argues for this position, also based on 1 Thessalonians 5:20–21, where prophecies are to be tested or discerned. It functions to prophecy as interpretation does to tongues.[106]

However, the discernment is not of prophecies but of spirits, so this gift is more likely the capacity to discern whether something is from the Spirit or a demonic source. In Hebrews 5:14, the term is used for the ability to discern good from evil. As such, here, the gift may be the ability to discern or distinguish between evil and good where spiritual things are concerned. The gift could include discerning a spiritual source of false teaching, spiritual snares, or evil situations.[107]

Tongues

The term γλῶσσα can mean the physical tongue or a language. Here, it indicates a Spirit-given capacity to speak in languages.[108] A minority of scholars hold that this is the same phenomenon as in Acts 2, whereby the Pentecost recipients of the Spirit spoke in known languages.[109] However, the descriptions in chapter 14 make this unlikely.[110] First Corinthians 13:1 may

---

105. BDAG, s.v. "διάκρισις," 231.

106. Fee, GEP, 171–72.

107. 1 Cor. 10:20–21; 2 Cor. 11:3–4, 13–15; Gal. 3:1; 4:9; Eph. 6:10; 2 Thess. 2:9; 1 Tim. 3:6–7; 4:1; 2 Tim. 2:26. See, similarly, Dunn, Jesus and the Spirit, 235–36. He concludes, "'discerning of the spirits' is best understood as evaluation of prophetic utterances, an investigating and interpreting which throws light on their source and their significance" (emphasis original). See also Carson, Showing, 41.

108. Acts 2:4; 10:46; 19:6; 1 Cor. 12:28, 30; 13:8; 14:5–6, 18, 22, 23; 14:39.

109. A good example who leans this way is Carson, Showing, 77–88. I am not convinced by this view for these reasons: (1) A tongues speaker speaks to God, and others cannot understand it (14:1); (2) the tongues speaker speaks mysteries in the Spirit that no one understands; (3) the illustrations of vv. 6–11 indicate tongues are incomprehensible sound; (4) tongues requires the power to interpret (v. 13); (5) the tongues are incomprehensible to the speaker whose mind is unproductive (v. 14); (6) tongues in song and prayer is with the spirit and not the mind (vv. 15–17); (7) tongues when encountered by unbelievers is seen as evidence of madness—this is highly unlikely if they were known languages (v. 23). However, the principles outlined in 1 Corinthians 14 concerning tongues and translation should apply with the use of known, translatable languages. See Mark J. Keown, "Implications of 1 Corinthians 14:1–25 for Multicultural Church Gatherings" (paper presented at the Annual Meeting of the Society of Biblical Literature, San Antonio, 2021).

110. The person also edifies him- or herself (v. 4), prays or sings in the spirit and not the mind (vv. 13–15), and others think the speaker is mad, suggesting an ecstatic gift (v. 23). Still, as Fee contends, whether it is an actual language or not is "irrelevant," as "Paul's whole argument is predicated on the phenomenon's unintelligibility to both speaker and hearer; he certainly does not envisage someone's being present who would be able to understand it because it was also an earthly language. Moreover, his use of earthly languages as an analogy in 14:10–12 implies that it is not a known earthly language, since a thing itself is not usually identical with that to which it is analogous." Fee, GEP, 173. See also Dunn, Jesus and the Spirit, 242–48. He also draws out parallels to the oracle of Delphi and Dionysus (esp. pp. 242–43). He rejects that these are known languages (p. 244).

indicate that some were considered angelic languages and others were recognized as known human ones.[111] Whatever is involved, they must be expressed with love for the edification of others or they are just profoundly annoying and meaningless noise (13:1). As the "clanging cymbal" was associated with paganism and especially the worship of Cybele, Paul may be suggesting that loveless tongues become the kind of idolatrous noise some of the Corinthians experienced in their pagan pasts (cf. 12:2).[112]

Tongues are a prayer language to God (14:2, 28). They can be used in church gatherings if translated or interpreted (14:1–25, 27). Their use in public gatherings without translation or interpretation is unacceptable because they do not build up others. However, where translated or interpreted, they are to be utilized in an orderly manner akin to prophecy. Presumably, Paul sees their private use outside of the church as a means of personal edification (14:4, 28). Even though there is no record of his doing so in Acts, Paul speaks in tongues (14:18). Some likely also prayed and sang in tongues (14:13–15). Tongues function as a sign of retribution for unbelievers as "they do not stimulate belief but instead seal unbelief."[113] The gift of tongues also fulfills Isaiah 28:11–12. Unlike love that remains, tongues are only required in this age and will pass away when the eschaton is consummated.[114] Presumably, believers will have a full ability to communicate and understand earthly languages. However, not all have the gift any more than they have gifts of apostle, prophet, teacher, and other expansive gifts (12:29). As such, they are certainly not the mark of being a Christian or of Spirit-reception.

The section on spiritual gifts in 1 Corinthians 12:27–31 ends with ζηλοῦτε δὲ τὰ χαρίσματα τὰ μείζονα, which can be indicative (you are seeking the greater gifts), a question (are you seeking the greater gifts), or imperatival (seek the greater gifts). While scholarship is split on this, the last seems self-evidently correct as it should be read in line with its chiastic parallel in 1 Corinthians 14:1: ζηλοῦτε δὲ τὰ πνευματικά μᾶλλον δὲ ἵνα προφητεύητε

---

111. The Corinthians likely saw the tongues in this way. The background for this might be T. Job 48–50. As Fee rightly says, this is not likely to indicate "speak eloquently" (so Martin, *The Spirit*, 43). Fee argues Paul does not see them as angelic tongues, but this cannot be ruled out with the background in T. Job. (see Fee, *GEP*, 200–201). Conversely, Dunn thinks Paul considered "glossolalia as speaking the language(s) of heaven." He may be correct. Dunn, *Jesus and the Spirit*, 244.

112. See E. Peterson, "ἀλαλάζω," *TDNT* 1:227–28; K. L. Schmidt, "κύμβαλον," *TDNT* 3:1037–39. Fee, *GEP*, 202, notes, "It makes one become like the empty, hollow noises of pagan worship." Corinthian bronze was also valued for its quality.

113. Garland, *1 Corinthians*, 648. Alternatively, they are a sign of the believers' madness in the eyes of unbelievers, which sees them reject the message and church, and are shut out from life. See also Dunn, *Jesus and the Spirit*, 231.

114. See on 1 Corinthians 13:8–10, Fee, *GEP*, 205–11. He rightly says of 13:9–10, "Convoluted as the argument may appear, Paul's distinctions are between 'now' and 'then,' between what is incomplete (though perfectly appropriate to the church's present existence) and what is complete, when its final destiny in Christ has been reached and 'we see face to face' and 'know as we are known.'"

(seek spiritual things, and especially that you may prophesy).[115] As people who cherish speaking skills, they should pursue the gifts that build others up, especially prophecy, before those that don't, like speaking in tongues.[116] In that God is the giver of the gifts, this implies praying for them and accepting what God in his wisdom chooses to give.

Interpretation or Translation of Tongues

The ερμηνευ- terms derive from Ἑρμῆς, Hermes, the messenger of the gods.[117] The terms are used for translations of Aramaic terms into Greek,[118] the interpretation of Scriptures, as with Jesus on the Emmaus Road (Luke 24:27), and explaining something (Heb. 5:12). Paul's only uses are his seven in 1 Corinthians 12 and 14, where they are always placed with tongues.[119] They can either mean, then, a translation of the utterance in tongues or their interpretation or explanation.[120] Which of these is in view is likely dependent on the nature of the tongues spoken. At Pentecost, the words spoken in tongues would have been translated. If a message in tongues is articulated out loud, it must be translated or interpreted to make it meaningful and edificatory for others (14:5, 26). If no one is present to interpret, the tongues speaker must pray for the interpretation or translation and provide it themselves (14:13). Dunn rightfully identifies two aspects here. First is the assembly's control over glossolalia; second is the vernacular interpretation or translation of what has been said.[121]

Through his instructions to the Corinthians, we can discern that Paul understood all gifts as coming from God and Son through the Spirit as God wills. An assortment of gift types is given to each believer to be used for the benefit of others.

1 CORINTHIANS 12:27-31

First Corinthians 12:12–26 introduces a range of important aspects of spiritual gifts in the church. As has been stressed in Romans 12:4–5, there is one body of Christ and multiple members who form the body (vv. 12, 19–20). All believers, regardless of ethnicity or social status, have received the same baptism of the Spirit (v. 13). Just as the parts of the human body

---

115. See the arguments in Fee, *GEP*, 106. Fee also rightly argues the present can be read "keep on eagerly desiring." Fee, *GEP*, 195–96.

116. Fee correctly rejects that Paul means here seeking the first gifts on the list. Fee, *GEP*, 195.

117. Silva, "ἑρμηνεύω," *NIDNTTE* 2:276–77.

118. Matt. 1:23; Mark 5:41; 15:22, 34; John 1:38, 41, 42; 9:7; Acts 4:36; 9:36; 13:8; Heb. 7:2.

119. 1 Cor. 12:10, 30.

120. See also Dunn, *Jesus and the Spirit*, 246–48. He agrees that it can be interpretation (loosely akin to the interpretation of the mantic utterances at Delphi) or translation.

121. Dunn, *Jesus and the Spirit*, 248. I think he goes too far in thinking any lingua franca utterance after the glossolalia message is in view. Instead, it is a specific interpretation or translation to ensure others understand.

are essential to its working, so it is with the body of Christ (vv. 14–17). God has put together the members of the body as he wills (v. 18). Each member needs the others (v. 21). Those members of the body (people and their gifts) who appear weaker and less desirable are to be honored more, as God has composed the human body like this. It must have no divisions (vv. 22–24a). Where there is suffering or rejoicing among members of the body, there must be empathy shown by others (v. 26). The Corinthians (and, by implication, all other churches) are Christ's body and individual members of it (v. 27).

Verse 28 introduces another gift list with a reminder that God appoints his church's leadership.[122] The list focuses on leadership and prominent ministry gifts, with Paul pointing out that not all believers are assigned gifts and offices in this way. The gifts are chosen due to their importance to Paul and Corinth, and the overall point is to show that tongues are being falsely elevated in the church over more important gifts. Furthermore, not all have the gift of tongues, so tongues are not the mark of receiving the Spirit.

The section can be broken into two parts: (1) the list of eight gifts and (2) questions demonstrating that all gifts are not given to every believer.[123] Two gifts in the list do not feature in the questions (helping and leadership), while interpretation is added. These gifts are more gifts of functions, perhaps indicating leadership roles in the church. Fee rightly notes that the first three gifts relate to people, the fourth and fifth to manifestations (as in 12:8–10), and the final two to deeds of service.[124]

While Paul uses "first . . . second . . . third," in light of the concern for humility and concern for the weaker in the chapter, it surely does not speak of a hierarchy but the order in which the first three gifts are used in the community—the apostle establishes, the prophet brings God's Word from day one, and the teacher instructs believers, particularly from the Scriptures.[125]

Apostle

It is widely agreed that the function[126] of apostle has its origins in the Jewish sending tradition in the OT. This idea is based on the extensive use of

---

122. Scholars debate whether "in the church" here is local gatherings (e.g., Dunn, *Jesus and the Spirit*, 262–63; Fee, *GEP*, 189) or the church universal (e.g., Martin, *Spirit*, 31). Clearly, Paul is writing to a local gathering, so it implies the local church first. However, the dichotomy breaks down and applies to the universal church in which these gifts function as well.
123. The implied answer to the questions in vv. 29–30, as indicated by the Greek negation μή, is "of course not." The Corinthians then should connect the dots and realize Paul's point: "Correct; so why don't you apply this to yourselves and your singular zeal for the gift of tongues?" Fee, *GEP*, 194.
124. Fee, *GEP*, 189.
125. Fee, *GEP*, 187: "As before, at issue is neither *instruction* about gifts and ministries, nor *ranking* them" (emphasis original). Limiting the first three to itinerant ministries is flawed. See Fee, *GEP*, 190; Martin, *Spirit*, 32–33.
126. Fee, *GEP*, 189. He considers these as functions rather than offices. In a sense, this is correct; the function must precede the office. However, the language here is of people recognized with the gift who are labeled "apostle," "prophet," and "teacher." Hence, I find the attempt to distinguish function from office

ἀποστελλ- language in the OT. It translates שׁלח- language used for the sending of people. The term ἀπόστολος itself is used sparingly for diplomatic sending. As Jesus selected the Twelve, it became the term for the group he sent into mission. In this use in 1 Corinthians 12:28–29, Paul may have just the Twelve and himself in view.[127] However, here and in Ephesians 4:11 (also Eph. 2:20; 3:5), he is more likely employing the term in a broader sense, including people with the apostolic group in churches.[128] This view is likely because while he uses "apostle" of himself and the Twelve,[129] elsewhere he uses it of James, the brother of Jesus (Gal. 1:19), his team (1 Cor. 4:9), himself, Silas, Timothy (1 Thess. 2:7), and Junia and Andronicus (Rom. 16:7).[130]

As I have argued elsewhere, two leaders (2 Cor. 8:23) and Epaphroditus (Phil. 2:25) may refer to local church apostles.[131] Others who established churches in the NT include Epaphras, who established the churches in the Lycus Valley (Col. 1:7; 4:13), and unknowns who evangelized other areas in Asia Minor (Acts 19:10), North Africa,[132] Illyricum,[133] Rome,[134] and elsewhere.[135] While it is uncertain exactly what the apostleship means, it makes sense to see this person as the pioneer missionary and church planter who establishes God's work in a given location. This perspective is supported by the ministries of the Twelve,

---

unhelpful. However, the gift must precede the appointment to the office, and not all who hold the office have the gift. It is God who appoints and gifts the person, and the church merely recognizes what he has done. As Fee says, "Thus in Paul the functional and positional usages nearly coalesce." Fee, *GEP*, 191.

127. In the Synoptic Gospels and apart from two exceptions in Acts 14, the term ἀπόστολος is used only of the Twelve (Matt. 10:2; Mark 3:14; 6:30; Luke 6:13; 9:10; 11:49; 17:5; 22:14; 24:10; Acts 1:2, 26; 2:37, 42–43; 4:33, 35–37; 5:2, 12, 18, 29, 40; 6:6; 8:1, 14, 18; 9:27; 11:1; 15:2, 4, 6, 22–23; 16:4. Peter uses it of himself (1 Peter 1:1; 2 Peter 1:1) and the Twelve (2 Peter 3:2) as do the authors of Jude (17) and Revelation (18:20; 21:14). Hebrews uses it of Jesus (3:1). John uses it in the sense of a messenger with the apostles in view (John 13:16). In Acts 14:4, 14 the plural "apostles" is used of Paul and Barnabas.

128. "It obviously includes the Twelve, but also goes considerably beyond them." Fee, *GEP*, 191.

129. Himself: Rom. 1:1; 11:13; 1 Cor. 1:1; 9:1, 2; 15:9; 2 Cor. 1:1; 12:12; Gal. 1:1; Eph. 1:1; Col. 1:1; 1 Tim. 1:1; 2:7; 2 Tim. 1:1, 11; Titus 1:1; The Twelve: 1 Cor. 9:5; 15:7, 9; Gal. 1:17.

130. Keown, *Congregational*, 170–84; Keown, *Philippians*, 2:38–45.

131. Contra Fee, *GEP*, 193. He states, "There is no other evidence of any kind that Paul thought of a local church as having some among it called 'apostles,' who were responsible for its affairs." He neglects Paul's designation of Epaphroditus as "your apostle" (Phil. 2:25) and the placement of "apostle" in the spiritual gift lists of churches. If there were prophets and evangelists in local churches, there were apostles. I agree that their concern was not the affairs of the church; rather, it was establishing new ones, as Paul planted churches through the empire.

132. The likes of the Egyptian and Cyrenian Pentecost pilgrims (Acts 2:10), the Ethiopian eunuch (Acts 8:27–40), Simon of Cyrene and his sons (Mark 15:21), and Niger and Lucius (Acts 13:1).

133. As I have argued, perhaps Luke led a team from Macedonia, while Paul went on to Athens (Acts 16:40). See Keown, *Romans and the Mission of God*, 49.

134. Roman Pentecost pilgrims, perhaps Junia and Andronicus (Rom. 16:7). See earlier chapter 2, "The Spirit Sets Apart and Sends Gospel Communicators."

135. Another group of apostolic workers may be those mentioned in Acts 2:8–11, including Pentecost pilgrims from eastern areas (Parthia, Media, Elam, Mesopotamia [modern eastern nations including Jordan, Saudi Arabia, Azerbaijan, and parts of Iraq and into Iran], Cappadocia, Pontus, Asia, Phrygia, Pamphylia [suggesting there were believers in modern-day Turkey before Paul got there]).

Paul, and others in his team establishing new churches. Also, the placement of the apostle first in this list and Ephesians 4:11 suggests an establishing role, with the work continued by the other gospel ministers.[136]

Fee contends that there is no evidence that apostleship is a charism of the Spirit because Paul's apostleship is received from Christ and by God's will (Rom. 1:4–5; 1 Cor. 1:1). This is patently flawed as it drives a wedge between the work of God and Jesus with the Spirit, as if the Spirit is not involved in the calling and equipping of a person for apostolic ministry. Furthermore, the passage deals with spiritual matters, and spiritual gifts are central to this. It seems strange to single out apostolicity as a non-spiritual matter when it plainly is.[137] Other gifts here are linked to the Spirit, including teaching (1 Cor. 2:13), healing (12:9), prophecy (see 12:10; 14:1), distinguishing between spirits (12:10), tongues (12:10), and interpretation (12:10). There is no clear reason for the gift of apostleship to be singled out as something not given by the Spirit.

Helping

The term ἀντίλημψις is a hapax legomenon. In wider Greek Jewish writings, it is used for God's help to people,[138] people helping others in different ways,[139] and the management of national matters (2 Macc. 11:26). The associated verb ἀντιλαμβάνω is used in the NT of God's help to Israel (Luke 1:54), leaders in the church helping the weak (Acts 20:35), and enslaved people giving benefit to their masters (1 Tim. 6:2).[140] The gift of "helping" suggests someone with an extraordinary ability to lend assistance to others in a range of ways—support, care, finance, hospitality, and so on.[141] It may relate to the gifts of generosity and merciful acts in Romans 12:8.[142]

1 CORINTHIANS 14:26

First Corinthians 14:1–25 directly addresses the problem in Corinth where the exercise of spiritual gifts is concerned. First Corinthians 14:26 speaks of the

---

136. I cannot fully agree with Dunn, who rejects the idea of local apostles exercising authority within the community. Dunn, *Jesus and the Spirit*, 274. He recognizes the role is as the "founder of that community" (p. 274). But he then mistakenly thinks the role is "within the local community"; instead, it is in the planting of new ones and then authority exercised within the new community of faith. This authority is then passed on to the appointed leaders and the apostle moves on.

137. Ephesians 3:5 also speaks of the revelation of God to apostles and prophets by the Spirit.

138. See 1 Esdr. 8:27; 2 Macc. 8:19; 15:7; 3 Macc. 5:50; Pss. 21:1, 20 (22:19 EVV); 83:6 (84:5 EVV); 88:19 (89:18 EVV).

139. 3 Macc. 2:33; 3:10; Pss. 82:9 (83:8 EVV); 107:9 (108:8 EVV); Sir. 11:12; 51:7.

140. In the LXX, the verb is diversely used of helping someone with timber (3 Kgdms. 9:11 [1 Kings 9:11 EVV]), military support (1 Chron. 22:17), helping prisoners (2 Chron. 28:15), help in sacrifices (2 Chron. 29:34), God's help to Israel (e.g., 2 Chron. 28:23; 2 Macc. 14:15; Pss. 3:6; 17:36 [18:35 EVV]; Wis. 2:18; Sir. 2:6; Pss. Sol. 16:3; Isa. 42:1), children helping fathers (Sir. 3:12), helping the poor (Sir. 29:9; cf. Ezek. 16:49), and helping a neighbor (Sir. 29:20).

141. See also Dunn, *Jesus and the Spirit*, 252–53.

142. Fee, *GEP*, 193.

gathered church (when you come together).[143] The sentence that follows should not be read as a limitation on the particular gifts to be used, nor in any sense an order of service.[144] Instead, these are examples of the gifts to be expressed in gathered worship.[145] It is not so much ad hoc as Fee asserts,[146] as another gift list carefully chosen for the Corinthians' situation. "Each one" indicates that all believers should come to the gathering prepared to share their particular gifts.[147] In so doing, Paul introduces another list of five spiritual gifts, two of which are the issue at hand (tongues and interpretation). Another is connected to a previous gift (teaching, also 14:6), one was mentioned in 14:6 (revelation), and the other was hinted at in v. 15 (song). Others could be added from the many spiritual gifts people have. The point is that Paul envisages the gathering as a pot-faith,[148] a spiritual smorgasbord, with people coming to the house church prepared to share something from their giftedness with others.

Song

The Greek ψαλμός can be limited to a song from the OT Psalter, but here more likely refers to any song brought to worship (cf. Eph. 5:19; Col. 3:16).[149] The gift of music is first mentioned in Scripture of Jubal (Gen. 4:21) and when Moses, Miriam, and Israel sing a song of victory and joy after the Exodus.[150] It is reflected repeatedly in the Psalter and in the musicians and singers of the Chronicles (e.g., 1 Chron. 15:16–28). The gift anticipates the importance of music, hymnody, and

---

143. Fee suggests that Τί οὖν ἐστιν, ἀδελφοί, "what then is to be, brothers and sisters" (my translation), is intended to tie together several loose ends. Fee, GEP, 48. However, it is better to see Paul effectively asking, "So what are we to do, brothers and sisters?" and applying the principles of 1 Corinthians 12–14:25 to the Corinthian worship practices.

144. Fee, GEP, 248. For others who make this point, see n. 678.

145. Fee rightly states this gift list is ad hoc, is not exhaustive, and is definitely not an order for their services. The gifts "represent various *types* of verbal manifestations of the Spirit that should occur in their assembly." While Fee is correct to state that tongues and interpretation are spontaneous, "revelation" may be the sharing of an experience outside of the gathering as much as within. Fee, GEP, 249–50.

146. It is ad hoc in a sense, but as Fee, GEP, 248, notes, they are verbal gifts for worship. They are no doubt carefully chosen to add to the other gift lists in instructing the Corinthians about the use of a diversity of verbal gifts, and not focusing on tongues and rhetoric.

147. Fee sums up the situation: "The first sentence, which describes what should be happening at their gatherings, echoes the concerns of chapter 12, that *each one* has opportunity to participate in the corporate ministry of the body." Fee, GEP, 248.

148. The term "pot-faith" is a variant of potluck that I began using years ago, as I did not like suggesting "luck" when people of faith gather together to dine spiritually and physically.

149. The translation "hymn" is inappropriate as it is tainted with contemporary ideas of a certain type of traditional song over contemporary song forms. Song is general, and could include spontaneous song creations, "hymns" as we know them, or other "contemporary" songs. It probably encompasses ψαλμοῖς καὶ ὕμνοις καὶ ᾠδαῖς πνευματικαῖς, ᾄδοντες (Eph. 5:18; cf. Col. 3:16). These are also "prayers" as Fee notes, but prayer is a wide category and should not be included in the clearly musical term here. There are plenty of injunctions to pray elsewhere in Paul, so there is no need to include it here. Fee astutely notices that there is no mention of leadership, meaning the Spirit effectively leads the worship of the church. Fee, GEP, 249. See further, Keown, "How Much Should We Sing?" 5–13.

150. E.g., Exod. 15:1–21.

song in the church up to the present day. It likely includes the skills of composition, musicianship, and vocalized singing. Those so gifted should bring music to share with others. This music may be previously known (e.g., psalms, Christian hymns, modern compositions) or others created spontaneously. Some may be performed solo, and others invite people to join in the songs.[151] I hold that this is the gift of music analogous to what we see in the church up to the present.

Revelation

The term ἀποκάλυψις speaks of something hidden that is unveiled, indicating something revelatory.[152] What Paul means exactly is a little vague. In that he uses the term in contrast to "prophecy" in this chapter (v. 6), it likely speaks of a different aspect of spiritual experience. He uses the term concerning his heavenly visionary experience in 2 Corinthians 12:1, 7 and his experience of seeing Jesus (Gal. 1:12), so it likely includes such extraordinary revelatory visions or experiences.[153] Fee agrees that the work of the Spirit is seen here in Paul's visionary and revelatory experience.[154] It is also likely that the use in Galatians 2:2 refers to the Agabus prophecy of future famines in Acts 11:28, and as such, the line between prophecy and revelation seems obscure.[155] It may include visions, as in 2 Corinthians 12:1.[156]

---

151. Some may have been spontaneous "charismatic hymnody" (cf. 14:15). Dunn, *Jesus and the Spirit*, 238; Fee, *GEP*, 231–32. There is, however, no basis to assume ψαλμός in 14:26 should be limited to spontaneous music, as Dunn and Fee aver. This could equally be prepared by musicians for corporate singing as much as "off-the-cuff." Nor is there any evidence the term includes "prayer" (Fee, *GEP*, 249); the term is specific to music.

152. Dunn considers that φανέρωσις, "manifestation," should be considered as a revelation of the Spirit. Dunn, *Jesus and the Spirit*, 212. However, the term is used once of "the manifestation of the Spirit given," suggesting it is another way of speaking of *charismata* or *pneumatikos* where it applies to gifts.

153. Other uses include eschatological revelation: the revelation of Jesus at his parousia (1 Cor. 1:7; 2 Thess. 1:7); the ultimate revelation of God's righteous judgment (Rom. 2:5); the revelation of the children of God (Rom. 8:19); the revelation of God in the gospel; the revelation of the mystery of the gospel (Rom. 16:26; Eph. 3:3); and the Spirit of wisdom and revelation (Eph. 1:17). It is by the Spirit that any such revelation is experienced. See also Dunn, *Jesus and the Spirit*, 214.

154. "Although not explicitly mentioned in this remarkable passage, the Spirit lies behind both the phenomenon and its narration ('whether in or out of the body' Paul does not know), as well as Paul's actually describing the phenomenon in terms of ἀποκαλύψεις ("revelations") in vv. 1 and 7 and in the final purpose clause, 'that the power of Christ might dwell in me' (v. 9)." Fee, *GEP*, 347. He rightly notes the difficulty of understanding the experience. However, this lies beyond the scope of this discussion. See his analysis at pp. 348–54.

155. Here I cannot agree with Fee, who outright rejects that the prophecy is in view in Galatians 2:2. He limits this to the Spirit's direction (and not the prophecy). Fee, *GEP*, 371–72. However, I see no reason why Agabus's prophetic revelation cannot be seen as this directing, or one aspect of the Spirit's work in the Antiochian church leading them to take a collection to Jerusalem. Indeed, Luke records that Agabus foretold the famine "by the Spirit" (Acts 11:28). Due to this, the disciples determined to send material relief to Judea as per their financial capacity. This was delivered by Barnabas and Saul (Gal. 2:1).

156. Second Corinthians 12:1 is the only use of ὀπτασία in Paul's letters, and as Fee asserts, "the 'revelation' in this case is but a synonym for 'vision.'" Fee, *GEP*, 350.

EPHESIANS 4:7-16

In Ephesians 4:1, Paul shifts from theological concerns to appropriate life in Christ. Verses 1–3 encourage the Ephesians to live up to their calling in God with humility, gentleness, patience, support for one another, love, and Spirit-created peaceful unity. This "oneness" is reflected in the oneness associated with God—one body, Spirit, hope, Lord, faith, baptism, and God. These verses set the scene for the gifts and imply that all gifts are to be shared through pneumaformed lives shaped by God, in Christ, by the Spirit.

In v. 7, Paul shares how each one has received the grace Christ distributes. Paul cites Psalm 68:18 of Christ's ascension to heaven with his people (captives) and his distribution of gifts to humankind (by the Spirit poured out at Pentecost and received at the moment of faith for each believer, cf. Eph. 1:14). The same Christ who descended and was incarnate is now supreme above all the heavens as Lord so that he will fill all things (vv. 9–10). As such, he distributes gifts.[157]

In v. 12, Paul now gives a list of vocational gifts and explains their purpose in what follows. These are not offices but charismatic functions God generates among those he selects in Christ.

Evangelist

The term ἐυαγγελιστής belongs to the ἐυαγγελ- nexus of terms and speaks of one who proclaims the good news of God, a gospel preacher. In that it is distinguished from the apostle, it likely refers to those who continue the work established by the apostle. It is also set apart from intrachurch speaking and leading gifts of the prophet, pastor, and teacher, suggesting that these people primarily continue the missional work of the church by proclaiming the gospel to unbelievers (and equipping others for the same, see v. 12). The only person designated an evangelist is Philip, who certainly fits the bill—evangelizing Samaria and large parts of Judea (Acts 8; also 21:8). Still, even this is a little uncertain as we find him domiciled in Caesarea Maritima with his four prophetess daughters, and so being an evangelist may include an intrachurch role.

Timothy is instructed to "do the work of an evangelist" in 2 Timothy 4:5. Although Paul does not give a clear context for the provenance of the second Timothy letter, he is likely in Ephesus as we saw was the case in 1 Timothy 1:3.[158] In the passage, Timothy is charged before God and Christ, who will judge all humankind, to "preach the word," indicating proclaiming the gospel.

---

157. "Paul is totally consistent with Luke in setting forth the propinquity of the Spirit's gifts within the context of Christ's exaltation (Eph. 4:8–10)." Habets, *Anointed Son*, 181.

158. Paul's statement that he is sending Tychicus to Ephesus rather than "to you" (2 Tim. 4:12) could indicate Timothy is not in Ephesus. However, the material in 2 Timothy 4:9–21 suggests Timothy is not in Thessalonica, Galatia, Dalmatia, Corinth, or Miletus. He can travel to Rome through Troas to pick up Paul's books and parchments en route to Rome (4:13). The mention of Alexander does suggest Ephesus (Acts 19:33; 1 Tim. 1:20) as does the mention of Priscilla and Aquila (with Corinth and Rome ruled out; 1 Cor. 16:19). So, while we cannot be certain, Ephesus is the best guess as to Timothy's whereabouts.

He is to be ready for this whether the preaching is producing immense fruit (in season) or, as sometimes is the case, is not (out of season).[159] The three aspects of his ministry then described must be read as a lead-in to v. 3, where Paul mentions false teachers. Dealing with such threats, Timothy is to correct (ἐλέγχω),[160] censure (ἐπιτιμάω),[161] and exhort (παρακαλέω)[162] false teachers and those coming under their spell.

Timothy must do so with "complete patience and teaching" because a time is approaching when people will not tolerate sound teaching that accords with the gospel. Instead, they will gather teachers who scratch their "itchy ears," preaching a gospel of their passions.[163] They will turn away from listening to the truth and follow the path of myths (vv. 3–4). In this setting, Timothy is to be "sober-minded, ensure suffering, do the work of an evangelist, fulfill [his] ministry."[164]

As such, in the NT, it seems that the evangelist follows on and continues the missional work begun by an apostle, working to further advance the gospel in such a setting through the proclamation and charismatic ministry and, if need be, to deal with false teachers as they arise, reasserting the gospel, and calling people back to it. It cannot be limited to a purely external gift, as is commonly held today. It involves preaching the gospel to strengthen and equip believers and to save the lost. Core to their job is equipping others for the task (Eph. 4:12).[165]

Pastor[166]

The ποιμήν was a "shepherd" of God's flock, his church. The language is employed for literal shepherds,[167] frequently of Jesus,[168] overseers and elders (Acts 20:28; 1 Peter 5:2, 4), Christian leaders (1 Cor. 9:7), and Christians who persevere (Rev. 2:27). It refers to leaders whose primary task is to care for the

---

159. For a solid analysis of this verse, see William D. Mounce, *Pastoral Epistles*, WBC 46 (Dallas: Word, 2000), 573.

160. Alternatively, "reprove" (BDAG, s.v. "ἐλέγχω," 315).

161. Alternatively, "rebuke, reprove" (BDAG, s.v. "ἐπιτιμάω," 384).

162. Alternatively, "appeal, urge, encourage" (BDAG, s.v. "παρακαλέω," 764).

163. The image portrays hearers as wanting a message that relieves the torment of an itchy ear. The message is then a balm relieving their pain. That is, they preach what people want to hear and not the authentic gospel.

164. In later Greek writings, "evangelist" is used by Papias of John the evangelist. See Michael William Holmes, *The Apostolic Fathers: Greek Texts and English Translations*, rev. ed. (Grand Rapids: Baker, 1999), 582. In the Christianized *Apocalypse of Sedrach* it is paired with apostle, showing the ministries were linked in some way (Apoc. Sedr. 15.2, 5). Eusebius uses it of Matthew (*Hist. eccl.* 1.7.10; 1.8.16.), John the apostle (*Hist. eccl.* 3.23.1; 3.25.3; 7.25.8; 7.25.10), the Synoptic writers (*Hist. eccl.* 3.24.8), and Philip of Caesarea (*Hist. eccl.* 3.31.5; cf. Acts 21:10).

165. See also the thoughts of Dunn, *Jesus and the Spirit*, 289.

166. Alternatively, "pastors who teach." However, the shift from μὲν ... δὲ ... δὲ ... δὲ to καὶ is likely due to the teacher being the last in the list. Furthermore, as Paul has clearly delineated the role of "teacher" in both Romans and 1 Corinthians, where he gives other lists, then this is likely that specific gift. Yet, if this is "pastors who teach," it does not change the outcome of my discussion particularly.

167. Luke 2:8, 15, 18, 20; John 10:12; 1 Cor. 9:7.

168. Matt. 9:36; 25:32; 26:31; Mark 6:34; John 10:2, 11, 14, 16; Heb. 13:20; 1 Peter 2:25; Rev. 7:17; 12:5; 19:15.

church (feeding them spiritually and protecting them). Paul may mean elders here; however, its range of uses in the NT shows it has a broader scope.

SPIRITUAL GIFTS IN PERSPECTIVE

The term χάρισμα is used elsewhere.[169] I will briefly discuss some of those uses and how Christians should approach spiritual gifts.

Romans 6:23

Through Romans 6, Paul argues that those declared righteous by faith and freed from enslavement to sin must now live as slaves of righteousness. Their previous lives as slaves of sin bore no fruit and, if continued, would end in physical and spiritual death (vv. 20–21). Now that they are free from sin and slaves of God, the fruit being born in their lives contributes to the sanctification of the saints. Implied here is the present work of the Spirit in two ways. First, "fruit" (καρπός) calls to mind "the fruit of the Spirit" (Gal. 5:22–23). Second, "sanctification" is suggestive of the work of the *Holy* [ἅγιος] Spirit. Paul goes on to state that the end of the sanctification process (τὸ δὲ τέλος) is eternal life (ζωὴν αἰώνιον).

Verse 23 sums up and contrasts the two paths open to humankind now that Christ has come. First, the way of sin that yields the fruit or wages of death.[170] Second, the gift of God (χάρισμα τοῦ θεοῦ) is eternal life in Christ, the believers' Lord. While one can argue, as does Fee, that Paul's use of χάρισμα demonstrates that the term does not necessarily imply a *spiritual* gift but an "endowment of grace" (as if the Spirit is not involved), here other factors come into play. First, as I have demonstrated above, v. 22 is suggestive of the work of the Spirit. Second, Paul sums up this new way of living in Romans 7:6 as "the new way of the Spirit." Third, other passages indicate the Spirit as the agent of resurrection.[171] As such, the χάρισμα τοῦ θεοῦ of sanctification and eternal life is indeed from God to those in Christ through the agency of the Spirit. Consequently, the ultimate spiritual gift is eternal life when believers are transformed from mortality and perishability to immortality and imperishability.

2 Corinthians 1:11

This complex verse[172] comes at the conclusion of a passage in which Paul blesses God for his comfort and informs the Corinthians of his team's

---

169. It is also used of the gift of salvation in Jesus and justification (Rom. 5:15–16; see also Dunn, *Jesus and the Spirit*, 206; Fee, *GEP*, 498); eternal life (Rom. 6:23; see also Dunn, *Jesus and the Spirit*, 206; Fee, *GEP*, 502–3); God's gifts to Israel (Rom. 11:29; Dunn, *Jesus and the Spirit*, 207, who confines this to election, and specifically rejects the law; this is way too narrow; Fee, *GEP*, 594); and the multiplicity of spiritual gifts given the Corinthians (1 Cor. 1:7; see Dunn, *Jesus and the Spirit*, 207; Fee, *GEP*, 86).
170. Death here spans the process of decay to human death and eternal destruction.
171. Rom. 1:3–4; 8:11; 1 Cor. 6:14; Eph. 1:19–20; 1 Tim. 3:16.
172. Fee describes this as a "terribly complex sentence." Fee, *GEP*, 286.

horrendous suffering in Asia Minor.[173] Verses 3–7 focus on God's comfort toward the Pauline group as they experience Christ's sufferings and toward the Corinthians. As discussed in chapter 8, although the Spirit is not mentioned, the passage is pregnant with the involvement of the Spirit. Verses 8–9 describe persecution and extreme distress in Asia Minor. However, the resurrection power of God delivered them from death (vv. 9b–10a). In v. 10b, Paul goes on to state his confidence that God will deliver them again.

The participle that launches v. 11, συνυπουργούντων, "join in helping," is likely one of attendant circumstances.[174] The present tense of the participle speaks of ongoing prayer. The means by which they join to help is their corporate petition to God for the deliverance of the Pauline group. The participle indicates that while God is the deliverer, the Corinthians' praying somehow will enhance the likelihood of their deliverance.[175]

The ἵνα clause in 11b states the purpose of their prayers,[176] namely, "so that thanks may be given on our behalf by many faces[177] for this gracious gift to us (τὸ εἰς ἡμᾶς χάρισμα), through the help[178] of many."[179] Whatever the complexities of this verse, the χάρισμα is deliverance. As the Spirit is not used, Fee considers this is not a spiritual gift and reinforces that χάρισμα means "endowment of grace." However, this gift from God is mediated in Christ through the Spirit.[180] So deliverance from danger is a "gift of the Spirit" given as God wills.[181] However, there is a difference in the type of gift—this is not a spiritual endowment for a vocational task within the body of Christ but God acting in history by his Spirit to deliver people from suffering.[182] When Christians face mortal

173. See for a fuller discussion, chapter 8, "The Spirit's Support in Suffering," in the section "Comfort and Peace in Suffering."

174. It could be causal, but that would make the Corinthians' prayers the cause of God's deliverance conditional, meaning God's deliverance is conditional on the Corinthians' prayers.

175. "Divine deliverance, when it occurs, is always an undeserved blessing (χάρισμα), but in some mysterious way it is intimately related to human intercession." Harris, *Second Epistle*, 160.

176. Harris, *Second Epistle*, 161.

177. I have kept this literal, as it implies faces beaming upward toward God and expressing thanks (otherwise the imagery is lost).

178. Alternatively, many prayers, or many praying people.

179. Similarly, Martin, *2 Corinthians*, 151.

180. Fee writes, "Some contextual reason must usually be present in order for us to understand this word as referring to the activity of the Spirit." Fee, *GEP*, 286. However, the passage presupposes the intimate connection of God, Christ, Paul and his team, and the Corinthians, which all implies the Spirit. God's power is at play in the passage as he reaches out to comfort his people in affliction and as they comfort each other (vv. 3–7). Deliverance also speaks of God's power being released through the Spirit to deliver his people from death. Indeed, this is the power that raised Christ from the dead (vv. 9–10). Prayer implies believers connecting with God through the Spirit, and God acting in response. This is an example of where Fee limits the Spirit's role through only seeing the work of the Spirit with regard to certain words chosen for the study. The Spirit's role is far greater and more dynamic.

181. Fee, *GEP*, 286.

182. See further in chapter 8, "The Spirit's Support in Suffering." See also Dunn, *Jesus and the Spirit*, 206.

danger and are delivered from it, it is the gift of God. If it ends in death, they receive the greatest of all gifts—eternal life (cf. Phil. 1:19–24).

1 Timothy 4:14 and 2 Timothy 1:6

In the letters to Timothy, Paul mentions "the gift (χάρισμα) of God" (1 Tim. 4:14) and "the gift (χάρισμα) that is in you" (2 Tim. 1:6). In the first reference, he urges Timothy not to neglect the gift—those who receive God's gifts must cultivate them by usage. It was also received "through prophecy with the laying on of hands by the council of elders" (LEB).

The notion of laying a hand on the head of someone to bless them is found as early as Genesis 48:14, where Israel (Jacob) places his right hand on Ephraim and his left on Manasseh.[183] Both receive a blessing, but using the right on Ephraim indicates a greater blessing. Doing this is surprising because it would be expected that Manasseh, the oldest, would receive the greater blessing. Hands are laid on sacrifices, indicating the conveying of the people's sins by the priest into the animal that then dies for them and releases the sinners from guilt (Lev. 8:14, 18, 22; 2 Chron. 29:23). Joshua is commissioned to lead Israel by the laying on of hands, as Yahweh has directed Moses (Num. 27:23). In Deuteronomy 34:9, Joshua is "full of the spirit of wisdom, because Moses had laid his hands on him" (NRSV), indicating the reception of God's wisdom for leadership through a similarly endowed leader by a successor near the end of his ministry.

The laying on of hands features in Christ's ministry. He lays hands on children, indicating that the Spirit moves through his hands into them and blesses them (Matt. 19:15; Mark 10:16). Many people are healed by Jesus putting his hands on them.[184] In Acts, the laying on of hands is used for commissioning people for specific ministries (Acts 6:6; 13:1). It is also used for the receipt of the Spirit after conversion (Acts 8:17; 9:17). It includes receiving spiritual gifts, such as unseen phenomena (in Samaria), healing (Paul), and tongues and prophecy (Acts 19:6).[185] The laying on of hands is considered one of the fundamentals of the faith to the author of Hebrews (6:2).

In 1 Timothy 4:14, the gift was received through prophecy and the presbyters laying hands on Timothy. This recollection suggests one or more elders speaks prophetic words over Timothy and this gift and aspects of his future ministry are received at this time. Paul also mentions times when prophecies are declared over Timothy in 1 Timothy 1:18, which may include the same event.

---

183. The metaphor of "laying hands" on someone can also mean to seize them (Matt. 26:50; Mark 14:46; John 7:30, 44; Acts 12:1).

184. Mark 6:5; 8:23, 25; Luke 4:40; 13:13.

185. In Acts 8:17–18, something was seen by Simon Magus indicating something happened; however, we cannot assume to know what it was. In Acts 9:17–18, Paul was healed of his Christ-induced blindness.

The gift not to be neglected is not explained. Still, it directly follows references to speaking (v. 12), public reading, exhortation, and teaching (v. 13).[186] As such, it is likely Timothy's gift as an expounder of the Scriptures in his exhortation and teaching.[187] Alternatively, it is another unspecified gift or the general gift of receiving the Spirit.

In 2 Timothy 1:6, Timothy is urged to rekindle the gift of God in him which has been received through the laying on of hands. Paul may be thinking of the same gift,[188] which Paul wants him to use by the Spirit who generates in believers enhanced courage and empowers the message of God to be efficacious for salvation (cf. 1 Cor. 2:1–5; 1 Thess. 1:5–6), love, and self-discipline (v. 7). While Paul's words here may indicate a failure of courage on the side of Timothy, equally it could simply mean to continue to use it with the same energy he has previously in his long and fruitful ministry with Paul.[189]

Romans 1:11

In Romans 1:11, Paul speaks of his yearning to come to Rome to impart to the Romans "some spiritual gift" (χάρισμα . . . πνευματικὸν).[190] Elsewhere, I have tentatively posited that this is partially fulfilled by the rise in evangelistic courage and enthusiasm reflected in Philippians 1:12–18a.[191] Still, Paul surely has more in mind than merely one such gift.[192] He understands that gifts are transmitted to others through prayer and the laying on of hands (further below). And, likely, he longs to pray for the Romans, asking that God would bless them with new experiences of his Spirit so that they can be more effective in ministry. His interest is general and not merely limited to one such gift.

---

186. Fee, *GEP*, 772, rightly rejects outright the idea that the gift was an office.

187. Similarly, Fee writes, "Thus it includes, but is not limited to, the 'public reading, proclamation/exhortation, and teaching' that Timothy is urged to 'devote himself to' in the preceding imperative. In the larger context of the letter it concerns the whole range of his ministry in Ephesus. Through the gift of the Spirit, Timothy has been especially gifted for a ministry similar to Paul's. Hence Paul can later urge him to 'guard the sacred trust by means of the Spirit who dwells *in us*' (2 Tim. 1:14)." Fee, *GEP*, 773 (emphasis original).

188. In my view, Fee's analysis is a little too pedantic as he questions whether the two refer to the same thing. They may not, but they may well with the differences due to the focus of the letters. Fee, *GEP*, 785–86.

189. On Timothy's supposed timidity, see Christopher R. Hutson, "Was Timothy Timid? On the Rhetoric of Fearlessness (1 Corinthians 16:10–11) and Cowardice (2 Timothy 1:7)," *BR* 42 (1997): 58–73. He correctly rejects speculating on Timothy's timidity and sees Paul's language as rhetorical.

190. Fee argues this should not be translated "some spiritual gift" but "some spiritual manifestation." He suggests gifts like those in 1 Corinthians 12 and Romans 12 are not in view, but "his understanding of the gospel that in Christ Jesus God has created from among Jews and Gentiles one people for himself, apart from Torah." Fee, *GEP*, 488. This is certainly one possible aspect of Paul's desire. However, with the diverse intent of the letter, it could include missional gifts, unity, and other gifts from God.

191. Keown, *Congregational*, 83–84.

192. "[Paul] is simply expressing his confidence that when they come together God will minister through him in a particular way for their mutual benefit." Dunn, *Jesus and the Spirit*, 207.

1 Corinthians 7:7

One's marital state is a χάρισμα ἐκ θεοῦ, "gift from God" (1 Cor. 7:7).[193] This suggests Paul's understanding of God's gifting extends beyond special spiritual endowments of grace to a person's wider life, over which God is sovereignly working by his Spirit.[194] A similar sense applies to 1 Corinthians 7:20–25 of a person's life situation, such as whether a person is circumcised, a slave, and so on.

As such, our theology of *charismata* must extend beyond the gifts listed to everything a person is. On a personal level, an example is my teaching gift reflected in decades of primary and tertiary teaching. Both my parents were teachers, as is my wife, as were an uncle and aunt, and my three daughters are all instructors in different ways in their vocations—clearly, the teaching gift is something God has endowed to my family.[195]

2 Corinthians 8:7

On the face of it, there is nothing to link this verse to spiritual gifts. However, the final clause indicates that giving to the Jerusalem collection is an act of grace, while in the first clause, Paul implies the things they excel in are also sourced in God's grace. The things listed should be seen as spiritual graces gifted to believers by the Spirit.[196] These are found in abundance among the Corinthians. Two of these are ethical virtues (eagerness and love,[197] cf.

---

193. This is the same for those who are single and those who are married. While the Corinthians were opting for celibacy, Paul's "celibacy was not singleness by choice, predicated as some of theirs was on the questionable grounds that marriage is sin, but by χάρισμα. . . . But lest he be understood to make celibacy a higher calling, he immediately qualifies, 'One χάρισμα of one kind, another χάρισμα of another kind.' Thus, if celibacy is χάρισμα, so is marriage." Fee, *GEP*, 138. I agree with Fee that Paul would reject seeing marital state as a Spirit manifestation *of the same kind* as those in 1 Corinthians 12–14. However, I aver he would see it as a gift of the Spirit, and a vital one at that, for it defines how a Christian will live his or her life. The Spirit is doing far more in a person's life than merely imparting a few gifts—God the Father, through Christ, and by the Spirit shapes our whole existence.

194. Fee notes of this text that this use of χάρισμα "functions along with the usage in 2 Cor. 1:11 and Rom. 6:23 as evidence that the concept of 'Spiritual gift' is ancillary to this word at best, not inherent to it." Fee, *GEP*, 138. However, I argue the converse. These gifts, too, are from God, mediated in Christ, and received through his Spirit. I disagree with Dunn, who sees the gift as celibacy and the ability to withstand sexual desire. It is Paul's marital state that is in question, although both of those are wrapped up in it. Dunn, *Jesus and the Spirit*, 206.

195. One can also notice the family continuity of ministry in the OT families of Aaron, the Levites, and the singers mentioned earlier.

196. Fee, *GEP*, 339. He rightly notes that aside from "earnestness" (σπουδή), the list is composed of things found elsewhere in the letter as Spirit ministries. He also observes that these are graces for the church if not necessarily gifts, and second, the combination of "word" and "knowledge" reflects 1 Corinthians 1:5. These are good graces but must be exercised in conformity with the cross. He adds, "Again, as so often in this letter, even though the Spirit is not mentioned by name, he would nonetheless be understood by the Corinthians to be the source of these 'graces' in their lives, in terms of their being manifestations of God's presence."

197. The love in view is either the Corinthian's love for Paul, or Paul and his team's love for the Corinthians. The more difficult reading, which speaks of the team's love for the Corinthians, is harder to account for than the alternative, which speaks of the Corinthians' love for the Pauline group (favored by Metzger,

Gal. 5:22), aligning more with the fruit of the Spirit than gifts. The four gifts are found earlier: faith (1 Cor. 12:8; 13:2), speech (1 Cor. 1:5), knowledge (1 Cor. 1:5; 12:8; 13:2, 8), and giving (1 Cor. 13:3).

1 Corinthians 13:1–8

In 1 Corinthians 12:31b, Paul shifts from the spiritual gifts to how they should be expressed by following the "still more excellent way" of love. This verse through 13:13 fills the center of the chiastic section and highlights that Paul's real concern is not just to teach the Corinthians about spiritual gifts but that all Christian service must be motivated and shaped by love for love's sake.

Verses 1–3 are formed by three conditional sentences couched in the first person, by which Paul begins to show them the most excellent way.[198] The hypothetical scenarios show the senselessness of possessing the greatest gifts imaginable without love—it is futile as they give no honor to the givers and gain them nothing.[199] The verses also function as a spiritual gift list, including seven gifts, of which the first six are linked to earlier gifts discussed and the final one is a gift not yet considered. The gifts are intentionally expressed hyperbolically, in the first person, and conditionally to emphasize the importance of love. They include tongues, prophecy, wisdom, knowledge, faith, giving, and martyrdom.

The final gift speaks of Paul (and, by implication, others) giving himself over to be burned,[200] indicating a preparedness to stand firm for his faith to the point of being burned to death rather than deny Christ. The purpose clause is disputed between (1) ἵνα καυχήσωμαι, "that I will boast," or (2) ἵνα καυθησομαι, "that I will be burned." The former is preferable because, at this time, there is no evidence believers were being burned for their faith. In contrast, boasting is a crucial theme in the Corinthian letters—both in content and tone. Paul finds boasting objectionable and critiques the Corinthians for engaging in it, even as he puts it to use ironically.[201] Boasting is also inherently unloving (13:4).[202] As

---

TCGNT, 512). However, ὑμῶν ἐν ἡμῖν is more widely attested and makes better sense in context as it seems nonsensical for Paul to commend the Corinthians for his love for them. Neither would Paul state that the love in the community derives from him (even if from the gospel); love is from God (as this verse actually implies—contra Harris, The Second Epistle, 574; Margaret Thrall, A Critical and Exegetical Commentary on the Second Epistle of the Corinthians, ICC [New York: T&T Clark, 2004], 2:529). Paul Barnett, The Second Epistle to the Corinthians, NICNT (Grand Rapids: Eerdmans, 1997), 389.

198. Paul uses three third-class conditional sentences, each signaled by ἐάν, "if," with the subjunctive and signaling a hypothetical situation. He uses the first person in his hypothetical scenarios.

199. As Fee puts it, "If not, that person's life before God adds up to zero." Fee, GEP, 200.

200. Fee sees this also as personal sacrifice. Fee, GEP, 203. However, the Spirit is involved in enabling a person to go through painful death for God.

201. See Metzger, TCGNT, 497–98. The arguments given by Metzger et al. are especially convincing. First, the alternate reading of καυθήσομαι is more likely to have entered later, when being burned for the faith became a reality; and second, καυθήσωμαι is a more difficult reading.

202. See 1 Cor. 1:29, 31; 3:21; 4:7; 5:6; 2 Cor. 5:12. Also 1 Cor. 9:15–16; 15:31; 2 Cor. 1:12, 14; 7:4, 14; 8:24; 9:2–3; 10:8, 13, 15–17; 11:10, 12, 16–18, 21, 30; 12:1, 5–6, 9.

the death of Jesus shows, there is nothing more significant than giving one's life for a cause. Yet, with boasting and without love, it avails nothing. With love, Christ's death has saved the world (Rom. 5:8). When we, motivated by love, die for him (whether through martyrdom or natural life expiry while in his service), we significantly aid his mission to save the world and we benefit through the Spirit and eternal life.

In 1 Corinthians 13:1–7, Paul establishes that love must be the motivating force for all spiritual gifts and explains aspects of love the Corinthians are to exhibit. In the chiasm of v. 7,[203] Paul stresses the power of love to endure in all present contexts. Verse 8a enhances v. 7, stressing that love is never defeated and always remains.[204] Having set the backdrop of the permanence of love, Paul contrasts it with the temporary nature of spiritual gifts. Like faith and hope (vv. 7, 13), they are required in this age but will become redundant in eternity when people will have complete knowledge and the fulfillment of hope, and will understand all speech and knowledge (vv. 8–13). In his exposition, Paul mentions three gifts already covered in the earlier lists: prophecy (Rom. 12:6), tongues (1 Cor. 12:10), and knowledge (1 Cor. 12:8; 13:2).

Prophecy will not be required, as believers in the eschaton will not require correction from prophetic words, will fully understand all things, and will be fully aware of the future. Tongues will also not be required, nor their interpretation, because the language confusion of Babel will be resolved (Gen. 11:7), and all will understand. Knowledge will go on, but now all will know and be known fully (v. 12). The three great Pauline virtues remain faith, hope, and love.[205] Of these, faith and hope also become redundant in the eschaton, whereas love will be a permanent feature of the consummated eschatological life.[206]

CONCLUSION

God is characterized by grace; he is a giving God. The Spirit is the gift of God, poured into believers to transform them into the image bearers God created them to be. God's giving is seen in our lives, shaped from before creation and the womb so that we are formed to serve him as we were created to do. Aside from salvation, sanctification, and the Spirit himself, believers also receive special gifts of grace to use in service of God's purposes and mission. Paul lists some of these gifts in his letters—prophecy, service,

---

203. Στέγει balances its synonym ὑπομένει ("endure"). In the center, the semantically overlapping πιστεύει ("trust, believe") and ἐλπίζει ("hope") stress confidence and hope. The fourfold πάντα emphasizes the power of love to empower others whatever the circumstances.

204. See the discussion in Fee, *GEP*, 205–6. He rightly notes the clause "love never fails" includes its never being defeated or passing away.

205. Paul commonly links the three virtues, e.g., Rom. 5:1, 5; 1 Cor. 13:13; Gal. 5:5–6; Col. 1:4–5; 1 Thess. 1:3; 5:8.

206. Some scholars consider that all three remain, but the greatest of these that remain is love. However, faith and hope are premised on doubt, both of which are removed in the perfection of the eschaton (as Paul indicates in vv. 8–10). See chapter 7, "The Greatest of These Is Love."

teaching, healings, speaking and/or interpreting tongues, apostleship, giving, and so on—and delves into how these gifts are to be expressed in the audience's given situation. The Corinthians, for instance, should not value tongues more than prophecy, but if people speak in tongues, there should be an interpretation so that the words edify the church.

The gifts are given to continue God's redemptive work in the world. None of these spiritual gifts are meant as a mark of being a Christian or having received the Spirit but are unique ways the Spirit's people act in community. They are to be used wholeheartedly to further his mission in our marriages and families, workplaces, social contexts, and above all, to strengthen the church and advance God's mission. The gifts are given to be passed on to others so they can contribute similarly.

THE SPIRIT AND MISSION

Somewhat surprisingly, when one considers how central the Spirit is to Luke's missiology (including Paul's mission), Paul himself does not often use πνεῦμα regarding mission. Still, when we deliberate on Paul's use of Trinitarian language, assuming that it is "by the Spirit" that Father and Son act, there is more to work with concerning the Spirit and mission in Paul's letters.[1]

Many passages speak of the Spirit's work in and through believers that, while focused on ethics, should be read to include mission. These include that they "serve [as slaves] in the new way of the Spirit" (Rom. 7:6), "walk according to/by the Spirit" (Rom. 8:4–5; Gal. 5:16), be "led by the Spirit" (Rom. 8:14; Gal. 5:18), "burn/be fervent in the Spirit" (Rom. 12:11),[2] "live by the Spirit"

---

1.   As I enter this discussion, I agree fully with the thesis of Gorman, *BGPPM*, 4, when he states in response to the critique that theosis rules out the possibility of mission, "The thesis of the present book is precisely the opposite: theosis—*Spirit*-enabled transformative participation in the life and character of God revealed in the crucified and resurrected Messiah Jesus—is the starting point of mission and is, in fact, its proper theological framework" (emphasis mine). Cruciformity/Christoformity by its very nature should generate mission, for God is a missionary God. Jesus was sent as a missionary to restore creation and save humankind, and the Spirit leads us in that mission as it goes on. Indeed, any discussion of cruciformity that does not see mission as an aspect of cruciformity is reductionist. Gorman himself said this earlier in *CPNSC*, 5: "*In the meantime, by the power of the Spirit of Father and Son, the new people, the new humanity bears witness in word and deed to that glorious future by participating now in the life and mission of the triune cruciform God*" (emphasis original).

2.   See Fee's discussion of this passage (*GEP*, 611–13). He considers both options—a person's spirit (fervent attitude) and the Spirit (be fervent [burn] in the Spirit)—difficult. He argues these things favor "of the Spirit" here: (1) the combination of ζέω and πνεῦμα; (2) the dative of πνεῦμα, which suggests "in/by the Spirit"; (3) a possible parallelism with the Spirit here and "serving *the Lord*"; (4) the emphasis on the Spirit in chapter 8; (5) and the mention of burning with Spirit that correlates the text with 1 Thessalonians 5:19 and 2 Timothy 1:6. Against seeing this as the divine Spirit is (1) the use of the article, which he always uses of the human spirit and rarely of the Holy Spirit; (2) the parallel with Acts 18:25, which Fee determines must mean "ardent of spirit" in the case of Apollos. He opts for the anthropological interpretation. However, I am not so sure. First, ζέων τῷ πνεύματι in Acts 18:25 could refer to the Spirit. Luke speaks of the work of the Spirit in people prior to Pentecost

(Gal. 5:25), "sow to the Spirit" (Gal. 6:8), and receive "the Spirit of wisdom and of revelation in the knowledge of him" (Eph. 1:17). All these apply equally to mission, worship, and intrachurch life.

Similarly, any number of passages speak of God's work in believers that should be read as being inclusive of missional engagement. For example, they speak of presenting one's members to God as instruments of righteousness (Rom. 6:13), bearing fruit for God (Rom. 7:14), and living by faith in the Son of God who lives in believers (Gal. 2:20). While it would be fruitful to explore the possibilities of these verses, my interest in this chapter is passages that more explicitly indicate the Triune God's involvement in missional engagement.

In a sense, this is an artificial chapter in that everything said of the Spirit's work in the believers' lives in earlier chapters includes missional engagement when believers leave explicitly Christian situations and enter the unbelieving world. God works in the world, exhibiting his glory in creation, wooing people to him, sending people to preach, saving them by the faith generated at the hearing of the word, filling new believers with his Spirit, and sustaining them to the end. The point of salvation in a person's life is not the end of the Spirit's work. From the moment of salvation and incorporation, the Spirit of the crucified and raised Christ begins shaping people into Christ, the image of God (pneumaformed Christoformity). As believers submit, their old patterns of sin are progressively overcome, and they exhibit the ethics, values, and virtues of God and his Son (chapter 7). Pneumaformity, by its very definition, will include the missional passion and purposes of the Spirit, into which God's people are drawn.

As considered in chapter 8, their incorporation in Christ is not an end in itself, but believers are transformed into missional beings who are cleaved into the mission of Christ to do their part in restoring his world and saving humankind. Together, individual believers from the body of Christ that continues the work of God's mission in the world led by the Spirit. As they are sent into mission, the Spirit leads them into times of suffering in the struggle of being poured out in a hostile and fallen world. At the same time, he comforts believers and delivers them from danger and difficulty. Yet, they are sometimes left in the struggle, and their lives are given (chapter 8). In addition, the spiritual gifts considered in the previous chapter (chapter 9) are not merely for the inward life of the church—the beneficial good and growth of the church includes new believers added to the church and their pneumaformation.

---

in his infancy narrative. There is no mention of Priscilla and Aquila imparting the Spirit to him. As such, I am not sure why he rejects outright Acts 18:25 referring to the Holy Spirit (see the excellent arguments of Ben Witherington III, *The Acts of the Apostles: A Socio-Rhetorical Commentary* [Grand Rapids: Eerdmans, 1998], 564–65). Second, use of the article is not determinative in that sometimes the article is used with the Holy Spirit.

With all this in mind, I will not go over all such ground again in this chapter. However, I will note those points where God's action is mentioned in explicitly missional contexts.

Unlike Paul's other appeals for prayer, in 1 Thessalonians 5 Paul simply asks the believers to "pray for us," without detail. While the scope of this prayer request is broad, as Paul's primary work is evangelistic mission, we can be confident that this can be rendered, "pray for our mission." Such prayers would include travel plans as in 3:11 where Paul asked God and Jesus to direct his team's path to Thessalonica. In other letters, as we will discuss, he gives more clarity concerning the things he has in mind.

Paul's letters repeatedly refer to his own prayers for his converts, indicating the importance of missionaries giving thanks for and praying for their converts. In these prayers, Paul speaks of God's role in guiding the mission and causing growth (Rom. 1:8–15, further below). Things prayed for include the following:

- The God of peace being with the Romans and filling them with joy, peace, and hope (Rom. 15:13, 33)
- Spiritual gifts, including speaking gifts (1 Cor. 1:6–7)
- God providing a way out of temptation (1 Cor. 10:13)
- Comforting and delivering missionaries in times of suffering (2 Cor. 1:3–11)
- God blessing converts with salvation and its many benefits, granting them enlightenment, wisdom, knowledge, and experience of Christ and God's love (Eph. 1:3–23; 3:14–21)
- Participation in mission with Paul, greater love, and righteous fruit (Phil. 1:3–11)
- Deeper knowledge, wisdom, and insight, to live in a way that pleases God, fruitfulness in good deeds (Col. 1:3–14)
- Gratitude for conversion, ongoing missional engagement, more love, blamelessness, and holiness[3]
- Flourishing faith, love, endurance in suffering, the fulfillment of every missional desire, further glorification of Christ, encouragement, hope, and hearts directed to God's love and perseverance in Christ[4]
- Christ's mercy shown to those like Onesiphorus, who make enormous sacrifices for the gospel mission and respond to those who harm God's people (2 Tim. 1:16–18; 4:14)
- More effective and Christ-aware fellowship in the faith (Philem. 6)[5]

---

3.   1 Thess. 1:2–10; 2:13–16; 3:12–13; 5:23.
4.   2 Thess. 1:3–4, 11–12; 2:16; 3:1, 5.
5.   In context, it speaks of Philemon continuing to be financially generous to mission and also generous in taking Onesimus back as a Christian brother and gospel worker without penalty.

THE SPIRIT IN THE MISSIONAL PROCESS TO CONVERSION

As discussed more fully in chapter 2, for Paul, God should be perceived by humankind through his creation, so much so that people are without excuse for choosing idolatrous worship of created things and beings rather than God (Rom. 1:19–25). The Spirit also sets apart, appoints, commissions, and sends people into his world to proclaim the gospel to others. The Spirit leads people in mission, as Luke so powerfully demonstrates in Acts.

The Spirit of God encounters unbelievers through his sent people, and faith is born as the gospel is heard. The word is a sword that pierces and circumcises the heart; it is the power of salvation. Faith declares people "justified," and the Spirit enters and begins God's sanctifying work. They are reconciled to God and his people. The Spirit floods the beings of new believers in Christ, sealing them and guaranteeing eternal life. The Spirit fills them with God's love, adopting them into God's family. New believers are baptized in the Spirit; drink of God; are washed, sanctified, adopted into God's family; and their pneumaformation begins instantly. Never again can they say, "Jesus be accursed"; instead, they proudly confess Jesus is Lord (1 Cor. 12:3). Often, this will be tested in a missional context. The process of pneumaformation begins with renewal by faith through the work of the Spirit (Gal. 3:3). Formerly dead in sin but now alive in Christ and new creations, believers become part of the temple of the Spirit. The church itself is a letter from Christ written with the ink of the Spirit. In that God is a missionary God, speaking into the world in and through his Son, by the Spirit, the new believer becomes a part of God's mission to the world.

FINDING THEIR PLACE IN THE MISSION

Paul hints at how he understands the involvement of people in God's mission. Clearly believers are, first of all, people made in the image of God. As mission is core to God's character and purposes, it should be central to ours. Some believers, like Paul, are instantly sent by God into vocational mission (Gal. 1:12, 15–17).[6] Of course, Paul was already a vocational religious leader on a mission to destroy the Christian movement in Syria. Now a Christian, Paul does not cease being missional, but God has directed his mission away from the destruction of the church to joining it and promoting it in the world.

Paul's commission coincides with his conversion. Is this the same for other Christians? Paul gives no indication he wants *all* Christians to give up their families, vocations, and ongoing lives to become vocational or bivocational (as he prefers) missionaries. Instead, he encourages his converts to remain in the call they had at their conversion. In 1 Corinthians 7:17, Paul tells the Corinthians to walk (περιπατέω) as "the Lord assigned" and as "God

---

6.   See also Acts 9:1–17; 22:1–21; 26:1–29. Paul of course was bivocational. However, he was certainly called to give his life to the mission of the proclamation of the gospel and establishment of God's church among the nations.

has called." Paul states this is a rule he applies across his churches. He restates it in v. 24, which, with v. 17, forms a chiastic frame around the passage. He applies the principle to the states of circumcision and uncircumcision, and slavery and freedom. Believers are to remain in these situations as God has placed them there. It seems reasonable to broaden this out to vocational and other social experiences (aside from the idolatrous and sinful) the believers find themselves in at the point of conversion.

That believers should remain in their vocational and social situations at conversion is tacitly supported by his injunctions to slaves to work whole-heartedly for their masters as if to the Lord (Eph. 6:3–8; Col. 3:23). His bivo-cational practice also lends support to this. Still, Paul recognizes that God calls people into vocational or bivocational missional roles. He uses a range of language to describe this.

People Sent

Paul's gospel is premised on God sending forth Christ, his Son, born of a woman under the law, in the likeness of human flesh to deal with sin and to redeem those under the law that they may be adopted as God's children (Rom. 8:3; Gal. 4:4–5). God, too, sends Christ's Spirit out from heaven into the hearts of believers, welcoming them into God's family by adoption (Gal. 4:6).

God, through Christ, by his Spirit, also sends people into mission, often with specific instructions. In 1 Corinthians 1:17, Paul recalls Christ doing this, sending him to preach rather than baptize. He is sent to clearly set forth the gospel of the crucified Messiah so that through his straightforward, unadorned words, God's power by his Spirit will generate faith. Preachers are also sent for the essential task of proclaiming Christ so that the gospel may be heard, faith generated, and people saved (Rom. 10:15).

Paul, as leader of his missionary team (no doubt constrained by the Spirit), sends coworkers for specific tasks. So, Timothy was sent to remind the Corinthians of Paul's faith expectations (1 Cor. 4:17), to Thessalonica to see how Paul's church was faring and to establish and encourage them in their faith (1 Thess. 3:2, 5), and to Philippi to hear of their news (Phil. 2:19, 23). Others sent include Tychicus, sent twice to encourage the readers of Paul's letters, especially in Asia Minor;[7] Epaphroditus, who had nearly died deliv-ering gifts to Paul (Phil. 2:25, 28); and Artemas (Titus 3:12). Paul tells the Corinthians he will send members of their church to take the collection up to Jerusalem (1 Cor. 16:3). On the collection trip, he sent several coworkers, including Titus, to Corinth in preparation for his coming.[8] While he does not name the Spirit regarding these sendings, his passion for doing God's will strongly suggests that his sending was Spirit-impelled. He also uses "we" language of his apostolic commission, drawing other preachers and members

---

7. Eph. 6:22; Col. 4:8; 2 Tim. 4:12; Titus 3:12.
8. 2 Cor. 8:18, 23; 9:3; 12:17–18.

of his team under his lead into his apostolic call—they, too, are called and sent to participate in God's gospel mission with Paul. The Spirit melds his team together in one Spirit (Phil. 1:27).

Ministries, Grace Gifted, and Authority

Δίδωμι (give) is sometimes used of the assigning of gifts for ministry. This usage is found concerning Jesus, whom God *gave* to the church as head over all things (Eph. 1:22). Paul also regularly speaks of "the grace given" as he describes his ministry as a gifted charism.[9] Both his and Apollos's ministries in Corinth are given by God (1 Cor. 3:5), as are the spiritual gifts Christians receive.[10] These gifts include the fivefold ministry gifts of Ephesians 4:11. The experience of this grace in the lives and ministry of believers is through the Spirit. Giving materially to those in need is also God's grace given to believers (2 Cor. 8:1). The ability to speak a particular message in each ministry moment is also the work of the Spirit (Eph. 6:19). Elsewhere, Paul speaks of Christ (the Lord) giving his authority to Paul to build up the Corinthians (2 Cor. 10:8; 13:10), and of God's gift of his stewardship to be a minister to complete God's Word (Col. 1:25).

Ministries Entrusted and Received

Paul sometimes uses the language of being entrusted in terms of ministry calls. He is entrusted with the stewardship of preaching the gospel (1 Cor. 9:17; 1 Tim. 1:11; Titus 1:3), the message of reconciliation (2 Cor. 5:19), the gospel to the uncircumcised (while Peter is entrusted with the gospel to the circumcised [Gal. 2:7]). In Ephesus, to deal with false teachers, Timothy is to guard what has been entrusted to him (1 Tim. 6:20; 2 Tim. 1:12) and is to entrust Paul's teaching to other faithful people who can teach others (2 Tim. 2:2).

Again, in 2 Corinthians 5:18, believers are reconciled to God "through Christ" (διὰ Χριστοῦ). Moreover, a "ministry of reconciliation" is also *given* to "us." "Us" could refer to the Pauline team or, more broadly, to all God-authorized ministers of reconciliation.[11] Alternatively, as all believers are reconciled to God in Christ (the first "us"), he may have in view all Christians.[12] Whatever the case, Paul recognizes that God gives to some or all Christians the ministry of proclaiming the gospel so that people can be reconciled to God by faith and reconciled to one another (2 Cor. 5:18).

As God gave the ministry of reconciliation "in Christ," the world is being reconciled to God. This idea speaks of the cosmic scope of the mission, which,

---

9.   Rom. 12:3; 15:5; 1 Cor. 3:10; Gal. 2:9; Eph. 3:2, 7–8. Dunn notes these same verses and rightly says, "In each case he is talking about some sort of commission or enabling for some service." For Paul it was "a continuing compulsion" of the Spirit. Dunn, *Jesus and the Spirit*, 203.

10. Rom. 12:6; 1 Cor. 1:4; 12:7, 8, 24; Eph. 4:7–8.

11. Harris, *Second Epistle*, 438–39.

12. Victor Paul Furnish, *II Corinthians: Translated with Introduction, Notes, and Commentary*, AYB 32A (New Haven, CT: Yale University Press, 2008), 317.

with our knowledge of the extent of the world in the first century,[13] presupposes multitudes of other Christians engaging in mission and not just Paul and his team. To these people, God entrusted "the message of reconciliation" (λόγον τῆς καταλλαγῆς, 2 Cor. 5:19).

Epaphras is described by Paul as a faithful minister of Christ, indicating Christ's call on his life to minister through Paul (on our behalf). The Colossians and perhaps Laodiceans heard the gospel from Epaphras (Col. 1:7; 2:1; 4:15, 16). Archippus has received a ministry call from Christ (the Lord), and Paul urges him to fulfill it (Col. 4:17).

Set Apart in the Womb

In Galatians 1:15, Paul states that God is the one who set him apart (ὁ ἀφορίσας με) from his mother's womb (ἐκ κοιλίας μητρός μου). The verb ἀφορίζω is used for exclusion (Luke 6:22), to separate oneself from something unholy (2 Cor. 6:17), and, as in Galatians 1:15, refers to people set apart for a specific ministry task (Acts 13:2). This includes God setting Paul apart for the proclamation of the gospel (Rom. 1:1).[14] In the OT, God also calls people to ministries in the womb, such as Samson (Judg. 13:7; 16:17) and Jeremiah, who was consecrated and appointed to be a prophet to the nations from the womb (Jer. 1:5). The Servant, whom NT writers believe to be Jesus,[15] was both formed in and called from the womb for his mission (Isa. 49:2, 5). In the NT, John is even filled with the Spirit while in his mother's womb, where he leaped for joy when Mary, pregnant with Jesus, greeted Elizabeth. Elizabeth then declared a blessing over the unborn Jesus (Luke 1:15, 40–44). These texts specifically refer to people with a special calling from God that is considered to have occurred from conception. In fact, with Paul's predeterminism, this occurred before conception. These moments point to the sovereign work of God by his Spirit on those he will set apart for mission, even on those who do not yet possess faith.[16]

People Appointed

Paul writes to Timothy and gives thanks to God for his ongoing strengthening, for considering Paul faithful, and for appointing (τίθημι) him to ministry. Τίθημι with God as subject and people as object speaks of God placing or putting people into a particular place or context and in a ministry

---

13. See Mark J. Keown, "An Imminent Parousia and Christian Mission: Did the New Testament Writers Expect Jesus's Imminent Return?" in *Christian Origins and the Establishment of the Early Jesus Movement*, eds. Stanley E. Porter and Andrew W. Pitts, TENTS; ECHC 4 (Leiden: Brill, 2017), 242–61.

14. Further, Keown, *Galatians*, 185–86.

15. John D. Barry summarizes the mentions of the Servant in the NT. John D. Barry, "Servant of the Lord," LBD.

16. Although we know nothing of Paul's mother's faith. She raised Paul in Tarsus in a home of Hebrews, and his sister's son warns him of a plot (Acts 23:16). It may be his sister has become a Christian by this time, although this is not certain. See the comments of Bruce, *The Book of the Acts*, 432.

context, appointing them for a role.[17] Paul employs the term of his own (and sometimes his team's) appointment to "the ministry of reconciliation" (2 Cor. 5:19); "to [God's] service" (1 Tim. 1:12); to be "a preacher and an apostle . . . a teacher of the Gentiles in faith and truth" (1 Tim. 2:7); and to be "a preacher and apostle and teacher" (2 Tim. 1:11). His ministry of reconciliation as an ambassador of Christ was a gift from God. Paul also employs τίθημι of God appointing people to the ministries of apostle, teacher, miracle-worker, healer, helper, leader, and tongue speaker (cf. 1 Cor. 12:18).

Proclamation

Dunn rightly argues of Paul: "Of central importance for Paul was his firm conviction that his own preaching of the gospel was charismatic."[18] He notes 1 Thessalonians 1:5, where Paul recalls his team's evangelism in Thessalonica—their gospel came "with word, power, the Holy Spirit, and deep conviction." The word was received in the joy of the Holy Spirit, indicating the Spirit's role in the reception and the life then generated (1:6).

Again, in 1 Corinthians 2:4, Paul's message was given not with rhetorical and philosophical dynamism but in the demonstration of the Spirit and God's power. Dunn notes that "the ἀποδείξει of his message was nothing to do with his skill as a rhetorician, nothing to do with arguments and proofs; it was ἀποδείξει of Spirit and power."[19] He rightfully adds that in contrast with the opponents focused on in 2 Corinthians, this power came through weakness.[20] Dunn adds a raft of other texts that speak of "the charismatic power of inspired proclamation."[21] The Spirit leads the mission of God in his people; central to this is the Spirit-led and empowered gospel proclamation.

The Spirit and Areas of Mission Influence

An intriguing aspect of the Spirit and mission is found in how Paul speaks of geographical spheres of activity. First, he clearly distinguishes between pioneering mission and that which follows. This distinction is seen in 1 Corinthians 3, where, as he repudiates the Corinthian factional preferencing of different preachers, he distinguishes between his role and that of Apollos and others who followed him. His pioneering ministry role is akin to "planting" a field (3:6) and "laying a foundation" (of Christ) to a building (3:10–11). Apollos and others "water" the field (3:6) or build on the foundation of Christ with other materials (3:12). Paul does not rank the roles—both are servants of

17. See in the wider NT, John 15:16; Acts 13:47; Heb. 1:2 [Jesus]; 1 Peter 2:6 [Jesus the cornerstone]). See also the use of Psalm 110:1 in the NT of God putting or placing people under Christ's feet (Matt. 22:44; Mark 12:36; Luke 20:43; Acts 2:35; 1 Cor. 15:25; Heb. 1:13; 10:13); God putting people into eternal destruction (Matt. 24:51; Luke 12:46; 1 Thess. 5:9; 1 Peter 2:8; cf. 2 Peter 2:6).
18. Dunn, *Jesus and the Spirit*, 226.
19. Dunn, *Jesus and the Spirit*, 226.
20. Dunn, *Jesus and the Spirit*, 227.
21. Dunn, *Jesus and the Spirit*, 227. He notes Rom. 1:16; 15:18; 2 Cor. 4:4–7; Gal. 3:5; Eph. 6:17; Col. 4:3.

God (3:6) and God's coworkers (3:9). Moreover, God brings the growth (3:6) and judges the quality of the work of both, bringing the appropriate reward or punishment (3:13–16).

While Paul often speaks of roles and gifts granted by the Spirit, he considers that all Christians are, in effect, assigned their role from conversion. If the earlier analysis of 1 Corinthians 7:17–24 is correct, believers should remain in the social and vocational situations they were in when they became believers. This context becomes their initial missional sphere, even if later they are called to vocational mission work.

In Romans 15, the power of Paul's apostolic ministry is the Spirit, and those Gentiles converted are an acceptable offering sanctified by the Spirit (15:16, 19). Paul mentions the sphere of his ministry—from Jerusalem to Illyricum—in which he has "fulfilled the ministry of the gospel of Christ" (15:19a). While there are varying interpretations of this, I concur with O'Brien, who argues this speaks of the establishment of churches that can continue the mission throughout the region from Israel to the western Balkans.[22] As with Apollos and Peter in Corinth, others who minister in them "water" and "build upon" what Paul has sown and founded. Next, Paul states his ambition to travel to places that have yet to hear the gospel and lay the foundation of Christ (15:20–21), including Spain via Jerusalem and then Rome (15:23–32). Paul here hints at his desire to go to fresh fields to preach the gospel, as he sees this as his primary work as an apostle. Others will come and build on the foundation of Christ.

Spheres of mission form an aspect in Paul's ironic boast against his opponents threatening the Corinthians. He boasts of the authority given to him by Christ (the Lord) for building up the Corinthians (2 Cor. 10:8). He will not boast immeasurably, but "only with regard to the area of influence God assigned to us, to reach even to you" (10:13). In coming as far as Corinth to preach the gospel, Paul and his coworkers (we) are not overextending their commissioned assignment of evangelizing the city (10:14). Paul hopes for further growth beyond their initial work so that he can push onto other regions beyond (e.g., Spain). He will not boast of the work of Christ done by others in their assigned places (10:16). All boasting must be "in the Lord," including in the sphere of ministry the Lord assigns to his workers by his Spirit (10:17). And in fact, it is the Lord's commendation that really matters and brings approval (10:18). This complicated passage supports the idea of the Lord, by his Spirit, assigning ministry roles and spheres to his workers.

Spheres of mission engagement granted by the Lord are reflected in Galatians 2:7–9. Essential to his apologia and *narratio* defending his gospel and ministry in the face of Judaizers, Paul recalls his visit to Jerusalem, where

---

22. On Romans 15:19a, see O'Brien, *Gospel and Mission*, 39–43. He identifies three interpretations: (1) fulfilment of OT eschatology; (2) fulfilment through Paul's preaching; and (3) fulfillment through the planting of churches through the region. The latter is undoubtedly correct. See also Keown, *Romans and the Mission of God*, 42 n. 39.

he encountered Peter, James, and John. At the meeting, it was agreed that the trio, under the leadership of Peter, were entrusted with the gospel to the circumcised (the Jewish people). They recognized that the coworkers under Paul's leadership were similarly entrusted to lead the mission to the uncircumcised (the Gentile world). Just as Peter, James, and John are pillars of the newly formed temple of God's Spirit to which Jews have been added by their ministry, Paul and his group are pillars of the same Spirit-indwelt building into which Gentile converts are being added (cf. 1 Cor. 3:16; Eph. 2:19–22). The trio urged Paul and his team to continue to remember the poor, which they were eager to do.[23]

PROVISION IN MISSION

While Paul recognizes churches should provision missional leaders in line with God's teaching, he prefers that those engaging in missions to new fields earn their living rather than expect payment from those to whom they minister. He has many reasons for this—not to burden them,[24] not to be seen as a peddler of the gospel, and not to place himself in social obligation to the giver. In 2 Thessalonians 3:6–12, he broadens his bivocationalism to something he did intentionally to set an example to his converts. They would then imitate his missional zeal while providing for themselves. Paul describes himself and other missional preachers as "servants/ministers of a new covenant" (2 Cor. 3:6). They do not minister in accordance with the letter of the law, as he did as a Pharisee and as opposing Judaizers do. Instead, God makes them adequate to minister in and by the Spirit who gives life where the gospel is heard, faith is generated, and the Spirit poured out (2 Cor. 3:8).

Paul's understanding of the God of nations and the cosmic scope of mission suggests the Spirit in the future generating a desire in many others to travel across land and sea to reach these Gentile nations with the gospel (see, e.g., Rom. 3:29; 2 Cor. 5:19). The notion of "far off" being "brought near by the blood of Christ" in Ephesians 2:13 suggests the Spirit's sending people to the "far off" that they may be joined to God's people.

In his defense of the right of preachers to receive their living from the gospel, using a question in the form of a first-class conditional sentence, Paul asks, "If we have sown spiritual things in you, is it a great thing[25] if you yourselves reap fleshly[26] things?" (my translation). Paul considers

---

23. With Longenecker, I consider this is the Antiochian collection visit referenced in Acts 11:29–30, and Paul and his team carried this on, including his western Antiochian collection mission through Galatia, Macedonia, and Corinth later (Rom. 15:24–32; 1 Cor. 16:1–4; 2 Cor. 8–9). Longenecker, *Galatians*, lxi–lxxxviii. See also Keown, *Galatians*, 14–27.

24. Keown, *Discovering: The Pauline Letters*, 327–30.

25. The neuter singular μέγα stands alone as "a great thing" as σαρκικά is plural. The verb "to be" is implied.

26. Σαρκικά should be translated "fleshly things" rather than "material things" or other alternatives as it is contrasted with πνευματικά, "spiritual things." Paul uses "fleshly" with the suggestion that things

those who benefit spiritually from others obligated to financially support those who minister to them. As in the previous, "spiritual things" include the gospel, and the language indicates the Spirit's work in imparting them through the Spirit-sent and Spirit-empowered preachers who minister to them.

SPIRITUAL GIFTS AND MISSION

The spiritual gifts have been discussed in the previous chapter. Here I will briefly consider the gifts that have an outward-facing dimension: prophecy (especially in the context of the interpretation or translation of tongues), service, teaching, generosity, and mercy. The "word of wisdom," healings and miracles, apostleship, martyrdom, and evangelism are also gifts that lead to missional engagement.

Romans 12:6–8

There is nothing limiting the exercise of gifts in Romans 12 towards believers only. The gifts also have a missional function. While prophecy is primarily an inward-facing gift, Paul speaks of its external function in 1 Corinthians 14:16–25, as his vision of church meetings includes the presence of unbelieving outsiders.[27] Paul disdains using tongues without interpretation as it leaves such people ignorant of what is said and of God and removes the possibility of their yielding to God due to what they hear. He prefers church members to prophesy and interpret/translate the message so it can then be understood. Then the unbelieving outsider may be convicted of sin by what is said, and recognizing God's presence in the church, fall before God in worship. In the presence of unbelievers, interpreted tongues and prophecies become evangelistic.

The second gift, διακονία, as discussed, may refer to ministry, deaconship, or as is likely here, service. Still, if Paul does have a ministry role in view, διακονία is used for a range of missional functions. These include the roles of pioneering evangelists, those seven selected for the distribution of food but of whom at least two were evangelistic, those in the "ministry of the word," Paul and his apostolic work, those with outward-working spiritual gifts, and Timothy and Mark in their ministries (2 Tim. 4:5, 11).[28] Hence, if διακονία here is a ministry gift, it includes ministering to nonbelievers.

---

required for the flesh to survive in this age, due to the fallenness of the flesh, are transient. In the age to come, all will be πνευματικά and nothing σαρκικά. In the meantime, those who preach the gospel should earn their living from it.

27. My own consideration of ἰδιώτης in the LXX (Prov. 6:8b), the Pseudepigrapha (Let. Aris. 288–289), Josephus, and Philo indicates it does not refer to a different category of unbelievers (e.g., an initiate), but the same group, that is, unbelievers who are outsiders from those of faith.

28. Alternatively, Mark helps Paul in his ministry.

The διδάσκω terms are also used for ministry beyond the church across the NT, including the teaching of Jesus (often),[29] early church teachers,[30] and Paul.[31] Similarly, while the παρακαλέω nexus of terms is primarily used for comforting, pleading with, and exhorting believers, it is used sparingly for proclamation, including by John the Baptist (Luke 3:18), Peter (Acts 2:40), and Paul (Acts 13:15; 2 Cor. 5:20).[32]

The other gifts mentioned may also occasionally have an outward focus. When encountering people in need, service, generosity, and mercy would be appropriate gifts to exercise missionally. These things marked Jesus's ministry to the world and his missional injunctions to the disciples.[33] Moreover, in what follows, Paul urges the Romans to exercise generosity toward others, including welcoming strangers (12:13),[34] blessing persecutors (which is not mere sentiment, see v. 20), living peaceably with all, and feeding enemies (v. 20).

1 Corinthians 12–14

Some of the gifts of 1 Corinthians 12–14 include missional activity. As noted in chapter 9, as σοφία- language is used in 1 Corinthians 1–4 of the message of a crucified Messiah,[35] the "word of wisdom" in 1 Corinthians 12:8 may refer to a message that articulates the deep wisdom of God in the gospel.

In that healing and miracles were an essential aspect of the evangelistic ministry of Jesus[36] and other early church missionaries in Acts, including Paul[37] and his letters,[38] these may have been an aspect of their evangelistic endeavor alongside the proclamation of the word.

---

29. Matt. 4:23; 5:2; 7:28, 29; 9:35; 11:1; 15:34; 21:23; 22:23; 26:55; Mark 1:21, 22, 27; 2:13; 4:1, 2; 6:2, 6, 34; 10:1; 11:17, 18; 12:35, 38; 14:49; Luke 4:15, 31, 32; 5:3, 17; 6:6; 13:10, 22, 26; 19:47; 20:1, 21; 21:37; 23:5; John 6:59; 7:14, 16, 17, 28, 35; 8:2, 20; 18:19, 20; Acts 1:1.
30. Inclusive of apostles', disciples', and false teachers' evangelistic endeavors: Mark 6:30; Acts 4:2, 18; 5:21, 25, 28, 42; 13:1; 15:35; 17:19; 18:11, 25; 20:20; 21:28; 28:31; 2 Peter 2:1; 1 John 2:27; 2 John 10; Rev. 2:14, 15, 20, 24.
31. In Paul, it at times is inclusive of evangelistic teaching (1 Cor. 2:13; Col. 1:28; 1 Tim. 2:7; 6:3; 2 Tim. 1:11; 2:2; 3:10, 16; 4:2; Titus 1:9; 2:7).
32. Possibly also 1 Tim. 4:13; 2 Tim. 4:2.
33. Examples include Jesus's servant ministry and the imperative to serve others (Matt. 12:18; 20:26–28; 23:11; Mark 9:35; 10:44–45; Luke 12:33; 22:26–27; John 13:1–16); giving freely and generously (Matt. 10:8; Mark 10:21; Luke 11:41); and Jesus's emphasis on compassion and mercy (Matt. 5:7; 9:36; 12:7; 14:14; 15:32; 20:34; 23:23; Mark 6:34; Luke 6:36; 10:37; 15:20).
34. While φιλοξενία here may refer primarily to the needs of the saints (see 12:13a), there is no limit placed, and other aspects of this passage and the next are outward facing.
35. 1 Cor. 1:17, 19–22, 24–27, 30; 2:1, 4–7, 13; 3:10, 18–20. The only other use aside from here is in 1 Corinthians 6:5 of wisdom to settle disputes in the church.
36. See Keown, *Discovering: The Gospels and Acts*, 468–74.
37. For the early church: Acts 2:22, 43; 3:1–9; 4:30; 5:12, 16; 6:8; 8:6–7, 13; 9:34; 10:38. Paul: Acts 14:3; 15:12; 16:16–18; 19:11–12; 28:8, 27.
38. Rom. 15:19; 2 Cor. 12:12; Gal. 3:5.

The outward nature of prophecy is regularly mentioned in this section (14:16, 24–25). As in 1 Corinthians 14:1–25, translated or interpreted tongues function effectively as prophecy in edifying those present; tongues could also include the same outward aspect on occasion.

The body metaphor in 1 Corinthians 12 in and of itself potentially includes mission. A body exists in a location in relation to other bodies, and communication is an essential aspect of being human. Paul mentions parts of the body, including the hand (v. 15), which potentially implies offering assistance to others, and there is no need to limit this to intrachurch life. Consistent with Paul's metaphor, one could suggest that the mouth is an aspect related to speech, even if not mentioned, and so includes speech within and beyond the church.

The gifts of vv. 27–30 include apostles who engage in pioneer mission and others whose missions reach beyond the church (prophets, teachers, healing, miracles, tongues, and interpretation). While Paul's injunction to seek greater gifts in v. 31 is only developed in the direction of speaking gifts, the principle potentially implies missional gifts that lead people to believe and join God's people (e.g., apostolicity, evangelism, healings, miracles, service, generosity, mercy, and so on). Indeed, using Paul's logic, one can argue that the pioneer missional gifts are the greatest gifts as they save people from eternal destruction into eternal life. To seek such gifts enhances God's mission, so his people should seek them.

Most of the gifts of 1 Corinthians 13:1–3 have been covered thus far (tongues, prophecy) or do not have an obvious external aspect (understanding all mysteries and knowledge,[39] faith). However, the gift of giving one's body over in v. 3 indicates martyrdom for the faith in a hostile context. Martyrdom, of course, applies to Jesus and, in the early church, the likes of Stephen (Acts 7), James the son of Zebedee (Acts 12:1–2), and Antipas (Rev. 2:13). Paul, also, at the time of writing, had been in multiple situations of extreme bodily threat, including his stonings in Derbe and Lystra that Luke records, the latter seeming to see him die and be raised to life (Acts 14:5, 19–20).[40] Such texts refer to Christian evangelism that excites opposition.[41]

Ephesians 4:12

As discussed in the previous chapter, Paul mentions five gifts active in the life of the Ephesus church and the other churches he addresses in Ephesians. The gift of apostleship speaks of the pioneering and church-founding ministries of the Twelve, Paul, Barnabas, Silas, Timothy, Epaphroditus, and others unnamed.[42] Prophets have a function in evangelism (1 Cor. 14:24–25), as do

---

39. Although, as argued, a message of wisdom or knowledge may include evangelism.

40. See also 2 Cor. 6:5; 11:23–27.

41. See, e.g., 1 Thess. 2:1–2. First Corinthians 14:26 refers to gifts to be used within the church gatherings and so will not be considered in this section.

42. Acts 1:26; 14:4, 14; Rom. 1:1; 1 Cor. 15:5; 2 Cor. 8:23; Phil. 2:25.

teachers. However, distinguishing teachers from evangelists in this passage may indicate that Paul is thinking more of the gift of teaching believers here.

The role of pastor or shepherd (ποιμαίνω) may be a gift exercised within the church—those specially gifted in feeding the people of the church with God's Word and pastoral care. In Acts 20:28–29, overseers shepherd the church of God (also 1 Peter 5:2–3) and protect the flock from false teachers. Yet, elsewhere in the NT, evangelism is implied in a couple of ways where the shepherding motif is used. First, the title of Jesus and his ministry includes evangelism of the shepherdless lost—his death for his sheep, reaching the "lost sheep," sheep yet to enter his flock, and people turning back to him.[43] Second, Jesus's injunctions to Peter to feed his sheep in John 21:15–18, read in the light of John 10:16, refer to his teaching and evangelistic ministry. Third, new sheep need to be carefully nurtured with milk and love and remain vulnerable when in an immature state. Pastoral and evangelistic ministries always overlap.

The other gift is that of the evangelist (εὐαγγελιστής). In the previous chapter, I suggested it is a Christian proclaimer of the gospel who continues the work begun by the apostle, seeking to advance the gospel among unbelievers and reasserting the gospel where false teaching threatens the church.

Each of these ministry leaders has the task of continuing the work for which they are called and gifted with the posture of Christ. They should also equip others for ministry in their specific areas. Where mission is concerned, apostles will identify others who are called by God to pioneer and have the wide range of gifts and exemplary Christian character necessary for such work. Recognizing God's call and the Spirit's equipping in them, the apostles will further train them and send them out, as Jesus did with the disciples and as Paul did with his coworkers. They will be concerned for them, as Paul was for lost Titus (2 Cor. 2:13) and sick Epaphroditus (Phil. 2:26–27). The evangelist will identify those called by God to preach the gospel to unbelievers, challenge false teachers, and strengthen believers in the face of their false teaching. They will equip the church for mission. The outcome of the work of these leaders is unity in Christ (Eph. 4:13), maturity (vv. 13–14), confidence in the gospel before false teaching (v. 15), confidence to speak out of the gospel of truth (v. 15), growth in converts and maturity (v. 15), Christlikeness, and a healthy worshipping, loving, and mission community (v. 16).

MISSIONAL GROWTH

The following passages clearly attribute the growth of the church to God, through Christ, by his Spirit. The people should be unified under Christ rather than letting ministry or mission divide them. Paul uses fruit metaphors and military invasion imagery to describe how God advances the gospel.

---

43.   See Matt. 2:6; 9:36; Mark 6:34; John 10:11–12, 16; 1 Peter 2:25; 5:4. See also Heb. 13:20; Rev. 2:28; 7:17; 19:15.

1 Corinthians 3:5–7

In his challenge to Corinthian factionalism based on preferred missionaries (Paul, Apollos, Cephas), Paul speaks of the different roles he and Apollos performed in the Corinthian church. Paul's function as the apostle was to establish the church on God's behalf. The foundation was Christ (1 Cor. 3:11), established through the proclamation of the gospel of Christ crucified and raised from death (2:2; 15:1–2). Later, after Paul had left Corinth, the firebrand Apollos of Alexandria, after preaching in Ephesus, came to Corinth. He preached in the community and city and also made converts (1:12; 3:4–6, 22). At some point, Peter, too, had been to the city, and some of those who loved his ministry had become a part of the Corinthian community (1:12; 3:22).

In 1 Corinthians 3:5a–b, as he challenges their divisions, Paul asks, "What then is Apollos? What is Paul?" He then answers his own question: "servants [διάκονος] through whom you believed" (3:5c). By identifying them both as servants, Paul ensures that there is no status differentiation, challenging anyone favoring one over the other. Then, in 3:5d, he continues, "and to as to the Lord gave" (LEB). Paul is here saying that Christ (the Lord) is the source of their beings, their ministries, and their ministry success. As such, as he has launched his long challenge in 1:12e, they should follow and favor Christ, not Paul, Apollos, Peter, or any other Christian leader. This principle applies to all ministries, but in terms of mission, it calls believers away from elitism and favor concerning the various ministries of God's witnesses.

Then, in v. 6, Paul states that he planted the church founded on Christ (v. 10). The image used in v. 6a implies the establishment of the Corinthians as one crop field (v. 9) made up of multiple plants (believers). Apollos came along after Paul and watered the field, giving water to help the plants shoot up (converting more people of Corinth). However, the punchline is v. 6c, where he states emphatically, "but God caused it to grow [αὐξάνω]" (NET). Here we have the missional truth that God, through Christ, by his Spirit, grows his community of faith. Christian apostles establish the church, and other workers come along. However, in reality, while, of course, their ministries are essential, compared to God, they are nothing (v. 7a). What alone really matters is "God who gives the growth" (v. 7b).

Colossians 1:6–10

The same Greek word, αὐξάνω, is used in Colossians 1:6. Here, Paul reminds the Colossians how the gospel had reached them and that it is "bearing fruit and growing" (NET). Both participles of καρποφορέω and αὐξάνω are present passive, indicating the continual agency of God by his Spirit in the ongoing growth of the Christian community. The growth spreads throughout the world through the apostolic witness of the likes of Epaphras, who evangelized the readers (v. 7). Consequently, the Colossians are to walk in a manner worthy of Christ and pleasing to him, "bearing fruit in every good deed, growing in the knowledge of God" (v. 10 NET). Read in context, this growth will include maturation, works of service, and further mission. Later in the same letter, Paul tells his readers that Christ, the head of the church, nourishes and knits together the body of Christ while God gives it growth (Col. 2:19).

Romans 1:13 and Philippians 1:22

"Fruit" (καρπός) is often used in Paul ethically.[44] However, he also uses it to describe missional conversions. For example, in Romans 1:13, Paul wants to go to Rome to preach in the city. He desires to gain "fruit" among the Romans as he has in the nations he evangelized between Jerusalem and Illyricum (15:19a). He next wants to go to Spain for the same (15:24, 28). His desire to produce more converts may also be in view in Philippians 1:22, where ongoing life after trial will mean "fruitful work" for him.[45] The image of fruit implies the work of God producing this fruit in and through believers as they engage in mission.

Philippians 1:12

God also advances the gospel as an invading military force. In Philippians 1:12, Paul uses προκοπή to speak of the gospel's advance in Rome, where he is imprisoned. The use of the military image is ironic. Paul is in prison due to his arrest in Jerusalem for his missional engagement for Christ and his subsequent appeal to Caesar. Yet, despite Paul's chains, the gospel is now spreading in the center of the empire among Nero's elite guards. The might of Rome, which has overpowered the whole region around the Mediterranean Sea, cannot stop the gospel's spread. The work of God is implied here as Paul goes on to speak of others in the context emboldened to proclaim Christ in the Lord (1:14). Paul then states that he is confident he will stand firm for Christ in his forthcoming trial due to the prayers of the Philippians and help of the Spirit (1:19–26). All these factors indicate the work of God, in Christ and by the Spirit, empowering the gospel's spread into the heart of the Roman world.[46]

MISSIONAL GUIDANCE

Luke's account of Paul's mission confirms that Paul's mission was Spirit-led. The collection and delivery of funds for the famine-facing Jerusalem church were catalyzed by a prophetic word through the Spirit to Agabus (Acts 11:28; cf. Gal. 2:2). Their first Antiochian mission was instigated by the Spirit summoning the Antiochian Christians to set Paul and Barnabas aside for the western mission (Acts 13:2, 4). At points in his missions, Luke describes Paul being filled with the Spirit bringing judgment (Acts 13:9), being carefully guided in his mission, imparting the Holy Spirit on new converts through

---

44. Rom. 6:21, 22; 7:4, 5; Gal. 5:22; Eph. 5:9; Phil. 1:11. He also uses it of material gifts such as the Jerusalem collection (Rom. 15:28; 2 Cor. 9:10) and of agricultural fruit, which symbolizes material gifts to preachers (1 Cor. 9:7; 2 Tim. 2:6).
45. Keown, *Philippians*, 1:245–48. See also Ware, *The Mission of the Church*, 214–15.
46. Further on this passage see Keown, *Congregational*, 71–106.

laying on hands (Acts 19:2, 6), being warned of impending trouble (Acts 20:23; 21:11), setting aside leaders in his churches (Acts 20:28), and recognizing that the Spirit spoke to the prophets like Isaiah (Acts 28:25).

As discussed more fully in chapter 7, while Paul reserves the language of being "led by the Spirit" for ethical living (Rom. 8:14; Gal. 5:16, 18, 25) and is not as explicit as Luke in terms of the Spirit guiding mission, he does indicate that the Spirit leads the mission in different ways.[47] Paul sees his ministry as an expression of God's will[48] and submits his ministry plans to the will or permission of God or the Lord, including mission in Corinth and Macedonia (1 Cor. 16:5–9; 2 Cor. 1:15–2:14), Rome (Rom. 1:10), and Spain (Rom. 15:32). His desire to evangelize in such places was a Spirit-impelled sense of obligation and necessity (cf. Rom. 1:15; 1 Cor. 9:16; 2 Cor. 2:12). He recognizes that God opens "doors" or great opportunities for the effective proclamation of the gospel, despite opposition (1 Cor. 16:9; 2 Cor. 2:12; Col. 4:3).

Paul's ministry was impelled by the Spirit, who led him to evangelize the region from Illyricum to Jerusalem, preaching, doing good deeds and signs and wonders, and planting churches. In 1 Thessalonians 3:11, Paul prays that God and Jesus will "direct (κατευθύνω) our way" to the Thessalonians. The verb κατευθύνω has the sense of "make/keep straight" (e.g., 1 Kgdms 6:12; Ps. 5:9) and means "lead, direct." It is used in the LXX of the Spirit rushing upon people (Judg. 14:6, 19; 15:14) and across Jewish Greek literature of God leading the affairs of his people and world. Paul's prayer from Corinth asks that God direct him and his team to Thessalonica. He would do this by the Spirit.

He subjects his plan to travel from Ephesus to Corinth to the Lord's will (1 Cor. 4:19). He had many times desired to come to Rome as long as God willed it. He speaks of being hindered from doing so, suggesting God's intrusions into his plans to thwart it (Rom. 1:10–13). In Romans 15:22–23, Paul's passion for evangelizing new fields, given to him by God (cf. Rom. 1:14), seems to be why he perceived that God wanted his focus on the Anatolian, Macedonian, and Greek regions before coming to the already-evangelized Rome. Having completed that work, and wanting to go to Spain, now was the time to visit Rome after delivering the collection. There he would strengthen the church through preaching, making new converts, and moving onto fresh fields to the west (1:13, 15; 15:24–32).

Still, his passion for going to yet-unevangelized areas points to the Spirit urging Paul and other believers to go to such places with the gospel so that their inhabitants might yield in the obedience of believing the message (Rom. 15:18–20; cf. Rom. 1:5). His desire for support from the Romans includes others joining him for the many challenges of the Spanish mission (Rom. 15:24).

---

47. See also, in the case of Paul, Acts 13:4; 16:6–7.
48. 1 Cor. 1:1; 2 Cor. 1:1; Eph. 1:1; Col. 1:1; 2 Tim. 1:1.

THE SPIRIT AS THE POWER OF MISSION

Paul not only considers the Spirit as the guide to mission but the one who empowers it. His ministry is conducted by "the power of God" as he carries weapons of righteousness in either hand (2 Cor. 6:7). He tells the Romans he will speak only of what Christ has done through him as he ministered "by word and deed, by the power of signs and wonders, by the *power of the Spirit*" (Rom. 15:18–19, emphasis mine). Paul's clear and unelaborate proclamation of Christ and him crucified sees God's power generate the faith of the Corinthians (1 Cor. 2:4). The spiritual truths preached did not have their source in human wisdom but were imparted by the Spirit (2:13). The Spirit gave them life through the preaching of the gospel (2 Cor. 3:6).

Even if Satan blinds people from understanding, the light of the knowledge of the glory of God invades people's minds, shining into open hearts from the face of Christ by the Spirit, and people believe (3:18; 4:5–6). The Galatians witnessed God pour out the Spirit and do miracles among them at the hearing of faith (Gal. 3:2, 5; 4:6). The Word of God, then, is the sword of the Spirit with which God cuts the human heart, killing and raising the hearer with faith (Eph. 6:17). Christ is the power and wisdom of God (1 Cor. 1:24). When the gospel concerning him is preached, that message is the power of God for the salvation of all people who believe (Rom. 1:16; 1 Cor. 1:18; 2:5).

In Philippians 2:12–18, Paul draws out implications of Christ's glorious example in the preceding Christ-hymn. God has elevated Christ to Lord so that all humankind will yield allegiance to him (2:10). This missional purpose in the Christ-hymn implicitly summons believers to participate in the mission of extending the gospel to the world so that people can voluntarily yield to Christ.[49] They are to continue to obey by working out their own salvation by God's power in them, that is, by his Spirit (2:12–13). By this power, they are to stop grumbling and arguing and be united with the virtues of Christ. This power will then shine through them, so they are lights in sinful Philippi, Macedonia's dark world, and beyond (2:14–15). The light of the gospel will extend from them into the darkness. They are to hold forth the word of life so that people can hear it, believe it, and receive the Spirit.[50] Philippians 2:13 indicates that the power for this is the Spirit.

This Spiritual power is reflected in 1 Thessalonians 1:5, where the gospel came to them "in power and in the Holy Spirit and with full conviction." It led to their joyful turn from idols to God, and their evangelization of the region (1:7–10), despite persecution.[51] The word of God is "at work in you believers" (2:13). The means of building up the Corinthians is "speaking in

---

49.   Keown, *Philippians*, 1:429–31. See also Keown, "A Missional and Liturgical Reading of the Christ-Hymn."

50.   On "hold forth," see chapter 4, "The Fellowship of the Holy Spirit."

51.   See earlier chapter 8, "Suffering in Service."

Christ" (2 Cor. 12:19). The power of the word means that while preachers like Paul can be bound in prison, "the Word of God is not bound" (2 Tim. 2:9). The gospel is an unstoppable Spirit-empowered force. The Scriptures also, being "God-breathed," are useful for correction and teaching in righteousness, so that believers are complete and equipped for every good work (3:16–17). Second Timothy 1:6–14 speaks of the Spirit given to believers, a Spirit who does not generate fear but empowers them, especially with love and self-control. As a result, Timothy is not to be ashamed to give witness "by the power of God" and to share in suffering for the gospel. He is to emulate Paul in this regard, to know God can guard him to the end, to trust in the Spirit, and to fan into flame his spiritual gift. The passage implies that every aspect of the mission is empowered by God's Spirit, including overcoming fear and perseverance in suffering.

Mission is spiritual to the core for a pneumaformed believer. The Spirit empowers mission, sends people he has formed in the image of God's Son, speaks into people's hearts as the gospel is shared, makes converts, and sends them back into God's mission field.

THE SPIRIT, FALSE SPIRITS, AND FALSE GOSPELS

By his Spirit, God through his Son is the initiator, empowerer, guide, and content of mission. Yet, as with the wider NT, while God is sovereign, the Spirit does not have all his own way in mission. While the NT has a muted apocalyptic tone compared with other apocalyptic literature of the time, Paul's letters indicate that he believes in opposing forces, unleashed into creation through human sin, that seek to thwart the mission.

Satan

At the head of this host of spiritual forces is Satan,[52] otherwise known to Paul as the devil,[53] Belial (2 Cor. 6:15), "the evil one" (Eph. 6:16; 2 Thess. 3:3), "the god of this world" (2 Cor. 4:4), "the tempter" (1 Thess. 3:5), "the serpent" (2 Cor. 11:3), and "the prince of the power of the air" (Eph. 2:2).[54] Although a case can be made that this being is merely a mythological personification of evil,[55] Paul stands in the Jewish tradition that believes in the existence of a supreme spiritual being, the head of myriads of evil spirits, opposed to God,

---

52. Rom. 16:20; 1 Cor. 5:5; 7:5; 2 Cor. 2:11; 11:14; 12:7; 1 Thess. 2:19; 2 Thess. 2:9; 1 Tim. 1:20; 5:15.

53. Eph. 4:27; 6:11; 1 Tim. 3:6, 7; 2 Tim. 2:26.

54. Paul does not use "Beelzebul." It is used ten times in Matthew, Mark, and Luke.

55. Especially considering Paul never mentions exorcism in his letters. However, Luke records Paul casting out demons (Acts 16:16–18; 19:12), and exorcisms likely fall into this category of "healings" (1 Cor. 12:9, 28–29). I consider the absence of exorcism in Paul and conclude that while he likely did perform them (based on Acts 16:18 and 19:11), it is possible he did not. He saw the cross as victorious over demons, and so conversion was sufficient. Mark J. Keown, "Paul, the Demonic, and Mental Health" (paper presented at the Annual Meeting of the Society of Biblical Literature, Denver, 2022). See also Fee, *GEP*, 679–80, and the brief mention in chapter 5, "Idolatry."

CHAPTER 10

hellbent on destroying his work and his people—even if God is sovereign over him and uses him for his purposes.

This being tempts believers into sins, including those of a sexual variety (1 Cor. 7:5). Where people become prey to vices like anger, Satan is given space to disrupt believers and relationships (Eph. 4:25). He has the capacity to exploit unforgiveness within the body of believers to create division and vulnerability to false ideas and teaching (2 Cor. 2:11). The devil can also disguise himself as an angel of God and so deceive people through false teaching (11:14).

False Teachers

Ongoing mission also involves engaging with converse ideas, false ideologies, and demonically sourced distortions of the gospel. In 2 Corinthians 10:3, Paul defends himself against the false teachers afflicting Corinth who claim he walks in the flesh. In his defense, Paul concedes he does walk in the flesh, in that he remains a fleshly creature. However, he does not minister by the flesh.[56] Instead, he stresses his team's reliance on divine power and not the flesh as they engage in spiritual warfare. Divine power implies the work of the Spirit. By the power of the Spirit, Paul destroys strongholds (v. 4)—ideas buttressed by demonic powers that oppose the knowledge of God, his Son, and the gospel. Empowered by the Spirit, believers capture false ideologies and thoughts to bring them into obedience to Christ (v. 5). The Corinthians are also prepared to punish disobedience among Christians if need be (v. 6). Paul's preparedness to expose and challenge false ideas dominates what follows in 2 Corinthians 10:7–13:9 and many parts of his other letters (all of Galatians, Philippians 3, Colossians 2, and significant parts of the Pastorals).

Judaizers

In Galatians, Paul never directly states that those preaching a Judaizing gospel are emissaries of Satan (as he does in 2 Corinthians). However, there are indications in the letter that he is thinking this way. The Judaizers are calling the Galatians to "a different gospel" (Gal. 1:6), disturbing them, and distorting the gospel (1:7; 5:10–12). Mention of the possibility of an angel proclaiming a different gospel calls to mind Satan as a fallen angel (1:8; cf. 3:19). In Galatians 2:4, the Judaizers are "false brothers" who use fraudulent means like spying on Paul and his group. The use of βασκαίνω in Galatians 3:1 speaks of his Galatian converts being bewitched by the opponents. The

---

56. "Paul, as well as all others, are 'in the flesh,' in the sense that in this 'between the times' existence we still live in the weaknesses and limitations of 'our mortal flesh,' through which, nonetheless, the life of Christ is fully manifested (4:11). But what we do not do, Paul insists, is 'walk in keeping with the flesh,' flesh now thought of in terms of human fallenness over against God in its self-centered, basically anti-God frame of reference. Nor do we carry on our warfare by means of 'weapons' that reflect such a perspective. To the contrary, since we walk by the Spirit our 'weapons' are 'powerful with reference to God.'" Fee, *GEP*, 341.

verb carries the sense of exerting an evil influence on another through the evil eye.[57] Silva notes that the "word group as a whole . . . enters the broader semantic domain of 'evil influence, envy, damage through hostile looks, bewitchment, sorcery.'"[58] The use of the term suggests Paul sees malicious satanic deception at work in Galatia.[59]

Paul also warns the Galatians that to yield to the Judaizers is to become subject again to τὰ στοιχεῖα τοῦ κόσμου, "the elemental spirits of the world" to which they were enslaved prior to their conversions (4:3, 8 LEB).[60] These he describes as "things which by nature are not gods" (v. 8 LEB), "weak and miserable" (v. 9 LEB). As such, he has in mind not merely religious systems and their ideologies but the idolatrous and demonic forces behind them. This view is consistent with the use of the term in the Testament of Solomon of evil spirits (T. Sol. 8:2; 15:5; 18:1). Having received God's Spirit and become his children (v. 6), the Galatians must not return to the miserable, enslaved existence that other religious systems offer (4:8–9).

Φαρμακεία is also a work of the flesh Paul rejects in Galatians 5:20. It is used in the LXX of magicians of Egypt (Exod. 7:11, 22; 8:3, 14; Wis. 18:13), Canaan (Wis. 12.4), and preexilic Judah (Isa. 47:9, 12).[61] Placed after εἰδωλολατρία, "idolatry," it adds to the sense that Paul considered the problem in Galatia to be, at least in part, spiritual.

Malicious Spirits and False Teachers

Paul links false teaching to the work of evil forces. As Paul directly refutes the false teachers, he speaks of his fear that the false teachers are leading the Corinthians away from Christ as the serpent deceived Eve in the garden (2 Cor. 11:3; cf. Gen. 3:4). He suggests that the Corinthians are allowing themselves to be open not only to false gospels but to receiving a different spirit (ἢ πνεῦμα ἕτερον, 2 Cor. 11:4). This likely refers not merely to an attitude, nor a nonexistent spirit in contrast with the Holy Spirit, but the malicious spirit(s)

---

57. BDAG, s.v. "βασκαίνω," 171. See Jerome H. Neyrey, "Bewitched in Galatia: Paul in Social Science Perspective," *CBQ* 50 (1988): 72–100. See also Buchanan, "Spirit," 89.

58. Moisés Silva, "βασκαίνω," *NIDNTTE* 1:491–92. See Diodorus Siculus, 4.6.4. In Sirach 14:8, evil is that which employs the evil eye toward another and turns away and despises other people, while in Testament of Solomon 18:39, the demon Rhyx Phtheneoth casts an evil eye on all people. It is used in the LXX of begrudging someone something (Deut. 28:54, 56; Sir. 14:6). In Josephus, it refers to envying (*Ant.* 10.250, 257; *Life* 425; *Ag. Ap.* 1.72; 2.286), as well as in Philo (*Agr.* 112; *Flacc.* 143).

59. See further Keown, *Galatians*, 296.

60. Used in comparative Jewish literature of basic elements, including the elements from which humans are made (4 Macc. 12:13); the elements by which the world and universe were made (Wis. 7:17; 19:18; Sib. Or. Prol. 102; 2.206; 3.80; 8.337, 447; T. Adam 1:3; Josephus, *Ant.* 3.183; *J. W.* 1.377; Philo, *Opif.* 38, 52; *Det.* 8; *Mos.* 1.96); the elements of language, the letters of the alphabet (Sib. Or. 5:15; 11:142, 154, 190, 196; 12:16, 97, 165, 238, 271; 14:183; Apoc. Dan 3:12) or grammar (Philo, *Opif.* 126); a mark on a forehead (T. Sol. 17:4); or evil spirits (T. Sol. 8:2; 15:5; 18:1–2). Josephus uses them of ethereal spirits of deceased heroes who join the stars (*J. W.* 6.47).

61. It is also used of poisoning with potions (Josephus, *Ant.* 15.47; *J. W.* 1.227, 452, 638; Philo, *Spec.* 3.94, 98).

driving the false teachers.[62] This influence has come from false apostles and deceitful workers, who disguise themselves as apostles of Christ (11:13). Their work is consistent with "the serpent" deceiving Eve by his craftiness (11:3). Paul is unsurprised at their cunning and deceitfulness, as he knows "Satan disguises himself as an angel of light" (11:14). Paul implies in 2 Corinthians 11:15 that the false teachers are Satan's servants who disguise themselves as "servants of righteousness." As such, preachers of a false gospel serve Satan, oppose God, and by the Spirit must be identified and exposed, and the church defended against them. This aspect of preaching is essential to form pneuma-form believers and churches.

Spiritual Powers

Ephesians 6 indicates that believers are to be extremely strong and reso-lute because of the evil one's capacity to disrupt Christian lives, churches, and mission. Paul uses military metaphors, imagining believers as soldiers bedecked in God's complete armor to enable them to stand against the evil one's stratagems. In fact, for Paul, the real enemies faced by believers are not people, however malicious, powerful, and opposed to the Christian move-ment, but spiritual forces of wickedness. While some identify these spiritual powers with the interior of fallen human institutions,[63] for Paul, they are ontic beings that work in and through fallen people and institutions.[64] Paul envis-ages evil days when believers are especially challenged (v. 13), including by attacks from Satan akin to the flaming arrows used in first-century warfare to set things ablaze. With the power of fire to destroy ancient structures, this speaks of consuming the person's life.

The believer is to "always be strong [ἐνδυναμοῦσθε] in the Lord [ἐν κυρίῳ] in the strength [κράτος] of his might [ἰσχύς]" (v. 10). The placement of the ἐνδυναμοῦσθε first gives it prominence and emphasis. It is passive and present tense and so speaks of being always strengthened by an external agent. The external agent is "the Lord." Paired with "in the Lord," Paul notes that the Spirit of the Lord is in the believer, generating strength to combat

---

62. Fee rightly rejects seeing "another spirit" as an attitudinal thing or "the spirit of the world" here. The problem is not worldview or merely a bad attitude—it is accepting a false gospel. He appears to say that Paul is not speaking of an actual spirit, but anything other than the Holy Spirit. However, I believe he is too hasty to rule out a "demonic spirit" here because while there is one Spirit, Paul associates idolatry and false teaching with demonic spirits elsewhere (1 Cor. 10:20, 22; Gal. 3:1; 4:3, 9; Col. 2:8; 1 Tim. 4:1). Further, he associates this particular teaching with the work of Satan (11:13–15). As such, I believe Paul is saying that in accepting the false gospel, they receive the teaching of false spirits. Compare with Fee, *GEP*, 342–45.

63. Walter Wink, *Naming the Powers: The Language of Power in the New Testament* (Philadelphia: Fortress, 1984).

64. Clinton E. Arnold, *Power and Magic: The Concept of Power in Ephesians* (Eugene, OR: Wipf & Stock, 1997).

enemy spiritual forces. "In the strength of his might" reinforces that the Lord by the Spirit provides the energy and strength required.

The Christian, whether Jew or Gentile, slave or free, male or female, old or young, is pictured as a soldier who is to put on the whole armor of God so that they can stand against the stratagems (μεθοδεία) of the devil. The term is perhaps a Pauline neologism, and the only other use in comparative literature is in Ephesians 4:14 of deceitful schemes that shipwreck the faith of an immature believer. Its use here suggests that the devil attacks through false teaching and no doubt uses other strategies to deceive, disrupt, and divert believers.

Verse 12 emphasizes the spiritual nature of the Christians' conflict. The battle is not with humans and their institutional creations but with ontic spiritual beings who seek to influence, disrupt, deceive, and destroy human life and affairs. Paul uses a range of language to describe these beings: plur. ἀρχή, "rulers"; plur. ἐξουσία, "authorities"; and plur. κοσμοκράτωρ, "cosmic powers." "Of this darkness" modifies all three categories, indicating the absence of light and their pure evil. These are clearly spiritual beings, not human authorities, not even governments, as they are "spiritual forces of wickedness in the heavenlies." They afflict and affect humans and the collectives they construct, but they are not to be confused with them.

As Paul's language rules out human authorities, the spiritual use of the three terms in the LXX, Pseudepigrapha, and NT will now be briefly considered. The common term ἀρχή in the LXX can mean "beginning,"[65] "first,"[66] "authority,"[67] "realm,"[68] "head," or "ruler,"[69] and is used in the latter sense spiritually of God,[70] the future Messiah (Isa. 9:5–6), and angelic or demonic forces.[71] "Αρχαί, "rulers," in Romans 8:28, neatly balances ἄγγελοι, "angels," and so likely speaks of fallen angels. Such spiritual beings cannot separate a person from God's love. The use in 1 Corinthians 15:25 undoubtedly includes spiritual and human political forces. Earlier in Ephesians 1:21 and Colossians 1:16, Jesus is exalted over all such forces, spiritual or human.[72] In Ephesians 3:10, through the newly established and spreading Christian

---

65. The term always means "beginning" in Matthew (19:5, 8; 24:8, 21); Mark (1:1; 10:6; 13:8, 19); John (1:1, 2; 2:11; 6:24; 8:25, 44; 15:27; 16:4); and sometimes in Luke-Acts (Luke 1:2; Acts 11:15; 26:4). It can also mean "corner" (Acts 10:11; 11:5). Paul uses this sense in Philippians 4:15 and probably Colossians 1:18 (which could alternatively mean "the ruler"). See also Heb. 1:10; 2:3; 3:14; 7:3; 2 Peter 3:4; 1 John 1:1; 2:7, 13, 14, 24 [2x]; 3:8, 11; 2 John 5; 2 John 6; Rev. 21:6; 22:13.

66. See Hebrews 5:12 of the elementary or first principles (στοιχεῖα) and Hebrews 6:1.

67. Luke 20:20.

68. Jude 6.

69. Human rulers (Luke 12:11). Paul also has this sense in Titus 3:1.

70. See Deut. 33:27; 1 Chron. 29:12; Esth. 4:17; Ps. 109:3; Job 37:3; Isa. 42:10; Dan. 2:37; Sib. Or. 3:743; 8:264.

71. In Testament of Solomon 20:11–17, there are three categories of angelic forces (ἀρχαί, "principalities or rulers," ἐξουσίαι, "authorities," and δυνάμεις, "powers"). Possibly also Isaiah 10:10 LXX.

72. It may be used of Jesus "who is the Ruler" (ὅς ἐστιν ἀρχή) in Colossians 1:18; however, it may here mean "the beginning." Similarly, in Revelation 3:14: "the Ruler of God's creation" or "the originator of."

church, the wisdom of God has been made known in the gospel to all such forces in the heavenlies. He has disarmed these principalities in the triumph of his death and resurrection (Col. 2:15).

The second term, ἐξουσία, with the essential meaning "authority,"[73] is used for God's authority,[74] the authority given to the one like a son of man (Dan. 7:14, 27) and his people (Dan. 7:27), Christ,[75] and angelic forces (T. Sol. 20:15).[76] It is also used of political rulers.[77] Elsewhere in the NT, Satan is "the ruler of the authority of the air" (Eph. 2:2 LEB), and unredeemed humankind is subject to his rule and "the domain of darkness" (Col. 1:13). Here in Ephesians 6, it is another descriptor of demonic forces (Luke 22:53; Col. 1:13), as in Ephesians 3:10. Colossians 1:16 likely includes both political and spiritual forces.[78]

The less common κοσμοκράτωρ, "world ruler," refers to evil spirits described as στοιχεῖα, "elemental spiritual forces" in the Testament of Solomon 8:2.[79] The final descriptor is πνευματικὰ τῆς πονηρίας, "spiritual force of evil." The adjective πνευματικός means "spiritual" and is used diversely, but only here in the Greek biblical texts of spiritual powers.[80] These are clearly evil, as the genitive of πονηρία indicates.[81] The locative ἐν τοῖς ἐπουρανίοις, "in the heavenlies," indicates these are spiritual forces that exercise their dominion against God's creation and his people, seeking to corrupt and destroy everything.

---

73. See Matt. 7:29; 8:9; 9:6, 8; 21:23, 24, 27; 28:18; Mark 1:22, 27; 2:10; 3:15; 6:7; 11:28, 29, 33; 13:34; Luke 4:32; 5:24; 7:8; 12:5; 19:17; 20:2, 8, 20; 23:7; John 1:12; 5:27; 10:18; 17:2; 19:10, 11; Acts 1:7; 5:4; 8:19; 9:14; 26:10, 12, 18; 1 Cor. 8:9; 9:4, 5, 6, 12, 18; 11:10; 2 Cor. 10:8; 13:1; 1 Thess. 3:9; Heb. 13:10; Rev. 11:6; 20:6; 22:14. Used substantively, it can speak of human political authorities (Luke 12:11). Its use of Christ's and believers' authority over demonic forces suggests they have some authority; however, Christ's authority over them is absolute (Matt. 10:1; Mark 1:27; 3:15; 6:7; Luke 4:36; 9:1; 10:19). Satan also has a level of global authority (Luke 4:6).

74. Esther 4:17b; Jdt. 8:15; 2 Macc. 3:24; Dan. 4:17, 31; 1 En. 9:5; Rom. 9:21; Rev. 16:9.

75. In the NT, it is used of Christ's authority over all rule, whether spiritual or political (1 Cor. 15:24; Eph. 1:21; Col. 1:16; 2:10, 15; 1 Peter 3:22; Jude 25; Rev. 12:10). Also of the authority over the nations given to the faithful believers (Rev. 2:26).

76. Including Semyaz, an evil angel (1 En. 9:7); angels including those who are upon the authorities (3 Bar. 12:3: ἄγγελοι <οἱ> ἐπὶ τῶν ἐξουσιῶν; also T. Ab. (A) 9:8; 13:11); and authorities in heaven with God (T. Lev. 3:8). See also Testament of Job. 16:2 of Satan's authority to act. See further on στοιχεῖα below.

77. In Paul, of governing authorities (Rom. 13:1, 2, 3; Titus 3:1). Also of worldly kings given authority (Rev. 17:12).

78. See Eph. 3:10.

79. In Testament of Solomon 8:1–12 these include deception, strife, fate, distress, error, and power. They change positions and dwell in different locales (e.g., Lydia, Olympus). Each one then describes their activity.

80. See earlier, chapter 3, "The Fellowship of the Holy Spirit."

81. The πονηρία nexus of terms indicate bad, corrupt, evil, wicked, and the like. Paul uses it in his vivid description of evil human sinfulness (Rom. 1:29), as does Mark (Mark 7:22). Matthew's Christ describes the Pharisees in this way (Matt. 22:18; Luke 11:39). Also Acts 2:36; 1 Cor. 5:8.

The readers are to take up the full armor of God and be clothed with truth, righteousness, faith, salvation, and the Word of God, always prepared to stand firm in the gospel of peace or move to share it with those who are not yet believers,[82] so that they can quench the flaming arrows of Satan (6:13–17). Living in such a way is to be bolstered by constant prayer and supplication "in [and by] the Spirit" (6:18).[83] For Paul, believers not only are in Christ by the Spirit but have joined God—Father, Son, and Spirit—in an ongoing conflict with spiritual forces of darkness that seek to destroy God's world and work. Paul's understanding of Satan indicates that God uses him in various ways, such as the destruction of the flesh in the case of an immoral Corinthian (1 Cor. 5:5), being taught not to blaspheme (1 Tim. 1:20), and imparting a thorn in Paul's flesh to keep him humble and dependent (2 Cor. 12:7). Still, Satan blinds the spiritual eyes of unbelievers so that they cannot see the light of the gospel (2 Cor. 4:4), attacks believers with deadly intent (Eph. 6:16), thwarts mission plans (1 Thess. 2:18), and before Christ's coming, through the son of destruction, will deceive people with false signs and wonders (2 Thess. 2:9), condemn people and ensnare them in disgrace (1 Tim. 3:6–7; 2 Tim. 2:26), and lead people astray (1 Tim. 5:15). The outcome is inevitable—all God's enemies will ultimately be subjected to Christ.[84] Still, Satan remains active, so, as discussed above, believers must defend themselves with God's armor (Eph. 6:11). They must be prayerful against the evil one (2 Thess. 3:3; above).

Unclean Spirit

Similarly, Paul warns the Thessalonians not to be shaken or alarmed by a spirit (πνεύματος) through which they hear of the imminent or recent return of Christ (2 Thess. 2:2). This speaks of a false prophetic message from an unclean spirit.[85] The spiritual gift of διακρίσεις πνευμάτων, "discernment of spirits," most likely includes a capacity to discern false gospels or ideas that skew the gospel and deceive (1 Cor. 12:10).

MISSION MOTIVATION

The love of Christ leads Paul and others to share their belief. Others are more malicious and self-serving in their missions, but Paul recognizes that the Spirit is still using them to share the news of God's love.

---

82. Keown, *Congregational*, 186–96.
83. On "in the Spirit" or "by the Spirit," see "Baptized in the Spirit," chapter 2.
84. Rom. 16:20; 1 Cor. 15:25, 27; Phil. 3:21; Eph. 1:22.
85. Fee, *GEP*, 71–75, believes "Spirit" here refers to a prophecy supposedly from Paul. If so, the prophecy does not exist, as Paul would not prophesy this. However, even if this is so, the false representation of Paul is spiritual and reflects a demonic distortion of his teaching. Hence, "spirit" here points to a false prophecy from a demonic source (whether attributed to Paul or not, not a true one). As such, this is a spiritual corruption, and hence, one can see why Paul used πνεύματος—the source is demonic.

2 Corinthians 5:11–14

The Spirit impels mission, as clearly seen in 2 Corinthians 5:11–14.[86] Paul explains to the Corinthians the hope of resurrection (5:1–5) and the need to be acceptable to God the judge as they await that hope (5:6–10). Then, in v. 11, he begins with a causal participle, εἰδότες, "because we know the reverential awe of the Lord." The knowledge here derives from their relationship with God. Due to this reverential awe, he and his team (we) attempt to persuade people, such as the Corinthians, to believe in Jesus Christ and remain faithful to him. Doing this, the Pauline team is revealed to God, indicating their intimate relationship with him by the Spirit who allows God to search their hearts and know their motives. Linked to the Corinthians by the same Spirit, Paul hopes that he and his heart for them will be revealed in their inner beings.

In v. 12, not for the first time, unlike the false teachers, Paul asserts that he is not seeking to commend himself to the Corinthians. There should be no need for letters of commendation, for the Corinthians themselves are his commendation (3:1–3). Rather (ἀλλά), he is giving them a reason to boast about the Pauline group before the opponents so that their doing so will answer the false teachers, who are concerned with outward appearance and matters and not the heart. This concern refers to their critique of Paul's unimpressive presence (cf. 10:10). Verse 13 likely indicates another of their charges, that Paul is out of his mind.[87] Paul responds—if so, it is for God, and if not, it is for the good of the Corinthians.

Verse 14 explains how the Spirit impels mission. The common verb συνέχω here has the sense of providing the impulse for an activity, "impel."[88] The much-discussed ἡ . . . ἀγάπη τοῦ Χριστοῦ is most likely a plenary genitive with the inseparable love Christ has for believers generating the response of love within them.[89] This love is from God, poured into their hearts at conversion, and compels them not only to love Christ but also to love others. One aspect of doing this is sharing the gospel and, in this case, calling the Corinthians back to God. This love controls them and leads them to conclude that Christ died for all people and that all who believe died. In v. 15, his death

---

86. Fee does not reflect on much of what I state here. He comments on 5:13, but in my view, the link of love and mission brings in the Spirit.

87. While a case can be made for referring to some kind of Spirit-ecstasy or experience (see Fee, *GEP*, 328–30), I am persuaded that there is nothing to suggest that Paul and his team being out of their minds (ἐξίστημι) is to be understood in terms of the Spirit (except in the broadest sense that he is serving God in the Spirit and is considered out of his mind for his approach and perspectives). Instead, this likely refers to criticisms of Paul from the false teachers blighting the church. Paul and his team's "out of mindedness" may have some link to the Spirit, but it is not directly related. Whatever is in view, Fee rightly asserts, "We need only note that nothing is added to our understanding of Paul and the Spirit that is not explicitly said elsewhere." Fee, *GEP*, 330.

88. With BDAG, s.v. "συνέχω," 971.

89. Wallace, *Greek Grammar*, 120.

is so that those who live (in him by the Spirit) should now live for the crucified and resurrected Christ, compelled to do so by his love.

Philippians 1:16

Philippians 1:16 also speaks of love as an appropriate motive for missional
engagement. In the passage, Paul is joyful that his presence in Rome has caused
the gospel to spread among the soldiers and others through his own witness.
Further, believers of Rome have become very emboldened to preach the word
fearlessly (1:12–14). However, vv. 15–18 indicate that not all are motivated
appropriately. Some are certainly sharing the gospel but are motivated by
envy, strife, selfish ambition, insincerity, and supposing they can cause Paul
worse suffering from the authorities. While they are motivated by malice and
personal gain, Paul is still delighted that they preach the gospel of Christ.

Conversely, others are well motivated. They are inspired because of goodwill (δι ᾽ εὐδοκίαν), from love (ἐξ ἀγάπης), and through knowing that Paul is
appointed by God for the defense of the gospel. Clearly, "love" in v. 16 belongs
to the well-motivated gospel witnesses. However, Paul does not clarify whether
God is the source of this love here, nor does he clearly define the object of this
love and goodwill. Undeniably, the source of their goodwill and love is God and
Christ through the Spirit. The object of their love and goodwill can be other
Christians, unbelievers, Paul, or God. Deciding between these options is probably unneeded, for if Paul wanted to state the object, he would have.[90]

God as the source of this love is confirmed in Paul's earlier prayer for
abundant, discerning love in 1:9–11. There, the subject is the Philippians,
but no object is stated. In the context of the letter, their love for each other is
in the foreground of this prayer; however, the absence of an object indicates
here that such love should shape every aspect of their lives—their worship
and service, their church relationships, their friendship with Paul and his
team, and their engagement with the world. Paul's prayer for love also indicates that while the goodwill and love of the well-motivated gospel sharers
are in view here, God is the source of this love. This goodwill and love are
derived from God by the Spirit, who pours forth love and other fruits of
righteousness from them.

God being the source is further confirmed in 2:1, where in his fourfold
protasis that resolves in the apodosis "complete my joy," Paul reminds the
Philippians of their "encouragement in Christ" (παράκλησις ἐν Χριστῷ),
"their comfort from *love*" (εἴ τι παραμύθιον ἀγάπης), "their fellowship
in the Spirit," and their "mercies and compassions" (εἴ τις σπλάγχνα καὶ
οἰκτιρμοί). These are all experienced through relationship with God, in
Christ, by the Spirit. The Philippians will complete Paul's joy by having the
same mindset (τὸ αὐτὸ φρονῆτε), having the *same love* (τὴν αὐτὴν ἀγάπην
ἔχοντες), being one-souled (σύμψυχοι), and being one in mindset (τὸ

---

90. For further discussion, see Keown, *Philippians*, 1:157.

ἐν φρονοῦντες). Their love flows from God and is to shape their worship, community relationships, and mission.[91]

Hence, in 1:15–18, these are commendable Christians who have goodwill and love for God, Christ, Paul, other Christians, and unbelievers. Paul does not critique the falsely motivated here because his eye is not on his situation and *their* behavior but that of the Philippians. The letter's content indicates that while he rejoices in their gospel proclamation, he is unimpressed with their motivations. Indeed, his letter is a passionate appeal that the Philippians embrace the ethics of the well-motivated in his setting. Such virtues will end the dispute between Euodia and Syntyche (4:2–3) and ensure that the Philippians shine like lights in the world (2:15) and that their moderateness is evident to the people of the perverse and corrupted Philippi, Macedonia, Roman world, and beyond (4:5). In the letter, as well, Paul embodies this love toward the Philippians. Separated from his converts by around 1,300 kilometers (807 mi),[92] Paul yearns for them "with the affection of Christ Jesus" (1:8), and they are his beloved (2:12; 4:1).

PRAYER AND THE SPIRIT IN MISSION

Paul often asks his churches to pray for his mission, which is linked to the Spirit. In 1 Thessalonians 5:25, Paul simply asks them to "pray for us" without detail. However, we can assume "pray for our mission" is implied. In other letters, he adds details that are a valuable source of information about the Spirit's work in response to prayers for mission.

Romans 1:8–15

The Spirit's role in shaping missional engagement in response to prayer is seen in passages like Romans 1:8–15. As he most often does after briefly praying for grace and peace, Paul begins his letters with thanksgiving and prayer. He thanks God for the Romans whose faith is being proclaimed in the world, indicating evangelistic engagement by the Romans and others (1:8). He calls the God he serves in gospel mission as a witness to testify that he has yearned for years to come to Rome (1:9–10). He states his desire to come and impart spiritual gifts and experience encouragement with the Romans (1:11–12). Paul restates his desire to come to Rome, explaining that he has been thus far hindered (1:13a). However, he has not given up, wanting to come and win new converts and strengthen Christians in Rome as he has in the empire to the east (1:13b). This is due to his obligation to all people (1:14–15).

Romans 9:2–3 and 10:1

Paul prays missional prayers for the Jewish people twice in Romans 9 and 10. He begins his explanation of the place of Israel in God's redemptive

---

91.   See further on this passage Keown, *Philippians*, 1:321–51.
92.   Assuming a Roman provenance. If Ephesus, this is still a substantial distance (550 km or 334 mi by sea and foot). If Caesarea, 2,000 km or 1,240 mi. by sea and foot.

purposes. He speaks of his inner being testifying in the Holy Spirit of his profound grief at the Jewish rejection of the gospel (9:2).

In 9:3, using εὔχομαι, "to pray," he asks that, if possible, he would be accursed and cut off from Christ for the sake of his fellow Jews. This verse has a couple of subtle plays on ideas. In Galatians 3:10–14, all humankind is under the curse of the law and imprisoned in sin with the consequence of death. However, Christ has become accursed on the cross to take the curse of the law and sin and save people through faith. In praying he would be accursed himself, Paul knows it is implausible and unnecessary for him to do so, as Christ has been accursed to save both Jew and Gentile.[93] Yet, his prayer reveals his grief and desire for the salvation of his people.

Paul states this prayerful desire more explicitly in 10:1, telling the Roman brothers and sisters that the desire of his heart and his prayer (ἡ δέησις) to God is for them to be saved. He clarifies in the passage how this salvation is achieved—through believing in Christ. So, we can surmise that pneumaformed believers should grieve and pray for their people (and all others, including Israel) who reject the gospel.[94]

Romans 15:27

This verse is set in the context of Paul's account to the Romans of the collection being taken from the Gentile churches for the Judean Christians.[95] As Paul wrote, he was in Corinth preparing to depart for Jerusalem with the collection. Paul mentions the pleasure the Gentile churches in Macedonia and Achaia had when they gave to the collection (v. 15:27a). In v. 27b, he explains why this is the case: "For if the Gentiles shared in their spiritual things [πνευματικοῖς], they are also obligated to serve them in fleshly things [σαρκικοῖς]" (my translation). Here, "spiritual things" relate to the matters of the gospel of Jesus that the Gentiles heard from Jewish preachers, that they believed, and so received salvation and its associated spiritual benefits.[96] These benefits include the receiving the Spirit. The fleshly things relate to the "material goods" Paul carries to Jerusalem.[97] Paul establishes a principle that when people receive the gospel and its benefits from another, they are obligated to reciprocate with material aid when required. This response is itself something the Spirit will engender in them.

Romans 15:30–33

Then, in Romans 15:30–33, Paul urges the Romans (παρακαλῶ) through "our Lord Jesus Christ and through the love of the Spirit" (LEB) to struggle

93. See Keown, *Romans and the Mission*, 316.
94. In 1 Timothy, Paul tells Timothy that believers should offer prayer for all people (1 Tim. 2:1), all of whom God wants to save, and for whom he sent the mediator Jesus (1 Tim. 2:5–7).
95. This verse is also briefly discussed in chapter 4 concerning "The Fellowship of the Spirit."
96. There is also no question that the nature of the prior πνευματικός sharing had to do with the sending out of the message of the gospel. Fee, *GEP*, 631.
97. Fee writes, "There can be no question that σαρκικός here refers to 'material goods.'" Fee, *GEP*, 631.

(συναγωνίσασθαί) with him in their prayers for him to God. The love poured into believers by the Spirit becomes a conduit through which they pray. The threefold content of the prayer, signaled by ἵνα, includes his deliverance from the disobedient people of Judea, that his ministry of bringing the collection to Jerusalem would be seen as acceptable to the saints, and that he would come to Rome joyfully, by God's will, and be restored with them (vv. 31–32, above on 1:8–15).

I have discussed the Spirit's role in God's missional will. While Paul sometimes emphasizes God's sovereignty, foreknowledge, and predetermining of history, he believes that Spirit-led and empowered prayer can bring to pass God's will, including the fulfillment of missional hopes and plans of pneuma-formed believers.

2 Corinthians 2:11

Here, in the context of Paul's intense description of his team's life-threatening experience in Asia Minor and expressing his hope of future deliverance, Paul assumes the Corinthians will join together in helping them in prayer. 2 Corinthians 2:11 presupposes that God is the agent of deliverance from precarious mission situations and that prayer affects such situations, enhancing the possibility of deliverance.

Ephesians 6:18–20

After appealing to the Ephesians to be strong soldiers of Christ, dressed in the armor of God, Paul appeals to the readers to be always prayerful in and by the Spirit (v. 18, see chapter 6). They are to pray for all God's holy people throughout the world (v. 18). In v. 19, they are also to pray for Paul, specifically his evangelistic ministry in the context of his Roman incarceration. The content is signaled by ἵνα, "that" clauses (6:19b, 20b). The first ἵνα clause urges them to pray that God will give him a message and boldness to speak it when he opens his mouth in his defense and whenever else he is given the opportunity to speak.

In v. 20, Paul describes himself as "an ambassador in chains," likening his ministry to a diplomatic post in which he represents his king, Jesus, and speaks on behalf of God's kingdom. With that in mind, he asks that they pray that he speak boldly and publicly (παρρησιάζομαι), which he must do, even while incarcerated by Rome. Paul believes that prayer enhances the power of the Spirit, giving those who evangelize increased boldness to preach the word.

This suggests believers sitting in the presence of God, connecting to him spiritually, articulating prayers, and hearing God's Spirit whispered into them and through his word (the sword). They are to persevere in praying this way for all the saints, that is, the believers in their context and worldwide. They are to pray for those like Paul who are called to be apostles or evangelists, God's ambassadors, praying that God would give them the words to freely speak as they share the mystery of the gospel, even in situations of persecution like the Roman incarceration Paul is in at the time of writing (6:18–20).

Colossians 4:2–6

At the same time that Paul sends the letter to the Ephesians, he also sends Colossians to the Christians in nearby Colossae.[98] In Colossians 4:2–6, Paul urges them to be devoted to prayer, always alert and expressing gratitude to God (v. 3). In v. 3, he implores them to pray for his team (us). With the first ἵνα clause, Paul specifies that the Colossians should pray that God will open a door for the message. This prayer refers to the Spirit's work among unbelievers, opening their hearts and minds to hear the gospel. It speaks of the Spirit enabling Paul and his group to recognize opportunities, take them, and preach the mystery of Christ (for which they are imprisoned).

The second ἵνα clause asks that they pray he will then make the message crystal clear (ἵνα φανερώσω αὐτὸ) to hearers. In some way, prayer clears the way for the Spirit to open avenues for the proclamation of the gospel. It enables God's people to recognize the opportunity and communicate the gospel unambiguously. As such, although the Spirit brings spiritual understanding, people can clear a straight path for this by clear, contextually appropriate, understandable preaching. Paul then speaks of the Colossians' missional engagement, urging them to live with wisdom among outsiders and speak the gospel to them graciously and flavorsomely. In so doing, the believers will know how to respond to inquiries (Col. 4:5–6).[99] No doubt, he wants them to pray for this, and in Rome, he will not only pray the same for them but act and speak in such ways.

Philippians 1:19

Philippians 1:12–13, written a year or so after Ephesians, indicates that Paul's prayer has come to pass, as Paul comforts his readers with news that the gospel is advancing in Rome even while he is being imprisoned for Christ. It is spreading throughout the whole Praetorian Guard and the others associated with his situation. Furthermore, the locals are being filled with courage to preach the gospel, even if some do so with poor motives.

After expressing his joy that the gospel is being preached in Rome, in Philippians 1:19, Paul expresses his joy that the prayers of the Philippians and the help of the Spirit will ensure he is saved (σωτηρία). "Saved" is a double entendre. As the passage unfolds, Paul clarifies that he knows he will be released. However, the noun points to a positive outcome even if he were to die—he would be saved

---

98. Based on the prominent mentions of Tychicus toward the end of both letters (Eph. 6:21–22; Col. 4:7–8), he may also have delivered Philemon on the same trip (although he is not mentioned).

99. On Colossians 4:5–6, see Mark J. Keown, "Engaging with Outsiders: Insights into Sharing the Gospel from Colossians 4:5–6," *Stimulus*, no. 2 (2022).

with Christ forever. The combination of "your prayers" and "the help of the Spirit of Jesus Christ" ensuring a positive outcome again brings together prayer and the power of the Spirit in God's mission through the likes of Paul.

2 Thessalonians 3:1–2

The other missional prayer request is in 2 Thessalonians 3, again showing that missional prayer is critical to pneumaformed Christian mission. From Corinth, Paul asks the Thessalonians to pray for his team. Two ἵνα clauses express the content of the prayer. First, he wants the word of the Lord to run and be glorified elsewhere as it is among the Thessalonians. The athletic metaphor recalls Psalm 147:15, where God sends his command to the earth, and his word runs swiftly. This image is evocative as ancient people often bore messages on foot. As such, it is a prayer that the gospel will move quickly through the world through Paul, his team, and others he inspires. The desire for the word to be glorified goes beyond its spread to it being received with faith and worship of God and his Son.

Second, Paul asks that he and his group be delivered from wicked and evil people. At this stage of his mission, Paul is in Corinth. Luke's record of his trip recalls Paul being urged by Christ in a vision to be fearless and to keep on speaking, for God is with him, and that he will not be harmed as God has many in the city who are his (Acts 18:11). Paul is then attacked by Jewish unbelievers who brought him before Gallio, the proconsul of Achaia. However, Gallio expressed disinterest in the case, seeing it as an internal Jewish issue. After this, one of Paul's converts, Sosthenes, is beaten up before Gallio (Acts 18:12–17). It may have been during such a time that Paul asks for prayer support. Connecting the dots, the prayers have been answered as he stayed for eighteen months before traveling to Ephesus.

These passages indicate that Paul considers prayer vital to pneumaformed missional engagement. For him, something happens when Christians pray for mission and those engaged in it. Through the Spirit and prayer, emboldened gospel proclaimers receive increased opportunities to share the good news and to share it clearly. The result is more converts and Spirit-produced fruit. Such evangelists are strengthened and encouraged in the face of trials, protected and delivered by God—either from their persecutions in their current state or via eternal salvation.

THE SPIRIT AND MISSIONAL UNITY

Paul speaks to the division in early churches and calls them to the undivided mind of Christ, unified spiritual gifts, the fellowship of the Spirit, and the one faith.

1 Corinthians

One of the primary concerns of 1 Corinthians is unity. The church, formed of people called into the fellowship of God's Son, Jesus Christ the Lord, lacks a unified mind and purpose and has become divided based on their preferences for one or another missional preacher (1:9–11). Paul challenges their divided-ness, and the Spirit plays a vital role in his appeal.

Paul reminds them of their conversion; when he preached the gospel of an undivided, crucified Christ, the power of God by his Spirit, released through the message, drew them into faith (2:1–5). The Spirit, at that time, revealed the deep things of God to them through Paul's Spirit-taught message so that together, as one people in Christ and the Spirit, they have the undivided mind of Christ (2:10–16). Now they are divided over their preferences for different preachers who are merely servants through whom God has built the temple of the Spirit in Corinth (3:1–16). Those who destroy this unity are in danger of themselves being destroyed (3:17). The Corinthians must stop boasting and destroying the oneness of God's Spirit-filled people, for they belong to Christ and God (3:18–23). They are to stop judging preachers, elevating one over another, and in oneness, recognize their service and support them (4:1–13). As their father in the faith, Paul is sending his faithful son Timothy to remind them of such things, and when he comes himself, they will see the power of God in Christ by his Spirit (4:14–21).

In chapters 5 and 6, the primary concerns are sexual immorality and Christians bringing litigation against one another in the Corinthian courts. Having been washed, sanctified, and justified in the name of the Lord Jesus and by the Spirit of God, the Corinthians are to turn away from such sins of the flesh that characterize the unrighteous. They are also to expel the rampantly sinful Christians in the hope of their salvation. Doing so shows that Paul's vision of inclusion does not include those who claim Christ's name but are unrepentantly and grossly sinful. Such sins violate the unity of believers and Christ, who are bound together in the temple of the Spirit (5:1–6:20).

Speaking as one who has the Spirit of God (7:40),[100] 1 Corinthians 8:1–11:1 concerns freedom in matters of idolatry. Although the Spirit is not mentioned explicitly, Paul urges the Corinthians (by the Spirit, implied, cf. 1 Cor. 13) to exercise love over liberty while renouncing idolatrous practices. They are to be motivated by a desire to do what is best to ensure the salvation of others and, in doing so, emulate Christ and Paul. If they do these things, their unity will be restored while they grapple with living in a pagan world.

Paul addresses the shame of their disunity being reflected in the prac-tice of the Lord's Supper, the very meal that symbolizes their oneness in the broken and resurrected body of Christ. They must eat and drink together, in

---

100. Fee writes, "This designates the Spirit as not simply from God, but as the way God himself is present in the apostle's ministry . . . he is one who lives in and by the Spirit and whom God regards as trustworthy (v. 25), the Spirit serves as the ultimate ground even for Paul's opinions on matters where there is no revelation. Thus 'having the Spirit,' even for an apostle, does not guarantee every word to be a word of revelation, nor does it allow even Paul to use the Spirit on such matters as a whip for his authority. The Spirit in this case is not the guarantor of Paul's words, but of Paul's life, which makes these words more than simply one man's personal opinion." Fee, *GEP*, 140.

unity, remembering Jesus's death and proclaiming it until he comes. The visual enactment of breaking the bread and drinking the wine in unity proclaims Christ and his oneness to the world.

As discussed fully in chapter 9, 1 Corinthians 12–14 concerns spiritual gifts that are being misunderstood in Corinth. Paul speaks of a range of spiritual gifts handed out to God's people by the Spirit that cause the church to grow. The same God—Father, Son, and Spirit—gives these gifts, which are to be exercised in unity as in the parts of the human body (12:1–30). Above all, they are to be exercised through and in the primary fruit of the Spirit, love (12:31–13:13). In chapter 14, Paul addresses the matter of speaking in other tongues, urging the Corinthians to prefer prophecy and tongues with interpretation (effectively making the tongues message prophetic). One reason he asks this is because of the presence of unbelievers in the church, whom he hopes will be convicted and worship God because of the messages given (1 Cor. 14:24–25). Their use in order and unity is vital, as in all Paul's churches.

First Corinthians 15 focuses on misunderstandings concerning the resurrection. Paul urges them to be united in their belief in not merely a spiritual resurrection but the complete reanimation and Spirit-transformation of the body into a "spiritual body" (15:44). The resurrection of Christ and the future resurrection of believers is an essential component of the gospel preached to them by Paul that they must continue to uphold (15:1–11).

As the glorious day is coming when, in the twinkling of an eye, God will make the perishable imperishable and the mortal immortal, the Corinthians must give themselves entirely to God's work in worship, in building up believers, and in taking the gospel to a world lost in sin and death. They do this knowing that their labor in Christ will not be in vain (15:50–58). The Corinthians are to be unified as a people and continue to give witness to the world, worshipping as one, loving one another, and offering the gospel to the world.

Philippians 1:27

Turning from prayer and then reporting on his circumstances in Rome (always with an eye on Philippi), Paul launches his direct appeal in the letter in Philippians 1:27. He urges the Philippians to "live in a manner worthy of the gospel of Christ." Then, whether he comes to them or hears through a third party, he will know that they are standing firm ἐν ἑνὶ πνεύματι. This phrase speaks of the role of the Spirit in binding believers together, what Paul calls "the fellowship of the Spirit" (2:1 LEB). They have experienced this fellowship from conversion; they are bound to God in Christ by the Spirit and joined together as one people across social status, gender, and race. Pneumaformed as one, they are to contend as "one soul" for the faith of the gospel. Even when opponents rise and attack them, they are not to be intimidated but stand together as one "army," tightly held together as a Greek phalanx or a Roman cohort, maniple, or legion. They must move together, defending the gospel when challenged and advancing it as Paul is doing in Rome (1:12).

Together, they are to shine as lights in the world as they hold forth the word of life (2:15–16a).[101] Based on this fellowship, the primary occasion for writing is to urge the coworking evangelists Euodia and Syntyche to lay aside their differences and adopt the same mindset in the Lord. In finding one-mindedness, same-mindedness in the Lord and being one-souled with the same love, Paul's joy will be complete (2:2).

Ephesians 4:1–16

Paul begins Ephesians 4 with an emphasis on the oneness of the Christian faith. As they live up to their noble calling, the Ephesians are to embody the full range of God's virtues—all humility, gentleness, patience, and love. As they express this ethic, they are to be eager to "maintain the unity of the Spirit in the bond of peace" as one body of Christ, bound together with one Spirit, called with one hope, worshipping one Lord, with one faith, participating in one baptism, and glorifying the one God and Father of all who penetrates all creation and time (Eph. 4:1–6). Into this one body of people, God, via Christ and by the Spirit, has poured gifts to each person (4:7–10). These spiritual gifts include the missional gifts of apostles, evangelists, and other church charisms. These charismatically endowed leaders are to equip God's people for the work of ministry, to build up the body, until all believers reach unity of faith and knowledge of the Christ, attaining full maturity. Such a body in which love is "truthed" becomes equipped to fend off false teachers, is joined together as one, with each part working in harmony, and continues to build itself up in love (4:11–16). The church grows inwardly and outwardly as people grow to maturity and more people become believers.

THE SPIRIT, SUFFERING, AND MISSION

Much of the material considered in the chapter on the Spirit and suffering (chapter 8) is set in the context of mission. Still, there is more to be said on suffering as it relates directly to mission.

Not only do believers experience the typical struggles of life, but as believers are sent into the world to communicate the gospel, they encounter opposition and persecution, and they suffer. They experience suffering in seeking to be the unified people of God serving the gospel. Yet, Paul also testifies to a God of comfort who comforts them (2 Cor. 1:4; 7:6), who strengthens them to endure suffering. He flips weakness on its head as through Christ, by the Spirit, anguishes become a means by which God's power is displayed through broken men and women (2 Cor. 12:9).

At times, God acts to deliver his workers (2 Cor. 1:10; 2 Tim. 3:11). Yet, at other times, they endure immense pain and even death on his behalf.[102] This can come through Gentiles (Phil. 1:12–18), Jews (1 Thess. 2:13–17), other

---

101. On "hold forth," see chapter 4, "The Fellowship of the Holy Spirit."
102. 2 Cor. 4:7–12; 6:4–10; 11:23–32; 12:10; Phil. 2:27; 2 Tim. 4:6–8.

malicious believers (Phil. 1:15–18a), and other Christians who distort the gospel and malign Paul (2 Cor. 10–12; Gal. 1:6–9). Yet God enables them to endure in his strength, builds character into them through suffering, and gives them hope through the Spirit of love (Rom. 5:3–5). Even in the face of death, he strengthens them to continue to give witness by the Spirit to God's goodness and grace in Christ (Phil. 1:19–20; 2 Tim. 4:17).

THE SPIRIT, MISSION, AND ETHICS

Much of what needs to be said on ethics is found in chapter 7. Still, as with the previous section, a few comments are in order. For Paul, in Christ's death for sinners, God's love is demonstrated (Rom. 5:8). Christ emulates God's love, prepared to give himself up for humankind as the ultimate final sacrifice for sin (Eph. 5:1). Believers experience this love, poured into their hearts (Rom. 5:5; Gal. 4:6). Love should shape their church relationships (Rom. 12:9–10), but cannot be limited to loving one another, for this love must extend to unbelievers (Rom. 13:8–10; 1 Thess. 3:10).[103]

Filled with the Spirit and the love of Father and Son, believers are compelled into mission (2 Cor. 5:14). They know God wants all people to be saved and come to a knowledge of the truth (1 Tim. 2:4–5) and are motivated to love them with the gospel in attitude, word, and deed. They are to do everything in love (1 Cor. 16:14). Paul emphasizes the importance of love by sandwiching 1 Corinthians 13 between chapters concerning the exercise of spiritual gifts (chap. 12, 14). He expounds what love looks like in different situations through a virtue list that is similar to the fruit of the Spirit list in Galatians 5:22–24. They are to be characterized by related virtues like patience and kindness, affection, compassion, humility, and gentleness (2 Cor. 6:6; Col. 3:12).

Furthermore, as Titus demonstrated among the Corinthians, Paul and the collection group behave with the utmost integrity where money is concerned (2 Cor. 12:18). They do not peddle the gospel or use their position of authority to line their own pockets (cf. 2 Cor. 2:17). Instead, they "walk in the same Spirit" and "take the same footsteps." As Fee has argued, this almost certainly is the Spirit rather than a reference to upright conduct.[104] Second Corinthians 12:18c and 18d together speak of engaging in mission in line with the leading of the Spirit and walking in the footsteps of Christ and others who emulate his

---

103. "In the spirit of conformity to Jesus, the church in the power of the Spirit must look again and again for new ways to love the world incarnationally and cruciformly in the interest of the world's salvation." Gorman, *BGPPM*, 132. He also rightly adds, "To be missional requires immense imagination." I would add that this is because love is not concrete but fluid, and must be expressed imaginatively in each new situation. Gorman agrees, writing, "It is the task of the Spirit to spark and sanctify the Christian imagination, so that together believers may discern what it means for them, in their particular contexts, to become the gospel in ways analogous to the praxis of the churches in Thessalonica, Philippi, and elsewhere." Gorman, *BGPPM*, 305.

104. Fee, *GEP*, 357–58.

example (cf. Phil. 3:17). Those who engage in mission must do so in the Spirit, embodying the virtues of God—pneumaformity.

Read on its own, Philippians 1:12–18a can be misread to think that what matters for Paul, whether or not people's motives are good, is that the gospel is preached. Indeed, he says nothing to confront those preaching the gospel with false motives (1:15, 17). However, that misrepresents the passage as his eye is on Philippi, not Rome. Paul spends the rest of Philippians summoning his readers in Philippi away from behaviors seen among the poorly motivated Romans and toward those of the well-motivated—goodwill, love, and the knowledge that Paul has been appointed to defend the gospel (1:16).[105] They are to embody the attitudes outlined through the letter especially articulated in 2:1–4: encouragement, comfort, love, close relationships in the Spirit, compassion, affection, humility, and selfless concern for the good of others, renouncing selfish ambition and empty glory.

Supremely, the Philippians are to take on the attitude of Christ who, although God in form and status, renounced all forms of self-aggrandizement and uses of rapacious force as he came to save his world (2:6). They are to emulate his self-emptying, voluntary enslavement, obedience, sacrifice, and if need be, death (2:7–8). If the believers work out their salvation by God's power, renouncing argument and grumbling, blameless in their relationships, and showing gentleness to all, they will shine like lights of the world, and the word of life they hold out will see some new names written into the book of life (2:12–16; 4:3–4).

When they lead others to Christ, like Paul, they are to be filled with affection for their converts.[106] Paul's coworker, Timothy, must also exercise his ministries with love and other core virtues (1 Tim. 6:11; 2 Tim. 3:10). Philemon is to continue to give joy and encouragement to other Christians, including God's workers like Paul (Philem. 7). Pneumaformed believers are Christoform and cruciform and take the ethics of God and his Son into the world as they engage with believers with love.

MISSIONAL GOOD WORKS AND THE SPIRIT

Paul is adamant that people are saved not through works but by grace through faith (Eph. 2:8–9; 2 Tim. 1:9; Titus 3:5).[107] Yet, he also has a robust theology of works—good deeds *will* flow from hearts transformed by the Spirit as believers work out their salvation with fear and trembling (Phil. 2:12–13). Indeed, Paul considers that new Christians are God's "creation, created in

---

105. We can assume that Paul wants the same from the Romans. Indeed, it is interesting to ponder how Philippians was understood as it was no doubt instantly accessible to the Roman church. I suspect Philippians 1:12–18a cut deeply.

106. 1 Cor. 16:24; 2 Cor. 2:4; 8:16; 11:11; 12:15; Phil. 1:8.

107. See also Paul's theology of justification by faith and not works of any sort, including those of the law (Rom. 3:28; 5:1; Gal. 2:16; 3:11, 24).

Christ Jesus for good works, which God prepared beforehand, so that [they] may walk in them" (Eph. 2:10 LEB). Reference to creation draws the Spirit's renewal work into view; the Spirit transforms people from the inside out to do good in the world. Moreover, God preparing works in advance speaks of the Spirit shaping the context and moving the believer into these actions. Those who sincerely believe in Jesus can rest assured in their salvation by grace through faith and not works. Trusting in God's grace, filled with gratitude, and overflowing with zeal, believers can follow the Spirit into the future works God has for them.[108]

The work they are to do encompasses mission. God is at work in those who engage in mission on his behalf, whether Peter, James, John, Paul, Barnabas, or Titus, and undoubtedly anyone else who works for him and his gospel (Gal. 2:3, 8). This mission is a work God has begun and will bring to completion (Phil. 1:6).[109] Paul describes the Corinthians as "my workmanship in the Lord" (1 Cor. 9:1). Ongoing life, if Paul escapes his situation in Rome, will mean "fruitful work," including the strengthening of the Philippians (Phil. 1:22).

Timothy carries out the Lord's work as he travels from Paul to Corinth (1 Cor. 16:10). Epaphroditus's great adventure taking money some thirteen hundred kilometers to Paul in Rome from Philippi[110] is "the work of Christ" that nearly killed him (Phil. 2:30). This work includes the Spirit working miracles among Paul's converts (Gal. 3:8). God's work includes the exercise of spiritual gifts that God "works" in all believers (1 Cor. 12:6).[111] The Spirit is at work in spiritual gifts, and believers are the vehicle of their expression (1 Cor. 12:11).[112]

At the core of the work of Christian leaders is equipping others for works of service, so they can expand the Spirit's work in the world (Eph. 4:12). Knowing that they will be raised from the dead at Jesus's return, believers are to abound in the work of the Lord (1 Cor. 15:58). God causes grace to abound to believers so that they "may overflow in every good work" (2 Cor. 9:8 LEB). Paul delights in the "work of faith" and "labor of love" exercised by the zealous Thessalonians, including the word of the Lord sounding forth from them in the region along with acts of love (1 Thess. 1:3, 8; 4:10; cf. 2 Thess. 1:11). He prays for their continued work, that God would fulfill their desires for goodness and work springing from their faith (2 Thess. 1:11) and encourage their hearts and strengthen them in every good work and word (2:17).

---

108. Similarly, deSilva, *Transformation*, 42.

109. On this interpretation, see Keown, *Congregational*, 216–24.

110. Or 550 km or 334 mi. by sea and foot from Ephesus; 2,000 km or 1,240 mi. by sea and foot from Caesarea.

111. Dunn cogently states that v. 6b indicates that for Paul, "all charismata are effected by divine power; *the utterances and actions he goes on to list are only charismata in so far as they are the action of God's Spirit in and through the individual.*" Dunn, *Jesus and the Spirit*, 209 (emphasis original).

112. Dunn rightly notes that this verse restates what I have quoted him as saying in the previous footnote. Dunn, *Jesus and the Spirit*, 209.

Believers are to work with their own hands, providing for themselves, so that they are not a burden on others (1 Thess. 4:11; 2 Thess. 3:10). Church leaders are to toil in their churches and experience love from those they serve (1 Thess. 5:13; 1 Tim. 3:1). Widows are to be well attested in good works and devoted to them (1 Tim. 5:10; cf. v. 25). The rich are not to hoard wealth but be generous in good works, sharing freely (6:18). All believers are to be prepared and equipped for every good work (2 Tim. 2:21; 3:17; Titus 3:1). With pneumaformed minds, they are to put into practice those things that they have observed in Paul and learned from him (Phil. 4:8–9). Such praxis includes bearing fruit in every good work (Col. 1:10). All such things are to be done in the name of the Lord Jesus and with gratitude to God (Col. 3:17). It is the Spirit who generates the desire to be concerned for the things of Jesus and others.

MISSIONAL COURAGE

Another aspect of the Spirit's work in believers is courage, which is often associated with mission. Although ἀνδρεῖα is one of the Greeks' four cardinal virtues, the language is only used once in the NT. This mention is in 1 Corinthians 16:13, where Paul's readers are to "be alert, stand firm in the faith, be courageous [ἀνδρίζεσθε], be strong, let all things be done in love" (my translation). The blend of military images of being alert, standing firm, and being courageous is instantly placed in the context of love. They are to be Christian "soldiers," shaped by love toward God, one another, and the world. Such love will restore the Corinthians' shattered relationships. This love will propel them into missional attitudes, works of service, and appropriate bold gospel speech.[113]

Paul's boldness in mission is seen in 1 Thessalonians 2:2 as he recalls his ministry in Philippi. Despite suffering and being shamefully treated in the nearby town, he came to the Macedonian capital and spoke the gospel of God to the Thessalonians boldly and openly (παρρησιάζομαι) during a great struggle (ἀγών). Earlier, in 1 Thessalonians 1:5, this proclamation came "in power and in the Holy Spirit," linking his courage in 2:2 with the work of the Spirit. In and by the Spirit,[114] the Thessalonians bravely welcomed the message amid great persecution and opposition (1:7; 2:14). The courage to share the message or receive it while opposition swirls around believers is the work of the Spirit.

Philippians 1:12–18a speaks of the Spirit's role in courageous witness. Paul is in Roman incarceration, facing trial. He is delighted that the gospel is advancing, including through the palace guard—even if it is the reason for his imprisonment. The palace guard's knowledge implies that Paul is preaching the gospel at every opportunity, and some believe it (cf. Phil. 4:22).[115] In 1:14, he speaks of the brothers and sisters in the context of his imprisonment becoming "confident in the Lord" by his chains. "In the Lord" speaks of the sphere of their life

---

113. I will be exploring courage in Paul's letters in a forthcoming book.
114. On the flawed binary "in the Spirit" or "by the Spirit," see "Baptized in the Spirit," chapter 2.
115. See Keown, *Philippians*, 1:189.

in Christ and implies the work of Christ by his Spirit emboldening them. The outcome is that they are "much more bold to speak the word without fear."[116] The circumstances of Paul's imprisonment and, more importantly, the work of Christ, have motivated these locals to share the gospel in their context without fear, despite the real danger. Paul goes on to reference two subgroups who are sharing the gospel. Some are well motivated; others are not so. Yet, Paul rejoices that people are preaching Christ (1:15–18a). Such people grasp the missional intent of God's Spirit but are not fully formed ethically. Ideally, the pneumaform believer shares God's Word with love.

Philippians 1:27–30 starts Paul's direct appeal to the Philippians. They are to live as citizens of heaven in a manner worthy of the gospel. This citizenship includes their standing firm as a military unit in the one Spirit of God. Unified as one soul by the Spirit, they are to contend for the faith of the gospel by defending it when false teachers like the "dogs" and enemies of the cross attack (3:2, 18–19). Together, they are to advance the gospel as the opportunity comes like Paul and the freshly motivated believers are doing in Rome (1:12–18a). They are not to be intimidated by the hordes of opponents coming at them in Philippi. God is with them in their suffering; he will save them and destroy their opponents if they do not yield to the gospel. When facing trial, the Philippians are to testify to Christ, as Paul is about to do in Rome, even if it brings his death (1:19–23).

Later in Philippians, Epaphroditus "nearly died for the work of Christ, having risking his life to complete what was lacking in [their] service to [Paul]."[117] The Spirit is not named in Philippians 2:25–30 and 4:14–20, where the gift Epaphroditus brought is mentioned. Yet the Spirit's presence is implied in various ways, catalyzing the sending of the gift and empowering Epaphroditus and others with him. First, he is identified as a coworker, fellow soldier, apostle, and minister, implying that God has set him apart to be an apostolic missionary in the early church. Hence, his ministry begins with the Spirit's work of calling, equipping, empowering, and urging him into works of service like the delivery of the gift (2:25). His recovery from near death in the delivery is accredited to God's merciful action (2:27). The work he has done is "for the work of Christ" indicating Christ's action in the situation (2:28). The gifts sent are a fragrant offering and acceptable sacrifice that pleased God, showing it was gathered and sent in the context of a relationship with God (4:18). Paul credits God as the supplier of his needs indicating the Spirit-impelled nature of the Philippians' giving. The right response is glorifying God.

CONCLUSION

The Spirit is urging God's people into mission. They do so through their work in the world outside God's church, working with God to fulfill their

---

116. Keown, *Philippians*, 1:193.
117. Keown, *Philippians*, 2:61.

image-bearing creation mandates to fill, subdue, care, and work the garden (Gen. 1:27–28; 2:15).[118] As they go about their vocational engagement, they share the faith in word and deed, pulsing with the ethics of God radiating from their core. They engage in mission toward one another, strengthening each other in the gospel. When they face difficulty and suffering, God enables them to endure in his strength, builds character, and gives hope. They can then have the courage of a victorious soldier. Where others are set apart for vocational roles in the church, others, overflowing with God's generosity in Christ, give to the mission and pray for the gospel to extend. When they encounter people in need, they love and do good to them as they long to be loved. The charismata of God define the believers' particular roles. Yet, whoever they are, if they are genuinely pneumaformed, they will be missional to the core.

---

118. Keown, *Discovering: The Gospels and Acts*, 435.

CHAPTER 11

THE SPIRIT AND THE ESCHATON

Before I conclude this study, this final major chapter considers the Spirit's work at the eschaton. Paul's eschatology seems to contain a few preceding events, including the conversion of the full number of Gentiles (Rom. 11:25)[1] and a final rebellion, including a lawless and destructive ruler who elevates himself as god (2 Thess. 2:1–10).[2] Then, in my view,[3] Paul expects Christ's return,[4] the resurrection of the dead to judgment,[5] the destruction of hostile spirits and the ungodly,[6] salva-

---

1. Keown, *Romans and the Mission of God*, 171 n. 12. See also Witherington and Hyatt, *Paul's Letter*, 273, who suggest it can mean either all the Gentiles to be saved or the full number of those yet to be saved when Romans was written. We agree that it certainly "does not mean the Gentile world as a whole."

2. While some see a clash here with 1 Thessalonians 5:2–4, it is unbelievers who are surprised by Christ's coming, while believers will not be surprised. As Wanamaker says, "Christians differ from outsiders in that they are *aware* of the imminence of the day of the Lord, while the day will overtake those who are ignorant about its coming like a thief." Wanamaker, *The Epistles*, 181.

3. It is possible Paul believes in the intermediate state whereby the believer dies and is with God in some form until his return when the body is raised. Some see evidence for this in Philippians 1:23 and 1 Thessalonians 4:14.

4. The coming of the Lord (1 Cor. 15:23; 1 Thess. 2:19; 3:13; 4:14–17; 5:23; 2 Thess. 2:1, 8); the Lord revealed (1 Cor. 1:8); the Lord appearing (2 Thess. 2:8; 1 Tim. 6:14; 2 Tim. 4:1; Titus 2:13). See also Phil. 3:20; Col. 3:14; 1 Thess. 1:10.

5. On judgment see Rom. 2:2–3, 5–16; 3:4, 6; 14:10–12; 1 Cor. 4:4–5; 5:13; 6:2–3; 2 Cor. 5:10; 2 Thess. 1:5; 1 Tim. 5:24; 2 Tim. 4:1, 8. See also wrath (Rom. 1:18; 2:5, 8; 3:5; 5:9; 9:22; 12:19; Eph. 2:3; 5:6; Col. 3:6; 1 Thess. 1:10; 2:16; 5:9); vengeance (Rom. 12:19; 2 Thess. 1:8); giving account (Rom. 14:12); executing a sentence (Rom. 9:28); bowing a knee (Rom. 14:11; Phil. 2:10); being accursed (Gal. 1:8–9). "The day" at times focuses on judgment (Rom. 2:5, 16; 1 Cor. 1:8; 3:13; 2 Cor. 1:14; Phil. 1:10; 2:16; 2 Tim. 1:18; 4:8) and at times seems broader to include the whole range of things that happen at Christ's return (Rom. 13:12; 1 Cor. 5:5; 2 Cor. 6:2; Eph. 4:30; Phil. 1:6; 1 Thess. 5:2, 4, 8; 2 Thess. 1:10; 2:2–3; 2 Tim. 1:12). Believers are raised never to die again (Rom. 8:11; 1 Cor. 6:14; 2 Cor. 4:14; 5:1; 1 Thess. 4:16; Col. 3:14). Paul speaks of this as a realized event in Ephesians 2:5–6. He uses "redemption" and "adoption" of this future salvation in Romans 8:23.

6. The destruction of Satan (Rom. 16:20); the subjugation of all powers (1 Cor. 15:25, 27; Eph. 1:22). On destruction expressed in different ways, see Rom. 2:5, 8–9, 12; 9:22; 1 Cor. 1:18–19; 3:17; 6:13; 2 Cor. 2:15; 4:3; Phil. 1:28; 3:19; 2 Thess. 1:8–9; 2:10.

tion[7]—including the gift of eternal life for believers[8]—the restoration of the cosmos,[9] and the inheritance of the kingdom.[10] How does the Spirit fit into this?

Clearly, Paul understands that the end has broken into the present. It has done so first in Christ's astonishing ministry that culminated in his death and resurrection. Second, the end has entered lives as the Spirit pours into the inner beings of those who hear the gospel and believe. Dunn rightly says of this, "So for Paul, the gift of the Spirit is the first part of the redemption of the whole man [person], the beginning of the process which will end when the believer becomes a spiritual body, that is when the man [person] of faith enters into a mode of existence determined solely by the Spirit."[11]

In the meantime, this Spirit bonds them to God the Father and other Christians; transforms them into the image of the Son, increasingly full of the fruit of the Spirit; and gives them gifts to be used to enhance God's work in worship, to build his church, and to evangelize and transform the world. The end will come when the mission presently led by God, through Christ, and by the Spirit, sovereignly and through his people, the church, is completed. Still, one more aspect of the Spirit comes at the culmination of the age when Jesus returns: the complete transformation of believers from sinfulness, decay, and death to ethical perfection and eternal life.

COMPLETING THE WORK

The Spirit is God's seal on the hearts of believers, a deposit of eternity that guarantees them this eternal life.[12] The intercession of this Spirit sustains believers (Rom. 8:26–27). The Spirit also generates strength and hope as they look forward to this reconciliation of the cosmos (Rom. 5:5; 15:13). The Spirit is the power that enables believers to eagerly await the hope of the final declaration of their justification at the final judgment (Gal. 5:5). Then the love poured into human hearts will transcend this age and feature in the age to come (1 Cor. 13:13).

---

7. Salvation seems a summary idea for the whole event of human deliverance from sin and its consequences. See especially Rom. 5:9–10; 10:9–10; 13:11; Phil. 1:28; 1 Thess. 5:9. This is a realized event in Ephesians 2:5–6. Similarly, redemption (Rom. 3:24; 1 Cor. 1:30; Gal. 3:13; 4:5; Eph. 1:7, 14; 4:30; Col. 1:14; Titus 2:14). Other ideas include "gain" (Phil. 1:21); "to be with Christ" (Phil. 1:23); the prize (1 Cor. 9:24; Phil. 3:14).

8. Rom. 2:7; 5:21; 6:22–23; Gal. 6:8; 1 Tim. 1:16; 6:12; Titus 1:2; 3:7.

9. The defeat of death (1 Cor. 15:26) and God all in all (1 Cor. 15:28). See also the reconciliation of all things (2 Cor. 5:19; Col. 1:20). All things are brought together under one head, Christ (Eph. 1:10).

10. This is the shared inheritance of the restored cosmos free of evil and totally and willingly under God's reign forever (1 Cor. 6:9–10; 15:50; Gal. 5:21; Eph. 5:5; Col. 1:12; 3:24).

11. Dunn, *Jesus and the Spirit*, 311.

12. 2 Cor. 1:22, also 3:3; 5:5; Eph. 1:13; 4:30; 2 Tim. 1:14.

2 Corinthians 4:16–5:5

In earlier chapters, Paul explains that God has given the Spirit to the Corinthians as a seal and guarantee of their future redemption (2 Cor. 1:23; also 5:5; Eph. 1:13; 4:30). The Spirit of the living God has penned the Corinthians as a letter from Christ delivered by Paul and his team (2 Cor. 3:3). Paul and his team minister in and by the Spirit, and their ministry, because of the glory of God, has more glory than the ministry under the old covenant (2 Cor. 3:8). The Spirit and Lord are seen as one, the Spirit being the means by which God in Jesus sets believers free and transforms them with ever-increasing glory into his image (2 Cor. 3:17–18).

Second Corinthians 4 begins with Paul speaking of his gospel ministry. Unlike his opponents, he and his team do not lose heart or use duplicitous methods (4:1–2a). Even if Satan has blinded many to the word's light, which shines the glory of Christ, the image of God, Paul and his group preach Jesus openly and consistently (4:2–6). The light images in the passage evoke the notion of God piercing the heart with the light shone by the Spirit.

In v. 7, Paul turns to the matter of suffering in ministry yet being sustained by God's power. He doesn't mention the Spirit, but the entire passage speaks of the Spirit's presence in mortal believers, sustaining them through the suffering they experience in mission.[13] While they suffer immensely, they are not defeated, destroyed, or despairing. The life of Jesus, by the Spirit, is manifest in their beings (v. 10).

In v. 14, Paul looks forward to the resurrection—just as God raised Christ, he will raise both the Pauline group and the Corinthians and bring them into his presence. He and his team do not lose heart despite suffering. Paul considers present suffering light and momentary compared to the eternal weight of glory prepared for believers (vv. 16–18). By the Spirit, he and his group look toward such things that are yet unseen (vv. 16–18).

In 2 Corinthians 5:1–5, which must be read in continuity with the previous passage, γάρ ("for," v. 1) signals that Paul looks toward the resurrection body that awaits believers when they die. Presently they groan, longing to be clothed in the heavenly dwelling and see the mortal swallowed up by life. This dwelling is prepared for them by God, and the Spirit guarantees this future resurrection.

As such, in v. 6, Paul states that he and his group are perpetually courageous despite suffering. Despite longing to be with the Lord in this final state, they continue to seek to please God, living by faith and not despairing at things seen. They know judgment is coming, and all people (including themselves and the lost) will appear before God, which motivates them to ensure they themselves live lives that please God. They are also motivated to ensure

---

13.   See chapter 8 at various points where I mention 2 Corinthians 4. See also Chapter 2, "The Spirit in Conversion: The Spirit and Faith (2 Cor. 4:13) and "The Spirit Who Brings Renewal: 2 Corinthians 4:16; and Chapter 8, "The Spirit of Suffering" where I discussed 2 Corinthians 4:7–20.

others are given the opportunity to pass through that judgment to eternal life by hearing the gospel. While there is no mention of the Spirit, v. 5 indicates the Spirit is the power by which they live this life despite the inevitable suffering life and mission bring.

Philippians 1:6

Although I hold to the view that Philippians 1:6 should be read in context as God bringing to completion his mission, I hold this view tentatively. Alternatively, this text may speak of the completion of God's salvation work in believers. Or the passage is intentionally ambiguous to encompass both ideas.[14] Whatever the case, this is an implicit reference to the Spirit in Philippians. If the mission is in view by the Spirit, the God who began the good work of bringing people to Christ in Philippi (in you) will bring his mission to completion on the day of Jesus Christ (his return and judgment). If Paul is thinking here of salvation, as many hold, this speaks of the Spirit completing the work of transforming the Philippians and other believers until the return of Christ.

Galatians 3:3

Earlier I discussed the implications of this passage for the Galatians continuing to live by faith and not works of the law.[15] The verse also points to the eschaton when the Galatians and all believers are "made complete" or "perfected." They will be whole, free of sin and its consequences. Importantly, it explicitly states that this perfecting is the work of the Spirit, as is ongoing life in Christ by faith. There is, then, direct continuity of life and Spirit-experience. While in the present it is partial, in the new creation it will be total. Paul laments the Galatians deserting the gospel of grace and faith for one based on works of the law. This means that rather than relying on the Spirit, they are relying on their own capacity to complete the work God began in them.[16] Achieving this is implausible as no one can fulfill the law to be justified before God. This verse implies that the Spirit began God's work in the Galatians when they heard the gospel, believed, and were gifted with God's presence. It also demands that they continue to walk in faith, rely on Christ, and complete the journey by walking in step with the Spirit and not the flesh. The completion of the Christian journey is the work of the Spirit.

---

14.   Keown, *Congregational*, 216–24.

15.   See also earlier on this verse in regard to "The Spirit Who Begins Growth" (chapter 3).

16.   Fee rightly notes that the issue here is not merely fleshly life but "to submit to circumcision is to put one's confidence before God in that which is merely an expression of 'flesh.' This becomes, therefore, *self*-confidence, rather than trust in Christ and him alone for a proper relationship with God." Fee, *GEP*, 386 (emphasis original).

Colossians 1:20

In Colossians 1:15–20, probably in the face of Judaizing and protognostic views of Jesus that saw him as something less than God (possibly an angel, cf. 2:18), Paul begins the body of the letter with a glorious description of Christ. He is the new Adam, the image of the invisible God, preeminent over creation, the means by which God created all things and all rulers, the one for whom things were created, preexistent, sustainer of all that exists, the head of the church and its beginning, the first to rise from the dead, and so, utterly supreme over the church and all things.

Of interest to this study is v. 19. Paul states that God was pleased to allow his fullness to dwell in Christ. This verse speaks of the completeness of God in Christ, by his Spirit. Jesus is the living tabernacle or temple of God and his Spirit.

Equally important is v. 20. Through Christ radiating fully with his Spirit, God has reconciled all things to himself. The use of the aorist (inf.) ἀποκαταλλάσσω has a range of possible interpretations. In that all things are not yet reconciled to God, as evidenced by the hostility of many people and spiritual beings, the ongoing problem of death, and the need to continue to proclaim the gospel, this can speak of the anticipated reconciliation that was completed at Christ's death and resurrection. Or it can speak of the inevitable process that began at Christ's resurrection and will be complete at the final destruction of God's opponents. Either way, it speaks of the reconciliation of "all things" and not merely people. As in Romans 8:19–23, God is redeeming the whole creation. This restoration will be complete when he returns and once and for all destroys his enemies, including death. Believers are swept up in God's redemptive work, including a concern for creation, building God's church, social transformation, and especially evangelism.[17]

2 Thessalonians 2:8

In this chapter, the work of the Spirit at the eschaton has mainly been restorative regarding believers and the whole creation. However, 2 Thessalonians 2:8 speaks of a lawless one being revealed after the power restraining him is removed, and the Lord Jesus killing and destroying (ἀναιρέω) him by the "breath of his mouth" (τῷ πνεύματι τοῦ στόματος αὐτοῦ) and by the appearance of his coming. This event will occur at the return of Christ mentioned in the previous chapter (1:7–8).

What is entailed by πνεῦμα here? Fee recognizes the parallel to Isaiah 11:4 (LXX) yet, surprisingly in my view, does not consider this to be the Spirit. For Fee, this overstates the metaphor and is unlikely because of the use of the definite article. He concludes, "It is extremely doubtful whether this text advances our understanding of the Spirit in Paul."[18] However, such a conclusion is not clear-cut.

---

17. Similarly, Habets, *Anointed Son*, 287. Liston, *Kingdom Come*, 132, aptly describes this as "pneumatologically enabled transformation."

18. Fee, *GEP*, 75–76 (quote on 76).

As discussed in chapter 1,[19] God is depicted frequently acting in judgment. Various body metaphors are employed, such as "the hand of the LORD"[20] and "the arm of the Lord,"[21] and the breath (πνεῦμα, רוּחַ MT) of God's anger ("nostrils" MT, Exod. 15:8). I also noted a range of other examples of God's πνεῦμα/רוּחַ bringing judgment. This material includes the Messiah, who is full of the Spirit, and God bringing a violent wind of judgment on the Gulf of Suez (Isa. 11:15). The Spirit is also involved in the deaths of Ananias and Sapphira in Acts 5:1–11.

Furthermore, here in v. 8, the use of the article is neither here nor there, as Paul quite commonly uses the article with the noun πνεῦμα.[22] More important, while this is a metaphor, it still speaks of the πνεῦμα that proceeds *from* Jesus,[23] in this case, his mouth. Thus, I argue "the Spirit/breath of Jesus" is in view. In that God's Spirit at times brings death and judgment, that the Spirit is active in resurrection and the restoration of the cosmos, and that this comes from Jesus's mouth, would seem to indicate it is the same Spirit referred to in other texts associating πνεῦμα with Christ.[24]

Considering this to be God's Spirit proceeding from Christ fits with the spiritual aspects of vv. 9–12. First, the parousia of the lawless one is in accordance with the working of Satan, his power, false miracles, and wicked deception among unbelievers.[25] Satan is, of course, a spirit being and God's primary antagonist. Second, God's sending of a deception speaks of the influence of false spirits, used by God[26] to deepen unbelievers in their falsehood and lack of belief to ensure the condemnation of unrighteous unbelievers.

The verb ἀναιρέω means to "kill"[27] or "destroy." Here, then, Christ by the Spirit will either kill the man, eschatologically destroy him, or, as is likely,

---

19. "The Spirit of Judgment."
20. E.g., Exod. 16:3; Deut. 2:15; Acts 13:11.
21. E.g., Exod. 6:6; 15:16; Deut. 4:34.
22. The article where it is not God's Spirit: Rom. 1:9; 8:16 (2nd); 1 Cor. 2:11 (1st), 12 (1st); 5:5; 7:34; 14:14; 14:15 (2x); 2 Cor. 2:13; 4:13; 7:13; 12:18; Gal. 6:18; Eph. 2:2; Phil. 4:23; 1 Thess. 5:23; 2 Tim. 4:22; Philem. 25. The article where it is God's Spirit: Rom. 8:2, 5 (2x), 6, 11 (1st), 16 (1st), 23, 26, 27; 12:11; 15:30; 1 Cor. 2:10 (2x), 11 (2nd), 12 (1st), 14; 3:16; 5:3; 6:11; 12:4, 7, 8 (2x), 9 (2x), 11; 2 Cor. 1:22; 3:8, 17 (2x); 5:5; 13:13; Gal. 3:2, 5, 14; 4:6, 29; 5:17 (2x), 22; 6:8 (2x); Eph. 1:13; 3:16; 4:3, 23, 30; 6:17; Col. 2:5; Phil. 1:19; 1 Thess. 4:8; 5:19.
23. While it is vaguely possible that στόματος αὐτοῦ is God or some other agent, by far the most likely referent is "the Lord Jesus."
24. Rom. 8:9; 2 Cor. 3:17–18; Gal. 4:6; Phil. 1:19. Also, 1 Cor. 15:45.
25. On this verse, see Fee, *GEP*, 76. He notes the parallel Mark 13:22 (Matt. 24:24).
26. Judg. 9:23; 1 Sam. 16:14, 15, 16, 23; 18:10; 19:9; 2 Chron. 18:22; Col. 2:8; 2 Tim. 4:1; Rev. 12:9; 19:20; 20:8, 10.
27. NT, Matt. 2:16; Luke 22:2; 23:32; Acts 2:23; 5:33, 36; 7:28; 9:23, 24, 29; 10:39; 12:2; 13:28; 16:27; 22:20; 23:15, 21, 27; 25:3; 26:10; LXX, Gen. 4:15; Exod. 2:14, 15; 15:9; 21:29; Num. 31:19; 35:31; Deut. 13:16; Josh. 9:26; 11:12, 17; 12:1, 7; Judg. 8:21; 9:45; 2 Kgdms. 10:18; 3 Kgdms. 2:25, 29, 31, 46; Tob. 2:4; Jdt. 1:12, 13; 16:4; 1 Macc. 6:46; 11:45; 2 Macc. 8:30, 32; 10:17; 13:15; 15:22; 3 Macc. 7:5, 14, 15; Job 5:2; 6:9; 20:16; Wis. 1:11; 14:24; Sir. 21:2; 22:2; Isa. 11:4; 14:30; 26:21; 27:1; 27:7, 8; 28:6; 37:36; 65:15; Jer. 4:31; 7:32; 18:21; 33:15, 19, 24 (26:15, 19, 24 EVV); 45:4 (33:4, 25 EVV); 48:8 (41:8 EVV); Ep. Jer. 12; Ezek. 26:6, 8, 11; 28:9; Dan. 1:16; Bel. 25; 4 Macc. 4:13; 5:3; 18:11; Odes Sol. 1:9. In the middle, it can

both (cf. 2 Thess. 1:7–9).[28] However, this killing, while an act of judgment, like all God's such actions, is a redemptive act—to save the world from evil. Indeed, that is why God will destroy all enemies—to free his creation from evil and to liberate his faithful people forever. This text, intriguingly, opens up the possibility of the Spirit's role in extinguishing evil as well as in renewal and imparting life. It may be then that the illness and deaths of those who abuse the unity of the church and the Lord's Supper in Corinth are the work of the Spirit (1 Cor. 11:30). If so, the purpose is redemptive—to discipline the offenders in the hope of their repentance and to purify the church.

NEW LIFE/RESURRECTION

Romans 8:11

In this chapter, Paul's focus is living by the Spirit rather than the flesh. Due to Christ's redemptive death, those justified by faith and "in Christ" are free from the law and its condemnation through "the Spirit of life" (Rom. 8:1–3). Paul then sets up the antithesis of flesh and the Spirit, summoning believing readers to live by Spirit and not flesh (vv. 4–8). They have received the Spirit of God, are "in the Spirit," and "belong to Christ." The body is subject to death because of sin, yet the Spirit generates life because they are justified by faith (vv. 9–10).

Verse 11 is a first-class conditional sentence, assumed true for Paul and the Roman believers for the sake of argument. The protasis lays down the premise: "if the Spirit [τὸ πνεῦμα] of him who raised Jesus from the dead dwells in you." The one who raised Jesus is God. It is God's Spirit who dwells in believers. Technically, the clause τοῦ ἐγείραντος τὸν Ἰησοῦν ἐκ νεκρῶν does not clearly state that the Spirit raised Jesus. However, the specific mention of Spirit in Paul's description indicates that the Spirit was involved in Christ's resurrection. Otherwise, the connection of God and Spirit in the verse does not work. Moreover, in the apodosis, it is "through his Spirit who dwells in you" that believers experience life. Hence, Paul here speaks of the Spirit's role not only (καί, also) in the resurrection of Jesus but in believers. The Spirit's indwelling in the protasis is true of all believers.

The apodosis draws out the implication "*then* he who raised Christ Jesus from the dead will also give life to your mortal bodies through [διά] his Spirit [αὐτοῦ πνεύματος] who dwells in you." The one who raised Christ is God, and he will make the mortal bodies of believers alive. He will do this "through" his Spirit, who dwells in them.[29] This clause clearly speaks of the future resurrec-

---

mean to "take for oneself" (Exod. 2:5, 10; Acts 7:21), "take up" (Num. 17:2; Josh. 4:3, 5), do away with something, as in an initial covenant (Heb. 10:9).

28. At times destruction is a better translation as in the case of Levi destroying Shechem (T. Levi 6:6) or the destruction of the light of the law (Isa. 28:6).

29. Fee, *GEP*, 552, prefers the accusative here. However, the genitive is preferable, and so this is likely a marker of agency.

tion, as Moo states: "Since reference to resurrection is so plain in the first part of the sentence, 'will make alive' must also refer to future bodily transformation—through resurrection for dead believers—rather than, for instance, to spiritual vivification in justification, or to the 'mortification' of sin in the Christian life."[30]

Romans 8:18–25

Living by the Spirit is the central theme of Romans 8:1–17. The foundation of the Spirit's work is that of Christ, who has died to release believers from the sin and death that for them is utterly inevitable (8:2–3). The counter to the "law of sin and death" is the "law of the Spirit of life" that speaks of the power of the Spirit to transform believers, to seal them for salvation, and to enable them to overcome the flesh that is beset with desirous sin.

In vv. 4–8, Paul contrasts two ways of being. Living by the flesh is the state of the unredeemed, which all believers continue to do to some extent. Paul here implicitly summons believers to turn away from fleshly impulses and submit to the inward summons of the Spirit and his desires for them in worship, toward others in the people of God, and in the world. Verse 9 states that the Romans and other readers (you) are in the Spirit, not the flesh. This truth means that while they are still fleshly beings, they have the Spirit in them. The Spirit is that of Christ, and those without his Spirit do not belong to him. Implied is the converse for the readers—the Spirit of Christ *is* in them. Notably, here is the Spirit of God *and* Christ, showing the unity of the Godhead working in the lives of believers again. As the Spirit of Christ, the Spirit morphs believers into his image and that of his Father.

In v. 10, Paul shifts from speaking of the Spirit to Christ being in believers (by the Spirit implied). They remain subject to sin and death; however, the Spirit generates life in them because they have been justified by faith. In v. 11, Paul turns from Christ in believers back to the Spirit, which is now "the Spirit of him who raised Jesus from the dead." This Spirit is of God, the agent of Christ's resurrection (Rom. 1:4; see also 2 Cor. 3:6; 1 Tim. 3:16).[31] Where the Spirit dwells in believers, this same God who raised Christ from the dead will give life to the fleshly bodies of believers by his indwelling Spirit. This vivification speaks of present inward spiritual transformation culminating in the final metamorphosis explored in 1 Corinthians 15. The future resurrection of believers, then, is the work of the Spirit.

In vv. 12–13, Paul draws out the implications for his Roman brothers and sisters. They are debtors not to the flesh and its impulses but are instead to live by the Spirit, putting to death those desires. If they persevere in seeking

---

30.   Moo, *Romans*, 515.

31.   At times, Paul speaks of God raising Christ and believers by his power (e.g., Rom. 4:24; 1 Cor. 6:14; 2 Cor. 13:4; Gal. 1:1). I would argue that "power" in such references refers to the Spirit. Also, see Romans 6:4, where Jesus was raised by the glory of the Father. "Glory" suggests the Spirit. See also 2 Cor. 4:14.

to do this, they will experience the fullness of life. Those pursuing sanctification are God's children who have been freed from the fear of condemnation and adopted into God's family. As Jesus cried out in the garden, they cry out "Abba! Father!" (vv. 14–15), and they experience the inward testimony of the Spirit assuring them of their status as God's children (v. 16). As children, they are to be heirs of all things with Christ (v. 17a–c). Ultimately, God, by his Spirit, will bring them through to the fullness of the glory of Christ (v. 17d).

I have spent time narrating Romans 8:1–17 to ensure that when vv. 18–25 are considered, readers do not divorce Paul's thinking from the Spirit. Indeed, he mentions the Spirit in v. 23 and follows the passage with the intercessory role of the Spirit in vv. 26–27. Hence, from this intentional framing, we can surmise that the transformation of the cosmos described in v. 21 is recognized as God's work, in Christ, by the Spirit.

As in 2 Corinthians 4:16–18, in v. 18, Paul states that the present sufferings, however extreme, cannot be compared to the glory to be revealed to believers at the eschatological climax of the age. Personifying creation—humankind and every aspect of the world, he vividly describes its present state. It longs for the day God's children (who have received the Spirit of adoption) are revealed (v. 19). Against its will, creation was subjected to futility by God (v. 20), it is enslaved to corruption (v. 21), and it groans in extreme travail like a woman in childbirth (v. 22). People, too, even believers who have the firstfruits of the Spirit,[32] groan in harmony with creation as they await their final adoption as God's children—their bodily redemption (so wonderfully described in 1 Corinthians 15; see above).

However long the wait is, all is not lost; the personified creation will be set free from its bondage and pain and experience the same freedom of God's children when redemption is complete. This redemption involves the glorious joy of being raised from the dead and receiving immortal bodies like that of the risen Jesus. Thus, then, Paul is intimating that the creation itself will be set free from the consequence of sin unleashed on it by human failings and demonic beckoning and be raised from the dead. Like God's people, it will be rebirthed. What a day that will be, when creation is entirely "in the Spirit," every vestige of evil's taint extinguished, nature humming with God's being. So, believers yearn in hope, patiently waiting for the redemption of their bodies and the world.

In the meantime, the Spirit prays in believers with noiseless groans and intercedes for them according to God's Word. He moves all things in the created order toward God's purposes for his called and loved people. He will transform them into the image of God's Son (vv. 26–28).

---

32. The firstfruit motif here speaks of the Spirit "as the first-fruits, that is, first sheaf of the harvest of the End, that is the beginning of the eschatological harvest of redemption." Dunn, *Jesus and the Spirit*, 311.

Paul's vision here is stunning. The Spirit will transform believers, flooding them with the totality of life, freed from sin, decay, and death forever (8:29; also 2 Cor. 3:18). By the Spirit, God will similarly flood the whole creation with the fullness of God's life, free from its corruption by human depravity and destruction. It will be beautiful. This vision is consistent with the hopes of Revelation 21–22.

1 Corinthians 6:14

In 1 Corinthians 6:12–20, Paul stresses the importance of the body, both in the present and for the future resurrection. In the passage, Paul uses a range of arguments to persuade the Corinthians to live as people who are washed, sanctified, and justified in Christ's name and by the Spirit. He begins challenging their slogan, "all things are lawful," in two ways. First, he states "not all things are helpful," and then adds that he will not be mastered by anything (as one freed from law and sin). In v. 13, he next challenges another slogan indicating that the Corinthians, like Stoics, believed that only soul and spirit survive death and that God will destroy body and stomach. This view led them to believe "that just as food is meant for the stomach and vice versa, so also sexual activity is meant for the body and the body for sexual activity. The stomach and the body are useless unless we eat and have sex. Such natural bodily processes have no abiding significance and are thus of no moral consequence."[33] Paul responds to their false understanding by applying it to the real issue, telling them that "the body is not for sexual immorality but for the Lord, and the Lord for the body." As such, this passage points to the Spirit's role in God bringing new life now and when Christ returns and his people are raised.

Paul then links this to the resurrection, demonstrating that the body is important eschatologically and in the present; and, anticipating chapter 15, he states, "And God raised the Lord and will also raise us up by his power." Somewhat surprisingly, Fee asserts that "it seems unlikely that Paul is here trying to say something about the Spirit."[34] He bases this on the premise "that nothing inherent either in this text or in Pauline usage elsewhere suggests that Jesus was raised by the power of the Spirit."[35] This assertion is strange and runs counter to his view of "power" in Paul's other letters and Romans 8:11, where "he who raised Christ Jesus from the dead will also give life to your mortal bodies through his Spirit who dwells in you." Fee also concedes that several texts point in that direction.[36] More importantly, Romans 8:11 (discussed above) indicates that by the Spirit, God will give life to mortal bodies, and as

---

33. Roy E. Ciampa and Brian S. Rosner, *The First Letter to the Corinthians*, PNTC (Grand Rapids: Eerdmans, 2010), 254.
34. Fee, *GEP*, 132.
35. Fee, *GEP*, 132.
36. See Rom. 1:3–4; 8:11; Eph. 1:19–20; 1 Tim. 3:16.

Moo says, this refers to "future bodily transformation."[37] As such, this passage points to the Spirit's role in God raising believers from the dead when Christ returns and his people are raised.

1 Corinthians 15:35–58

First Corinthians 15 begins with Paul appealing to the Corinthians to remain faithful to the gospel they received (vv. 1–2). At the gospel's heart is the resurrection of Christ, which is attested by multiple appearances to a range of early believers, including Paul (vv. 3–11).

Verse 12 indicates that while the Corinthians believe in the resurrection of Christ, in some way, they have misunderstood their own future resurrection. While some theologians have posited that an over-realized eschatology like that of Hymenaeus and Philetus in Ephesus blights them (2 Tim. 2:18), more likely they have syncretized the gospel of bodily postmortem existence for believers with the Greek understanding of resurrection as a purely spiritual experience.[38] While they accept Christ was raised (and so are believers, unlike those mentioned above), the Corinthians do not fully grasp that their own resurrection will involve the complete spiritual reanimation of their corpses.

Paul responds to their misunderstanding by reminding that Christ's resurrection anticipates their own bodily transformation. Working on the logic that if they are to be raised spiritually, then such a spiritual resurrection must be true of Christ, as Paul sees his resurrection as the first harvest to come (below). Working with this false assumption, he explains the futility and hopelessness of faith and mission if Christ had not been raised in a full bodily way (15:13–19).

In vv. 20–28, Paul explains that Christ was raised from the dead (bodily) and is the firstfruits of the resurrection of believers who have died in history. By him, the resurrection of the dead has come to all born of Adam who believe in the new Adam. Christ is now raised, but at his coming, "those who belong to Christ" (by faith implied, and having received the Spirit, cf. vv. 1–2) will also be raised. At this point, Christ will destroy all spiritual beings and humans that oppose God, including death, and hand them to the Father so that God is all in all.

---

37. Moo, *Romans*, 515. See my earlier discussion of Romans 8:10–11, chapter 3, "The Spirit Who Gives Life."

38. See Thiselton, *The First Epistle*, 1172, who summarizes a range of studies identifying a range of options, including that some in Corinth did not believe (1) in any postmortem existence, (2) that the resurrection had occurred (2 Tim. 2:18), or (3) in the resurrection of the body. I am persuaded by the view of Wright, who states that 15:12 refers to a "spiritual experience or event," and so they are "denying that there would be a future bodily resurrection." N. T. Wright, *The Resurrection of the Son of God*, COQG (London: SPCK, 2003), 316. See also pp. 32–84, which summarizes the Greco-Roman view that the Corinthians are importing. Here I diverge from Fee, *GEP*, 262, who sees it as an over-realized eschatology based on their view that as πνευματικοί, they had a "triumphalist, over-realized, and anti-physical spirituality." Fee, *GEP*, 100, 150, 824.

First Corinthians 15:29–32b speaks of the futility of present activities, such as various forms of baptism and the dangers and struggles of mission, if Christ (and so the dead believers) were not to be raised. If there is no bodily resurrection, believers may as well stop their baptismal practices, suffering for the gospel, and wasting their time engaging in mission, and enjoy life's pleasures without restraint.[39] However, as the dead are to be raised, as demonstrated by Christ's bodily resurrection, the Corinthians must stop debauching the body (vv. 32c–34; cf. 6:13–14).

In vv. 35–37, Paul likens the present body to a seed that dies and then grows into a plant. The type of plant or body produced by the seed is God's creative work. Paul extrapolates this into the various types of fleshly beings and astral bodies he created. God giving to each its own body and the image of growth implies the resurrectional work of God by his Spirit in creation (cf. Gen. 1).

Then, in vv. 42–49, Paul focuses on the effect of the resurrection. The seed in the passage is people's present bodies that are perishable, dishonorable, and weak due to sin and its inevitable consequences of decay and death. However, the body of the resurrected believer will be raised imperishable, in glory and power. The use of "power" in v. 43 draws our attention to God's creative action by the Spirit. The body is "a natural body" (v. 44), bearing the image of Adam's body, alive by God's breath yet dying due to Adam's sin. It is a body of dust, formed from dust (v. 45; cf. Gen. 2:7), animated by God's breath (his Spirit) yet subject to decay and death, to return to dust.

However, this body of dust will be raised as "a spiritual body" (v. 44).[40] To suggest Paul has in mind here a purely spiritual existence completely misses his point. It means that, as in the case of Christ's resurrection, the same body will rise fully animated by the Spirit, no longer infected with sin and subject to death and decay. This liberation is because "the last Adam became a life-giving spirit" (v. 45). This does not mean Jesus is no longer corporeal and is merely a spirit; Paul has refuted that idea earlier in the chapter. It means that by his Spirit, just as God breathed life into the earth-formed Adam (Gen. 2:7), and as he raised Jesus, God will raise the dead.[41] The description of Jesus as a "life-giving Spirit" is another one of the few

---

39. Fee rightly notes this is an oxymoron with power to shock the Corinthians away from a purely spiritual postmortem existence to a bodily one that is fully spiritual. Fee suggests that the new body is spiritual "in the sense that it belongs to the final world, the world of the Spirit, of which the Spirit also presently serves as God's down payment or firstfruits in the life of the believer." Fee, *GEP*, 263. While this is true, Paul is going beyond this to speak of the Spirit who raised Jesus, fully transforming the believers' bodies to be like his (remembering that Fee does not consider the Spirit raised Jesus; see earlier chapter 3, "The Spirit Who Gives Life").

40. Fee rightly calls this an oxymoron, that this links back to the contrast between πνευματικόν and ψυχικόν in 2:14–15. Fee, *GEP*, 263.

41. Fee, *GEP*, 265, notes that this reflects the language of Genesis 2:7 (LXX) and recalls God raising the dead in Ezekiel 37:14.

Pauline texts that blur the clear distinction made between Christ and the Spirit (esp. 2 Cor. 3:18).[42] This should not lead us to a binitarian understanding but shows the perfect unity of the work of Christ and the Spirit (and God the Father). It implies that Christ, through the Spirit, is the agent by which God raises the dead.[43]

The spiritual bodies of believers will be raised by God's agency, through Christ, by the Spirit. No longer blighted by sin, they will experience the fullness of God's Spirit, animating them not merely to spiritual life in a body of death nor some disembodied spiritual nirvana but eternal life in bodies radiating with the pure goodness and life-power of God.[44] There is a sequence—the natural body of dust (like a seed) and then the spiritual body (the fully formed plant that grows from the seed). This renewed living body will not bear the image of Adam but the new Adam,[45] Christ. Notably, Jesus here is described as a "man," implying he retains his incarnate state as human. Believers are "those of heaven" and will be transformed by the power of the Spirit to be like the resurrected man Jesus.

Verse 50 explains that flesh and blood cannot enter the final state of God's kingdom. This prohibition implies no fleshly creature subject to death and decay, including humankind, can do this.[46] Death cannot feature in the world to come. It must itself be destroyed, and Paul has already assured readers it will be (v. 26). That which is perishable cannot inherit the imperishable realm of God.

---

42.   Fee correctly says here, "Christ is not *the* Spirit." Fee, *GEP*, 266.

43.   I find it strange that Fee here acknowledges Christ's "function in this role [as 'life giving πνεῦμα'] will take place at the resurrection of believers," yet does not see the Spirit's agency in any way. Fee, *GEP*, 265.

44.   Here, I diverge from Fee, who writes, "The new body will be πνευματικόν, 'spiritual,' in the sense that it belongs to the final world, the world of the Spirit, of which the Spirit also presently serves as God's down payment or firstfruits in the life of the believer." Fee, *GEP*, 263. He also rejects the Spirit's role in the resurrection of Jesus and believers (p. 553), which I affirm (see chapter 3, "The Spirit Who Gives Life"). I believe it is spiritual because God, through Christ, and by the Spirit, raises believers and frees them forever from sins and its consequences, and fills them completely. I also think translating πνευματικόν as "supernatural" is flawed and loses the flesh-Spirit and natural-spiritual antitheses. Fee, *GEP*, 264. See also Habets, who says, "But one day we too will have a 'spiritual body' (15:44, 46), one like Christ, one in which the sovereignty of the Spirit will reign supreme." Habets, *Progressive Mystery*, 85.

45.   Fee's sharp distinction between the christological/ontological and soteriological aspects of Jesus as the last Adam is overstated. Christology and soteriology are intertwined in Paul's "in Christ" theology. While he is right to see it as secondary at one level, it becomes primary as believers are raised in Christ, who is the last Adam, and so in him resurrected humankind will fulfill the vocation of Adam. He rightly links this passage to vv. 21–22 but neglects the use of "in Christ" in v. 22. Fee, *GEP*, 264. See also Habets: "Rather than treat them separately or to disregard a *pneumatologia crucis* altogether, as has been common in classical Christology, a Spirit Christology holds them together, for one without the other is a distorted view of the cross work of the Trinitarian God." Habets, *Anointed Son*, 166.

46.   This then applies to animals, which are also liable to decay. If they are to exist eternally, they will need to be similarly transformed. This is not to be ruled out as many OT passages expect animals in the eschatological realm (e.g., Isa. 11:6–7; 65:25). The restoration of the cosmos portrayed in Romans 8:19–22 may include the resurrection of the animals of history.

To become imperishable, humankind must experience the mysterious moment and process of spiritual transformation (vv. 51–53). Some believers will be alive (not sleep) when Jesus returns, and believers who have died in the Lord will be resurrected. However, all the dead in Christ, and the living at his return, will be transformed. This metamorphosis will be instantaneous, at the last trumpet of God that heralds the end. The dead will be raised in a twinkling of an eye whereby their perishable and mortal bodies are imperishable and immortal.

At this point, the hopes of the prophets Isaiah and Hosea will be fulfilled. While people dine on the finest fare at God's great eschatological feast, God devours death in the victory of the resurrection. The sting of death is removed, and the law is no longer a force that enslaves people into sin and the knowledge of it (vv. 54–56; cf. Isa. 25:8; Hos. 13:14). Not surprisingly when one considers the gravity of what he has just shared, Paul ends with eucharist, crying out his thanks for God's victory given to believers in Jesus Christ their Lord (v. 57).

The final verse (v. 58) draws out the implication for life in the present. The beloved brothers and sisters of Corinth are to stand firm without compromising their faith in Christ crucified, buried, and risen. They must continue to abound in the work of the Lord, knowing that their labor in the Lord is not in vain—eternal life awaits. For this reason, they are to do as Paul does and continue to serve with all they have. It is implied they do so by the Spirit, who will complete their pneumaformation at the consummation.

Galatians 6:8

Paul urges the Galatians to sow to the Spirit and not the flesh.[47] That is, they are not to fall prey to the things listed in the works of the flesh in 5:19–21. Instead, they are to yield to the Spirit's work to produce in them the things listed in the fruit of the Spirit in Galatians 5:22–24.[48] Those who have the Spirit are led by the Spirit, walk in the Spirit, keep in step with the Spirit, and sow to the Spirit. Sealed with the Spirit, they will reap eternal life "from the same Spirit." Here, eternal life is granted as a further work of the Spirit.[49] In Ephesians 2:18, the Spirit is the means by which believers have access to the Father. Likely, Paul imagines their full access in the eschaton is through the same means.

---

47. I am not fully persuaded by Buchanan, who argues that flesh here refers not merely to individual flesh but to flesh in a cosmic sense. Although, overall, the theological point is reasonable. Buchanan, "Spirit," 180–82.

48. Fee rightly says, "To 'sow unto the Spirit' is but another way of pressing the imperatives, expressed and implied, that dominate vv. 16–26: 'walk by the Spirit,' 'being led by the Spirit,' bearing the 'fruit of the Spirit,' 'conforming one's life to the Spirit.'" Fee, *GEP*, 465. He also rightly repudiates the idea that the human spirit is in view.

49. Contra Fee, who constantly rejects the idea. Yes, it is God's work in Christ, but through the agency of the Spirit.

ETERNITY

Philippians 1:19–26

Paul states his knowledge (οἶδα) that his incarceration will turn out for "salvation" (σωτηρίαν) through the combined effects of the prayers of the Philippians and the help (or supply) of the Spirit of Jesus Christ. Scholars are divided concerning whether σωτηρίαν should be understood as "deliverance" from prison or eternal salvation. The latter is almost certainly correct, as Paul only ever uses σωτηρία of eternal deliverance.[50] Still, it is also a double entendre as, later in the passage, he speaks of his certainty of deliverance. Assuming this is correct, Paul considers that the Spirit will enable Paul to stand firm in the forthcoming trial. And ultimately the Spirit will bring him to eternal salvation.

Philippians 3:21

Philippians 3:20–21 complete a lovely sequence of transformational ideas implied across chapters 2–3 of the letter. In Philippians 2:6–8, Paul traces Christ's movement in his incarnation and service. First, Christ is the preexistent one who exists eternally "in the *form* [μορφή] of God" with the status of "equality with God" and all that implies. However, rather than exploit his divine status and power to subjugate humankind, he took on the form (μορφή) of a slave, in human form (σχῆμα), emptying himself for the world. This self-emptying describes his life of service to the point of death succinctly. The Son of the God of the world, fully God, humbled himself into full humanness and service to the point of death by crucifixion. Elsewhere Paul explains that this death deals with the problem of sin, decay, and death; here, he assumes the Philippians know this. Consequently, God raised Jesus and exalted him to supreme lordship over the cosmos. So, the one in the form of God is now the world's Savior who will continue his eternal divine state as a human!

Then, in Philippians 3, combatting Judaizing challenges, Paul traces the same movement of Jesus concerning his own life. He elevates his status regarding his Jewish heritage—he has greater claims before God than any of his generation. Yet, he then writes them off as rubbish (or dung) and loss and speaks of his longing to deepen his connection with Christ (3:4–9). He states his desire to know him, to live his life of present suffering and even death by the power that raised Christ from the dead—the Spirit. Paul wants to be conformed (συμμορφίζω) to Christ and participate in his suffering and death (3:10). He speaks of his hope of the resurrection, how he presses on toward that prize for which he is called in Christ and urges the Philippians to take on the same mindset (3:1–17).

---

50.   Keown, *Philippians*, 1:227–30.

In Philippians 3:20–21, believers (we) are citizens of heaven. From there, Jesus the Savior is coming, and believers wait and yearn for this day. In the present, they live on in bodies of humiliation. This attributive genitive describes bodies beset with death, subject to decay, and destined for destruction.[51] However, when Jesus returns, they will not end up being destroyed for all eternity. Christ will transform (μετασχηματίζω) believers so that their bodies conform (σύμμορφος) to his glorious body. Notably, Paul here draws language connected to the Christ-hymn (μορφη, σχῆμα) to link the transformation of believers to that of Christ's descent into human form and "slavery." Having been conformed to Christ-in-his-incarnation (3:10), believers experience the "ascent" into bodies with the same glory as the resurrected Jesus. This metamorphosis is the same process described more fully in 1 Corinthians 15. Jesus will do this because of his unrivaled power to subjugate all things (v. 21). This speaks of Jesus's spiritual power to bring the whole creation under God's unopposed rule and transform people to imperishability and immortality.

1 Corinthians 13:13

Paul ends his lovely "aside" on "the most excellent way," love (1 Cor. 12:31–13:13) with one of the great maxims in his letters. It draws together the three great virtues of Paul: "But now, these three things remain: faith, hope, love. But the greatest of these is love" (my translation).[52]

The context is eschatological.[53] In v. 8, Paul indicates that the gifts mentioned (prophecy, tongues, and knowledge)[54] will pass away at the culmination of the age. Verse 9 explains that in the present age, knowledge and prophecy are partial—fragmentary glimpses of the fullness of knowledge to be experienced in the eschaton. In v. 10, Paul speaks of the perfect (τέλειος) coming. When the new era begins and the world is fully renewed, that which is incomplete will pass away, superseded by the perfect and completeness of the age to come when God is all in all.

Verses 11–12 use two analogies to contrast the two ages. First, using the first-person singular, Paul likens life in the present age to childhood. Although he is a believer with the Spirit, living in the present age is like Paul's childhood when he was immature in his speaking and thought. Life eternal is likened to mature adulthood, whereby those childish ways are given up. Verse 12 likens

---

51. Keown, *Philippians*, 2:280–83.

52. The triad is found in Paul in Rom. 5:1–5; Gal. 5:5–6; Eph. 4:2–5; Col. 1:4–5; 1 Thess. 1:3; 5:8. He also notes Heb. 6:10–12; 10:22–24; 1 Peter 1:3–8; Barn. 1:4; 11:8; Pol, *Phil.* 3:2–3. See further Fee, *GEP*, 212n505. See also faith and love together (1 Cor. 13:2; 2 Cor. 8:7; Eph. 1:15; 3:17; 6:23; 1 Thess. 3:6; 2 Thess. 1:3; 1 Tim. 1:5, 14; 2:15; 4:12; 6:10; 2 Tim. 2:22; 3:10; Titus 2:2; 3:15; Philem. 5; also, James 2:5; Rev. 2:19). See also faith and hope together (2 Cor. 10:15; Col. 1:23; also 1 Peter 1:21).

53. See Fee, *GEP*, 211–14, for a discussion of the complexities. He is right that "and now" is eschatological referring to "the present state of things"—now that Christ has come.

54. This is not knowledge per se, but a special ability to impart a "word of knowledge." See 12:8.

present life to seeing a reflection in a mirror dimly or as in a riddle.[55] This idea relies on recognizing that ancient mirrors gave a poor-quality reflection. Life in the eschaton will involve seeing "face to face," with full knowledge. He concludes by stating that presently he has partial knowledge, but in the eschaton, he will know fully, even as now he is fully known by God.

This contrast of now . . . then carries into v. 13. Paul sees the three great virtues as a concise summary of the Christian life. By faith, believers are declared righteous in God's sight. They must continue to walk in faith to their dying breath or the return of Christ. However, as the previous verse indicates, faith will be superseded by knowledge in the age to come. In the present age, hope sustains believers as they yearn for the return of Christ, their resurrection and eternal life, and the renewal of the cosmos. Once in the new, all hopes will be fulfilled, and hope will be unnecessary. The third virtue, love, will go on as the defining virtue of God, the Son, the Spirit, and his people. Just as Father, Son, and Spirit existed in pure love prior to creation, believers will exist in an environment of complete love.[56]

Love, then, is the culmination point of the process of pneumaformation. The Spirit raises believers, and the supreme virtue of God will envelop them and radiate from them without hindrance. They will be love incarnate, as Christ always was, is, and ever will be. The undefiled creation will hum with love. All idolatry will be defeated, and believers' love for God will be absolute and unhindered. They will live to serve and will love to do so. Nothing will hold them back. They will love one another with an untarnished love, sincere, pure, and whole. Seeing others flourish will be their reason for living. They will no longer need to love the lost, for those among the lost who want to be found will be so. They will love themselves, completely whole in their souls, without doubt, self-recrimination, and feelings of worthlessness. Their love for creation will be complete as they live in a restored world free from its bondage to decay and death.

However, we are not there yet. In the meantime, Paul subtly urges those being pneumaformed to continue believing and hoping while loving. God will enable them to do so by his Spirit. And, by the Spirit, they yearn in hope for the day. The Spirit is deposited in their beings, their hearts sealed and signed, and this Spirit will meet them in their moment of need with hope. The Spirit is a deposit of the eschaton in them. They eagerly await Christ's return, and the present deposit of the Spirit enables and strengthens them to do so

---

55.   On the options here and the background in Numbers 12:6–8, see Garland, *1 Corinthians*, 623–25.

56.   Fee discusses the meaning of "remain" or "abide." He correctly states, "Along with the gifts, these three 'remain' as long as present life endures. But in the immediate context the greatest of these is love, both because the emphasis lies here, with the ethical dimension of life in Christ, and because it precedes them on into the final glory. Love will still remain when faith and hope have been realized; hence 'the greatest of these is love.'" See Fee, *GEP*, 213.

while at the same time giving a hopeful glimpse of what God has prepared for those who love him.

CONCLUSION

Pneumaformity is a past event in that, at the moment of conversion, the Spirit has entered a person's life and begun their transformation. Pneumaformity is also a present process whereby as believers walk with God by the Spirit, they are transformed to be more fully God's image bearers. Pneumaformity is a future moment when the believers meet Jesus as he returns and they experience their final transformation.

This future experience is believers' full and complete metamorphosis. The mind is fully transformed—their thinking, feeling, imagining, and relating are aligned with God's mind. This transformation includes their hearts being totally yielded to God who forever shapes their feelings, attitudes, and motivations. Final pneumaformation sees the mortal, perishable body of humiliation set free from its bondage to decay and made forever imperishable and immortal. The desires of the flesh no longer war against those of the Spirit; believers are finally freed from sin and all its consequences. They *are* people of the Spirit.

Final pneumaformation is not merely an individual experience. Those faithful to the end are freed from all that previously divided them, oppression is ended, and they find that God is all in all. God's people will be his children in the fullest and best sense, the body of Christ will be free of all cancer and illness, and the temple of the Spirit will be utterly pure in every sense of the word.

But wait, there is more—the whole creation will also be liberated from its bondage to decay and death. The world will be radiant with life; death will be no more. God and his people will inhabit creation in complete harmony, living united in the Spirit, loving sincerely, and the world will know God's shalom in every way.

In the meantime, those being pneumaformed, led by the Spirit, must work with all they have in submission to God, seeking to see others pneumaformed and expressing pneumaformation in family, church, and world. We do so always encouraging one another as we await the day when Jesus returns, evil is destroyed, the world is renewed, and God's Spirit-filled people dwell with him and Jesus the Son forever.

CHAPTER 12

LIVING BY THE SPIRIT

Any such biblical study must end with, So what? In this case, the answer is obvious. Christian life for Paul is living in total submission to God's Spirit. For Paul, there is no other life. I can almost hear him say, "Children of God. Be led by the Spirit!"

As such, we who are God's people must live our lives intentionally at all times, whether awake or asleep. From the second we hear God's call in Christ, believe, and receive the Spirit, we live by the Spirit's impulses. There is simply no other way to live. All other roads lead to death. Our existence is to be pneumaformed, with us as willing participants in God's redemptive purposes flowing through creation by his Spirit. To be so is to be Christoformed, cruciformed, and theoformed. What does such a pneumaform life look like?

UNDERSTANDING THE WORK OF THE SPIRIT

We understand the essence of what the Spirit is doing in us. The Spirit is not a magical being performing miracles at our behest, making us wealthy, or fulfilling our worldly potential. More than such profane things, the Spirit is doing that of God and his Son, and by the Spirit, God is transforming us into the image of the one true image bearer, Jesus Christ. For such a transformation, we have been predestined before the world's creation, called to believe and be his people, and justified (declared righteous). Ultimately, when our pneumaformation is complete, we will experience his glorification.

As the Spirit is that of Jesus, Jesus is our everything. As such, the Spirit in us will move us to seek him, gain him, be found in him, know him, and participate in the fullness of his experience of being a Spirit-led human, including suffering and death. Like Paul, while we do not seek suffering as we serve God, we delight in participating in suffering—not for its sake but for his sake, giving our mortal existence to his service, rejoicing in persecution, for through it, we are being conformed to his death. We delight in the struggle because we know that our citizenship is in heaven, and here on earth, as we toil in the work of the Lord, our Savior is coming. In the twinkling of an eye, he will transform our humble, decay-ridden bodies into glorious bodies like his.

HEEDING THE CALL OF THE SPIRIT

Keeping in step with the Spirit involves hearing the summons of God by the Spirit in and through his creation, his call to us through his Word, and then yielding to it. The first moment may come when a faithful believer preaches the Word. Alternatively and rarely, God might meet us dynamically and decisively by his sovereign power as he did Paul. Either way, true hearers and seers *believe* in God, his Son, and his Spirit. Believing means yielding to Christ's lordship, accepting his invitation into his life, gratefully trusting in him to be our Savior, and committing to his service. Such faith is not a one-off moment at an altar call or saying the sinner's prayer. It is an allegiance and commitment to obedience that, while it may waver at times, holds firm from conversion to the day we meet Jesus face to face. This faith, itself a gift of God, will be sustained by the Spirit in the willing. As such, we must be willing to be willing.[1]

ACKNOWLEDGING THE SPIRIT

The pneumaform life acknowledges the Spirit's presence from beginning to end. So, we regularly pause and acknowledge that God, in his mercy and grace, through his Son, has sent his Spirit into our beings and allowed us to share in Christ's anointing. Doing so, he has sealed us for the day of redemption, and the Spirit is the guarantee and firstfruit of our total transformation when God will complete his mission of cosmic restoration. We acknowledge that in Christ, by the Spirit, we are justified and seek to live righteous lives; cleansed, to live in purity; and sanctified, to be holy as he is holy. We care deeply about who we are, for our bodies are temples of the Spirit, and we behave accordingly. Often, we do this more when we become anxious and fearful. Knowing God is near to hear our prayer, we bring him our anxieties, and he meets us with a peace that surpasses all understanding. He reshapes us and history in conformity with his will, and we have peace.

LIVING TOGETHER WITH OTHERS BY THE SPIRIT

The pneumaformed push against the rampant individualism of the age and acknowledge that when we were redeemed from sin and its horrific consequences, we were swept up into God and his people. We are adopted into his family, and others, whatever ethnicity, gender, and social class, are our brothers and sisters. There is no slave and free; we are all citizens. We show no prejudice. We repudiate stereotypes, sexism, racism, ethnocentricism, and

---

1. I heard this in a sermon in my earliest days of my faith. It was by an African preacher I would acknowledge if I could.

elitism. While there are leaders, we are never comfortable with a clergy-laity divide.

Our pattern is that of Christ, who emptied himself for the world despite being God the Son, the clergyman of all clergy people. We commit to other believers, for Jesus has given his life for them. We recognize that we are a people first and individuals second. By the Spirit, we commit to engaging with other Christians, being involved in church (despite the pain that can bring), and working with our gifts to see God's family, the body of Christ, the temple of the Spirit, grow. We push against denominationalism and factionalism, the brokenness that pervades God's family. We expose injustice, oppression, and elitism in our church by seeking humility and Spirit-impelled service of others. We seek out the marginalized and bring them in. We remember the summons of the Spirit for the "strong" to curb their liberty out of love for the "weak." We thus expose injustice and oppression and, in humility, esteem others above ourselves. Always living out of the gospel and where need be, defending it, we work for unity with love.

PRAISE BY THE SPIRIT

We constantly pause, especially during our busy days, yield afresh to the Spirit's yearning toward God, and join the Son and Spirit's intercession for the world. We self-consciously quiet ourselves and allow God's Son, by the Spirit, to lead us in worship, praise, gratitude, confession, prayer, song, and supplication. We move beyond such things as church political intrigue; "Corinthianizing" by following this or that preacher, theologian, or tradition; the overemphasis on singing or the style of song; the supposed deficiencies in denominational expressions of the sacraments; problems with the lectionary; liturgical imbalances; concerns at the decline of the church; minor theological disagreements; and our previous hurts from immature Christians or because of our immaturity at the time.

Instead, by the Spirit, we do what we were created to do: praise and adore our Triune God. We love God—Father, Son, and Spirit. We delight in worship, hunger for more prayer, rush to prayer meetings, thank God even in suffering, and rejoice in the Lord always. We dispense with those idols stealing our hearts and time, connecting by the Spirit to the one who created us. As we leave the physical church, we continue to worship in our service, pouring ourselves out as drink offerings on the sacrifice of others. We come together again in homes, church buildings, prayer meetings, and more to be replenished in worship again.

NOT BY THE FLESH BUT BY THE SPIRIT

Being formed by the Spirit, as we seek conformity with Christ, we determine to live by the Spirit and not the flesh and its wicked allies—evil spirits, the corporate evil of the fallen world. Knowing God loves us as his children, unafraid and yearning for his discipline, we ask God, in Christ, by the Spirit, to reveal our fleshliness. We want him to expose aspects of our life that are corrupted. We want the Spirit to make us aware of the sins and additions that developed within us as as result of our experiences in a broken and, at times, hostile world. We determine never to grieve or quench the Spirit with fleshly immaturity. We pray fervently, in and by the Spirit, that he will give us victory over these works of the flesh, our selfishness, and our desire for our way and that he cultivates in us the fruit of the Spirit. We ask him to expose false ideas and keep us in line with the gospel. We never give up on joyfully and gratefully entering into this process day by day. However, we don't take this struggle on alone; we seek fellowship with others, prayer, and Spirit-led counseling, unafraid to humble ourselves so that we can be the people God created us to be. We do all this because "it requires ongoing attention, discernment, and commitment to continue to lay aside what is not from the Spirit and to take up what is."[2]

HEARING THE SPIRIT

As those determined to live by the Spirit, we devote ourselves to learning to hear the Spirit. Hearing the Spirit is one of the challenges of being a pneumaform believer. The world, especially in its cities, is full of noise, and we grow up bombarded by sounds and images. We are surrounded by audio and audio-visual stimuli. God's Spirit is a breath, so we must learn to hear his wordless breathings in our beings. He inhabits the center of our beings, which we know to be our minds. Hence, often he speaks by way of what seems a thought (rather than a voice). We must become trained to recognize these murmurings.

Key to this are the Scriptures written by Spirit-filled people through whom God breathed his Word into the writings that shape us. We read them as Spirit-filled people, so each time we do so, there is an encounter between God, the Word, the Spirit, and us. The breathed thoughts of God never violate the breathed canon, which is to be read through the lens of the one of whom God said, "Listen to him."[3]

As pneumaform people, we live in the Scriptures; we delight in reading them with others and hearing fresh perspectives. We listen and watch great sermons, biblical exposition, and theological explorations premised on Scripture. We test everything against Scripture and consider it in prayer with others. The most important parts of our daily prayer times are reading, studying, reflecting on the Word, sitting in silence, and listening to God's voice. We should do this with a pen, ready to write down what he tells us. We do this not only alone but also with others, knowing that God has called us to be a

---

2.   DeSilva, *Transformation*, 54. He rightly notes it takes the perservance of an athlete, as in the case of Paul (1 Cor. 9:24–27).

3.   See also the excellent comments of deSilva, *Transformation*, 56, concerning spiritual disciplines of reading Scripture, prayer, self-examining, and holy conferencing.

people. The pneumaformed are those who rise and allow the Spirit's guidance to shape their day.

We also delight in the sacraments, especially baptism and the Lord's Supper. While Spirit baptism is determinative for Paul, he never for a moment imagined believers forsaking water baptism. We have a fresh encounter with God's Spirit when we are baptized. When we observe another's baptism, the death, burial, and resurrection of ourselves and other believers are reenacted. The Spirit reminds us of who we are in Christ and summons the not-yet-saved to believe. The Lord's Supper, for Paul, is to be celebrated every time we meet. It is a proclamation of the death of Jesus. We experience God by the Spirit, renewing us by his grace and reminding us of the centrality of Christ and him crucified.

We also reject the false dualism of mind and heart that can deceive us into thinking we only hear and feel the Spirit in our feelings or emotions. The pneumaformed believer knows that as we walk with God, the Spirit permeates our every part. He shapes our thinking so that as we mature, we begin to think the thoughts of God. Yet this never leads us to arrogance, for we are people dependent on God's breath and Spirit for physical and spiritual life. He moves in our emotions and feelings for sure, but consistently with our minds and in line with his Word. He knows our minds and thoughts. He fills our bodies, for we are embodied people. We have a holistic understanding of the Spirit's presence and lead and walk in it with every part of our being. He inhabits us and is sustaining and shaping the world around us. Hence, we sense him moving in others, in situations, and in circumstances.

Furthermore, God knows us in our individuality and meets us that way. As such, we must beware of taking our own experiences of the Spirit and making them determinative. We resist that, knowing the wind blows where it wills it wills. God meets us in our individuality and personality; how naive would we be to think he encounters others in an identical way and gives them exactly the same experience!

Knowing that the Spirit inhabits our whole being and God meets us as we are means that we don't have to continually seek the next spiritual buzz or high. God is with us during those times of ecstatic experience; he is equally with us in moments of pain and when he seems far away. Indeed, we can relax and allow the Spirit to testify to our own spirits that we are God's children. We then live out the life he calls us to confidently, yet humbly, individually and corporately.

SUFFERING IN THE SPIRIT

Pneumaformed people recognize that their path to glorification is paved with suffering. One of the hideous misunderstandings of the Spirit in the church today is the idea that if we just have enough faith and are led by the Spirit, we will be freed from suffering—we will be prosperous and always healthy. That all that is needed is faith, obedience, and the Spirit.

Believers are still humans, broken and sinful, living in a world blighted by sin and corruption. We suffer the same things as others—relational problems, sickness, mental ill-health, injuries, tragedies, economic challenges, and death. Such suffering is the human condition. In addition, as I showed in chapter 8, living by the Spirit brings further suffering, not less. There is the pain of conversion, the struggle to live by Spirit and not flesh, the challenges of church life, and the rejection and persecution that comes with sharing the faith. Yet, those seeking pneumaformity recognize that through these experiences, God shapes us into the image of his Son as we walk in the pattern of his Son. As we mature, we boast in our hardships, not before others (unless forced to, as was Paul to the Corinthians). We pray in suffering and know God sometimes intervenes and delivers us, he always strengthens and comforts us, and that he will bring us through to eternal life. The Spirit is God's limitless resource as we take up our crosses and follow Jesus. We also know that we do not suffer alone, for we are part of a great family, which, if it is pneumaform, will surround us with God's love, comfort, and strength. We know God will bring us through.

ENGAGING IN MISSION BY THE SPIRIT

Pneumaformity calls us to participate in God's mission by being obedient to our call and using our gifts with a posture of love. Christ is redeeming a whole world, and that is a big job. It will involve us finding our identity in him and walking with him in the life he has for us. Our vocations in this will vary, with many rising daily to do what appear to be mundane jobs. They are not, for God has led people into these spaces. In the wide range of places God's people are found, they build, shape, and restore God's world.

Our marriages and families are to be pneumaformed. If we are married Christian men, we are not concerned about debates over the meaning of *kephalē*, the submission of women, or who can and cannot preach and lead. Instead, we focus on our call to love our wives as Christ loved the church and gave himself for them. We honor the giftedness of other image bearers and are always teachable. We take our job of bringing our children up in the Lord seriously. Living faithfully with our spouses by the Spirit, we lovingly raise our children to desire pneumaformity. We share the story of our amazing God and his world in our homes. We invite our family members to be God's children. We have no control over their response other than to pray and share the gospel with godly character, winsome conversation, and deeds of grace.

And if we are single, we emulate Christ and Paul, seek celibate purity, delight in the gift of singleness, and live to serve God, his people, and his mission. Where a believer is married to an unbeliever, for whatever reason, the pneumaformed believer will be faithful and loving toward the unbeliever.

Those who have the privilege of a full-time role serving God in a church or one of its many offshoot organizations (as is my privilege) are to do so with the posture of Christ—humility, servanthood, selflessness, sacrifice, suffering—love. Knowing this is God's creation and realizing the Spirit's work is to reconcile it, we care for creation. We spend ourselves on behalf of others that they may know God's joy.

Knowing God has exalted Jesus to the highest place so that the world might yield to him as Lord, we join God's mission to save those who do not believe. We love, befriend, serve, and do good work among them. We pray for them to open their hearts to the gospel. We also pray for the right way to share God's Word with them and then, listening to the Spirit, we share Christ with them as led. On a Sunday, while we give our full attention to those who fill the church's pews, we also notice the empty seats and pray and work for them to be filled.

HOPING IN THE SPIRIT

Pneumaform people yearn with great eagerness for Christ's return. We look forward to that day. We feel the tug of eternity in our hearts and grieve the delay. But as Paul's friend Peter said, we count the delay of Christ's return as his patience, for he wants all to come to repentance and the knowledge of the truth. And when he comes, we will be completed. Sin will be ripped out of us, corruption obliterated, decay halted, and we will be fully alive in him. The world will be restored, and we will know the fullness of our God, his Son, the Spirit, and a restored world.

In the meantime, we allow the Spirit to lift our hearts upwards toward our heavenly home, and we continue to do his work here. May God fill us with his Spirit so we can walk in the fullness of life he has for us. *Maranatha*, our Lord, come! In Christ's name, by the Spirit, Amen!

APPENDIX 1

OTHER TERMS USED TO TRANSLATE רוּחַ IN THE LXX

Sometimes instead of πνεῦμα, the LXX opts for other terms for רוּחַ. These include δειλινός, "the afternoon, the windy cool of the day" (Gen. 3:8); ἐρίζουσαι, "quarreling" for "bitterness of spirit" (Gen. 26:35); ὀλιγοψυχίας, "small souled, fainthearted" for a "broken spirit" (Exod. 6:9; 1QS XI, 1), and similarly, ὀλιγόψυχος (Prov. 18:14; Isa. 54:6); commonly ἄνεμος, "wind" (Exod. 10:13, 19; 14:23; 2 Kgdms. 22:11; 1 Chron. 9:18; Job 21:18; 28:25; Pss. 1:4; 17:11 [18:10 EVV]; 17:43 [18:32 EVV]; 34:5 [35:5 EVV]; 82:14 [83:13 EVV]; 134:7 [135:7 EVV]; Prov. 11:29; 25:14, 23; 27:16; 30:4; Eccl. 5:16; 11:4; Zech. 2:6; 6:5; Isa. 17:13; 41:16; 57:13; 64:6; Jer. 5:13; 13:24; 14:6; 18:17; 22:22; 25:16 [49:36 EVV]; Ezek. 5:10, 12; 12:14; 17:10, 21; 19:12; Dan. 8:8; 11:4); καρδία, "heart" (Exod. 35:21; Ezek. 13:3); φρόνησις, "wisdom, intelligence" (Judg. 5:1); ἡ σκληρὰ ἡμέρα, "who has had a hard day" for "troubled in spirit" (1 Sam. 1:15); ἐξ ἑαυτῆς ἐγένετο, "she was beside herself" because of the absence of breath (2 Kgdms. 22:16; 3 Kgdms. 10:5; 2 Chron. 9:4); θυμός, "anger" (Job 6:4, 15:13; Prov. 17:27; 29:11; 59:19; Zech. 6:8; Ezek. 39:29); similarly, θυμόω, "angry" (Job 21:4); ψυχή, "soul" (Job 7:11); ἀναπνέω, "draw breath, revive" (Job 9:18); ἔμπνευσις, "breathing" (Ps. 17:16 [18:15 EVV]); στόμα, "mouth" (Ps. 31:2 [32:2 EVV]); καταιγίς, "squall, storm" (Ps. 54:9 [55:8 EVV]); πνοή, "breath" (Prov. 1:23; 11:13; Isa. 38:16; 57:15; Ezek. 13:13); ὕβρις, "arrogance" (Prov. 16:18); ταπεινόω, "lowly in spirit, humble" (Prov. 16:19; 29:23); νοῦς, "mind" (Isa. 40:13); ἀνεμόφθορος, "blasted by the wind" (Hos. 8:7); πνευματοφόρος, "bearing the divine spirit" (Hos. 9:7). Commonly, רוּחַ is not translated in the Greek (1 Kgdms. 18:10; Job 6:26; 19:17; 21:4; 26:13; 30:15; Prov. 14:29; 15:13; 16:2, 32; 17:22, 27; 25:28; Isa. 31:3; 32:2; 40:7; 41:29; 66:3; Jer. 10:13; Ezek. 42:16, 17, 18, 19, 20; Dan. 2:1). Some LXX texts include πνεῦμα without Hebrew equivalence (Num. 23:7; 2 Kgdms. 13:21, 39; Job 7:15; 13:25; Zech. 1:6; Isa. 38:12; Jer. 52:23; Dan. 3:39, 50, 65, 86; 5:4, 12, 23; 6:4; 10:8, 17).

425

πνεῦμα AND THE SPIRIT IN JEWISH LITERATURE

Aside from those situations where πνεῦμα is used for the Spirit of God, there is a range of other uses in Jewish literature.

πνεῦμα is an essential element of creation (Sib. Or. 8:451). For Philo, the term is used of air (*Opif.* 29), which is the breath of God (*Opif.* 30; see also *Cher.* 111; *Sacr.* 97; *Gig.* 10; *Ebr.* 106; *Her.* 208).[1] Philo speaks of the air flowing over the earth, the third element with water and earth (*Gig.* 22).

It is used for spiritual beings in heaven (1 En. 15:7, 8, 10), all heavenly spirits (T. Ab. (A) 4:9), the spirits of the air (T. Sol. 16:3; 18:3; 22:1), and invisible spirits (T. Levi 4:1). Spirits are like air (T. Sol. 24:4). Similarly, a spirit like a wind, the spirit of the wind (T. Sol. 22:3, 10, 13, 15).

Angels are spirits (Ps. 103:4 [104:4 EVV]), or spiritual beings (Odes Sol. 7:20; 8:65, 86). Job speaks of a spirit beyond understanding (Job 20:3). Angels are spirits who minister to God (1 En. 19:1; 20:3; Jub. 2:2). There are angels of the spirit of fire; angels of the spirit of the winds; angels of the spirit of the clouds, darkness, snow, hail, and frost; angels of the spirits of cold, heat, winter, spring, harvest, and summer (Jub. 2:2). There is also an angel of the Holy Spirit (Mart. Ascen. Isa. 3:16). Similar is the idea of spirits of those bringing God's judgment (T. Levi 3:2).

In the pseudepigraphal writings, πνεῦμα is used widely for inimical spiritual powers. Demons used to be spiritual (1 En. 15:4, 6). It is employed for evil spirits, deceitful spirits, spirits of error; spirits from Beliar; spirits from Satan; unclean spirits; a three-pronged dragon spirit; other dragon-like spirits; Ruax; a spirit in Arabia (Ephippas), and a hostile winged spirit (1 En. 15:9; Apoc. Dan 12:1; T. Reu. 2:1, 2, 3; 3:2; T. Sim. 3:5; 4:9; T. Levi 3:3; 5:6; 18:12; T. Jud. 16:1; T. Iss. 7:7; T. Zeb. 9:7; T. Dan 1:7; 5:5; 6:1; T. Naph. 3:3; T. Ash. 6:5; T. Jos. 7:4; T. Benj. 3:3, 4; 5:2; T. Sol. 3:7; 8:1; 11:1; 12:2; 13:6; 14:2, 4, 6, 7; 15:1, 8, 11, 15; 16:1; 17:1; 18:4; 22:2, 12, 15, 17, 19; 24:2, 4; 25:2; Apoc. Mos. 32; Josephus, *Ant.* 6.211, 214, 223; *J.W.* 7:185; *m. Sabb.* 2:5A; *m. Erub.* 4:1B; *m. Ker.* 1:1F;

---

1.   Philo also cites Heraclitus's view that breath is the soul. Philo, *Aet.* 111.

1QapGen ar XX, 16, 20, 25, 28, 29). A spirit can be made into a body (T. Sol. 4:4). Beliar is spirit (T. Benj. 6:1), as is Satan (T. Job 27:2). Josephus speaks of soldiers inspired by the spirit of Arēs, god of destruction (J. W. 3:92).

Sometimes πνεῦμα refers to a negative spiritual influence including a spirit of jealousy (Num. 5:14, 30); a "different spirit" in Caleb (Num. 14:24; cf. 2 Cor. 11:4); a spirit of straying (Isa. 19:14); an evil, deceitful, wicked, or unclean spirit (Judg. 9:23; 1 Kgdms. 16:14–16, 23; 19:9; 2 Kgdms. 22:21–22; 4 Kgdms. 19:7; 2 Chron. 18:20–23; Tob. 6:8; Job 4:15; Zech. 13:2; Isa. 37:7; Jer. 4:11; T. Ash. 1:9; 1QS IV, 9; 1QS V, 26); a hardened spirit (Deut. 2:30); a spirit of promiscuity or fornication (Hos. 4:12; 5:4; T. Reu. 3:3; 5:3; T. Levi 9:9; T. Jud. 13:3; 14:2; T. Dan 5:6; Mart. Ascen. Isa. 3:28); a spirit of stupor or deep sleep (Isa. 29:10); a spirit of weariness (Isa. 61:3; Bar. 3:1); a spirit of error (Pss. Sol. 8:14); a frenzied spirit (Sib. Or. Frag. 3:40); a spirit of procreation and intercourse (T. Reu. 2:8); a spirit of sleep (T. Reu. 3:1); a necromancer or medium (m. Sanh. 7:4 D; m. Ker. 1:1 F; cf. Lev. 20:6); a spirit of desertion (1QS VIII, 12); a stray spirit (1QS iX, 3). A flawed person has a spirit of something false, or their spirit projects a negative attribute such as "arrogance of spirit" (Eccl. 7:9). An arrogant person is haughty of spirit (1QS XI, 1).

In the Pseudepigrapha, these are actual spirits: a spirit of instiability (T. Reu. 3:4), of strife (T. Reu. 3:4), of flattery (T. Reu. 3:4), of trickery (T. Reu. 3:4), of arrogance (T. Reu. 3:5), of lying (T. Reu. 3:5), of injustice (T. Reu. 3:6), of jealousy (T. Sim. 2:7; T. Dan 1:6), of deceit and jealousy (T. Sim. 3:1), of envy (T. Sim. 4:7; T. Jud. 13:3), of error (T. Sim. 6:6; T. Levi 3:3; 14:8; T. Jud. 20:1; 25:3; T. Iss. 4:4; T. Zeb. 9:8; T. Ash. 6:2; Mart. Ascen. Isa. 3:28), a spirit of unrighteousness (T. Levi 16:7), a spirit of contention (T. Levi 16:7), a spirit of desire (T. Jud. 16:1), a spirit of debauchery (T. Jud. 16:1), a spirit of sensuality (T. Jud. 16:1), a spirit of greed (T. Jud. 16:1), a spirit of pretension (T. Dan 1:6), a spirit of anger (T. Dan 1:8; 2:1, 4; 3:6; 4:5), a spirit of falsehood (T. Dan 2:1), a spirit of hatred (T. Gad 1:9; 3:1; 4:7; 6:2). Death is a high spirit (T. Ab. (B) 13:7). Others include deception (T. Sol. 8:3), strife (T. Sol. 8:3), fate (T. Sol. 8:3), distress (T. Sol. 8:3), error (T. Sol. 8:3), power (T. Sol. 8:3), the worst (T. Sol. 8:4), murder (T. Sol. 9:5), a spirit of vainglory (Mart. Ascen. Isa. 3:28), and the Spirit of the love of money (Mart. Ascen. Isa. 3:28).

πνεῦμα can be used for the spirits of all creatures on heaven and earth (Jub. 2:2). It can more specifically refer to the spirit of a person or people (Judg. 8:3; 15:19; 1 Kgdms. 30:12; 2 Kgdms. 13:21, 39; 3 Kgdms. 20:4–5; 1 Chron. 5:26; 28:16; 2 Chron. 36:22; 1 Esd. 2:1, 5; 2 Esd. 1:1, 5; Esther 5:1e; Jdt. 7:19; 1 Macc. 13:7; 2 Macc. 7:23; 14:46; 3 Macc. 6:24; Pss. 76:7 [77:6 EVV]; 77:8 [78:8 EVV]; 105:33 [106:33 EVV]; 141:4 [142:3 EVV]; 142:4 [143:4 EVV]; 142:7 [143:7 EVV]; Job 10:12; Eccl. 3:21; 7:9; 10:4; Wis. 1:5; Sir. 9:9; Mal. 2:15, 16; Isa. 19:3; Jer. 28:11; Ezek. 20:31; 21:12; Dan. 2:3; 3:86 LXX; 10:8 LXX; 1 En. 13:6; Odes Sol. 5:9; 9:27; 11:12; 5:3; 7:23; T. Sim. 5:1; T. Naph. 2:2; T. Jos. 7:2; T. Job 43:2; T. Ab. (A) 17:3, 19; 18:8; 19:2; T. Sol. 16:5; 26:7; Jos. Asen. 19:3; Apoc.

Mos. 42; Jan. Jam. 5:39; Hist. Rech. 2:2; 6:7; T. Gad 5:9; Josephus, *Ant.* 11:241; *m. Yoma* 8:5A; Philo, *Spec.* 1:277).

In regard to people, at times πνεῦμα has the sense of courage (Josh. 2:11; Esther 8:12m; 1 Macc. 13:7; 2 Macc. 6:24; Pss. 75:13 [76:12 EVV]; 76:4 [77:3 EVV]; Hag. 1:14; Dan. 10:17). God is the Lord of the Spirits of all people and all things (2 Macc. 3:24). The alternative, being humbled, crushed, or broken of spirit, is also a common thread (Pss. 33:19 [34:18 EVV]; 50:19 [51:17 EVV]; Prov. 15:4; Dan. 3:39 LXX)

The spirits of people are given by the creator (Sib. Or. Frag. 1:5). Fourth Maccabees 7:14 speaks of being young again in spirit through reason. In the Pseudepigrapha, it is also used for the spirits of giants conceived of angels and women (1 En. 15:11, 12). In Job, the spirit is distinguished from the bones (Job 7:15). It is also employed of the spirits of the souls of the dead (1 En. 22:3, 6–7, 9, 11–13). The resurrection of the dead is through breath given to them (Sib. Or. 2:221, see also Sib. Or. 4:46, 189). In eternal destruction, the wicked are burned in spirit forever (Sib. Or. 7:124).

Very commonly, πνεῦμα refers to the wind, although often this has a double meaning, a God-sent wind or a spirit (3 Kgdms. 19:11; 4 Kgdms. 3:17; Pss. 10:6; 30:6 [31:5 EVV]; 102:14 [103:14 EVV]; Eccl. 1:6, 14, 17; 2:11, 17, 26; 4:6, 16; 6:9; 8:8; 11:5; Job 8:2; 16:3; 17:1; 32:18; 41:8; Wis. 5:11, 23; 13:2; 17:17; Sir. 39:28; 43:17; Hos. 4:19; 12:2; Amos 4:13; Jonah 1:4; 4:8; Hab. 1:11; Zech. 5:9; Isa. 7:2; 29:24; 65:14; Jer. 30:27; Ezek. 1:4, 12, 20, 21; 5:2; 13:11; 27:26; Dan. 3:50 LXX, 65 LXX; Ep. Jer. 60; Odes Sol. 4(B):18); breathing (Jdt. 14:6; 4 Macc. 11:11; Job 1:19; 13:25; 30:15; Jdt. Sib. Or. 3:102; 7:102; 8:297; Let. Aris. 86; Josephus, *Ant.* 17:169; 1QpHab 4, 9; 1Q33 VI, 12; 1QHa IX, 12; 1QHa XIV, 23; 1QHa XV, 23; 3Q15 XI, 16; 4Q185 I, 11, 12; 4Q210 1 II, 4–9; 4Q223–224 2 II, 12; CD–A VIII, 13; CD–B XIX, 25; 4Q385 Frag 2, 7; 4Q427 Frag. 6, 4; 4Q427 Frag. 6, 4; 4Q429 2 II, 2; 4Q554a 3; 11Q10 XVI, 4). The term is used for directions or the sides of things (e.g., east side), which are defined by the wind direction (3Q15 VII, 5; 3Q15 XI, 16; 4Q209 23, 4; 4Q554 1 II, 14; 4Q554a 3; 5Q15 1 II, 6; 11Q5 XXVI, 15; 11Q18 12 I, 5). For Philo, the wind is spiritual, holding the land together (*Opif.* 131). Josephus also speaks of the blasts of fire in an eruption (*Ant.* 4:55). Other associated ideas include windy knowledge (Job 15:2), to speak wind (nonsense) (Mic. 2:11), a wind of salvation (Isa. 26:18), and a bladder full of air (Philo, *Prob.* 97).

Similarly, it can mean breath (2 Macc. 7:22; Job 7:7; Isa. 25:4; 26:9; 33:11; T. Ab. (A) 20:5; Let. Aris. 70; *Leg.* 3:14; *Gig.* 10; *Deus* 84; *Mos.* 1:93; *Decal.* 33; *Praem.* 144; *Aet.* 128; *Legat.* 63, 125, 188, 243; Josephus, *Ant.* 3:291). Philo uses it commonly in this regard (*Opif.* 41, 58, 80, 113; *Leg.* 3:53; 3:223; *Cher.* 13, 37, 38; *Post.* 22; *Deus* 26, 60, 98, 175; *Agr.* 174; *Migr.* 148, 217; *Cong.* 133; *Somn.* 2:13, 67, 85, 86, 143, 166; *Abr.* 43, 92, 160; *Ios.* 33; *Mos.* 1:141, 179; 2:104; *Spec.* 1:26, 92, 301, 322, 228, 338; 2:71, 153, 191; 4:27; *Praem.* 41; *Aet.* 11, 139; *Flacc.* 155; *Legat.* 177; *Prov.* 2:43, 45, 47; cf. Josephus, *Ant.* 2:343, 349; 8:346; 9:36, 210; 10:279; 12:75; 14:28; 16:17, 20, 62; *J.W.* 3:422; 4:77, 477). The Lord's anointed (the King) is "the breath of our nostrils" (Lam. 4:29).

Positive attributes in a person are defined with a genitive, such as a spirit of reason (4 Macc. 7:14); a right spirit (Ps. 50:12 [51:10 EVV]); a generous spirit (m. Pirqe Abot. 2:9 B); a spirit of grace and mercy (Zech. 12:10); exciting the spirit (Ps. 118:131 [119:131 EVV]). The senses are attached to spirits in the Testament of Reuben: a spirit of seeing (T. Reu. 2:4), of hearing (T. Reu. 2:5), of smell (T. Reu. 2:5), of speech (T. Reu. 2:6), and of taste (T. Reu. 2:7). Philo speaks of the spirit of a great athlete (Philo, *Prob.* 26).

In Qumran, the foundation of the spirit of the sons of truth in the world is a range of attributes created by the spirit, including meekness, patience, generous compassion, eternal goodness, intelligence, understanding, potent wisdom that trusts in all, the deeds of God, dependence on his abundant mercy, knowledge in all the plans of action, enthusiasm for the decrees of justice, holy plans with firm purpose, generous compassion with all the sons of the truth, magnificent purity that detests all unclean idols, careful behavior, wisdom concerning everything, and concealment concerning the truth of the mysteries of knowledge (1QS IV, 1). The spirit of holiness is established after atonement (1QS IX, 3).

BIBLIOGRAPHY

Aland, Barbara, Kurt Aland, Johannes Karavidopoulos, Carlo M. Martini, and Bruce M. Metzger, eds. *The Greek New Testament*. 5th rev. ed. Stuttgart, Germany: Deutsche Bibelgesellschaft, 2014.

_____. *Novum Testamentum Graece*. 28th ed. Stuttgart: Deutsche Bibelgesellschaft, 2012.

Appian. "Appian's Roman History," edited by T. E. Page, E. Capps, and W. H. D. Rouse. *Loeb Classical Library*. London; New York: William Heinemann; The Macmillan Co., 1912.

Arndt, William, F. Wilbur Gingrich, Frederick W. Danker, and Walter Bauer. *A Greek-English Lexicon of the New Testament and Other Early Christian Literature: A Translation and Adaption of the Fourth Revised and Augmented Edition of Walter Bauer's Griechisch-Deutsches Worterbuch Zu Den Schrift En Des Neuen Testaments Und Der Ubrigen Urchristlichen Literatur*. Chicago: University of Chicago Press, 1979.

Arnold, Clinton E. *Ephesians*. ZECNT. Grand Rapids: Zondervan, 2010.

_____. *Ephesians: Power and Magic; The Concept of Power in Ephesians in Light of Its Historical Setting*. SNTSMS 63. Cambridge: Cambridge University Press, 1989.

_____. "The Exorcism of Ephesians 6:12 in Recent Research." *JSNT* 30 (1987): 71–87.

_____. *Power and Magic: The Concept of Power in Ephesians*. Eugene, OR: Wipf & Stock, 1997.

Balz, Horst Robert, and Gerhard Schneider. *Exegetical Dictionary of the New Testament*. Grand Rapids: Eerdmans, 1990.

Barnett, Paul. *The Second Epistle to the Corinthians*. NICNT. Grand Rapids: Eerdmans, 1997.

Barrett, C. K. *The First Epistle to the Corinthians*. HNTC. New York: Harper & Row, 1968.

Barry, John D. "Servant of the Lord." *LBD*. Bellingham, WA: Lexham, 2016.

Bartchy, S. S. Μᾶλλον χρῆσαι: *First-Century Slavery and the Interpretation of 1 Cor. 7:21*. SBLDS 11. Missoula, MT: Scholars Press, 1973.

Barth, Markus. *Ephesians*. ABC. 2 vols. New York: Doubleday, 1984.

Bauckham, Richard. *Gospel Women: Studies in the Named Women of the Gospels*. Grand Rapids: Eerdmans, 2002.

Bauer, Walter, Frederick W. Danker, William Arndt, and F. Wilbur Gingrich. *A Greek-English Lexicon of the New Testament and Other Early Christian Literature*. 3rd ed. Chicago: University of Chicago Press, 2000.

Beasley-Murray, George R. *Baptism in the New Testament*. Grand Rapids: Eerdmans, 1962.

Berkhof, Hendrikus. *The Doctrine of the Holy Spirit*. London: Epworth, 1965.

Best, Ernest. *A Critical and Exegetical Commentary on Ephesians*. ICC. Edinburgh: T&T Clark International, 1998.

Betz, Hans Dieter. *Galatians: A Commentary on Paul's Letter to the Churches in Galatia*. Hermeneia. Philadelphia: Fortress, 1979.

Bockmuehl, Markus. *The Epistle to the Philippians*. BNTC. London: Continuum, 1997.

Bowers, W. Paul. "Church and Mission in Paul." *JSNT* 44 (1991): 89–111.

Brown, Francis, Samuel Rolles Driver, and Charles Augustus Briggs. *Enhanced Brown-Driver-Briggs Hebrew and English Lexicon*. Oxford: Clarendon, 1977.

Bruce, F. F. *1 & 2 Corinthians*. NCB. Grand Rapids: Eerdmans, 1980.

———. *1 and 2 Thessalonians*. WBC 45. Dallas: Word, 1982.

———. *The Book of the Acts*. NICNT. Grand Rapids: Eerdmans, 1988.

———. *The Epistle to the Hebrews*. NICNT. Grand Rapids: Eerdmans, 1990.

Buchanan, Grant David. "The Spirit, New Creation, and Christian Identity in Galatians: Toward a Pneumatological Reading of Galatians." PhD diss., University of Divinity, Melbourne, 2021.

Burns, Joshua Ezra. "Conversion and Proselytism." *EDEJ*. Grand Rapids: Eerdmans, 2010, 484–86.

Carson, D. A. *The Gospel according to John*. PNTC. Grand Rapids: Eerdmans, 1991.

———. *Showing the Spirit: A Theological Exposition of 1 Corinthians 12–14*. Grand Rapids: Baker, 1987.

Chafer, Lewis Sperry. *Systematic Theology*. Grand Rapids: Kregel, 1993.

Charles, J. Daryl. "Vice and Virtue Lists." *DNTB*, 1252–57.

Charlesworth, James H. *The Old Testament Pseudepigrapha*. 2 vols. New Haven, CT: Yale University Press, 1983.

Ciampa, Roy E., and Brian S. Rosner. *The First Letter to the Corinthians*. PNTC. Grand Rapids: Eerdmans, 2010.

Collins, John J., and Daniel C. Harlow, eds. *The Eerdmans Dictionary of Early Judaism*. Grand Rapids: Eerdmans, 2010.

Cosgrove, Charles H. *The Cross and the Spirit: A Study in the Argument and Theology of Galatians*. Macon, GA: Mercer University Press, 1989.

Cranfield, C. E. B. *A Critical and Exegetical Commentary on the Epistle to the Romans*. 2 vols. ICC. London: T&T Clark International, 2004.

DeSilva, David A. *The Letter to the Galatians*. NICNT. Grand Rapids: Eerdmans, 2018.

_____. *Transformation: The Heart of Paul's Gospel*. Bellingham, WA: Lexham, 2014.

Dickson, John P. *Mission Commitment in Ancient Judaism and in the Pauline Communities*. WUNT 2. Tübingen: J. C. B. Mohr [Paul Siebeck], 2003.

Dunn, James D. G. *Jesus and the Spirit: A Study of the Religious and Charismatic Experience of Jesus and the First Christians as Reflected in the New Testament*. Philadelphia: Westminster, 1975.

_____. *Romans 1–8*. WBC 38A. Dallas: Word, 1988.

Eadie, John. *A Commentary on the Greek Text of the Epistle of Paul to the Ephesians*. Edited by W. Young. Edinburgh: T & T Clark, 1883.

Edwards, James R. *The Gospel according to Luke*. PNTC. Grand Rapids: Eerdmans, 2010.

Evans, Craig A., and Stanley Porter E. *Dictionary of New Testament Background: A Compendium of Contemporary Biblical Scholarship*. Downers Grove, IL: InterVarsity Press, 2000.

Fee, Gordon D. *The First Epistle to the Corinthians*. Rev. ed. NICNT. Grand Rapids: Eerdmans, 2014.

_____. *The First and Second Letters to the Thessalonians*. NICNT. Grand Rapids: Eerdmans, 2009.

_____. *God's Empowering Presence: The Holy Spirit in the Letters of Paul*. Grand Rapids: Baker Academic, 2011.

_____. *Paul's Letter to the Philippians*. NICNT. Grand Rapids, MI: Eerdmans, 1995.

Fowl, Stephen E. *Ephesians: A Commentary*. Edited by C. Clifton Black, M. Eugene Boring, and John T. Carroll. NTL. Louisville: Westminster John Knox, 2012.

Furnish, Victor Paul. *II Corinthians: Translated with Introduction, Notes, and Commentary*. AYB 32A. New Haven, CT: Yale University Press, 2008.

Gardner, Paul. *1 Corinthians*. ZECNT. Grand Rapids: Zondervan, 2018.

Garland, David E. *1 Corinthians*, BECNT. Grand Rapids: Baker Academic, 2003.

_____. *2 Corinthians*. NAC 29. Nashville: Broadman & Holman, 1999.

Gatumu, Kabiro wa. *The Pauline Concept of Supernatural Powers: A Reading from the African Worldview*. PBM. Milton Keynes: Paternoster, 2008.

Gorman, Michael J. *Becoming the Gospel: Paul, Participation, and Mission*. GOCS. Grand Rapids: Eerdmans, 2015.

_____. "Cruciform or Resurrectiform? Paul's Paradoxical Practice of Participation in Christ." *Ex Auditu: An International Journal for the Theological Interpretation of Scripture* 33 (2017): 60–83.

_____. *Cruciformity: Paul's Narrative Spirituality of the Cross*. Grand Rapids: Eerdmans, 2001.

_____. *Inhabiting the Cruciform God: Kenosis, Justification, and Theosis in Paul's Narrative Soteriology*. Grand Rapids: Eerdmans, 2009.

Grayston, K. "Not with a Rod." *ExpT* 88 (1976): 13–16.

Green, Gene L. *The Letters to the Thessalonians*. The Pillar New Testament Commentary. Grand Rapids; Leicester, England: W. B. Eerdmans Pub.; Apollos, 2002.

Green, Joel B., Jeannine K. Brown, and Nicholas Perrin, eds. *Dictionary of Jesus and the Gospels*. 2nd ed. Downers Grove, IL: IVP Academic, 2013.

Gundry, Robert H. Sōma *in Biblical Theology with Emphasis on Pauline Anthropology*. SNTSMS 29. Cambridge: Cambridge University Press, 1976.

Habets, Myk. *The Anointed Son: A Trinitarian Spirit Christology*. PTMS. Eugene, OR: Pickwick, 2010.

_____. *The Progressive Mystery: Tracing the Elusive Spirit in Scripture and Tradition*. Bellingham, WA: Lexham, 2019.

Hamilton, N. Q. *The Holy Spirit and Eschatology in Paul*. SJTOP 6. Edinburgh: Oliver & Boyd, 1957.

Hansen, Walter G. *The Letter to the Philippians*. PNTC. Grand Rapids: Eerdmans, 2009.

Harden, J. M. *Dictionary of the Vulgate New Testament*. London: SPCK, 1921.

Harrington, Daniel S. J. "Ethics." *EDEJ,* 605–9.

Harris, Murray J. *The Second Epistle to the Corinthians: A Commentary on the Greek Text.* NIGTC. Grand Rapids: Eerdmans, 2005.

Harrison, Everett F. "Romans." *The Expositor's Bible Commentary: Romans through Galatians,* edited by Frank E. Gaebelein. Vol. 10. Grand Rapids: Zondervan, 1976.

Hawthorne, Gerald F. *Philippians.* Rev. ed. WBC 43. Dallas: Word, 2004.

Hawthorne, Gerald F., Ralph P. Martin, and Daniel G. Reid, eds. *Dictionary of Paul and His Letters.* Downers Grove, IL: InterVarsity Press, 1993.

Hellerman, Joseph H. "The Humiliation of Christ in the Social World of Roman Philippi, Part 2." *BSac* 160, no. 640 (2003): 427–30.

Hengel, Martin. *Crucifixion.* Philadelphia: Fortress, 1977.

Hoehner, Harold W. *Ephesians: An Exegetical Commentary.* Grand Rapids: Baker, 2002.

Hoehner, Harold W., and J. K. Brown. "Chronology." *DJG2* 134–38.

Holmes, Michael William. *The Apostolic Fathers: Greek Texts and English Translations.* Rev. ed. Grand Rapids: Baker, 1999.

Hutson, Christopher R. "Was Timothy Timid? On the Rhetoric of Fearlessness (1 Corinthians 16:10–11) and Cowardice (2 Timothy 1:7)." *BR* 42 (1997): 58–73.

Jewett, Robert. *Paul's Anthropological Terms: A Study of Their Use in Conflict Settings.* AGJU 10. Leiden: Brill, 1971.

Jongkind, Dirk, ed. *The Greek New Testament.* Wheaton, IL: Crossway, 2017.

Justin Martyr. *The Second Apology of Justin* 2.6. In A *ANF*[1].

Käsemann, Ernst. *Commentary on Romans.* Grand Rapids: Eerdmans, 1994.

Kellner, Menachem. "Ethics of Judaism." *EJ,* 1:150–59.

Kelly, J. N. D. *The Pastoral Epistles.* BNTC. London: Continuum, 1963.

Kempthorne, R. "Incest and the Body of Christ: A Study of 1 Corinthians VI.12–20." *NTS* 14 (1967–68): 568–74.

Keown, Mark J. "The Apostolic Green Imperative." In *Living on the Planet Earth: Faith Communities and Ecology,* edited by Neil Darragh, 33–39. Auckland: Accent, 2016.

———. "A Biblical View of Marriage." *Candour* (2013): 10–12.

———. "The Christ Pattern For Social Relationships in Philippians and Beyond." In *Paul and His Social Relations,* edited by Stanley E. Porter and Christopher D. Land, 301–31. Pauline Studies 7. Leiden: Brill, 2012.

_____. *Congregational Evangelism in Philippians: The Centrality of an Appeal for Gospel Proclamation to the Fabric of Philippians*. PBM. Milton Keynes: Paternoster, 2008.

_____. "Did Paul Plan to Escape from Prison? (Philippians 1:19–26)." *JSPL* 5, no. 1 (2015): 89–108.

_____. *Discovering the New Testament: An Introduction to Its Background, Theology, and Themes: The Gospels and Acts*. Vol. 1. Bellingham, WA: Lexham, 2018.

_____. *Discovering the New Testament: An Introduction to Its Background, Theology, and Themes: The Pauline Letters*. Vol. 2. Bellingham, WA: Lexham, 2021.

_____. "'Do Not Go Beyond What Is Written' (1 Cor. 4:6)." *Stimulus* (2015): 45–47.

_____. "Engaging with Outsiders: Insights into Sharing the Gospel from Colossians 4:5–6." *Stimulus* 29, no. 2 (2022). https://hail.to/laidlaw-college/publication/iOXHXeW/article/Puacv39.

_____. *Galatians: A Commentary for Students*. Auckland: Morphe, 2020.

_____. "Holding Forth the Word of Life." In *Holding Forth the Word of Life: Essays in Honor of Tim Meadowcroft*, edited by John de Jong and Csila Saysell, 98–117. Eugene, OR: Wipf & Stock, 2020.

_____. "How Much Should We Sing?" *Colloq* 19, no. 3 (2012): 5–13.

_____. "An Imminent Parousia and Christian Mission: Did the New Testament Writers Expect Jesus's Imminent Return?" In *Christian Origins and the Establishment of the Early Jesus Movement*, edited by Stanley E. Porter and Andrew W. Pitts, 242–61. TENTS. ECHC 4. Leiden: Brill, 2017.

_____. "Implications of 1 Corinthians 14:1–25 for Multicultural Church Gatherings." Paper presented at the Annual Meeting of the Society of Biblical Literature, San Antonio, 2021.

_____. "Initial Discipleship and Sexual Holiness." Paper presented at the Evangelical Theological Society 2022 annual meeting.

_____. "A Missional and Liturgical Reading of the Christ-Hymn." Paper presented at Tyndale NT Study Group, 2021.

_____. "Notes of Hope in the Face of Suffering (Rom. 8:18–39)." *Stimulus* (2020).

_____. "Paul, the Demonic, and Mental Health." Paper presented at the Annual Meeting of the Society of Biblical Literature 2022, Denver, 2022.

_____. "Paul's Answer to the Threats of Jerusalem and Rome." In *The Gospel in the Land of Promise: Christian Approaches to the Land of Promise*, edited by Philip Church, Peter Walker, Tim. Bulkeley, and Tim Meadow-croft, 28–45. Eugene, OR: Pickwick, 2011.

_____. "Paul's Use of εἴτε . . . εἴτε: Constructions and the Proclamation of the Gospel (Phil. 1:18a)." *Colloq* 48, no. 2 (2016): 195–208.

_____. "Paul's Vision of a New Masculinity." *Colloq* 47, no. 1 (2016): 47–60.

_____. "Philemon and Restorative Justice." *Stimulus* 25, no. 1 (2018): 12–19.

_____. *Philippians*. 2 vols. EEC. Bellingham, WA: Lexham, 2017.

_____. "Preaching Christ Crucified: Cruciformity in Content and Delivery." In *Text Messages: Preaching God's Word in a Smartphone World*, edited by John Tucker, 217–29. Eugene, OR: Wipf & Stock, 2017.

_____. "Redeeming Paul." In *Scriptural Sexuality*, edited by Zohar Hadromi-Allouche, Nirmal Fernando, and Keren Abbou Hershkovits. Forthcoming.

_____. *Romans and the Mission of God*. Eugene, OR: Wipf and Stock, 2021.

_____. "The Use of the OT in Philippians." In *All the Prophets Have Declared*, edited by Matthew R. Malcolm, 139–65. Milton Keynes: Paternoster, 2015.

_____. "The Vision for Intercultural Church in Ephesians 2 and Colossians 3." Paper presented at the Annual Meeting of Society of Biblical Literature, Denver, 2022.

Kittel, Gerhard, Geoffrey W. Bromiley, and Gerhard Friedrich, eds. *Theological Dictionary of the New Testament*. Grand Rapids: Eerdmans, 1964.

Koehler, Ludwig, Walter Baumgartner, M. E. J. Richardson, and Johann Jakob Stamm. *The Hebrew and Aramaic Lexicon of the Old Testament*. Leiden: E. J. Brill, 1994–2000.

Köstenberger, Andreas J. *John*. BECNT. Grand Rapids: Baker Academic, 2004.

Laertius, Diogenes. *Lives of Eminent Philosophers*. Edited by R. D. Hicks. Cambridge, MA: Harvard University Press, 2005.

Liddell, Henry George, Robert Scott, Henry Stuart Jones, and Roderick McKenzie. *A Greek-English Lexicon*. Oxford: Clarendon Press, 1996.

Lightfoot, Joseph Barber. *Notes on the Epistles of St Paul from Unpublished Commentaries*. London: Macmillan, 1895.

_____. *Saint Paul's Epistle to the Philippians*. CCGNT. London: Macmillan, 1913.

Lincoln, Andrew T. *Ephesians*. WBC 42. Dallas: Word, 1990.

Liston, Gregory J. *Kingdom Come: An Eschatological Third Article Ecclesiology*. London: T&T Clark, 2022.

Long, Phillip J. "Holy of Holies." *LBD*.

Longenecker, Richard N. *The Epistle to the Romans: A Commentary on the Greek Text*. NIGTC. Grand Rapids: Eerdmans, 2016.

_____. *Galatians*. WBC 41. Dallas: Word, 1990.

Louw, Johannes P., and Eugene Albert Nida. *Greek-English Lexicon of the New Testament: Based on Semantic Domains*. New York: United Bible Societies, 1996.

Malherbe, Abraham J. "The Beasts at Ephesus." *JBL* 87 (1968): 71–80.

_____. *The Letters to the Thessalonians: A New Translation with Introduction and Commentary*. AYB 32B. New Haven, CT: Yale University Press, 2008.

Man, Ronald E. "The Value of Chiasm for New Testament Interpretation." *Bibliotheca Sacra* 141 (1984): 146–54.

Marshall, I. Howard. *1 and 2 Thessalonians*. NCB. Grand Rapids: Eerdmans, 1983.

Marshall, I. Howard, and Philip H. Towner. *A Critical and Exegetical Commentary on the Pastoral Epistles*. ICC. London: T&T Clark, 2004.

Martin, Ralph P. *2 Corinthians*. 2nd ed. WBC 40. Nashville: Thomas Nelson, 2014.

_____. *The Spirit and the Congregation: Studies in 1 Corinthians 12–15*. Grand Rapids: Eerdmans, 1984.

Martin, Ralph P., and Peter H. Davids, eds. *Dictionary of the Later New Testament and Its Developments*. Downers Grove, IL: InterVarsity Press, 1997.

McKnight, Scot. *Pastor Paul: Nurturing a Culture of Christoformity in the Church*. TECC. Grand Rapids: Brazos, 2019.

Metzger, Bruce Manning. *A Textual Commentary on the Greek New Testament, Second Edition: A Companion Volume to the United Bible Societies' Greek New Testament (4th rev. ed.)*. London; New York: United Bible Societies, 1994.

Montanari, Franco. *The Brill Dictionary of Ancient Greek*. Leiden; Boston: Brill, 2015.

Moo, Douglas J. *Galatians*, BECNT. Grand Rapids: Baker Academic, 2013.

_____. *The Letter to the Romans*. 2nd ed. NICNT. Grand Rapids: Eerdmans, 2018.

_____. *The Letters to the Colossians and to Philemon*. The Pillar New Testament Commentary. Grand Rapids: William B. Eerdmans Pub. Co., 2008.

Morris, Leon. *1 and 2 Thessalonians*. TNTC. Downers Grove, IL: InterVarsity Press, 209.

_____. *The Epistle to the Romans*. PNTC. Grand Rapids: Eerdmans, 1988.

Moulton, James Hope, and George Milligan. *The Vocabulary of the Greek Testament*. London: Hodder and Stoughton, 1930.

Mounce, William D. *Pastoral Epistles*. WBC 46. Dallas: Word, 2000.

Murray, G. W. "Paul's Corporate Witness in Philippians." *BSac* 155 (1998): 322–23.

Murray, John. *The Epistle to the Romans: The English Text with Introduction, Exposition, and Notes*. Vol. 2. NICNT. Grand Rapids: Eerdmans, 1965.

Neusner, Jacob. "The Shema," in "Liturgy of Judaism." *EJ* 2:816–19.

Neusner, Jacob, Alan J. Avery-Peck, and William Scott Green, eds. *The Encyclopedia of Judaism*. Leiden: Brill, 2000.

Neyrey, Jerome H. "Bewitched in Galatia: Paul in Social Science Perspective." *CBQ* 50 (1988): 72–100.

Nikkanen, Markus. "Response to Gorman." *Ex Auditu: An International Journal for the Theological Interpretation of Scripture* 33 (2017): 84–91.

O'Brien, Peter T. *Gospel and Mission in the Writings of Paul: An Exegetical and Theological Analysis*. Grand Rapids: Baker, 1995.

_____. *Introductory Thanksgivings in the Letters of Paul*. NovTSup 49. Leiden: Brill, 1977.

Oropeza, B. J. *1 Corinthians: A New Covenant Commentary*. NCCS. Eugene, OR: Cascade, 2017.

Owen, John. *An Exposition of the Epistle to the Hebrews*. Edited by W. H. Goold. *Works of John Owen* 19. Edinburgh: T&T Clark, 1862.

Pao, David W. *Colossians and Philemon*. ZECNT. Grand Rapids: Zondervan, 2012.

Parratt, J. K. "Romans 1:11 and Galatians 3:5—Pauline Evidence for the Laying On of Hands?" *ExpT* 79 (1968): 151–52.

Peterman, G. W. "'Thankless Thanks': The Epistolary Social Convention in Philippians 4:10–20." *TynBul* 42 (1991): 261–70.

Philo. Translated by F. H. Colson, G. H. Whitaker, and J. W. Earp. *The Loeb Classical Library*. Cambridge, MA: Harvard University Press, 1929–1962.

Porter, Stanley E. *Idioms of the Greek New Testament*. Sheffield: JSOT, 1999.

_____. "Tribulation, Messianic Woes." *DLNTD* 1179–82.

Roberts, Alexander, James Donaldson, and A. Cleveland Coxe, eds. *The Apostolic Fathers with Justin Martyr and Irenaeus*. ANF[1]. Buffalo, NY: Christian Literature, 1885.

Robertson, A. T. *A Grammar of the Greek New Testament in the Light of Historical Research*. 3rd ed. Bellingham, WA: Logos Bible Software, 2006.

Rogers, C. "The Dionysian Background of Ephesians 5:18." *BSac* 136 (1979): 249–57.

Schnackenburg, Rudolf. *Ephesians: A Commentary*. Edinburgh: T&T Clark, 1991.

Schreiner, Thomas R. *Romans*. BECNT. Grand Rapids: Baker Academic, 1998.

Scott, James M. "Adoption, Sonship." *DPL* 15–18.

Shogren, Gary Steven. *1 & 2 Thessalonians*. ZECNT. Grand Rapids: Zondervan, 2012.

Silva, Moisés, ed. *New International Dictionary of New Testament Theology and Exegesis*. Grand Rapids: Zondervan, 2014.

_____. "Old Testament in Paul." *DPL,* 631–42.

_____. *Philippians*. 2nd ed. BECNT. Grand Rapids: Baker Academic, 2005.

Smith, Gary. *Isaiah 40–66*. NAC 15B. Nashville: Broadman & Holman, 2009.

Swanson, James. *Dictionary of Biblical Languages with Semantic Domains: Greek (New Testament)*. Oak Harbor WA: Logos Research Systems, 1997.

Tacitus: The Histories and The Annals: English Translation. Edited by G. P. Goold. Translated by Clifford H. Moore and John Jackson. Loeb Classical Library. Cambridge, MA: Harvard University Press, 1925–1937.

Taylor, Mark. *1 Corinthians*. NAC 28. Nashville: B&H, 2014.

Taylor, Richard A., and E. Ray Clendenen. *Haggai, Malachi*. NAC 21A. Nashville: Broadman & Holman Publishers, 2004.

Tesh, S. Edward, and Walter D. Zorn. *Psalms*. CPNIVC. Joplin, MO: College Press, 1999.

Theissen, G. *The Social Setting of Pauline Christianity: Essays on Corinth*. Translated by J. H. Schütz. Philadelphia: Fortress. 1982.

Thielman, Frank. *Ephesians*. BECNT. Grand Rapids: Baker Academic, 2010.

Thiselton, Anthony C. *The First Epistle to the Corinthians: A Commentary on the Greek Text*. NIGTC. Grand Rapids: Eerdmans, 2000.

Thrall, Margaret. *A Critical and Exegetical Commentary on the Second Epistle of the Corinthians*. 2 vols. ICC. New York: T&T Clark International, 2004.

Twelftree, Graham H. "Healing, Illness." *DPL* 378–81.

Wallace, Daniel B. *Greek Grammar Beyond the Basics: Exegetical Syntax of the New Testament*. Grand Rapids: Zondervan, 1996.

Wanamaker, Charles A. *The Epistles to the Thessalonians: A Commentary on the Greek Text*. NIGTC. Grand Rapids: Eerdmans, 1990.

Ware, James P. *The Mission of the Church in Paul's Letter to the Philippians in the Context of Ancient Judaism*. NovTSup 120. Leiden: Brill, 2005.

_____. "The Thessalonians as a Missionary Congregation: 1 Thessalonians 1, 5–8." *ZNW* 83 (1992): 126–31.

Watts, John D. W. *Isaiah 1–33*. WBC 24. Dallas: Word, 1985.

Weima, Jeffrey A. D. *1–2 Thessalonians*. BECNT. Grand Rapids: Baker Academic, 2014.

Wink, Walter. *Naming the Powers: The Language of Power in the New Testament*. Philadelphia: Fortress, 1984.

Winter, Bruce W. "'The Seasons' of This Life and Eschatology in 1 Corinthians 7:29–31." In *"The Reader Must Understand": Eschatology in Bible and Theology*, edited by K. E. Brower and M. W. Elliot, 323–34. Leicester: Apollos, 1997.

Witherington, Ben III. *The Acts of the Apostles: A Socio-Rhetorical Commentary*. Grand Rapids: Eerdmans, 1998.

_____. *Conflict and Community in Corinth: A Socio-Rhetorical Commentary on 1 and 2 Corinthians*. Grand Rapids: Eerdmans, 1995.

_____. *Women in the Earliest Churches*. Cambridge: Cambridge University Press, 1988.

Witherington, Ben III, and Darlene Hyatt. *Paul's Letter to the Romans: A Socio-Rhetorical Commentary*. Grand Rapids: Eerdmans, 2004.

Wright, N. T. *Pauline Perspectives: Essays on Paul, 1978–2013*. Minneapolis: Fortress, 2013.

_____. "Romans." In *The New Interpreter's Bible: A Commentary in Twelve Volumes*, edited by Leander E. Keck et al. Vol. 10. Nashville: Abingdon, 2002.

_____. *The Resurrection of the Son of God*. COQG. London: SPCK, 2003.

Young, F., and D. F. Ford. *Meaning and Truth in 2 Corinthians*. Grand Rapids: Eerdmans, 1987.

Zuntz, Günther. *The Text of the Epistles*. London: British Academy, 1953.